MAKING SENSE OF SPORTS

Updated, revised, and enhanced with new features, the fifth edition of *Making Sense of Sports* is the strongest yet.

Ellis Cashmore's unique multidisciplinary approach to the study of sports remains the only introduction to combine anthropology, biology, economics, history, philosophy, psychology, and sociology with cultural and media studies to produce a distinct unbroken vision of the origins, development, and current state of sports. New chapters on exercise culture and the moral climate of sports, supplement a thoroughly overhauled text that includes fresh material on Islam, depression, crime and deviance, and the interdependence of sport, culture, and consumerism.

Now packed with teaching supplements, including access to a dedicated online resource headquarters with podcasts of interviews with self-assessment quizzes, the new edition contains a glossary of sports terms as well as guides to further reading, capsule explanations, and model essays. In short, *Making Sense of Sports* is an all-purpose introduction to the study of sports.

Ellis Cashmore is Professor of Culture, Media, and Sport at Staffordshire University's Faculty of Health. Prior to this he was Professor of Sociology at the University of Tampa, Florida, and Lecturer in Sociology at the University of Hong Kong. Previous publications include, *Martin Scorsese's America* (Polity Press, 2009), *Sport and Exercise Psychology: The Key Concepts* (Routledge, 2008) and *Celebrity/Culture* (Routledge, 2006).

MAKING SENSE OF SPORTS

Fifth edition

UniversityCampus
Oldham

Library & Resource Centre: 0161 344 8888
UCO Main Reception: 0161 344 8800
University Way, Oldham, OL1 1BB

**Text renewals: text RENEW and your UCO ID number to
07950 081389.**

Shelfmark: 306.483 CAS

This book is to be returned by the date on the self-service receipt.
Your library account can be accessed online at:
http://library.oldham.ac.uk/heritage/

Follow UCO Library on Twitter: @ucolrc

Routledge
Taylor & Francis Group

LONDON AND NEW YORK

First published 2010
by Routledge
2 Park Square, Milton Park, Abingdon, Oxon OX14 4RN

Simultaneously published in the USA and Canada
by Routledge
711 Third Avenue, New York, NY 10017, USA

Routledge is an imprint of the Taylor & Francis Group, an Informa business

Typeset in Adobe Garamond and Frutiger
by Keystroke, Tettenhall, Wolverhampton

British Library Cataloguing in Publication Data
A catalogue record for this book is available from the British Library

Library of Congress Cataloging in Publication Data
Cashmore, Ernest.
Making sense of sports / by Ellis Cashmore. — 5th ed.
p. cm.
1. Sports—Social aspects. I. Title.
GV706.5.C38 2010
306.4'83—dc22
2010001995

ISBN: 978–0–415–55220–2 (hbk)
ISBN: 978–0–415–55221–9 (pbk)
ISBN: 978–0–203–87269–7 (ebk)

CONTENTS

LIST OF ILLUSTRATIONS

FIGURES

TABLES

BOXES

ABBREVIATIONS

AA	American Association (baseball)
AAA	Amateur Athletic Association
ABA	American Basketball Association
ABC	American Broadcasting Company
ABL	American Basketball League
ACB	Australian Cricket Board
ADHD	attention deficit hyperactivity disorder
ADP	adenosine diphosphate
AFC	American Football Conference
AFL	American Football League
AIBA	International Boxing Association (Amateur)
AL	American League (baseball)
ANC	African National Congress
ANS	autonomic nervous system
ASA	Amateur Swimming Association
ATP	adenosine triphosphate
ATP	Association of Tennis Professionals
BAF	British Athletics Federation
Balco	Bay Area Laboratory Co-operative
BBBC	British Boxing Board of Control
BBC	British Broadcasting Corporation
BCE	Before the Common Era (before the Christian Era)
BDO	British Darts Organization
BRS	Blue Ribbon Sports
BSkyB	British Sky Broadcasting
CBS	Columbia Broadcasting System
CE	Common Era
CERA	continuous erythropoiesis receptor activator
CNS	central nervous system
CPUs	central processing units
EA	electronic arts
ECB	England and Wales Cricket Board
EPO	erythropoietin
ESPN	Entertainment and Sports Network

F1	Formula One (motor racing)
FA	Football Association
FAME	Falk Associates Management Enterprises
FCC	Federal Communications Commission
FDA	Food and Drugs Administration
FIBA	Fédération Internationale de Boxe Amateur
Fifa	Fédération Internationale de Football Associations
Fina	Fédération Internationale de Natation (swimming)
HBO	Home Box Office
hGH	human growth hormone
HRM	heart rate monitor
IAA	Intercollegiate Athletic Association
IAAF	International Amateur Athletics Federation
IBF	International Boxing Federation
ICC	International Cricket Conference
IGH	insulin growth hormone
ILTF	International Lawn Tennis Federation
IPL	Indian Premier League
ITF	International Tennis Federation
ITV	Independent Television
LAN	local area network
LH	luteinizing hormone
MCC	The Marylebone Cricket Club
MHR	maximum heart rate
MLB	Major League Baseball
MLS	Major League Soccer
MMA	Mixed Martial Arts
NABP	National Association of Base Ball Players
NASA	National Aeronautics and Space Administration
NASL	North American Soccer League
NBA	National Basketball Association
NBC	National Broadcasting Company
NCAA	National Collegiate Athletic Association
NFC	National Football Conference
NFL	National Football League
NHL	National Hockey League
NL	National League (baseball)
NYSAC	New York State Athletic Commission
OHL	Ontario Hockey League
PEG	percutaneous endoscopic gastrostomy
PES	Pro Evolution Soccer
PFC	perfluorocarbon
PLO	Palestine Liberation Organization
PNS	peripheral nervous system
ppv	pay per view
Push	People United to Save Humanity

RAF	Royal Air Force
RAS	reticular activating system
RFU	Rugby Football Union
ROM	read-only memory
RSPCA	Royal Society for the Prevention of Cruelty to Animals
SANROC	South African Non-Racial Olympic Committee
SARU	South African Rugby Union
TBS	Turner Broadcasting System
T–E ratio	testosterone to epitestosterone ratio
TNT	Turner Television Network
TOP	The Olympic Partner program
UCI	Union Cycliste Internationale
UDI	Unilateral Declaration of Independence
Uefa	Union des Associans Européenes de Football
UFC	Ultimate Fighting Championship
USATF	USA Track and Field
USOC	United States Olympic Committee
VO^2_{max}	Maximum oxygen uptake
WADA	World Anti-Doping Agency
WBA	World Boxing Association
WBC	World Boxing Council
WHO	World Health Organization
WNBA	Women's National Basketball Association
WPBSA	World Professional Billiards and Snooker Association
WWE	World Wrestling Entertainment (formerly WWF)
WWF	World Wrestling Federation
Zanu PF	Zimbabwe African National Union – Patriotic Front
ZCU	Zimbabwe Cricket Union

CHAPTER 1

Introduction

KEY ISSUES

▌ How do we express our identities through sport?

▌ What would a world without sport be like?

▌ When life becomes too organized, what do we do?

▌ Where is spitting melon seeds considered a sport?

▌ Why do so many of us spend money, time and energy on something that makes no material impact on our lives?

▌ . . . and is being a sports fan a form of madness?

A WORLD WITHOUT SPORT

Just think of a world without sport. Almost unimaginable, isn't it? No sports to provide us with those ritualistic actions that bring us together, or the traditions that transfer customs and beliefs from one generation to the next. Where would we look for the dramatic spectacles that set the adrenaline pulsing through our system, the savage, gladiatorial conflicts that have no counterpart in any other area of entertainment? Our pantheon of heroes would be seriously diminished without figures like Muhammad Ali, Babe Ruth, or Stanley Matthews. How we'd miss savoring the delicate skill, the unconquerable combativeness, and the occasional moment when art intrudes into the realm of competition and elevates a contest into an expression of sublime creativity. Sport can be overrated. But not by enthusiasts.

If we had to reconstruct history without sport, it would leave unbridgeable gaps. Jesse Owens' four gold medals at the Berlin Olympics of 1936 would be missing. The "Rumble in the Jungle" of 1974, when Muhammad Ali reclaimed the world heavyweight title wouldn't have happened. Tiger Woods' historic Masters win in 1997 just wouldn't exist. Numberless people would have been destined to live in poverty if denied their only opportunity for advancement. There would be no camaraderie, or the filial relationships, the ritual bonding, the common causes that unite people. The peaks of triumph, the troughs of failure, the ecstasy and despair: we would never have experienced how sport can elicit all these. The color would be erased from otherwise monochrome lives. The commerce, industries, media of communications, and employment sectors that have organized around sport just wouldn't have materialized.

Surely, we would be worse off without sport. Wouldn't we? Not according to some: they insist the world would be a better place. They'd argue that the clasp that sports have had on our hearts and minds has been unhealthy and led to all manner of despicable incidents. Sport may not have been the cause of the Munich atrocity of 1972, when eleven Israeli athletes were taken hostage and killed, but it provided a global forum. The 95 football fans who were crushed to death at the Heysel Stadium in Brussels, in 1985, were gathered for one purpose – to watch a sporting competition: they surrendered their lives for a pointless game. Countless young people illicitly procure dubious substances and ingest them, often in dangerously high doses, for one simple reason: to win sports contests.

These are the kinds of reminders that should make us scratch our heads and wonder: is this madness? Should lives be lost or ruined because of something that's meant to bring joy? The answer is, of course, no. So have we lost the ability to make rational choices? Let's consider one sports event that seems to offer an answer. Since its inaugural race in 1903, the Tour de France has been responsible for at least 30 deaths, of cyclists as well as spectators. And riding a cycle over 2,130 miles along a track that takes in Champagne country, the Alps, the Pyrenees and the Atlantic coast has no obvious utility. Yet, every year, 15 million spectators crowd along the cyclists' path. All they see is a brief blur of 198 cyclists hurtling past en route for Paris.

The Tour de France is an exceptional event, of course: it remains one of those competitions that excite people from around the world, turning rationality on its head. They forget the purpose of the epic ride – which was actually to promote a magazine – and flock to whatever vantage point they can just to catch sight of the competitors whizzing past. Spectators are familiar with the brutal side of this sport, but there is a momentary frisson at the sight of fit and doughty young men submitting their bodies to what is an almost inhuman ordeal, not for 90 minutes, or 3 hours, or even for the 5 days test cricket sometimes takes, but for 3 weeks, with only a couple of rest days.

Most major competitions are over in a fraction of Tour's duration time, and take place in confined spaces that can accommodate thousands rather than millions. But, thanks to television, anyone who's interested can watch from anywhere in the world. Association football's World Cup is actually longer than the Tour and draws an overall audience of 30 billion over 25 days, the final game alone drawing 1.7 billion people to their tv sets. That's about a quarter of the world's population. A figure like this makes the NFL's Super Bowl seem like a private gathering of 200 million.

Well, all this certainly looks like madness. After all, the sight of grown men cycling at breakneck speeds for 3 weeks, or 11 supremely fit and trained men trying to move a ball in one direction while another 11 supremely fit and trained men try to move it in the opposite direction serves no obvious function. Nor will the fruits of their labors bring any lasting benefit to civilization. It's not as if they'll take us anywhere nearer curing cancer, or bringing peace on earth or saving the planet. And unless we've staked a substantial wager on the outcome, we don't stand to gain anything in material terms. In fact, we will, for the most part, be out of pocket. Enthusiasm for sports is truly universal and seemingly unquenchable: no matter how much we get, we thirst for more. And there's no apparent let-up to our spending.

We pay out inordinate amounts of money either to watch or to bet on events; we travel often great distances; in some cases, we even fight – to the death – over sports.

We should properly feel at least slightly uncomfortable about this. Challenge is important to the human condition: it's one of the oldest preoccupations. Where obstacles – natural or artificial – exist, we always attempt to surmount them. And, where they don't exist, we invent them. Countless episodes of triumph or folly and, sometimes, disaster have followed our attempts to conquer obstacles. Witness the yearly catalog of deaths resulting from mountaineering expeditions.

The human tendency to rise to challenges rather than just accept them is no doubt part of our evolutionary adaptation. If we didn't rise, we wouldn't have survived as a species. Sports kick in when we've taken on all the challenges germane to our survival and then lust for more; when the challenges no longer exist, we invent them. Sporting competition has everything: the challenge, the confrontation and the climactic finality of a result. Someone, or something, always wins, loses or draws. And this goes some way toward understanding our fundamental fascination with sports. But we still need to dig deeper for the sources.

No human institution is immune from critical investigation. Not even ones that provide us with so much pleasure – in fact, you could argue that these are especially worthy of critical investigation. This is why there are theories of and investigations into art, humor and, of course, sex. Ask anybody why he or she likes any of these and odds are you will get a stock response along the lines of "they're good fun" or "because they give us pleasure." Fair comment. But the analyst of sports uses this only as the starting point of his or her examination.

Often, there's resistance to approaching sports on any other terms other than those of the fan, the reporter or the athlete. Sports practitioners and journalists have warned off those who bring too much intellect to what is, after all, a joyous human activity. Theoretical contemplation is all very well; but sports are for doers, not thinkers. If you intellectualize over an activity too much you lose sight of the basic reason why people like it. That was the jaundiced view once encountered by sports analysts. Now it's changing.

Sport as an institution is just too economically big, too politically important, too influential in shaping people's lives not to be taken seriously as a subject for academic inquiry. I should distinguish between sport and sports: *sport* refers to the entire institution and is preferred in Britain to the plural *sports,* which describes the various activities and organizations and is more popularly used in the United States. In practice, the two are used interchangeably.

Those whose emotions are left undisturbed by sports, are often bewildered and sometimes disgusted by the irrational waste involved in sports. Readers of this book will probably not be among this group. But they'll be looking for explanations: they'll want to make sense of what is, on the surface at least, a senseless activity. This book, as its title suggests, tries to do exactly that. In the chapters that follow, we'll go beyond surface appearances to reveal new perspectives on sports.

None of what follows denies the validity of the views of the fans, the athletes, the sports journalists, nor indeed the cynics: they all provide us with pieces of a jigsaw, a puzzle that can only be assembled by fitting the various different-shaped pieces together. To this end, I'll integrate as many different perspectives as necessary in the attempt to make sport comprehensible as an enduring, universal phenomenon. The reader will find contributions from a range of behavioral and physical sciences, such as anthropology, biology, history, psychology, and sociology, and more from humanities, including history, philosophy, literature, and film. None of these disciplines has been able to supply a single unifying answer to the question of why people are so drawn to sports. But, by piecing together various contributions, we can approach a fuller comprehension.

IDENTITIES AND DISTINCTION

We know what we want from sports, don't we? We want the incomparable enjoyment that comes from competition. We want healthy physical exercise that leaves us drained. We want the camaraderie and mutual trust of our team and the respect of our opponents. We want identities. Wait. *Identities*?

Maybe it doesn't top the list of demands we make of sports and it probably never occurs to us when we're actually training, competing, or watching. But, according to many contemporary researchers, identities thrive in sports. For example, Daniel Burdsey argues that football constitutes "an arena for British Asians to articulate their identities, but it is also a social space in which those identities are met with some of the most severe forms of discrimination" (2007: 3).

This is a perplexing observation, but worth unpicking. When Burdsey uses "articulate," he presumably means players communicate or express themselves visibly, through body and speech. His use of "identities" is less clear, though it's likely he means the relatively stable conceptions we have of ourselves, as individuals. Put simply: the way we think about ourselves as people who are unique yet connected to others. We're continuously aware of our distinctness and singularity as well as our connectedness, and, in Burdsey's view, football provides a social space in which British Asians can express this.

In Burdsey's study, young men (not women) from Asian backgrounds and descent, meet rebuffs and disapproval in a sport about which they feel passionate. As a consequence, their identities are ambiguous and uncertain. Identity isn't an end in itself, but a quest for distinction. None of us ever settles for one particular identity; we're always changing the way we think about ourselves and sport plays a role in this.

John Harris and Andrew Parker reinforce Burdsey's point: "Sport certainly provides an environment where identities can be established" (2009: 169). Identities are forged and developed as well as articulated in the context of sport. Harris and Parker are actually referring to a particular kind of identity. *Social identity* is a conception reflected from the images others have of a person. In practice, there is a close, if not exact, resemblance: the conception we have of ourselves is, in large part, a mirror of how others see us (the word itself is taken from the Latin *identitas*, meaning same).

Harris and Parker believe sport contributes to the creation of identity in four ways: (1) it is a court in which we can test who we are and who we aren't (what Harris and Parker call similarity and difference); (2) it offers a group, team or collectivity of others with whom we can identify (belonging and recognition); (3) it forms a network of likeminded individuals (attachment and affiliation – what we called connectedness);

(4) it provides the basis of collective action in the search for justice (inequality and social justice) (2009: 169).

It seems an impressive catalog of qualities for an activity that was once intended only to test one person's or group's mettle against another's. But perhaps sport has never been *just* that: close inspection indicates that the magnetic pull of sports over the centuries can't be understood in simple terms. And maybe it can't be understood solely in terms of providing a space in which we can cultivate a sense of selfhood. But it's a serviceable way to start. Think, for example, of the kinds of identities played out through sport.

Athletic identity is, according to Diane Groff and Ramon Zabriskie, "the degree to which an individual identifies with the role of an athlete and will look to others for confirmation of that role." Groff and Zabriskie investigated "individuals who access their sense of self within the context of sport" (2006).

In a separate study, Elizabeth Daniels *et al.* observe: "Individuals with a strong athletic identity view statements such as 'I consider myself an athlete' and 'sport is the only important thing in my life' as highly representative of themselves" (2005). In both research projects, the way in which competitors approached their sport was affected by their conceptions of themselves, whether as athletes or, for example, as people who just happened to be involved in sports. But sport was an integral part of the way they saw themselves.

In the Groff–Zabriskie study, the active competitors all had physical disabilities, suggesting how sport can effectively provide disabled and impaired persons with identity.

We might expect this to be a good thing: regarding oneself as essentially a competitor, sport being an integral part of how we see ourselves and how we assume others see us. But what happens after a serious injury, or when age takes its toll? An enforced departure from sport can have far-reaching consequences, as William Webb *et al.* point out: 'Retirement subsequently denies opportunities to foster and maintain this identity." If forced out of sport, someone who is an individual with a strong, centralized athletic identity often has problems redefining his or herself.

Yet alternatives in sport are always available: a transition to coach, manager, or even just fan maintains an attachment. The implication is that sport can provide identities for groups at any stage of the lifecycle, perhaps for an entire life.

Daniel Wann and Frederick Grieve write about *fan identity*, which, they argue, is fostered by "both in-group favoritism and out-group derogation."

This resonates with Harris and Parker's points (2) and (3). A strong sense of attachment to other fans can be a salient part of fans' identities (salient means the most prominent or important). As the other forms of identities can be threatened by injury, retirement, or poor performance, so the fans' identity can be vulnerable to, for instance, the results of the team they support, the behavior of rival fans or sheer geography (i.e. relocating to faraway places).

Instead of a unique, singular sense of individuality, fan identity is a collective type of identity that bonds individuals together into a unit. As such, it's usually unstable, with people joining and leaving and perhaps rejoining, shuttling back and forth into the collectivity. It's the kind of *social identity* that Harris and Parker have in mind when they refer to negotiating boundaries: sport provides lines of demarcation that enable us to think of ourselves as on the inside, with all others outside. The meaning of being inside might be assembled through a combination of memory, fantasy, and myth, but, as long at it unifies individuals into a group, it remains a potent force.

The 2009 film *The Firm* (directed by Nick Love) makes us privy to the double-life of London anti-hero Bex, who earns a living charming customers into buying houses, but articulates his salient identity when he puts on his Ellesse tracksuit and becomes a baseball bat-wielding, head-butting West Ham United fan who relishes a "meet" with rival fans.

Some scholars, such as Bradley J. Cardinal, and Marita K. Cardinal, have researched what they call *exercise identity*, describing how committed gym-goers build exercising into their self-concepts (see also Anderson and Cychosz, 1995). It's an odd thought: sport and, for that matter, exercise as, to use Harris and Parker's phrase, "the crucible in which many young male (and female) identities are forged" (2009: 172). Not just young either: all ages, all abilities, all over the world; sport is an all-purpose source of identities.

Why? Because life's too predictable

Life has deficiencies. Sports are a way of compensating for those deficiencies. He might not have been the first scholar to notice this, but A. A. Brill (1874–1948) was the first to organize an argument around the observation in 1929.

"The why of a fan" is the title of Brill's classic article published in the *North American Review*. "Life organized too well becomes monotonous; too much peace and security breed boredom; and old instincts, bred into the very cells of the body. . .still move the masses of normal men," argued Brill (1929: 431).

Brill wrote in terms of the "restrictions of modern life" depriving people of their "activity and scope, the triumphs and *réclame*" which were achievable through physical prowess under "more primitive conditions" (*réclame* means renown or notoriety – what we'd now regard as celebrity, as we'll see in Chapter 17*)*. In explaining the fans' attraction to sports, Brill exposed what he took to be a dark truth about human nature; he described the human being as "an animal formed for battle and conquest, for blows and strokes and swiftness, for triumph and applause" (1929: 434).

As the civilizing process and rise of governing states removed the necessity for physical struggle and modernity brought with it order, stability, and security, so the nasty and brutish qualities were made superfluous – but not irrelevant. They were of great use in sports. The sports that began to take shape in the middle of the nineteenth century required physical prowess. Of course, not everyone could excel in physical activities; but the ones who couldn't, were able to identify with those who could.

In Brill's view, this enabled them to recover something resembling their natural state: they could "achieve exaltation, vicarious but real" and be "a better individual, better citizen." Sports, or at least its precursors, actually contributed to building a better citizenry for the modern nation state.

Improbable as Brill's argument might have been as a total theory of sports, it offered a timeless insight about the drabness and uniformity ushered in by modernity, which is often thought to have begun in the Enlightenment of the eighteenth century and had effects across all facets of society – as we will see. One of the effects of the modern effort to bring shape and coherence to human affairs was that life became more directed, more patterned, and more predictable.

BOX 1.1 MODERNITY

From the Latin *modernus*, meaning "just now," modernity refers to the state of the present and recent times, a period beginning, according to some, in the 1500s. The scientific revolution of the seventeenth century, the Enlightenment of the eighteenth, and the industrial revolution of the late eighteenth and early nineteenth centuries instigated changes that brought an age in which modern values predominated. Modernity was characterized by a confidence in scientific knowledge and the explanatory power of theories (such as those of Darwin, Freud, and Einstein), a decline in the social importance of religion and the emergence of a more secular culture (i.e. more worldly rather than sacred), and a striving toward universal standards, absolute principles, and uniformity. The bureaucracy exemplified modern life: a large organization run by a central administration, it operated on rational rules and hierarchies and became a slogan for sameness, lack of imagination, and an absence of spontaneity.

The German social theorist Max Weber (1864–1920) used the term *calculability* to capture the ethos of modern bureaucracy; he meant that the workings of the complex organizations that had proliferated all around him (he was writing around 1904–20) strained towards regulation. Their rules and procedures were designed to minimize the intrusion of the personal emotions or whims of those who administered its policies. As a result, the performance of a bureaucracy was highly predictable. (We'll return to Weber's theories in Chapter 5.)

Once the applicable regulations and procedures are known, it's possible to calculate exactly how a bureaucracy is going to deal with a matter and predict the likelihood of a certain kind of outcome. So bureaucracies stabilize a society, order its policies, regulate its citizens and make it reliably predictable. All this makes for a rational and smooth-running society. It also affects the mentality of the people who live in such a society.

Calculability is an organizing principle in all contemporary societies, apart from those in the throes of upheaval. Spontaneity and randomness may be pleasant diversions but, in large doses, they can prove disruptive and threaten the citizenry's sense of security. Still, there's a residual attraction in the unplanned, surprise happening; everyone knows the pleasant sensation of an unexpected gift or a turn of events that are completely unexpected. On an occasional basis, surprises are fine; were they to invade our working, or public lives, they would lead to disruption and, possibly, disorientation.

In the main, we try to confine the fascination for the unpredictable to our private lives. Office workers can approach their daily tasks with a strangulating regard to rationality and precision. Once out of the office, they might retreat to the tumult of home where chaos, clutter, and utter confusion reigns. One set of the rules for work, but another for home.

The separation of life into public and private spheres is itself a product of the modern age. It has the advantage of allowing the individual to compensate in one sphere for the tensions and frustrations that build up in the other. How many of us have quietly boiled in rage during a lecture or at work? We might keep a lid on it, but explode once we're in a different context. Most of us experience bureaucracies, if only indirectly, and, equally, most of us have been irritated or angered by them; but we typically don't scream or assault people. Instead, we find outlets for these emotions elsewhere – like in sports.

Kicking or throwing balls, riding horses in a circle or inflicting damage on others might look like irrational pursuits. But, that's precisely the point: whether watched or performed, they guide the participant clear of the formal limits of bureaucracies and into areas where the outcome of situations are wholly unpredictable; the opposite of bureaucracies.

For all of the layer-on-layer of organization that sports have acquired, especially in recent years, the actual sporting activity has retained one special nucleus: *indeterminacy*. You can never predict the result with unerring success. That is, unless the result is fixed; but then it ceases to be a genuine sport and becomes a fake or just plain theater. The indeterminate qualities of sports make them constant challenges to the bureaucratic spirit of predictability. The result of a competition can never be determined in advance, even when the odds overwhelmingly favor one party over another. Athletic competition is an area where fairytale endings occasionally do come true. Every underdog has a shot at winning.

In a world in which certainty has become the norm, uncertainty is a prized commodity. And, of course, sports are commodities in the sense that they are packaged, visually moving, and colorful displays that excite our senses. Not that they would excite us if their outcomes were known ahead of schedule: contrast the rush of watching an event as it happens to watching a tape delay transmission once the result is known. It's not knowing what will happen that makes sports attractive. They can't be determined, their outcomes are uncertain and, calculate as we may, the formbook will never tell us what is going to happen once the competition begins.

Bureaucracy predominates in most countries where there are organized sports and the shift from goods producing to service economies promises no significant reduction in organization and standardization. As economies develop, so do sports and, for that matter, religion, education, science and many of the other important institutions that have been subject to bureaucratic imperatives.

The irony here is that, while sports are exciting because of their separation from other parts of life, the organizations that govern and administer sports have increasingly reflected those other parts. For example, sports have accumulated their own bureaucracies and some of their policies have resulted in administrative decisions that seem to go against the grain of sports. Boxing champions have had their title stripped from them without even fighting in the ring; European soccer teams have been made to play games behind locked doors with no fans allowed in. Track athletes are suspended for taking products bought over the counter of a pharmacy to ease nasal congestion.

We might rail against the rulings, but most sports have become so vast that they need complex, bureaucratic organizations to function effectively and policies to maintain continuity. Imagine the amount of intricate organization and planning that goes into an event like the four-week World Cup championship, or the summer Olympic Games, both of which occur every four years.

Even the day-to-day activities of sports performers have come to resemble those of other workers. Divisions of labor; deadlines; monotonous regimes; computer-enhanced analyses: these are all elements of work that have infiltrated sports. Much of sports today is routine and predictable. But not everything: the uncertainty that hangs over the actual competitive matchup can never be eliminated. Nor can the inspiration, innovation, vision, and moments of bravura skill that emerge in the competitive encounter. These are like lightning bolts that interrupt an otherwise continuous skyline. The unpredictability of sports provides an agreeable, perhaps even necessary, divergence from the certainty that prevails in much of our everyday lives.

At safe distance

The British writer Howard Jacobson has offered a short but provocative account of our fascination with sports. Like Brill, he relies on a primitive model of the human being as engaged in a sort of struggle against the civilizing influences of contemporary life. Sport is an outlet for our lust for killing, "the aestheticization of the will to murder," as Jacobson calls it in his article "We need bad behaviour in sport, it's the way to win" (in the *Independent*, June 6, 1998).

Jacobson appeals to Darwin's theory of natural selection: he believes that life is itself a form of competition, though human society cannot function on a win-at-all-cost principle. So, we've devised manners, customs, protocols, the patterns of restraint by which we live in civil society. "Which is why we have invented sport," writes Jacobson.

Our primary instincts incline us toward competition in order to survive yet civil society forces us to curb those instincts or at least channel them into "the means whereby we can obey our primary instinct to prevail while adhering to the artificial forms of civilized behaviour." Jacobson goes on: "We watch sport in the hope that we may see someone die, or failing that, humiliated. We give up our weekends to witness rage, violence, unreason . . . to be part of the unrelenting hysteria of species survival, but at a safe distance."

In other words, it is blood letting by proxy: we let others – the athletes – play out our instinctual impulses. This is why we feel indifferent about some sports performers who are technically good, but "nice," yet we give our hearts to headcases who seem to epitomize the rage we sometimes feel inside us.

On this admittedly extreme view, a pool table or a tennis court, a football field or a baseball diamond is a symbolic killing field; a refined Roman coliseum, where real deaths actually did occur. All fulfill the same function: providing a stage on which one can mount a ritualized Darwinian survival of the fittest. We the spectators are effectively electing others to do the dirty work for us. This makes for an attractive spectacle; murder rendered aesthetically pleasing for the masses.

Jacobson's perspective is open to many objections, not least because it crudely reduces a complex series of activities to a basic survival impulse. Yet, it provides an intriguing starting point for discussion: sports as symbolic expressions of an impelling force that has its sources in our survivalist instincts. If we didn't have sports, we might be still splitting each other's heads open.

Sigmund Freud explained that civilization is a sort of mutilation that the civilized being never completely accepts; the civilized individual unconsciously tries to recover a natural wholeness. It is the pursuit of this wholeness that endangers him or herself as well as others. It is a form of primitive death wish.

We stand as privileged citizens of a world that has taken over a millennium to reduce the despotism, poverty, ignorance, and barbarity that were features of primitive cultures. But, on this view, we've renounced some part of our natural selves. We'll see in later chapters how the conversion from barbarity to civilized culture has formed the basis of more elaborate and sophisticated theories of sport.

Both perspectives covered so far consider that life has become too organized and too laden with rules for our own good. There is something primeval inside us being stifled by the containing influences of modernity. Complementing this is the view that the massive changes wrought over the past two centuries have made life, not only predictable and rule-bound, but also safe.

Of course, there are road deaths, unconquerable diseases, homicides, fatal accidents, and other unseen malefactors lurking in society, especially since 2001. Whether life is safer or less safe as a result, not so much of the September 11 attack as the response to it, remains an unanswered question. One thing is certain: the intricate security arrangements that have developed since that fateful day have been designed to safeguard life rather than expose it to more risk.

Even allowing for 9/11 and its aftermath, our lives are a lot more secure than they were even forty years ago, let alone in the days of barbarism. Of course, we also create new perils, like environmental pollution and nuclear energy plant catastrophes. It seems the more we find ways of minimizing danger in some areas, we reintroduce them into others.

The sociologist Frank Furedi argues that, by the end of the twentieth century, societies all over the world had become preoccupied, if not obsessed, by safety. Risk avoidance became an organizing principle for much behavior. Safety was not something that people could just have: they needed to work toward getting it. So, human control was extended into virtually every aspect of cultural life: nothing that was potentially controllable was left to chance.

The title of Furedi's book *Culture of Fear* describes an environment in which risks are not so much there – they are created. We started to fear things that would have been taken-for-granted in previous times: drinking water; the nuclear family, technology; all came to be viewed as secreting previously unknown perils. Furedi despairs at this "worship of safety," as he calls it. The most significant discoveries and innovations have arisen out of a spirit of adventure and a disregard for perils.

While we avoid risks that lie outside our control, we're quite prepared to take voluntary risks. The so-called "lifestyle risks" such as smoking, drinking, and driving are examples of this. But sports present us with something quite different: manufactured risks that are actually designed in such a way as to preserve natural dangers or build in new ones. Horseracing always contains some risk for both jockey and horse, particularly in steeplechases. Lowering fences would reduce the hazard; but the governing associations have resisted doing so.

On the other hand, boxing, especially amateur boxing, has done its utmost to reduce the dangers that are inherent in combat sports. Yet both sports are fraught with risk and both continue to prosper. According to Furedi's thesis, it is probable that they would continue to prosper with or without safety measures. He cites the example of rock climbing which had some of its risks reduced by the introduction of improved ropes, boots, helmets, and other equipment. Furedi writes: "The fact that young people who choose to climb mountains might not want to be denied the buzz of risk does not enter into the calculations of the safety-conscious professional, concerned to protect us from ourselves."

Furedi is one of a number of writers who have speculated on the rise of what Ulrich Beck calls the *Risk Society* (1992). Beck believes that advances in science and technology have expanded our knowledge not only of how the world works, but of the perils it holds. Many of the perils have actually been fostered by our desire to know more. In other words, many of the anxieties we have have been produced by knowledge not ignorance.

Author of the book *Risk,* John Adams believes we have inside us a "risk thermometer" which we can set to our own tastes, according to our particular culture, or subculture: "Some like it hot – a Hell's Angel or a Grand Prix racing driver, for example; others like it cool . . . But no one wants absolute zero" (1995: 15). We all want to restore some danger to our lives. How we do it is quite interesting: for instance, the same people who go white-water rafting or bungee-jumping will probably steer clear of a restaurant declared unsafe by state sanitary inspectors.

A game of chess or pool might offer no hint of danger, but skiing, surfing, Xtreme sports, and all motor and air sports certainly do. Even sitting in a crowd watching these sports carries a sense of danger. And, if the crowd happens to be at a game of soccer, the danger may be not be just vicarious. The risk in some sports may be tiny; but its presence is what counts; and where it doesn't exist, we invent it.

Seekers for the source of our attraction to sports have found it in the ways culture has changed. Complex industrial societies and the maize of bureaucratic rules and procedures they brought stifled our natural spontaneity and made life too boring, according to Brill. Our primitive urges to do battle were suppressed by the development of civility and good manners in Jacobson's view. And, for others, contemporary life has become organized in such a way as to minimize risks. Sports re-inject these missing elements back into our lives. None of us is willing to sacrifice the benefits of an orderly life in which we are relatively safe and can go about our business without having to wonder what tomorrow will bring. At the same time, we need activities that give vent to what some writers believe to be natural impulses.

It seems that humans are bored: they yearn for the uncertainty, risk, danger, life lived because of instinct and passion. Sport provides an occasion for exhibiting the excesses that are prohibited in other aspects of life. It has parallels with the North American Indian Potlatch ceremonies and in the carnivals of the middle ages (in which competitions featured, as we will see in later chapters). Both presented occasions for breaking rules. In particular, the "carnivalesque," written of by Mikhail Bakhtin, presented an occasion for violating rules (1981). The penalties for such offenses would be severe in any other context. The carnival was an escape from ordinary life.

Sports have obviously morphed over the years, but we can still find in them the kinds of escape attempts that inspired early industrial workers in the nineteenth century to enrich their laborious lives by organizing games. Their efforts were gropings toward what we now regard as legitimate sports. Their pursuits were as lacking in purpose as today's sports: they were simple activities enjoyed purely for their own sake. Professionalism has ensured that sports are no longer as simple as that; today's athletes compete for money, gamblers bet for the same reason and there are an assortment of others, including agents, coaches, and owners, whose motives may include a pecuniary element. But, for the overwhelming majority of fans and amateur players, sports still have an *autotelic* quality—the act of competing is the main pleasure. Their function lies in avoiding what we do during the rest of working week.

Sports, at least those of today, have nothing to do with anything at all, certainly not work. They do not resemble anything, represent anything and it does not actually do anything apart from providing a momentary release from other, less pleasurable, facts of life. We savor sports as ends-in-themselves.

Even sports, which appear plain stupid, have stood the test of time and measure up to the strict criteria of sport. There has even been a campaign to have melon-seed spitting in the Olympic program: every August in Le Frechou, France, about 50 well-trained competitors line up for this traditional country contest. Before we dismiss it as a huge prank, we should take note that spitters regularly make distances over 30 feet, suggesting that there is technique involved. While on the subject of distances, the world record for cow-dung throwing is 266 feet. Every year in Beaver, Colorado, championships are held and rules applied (like the "chips," as they are known, being 100 percent organic and non-spherical in shape!). There is even a World Dwarf Throwing Authority that has defied political correctness and still holds its 100-year-old championships in Australia. Wacky they may seem, but they are only as irrational and purposeless as the competitions we take seriously and, in many cases, fight over.

There is symmetry between our enthusiasm for sports and our embrace of other gestures, displays, and even fantasies that have no underlying reference points. We visit theme parks, like DisneyWorld in Florida, and Alton Towers, in England, and surround ourselves with artificial articles that have no reality outside themselves. We decamp to fantastic communities where image is everything. Our voyages into cyberspace can also be seen as flights away from the gray mundanity and toward a lusciously unrestricted universe where former identities are swapped for new ones.

At various points in history, sports have held practical value, military, industrial, and commercial; now sports beckon as a way of restoring excitement. This makes them no less powerful or compelling than they once were. Far from it: sports are more arresting now. As John Hannigan writes in his *Fantasy City: Pleasure and profit in the postmodern metropolis*: "Sports has become a defining part of our life and culture, infusing a wide range of events, activities and institutions . . . professional sports have taken the role of a common cultural currency" (1998: 142).

Cultural currency is an interesting choice of terms. If sport is such a currency, it is exchanged by more people than at any time in history. Sports are watched by more people, turn over more money, and probably bear more responsibility for hope and heartache than ever before. The precise reasons for this remain obscure, but we will reveal them in the chapters to come.

OUTLINE OF THE BOOK

This book should make you wonder: why am I interested in sport? For that matter, you should ask: why is almost everyone I know interested? Fantasy, friendship, feverishness? Sport provides all of these and more: the gratifications are many. Trouble is: this is an answer that springs another question. Why do we find it gratifying? By now, you'll be getting the hang of this book. Every time you respond to one question, there is another "Why?"

In fact, there is always a *how*, *what*, *when*, and *where* too. At the start of this and every subsequent chapter I'll advance a few questions that I intend to answer in the pages that follow. Even then, I hope the reader will find some more questions to ask. The kinetic power of the book is in the readers' curiosity. How? What? When? Where? And above all: Why? Even if you don't find all the answers in this book, you'll acquire the capacity to ask more questions.

The eclectic approach of this book is a little strange; most serious books on sports opt to study it through a single lens. So there is sociology of sport, sports psychology, biology of sport, philosophy of sports, sport history, and so on. But this book has a wider scope. It may not be for purists who prefer a single-subject examination, but my belief is that sport is too old, too substantive, and too pervasive to be understood with a single perspective. Reality-congruent knowledge, as Norbert Elias called it, comes from many sources (I deal with Elias's theory of sport in Chapter 5).

After this introduction, there is a succession of 19 chapters, plus an additional chapter that is available exclusively online. The logic guiding the chapters is simple and systematic: all sports are, when distilled, performance – human actions aimed at accomplishing a task or function. So, the first thing we need to understand is the human being, specifically how humans are different from other animals, why they are capable of behaviors we recognize as skills and what kind of equipment they need to be able to complete the complex actions necessary for competitive pursuits. So the human animal occupies most of the attention for the first four chapters.

Immediately after Chapter 4, there is the first of a series of responses to burning questions, this one being "How old are sports?" The others, which appear at intervals throughout the text, revolve around gay athletes, cheating, gambling, and left-handedness. They are designed to answer questions with evidence, opinion, and rational argument.

One of the questions students and aficionados of sport often ask is: what use is theory? Sport is about practical action, not contemplation. It's a valid question. In Chapter 5, I offer an answer. Theory, as I point out in the chapter, is supposed to enlighten, illuminate, and explain. It should not obscure, bewilder, and make things unintelligible. That applies to sport psychology too.

Often dismissed as over-intellectualized mumbo-jumbo or, at the other extreme, statements-of-the-glaringly-obvious-dressed-up-in-psycho-gobbledygook, sport psychology is actually central to our understanding of organized human competition. In Chapter 6, I explain why a comprehension of, for want of a better word, the mind is so important. But minds don't exist in a cultural vacuum: the reason why much sport psychology elicits sneers is that it focuses too specifically on individuals and not enough on the circumstances in which those individuals operate.

If there is a motif, or recurring theme, in this book, it is this: no understanding of sport, whether historical or contemporary, physical or social, is possible without close attention to the changing contexts in which sport occurs. So, when I move to the analysis of exercise and the fitness culture that gives it meaning and purpose, I am careful not to see exercise in isolation – as an activity that has been around for decades, even centuries and which has been practiced in the same way, for the same reasons by one generation after another. It may surprise many to discover that exercise – certainly in the way we understand it today – is a recent phenomenon and one closely associated with an entire fitness industry that has developed around it.

BOX 1.2 CONTEXT

The circumstances in, or conditions under which an event happens and which assist in fully understanding it. Knowledge of context assists in accounting for and evaluating the meaning of an event. The origins of the term are revealing: from the Latin *contextus,* from *con*, together and, *texere*, to weave, it suggests the reconstruction of something.

Contexts include both time and place and, as such, involve events preceding and following, surrounding objects and people (including their beliefs), and other background factors that are pertinent. The analyst needs to establish what level of context is relevant.

For example, Seymour Feshbach distinguishes between the *interpersonal context*, that is, the immediate situation in which an interaction takes place, *historical context*, meaning the broader background factors that impinge on the interaction, and *dramatic context*, in which "the individual may be alone." We might add that the *global context* is often regarded as being relevant to many events. The term *social context* is used in a variety of ways, but always making reference to the characteristic features of a particular social group, culture, or wider society. These can include all or some of the following: people, values, beliefs, mores, institutions, conventions, and other organized activities specific to a particular place during a particular period.

The group of chapters that follow the "Burning question" feature "Why don't more gay athletes come out?" are about the body: not its structure and functions; these are covered in Chapter 3. But our conceptions of the body and the uses to which it can be put have changed over time. Again, the cultural context in which we experience the body comes to the fore. The body is made of flesh, blood, tissue, and other materials, but that's not all. In Chapter 8, I reveal how our experiences and conceptions of the human body have changed, often dramatically, over the years. Did you know, for example, that the division of the world into men and women based on sex is a relatively new convention? Imagine what it was like when there were no sexes – just people, some of whom could have children, others of whom could not, but no real understanding of why they were different.

The next two chapters concern groups that have been designated minorities – minorities, that is, not in a numerical sense, but in the sense that they haven't had a predominance of authority or decision-making capabilities. The textbook cliché is that sport presents a mirror image of society and, the experience of women historically appears to confirm this. Women have been undervalued and underrepresented in both. But this has changed dramatically since the 1990s to the point where, as I argue, sport has been "emasculated."

When you think of black people and sport, you imagine indomitable champions who have helped define their sports: Muhammad Ali, Michael Jordan, Tiger Woods. So much so that many scholars have been tempted to argue the source of their excellence is natural, rather than cultural. I evaluate this argument in Chapter 10.

Is cheating endemic in professional sports? This is a question that I consider immediately after the chapter and which forms a foundation for the subsequent group of chapters, each of which analyzes a facet of rule breaking. One of the challenges I set readers of this book is to express doubts about orthodoxies. The consensus orthodoxy when analyzing the issue of drugs in sport is that it is wrong. Remember the key question that informs every chapter – why? In Chapter 11, I ask and answer it.

The next cluster of chapters focus on the growing presence of the media in sport, beginning with an overview of how sports have been visualized and represented by artists and filmmakers over the years. This is the start of an understanding of the fascination of sport for people who may never participate in or even attend sports events. These include gamblers, television viewers and, perhaps in the near future, computer screen gogglers. The rationale behind these chapters is that sport is consumed in a number of different ways: various media have delivered a kind of parallel reality in which consumers can enjoy the thrills and gratifications of competition without being proximate to the actual competitive activity.

"If you build it, he will come," somebody must have whispered to a television executive in the 1950s. The saying is from *Field of Dreams*, of course, though it might easily have applied to the sports fan. Build a television capable of transmitting images of baseball, football, boxing or any of the other major sports and he – the fan – will go to it. Most sport today is watched on screens of some sort. Sport has metamorphosed as a result of the media's interest in it: it has changed completely in form and nature. It still evokes excitement, perhaps even more so. But, as we will see, since the 1960s, the media has utterly changed sport.

One of the more recent aftereffects has been the dramatic change in the status of athletes. Once great champions and upholders of hallowed values, they are now celebrities, much like rock stars, or movie actors. They enjoy all the benefits, but inherit the obligations too. In a sense, celebrity athletes have become our property. Chapters 16 and 17 explain how this came about, first by investigating how marketing contributed to sport's rise, and then by exploring how consumers responded. In between the two chapters, there is a final "Burning question," this one pondering whether being left-handed is an advantage in sport.

Can we learn anything from sport? We once thought so. Sport was supposed to contain human verities, true principles of fundamental importance. Its moral code was considered laudable, serving as a desirable model for the rest of society. This sounds like a fairytale; today sport is a cutthroat affair with greedy, devil-may-care competitors doing their utmost, by fair means or foul, to win – at any cost. Too harsh? Possibly. But sport has lost its place as a moral exemplar. This doesn't mean there are no moral lessons to be learned from sport. Chapter 18 discloses some of these lessons.

Here is one of the great paradoxes of sport: it's supposed to remain above and beyond politics, yet is, in its very nature, political. Anyone who believes sport and politics can be kept separate is seriously adrift. Politics is a major presence in sport: even a cursory observation of the sporting landscape reveals the ubiquity of politics in sport. This is both good and bad. Good if spelling out a political message through the medium of sport brings changes that benefit humanity. Bad if lives are lost in the process. Chapter 19 looks at the landscape.

Finally, the book – at least the paper version – closes with a question: what will happen next? In this flashforward chapter, I extrapolate from available data what sport might be like in years to come.

H. G. Wells' delirious blast through future-historical possibilities, *The Time Machine* (1895) has provided me with an organizing device. In the late nineteenth and early twentieth centuries, Wells wrote books that pushed the envelope of technological possibility issuing warnings about the power of science and indeed modernity. I've imagined what Wells might think about sports through the ages. The first we hear of Wells is at the start of the next chapter.

OF RELATED INTEREST

"The why of a fan" by A. A. Brill is still worthy of serious attention, despite its age. Published in the *North American Review,* in 1929, it retains its relevance to our attempts to explain contemporary sports and is full of piercing insights.

Culture of Fear by Frank Furedi (Cassell, 1997) is a strong argument that explains our continuing fascination with danger and may profitably be read in conjunction with Michael Bane's *Over the Edge: A regular guy's odyssey in extreme sports* (Gollancz, 1997) and an interesting study published in the journal *Physician and Sportsmedicine*, "Why do some athletes choose high-risk sports?" by D. Groves (vol. 15, no. 2, 1987). *Risk* by John Adams (UCL Press, 1995), while not about sports, is full of insights about how our obsession with security has created as many problems as it solves.

"Introduction: immersed in media sport" by David Rowe opens the 2nd edition of his *Sport, Culture and the Media* (Open University Press, 2004) and discusses "the extent to which sport has insinuated itself into the warp and weft of everyday life."

Sport Sociology edited by Peter Craig and Paul Beedie (Learning Matters, 2008) and *Sports in Society: Issues and controversies*, 10th edition, by Jay Coakley (McGraw-Hill, 2009) are both texts on sociology of sport, the former taking a British perspective, the latter American. Both cover a wide terrain, including class, gender, the media, and the body. Craig and Beedie's volume also has a chapter on adventure sports.

Sport and Social Identities edited by John Harris and Andrew Parker (Palgrave Macmillan, 2009) is a collection of essays, all exploring the different ways in which participating in or just following sports contributes to the ways we think about ourselves.

Encyclopedia of International Sports Studies edited by Roger Bartlett, Chris Gratton, and Christer G. Rolf (Routledge, 2009) is a multidisciplinary reference work with over 1,000 essays on aspects of sports studies; as such, it makes a valuable resource.

ASSIGNMENT

Reviewing a previous edition of *Making Sense of Sports*, Timothy Chandler, of Kent State University, Ohio, wrote: "I was surprised to find that Cashmore had not attempted to make sense of sports as a ritual sacrifice of human energy" *(Culture, Sport, Society*, vol. 1, no. 1, 1998). Make the attempt.

CHAPTER 2

Back to Nature

KEY ISSUES

▌ How do we decide whether athletes are born or made?

▌ What does the human genome project teach us about sport?

▌ When did *Homo sapiens* appear?

▌ Where do we draw the line between nature and nurture?

▌ Why is the brain our most important piece of sports equipment?

▌ . . . and is it possible to synthesize an athlete genetically, as in the *Species* movies?

BORN OR MADE?

To . . . e.e. cashmore@staffs.edu
From . . . h.g.wells@timemachine.org
Subject: nature or nurture?

Professor Cashmore: I recently stopped off in the late twentieth century and had the opportunity of reading the fourth edition of your book *Making Sense of Sports* in which you make reference to the *Back to the Future* films and venture to imagine what sports might have been like in 1880. Before we continue, I should perhaps point out that in 1898, I wrote a book entitled *The Time Machine,* which was popularly thought to be a work of fiction. You are probably already anticipating that this was not the case: it was based on factual experience. I was visited by a time traveler who had constructed an appliance capable of carrying her through the fourth dimension of time and who kindly allowed me to journey with her, at first to the year 802701, where I made the observations that were recorded in my book.

You can understand why I was so confident about my various predictions, such as lasers, which I describe in *The War of the Worlds* (which was published in 1898), or genetic engineering, which I portray in *The Island of Dr Moreau* (1896). When I wrote

The First Men in the Moon (1901), people thought it was science fiction. You'll have to wait awhile to see – or not see – the inspiration behind *The Invisible Man* (1897)

I have undertaken voyages into the distant future, when the sun no longer shines, and to what is, to you, the recent past. All of which leads me to the point of this communication: why are you still agonizing over what seems to me an unanswerable question – are we products of nature, or are we shaped, influenced, perhaps even determined by our environments? People have been struggling with this since the days of Plato (429–c.347 BCE). There's no such thing as nature, plain and simple. And, in order to talk about an environment, you have to have surroundings and conditions that promote growth and development, and these are ultimately parts of the natural world, aren't they? So maybe the whole nature versus nurture argument is based on a fallacy. Try thinking in terms of nature through nurture and see where this line of argument gets you. I'll write to you again soon, next time with some observations from the future.

Cordially,
H.G.Wells

Since Plato started to muse on the question in the fourth century BCE, scholars have tried to fathom which exerts most influence on us: nature or nurture, genetics or the environment? Thibaud Gruber and his colleagues didn't come up with the answer, but their research offered a new slant on the age-old question. Gruber *et al.* presented two genetically similar groups of wild East African chimpanzees with a simple, but unfamiliar challenge under identical ecological conditions: how to get honey from a hole drilled in a log.

What do you imagine happened? Readers who lean toward the nature view will probably predict that the chimpanzees, being genetically similar, would adapt to the task in exactly the same way. Natural instincts would incline the chimpanzees toward the same response in the same environmental circumstances. Wrong. Chimps from the equatorial Kibale rainforest in western Uganda used sticks to extract the honey, while those from the Budongo forest, 112 miles (180 km) away, opted to use leaves as sponges to soak up the sweet, sticky stuff.

The researchers ruled out basic stimulus and response acquired through trial-and-error. "Our results suggest that chimpanzees rely on their cultural knowledge," concluded Gruber *et al.* (2009: 5). Cultural knowledge is acquired through experiences: it consists of theoretical ideas, practical skills, and an awareness or familiarity gained by practical encounters with and observation of actual situations.

Crucially, it is context-specific, that is, linked to particular communities, fields, or traditions. The chimpanzees in the study applied their cultural knowledge in a way that allowed the researchers to identify how cultural differences influence the behavior of neighbors.

We'll discover later in this chapter that, genetically speaking, we share much more with chimpanzees than most people suspect, though there are still dangers in generalizing from experiments with apes to observations about humans. But we shouldn't cut this research adrift: it suggests a way of approaching the first task of this chapter; to establish whether or not athletes are, as some people propose, naturals. Certainly, some appear to be. Take the case of Usain Bolt.

At 6 feet 5 inches, Bolt seemed too tall to be a sprinter; what's more the casualness of his approach contrasted with the zone-locked concentration of his rivals. Yet, he didn't just cruise to a world 100 meters record in 9.69 seconds: he also ran 200 meters in 19.30 seconds to beat a 12-year world record of 19.32. At 21, Bolt had lowered the 100 meters best time only months before, the incredible feature of this race being that Bolt was running only his fifth 100 meters race. So, at the time of his Olympic feat in 2008, Bolt was, in athletic terms, a novice.

Rational explanations poured out. While traditionally understood as a handicap for sprinters, long limbs might actually confer a mechanical advantage on Bolt, especially when combined with the fast-twitch fibers typically associated with shorter, more compact athletes – mesomorphs.

There are other athletes who seem to have qualities that suit them ideally for a successful career; qualities that might even be seen as wondrous or peculiar, that no amount of training can duplicate in lesser beings. Bernard Malamud's allegorical novel *The Natural* was the story of one such athlete, Roy Hobbes, an invincible baseball player who brandished his bat like King Arthur's Excalibur. Barry Levinson's 1984 movie of the book emphasizes the mythological aspects of the "natural."

The world of fact is not too far away from the world of fiction. Like Bolt, Roger Federer looked naturally suited to his sport, in his case tennis. When in flight, Yelena Isinbaeva appeared to be a natural extension of her pole. Sports history is crowded with athletes who seem to have been born to their sports. Juan Manuel Fangio, who was unbeatable in the 1950s, was acknowledged as the best ever racing driver before the advent of Michael Schumacher, who, many believe, surpassed him. Winning the Tour de France seven times established Lance Armstrong among the crème de la crème of cyclists. In her prime, Martina Navratilova was untouchable on grass, clay, carpet, or hard tennis courts. These performers all appeared so accomplished and superior to their opponents that they just *had* to be as naturally suited to their events as Bolt, it seems, was to sprinting.

BOX 2.1 BODY TYPES

Mesomorph: a person with a compact and muscular body. *Ectomorph*: a person with a lean body. *Endomorph*: a person with a soft round body with a high proportion of fat tissue.

Yet, we're all "naturals" in one way: endowed with some capacity for a sporting activity. Yet, in another way, none of us is natural. Let me explain the apparent contradiction: some people clearly possess great mechanical efficiency and skill in performing certain tasks and will refine these to the point where their expertise appears effortless; so effortless in fact that it appears to be the product of a gift. Federer, for example, swept his racket as fluently as a conductor motioning his baton. Michael Phelps flowed eel-like through water; there appeared to be no great exertion. On closer inspection, their actions, like those of any other athlete were the result of painstaking training rather than inborn ability – though, of course, nature does have a role to play, as we'll soon see.

Rejecting the old adage, "great sportsmen are born, not made" (and the sexism it implies), takes us so far in explaining why certain consummate performers have risen to the top. They have worked harder, have more determination to succeed, are resilient enough to withstand defeat and can get focused at precisely the right time in a competition, that is, in the "clutch."

Yet, athletes are simply not born equal: a 5 foot 4 inch South Korean, no matter how hard he practices throwing hoops, is not going to prove much of a match for LeBron James. A native of Nairobi, who works out over a mile above sea level, will not threaten Lindsey Vonn on the alpine slopes. In the first case, training will simply not provide what genetics has not. In the second, environment prohibits the development of skills that are integral to some sports.

All human beings have some natural ability: sports express this in exaggerated and often extravagant forms. They provide opportunities to wring from our natural mental and physical equipment behavior that deviates dramatically from normal responses. The deviation has, it seems, no limits. Runners, rowers and swimmers cover distances faster and faster; gymnasts perform with staggering technical proficiency; tennis players hit with ever-greater velocity.

Those who can't squeeze such efforts from their bodies – and that's most of us – are often drawn to watch, admire, and be awed by the efforts of others, efforts that sometimes last for only a few seconds. A Guo Jingjing dive from the 3-m springboard, spectacular as it was, took less than 1.5 seconds. Shaquille O'Neal slam-dunked in two seconds tops. Allyson Felix ran 100 meters in the time it takes to start a car. Alex Rodriguez could steal a base while spectators are taking a swig of beer. No matter what the sport, fans will go to great lengths and pay money to witness a human performance that may well be fleeting.

We *learn* to appreciate sports performances, just as competitors learn basic techniques and styles on which they later innovate. The sports fan is like the art critic who acquires a knowledge of what to look for, how to evaluate, the meaning of certain properties, and so on. The athlete needs not just knowledge, but a physical mastery; in other words, a skill. This involves a lengthy and, sometimes, complex process in which he or she is made to call into service devices, ingenuity, and powers that might have gone undiscovered had the athlete not been urged or even forced to develop them. During this time, a sports competitor changes, physically and mentally: he or she learns how to control bodily movements, in many cases calibrating those movements with inanimate objects, like bats and balls.

Looked at this way, sports are learnt. But they're also completely natural: without the basic anatomical and behavioral apparatus, we couldn't perform even the simplest of operations, let alone the more complicated maneuvers need for decent sporting action. There are what we might call limiting "givens" in the physical makeup of humans, just as there are in those of other animals (a given is an established reality, or a certainty).

Humans have succeeded in overcoming all kinds of limitations set by nature, basically by creating and employing technologies. Not that we are totally alone in this: some other species use rudimentary technologies, though not on anything like the scale of humans. Capuchin monkeys, for example, use heavy rocks to crack open large palm nuts. Beavers gather sticks, mud, rocks, and other available materials to make dams, which are integral to their safe environments.

Technology has assisted sports performance and been integrated into most spheres of sports. As artifacts, technologies are manufactured items that we create and use to assist us. Poles help us vault higher, surfboards help us travel across the ocean surface. We monitor the results and modify the technologies, then transmit them to successive generations. This is not only true of sports technologies, of course: we're constantly passing on information about technologies in the effort to improve life.

Our ability to use technology derives from natural abilities: specifically, a brain large and complex enough to imagine a product, movable limbs, and prehensile hands and feet to create and utilize it, and an acute sense of sight to envisage the product and gauge distance. These are not properties unique to humans, but the way in which they're combined in the human species is very particular and is resembled only in other higher primates, namely monkeys and apes. The question is: what is it about the special combination in humans that enables them to develop the potential of their animal nature to levels far removed from those of other species?

BOX 2.2 TECHNOLOGY

Any practical application of knowledge is technology, the word deriving from the Greek *technologia*, meaning systematic treatment of an art or skill, from *technē*, craft, or skill and -ology for a branch of knowledge. Technology provides capability and so assists natural endeavor. Thus technologies do not just extend the capabilities of living organisms that develop them, but create new ones.

Sports, as I will argue in detail later, have only been possible because of such advanced developments; other animals engage in activities that look like sports, but aren't. Pursuing this logic, not only sports but religion, industry, warfare, education, and so on – all conventionally regarded as social institutions – are grounded in our animal origins. The entire discipline of physical (sometimes called biological) anthropology is dedicated to the task of assessing the relative contributions to social life made by heredity and environment.

Different subjects examine the same things, but in different ways. Humanities and social sciences generally find natural science approaches too reductionist in their attempt to break down, or reduce, phenomena into their constituent parts to understand how they work. For example, the sociologist sees the human effort to challenge, manipulate, or transcend the physical and biological facts of life giving rise to distinct patterns of thought and behavior. These are cultural patterns and can't be explained by reference to biological factors alone. The interaction between human beings and their natural environments results in events and processes that defy explanation in purely biological terms.

Between the two extremes, there's a whole range of diverse attempts to describe and analyze human behavior, each with its own version of why we do the things we do. In the course of this book, I'll consider several of them and assess what contributions they may make to our comprehension of just one element – sports.

BOX 2.3 REDUCTIONISM

This is a method for analyzing phenomena based on the philosophy that matter is best understood once divided into its component parts. So, human societies can be approached in terms of individual beings, who, in turn, may be reduced to genes, which, in turn, may be reduced even further, and so on. In other words, complex wholes can only be fully understood by isolating their parts. Critics argue that the "sum of the parts" is frequently not the same as the "whole" and that there are *emergent* qualities produced when all the elements come together; these are distinct and need to be analyzed in terms of the whole. "How can one understand something like fashion by reducing it to its constituent parts?" they might ask, adding that it becomes meaningful as fashion only when people act together in a collectivity, however loosely assembled. This approach is known as holism.

SEVEN KEYS

Stripped to their bare elements, human beings are mobile, multi-celled organisms that derive their motive force from eating other organisms. In taxonomic terms, humans are *Animalia*, as distinct from members of the plant kingdom, these being bacteria, single-celled organisms, and fungi. So, we have a great many characteristics in common with other animals, especially those with whom we share common ancestors, our closest evolutionary relatives being other primates, a taxon that includes monkeys, apes, lemurs, tarsiers, and others (a taxon is the unit of classification used in biology).

There are seven key characteristics of primates that set them apart from the rest of the living world and afford them special advantages for survival. Humans have extra-special advantages, but, for the moment, we'll focus on similarities. The seven features are: an ability to grip and control; relatively great strength of limb; stereoscopic eyes positioned at the front of the head; small numbers of offspring; a high degree of interdependence and a corresponding tendency toward living in groups; a use of reliable, efficient communication systems; and a large brain relative to body size. Now, let's deal with each of these key characteristics in more detail.

Grip

All primates have prehensile hands and feet: they can catch, grip, and hold, thanks to relatively long, flexible digits. The ability to grip and control is enhanced by opposable thumbs or big toes which make it possible to lock around objects rigidly and so control an object's movement, as a golfer carefully guides the arc of a club's swing. From an evolutionary point of view, the origins of prehensility (the capability for grasping) are not difficult to trace: distinguishing primates from other mammals was their tree-dwelling capacity. Prehensile hands and feet were useful for climbing up and down and to and from trees in forests, and additionally for plucking fruits and berries and overturning stones to pick up insects to eat.

The ability to grip is complemented by a strong versatile set of forelimbs. Suspending full body weight and swinging needs extremely powerful, long arms and legs. The very specialized functions of arms and legs for primates are reflected not only in the size and heavy muscle of the limbs, but in their range of movement: they can flex (bend), extend, and rotate. Combined with the dexterity of the hands and feet this assists fast, multidirectional travel sometimes over great distances. Gymnasts offer examples of how this ability has not been completely lost despite the human's transition from the trees to the ground.

Stereoscope

Related to this mobility is the position of the eyes, which are typically to the front rather than the sides of the head. Two eyes enable stereoscopic vision that permits reasonably accurate estimates of distances. The sense of vision is highly developed in primates, as opposed to, say, dogs which see the world in monochrome, but have sensitive snouts and use their acute sense of smell as their chief source of information about their environments. It's no accident that no sport is based on smelling or sniffing ability, whereas a great many are organized around the ability to gauge distance and coordinate hand movements accordingly: archery and shooting being obvious examples. (It seems feasible to imagine that if humans were sensitive to smell we might have devised a sport in which an acute sense of smell was employed in conjunction with other capacities; a modified form of orienteering perhaps.) We'll return to the human capacity for making and using tools and technology in the concluding chapter.

Small families

With other primates, humans share a tendency to give birth to one or two infants at a time; larger births are known, of course, but they are deviations from the norm. Mammals that have large litters lose some offspring at, or shortly after, birth. Primates have a smaller number of births, usually after a relatively long pregnancy, and accentuate the role of the mother in caring for and protecting the infant in an environment uncomplicated by the kind of competition that comes from large litters.

Interdependence

One very important consequence of having small families with intense mother–infant contact is that primates learn interdependence. They rely on each other far more than members of many other species, which are abandoned at a young age and learn to adapt and survive individually, or else perish. Primates, by contrast, never learn the skills associated with lone survival. Having a protective mother, the infant has no need of such skills. What an infant does acquire is an ability to cooperate and communicate with others. And this helps explain why primates spend their lives in groups, caring for and cooperating with others.

Gregariousness

Individual survival for humans as well as other primates is a matter of communicating effectively in groups. So, all primates are gregarious: they grow and mature socially and not in isolation. Sports reflect this; most activities are organized in terms of a club structure with high degrees of interdependence and mutual cooperation needed. Even the famously lonely long-distance runners need coaches to plan their training and other competitors to make their racing meaningful.

Communication

A lifetime spent in the company of others on whom one has to depend for survival necessitates a high degree of communication. The process of inculcating communication skills begins with the passing of auditory, visual, and tactile (touch) signals from mother to infant. It continues through life; in fact, group life is contingent on the successful storage and transmission of large volumes of information. At its simplest level, the warning conveys perhaps the single most important communication for survival. The human cry of "Fire!" imparts much the same effect as a screech of a panicking baboon. In both cases, the first communicator supposes the recipients have some facility for recalling the image of impending danger.

Big brains

It seems that the necessity of communicating and the ability to do so quickly and efficiently has a connection with the large size of the brain of the primate compared to other mammals. Human beings have the largest brains and are clearly the most adept at communicating. They are, as a direct result, most developed socially. A growth in the size of the human brain can be traced back to two periods. The first, between 1.6 and 2 million years ago, witnessed a rapid expansion in cranial capacity, a change that accompanied the origin of what we now call *Homo erectus* (probably in Africa) and the use of new types of primitive tools. Bipedalism emerged as a result of a transference from the trees to the ground; the change in habitat necessitated a behavioral adaptation in posture and, eventually, an anatomical change of great significance, particularly in relation to arms and hands which were no longer employed to suspend the body and could be used for many other purposes, like making tools, building, and generally shaping the material environment to suit one's own purposes – often using technologies to do so.

Anthropological evidence suggests that the size of the typical skull then remained stable for about 1.3 million years, before a second, sudden, increase in brain size. The appearance of *Homo sapiens* (which, in Latin, means wise man) about 0.2 or 0.3 million years ago was followed by a burst of cultural change in the spheres of manufacture, settlement, and subsistence. This is important, as there is much contention about the precise relationship between the growth of what is now the human brain and changes in habitat and activity. What is absolutely certain is that there is some form of close relationship, though the direction and way in which it worked is still in dispute. Let me expand on this.

The idea of a spontaneous expansion is not supportable. More plausible is a scenario in which the actual size of the brain after the advent of *Homo erectus*, who appeared between 1.8 and 0.3 million years ago, stayed the same, but the number of brain cells and neural pathways between them continued to increase. This made it possible for *Homo erectus* to become a more effective bipedal hunter and gatherer, operating at the time of day when other predatory creatures (and, therefore, competitors) were sheltering from the intensely hot midday sun.

Growing extra brain cells, in this interpretation, was a defense mechanism against the harmful effects of the sun's rays on the brain; that is, the humans grew bigger brains, leaving many of the cells redundant, as mere "fail safe" devices in the tropical heat. (There are other explanations, which we'll consider in Chapter 4.) This might well have established a neural potential for more sophisticated communication and imaginative thought, which, in turn, stimulated a phase of modifying physical environments rather than adapting to them. The phase marks the beginning of sports, as we'll see later in Chapter 4. One often hears of triathletes, who swim, cycle, and run for seven hours or more, sometimes in hot atmospheres, described as "mad." Ironically, they may be demonstrating the extraordinary adaptive brilliance of the human brain in acquiring an ability to function effectively all day in extreme climates. The adaptation dates back to *Homo erectus's* pursuit of game animals.

THE HUMAN EDGE: LANGUAGE

The human brain is the organ responsible for the difference between *Homo sapiens* and the rest of *Animalia*. The enlarged neural capacity introduced the possibility of ever-more elaborate forms of communication. The physiology of the human ear and vocal tract meant that audible messages could be sent with a high probability that they would be received with reasonable efficiency. These elements, combined with the enhanced capacity for imaginative thinking, laid the foundations for human language and, by implication, new systems of word-associated thought.

Language assists the accumulation of information to be stored in the brain and confirms the awareness that other humans have similar stores of information. At the blandest level, we might ask how a game of hockey would be possible unless the players were cognizant of the rules and aware that all other players had the same knowledge. Any sport has the same prerequisite. Without language or, at least, some derivative communication system, abstract rules wouldn't be possible; so there would be no sports.

Humans aren't alone in being able to pass on knowledge from one generation to another and so perpetuate cultures, but they have the special ability to add to, or recreate, cultures whereas other primates merely inherit and receive. A verbal language as opposed to sign-based systems of communication makes this possible. Culture, we should note, refers to anything acquired and transmitted by learning and not by physical inheritance. While other animals most certainly maintain recognizable cultures, even higher apes are quite limited in their capacity to communicate and, as a result, do not pass on a vast amount of experience to new generations. The transmission has to be direct and immediate (for example, modeling and imitation); apes lack the linguistic capability to standardize, encode, classify, and concentrate meanings and experience.

BOX 2.4 CULTURE

From the Latin *cultivara (terra)*, meaning land suitable for growth, this is often used in contrast to *nature* and refers to the learned traditions that are acquired socially and appear among mammals – especially primates. Human culture means the lifestyle of a group of people, including their repetitive, patterned ways of thinking, behaving, and even feeling. These ways are picked up through learning processes rather than through natural inheritance. The anthropologist Edward B. Tylor (1832–1917), in his classic text *Primitive Culture* (first published in 1871), proposed a definition of human culture that included "knowledge, belief, art, morals and habits acquired by man as a member of society." This is a very inclusive definition and others prefer to restrict the use of "cultural" to refer to rules for thought and behavior, the ways those rules are put into practice, and the manner in which they are represented or portrayed. Many contemporary scholars emphasize the human capacity to *represent* experiences through symbols, i.e. material objects endowed with meaning. A symbol is something that represents or stands for something else. While other animals can emulate, humans externalize thoughts and emotions through representations and so have a capacity to learn and adapt through signs as well as imitation or rote.

By contrast, humans can transmit sometimes quite abstract meanings through several generations without any significant loss of informational accuracy. Ancient Greeks, as we will see in the next chapter, left a largess of information about themselves in the form of inscriptions, mostly on walls or clay tablets. A comprehension of these inscriptions tells us that the Greeks pursued athletics in a recognizable, rule-governed form more than any other ancient culture. Language, which articulates this information, is such that we can actually use it to project into the future.

A future tense permits the communication of imaginative schemes and the transmission of such activities as sport. The unique elements of human language that provide for this type of knowledge of ancient cultures almost certainly arise from our genetic adaptations related to social cooperation and interdependence and changing patterns of subsistence. We have the neural equipment for picking up language; that much is clear. Less clear is the reason for the bewildering diversity of human cultures. Our biological equipment scarcely changes at all over time and space; languages, customs, religions, laws, etc. vary greatly from society to society and from one time period to another.

The suggestion is that, once acquired, the developed language, and the new styles of thought it ushers in, launches its users into all manner of trajectories. Humans plan and create complex organizations and institutions of a quite different quality and order than those found among other animals. Obviously these elaborate phenomena are ultimately dependent on biological factors; but their accomplishment can't be exclusively traced to biological equipment and inheritance. The often extraordinary transformations in human performance engendered by an inspirational coach, for example, remind us that we should approach biology as a license not a limit.

My prehensility and neural circuitry make it possible for me to write this book, but there are countless other non-physical influences on my ability and disposition to write – and on your willingness to read. The very concept of a book to be produced and used reflects an extremely sophisticated and unique level of communication. Books are needed for records, and records have been vital to the evolution of sport. Any balanced comprehension of sports clearly needs a range of scientific approaches: one "-ology" isn't enough. We must refer to hereditary nature; equally, though, we must examine environmental life experience, how organisms react to physical conditions surrounding them. Between the gene and the environment there are all sorts of intervening factors and processes that must be studied if we are to reach an understanding.

BOX 2.5 NATURAL SELECTION

The process in which forms of life that possess characteristics that make them better adapted to environmental pressures (such as predators, climates, or competition for food) tend to survive, reproduce, increase in number, and so transmit and perpetuate their characteristics to succeeding generations. Those that can't adapt to the environment perish and become extinct. Hence the process is often known as "survival of the fittest" – fittest, in this sense, meaning the ability to effect a successful adaptation to environments. So, natural selection is the primary mechanism for evolution. First presented by Charles Darwin (1809–82) in classic works *On the Origin of the Species* (1859) and *The Descent of Man* (1871), the theory of evolution suggests that change is gradual, taking place over thousands or millions of years. The theory also contends that the millions of species that have survived arose from a single original life form, which then branched off and formed new and distinct species – a process called *speciation*.

The biological characteristics, which distinguish humans from other animals – bipedalism, prehensility, large and more complicated brains, and language – are necessary conditions for culture building. Necessary, but by no means sufficient. Yet in recognizing this, we must at least begin our analysis of sports with a scenario: creative human beings striving to satisfy at least the minimal requirements for subsistence while subjected to the physical constraints imposed by their own biology and the material world around them. Their primary needs are to produce food, shelter, tools, and to reproduce human populations. Unless they can complete these tasks, they will have no opportunity to believe in religions and ethics, create political and economic systems, engage in war, or perform any of the other activities associated with culture. These activities, almost by definition, depend to some extent on genetically predetermined capacities. But, what does "to some extent" actually mean?

GENOME: NATURE VIA NURTURE

We know that we share many characteristics with chimpanzees and other apes, but it's still a bit of an indignity to be reminded that we are about 98 percent the same. Well in one sense, anyway: we share that amount of genetic material. Of course, the genetic bits we don't share are important, though perhaps not important enough to account for the colossal differences between apes and humans.

In nearly every cell of every living organism there is a complete set of instructions for creating that organism and regulating its cellular structures and activities over a lifetime. The set of instructions is called a *genome*. Imagine the genome as a vast library inside which there were once thought to be thousands and thousands of units called genes. Genes themselves are sequences of deoxyribonucleic acid, which is usually

BOX 2.6 GENETIC TERMS

Gene: unit of heredity that is transferred from parent to offspring and determines some of the characteristics of the offspring.

Chromosome: threadlike structure of nucleic acids and protein that carries the genetic information in the form of genes. Each chromosome consists of:

DNA: self-replicating material present in nearly all organisms, this consists of two strands coiled around each other to form a double helix;

Genome: the complete set of genes or genetic material present in an organism or cell;

XX/XY: humans have 22 pairs of chromosomes plus 2 sex chromosomes – 2 X chromosomes in females (XX) and 1 X and 1 Y (XY) in males.

abbreviated to DNA, and this is like two rubbery ladders twisted together to form a spiral. It's called the "double helix" and there are about 3.5 billion of them in the human genome. To get some idea of the size of DNA, think of the genome library as 100 miles wide and the DNA as the size of a filament of a spider's cobweb in the corner of a shelf. If human DNA was uncoiled and stretched out, it would measure six feet.

Genes themselves are units in the thread-like structure known as the chromosome and they carry the instructions for producing proteins. Proteins perform a variety of physiological functions, such as facilitating digestion, breathing, immune responses, and the movement of fluids. Most members of a species have the same collection of genes, differences resulting from very slight variations in the sequences of nucleotides. Your own DNA will probably be only 0.1 percent different from the person closest to you. So: chromosomes carry the genes, which are arranged into sequences of DNA, all housed in the genome, which is the total complement of DNA genes.

Mention of genes returns us to the eternal question with which we opened this chapter? Genetic reductionists favor the nature argument, believing that our genes fix the instructions for our development. Genes have been discovered that are allegedly responsible for all manner of human conditions, ranging from intelligence to alcoholism. Some even claim that there is a "gay gene." Following this line of thought, we'd be drawn to the conclusion that we could theoretically isolate genes that determine attributes that lead to sporting excellence, such as muscular strength or speed. We'll return to this idea shortly.

The DNA double helix was discovered in 1953 by Francis Crick and James Watson and, following the discovery, it was widely assumed that the DNA was a kind of absolute monarch of inherited development: its rule was total. The assumption reduced inheritance, a property that only living things possess, to molecular dimensions. What we look like, what we do and, indeed, who we are were seen as the product of inherited traits and DNA genes had unique, complete control over that inheritance. If the suspected 100,000 or so genes stitched into 23 pairs of chromosomes that were thought to make up the genome act as a script for the body to make proteins, then nature rather than nurture, or upbringing, seemed to make the decisive contribution to directing, or shaping us.

The surprise was that, 25 years later, further research revealed that the human genome was not as chock-full as imagined: we have only around 30,000 or 40,000 genes – about twice as many as a worm or a fly and only about six times as many as baker's yeast. In terms of genetic profile, we humans were found to be astonishingly similar: every human being on the planet was 99.9 percent the same – and 98 percent the same as chimps, of course. Yet, the evidence of our senses tells us that there is an overwhelming diversity among the human population, a diversity that manifests culturally as well as psychologically and physically; and, of course, we're very different from chimps.

The Human Genome Project began as an attempt to decode the more than three billion letters of the complete human genome. What it showed was that there are far too few human genes to account for the complexity of our inherited traits or for the huge inherited differences between people and other life forms, even plants. In this sense, the project delivered a body blow to the nature thesis, offering fresh hope to the proponents of nurture. As Barry Commoner puts it in his article "Unraveling the DNA myth": "There are far too few human genes to account for the complexity of our inherited traits or for the vast inherited differences between plants, say, and people" (2002: 39).

Genetic engineers were less concerned about the philosophical implications of the breakthrough and more concerned with what could be done with genes. They sought to modify an assortment of life forms, including a rhesus monkey that carried the gene of luminescent jellyfish (which made it glow), pigs with bovine growth hormone, a mouse with a human ear and, perhaps most famously, Dolly, the fatherless sheep who was cloned from her mother's cells. Why not introduce a gene for muscular development into an aspiring sprinter, or even clone another Muhammad Ali from the DNA of the Greatest? These are questions some geneticists pondered, though, obviously, the more immediate questions revolved around how to screen for and control disease-causing variant genes.

Of the more fantastical and maybe nightmarish applications was the attempt to synthesize DNA, as in *Species* movies, in which a scientist does exactly this, downloading information on the sequencing from extraterrestrial sources and creating a fast-maturing athletic female. Escaping the confinement of the lab, she goes in search of a mate and develops the upsetting habit of killing every man who fails to live up to her exacting standards. Used more beneficially, genes, whether real or, as in the movie, manufactured, could be introduced into the body like a rescue squad to help the body fight a faulty gene that causes, for example, cancer, Huntington's disease, or premature Alzheimer's. Duchenne muscular dystrophy, a fatal wasting disease,

BOX 2.7 GENETIC ENGINEERING

The deliberate modification of the characteristics of a life form by manipulating its genetic material has been made possible by scientific advances, though the ethical issues rising out of the science have not been settled. While it's fanciful to think about shopping for children in a genetic supermarket or designing people the way we design cars, it's likely that we will develop the ability to make changes in the human genome that may significantly affect the physical and mental health, opportunities and life prospects of future generations. Identifying the gene(s) responsible for inherited diseases and removing them is one application that typically meets with approval. Introducing genes responsible for the development of a desired trait is more controversial. Something similar has been tried before. Eugenics describes the production of human (or other animal) offspring by the improvement of inherited qualities and was popularized in the nineteenth century by Francis Galton (1822–1911). *Eu* is Greek for well or good. While eugenics was practiced in Europe and the United States through sterilization programs (to remove the genes of those thought to be mentally deficient, criminally inclined, dangerously ill, etc., from future populations), it was used by Nazi Germany to justify the killing of whole categories of persons.

was among the targets for the technique. The more people learn about genes, the greater their chances of isolating them and controlling them. There is another sci-fi movie that explores the consequences of this: Andrew Niccol's 1997 *Gattaca*, in which perfect health is the norm and those with physical imperfections are consigned to an underclass.

Genetic enhancement, which has the aim of improving physical health, appearance, mental, or athletic abilities, is one consequence of the genetic discoveries of recent decades. Another is the recognition of the inadequacy of trying to explain overall human development by reference only to genes. If we humans are so genetically close to other life forms, say, dogs, which share about 95 percent of our genome, why do we turn out to be so different? The differences are obvious and pronounced, leading to the strong suspicion that they aren't caused solely by genetic dissimilarities. Then what?

Matt Ridley has remarked: "The more we lift the lid on the genome, the more vulnerable to experience genes appear to be" (2003b: 59). He suggests dumping the age-old nature versus nurture dispute and replacing it with *Nature via Nurture*. Genes don't determine our development any more than PowerPoint or Mozilla Firefox determine what our computers can do. They actually enable us to develop, like the computer applications enable us to open more files, search websites, check email and so on. So, the metaphor of genes as supplying a set of instructions is misleading, according to Ridley; they make things happen, but don't decide how they happen. Nature works by way of the cultural circumstances in which we find ourselves – which is why Ridley prefers *via* (meaning through) instead of *versus* (which is Latin for against, or toward).

When it comes to talent, athletic or any kind, Ridley argues that the original genetic differences between us may be very slight. "Practice has done the rest." This might seem as if he is heading full-tilt for nurture, but here's the twist: the appetite for nurturing talent may itself be an instinct, that is, something natural, in the genes. A young schoolgirl might discover she is usually more accurate when throwing a ball at a target than her peers and this intensifies her desire for throwing the ball. She enjoys demonstrating her pre-eminence and practices; her throwing improves, which intensifies her appetite even further. So, although her initial edge over others was small, it becomes considerable after practice. But, that practice itself may depend on an instinct that dictates that, as Ridley puts it: "Enjoy doing what you are good at; dislike doing what your are bad at."

Ingenious as this argument is, it's not provable. Still, it suggests a way of recognizing the crucial part played by cultural factors without dismissing the role of genes in making us. Athletes are often described as talented or multi-talented, meaning they are highly proficient in a particular skill or set of skills. While the term talented might once have been used uncritically to suggest a genetic basis for skill, we now have the knowledge to recognize that genes provide only the potential for achievement, often called *aptitude*. Converting that potential into actual capacity, or capability (both meaning undeveloped faculty) and eventually skill depends on the routine performance of the skill – practice makes perfect. That inclination to practice may itself be genetically based, as Ridley argues. Maybe nature/nurture is not such a puzzle after all.

Extending the *Species* scenario, we might imagine a top coach who receives mysterious information through his email that describes the genome of an unknown organism. With the help of friendly genetic engineers, he helps synthesize the DNA described in the messages and the resulting creature turns out to be a ringer for Pelé, the Brazilian player widely credited as being the best of all time. Test results show that the newly created organism is genetically the same as the great soccer player. The thrilled coach takes him out on the practice field, tosses him a ball, only to see him fall clumsily to the ground in his awkward attempt to trap it. The creation may have Pelé's genes, but he doesn't have his upbringing in the streets of Brazil, his motivation to succeed, his determination to overcome serious injuries, or any of the other social and psychological experiences that affected his eventual ability to play soccer.

Nature operates through nurture. Every gene has potential, but it's only that – potential. Whether it will realize that potential depends on what it's allowed to do, by other genes, the rest of the cell, the body and, crucially, the entire physical and social environment at large.

The Human Genome Project confirmed what we already know: that we are all natural. But, it also disclosed something else: we're not *just* natural; there are a great many other factors involved in making us human. While its remit wasn't to explain sporting prowess, the project actually reminded us of the limits of biology and necessity of bringing history, culture, and the whole gamut of other forces that affect human development.

OF RELATED INTEREST

Culture, People, Nature: An introduction to general anthropology, 7th edition, by Marvin Harris (Addison-Wesley, 1997) is an introduction to general anthropology and a model of clarity. Harris favors a materialist approach, which complements the one taken in this book. His view is that the shaping of thought and behavior is the outcome of adaptations to ecological conditions. Taking a Darwinian starting point, Harris argues: "As a result of natural selection, organisms may be said to become adapted to the needs and opportunities present in their environments." And further: "All individuals are the products of the interaction of their genes and their environment." More extreme versions of materialism would insist that thought and behavior can be understood by studying the constraints to which human existence is subjected; these constraints arise from the need to produce food, shelter, tools, and machines, and to reproduce human populations within the limits set by biology and the environment. Harris replies to critics of his approach in *Theories of Culture in Postmodern Times* (AltaMira, 1998).

So Human an Animal: How we are shaped by surroundings and events by Rene Dubos (Transaction, 1998) is, as its subtitle suggests, an argument about how our human "nature" is something of a misnomer. It contrasts nicely with E. O. Wilson's *Sociobiology: The new synthesis* (Harvard University Press, 1975), a hugely ambitious attempt to explain differences and similarities in living forms by reference to the tendency to optimize reproductive success; the theory has been criticized by many who oppose Wilson's emphasis on biological factors rather than social, or cultural ones.

Nature via Nurture: Genes, experience and what makes us human by Matt Ridley (HarperCollins, 2003b) is one of a number of contributions by one of the most illuminating writers on genetics. Among his others are: "Sex, errors, and the genome" (pp. 45–51 in *Natural History*, vol. 110, no. 5, 2001a), "The genome is decoded; be happy" (p. A22 in the *Wall Street Journal*, February 14, 2001b), and "Listen to the genome" (pp. 59–65 in *The American Spectator*, vol. 36, no. 3, 2003). The website for the Human Genome Project is at:www.ornl.gov/sci/techresources/Human_Genome/project/timeline.shtml.

"Designer people" by Sally Deneen in *E: The Environmental Magazine* (vol. 12, no. 1, 2001) explores the possibilities and dangers of genetically engineering humans. Athletic ability and intelligence, she writes, rely "to a significant degree on nurture instead of nature."

Smithsonian Intimate Guide to Human Origins by Carl Zimmer (HarperCollins, 2005) begins with the reminder that genetic studies have shown that human populations are very, very closely related. This is an accessible, illustrated guide.

Genes, Culture, and Human Evolution: A synthesis by Linda Stone, Paul F. Lurquin, and L. Luca Cavalli-Sforza (Wiley-Blackwell, 2006) takes a holistic approach to the relationship between culture, evolution, and genetics, emphasizing that none of these can be studied independently of the others. Complementing this is *Human Evolution, Language and Mind: A psychological and archaeological inquiry* by William Noble and Iain Davidson (Cambridge University Press, 1996) which examines the critical role played by the distinctly human trait of symbol-making in communication; other primates use utterances that are like symbols, but probably not with intentions.

"The animal cultures debate" by Kevin N. Laland and Vincent M. Janik (in *Trends in Ecology and Evolution*, 2006) examines the balance between genetic, ecological and social influences on animal behavior and argues: "Clearly, behavioural differences can simultaneously result from genetic, ecological and cultural variation . . . the prime issue in the animal cultures debates is not whether a given behaviour is learned socially or asocially [without social interaction], but rather how much of the variance in the behaviour can be attributed to social learning." The article can be read in conjunction with the Gruber *et al.* study.

ASSIGNMENT

"Between the gene and the environment there are all sorts of intervening factors and processes that must be studied" (see p. 28). List as exhaustively as possible the factors and processes that contribute to the creation of what we might regard as "natural" sports performers; in other words, the kinds of factors and processes that show that performers learn and develop as much as they inherit.

CHAPTER 3

Built for Action

KEY ISSUES

▨ How does the body compare to well-engineered machinery?

▨ What are the materials our bodies are made of?

▨ When does oxygen debt start to affect us?

▨ Where *isn't* the nervous system?

▨ Why do athletes often tear their anterior cruciate ligaments?

▨ . . . and what happens to the body of a swimmer when she's breaking a world record?

ALL SYSTEMS "GO" – FOR 3 MINUTES 59.15 SECONDS

July 26, 2009: the body of Federica Pellegrini breaks the water of the pool in Rome. She takes the lead from Jo Jackson at the 100-meter point and, at 300 meters, turns inside her own world record. Jackson remains in second place, 0.5 seconds behind. Pellegrini has set in motion processes and mechanisms of immense complexity: every one of her 600 muscles has contracted, stretched, and twisted; her lungs have filled and emptied repeatedly; her heart has pumped at least 50 gallons (227 liters) of blood into all areas of the body. All this has been made possible by the intricate organizing and synchronizing capacity of her brain, which has submitted her entire body to one purpose for the duration of the race. Pellegrini touches in 3:59.15 to become the first woman in history to break the 4-minute mark for 400 meters.

Question anyone who has witnessed a sports event first hand, or even on television, and they'll identify the actual performance as the most exciting aspect of sport. The performance is the moment when competitive humans bring to an end their preparations and make visible their self-willed mastery of a particular set of skills. It is an engaging experience that easily surpasses reading reports, watching interviews, studying form, or any of the other ancillary activities associated with sports.

The performance itself always occupies center stage in sports. And while the stage itself – its structure, scenery, and props, and the audience – will occupy our attention in the pages to follow, we must provide some analysis of the performance before progressing. The body will command a great deal of attention in this book: how our perceptions of it have changed, how it relates to gender and race, how it responds to drugs, how it has been visualized by artists, how it will become "cyborgized" and augmented with prosthetics and so on. We can't address the questions without at least a basic understanding of how it works.

When we watch sports, we watch bodies move. That's what excites us. The thrill of anticipation, the arousal of the build-up and the tension of the preliminaries are all pleasurably stimulating; but nothing beats action. Even in a chess game, the peak moments are when the players extend their arms to propel pieces across the board.

Obviously, we all control our bodies; the sports performer just controls his or hers in a particular kind of way. The more control they have, the better their chances of imposing their wills to bring a ball under control, make a vehicle travel faster or lift their legs off the ground – and the more likely the chances of success. So, what enables us to control our bodies? It seems a ludicrously obvious question, but one that needs an answer if we're to understand better the complexities of sport.

Imagine Pellegrini as a series of systems, interacting so as to produce motion. When the starter's gun fires, her central nervous system receives the signal and very rapidly relays messages to her muscular system which is stimulated to move by electrical impulses. Muscular contractions move her limbs mechanically, this being made possible by the fact that the muscles are attached to the bones of Pellegrini's skeleton, which is yielding, yet tough enough to withstand the stress of movement without fracturing. Fuel is needed for the athlete to be able to repeat the motion and this comes via breathing, circulation, and digestion; once burned up, the waste matter of fuel has to be disposed of.

Viewed as a lump of matter, Pellegrini's body is a bundle of about 60 billion living units called cells, each of which has the same basic structure, comprising membrane (which holds the unit together), ribosomes (which manufacture proteins), lysosomes (which destroy harmful substances and diseased parts of the cell), golgi complex (which stores endoplasmic substance), reticulum (which transports substances throughout a cell), cytoplasm (which is the liquid in which the other elements float), mitochondria (which are powerhouses, where oxygen and food react to produce vital energy to keep the cell alive) and a nucleus (which contains the chromosomes carrying coded instructions for the workings of the cell).

Cells often cluster together to form other substances, such as tissue and muscle (which comprises 50 percent of cells, being a type of tissue) and these tissues can also work in groups to become organs (heart and lungs, for instance). When organs operate together to perform a particular function, like transporting blood around the body, we usually talk in terms of systems.

For an elite swimmer like Pellegrini to perform at her maximum, all her systems need to be working maximally and synchronously. We'll probe the body as if it was a series of interlocking systems. A logical first step is to ask how a swimmer, or indeed any living animal, is able to move at all and here we're drawn to an examination of the skeletal and muscular systems.

BOX 3.1 MITOCHONDRIA

These are found in most cells, often known as the power stations of a cell where glucose and oxygen react together to create energy which converts the chemical adenosine diphosphate (ADP), which is like a flat battery, to charged-up adenosine triphosphate (ATP). This then supplies the rest of the cell with power. As its energy is used up, the ATP reverts to ADP and returns to the mitochondria for recharging. ATP is most likely the supplier of energy for every activity in animals and plants. Energy, of course, is needed for muscular movements, but also for nerve conduction and other functions.

MOVING THE SKELETON

The skeleton isn't just a framework, an elaborate coat hanger on which we drape skin and muscle. It's a rather elaborate, living structure that serves four important functions: protection, support, storage, and movement. Structurally, it has two aspects: the axial comprises the skull, backbone, ribs and sternum; the appendicular refers to appendages (legs and arms), the pelvic girdle (to which the legs are attached), and the pectoral girdle (to which the arms are connected). In total, there are over 200 bones.

The human brain is disproportionately large compared to those of other mammals and, together with the spinal cord, controls in large part the movements of the whole body. As a complex, yet delicate, piece of equipment, it needs maximum protection: this is why we have a skull (or cranium), a resilient helmet composed of plates of bone fused together to form a hard casing around the brain. The interstices between the bones are called sutures and allow growth in the size of the brain until around the age of 20, after which they weld together. The skull affords sufficient protection for the brain in most activities, although motor sports, hang gliding and other sports in which the risk of direct collision is high (e.g. football, cricket, and cycling) use headgear for additional protection.

The other main part of the central nervous system, the spine, also needs the protection of bone; in this case a long, flexible column of vertebrae separated by discs of cartilage. In functional terms, the spine represents a remarkable adaptation, affording protection to a sensitive cable of nerves that runs from the brain to all areas of the body. The spine is articulate so as to permit the movement and flexibility so necessary to survival.

This flexibility is bought at a cost, for in certain parts of the back the spine has little or no support. Hence weightlifters strap broad belts around their waists so as to maintain rigidity in and give support to the vulnerable areas of their lower back when it is likely to be exposed to stress. Some other sensitive organs, like the lungs and heart are also given skeletal protection, but, unlike some vertebrates (armadillos and tortoises), humans have discarded external physical protection and rely more on the wit and ingenuity that derive from the large brain, and the fleetness of foot made possible by bipedalism to protect themselves.

The conventional notion of the skeleton as a means of support is true for the majority of bones. But this needs qualification. The bony material itself is not solid, but is a composite of collagen protein fibers and inorganic mineral crystals ordered in a meshwork of cylindrical layers. This honeycombed arrangement prevents brittleness and gives bone some degree of elasticity: should stress be applied, bone distributes it to prevent a concentration. Excessive stress will cause cracks or breaks, of course, but bone's yielding capacity, or "give," reduces the danger of breakage. These qualities make it ideal as a supporting apparatus because it combines tensile strength with the yield needed for a wide range of motions.

As a rule, the heavier the load a bone must bear, the greater its diameter must be. Human thighbones, or femur, are large, as are tibia and fibula connecting the knee to the foot; they are responsible for supporting the upper body weight. But, while the femur has some protection from the quadriceps, the tibia and fibula are exposed and may need artificial cushioning from direct knocks in sports like soccer and hockey.

The skeleton can support effectively only if it grows in correspondence with the rest of the body. And bone does grow; it receives food and oxygen from blood vessels. New layers of tissue encircle existing material and form new bone, thus increasing the diameter (growth in length ceases before the age of 20). Bone grows in response to force, as does muscle. Bend, twist, compress, load, or combine these and, over time, the bone will grow to meet its task and fulfill its function, within limits of course. It will react to certain pressures or movements by fracturing, breaking, or shearing. (When this happens, cells in the outer layer of the bone, the periosteum – multiply and grow over the break, joining the two parts together.)

At the other extreme, bone will lose mass if deprived of function. Stored inside bone are the minerals calcium and potassium, which are delivered to the cells by blood (and which give bone its hardness) and marrow, a soft jelly-like tissue that produces red and white blood cells.

The fourth major function of the skeleton – and the most important for our purposes – is that of providing mechanical levers for movement. Bones are connected to each other at joints, which serve as axes for rotation. For instance, the forearm, the upperarm bone or the humerus, acts as a fulcrum, and the radius and ulna as a lever. The elbow joint, which is a hinge, makes possible a simple range of movement; flexion (bending) and extension (stretching). Other joints, like the biaxial (between forearm and wrist and at the knee), the pivot (at the wrist), and the ball-and-socket (at the shoulder and hip) are more complicated arrangements and permit multiple movements in different planes and directions.

Were the joint a manufactured piece of equipment, the articular surfaces would grind together and need WD-40 or some other lubricant sprayed onto them. The human body takes care of this by interposing a film of lubricating fluid between opposing bone surfaces (in which case, they are called synovial joints), or by sandwiching a tough pad of gristle between articulating bones (cartilaginous joints). An engineer would love this natural bearing, which reduces friction.

Cartilage belongs to a class of connective tissues which, as the name suggests, joins or ties together the various parts of the body and makes movement smooth. Its capacity isn't limitless, however, and cartilage can wear out. Ligaments, which are flexible collagen bands that connect and support joints, are also liable to wear-and-tear, especially amongst sports performers, such as throwers or shot putters, who maximize the intensity or repetition of stresses on shoulder and elbow joints and are therefore prone to sprains (torn ligaments) and dislocations of joints.

BOX 3.2 ANTERIOR CRUCIATE LIGAMENT INJURIES

Michael Owen and Tom Brady were among the countless athletes to be sidelined by a torn anterior cruciate ligament. The ACL, as it is known, is one of the four main ligaments of the knee, the others being the medial collateral ligament (MCL), lateral collateral ligament (LCL), and posterior cruciate ligament (PCL). The ACL is about 1.5 inches, or 35 mm and is behind the kneecap (patella) and in front of the PCL. It's the second strongest ligament in the knee and stabilizes the joint, connecting the thigh bone (femur) and the leg bone (tibia). It prevents forward movement of the tibia from underneath the femur. A torn ACL usually occurs through a twisting force being applied to the knee while the foot is planted on the ground (as in Owen's case), or as the result of a blow to the knee (as in Brady's case). While this type of injury finished many athletes' careers (Brian Clough never played again after he sustained such an injury in 1962), full recoveries are commonplace nowadays. Athletes usually opt for a reparative procedure involving grafting tissue from hamstring tendons or the kneecap and then attaching to the bones above and below the knee. Graduated exercise can start about six weeks after the procedure, with a return to full range of movement between 3 and 6 months (see Figure 3.1).

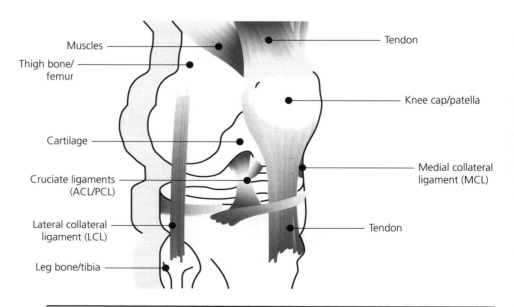

Figure 3.1 The knee

Perhaps the most troublesome connective tissue for sports competitors is tendon, which is basically a collagen cable that joins muscle to bone and so transmits the pull, which makes the bone move. Tendons make it possible to use a muscle to move a bone at a distance. In the case of fingers, which are clearly vital in dexterous activities (e.g. table tennis, darts, and spin bowling in cricket), we need muscular control of the fine movements without the invasive presence of muscles at the immediate site. Were the necessary muscles attached directly to the finger bones, the size of the digits would be so large that catching, holding, or even forming a fist would be a problem. Without the action permitted at distance by slender tendons, primate prehensility would be severely restricted. Special nerves in the tendon are designed to inhibit over-contraction, but tears do occur often when fatigue or poor skill impairs co-ordination. Tendon tears may be partial or complete and, although any muscle tendon is at risk, those subjected to violent or repetitive stresses, such as the Achilles tendon and shoulder tendons are most frequently involved.

The way the skeleton is framed and its levers fitted together give the body the potential for a great variety of movements through all planes. But we still need to analyze the source of its motion. Plainly stated, muscle moves our bones; it does so with two actions, contraction and relaxation. Usually, the arrangement features tendons connecting bones to one or more muscles which are stimulated by nerves to contract, causing the tendons to tighten and the bone to move. (Some muscles appear to be attached directly to bone, obviating the need for tendons, but motion is accomplished by basically the same process.)

Muscle use is present in every sporting activity, right from sprinting where muscles are maximally in use, to playing chess where muscles function perhaps only to position eyeballs in their sockets or to move a finger by inches. The various types of muscle present in humans differ in structure and properties, but the striated muscle, which acts as the motor of the skeleton, is our chief concern. Striated muscle is under our control in the sense that we voluntarily induce its contraction and hence movement. Other types of muscles contract in the absence of nerve stimulation: cardiac (heart) muscle, for example, contracts independently of our will and has the property of "inherent rhythmicity" (we'll return to this).

Skeletal muscle consists of fibers, which are long tubes that run parallel to each other and are encased in sheaths of the ubiquitous collagen. Each fiber is made up of strands called myofibrils, which are themselves composed of two types of interlocking filaments. Thick filaments are made of a protein called myosin and thin ones of actin, and they are grouped in a regular, repeated pattern, so that, under the microscope, they give a striated, or streaky, appearance. The lengths of myosin and actin filaments are divided into units called sarcomeres, the size of which is recognized as the distance between two "Z-lines" (the structures to which the actin filaments are attached).

Although the filaments can't change length, they can slide past each other to produce the all-important contraction. We'll see later how messages from the central nervous system are taken to muscles by nerve impulses. When such an impulse reaches a muscle fiber with the instruction "Move!" energy is released in mitochondria and the filaments move closer together, shortening the muscle. As they pass, a chemical reaction occurs in which: (1) calcium is released from storage in the tubular bundles; (2) in the calcium's presence, myosin molecules from the thicker filaments form bonds with the actin filaments; (3) the myosin molecule is then thought to undergo a change in shape, yanking the actin filaments closer together; (4) the contraction of the muscle fiber ends when the calcium ions are pumped back into storage so as to prevent the formation of new chemical bonds.

The effect of the contraction is a pull on the bones to which the muscles are attached and, as the four phases take no more than a few thousandths of a second, we are capable of mechanical movements at very high speed. The flexion and extension of, for example, boxer Manny Pacquiao's left hook took a few hundredths of a second. Such a punch, which had a concussing effect, required a great force of movement, so many fibers would have been required to contract together at speed. An 8-ft putt, by contrast, would involve fewer fibers.

In both instances, opposing, or antagonistic pairs of muscles would be working to allow free movement. For the hook or the putt, biceps muscle would contract to bend the elbow, which its opposing member, the triceps, would relax. To straighten the arm in the action of a shot putter the triceps need to contract, while biceps relax. Muscles are equipped with special receptors that let the brain know the extent of contraction and the position in three-dimensional space without having to look constantly to check. We can close our eyes, but know the movement and position of our limbs. This is known as proprioception.

BOX 3.3 PROPRIOCEPTION

This refers to stimuli produced and perceived within an organism; it describes the actions of sensory systems involved in providing information about the position, location, orientation, and movement of the body. The main groups of proprioceptors are: (1) in the vestibular system of the inner ear and (2) the somatosenses, comprising the kinesthetic (associated with muscles and joints) and cutaneous (relating to skin) systems. Kinesthesia (or kinaesthesia) is often used interchangeably with proprioception, though it specifically describes the awareness of the position and movement of parts of the body by means of sensory organs in the joints and muscles.

The 206 bones of the adult skeletal system form a protective casing for the brain and the spinal cord, a sturdy internal framework to support the rest of the body, and a set of mechanical levers that can be moved by the action of muscles. All of these make the human body a serviceable locomotive machine for walking, running, and, to a lesser degree, swimming, climbing, and jumping. But, like other machines, the body depends on fuel supply for its power, a method for burning the fuel, and a system for transporting the waste products away. Again, the human body has evolved systems for answering all these needs.

NOT BY FOOD ALONE: ENERGY

As a living organism, the human being depends on energy. Plants get by with light and water; animals need food. In particular, humans need protein (built up of chemical units called amino acids), carbohydrates (comprising sugars which provide most of our energy), lipids (or fats for storage and insulation), vitamins (about 15 types to assist various chemical processes), minerals (like iron and zinc), and water (to replace liquids). These provide raw energy sources that drive the machinery of the body; that is, making the compounds that combine with oxygen to release energy, and ensure the growth and repair of tissues.

Obtaining food is of such vital importance to survival that the entire plan of the human body is adapted to its particular mode of procuring food. Sports, as I'll argue later, reflects our primitive food-procurement even to this day. For the moment, we need to understand not so much the way in which food is obtained, but how it's used. In their original forms, most of the above substances are unusable to human beings. So we've evolved mechanisms for rendering them usable as energy sources. Processing food is the function of the digestive system, which consists of a long, coiled tube, called the digestive tract, and three types of accessory glands.

Although in extreme cases food can be introduced directly into the stomach via a feeding tube, a procedure known as percutaneous endoscopic gastrostomy (PEG), or intravenously by feeding through a vein, the obvious way most of us take our food is through our mouths. By chewing, the food becomes mixed with saliva and turned into a pulp in a process of ingestion. After being formed into lumps, we swallow it, after which it drops into the pharynx (throat) and, then, to the epiglottis, which is a small valve that closes off the windpipe. Water falls under the force of gravity, but food is ushered along by a wave of muscular contractions called peristalsis. Fibers in the wall of the esophagus tube (gullet) push the food downward to the stomach (which explains why cosmonauts can still eat in the absence of gravity).

From here, the food passes into the stomach, a sausage-shaped organ that can expand to about a two-pint capacity. At this stage, a churning process starts in which the food is mixed with mucus, hydrochloric acid, and enzymes (chemical substances that speed up processes – in this instance, the breaking up of protein). The effect of this is to liquefy the food, so that after between three and four hours the churned-up mass (called chyme), which now resembles a cream soup, gets transferred, via peristaltic waves, to the stomach's exit point and then to the duodenum which is the first chamber of the small intestine. Contrary to popular belief, it's here rather than the stomach, where most of the chemical digestion gets done: bile from the liver and enzymes from the pancreas are released. (An exception is alcohol, which is readily absorbed in the stomach and doesn't pass through.)

A note here about the role of the brain in regulating the discharge of naturally secreted juices that aid digestion: seeing, smelling, tasting, or even thinking about food can stimulate the brain to send messages to the glands in the mouth and stomach to release a hormone called gastrin that is quickly absorbed into the blood and then to glands where it triggers the release of gastric juice. So athletes who chew gum to enhance their concentration are usually doing a disservice to their stomachs by producing gastric juices when there is no food. Gastric juices have enough acidity and protein-splitting capacity to burn human flesh. The stomach has natural protection against this, although resistance can be lowered by alcohol or aspirin and by overproducing the juices when no food is available. A possible result is an open sore in the wall of the stomach, or a duodenal ulcer.

Basically, the idea is to reduce the parts of the food that can be profitably used by the body (the nutrients) to molecular form and allow them to seep through the cells lining the long digestive tube, through the minuscule blood or lymph vessels in the stomach wall and into the blood or lymph. All the cells of the body are bathed in a fluid called lymph. Exchanges between blood and cells take place in lymph. Lymph is derived from blood, though it has a kind of circulatory system of its own, filtering through the walls of capillaries, then moving along channels of its own (lymphatics), which join one another and steer eventually to the veins, in the process surrendering their contents to the general circulatory system. Food is absorbed through the wall of the intestine, which is covered in *villi*, tiny absorbent "fingers" that give the tube a vast surface area. Not all food passes directly into blood vessels: the lymphatics are responsible for collecting digested fats and transporting them to the thoracic duct which empties into one of the large veins near the heart.

BOX 3.4 LYMPH

From the Latin *lympha*, for water, this is a body fluid derived from the blood and tissue and returned to the circulatory system in lymphatic vessels. At intervals along the vessels there are lymph glands, which manufacture antibodies and lymphocytes that destroy bacteria. The lymph system has no pump like the blood system and the movement of lymph is brought about largely by pressure from contracting skeletal muscles, backflow being prevented by valves. The lymph system doubles as the body's immune system in that it produces proteins called antibodies, lying at the surface of certain white blood cells (lymphocytes). When needed, antibodies and cells rush into the bloodstream and "round up" the harmful bacteria and viruses. While the lymph system can make thousands of antibodies, its vital adversaries are constantly mutating so as to find ways of defeating it, as the Aids pandemic indicates. If the flow of lymph is dammed up behind damaged or blocked drainage routes, fluid accumulates in surrounding tissues and swelling occurs. Lymph drainage is a style of massage that stimulates circulation of lymph through the lymphatic system.

Once absorbed the nutrients are carried in the blood and lymph to each individual cell in the body where they are used up; that is, metabolized. The residue of indigestible or unabsorbed food is eliminated from the body by way of the large intestine. En route, bacteria in the large intestine feed on vestiges and, in return, produce certain vitamins, which are absorbed and used. Some of the unwanted water is converted to urea and passed out via the bladder. The body has precise control over what it needs for nutrition, growth, and repair. One of the many functions of the liver is to store surplus nutrients and release them together to meet immediate requirements. This large abdominal organ receives digested food from the blood and reassembles its molecules in such a way as to make them usable to humans. Different cells need different nutrients, so the liver works as a kind of chef preparing a buffet for the blood to carry around the rest of the body.

A supply of glucose is needed by all body cells and especially brain cells, especially as they have no means of storage. If, after a sugar-rich meal, the body has too much glucose in the blood, the liver cells remove it and store it, later pushing it back into the blood when the glucose level drops. After a carbohydrate-rich meal, the level may increase briefly, but the liver will take out the surplus for later use. Muscle cells are also able to store large amounts of glucose molecules, packaged as glycogen, which is why endurance-event competitors, like marathon runners, try to pack muscle and liver cells with stored glycogen prior to competition in the expectation that it will be released into the blood when levels fall. After the glucose is used up, liver cells start converting amino acids and portions of fat into glucose and the body shifts to fat as a source of fuel.

Metabolism refers to all the body's processes that make food usable as a source of energy. The success of these depends on how effectively the body can get the nutrients and oxygen it requires to the relevant parts of the body and, at the same time, clear out the unwanted leftovers like carbon dioxide. The substance employed for this purpose is blood, but it's actually more than just a convenient liquid for sweeping materials from place to place. Cells, cell fragments (platelets), proteins, and small molecules float in liquid plasma, which is mainly water (and makes up about 60 percent of the blood's composition). The plasma contains red and white blood cells; the latter are capable of engulfing bacteria and combating infections with antibodies. Red cells are more numerous and contain hemoglobin, a chemical compound with a strong affinity for oxygen.

BOX 3.5 MUSCLE-PACKING OR MUSCLE-LOADING

Carbohydrates (carbs) provide most of our energy and can be ingested in many forms, after which they are reduced to simple sugars before being absorbed into the bloodstream. Carbs are an economical source of fuel. Liver and muscles store carbohydrates in the form of glycogen, which converts rapidly to glucose when extra energy is needed. Mindful of this, endurance performers sometimes seek to "pack" or "load-up" their muscles with glycogen by consuming large amounts of carbohydrate foods such as bread, cereals, grains, and starchy products for about 72 hours preceding an event. The idea is to store as much glycogen as possible, making more glucose available when energy supplies become depleted.

Hemoglobin allows blood to increase its oxygen-carrying capacity exponentially. Long- and middle-distance runners have exploited the advantage of having more hemoglobin in their blood by training at high altitudes, where there is less oxygen naturally available in the air. Their bodies respond to the scarcity by producing a chemical that triggers the release of larger numbers of red cells in the blood. After descending to sea-level (or thereabouts), the body will take time to readjust and will retain a high hemoglobin count for some weeks, during which an athlete may compete and make profitable use of a generous supply of oxygen to the muscles (blood doping, as we will see later, involves extracting hemoglobin-packed blood during altitude training, saving it, and administering a transfusion to the athlete immediately prior to a race). At the other extreme, excessive bleeding or an iron-deficient diet can lead to anemia, a condition resulting from too little hemoglobin.

So, how do we manage to circulate this urgently required mixture throughout the body? The internal apparatus comprises the heart, blood vessels, lymph, lymph vessels, and some associated organs, like the liver. These form a closed system, meaning that the blood that carries the vital substances all over the body is confined to definite channels and moves in only one direction, rather than being left to swim about. It travels in three types of tubes. The thickest are arteries in which blood moves at high pressure from the heart to the body's tissues. These arteries split over and over again to form microscopic vessels called capillaries that spread to every part of the body.

A single capillary is only about half a millimeter long and a single cubic meter of skeletal muscle is interlaced with 1,400 to 4,000 of them. Laid end-to-end the length of all the body's capillaries would be about 60,000 miles or 96,500 kilometers – twice the earth's circumference. While coursing around, oxygen and nutrient-rich liquid,

▌ BOX 3.6 BLOOD DOPING

Otherwise known as induced erythrocythemia, this describes the intravenous infusion of an athlete's own blood. It involves: (1) training at altitude – say in Ethiopia, 7,500 feet above sea level, or Colorado, 6,800 feet – where the natural oxygen scarcity prompts the body to adapt by increasing the number of hemoglobin, or red blood cells, which are produced in response to greater release of the hormone erythropoietin (EPO) by the kidneys. Red cells carry oxygen from the lungs to muscles. More red cells means blood can carry more oxygen to compensate for the shortage of oxygen in the air. (2) Before leaving the altitude training, 2 or 3 units of an athlete's blood (1 unit = 15 fluid ounces, or 450 ml) are withdrawn and frozen. (3) The day before competition, the blood is thawed and injected back into the athlete. This is known as *autologous* blood doping, as opposed to *homologous* doping, which means that the injected blood is taken from another person. Similar effects can be obtained from CERA (continuous erythropoiesis receptor activator), a variant of synthesized EPO. All three are banned by WADA. Andreas Kloeden, who was expelled from the 2006 Tour de France, is among several athletes disqualified from competition for blood doping. Martti Vainio returned a positive dope test after the 10,000 metres at the 1984 Los Angeles Olympics. Before the Games the Finn had reinfused stored blood. He might have escaped a ban, but the blood contained traces of anabolic steroids.

plasma seeps through the ultra-thin walls of the capillary. At the same time, capillaries, like vacuum cleaners, suck up waste products from cells. Gradually, capillaries merge together to form larger vessels that turn out to be veins; these keep blood at a lower pressure as they deliver it back to the heart.

A fist-sized muscle weighing less than a pound, the heart is a four-chambered pump that pushes blood into the arteries, gets it back from all parts of the body (except the lungs), pumps it out of the lungs, takes it back from the lungs, then returns it to the body. The chambers of the right side of the heart consist of one atrium and one ventricle. Connected to the right atrium are two large veins, one of which brings blood from the upper body and one from the lower. Blood flows from the right atrium into the right ventricle via a one-way valve; it leaves this chamber through a pulmonary artery that branches and services the lungs. Another valve stops any backflow. Blood returns from the lungs via pulmonary veins which drain into a left atrium and, then, to a left ventricle.

From here, the blood is squeezed into the aorta, the single largest artery of the body, which runs into several other arteries connected to head, arms, and the upper chest, and, later, to abdominal organs and body wall. In the pelvis, the aorta branches and sends arteries into the legs. Blood returns to the right atrium of the heart through veins. The direction of the blood is ensured by a series of valves (blood, controlled by the valves, moves in one direction only). We call the movement away from ventricles systole and its opposite diastole. At any one time, there are about 1.5 gallons of blood in the mature human body. It takes less than a minute for the resting heart to pump out this amount and considerably less for the exerting sports performer, who can push out as much as 6.6 gallons per minute when active.

As mentioned before, the heart muscle has inherent rhythmicity and the pump acts independently of our volition. It will (given a suitable atmosphere) pump even outside the body, and with no stimulation; this makes heart transplants possible. Not that the heart is indifferent to outside influences; a sudden shock, for example, can cause sufficient stimulation to slow down, or skip, the heartbeat.

During exercise or competition the action may accelerate to over 200 beats per minute. The heart muscle itself would stretch and automatically increase its strength of contraction and flow of blood. Athletes work at increasing blood flow without the corresponding heartbeat. The extra blood flow results in a heightening of the pressure of blood in the arteries of the chest and neck, which are detected by special sensory cells embedded in their walls. Nerve impulses are sent to the brain, resulting in impulses being relayed back to the heart, slowing its beat rate and lowering potentially harmful blood pressure levels. So, the brain has to monitor or feed back what is going on during intense physical activity.

The rate of heart action is also affected by hormones, the most familiar in sports being adrenaline which causes an immediate quickening of the heart in response to stressful situations. The reaction is widespread; amongst other things, blood vessels in the brain and limbs open up, and glycogen is released from the liver. In this type of situation, the skeletal muscles might receive up to 70 percent of the cardiac output, or the total blood pumped from the heart. Under resting conditions, the liver, kidneys, and brain take 27, 27, and 14 percent respectively. Immediately after eating, the digestive organs command great percentages (to carry food away), thus reducing the

BOX 3.7 ADRENALINE RUSH

The sudden sensation of excitement and power that often occurs in stressful situations is described as an adrenaline rush, adrenaline (sometimes called *epinephrine*) being one of the two main hormones released by the medulla of the adrenal gland which covers part of the kidney – the word adrenaline derives from the Latin for "toward the kidney," *ad* meaning to and *renal* kidney. In competition, the rush of adrenaline into the system can act as a spur to athletes, often at unexpected moments. The reason is that adrenaline causes profound changes in all parts of the body.

The release of the hormone effectively mobilizes the whole body for either *fight or flight*: by stimulating the release of glycogen (which serves to store carbohydrates in tissues) from the liver, the expansion of blood vessels in the heart, brain, and limbs and the contraction of vessels in the abdomen. It diminishes fatigue, speeds blood coagulation, and causes the spleen to release its store of blood. The eyes' pupils dilate. Sweat increases to cool the body and sugar is released into the bloodstream to provide more energy for vigorous muscular activity. The value of adrenaline release to the sports performer is obvious, which is why many often reflect on good performances as happening when the "adrenaline was pumping" or try to break a *slump* during a competition by "getting some adrenaline going." The effects are similar to the stimulation of the sympathetic division of the autonomic nervous system (ANS).

Under certain, usually dangerous, conditions, the skeletal muscles might receive up to 70 per cent of the cardiac output, that is, the blood pumped from the heart. More blood is fed to muscles than need it at the expense of the viscera, especially the abdomen, where the needs are not urgent. Feelings of pain and tiredness are minimized and the body is prepared for extraordinary feats.

The whole process is mobilized by the sympathetic division of the ANS, which regulates heartbeat, breathing, digestion and other internal processes. The sympathetic division stimulates the body and causes it to expend energy. Once the adrenaline rush subsides, the parasympathetic division of the ANS kicks in to bring the body's function back into balance; for example, breathing and heartrate slow down and digestion increases.

While competitors consciously hope for an adrenaline rush at some point during a flaccid performance, the surge typically occurs in the context of events that use natural conditions rather than synthetic environments, such as a stadium or an indoor arena. Long-distance swimming, orienteering, car rallying and rock climbing are examples of sports in which the performers' lives may occasionally be in jeopardy. Risk creates perfect conditions for an adrenaline rush. The sense of exhilaration and might are difficult to reproduce artificially, of course; though part of the summer Olympics triathlon course in 2000 was held in Sydney harbor and it was speculated that the sharks that habitually lurk in the waters might hasten triathletes to personal bests.

Actually an answer of sorts comes from K. C. Hughes, writing for the military magazine *Armor:* "in times of pure terror or crisis, the body might release endorphins . . . These chemicals cause soldiers to ignore pain and give the 'out-of-body' feeling that is described by many during traumatic events. This survival technique is called emotional numbing."

Athletes, particularly boxers, have reported similar desensitizing when enduring what might in non-competitive circumstances be an unbearably painful injury and completing a contest. Research by Pamela Smith and Jennifer Ogle reported how cross-country runners strove to achieve a similar awareness in their training: "The sensation of healthfulness was most discussed within the context of running and was described as a feeling of euphoria or an 'adrenaline rush' that a 'hard run' could incite."

One of the properties of the drug pseudoephedrine, which is found in many cold remedies and decongestants, is that it mimics the adrenaline rush. It is on most sports' lists of banned substances. Five different types of the stimulant were found in the urine of Argentina's soccer player Diego Maradona when he was tested at (and subsequently banned from) the 1994 World Cup championships.

supply to the muscles. So, activity after a meal tends to be self-defeating; you can't get as much blood to the muscles as you would if you waited for three hours or so.

I mentioned before that food alone does not give the body energy, but needs the addition of oxygen, which is, of course, inhaled from the surrounding air, taken to the lungs, and then transferred to all parts of the body via the blood. Once it arrives at cells, the oxygen reacts with glucose, supplied by courtesy of digested carbohydrates, and produces energy at the mitochondria sites. During this process of respiration, unwanted carbon dioxide and water are formed in the cells. Exhaling gets rid of them.

Lungs and windpipe make up the respiratory system, though the actual process of breathing is controlled by the contractions of muscles in the chest, in particular the diaphragm muscle beneath the lungs and the muscles between the ribs. The diaphragm moving down and the ribs expanding create space in the lungs. Air rushes in mainly through the nostrils where it is filtered, warmed, and moistened, and then into the lungs via the windpipe, or trachea. To reach the lungs, the air travels along tubes called bronchi which, when inside the lungs, divide into smaller and smaller tubes, ending in small bunches of air sacs called alveoli. Oxygen seeps out of the alveoli and into surrounding capillaries, which carry hemoglobin, a compound which, as we noted, readily picks up oxygen. While oxygen leaves alveoli, carbon dioxide, produced by the body cells, enter ready to be exhaled, a motion initiated by a muscular relaxation of the diaphragm and ribs. Air rushes out when we sigh "Phew!" to denote relief and relaxation; the ribs close in and diaphragm lifts up.

The motions are more pronounced during continuous physical exertion; the body makes a steady demand for more oxygen and to meet this we breathe more deeply and more fully. The heart responds by pumping the oxygen-rich blood around the body faster. The process involves sustained use of oxygen in the breakdown of carbohydrates and, eventually, fats to release in the mitochondria of cells where the raw fuel ADP is energy charged up as ATP. This is why the name aerobic (meaning "with air") is applied to continuous activities, such as cycling, swimming, and running over distances. In contrast, weight lifting, high jumping, and other sports requiring only short bursts of energy are anaerobic. In this case, food is not broken down completely to carbon dioxide and water, but to compounds such as alcohol or lactic acid. An incomplete breakdown means that less energy is released, but what is released can be used immediately.

"Oxygen debt" affects many sports competitors, particularly ones whose event requires explosive bursts, but over a reasonably sustained period. Four hundred-meter runners often tie up in the home straight; they can't get the oxygen and glucose round their bodies fast enough, so their muscles use their own glycogen stores for releasing ATP anaerobically (without oxygen).

The product of this process is lactic acid, which needs oxygen to be converted into carbohydrate to get carried away. As runners need all the oxygen they can process for the release of energy they "borrow" it temporarily, allowing the lactic acid to accumulate in the muscles and cause fatigue. After the event, the debt has to be repaid, so rapid breathing invariably carries on. Shorter-distance sprinters also incur oxygen debts, but the buildup of lactic acid in their muscles is not usually great enough to hinder contraction. Longer-distance performers tend to get second winds: an increase in heart beat rate and breathing enables the runner to take in enough oxygen to convert and dissipate the lactic acid without over-extending the oxygen debt.

BOX 3.8 HYPERVENTILATION

Carbon dioxide (CO_2) is a waste product and needs to be flushed out of the blood. Even a small increase in CO_2 content of the blood stimulates deep and, later, more rapid breathing to reduce the CO_2. The action is brought about involuntarily, usually during physical activity because of the fast breakdown of carbohydrates to release energy (impulses are sent to the medulla, resulting in increased breathing). Occasionally, this can lead to an over-reduction and a loss of consciousness. When this happens, hyperventilation is said to occur.

COMMUNICATIONS AND CONTROL

Let's return to Federica Pelligrini for a moment. We now have an idea of how her movements are possible: how the supporting scaffold of her skeleton is urged into motion by the contraction of muscles; how those muscles are fed a supply of fuel to turn into energy; and how that fuel, in the form of food and oxygen, is pushed to its destination by blood which, at the same time, picks up waste products to dispatch. Although we've examined these processes separately, this is a device; in actual performance, all the processes are closely connected and dependent on each other.

The digestion of food, for instance, would be of no value without a bloodstream to absorb it and to distribute the products; release of energy in a contracting muscle would cease if the lungs failed to supply oxygen via the circulatory system; a contracting muscle has to be connected to articulated bone to get a movement. The working together of these is no haphazard affair. During strenuous activity, when muscles need to lose excess carbon dioxide and take in more glucose and oxygen, the rate of breathing increases automatically and the heart beats faster, so sending a greater amount of oxygen-rich blood to the muscles.

Crudely stated, the information we receive about the environment arrives by way of cells called receptors, which respond to changes in, for example, light and sound. They produce pulses of electricity which travel along nerves to the brain, which quickly interprets the meaning of the changes and issues instructions to the relevant other parts of the body (e.g. "loud noise – cover ears"). Some of the information received by the brain is stored for future use, a facility of crucial importance in the acquisition of skill, which involves the capacity to react in precisely the same way to similar stimuli time after time.

The two components of the whole nervous system are: (1) the central nervous system (CNS), comprising the control center of the brain and its message conduit, the spinal cord; and (2) the peripheral nervous system (PNS), which is the network of nerves originating in the brain and spinal cord and which is responsible for picking up messages from the skin and sense organs (sensory nerve cells) and carrying messages from the CNS to the muscles (motor nerve cells).

BOX 3.9 HEART RATE MONITOR (HRM)

A device comprising a chestband transmitter and a wrist-worn receiver that indicates how fast the heart is beating. The principle of exercising within a certain percentage of maximum heart rate has been known for years; but only with the advent of the HRM has the ability to apply those benefits been available to athletes. It is necessary to know the maximum heart rate (MHR) of the athlete and the threshold heart rate, the point at which exercise moves from aerobic effort to anaerobic. By exercising at slightly below the threshold, one can gradually force it up.

Nerves are spread throughout the entire body; each one consists of a bundle of minute nerve fibers and each fiber is part of a nerve cell, or neuron, of which there are about 100 billion woven into each body in such a way as to bypass the packed body cells. To do this, the network needs a shuttle service provided by connector neurons that carry signals back and forth. Further physical facts about signals are, first, that the nerve fibers that pick up sensations from receptors and deliver them to the CNS, do so with electrical impulses that are chemically charged; changes in the balance of the minerals sodium and potassium in the cells cause the impulse. Second, the speed of the impulse varies from fiber to fiber and with environmental conditions. And third, fibers covered in sheaths of myelin (a fatty substance) conduct impulses faster than naked fibers.

Perhaps the clearest way of depicting the role of the nervous system is by tracing its stages. Suppose you are a gun marksman (or woman); you must use primarily the senses of sight and touch when focusing on the target and aligning the gun and make adjustments to these environmental factors. A first step is made by bringing the target into focus: the eyes are, of course, sense organs (i.e. an assembly of receptors) and their surface, known as the retina, will react to rays of light by changing its chemical structure; this triggers off an electrical impulse that travels along nerve cells, or neurons, to the brain.

There are no direct connections between neurons, so the impulse may have to travel a circuitous route. The tiny gaps between neurons are synapses and these are bridged by a chemical neurotransmitter that takes the impulse across the synapse to the next neuron. The points of connection with the next neuron are called dendrites, which are in effect short, message-carrying fibers. One long fiber called an axon carries messages away from one neuron to the dendrites of the next. It takes only fractions of a second for the impulse to make its way through the synapses and neurons to the brain.

The fine web of nerves running through most of the body pales beside the densely complex mesh of neurons in the brain. Senses gleaned from our contact with the environment provide inputs that are sent to the brain; this processes the information before sending out instructions to muscles and glands. Most of our behavior in and out of sports is controlled in this way. A fast pitcher in a baseball game may choose to do many different things based on his sense impressions, mostly picked up by his vision and touch. He may notice a shuffle in the hitter's gait; he may feel moisture rising in the air that may affect the trajectory of his ball. His brain sends messages to his muscles so that he deliberately pitches a fast, curving delivery.

But not all of our behavior is produced by such a process: the receiving hitter may not expect the fast ball which zips sharply toward his head, prompting him to jerk his head away almost immediately to protect it from damage – as we'd withdraw a hand inadvertently placed on a hot iron. The spinal cord section of the CNS controls this type of reflex action. The nervous impulse defines an arc that short-circuits the brain, so that the message never actually reaches it.

The behavior resulting from the reflex arc is sudden and often uncoordinated because all the muscle fibers contract together to avoid the danger. A boxer drawing away from a punch, a goalkeeper leaping to save a short-range shot, a volleyball player blocking an attempted spike; all these suggest automatic responses that need not involve conscious will for their successful completion. We hear much about reflex movements in sports and, clearly, sports in which fast reaction is crucial do exhibit such responses. But most sports action is governed by the brain and, for this reason, we need to look in more detail at the structure and functions of this most vital of organs.

While the brain itself is an integrated unit which, like any other living organ, needs a continuous supply of food and oxygen to produce energy, it can be seen in its component parts, each of which has specific functions. The medulla, for instance, controls involuntary activities that we can't control consciously, but which are essential for survival (such as breathing and heartrate). Also of interest for athletic performance is the cerebellum, which receives messages from the muscles, ears, eyes, and other parts and then helps coordinate movement and maintain balance so that motion is smooth and accurate. Injury to this component doesn't cause paralysis, but impairs delicate control of muscle and balance; for instance, the ability to surf or skate would be lost. All voluntary and learned behavior is directed by the cortex, the largest portion of the brain; this forms the outer layer of the area known as the cerebrum lying at the fore of the brain.

The cerebrum is divided into two halves, or hemispheres, each of which is responsible for movement and senses on its opposite side. Nerves on the two sides of the body cross each other as they enter the brain, so that the left hemisphere is associated with the functions of the right-hand side of the body. In most right-handed people, the left half of the cerebrum directs speech, reading, and writing while the right half directs emotions; for left-handers, the opposite is true. So, Marat Safin's service would have been controlled by the right side of his brain, while his emotional outbursts would be associated with the left. Physical movement is controlled by the motor area: motor neurons send impulses from this area to muscles in different parts of the body. The more precise the muscle movements, the more of the motor area is involved; so a hammer thrower's actions wouldn't use up much space while a dart player's would, as he or she would be utilizing fine movements of the fingers.

The only other zone of the brain I want to note at present is the thalamus, which is where pain is felt. Pain, of course, is principally a defensive phenomenon designed to warn us of bodily danger both inside and outside the body. Impulses originating in the thalamus travel to the sensation area so that a localization of danger can be made. This is a mechanistic account of our reactions to pain: it's actually affected by all manner of intervening factors, including self-belief. In other words, if people do not believe they will feel pain, they probably won't – at least under certain conditions. There are also cultural definitions of pain: we learn to interpret pain and react to it and the thresholds may differ from culture to culture.

Such is the nature of competitive sports nowadays that few concessions to pain are allowed. Inspirational coaches encourage performers to conquer pain by developing a kind of immunity, just ignoring pain. Chemical ways of "tricking" the brain have been developed. Some drugs, for example, cause nerve cells to block or release a neurotransmitter (the chemical that carries nerve impulses across synapses to the dendrite of the adjacent neuron), the idea being to break the chemical chains linking brain to cell. We'll look at the use of drugs more closely in Chapter 11. The point to bear in mind for now is that the CNS generally, and the brain in particular, play a central role, not only in movement, but in the delicate sensory adjustments that have to be made in the operation of all sports, even those such as power lifting, which seem to require pure brawn. The lifter's cerebellum enables him or her to control the consequences of the lift; without this, initiation might be possible but corrective feedback coordination would be absent. In short, there would be no balance and no instruction to the opposing (antagonistic) muscles to make a braking contraction on the lift's completion. The whole operation would collapse.

BOX 3.10 PAIN BARRIER

Most frequently refers to the physical feelings experienced because of the sensation of crossing certain thresholds of endurance. Crossing the pain barrier relates to pain tolerance and training for endurance events particularly is geared to instilling in an athlete the ability to tolerate pain for long periods. The pain in question is not chronic, of course; but it is a dispersed discomfort that distance runners and triathletes especially have to assimilate (chronic pain is long-lasting and intractable). Tolerance to pain may have a biological component, but its variability and susceptibility to change indicate that it also has a significant psychological component. In training, athletes are implored to "bite the bullet" or similar when approaching the pain threshold. Bodybuilders famously remind others of the "no pain, no gain" principle. Brazilian jujitsu fighters prepare for contests by a type of pain inoculation, inducing pain in training so as to safeguard against it during competition.

In his 2007 article on training processes leading to elite athletic performance, David Smith includes "the aptitude to tolerate pain and sustain effort" as part of the "solid psychological platform" that an athlete needs to build, suggesting that the resistance is acquired.

Mark Anshel examines the manner in which the construction is done: "Elite athletes tend to use one of two mental techniques in coping with physical discomfort, *association* and *dissociation*" (1997). The goal of the first is to remain "in touch with one's body" and maintain the necessary motivation to meet challenges: weight lifters "associate with" their muscles as they lift; runners concentrate on planting their feet with each stride. This strategy can backfire if the athlete's concentration wavers and he or she begins focusing on the area of pain rather than the bodily functions that enhance performance. Dissociation entails externalizing projecting feelings and sensations outward to surrounding events rather than inward to internal experiences. Both are examples of pain endurance.

John Draeger *et al.* suggest that pain can take on a compulsive character. In their study of exercise dependence, they note how some individuals experience physical pain as a habitual part of their compulsion yet feel obliged to endure it in order to continue exercising (2005).

While we exert a large degree of control over our bodies through the CNS, many vital activities, such as heartbeat, peristalsis, and functioning of the kidneys simply can't be controlled voluntarily. Handling these is a secondary system of nerves called the autonomic nervous system (ANS). Many of the cell bodies of the ANS lie outside the brain and spinal cord and are massed together in bunches, each bunch being a ganglion. These ganglia receive information from receptors in the various organs of the body and then send out the appropriate instructions to muscles, such as the heart, and glands, such as salivary glands. The instructions are interesting in that they are twofold and antagonistic.

Unlike skeletal muscle which is either stimulated to contract or not (it needs no nerve impulse to relay), cardiac muscle and the smooth (as opposed to striated) muscle of other organs must be stimulated either to contract more than usual or to relax more than usual. To achieve this the ANS is divided into two substrata: the sympathetic system (more centrally located) and the parasympathetic system (more dispersed). The parasympathetic system constricts the pupil of the eyes, increases the flow of saliva, expands the small intestine, and shrinks the large intestine; the sympathetic system has the opposite effect. Impulses are propagated continuously in both systems, the consequences of which are known as *tone* – a readiness to respond quickly to stimulation in either direction. (Sympathetic derives from the Greek *sym* for have and *pathos* for feeling.)

Tone is rather important in certain sports: for instance, a panic-inducing visual stimulus will cause an increase in sympathetic impulses and a decrease in parasympathetic impulses to the heart, eliciting a greater response than just a sympathetic stimulation. Impulses from the two systems always have antagonistic effects on organs. The name autonomic nervous system implies that it's independent and self-regulated, whereas, in fact, the centers that control ANS activity are in the lower centers of the brain and usually below the threshold of conscious control. The appeal of bringing ANS functions under conscious control is fascinating; yogis have for centuries been able to slow heartbeat quite voluntarily, with corresponding changes to the entire body. The potential for this in sports, particularly in the areas of recovery and recuperation, is huge.

In sports, responses to change in the environment have usually got to be swift and definite. Consequently, our treatment of the nervous system has focused on its ability to direct changes and issue instructions to the relevant parts of the body in order that they react quickly. The quickest communication system is based, as we have seen, on electrical impulses. But the body's response to an internal change is likely to occur over a period of time and be brought about by chemical adjustments. The substances involved are hormone molecules and they are manufactured by a group of cells called endocrine glands, the most important of which is the pituitary attached to the hypothalamus on the underside of the brain. This produces a growth hormone by regulating the amount of nutrients taken into the cells. Hormones themselves are messengers, secreted into the blood in which they travel to all body parts, interacting with other cells and effecting a type of fine-tuning.

Because some hormones have very specific effects – many of them local rather than body-wide – they have been of service to sports performers seeking to enhance performance (as we'll discover in later chapters). The male testes secrete the hormone testosterone, which regulates the production of sperm cells and stimulates sex drive. Testosterone has been produced chemically and the synthetic hormone introduced into the body of competitors. Among the alleged effects are an increase in muscle bulk and strength and a more aggressive attitude.

Adrenaline is another example: as we have seen, it pours into the blood, stimulating the release of glycogen from the liver, expansion of blood vessels in the heart, brain, and limbs, and contraction of vessels in the abdomen. Fatigue diminishes and blood coagulates more rapidly (which is why boxers' seconds apply an adrenaline solution to facial cuts). Competitors pumped-up with adrenaline will usually have a pale

BOX 3.11 NERVOUS SYSTEM

The physical arrangement of neural tissue in vertebrates is the nervous system and its basic function is to receive information about the environment, and process, store, retrieve, and respond to it in appropriate ways. In all forms of physical activity, responses to change in the environment, to be effective, have to be swift and definite. Possessing a skill means being able to respond relevantly to surrounding changes and maintain control over one's body.

The human nervous system comprises: (1) the central nervous system (CNS), which is the control center of the brain and its message conduit, the spinal cord; and (2) the peripheral nervous system (PNS) which is the network of nerves originating in the brain and spinal cord and which is responsible for picking up messages from the skin and sense organs (sensory nerve cells) and carrying messages from the CNS to muscles (motor nerve cells).

While humans exert a large degree of control over their bodies through the CNS, many vital activities, such as heartbeat, peristalsis, and functioning of the kidneys are involuntary. Regulating these is a secondary system of nerves called the autonomic nervous system (ANS). Many of the cell bodies of the ANS lie outside the brain and spinal cord and are massed together in bunches called ganglia, which receive information from receptors in the various organs of the body and then send out appropriate instructions to muscles, such as the heart, and glands, such as salivary glands. Activation of organs and mechanisms under the control of the ANS will affect levels of arousal, which is crucial to athletes.

The ANS is divided into two strata: the sympathetic system (more centrally located in the body and responsible for changes associated with arousal) and the parasympathetic system (more dispersed). The parasympathetic system constricts the pupils of the eyes, increases the flow of saliva, expands the small intestine, and shrinks the large intestine; the sympathetic system has the opposite effect and is much slower. This is why bodily changes that occur after a sudden fright are rapid, but the process whereby they resume normal functioning is gradual.

The name autonomic nervous system implies that it is independent and self-regulated, whereas, in fact, the centers that control ANS activity are in the lower portions of the brain and usually below the threshold of conscious control. In sport, the appeal of bringing ANS functions under conscious control is obvious: the potential, particularly in the areas of relaxation, recovery from injury and perhaps even skill acquisition (among others) is great.

complexion, on account of their blood being diverted from skin and intestine and dilated pupils; hearts will be pounding and the breathing will be fast. The muscles will have the capacity to contract quickly and effectively either for, as the expression goes, fight or flight. This is an unusually fast hormonal change and most influences are long term, concerning such features as growth and sexual maturity. When they pass through the liver, the hormones are converted to relatively inactive compounds that are excreted as waste product, or urea, by the kidneys; this is why urinalysis is the principal method of detecting banned substances. It determines hormonal products in urine.

The chemical fine-tuning of the body is extensive and, in the healthy body, works continuously to modify us internally. Sweat glands are largely responsible for our adjustment to heat and, as many sports activate these, we should recognize their importance. The glands' secretions cover the skin with millions of molecules of water and they begin rising to the surface (epidermis) when external temperatures exceed about 25°C/77°F, depending on weight of clothing or the rigor of the activity performed. When blood reaching the hypothalamus is 0.5–1°C/33°F above normal, nerve impulses conveyed by the ANS stimulate sweat glands into activity.

Fluid from the blood is filtered into the glands and passes through their ducts so that a larger amount of moisture is produced on the skin surface. As it evaporates, the heat in the molecules escapes, leaving coolness. The internal temperature of the body is kept within acceptable limits, as long as the sweat continues to take away the heat. (When temperatures drop, a reflex action is to shiver, which is a spasmodic muscular contraction that produces internal heat.) Most, but not all, sweating results from the eccrine glands; secretions around the armpits and nipples of both sexes and the pubic area of females come from apocrine glands, which discharge not only salt and water, but odorless organic molecules that are degraded by skin bacteria and give off distinct smells. In mammals, the smell has a sexual function, though the lengths to which humans go in trying to suppress or disguise the smell suggests that the function have been discarded in our species.

A general point here is that sweat is not just water but a concentration of several materials and profuse sweating may deprive the body of too much salt. Heat prostration and sunstroke are curses to marathon runners and triathletes and their efforts to conquer them include swallowing salt tablets before the race, drinking pure water at stages during the race, and taking Gatorade or other solutions of electrolytes (salt and other compounds that separate into ions in water and can therefore help in the conduction of nerve impulses and muscle contraction). Problems for these athletes multiply in humid climates where the air contains so much vapor that the sweat can't evaporate quickly enough to produce a cooling effect; instead, it lies on the skin's surface forming a kind of seal. The result is known as heat stagnation. Even more dangerous is the situation when, after prolonged sweating due to activity in hot atmospheres, sweat production ceases and body temperatures soar to lethal levels.

Sweat glands perform a vital compensatory function in minimizing the effects of heat during physical activity and, under instruction of the brain, try to stabilize body temperature at around 37°C/98.6°F. But their thermostatic powers have clear limitations when tested by athletes, for whom 26 miles is but the first station of the advance toward the boundaries of human endurance.

The journalist who coined the now-clichéd term "well-oiled machine" to describe some highly efficient football team actually, and perhaps unwittingly, advanced a rather accurate description of the collection of trained and healthy individuals in question. Machines in the plural would have been more correct because, when examined in one perspective, that's what human beings are: a functioning series of systems made of cells and based on principles that any engineer, biologist, or chemist would find sound. But this is a partial and inadequate description and this chapter has merely set up a model; now it must be set in context and seen to work. We now have a grasp of the basic equipment and capabilities of the body; we still know little of its properties and motivations. Sports as activities, derive from natural faculties, but the particular form or shape they have taken and the way they has been perpetuated and mutated over the centuries is not understandable in purely biological terms. It needs explanation all the same and this will be the task of the following chapters.

OF RELATED INTEREST

Introduction to the Human Body: The essentials of anatomy and physiology, 2nd edition by Gerard J. Tortora and Bryan H. Derrickson (Wiley & Sons, 2006) is a reliable and comprehensive 700+ pages primer on the structure and functions of the body.

The Biophysical Foundations of Human Movement, 2nd edition, by Bruce Abernethy, Stephanie Hanrahan, Vaughan Kippers, Laurel Mackinnon, and Marcus Pandy (Human Kinetics, 2005) takes a multidisciplinary approach to biophysics, integrating contributions from functional anatomy, exercise physiology, and other disciplines.

Introduction to Kinesiology: Studying physical activity, with Web Study Guide, 3rd edition, by Shirl Hoffman (Human Kinetics, 2009) explains the evolving discipline of kinesiology, demonstrating how its many subject areas integrate into a unified body of knowledge. Kinesiology is the study of the mechanics of body movements. This all-inclusive approach gives students a solid background in the field and prepares them for further study and course work. Engaging and jargon-free, this outstanding text also introduces students to the available job prospects and areas of study and professional practice in kinesiology.

Structure and Function of the Musculoskeletal System, 2nd edition, by James Watkins (Human Kinetics, 2009) offers readers a clear conception of how the components of the musculoskeletal system coordinate to produce movement and adapt to the strain of everyday physical activity and the effects of aging. Musculoskeletal denotes that the two systems are considered integrally – integrating anatomy and biomechanics to describe the intimate relationship between the structure and function of the musculoskeletal system. This unique reference thoroughly explores the biomechanical characteristics of musculoskeletal components and the response and adaptation of these components to the physical stress imposed by everyday activities.

In the seventeenth century, the French philosopher René Descartes (1596–1650) tried to explain living processes like digestion, growth, and reproduction in terms of a mechanical model, i.e. the human as a machine. Repeat the exercise: break the human body down into its component parts and analyze the relationships between them as if you were studying a machine, then do a specification sheet (rather as car manufacturers do), incorporating dimensions, safety ratings, replacement parts, insurance, maintenance costs, unique features, etc.

Finally, create some copy for a possible advertisement, for example: "Beneath the sleek contours of its outer shell is an engine incorporating all the latest technological advances – from electronic microchip management systems controlling hybrid synergy fuel system and timing through to the latest 6-valve VVT-I system with turbo charger and intercooler together with 170-brake horsepower. With an acceleration of 0–60 mph in 9 seconds and a top speed of 120 mph the machine runs well with no noticeable adjustment on unleaded fuel and indigenously generated electricity (the sealed 168-cell nickel metal hydride rechargeable battery providing 201.6 volts). Lower drag coefficient at 0.29 reduces air resistance, especially at higher speeds. The fully independent multi-link suspension, disc brakes on all wheels, power steering, and electronically controlled 4-wheel antilock brake system combine to offer precise handling.

Regenerative braking, a process for recovering kinetic energy when braking or traveling down a slope and storing it as electrical energy in the traction battery for later use while reducing wear and tear on the brake pads. Climate-control air conditioning powered by solar-paneled sun roof. Its leather interior and 6-speaker radio/cd/MP3 player provides comfort, while ABS and front and side airbags afford security. 3-D mapping, voice-guidance satellite navigation is standard."

CHAPTER 4

A Very Different Animal

KEY ISSUES

▌ How old is sport?

▌ What pleasure did people take from being cruel to animals?

▌ When did we stop hunting and start rearing animals?

▌ Where were the first Olympic Games held?

▌ Why has the sight of human combat thrilled us for two thousand years?

▌ . . . and what impact did industrialism make on sport – and on us?

THE TASTE FOR BLOOD

Recognize anything in the following activity that would make you call it sport? Time: early-1800s. Place: Birmingham, England. Players: a tied-up bull and a ferocious dog.

> Sometimes the dog seized the bull by the nose and "pinned" him to the earth, so that the beast roared and bellowed again, and was brought down upon its knees. . . The people then shouted out "Wind, wind!" that is, to let the bull have breath, and the parties rushed forward to take off the dog . . . However, the bulls were sometimes pinned between the legs, causing [them] to roar and rave about in great agony.

The passage is from Richard Holt's book, *Sport and the Working Class in Modern Britain*, which is full of other lurid details of what passed as sports in the eighteenth and nineteenth centuries (1990: 16). The bull sometimes had hot pepper blown in its nostrils to irritate it and the dogs were trained specifically to go for the bull's head. Sometimes a hole was dug in the ground so that the bull could protect its head while the dogs attacked. Bears were sometimes chained by the neck or ankle and made to defend themselves against ferocious dogs.

Bearbaiting and bullbaiting and the variations on these "sports" began to decline in popularity, although very slowly, from the late seventeenth century onward. They were banned in England by the Puritans during the Civil Wars and Commonwealth

(1642–60) and were permanently outlawed by act of Parliament in 1835, by which time they had also been outlawed in most countries in northern Europe.

As well as baiting, there was cockfighting, which involved pitting two highly trained fowl together, and dogfighting, which goes on in Britain and the United States today, albeit in an illicit way. These types of activities in which animals were made to fight, maim and often kill each other, were regarded as sports. It sounds monstrous to compare these kind of cruel, barbaric spectacles with today's sports. But think of the similarities. There are five obvious ones.

1 *Competition* for no reason apart from competition itself: unlike animal fights in other contexts, there were no evolutionary functions (such as "survival of the fittest") served by the fights.
2 *Winning* as a sole aim: spectators were interested in a result rather than the actual process of fighting, and animal contests typically ended with one either dead or at least too badly injured to continue. Holt adds to his description of the Birmingham bullbait: "Blood would be dropping from the nose and other parts of the bull" (1990: 16).
3 *Spectators*: the tournaments were set up with an audience in mind – in specially dug pits around which a crowd could stand, in barns, or other public places where the action was visible to spectators.
4 *Gambling*: the thrill of watching the contest was enhanced by wagering on one of the animals and money frequently changed hands among the spectators.
5 *Animals* were trained and used: although the contests were unacceptably cruel by today's standards, we still train and employ animals in sports, such as horse- and dogracing, pigeonracing, polo, and (though repugnant to many) bullfighting. And the Staffordshire bull terrier remains consistently one of the top five most popular breeds of dog in the world. In fact, I write this from the part of the world where the breed was first developed in the seventeenth century, partly as a result of the decline in bullbaiting and the rise in interest in dogfighting.

Perhaps the most remarkable legacy is the Iditarod, a 1,180-mile race through Alaska featuring packs of huskies pulling a person in a sled. The original trail was forged by dog sleds carrying freight to miners and prospectors; the latter-day contest recreates the hunger and exhaustion of driving for eight days and nights at temperatures of –60°F/–51°C.

All five elements are present in human cultures that extend far beyond the Industrial Revolution of the late eighteenth and early nineteenth centuries, which is the conventional starting point for studies of sports. True, the distinct shape, or form of sports developed in that crucial period and the organizational structure that distinguishes sports from mere play was a product of the industrial age. But we can go back much further: it's possible to trace the origins of contemporary sports back to primitive matters of survival; which is precisely what I intend to do in this chapter.

The methods we once used for getting nutrition have been reshaped and refined, but are still vaguely discernible. Track and field events such as running and throwing are virtually direct descendants of our ancestors' chase of prey and their attempts to stun or kill them with missiles; some events still consciously model themselves on the disciplines and aptitudes associated with hunting, modern pentathlon (riding, fencing, shooting, swimming, and running) being the clearest example. Today's versions are, of course, more enjoyable than the originals in which hunters might return from a day's pursuit minus a couple of their associates.

More advanced tool use, which enhanced the ability to survive and improved nutrition, also generated a new adaptation that we see reflected in current sports. Tools that were once used for killing or butchery have been transformed into symbolic instruments like bats, rackets, and clubs and used in a fashion, which disguises the functions of their predecessors. The origins of others, such as epées, are more transparent. The purpose of this chapter is to provide an account of the beginning of sports and its subsequent development up to the last century.

BOX 4.1 PLAY AND GAMES

"A free activity standing quite consciously outside 'ordinary' life as being 'not serious,' but at the same time absorbing the player intensely and utterly. It is an activity connected with no material interest, and no profit can be gained by it." This is the serviceable definition of Johann Huizinga in his text *Homo Ludens* (Man the Player). A game is a form of play, which is played according to rules. In his *Man, Play, and Games*, Roger Callois divides games into four types: games of chance, in which the outcome is decided by luck, competition, in which skill is the determining factor, mimicry, in which the roles or actions of others is copied, and vertigo, which is sensation or thrill-seeking behavior.

The model of sports I'm building suggests the entire phenomenon has human foundations that were established several thousand years ago. It follows that any chronicle must track its way back through history to discover the reasons for the human pursuit of what are, on this account, mock hunts and battles and the purposes they serve at both individual and social levels. The latter point will be answered in the next chapter, but the immediate task is to unravel the mystery of ancestry: how did sports begin? It's a question that requires an ambitious answer, one that takes up deep into history for a starting point.

AFTER THE PLANET OF THE APES

The popular image of humans emerging from their caves before progressing to ever-higher levels of civilization has given filmmakers some wonderful raw material. Kevin Connor's *The Land That Time Forgot* (1974), featuring marauding ape-men, Don Chaffey's *One Million Years BC* (1966), made memorable by a young Raquel Welch clad in animal skin bikini, and *10,000 BC* (2008), Roland Emmerich's tale of a mammoth hunter who staves off the attacks of saber-toothed tigers, are three of several films that have capitalized on appealing but erroneous premises. As historical documents the films are about as accurate as the *Ice Age* films. Our species developed in a series of relatively sudden lurches. Traveling on two legs is one of them; tripling of brain size is another.

Homo sapiens first appeared 100,000 to 200,000 years ago. In evolutionary terms, this is an eyeblink. Several discoveries of remains have undermined efforts to trace what used to be called the "missing link" – the creature that was more intelligent than apes but had not yet become the finished human article. In all probability, such a creature didn't exist at all. The more we know, the less simple it seems.

Every new find indicates that there is no single line of descent with a few evolutionary dead-ends branching off it. For hundreds and thousands of years, a bewildering number of different species and subspecies of ape-like and then human-like (hominoid) animals adapted, migrated, and then perished. Only one thing is clear: the species we call human beings came out of Africa, not in a single process of migration, but after a series of waves of migration.

The earth was once like the *Planet of the Apes* movies: apes were everywhere ten million years ago. There were about fifty different ape-like species, some of them tree-dwellers, others living on the thickly forested ground. And, although they didn't talk or dominate humans as in the movies, some might have even used sticks and stones as crude tools. Then, they began to die out, leaving only the most adaptable and so most intelligent species. Exactly why so many species perished is not absolutely clear, but the strong likelihood is that, around eight million years ago, there was a dramatic environmental change that turned much of the earth's surface to grassland. Remember the natural selection mechanism we discussed in the previous chapter: the species that could adapt successfully to this survived, leaving other forest-dwellers to die out.

It's probable that, out of all the survivors, several species were bipedal, walking erect across the grassy, flat terrain. Many of these would have perished, leaving those best-equipped species to remain and propagate. One of these species was a hominoid that emerged 4.4 million years ago, stood about 4 feet tall with a muscular, hairy body that weighed about 110 lb. She is the earliest known member of the human lineage; she had long, powerful arms that made climbing relatively easy, and had opposable big toes for grip. The interesting feature about this ape-like creature, known as *Ardipithecus ramidus*, was that she was the first known human ancestor who walked upright rather than using knuckles for support.

Australopithecus afarensis, which emerged about 3.2 million years ago, was also bipedal but had lost the adaptation that allows apes to climb trees. Lucy, as her discoverers named her, had an unusual pelvis that enabled her to move on two legs. This had important evolutionary consequences: the two upper limbs used by other species for locomotion were unhindered, allowing the 3 foot (1 meter) tall Lucy, to use the arms for other purposes.

Prior to the discovery of Lucy's fossil in 1974, it had been thought that big-brained creatures started using tools, and, to free up their hands, began to walk upright. Lucy, whose brain was about the third of the size of a human brain (i.e. not much bigger than a chimp's), walked on two feet and even had "modern" hands, yet showed no evidence that she'd used tools. *Australopithecus* is the generic name of small-brained fossils.

Yet, there were larger-brained creatures around and the discovery of skull KNM-ER 1470 (it's always been known by its museum classification) with a cranial capacity of 785 cc (compared to a human's 1,400 cc), suggested a coexistence of bipedal species. There may have been several other two-legged creatures for which the grassland was, at first, suitable, but which failed to make later adaptations and died out.

By contrast, one of the most successful creatures in evolutionary terms, *Homo erectus* arrived on the scene in East Africa and, later, spread to Asia and Europe between 1.5 to 2 million years ago and survived up to about 100,000 years ago. According to some theories of evolution, *Homo erectus* instituted some significant adaptations and evolved into the earliest members of our species *Homo sapiens*, who were succeeded in Africa by the anatomically modern *Homo Sapiens sapiens* and in Europe by *Homo Sapiens neandertalensis*, or Neanderthals. (*Sapiens* is Latin for wise.)

Homo erectus was a respectful and cautious scavenger, though much evidence points to males banding together in predatory squads and becoming proficient hunters of large animals like bears, bison, and elephants and using equipment such as clubs and nets. Layers of charcoal and carbonized bone in Europe and China have also suggested that *Homo erectus* may have used fire. Physically, the male of the species might have stood as tall as 5 feet 11 inches (1.8 meters) and, while his brain was smaller than our own, the animal had enough intelligence to make primitive tools and hunting devices. The expansion of brain size came along long after the evolution of upright walking on two legs.

Neanderthals, who were well established in Ice Age Europe by 70,000 BCE, certainly had sufficient intellect to use fire on a regular basis and utilized a crude technology in making weapons, which, as predatory creatures, they needed. Their name comes from the name of a region in Germany where remains were found and their distinct features are familiar: prominent brows and sloping forehead, giving them a brutish countenance. As their prey were the large and mobile bison, mammoth, and reindeer, they made good use not only of physical weapons but also of tact, or stealth. They'd hunt in packs and allocate assignments to different members – like a proper team. Other hints of social life are found amongst Neanderthals. Evidence of burials, for example, indicates an awareness of the significance of death; ritual burials are not conducted by species other than humans. Archeological research indicates that the majority of Neanderthals were right-handed – the relevance of which will become clearer on pp. 433–6 (Llaurens *et al.*, 2009)

BOX 4.2 THE ICE AGE

This was actually a series of fluctuations in climate that caused cold periods when much of the earth was glacial with warmer interglacial spells, and lasted from 1,640,000 to about 10,000 years ago. The whole span is known as the Pleistocene period.

There's also something uniquely human about the rapport with other species: the relationships humans have with other animals is an unusual one and Neanderthals may have been the first to forge this special link. It's possible that Neanderthals attempted to domesticate as well as hurt other species. The cartoon depiction of Fred Flintstone adorned in bearskins is a bit more accurate than it seems: it's quite probable that the wearing of skins was thought to invest the wearer with some of the animal's qualities (such as strength of the mammoth or speed of the deer). The close association between many sports and animals is undoubtedly connected to this type of belief.

Some see Neanderthals as distinct from and having no breeding with *Homo sapiens*, while others see them gradually replaced by *Homo sapiens* after long periods of genetic mixing. Whether or not they were replaced or just became extinct, two facts are clear: one is technological, the other cultural. Neanderthals exploited raw materials for tool manufacture and use; they also displayed collective behavior in the division of labor they used to organize and coordinate their hunts. Related to these two activities is the fact that the reciprocal obligations systems used in hunting were carried over into domestic life. Neanderthals were cave dwellers and so used a home-base arrangement; this leads to the suggestion that they most probably constructed a stable pattern of life, possibly based on role allocation.

Homo sapiens shared these features: they used tools, hunted in groups, and had division of labor at the home base and especially in the hunting parties. Accepting responsibility for specific duties had obvious advantages for survival: coordinating tasks as a team would have brought more success than pell-mell approaches. Signals, symbols, markers, and cues would have been important to elementary strategies. Complementing this was the sharing of food at the central home base. Maybe this awakened humans to the advantages of pair bonding and the joint provisioning of offspring: the mutual giving and receiving, or reciprocity, remaining the keystone of all human societies.

HUNTERS: FORERUNNERS OF SPORT

The hunter-gatherer mode of life is central to our understanding of the origin of sports. It began with foraging and scavenging as long as three million years ago; hunting as a regular activity followed a period of feeding off carcasses or spontaneous picking. Including more meat in the diet brought about nutritional changes, but also precipitated the invention of more efficient means of acquiring food. The response was to hunt for it – and this had widespread behavioral repercussions, not only in terms of social organization but also in physical development.

Covering ground in pursuit of quarry required the kind of speed that could only be achieved by an efficient locomotion machine. The skeleton became a sturdier structure able to support the weight of bigger muscles and able quickly to transmit the force produced by the thrust of limbs against the ground. Lower limbs came to be more directly under the upper body, so that support was more efficient in motion; leg bones lengthened and the muscles elongated, enabling a greater stride and an ability to travel further with each step. The human evolved into a mobile and fast runner, and, though obviously not as fast as some other predators, the human's bipedalism – using only two legs for walking – left upper limbs free for carrying.

Where quarry was near enough to be approached, but also near enough to be disturbed, hunters would need short bursts of explosive speed, an ability to contract muscles and release energy anaerobically. In short, they needed the kind of power which modern sprinters possess. Hunts might take up an entire day and would demand of the hunter stamina, endurance, and the capacity to distribute output over long periods – precisely the type of aerobic work performed by middle-distance and marathon runners, not to mention triathletes.

Effective synthesis of ATP (adenosine triphosphate) from ADP (adenosine diphosphate), as discussed in Chapter 3 and the removal of waste lactic acid was enhanced by respiratory evolution. Ribs expanded and the muscles between them developed to allow the growth of lungs, which permitted deeper breathing to take in more and more air. Since the sustained release of energy depends on a supply of glucose and other foods, the hunter's diet was clearly important. While we can't be certain exactly what proportion of the diet was taken up by meat, we can surmise that this protein-rich food source played a role in balancing the daily expenditure of energy and providing enough fats and proteins for tissue repair.

Habitual meat eating was not unqualified in its advantages – and I'm not referring to the development of a meat-centered diet and the associated problem of high cholesterol. It introduced the very severe disadvantage of bringing humans into open competition with the large mammalian carnivores and scavengers like hogs, panthers, and tigers, which roamed the savannas looking for food. Ground speed was, in this instance, a requisite quality for survival, the clawless, weak-jawed biped being ill equipped to confront the specialist predators.

In time, evolution yielded a capacity to make and use not only tools but also weapons like clubs and stones, which at least evened up the odds. The physical clash with other animals continues to fascinate elements of the human population, a fact witnessed in such activities as bearbaiting, which still goes on in some parts of Asia, boxing kangaroos, and the type of man *vs.* horse races in which Jesse Owens performed during the undignified twilight of his career (as we will see in Chapter 10). A big advantage that tilted the balance was the increase in the human's most important asset.

Compared to body size, our brain is a truly exceptional organ; it's one of the most obvious physical features that distinguish us from the rest of the animal world. How did we acquire our large brains? One theory holds that cooking our food enabled us to digest nutritionally rich vegetables with thick skins that could not be eaten raw. Cooking food made it more easily available, cracking open or destroying physical barriers such as thick skins or husks, bursting cells and sometimes modifying the molecular structure of proteins and starches; all of which gave us the extra calories necessary for brain growth – food for thought, so to speak.

This view opposes the more traditional view of meat as the trigger behind brain development. The larger brain, with its larger neurons and denser, more complex circuitry of dendrite branches, may well have been related to the long days spent beneath the hot sun, hunting in comparative safety while the bigger predators sought shade and rest. As carnivores, we would scavenge what the big cats left behind. The meat gave us energy and the effect of the sun on our heads caused the brain to swell.

It was once thought that bipedalism was a prime mover of brain expansion: freeing up arms, enabled our ancestors to explore and discover, prompting further curiosity about the world and a desire to re-shape it in a way we desired. The results of our handiwork stimulated further enquiry, the development of knowledge and technology and an evolutionary cerebral adaptation. The discovery of *Ardipithecus ramidus*, which walked fully upright undermined this view: it would be another couple of million years before this creature's descendants developed the large brains and higher intelligence that separates humans from the rest of the animal kingdom, suggesting that the brain expansion occurred independently of upright walking.

Obscure as the relationship between brain growth and behavioral change may remain, we should at least recognize that neither is independent of the environment in which the processes take place. For instance, survival success would have depended on the ability to identify in the surrounding environment things that were needed: rocks for tools and weapons, tracks of game and competitive predators, sources of vegetable. The need to discriminate perceptually encouraged larger brains and better communication skills, which in turn occasioned bigger and improved brains; these more complicated organs needed nourishment in terms both of food and social stimulation, and this would have been reflected in subsistence methods and social arrangements. The process had no "result" as such, for the brain constantly developed in response to behavioral change but at the same time led to new thoughts that were translated into action: a continuous feedback motion.

Hunting, gathering, and, to a decreasing degree, scavenging were the main human adaptations. Among their correlates were division of labor, basic social organization, increases in communication, and, of course, increase in brain size. Slowly and steadily the species evolved ways of satisfying basic biological drives and needs: food supply, shelter against the elements and predators, sex, and reproduction. In the process, a prototype emerged: "man the hunter" (and I choose the phrase with care, as evidence suggests that the more robust males assumed most responsibility in catching prey).

The species' greater brain capacity gave them the advantage of intellect, an ability to both devise methods of tracking and capture, to utilize cunning and stealth as well as force and to innovate with hunting tools. Lightweight throwing spears and bows and arrows were easily portable weapons and the improvement of cutting tools and animal cleaning processes made for more effective butchery

The intellectual demands were many: concentration became important; intelligence enabled our ancestors to ignore distractions and fix attention, or focus, on the sought-after game. Hunts, especially for large animals, would be more effectively performed in squads and these required a level of coordination, synchronization, and communication. Cooperation and reciprocity were qualities of great use in hunting and at the home base, where the spoils would be shared.

The accumulated experience of the hunt itself would impart qualities – like courage in the face of dangerous carnivores who would compete for food. Risks were essential to reproductive success; if they hadn't been taken, the species would still be picking fruit. Among the specific skills refined in this period would have been an ability to aim and accurately deliver missiles, a capacity to judge pace in movement, and to overwhelm and conquer prey when close combat was necessary. We should also take note of the fact that humans became impressively good swimmers and divers, evolving equipment and functions that aided deep diving and fast swimming; this aquatic adaptation may have been linked to hunting for fish.

By now, you'll have detected where I'm headed with this argument. All these features are responses to the manner in which the species procured its food: this is essential to life and so has a strong, if not determining, effect on every aspect of both lifestyle and personality. If an existing method of obtaining food doesn't yield enough nutrition, then bodies suffer and the species either perishes or makes new adaptations, perhaps formulating alternative methods. In the event, what seems to have happened in the case of *Homo sapiens* is that they hit upon a novel way of guaranteeing a food supply that eliminated the need for many of the activities that had persisted for the previous 2 million years or more, and had carved deeply the features of human character and capacities. As recently as 10,000 years ago, *Homo sapiens* devised a way of exploiting the food supply, which was to remove the necessity of hunting and release humans to concentrate on building what is now popularly known as *civilization.*

Instead of exploiting natural resources around them, the species began to exploit its own ability. In short, the ability to create a food supply. This was accomplished by gathering animals and crops together, containing them in circumstances that permitted their growth and reproduction, then picking crops or slaughtering animals as necessary, without ever destroying the entire stock. In this way, supply was rendered a problem only by disease or inclement weather. The practice of cultivating land for use, rather than for mere existence, gave rise to farming.

ENTER THE FARMER

Although now open to debate, the beginnings of agriculture are seen in orthodox teaching to coincide with the end of what's called the Paleolithic Age – the early phase of the Stone Age, lasting about 2.5 million years, when primitive stone instruments came into common use. Some see the transition as swift and dramatic, though this view has been challenged by others who accentuate the uneven process of development over periods of time. For example, in Europe, following the recession of the Ice Age, there appears to have been an interlude in which certain animals, especially dogs, were domesticated, some cereals were harvested, and forms of stock management were deployed, but without the systematic approach of later agriculturists.

Obviously, regions differed considerably ecologically, and the period characterized by the transition from hunter-gatherer to farmer was neither smooth nor uniform. But it was sudden – in evolutionary terms, that is. We started the systematic domestication of animals – a process central to agriculture – only 10,000 years ago. It may have taken the form of controlled breeding or just providing fodder to attract wild herds, but the insight was basically the same: that enclosing and nourishing livestock was a far more effective and reliable way of ensuring food than hunting for it. It was also safer, of course.

BOX 4.3 PALEOLITHIC AGE

From *palaios*, the Greek for ancient times, and *lithos*, meaning stone, this describes the period in which primitive stone implements were used. Beginning probably more than 2.5 million years ago when our ancestors put an edge on a stone, pressed its thick end against the palm of the hand and realized its power to strike and cut, this age saw the arrival of the hunter-gatherer, as opposed to the simple forager cultures. It ended as recently as 10,000 years ago, when the domestication of animals and cultivation of plants started.

Complementing this discovery was the realization that planting and nurturing plants and harvesting only enough to meet needs so that regrowth was possible was an efficient exploitation of natural resources compared to the cumbersome and less predictable gathering method. The breakthroughs led to all manner of toolmaking and other technologies that added momentum to the agricultural transformation that's loosely referred to as the Neolithic Age (from the Greek *neo* meaning new and *lithos* meaning stone: a period when ground and polished tools and weapons made out of stone were introduced).

Remember: hunting and gathering had been dominant for more than two million years before. During that period the lifestyle and mentality it demanded became components of our character. Chasing, capturing, and killing with their attendant dangers were practiced features of everyday life. The qualities of courage, skill, and the inclination to risk, perhaps even to sacrifice on occasion, were not heroic but simply human and necessary for survival. What we'd now regard as epic moments were in all probability quite ordinary. The coming of farming made most of these qualities redundant. The hunting parties that honed their skills, devised strategies, and traded on courage were no longer needed. Instead, the successful farmer needed to be diligent, patient, responsible, regular, and steadfast. A farmer's tasks included cultivating soil, growing crops, and rearing animals to provide food, wool, and other products. Not hunting and killing them. The transition from hunter to farmer introduced strains.

Hunting and gathering affected us not only culturally but perhaps even genetically, so long and sweeping was its reign. No organism is a product purely of hereditary nature or of environmental experience. Humans are no different in being products of the interaction between genes and the environment: nature via nurture, to revive the phrase used in Chapter 2. But the kind of evolutionary change we're interested in advanced at different levels: the human way of living changed, but not in such a way as to incur an automatic switch in human beings themselves. After all, even rough arithmetic tells us that the 10,000 years in which agriculture has developed represents at most 0.5 percent of the period spent hunting and gathering. Imagine watching a five-set tennis match for three hours. If this represents the whole period in question, then the time it takes to play the very last winning point is the farming period, the foregoing time being the hunter-gatherer portion of human existence.

So, did we make a smooth adjustment, or are we still making appropriate changes to our way of life? Sport is the evidence that we're still making adaptations. It's as if cultural evolution sped ahead of biological evolution: we didn't completely change from one type of organism into another as quickly as the cultural pace required. There was – perhaps *is* – still too much of the hunter-gatherer in us to permit an easy settling down to breeding animals and sowing crops. Sport, in this scenario, is an accommodation: a way of incorporating the thrills and the prowess associated with the chase and the kill into a culture that no longer needs hunting.

In other words, sport is our sometimes elegant, sometimes unwieldy attempt to re-enact the hunt: imitate the chase, mimic the prey, copy the struggle, simulate the kill, and recreate the conditions under which such properties as bravery, fortitude, and resolve would be rewarded. It's a minor but important adaptation in which the customary skills, techniques, and habits were retained even when their original purpose had disappeared.

OK, it made far more sense to enclose, feed, and domesticate animals than to hunt them, as it did to sow crops rather than gather wild fruits and grains. It was perfectly possible to acknowledge this, while growing bored by it. How many times have you wanted and chased something or someone and when you finally get it or them, you feel an anticlimax and yearn for the excitement the chase? Maybe the tyro farmers craved the excitement the hunts used to bring. How could the spirit of the hunt be recaptured?

The answer was, as we now know, to keep it going: hunt for its own sake rather than for food. No matter that hunting served no obvious purpose any longer, let people engage in it for the sheer pleasure or tingle it generated. We throw javelins, race on horseback, hurl missiles at targets; these once had purpose. Now, they are play: we don't direct efforts to meeting the immediate material needs of life, or acquiring necessities. We do them because they bring joy. Hunting has become an *autotelic* activity, having no purpose apart from its own existence.

BOX 4.4 AUTOTELIC

From the Greek *auto*, meaning by or for itself, and *telos*, meaning end. An autotelic activity is one which has an end or purpose and is engaged in for its own sake.

Once detached from the food supply, the pseudo-hunt took on a life of its own. When survival no longer depended on killing game, the killing became an end; what was once an evolutionary means to an end became an end in itself. The new hunt no longer had as its motive the pursuit of food but rather the pursuit of new challenges. Although in behavioral terms much the same activity as hunting, the new version was an embryonic sports or at least an expression of the drive or impulse underlying sports right to the present day. Stripped of its original purpose, the mechanical aspects of the activity came to prominence. Team coordination, stealth, intelligence, daring, physical prowess, and courage in the face of danger were valued more than the end product and, over time, these became integrated into a series of activities, each in some way mimicking the original activities.

It sounds trite to say that the roots of sports lie in our primeval past when so many of today's sports operate not in response to survival but as adjuncts to commercial interests. At the same time, we should recognize that the impulses that make sports attractive enough to be commercially exploited are part of our evolutionary make-up. Why else would we pay to watch grown men kick a ball or fight each other or run around a track? There's nothing intrinsically entertaining about any of these activities. We, the spectators, are the ones that make them exciting.

If sport was the result of the attempt to reintroduce the thrill of the hunt into lives that were threatened with mundane routines in unchallenging environments, it was and remains both precious and profound. It may owe nothing to the hunt nowadays; but it still owes a good deal to the attempts at replacing the hunt with something comparably as stirring, invigorating and dramatic.

So, there is perfect sense in Gerhard Lukas's claim that "the first sport was spear throwing" (1969). Javelins, darts, blowguns, and bows and arrows were modifications of the basic projectile and unquestionably featured in mock as well as genuine hunts. The use of the bow is especially interesting in that it simulates the construction of an artifact, the target, the bull's eye, which, as its name implies, represented the part of the animal to be aimed at. Archery, as a purely autotelic behavior, actually had the quality of compressing a symbolic hunt into a finite area and allowing a precise way of assessing the results. As such, it had potential as an activity that could be watched and evaluated by others, who wouldn't participate except in a vicarious way. That is, they might experience it imaginatively through the participants – which is what most sports spectators do, even today. This vicariousness was, as we now realize, absolutely crucial to the emergence and development of spectator sport.

The facility for bringing the rationality and emotion of a hunt to a home base made it possible to include dozens, or hundreds, of people in the whole experience. Just witnessing an event offered some continuity, however tenuous, within change: spectators could "feel" the drama and tension of a supposed hunt from another age, through the efforts of the participants.

The obvious acknowledgment of this came with the custom-built stadium. Stadiums, or stadia (as some prefer the plural), came with the clustering together of human populations and the creation of city-states, i.e. cities that with their surrounding territories formed independent states. Irrigation was crucial to farming, of course, so most of the earliest known civilizations had their urban centers near rivers, as in China, India, and the Near and Middle East. Richard Mandell, in his *Sport: A Cultural History* urges caution in gleaning evidence of what we now call spectator sports in ancient civilizations (1984). But he does show that the Mesopotamians, for example, left traces of evidence that suggest physical competitions (Mesopotamia was an ancient region of southwestern Asia in what is today Iraq). These might have been tests of strength and skill; though they may also have been more military training regimes than amusements for the masses.

The seminal Egyptian civilization of some 5,000 years ago left much material in the form of documents, frescos, tombs, and bric-a-brac. In these we find depicted one of the most essential, enduring, and unchanging activities, and one which we will consider in the next section: combat.

IN PURSUIT OF ÁTHLON

At some stage in ancient history, the idea of rivalry seems to have struck chords. The straightforward drive of the hunt, in which packs pursued game, acquired a provision. The object was not merely the climax of a kill, but in administering the kill faster or more effectively than others. Competition between individuals or groups added a new and apparently appealing dimension to an already perilous activity, turning it into a game with some semblance of organization and a clear understanding of what constituted an achievement. The amusement value, it seems, was boosted by the introduction of a human challenge and by spectatorship.

It's probable, though undocumented, that physical combat activities between humans and perhaps animals coexisted with the autotelic hunts.

We needn't invoke the Cain and Abel fable to support the argument that intra-species fighting, for both instrumental and playful purposes, existed throughout history. It is one of the least changeable aspects of *Homo sapiens*. Combat has many different forms, ranging from wrestling to fencing; stripped to its basics, it expresses the rawest type of competition. As such, it seems to have held a wide appeal both for participants seeking a means to express their strength and resilience and for audiences who to this day are enraptured by the sight of humans disputing each other's physical superiority.

The hunt, or at least the mimetic, or imitative activity that replaced it, would have satisfied a certain need for those closely involved, but the actual behavior would have been so fluid and dispersed that it would not have been closely observed, certainly not as a complete and integrated action. Today's equestrian events in which riders on horseback traverse over obstacles, ditches, and hedges designed to resemble hunting (dressage was originally developed during the Renaissance as a method of training).

Spectators would have been much more easily accommodated at a permanent base where combat competitions could be staged in much the same way and with a similar purpose to hunting-inspired events: to break up tedious routines and raise emotions with brief but thrilling and relatively unpredictable episodes of violent action. Fighting has fascinated us over the centuries: whether between animals, unarmed humans, or armed humans pitched against large animals such as bears or tigers, violence in a controlled environment exerts a particular hold over our imaginations.

A fresco excavated from the tomb of an Egyptian prince and dated to about 4,000 years ago looks similar to a modern wall chart and shows wrestlers demonstrating over a hundred different positions and holds. Mandell suggests that there may have been professional wrestlers in the Egyptian civilization. Artwork shows fighters also using sticks about 1 meter long; even today, stick fighting persists in parts of Egypt, though in a more ritualized form. It's quite possible that the proximity to the Nile encouraged competitive swimming and rowing. In the plains of the Upper Nile region, hunting of large game, including elephants, was commonplace, the chariot being an effective vehicle for this purpose. Pharaoh Tutankhamen (fourteenth century BCE) is shown on one fresco hunting lions from his chariot. Amphibian Nile dwellers like crocodiles and hippopotamuses were also hunted. Crete (to the south of Greece in the Aegean Sea) had trade contacts with Egypt and some kind of cultural cross-fertilization is possible.

Certainly, Cretans were avid hunters and their relics suggest they were combat enthusiasts also, though the form of fighting they favored seems more akin to boxing than wrestling. According to J. Sakellarakis: "One finds in Crete, the first indications of the athletic spirit which was to evolve and reach a high pitch in subsequent centuries" (1979: 14).

The games that had been played in Egypt and to the East developed into more exacting performances with codified rules. We also have evidence of a version of bullfighting, and a type of cattle wrestling that resembles the modern rodeo in the United States. Bull leaping was a dangerous game that involved grasping the horns of an onrushing bull and vaulting over its body. Bull games are still popular today, of course.

The mythical and the mundane are intertwined in our knowledge of Greek civilization, popularly and justifiably regarded as the first culture to incorporate sports or, more specifically, competition, into civic life. The compulsion to pursue public recognition of one's supremacy through open contest with others was known by the Greeks as *agôn*. Athletic excellence achieved in competition was an accomplishment of, literally, heroic proportions. Myths of Hercules sending discuses into oblivion and Odysseus heaving boulders are important signifiers of the high value Greeks placed on physical feats, but the less spectacular evidence shows that they approached, organized, and assessed the outcomes of activities in a way, which is quite familiar.

"The spirit of competition and rivalry extended to every area of Greek life," writes Manolis Andronicus (1979: 43). The Greeks' approach was to win, and here we find the precursor of the obsessive drive for success that characterizes contemporary sport: winning was quite often at any cost and scant respect was paid to such things as "fairness."

Some may argue that the search for supremacy is a primordial competitive instinct. It's more likely that particular social arrangements in which inequality and distinct strata are key components encourage individuals to strive hard and better themselves by whatever means they can. Athletic prowess was one such means in the ancient civil society of Greece. Victors could acquire *arête*, the pinnacle of excellence, the ultimate attainment. Greeks were also very keen on physical perfection and part of the purpose of athletic competition was to display the brawny bodies of men, but not women. One of the ideals embedded in Greek games was *kalos kagathos*, meaning the "good and beautiful man."

In terms of organization, Greeks created events that exist today without major modification. They are credited with being the first organizers of sports on a systematic basis, the Olympic Games, which began in 776 BCE, being the clearest expression of this. This event integrated sports into a wider religious festival, drawing disparate competitors and spectators together at one site every four years in an effort to convince themselves they were in some sense united – even in times of conflict.

Greeks were also influential in their attempts to determine outcomes. Despite aphorisms about competing being more important than winning, victory was crucial and systems were designed to ensure accurate assessment of performance.

Exact distances were measured and staggers were introduced on racing circuits. Tallies of points were kept in multidisciplinary events like the pentathlon (the Greek *(thlon* meant award, or prize, from which came the noun *athlétés* to describe those who competed for the award*)*. Records of performances were kept (each Olympiad took the name of the victorious sprinter at the previous festival). The Games may have been less important as a spectacle than they were as a focal point around which to organize training. Physical fitness, strength, and the general toughness that derives from competition were important military attributes, and so the process was tuned to producing warriors as much as sports performers.

Sparta is the best-known city-state in this context: it was a site of phalanx training in which youths would be taken from their families and reared in an austere garrison where they would be honed for combat. Spartans provide the clearest historical evidence of a culture in which physical exercise was of paramount importance, though for military rather than aesthetic purposes. There was also a religious element to competition, for the Greeks believed that athletic victory indicated that the winners of events would be favored by the capricious gods in whom they believed.

It's important to remember that, while today's Olympics bear the same name as their ancient forerunner, they were not games in the way we understand them – competitive activities in which winners, no matter how single-minded, find time to shake the hands of their rivals and show their respect. Winning was ruthlessly pursued and no prisoners were taken. There were no silver or bronze medals and only winners were recorded. If competitors died or were seriously injured, it went with the territory. Winners were competing not simply for glory but for the grace of the gods and this was a powerful motivation.

We can be sure that the Greeks went to great lengths in their preparations and so provided something of a prototype for what we now call training. Spartans in particular used a cyclical pattern of increasing and decreasing the intensity of preparations which is used in most modern sports. The very concept of preparation is important: recognizing that excellence does not spring spontaneously but is the product of periods of heavy labor and disciplined regimes prompted the Greeks to provide facilities. So, in the sixth century BCE, we see a new type of building called a *gymnasium* (meaning, literally, an exercise for which one strips).

By the time of the Greeks' refinements, sports had undergone changes in purpose and, indeed, nature. While the content showed clear lines of descent connecting it with more basic hunting and combat, the functions it served were quite novel: it was seen as a military training activity, as a vehicle for status-gaining, or what we might now refer to as social mobility, and as a way of securing divine favor. This doesn't deny that the impulses associated with hunting and gathering were present, but it does highlight the autonomy of sport once separated from its original conditions of creation and growth. The Greek adaptation was a response to new material and psychic requirements.

Powerful Greek city-states needed defense against outside attacks and they ensured this by encouraging and rewarding warriors. Accompanying the development of the *polis* was the growth of the state's control over human expressions of violence; sophisticated social organization and internal security were impossible without some regulation of violence. The state's response was to obtain a legitimate monopoly over violence and establish norms of behavior, which discouraged the open expression of violence by citizens and encouraged saving violence for the possible repulsion of attacks from outside powers. Contests, challenges, and rivalries were ways in which the impulse could reassert itself, but in socially acceptable forms.

The value of athletic competition earned it a central place in Greek civilization and the importance of this is reinforced by writers such as Johann Huizinga and Norbert Elias, who stress that the process of becoming civilized itself implicates a culture in controlling violence while at the same time carving out "enclaves" for the "ritualized expression of physical violence." We'll return to the theory in Chapter 5 but should note the observation that sport serves as a legitimate means through which primitive, violence-related impulses and emotions can simultaneously be engendered and contained.

Much of what the ancients would have regarded as expressions of civilization would be seen as barbarous from the standpoint of the late twentieth century. Gouging, biting, breaking, and the use of spiked fist thongs were all permissible in Greek combat. But these were occasions for the exhibition of warrior-like qualities and mercy was not such a quality. While victory was a symbolic "kill" it was also, at times, a quite literal kill.

Much of the glory and honor that Greeks had invested in athletic competition was removed by the Romans, who finally conquered Greece at the Battle of Corinth in 146 BCE. For Romans, part of the appeal of sports lay in the climax of killing. One of their innovations on Greek sports was in establishing preparatory schools exclusively for gladiators, who would eventually be publicly applauded or slaughtered. The actual events would be staged in hippodromes, cavernous stadia where spectators would joyously witness the death of one human being either by another or by beasts. Scenes such as these are vividly depicted in Ridley Scott's movie *Gladiator* (2000).

Influenced by some Greek activities, Romans held footraces, chariot races, and many types of one-to-one combat in the centuries either side of the start of the Christian era. They were also aware of the immense military advantages of having a fit, disciplined, and tempered population. It was expensive to train gladiators, especially if they were all to be killed, so convicted prisoners and slaves were virtually sacrificed.

Adding to the extravagance was the cost of importing animals: wild beasts from throughout the world were captured, transported, and nourished. For five or more centuries, hundreds of thousands of beasts were brought into the coliseum and other stadia and, watched by massed audiences, pitched against each other or against humans. Death seems to have been an accepted part of this activity. There was nothing curious about the Romans' apparent lack of fascination when it came to hunting (no artifacts to suggest much interest). They had no need to leave their cities: the hunts were effectively transferred to the stadia where audiences could satisfy their appetites for violence, or their "blood lusts," as some might say. Gladiatorial conflicts featuring wild animals were comparable to the primitive hunts; the comparisons between human combat and today's fighting sports are clear.

Nowadays, there are few deaths to observe in sporting combat, and when tragedy does strike it leads to a period of earnest self-reflection as well as attacks from medical authorities on the "barbaric" nature of such activities. The fact remains: audiences are amused and excited by the prospect of human combat, as they are by animal conflict – about which there is far less restraint, as the slaughter in bullfighting and harecoursing suggests. The threshold of tolerance has dropped, but this is largely a function of the cultural forces that emanate from civilization: the human proclivity to watch, enjoy, and appreciate the infliction of damage during combat does not seem to waver. Perhaps we're not so dissimilar to our Roman ancestors who wallowed in the bloodletting and cheerfully pointed their thumbs to the floor to answer the question, life or death? As Mike Tyson told a journalist from the *Albany Times* back in January 1986: "When you see me smash somebody's skull, *you enjoy it.*"

The gladiatorial schools finally closed after Christian opposition in the year 399 of the Christian Era. In the following century, the combat grew less deadly and was superseded as an entertainment by less expensive chariot racing, which was arguably the first mass spectator event, drawing crowds of up to 250,000 to the Circus Maximus (in ancient Rome, the Circus meant a round or oblong-shaped arena lined with banks of seats, much like today's sports stadiums).

Chariot racing required teams, each team wearing different-colored uniforms and the winners receiving prize money as well as garlands. It's been argued that Roman sports assumed a political character in this period. With no genuinely democratic means of representation, the populations may well have grown restless and demanded change, were it not for the diverting effect of the combat and racing.

Reflecting on the way his countryman in the first century of the common era flocked in hundreds of thousands to the coliseum and assigned celebrity status to gladiators, the Roman poet Juvenal coined the phrase *panen et circenses*. Translated as "bread and circuses" it described the way in which ancient Roman leaders would provide food and entertainment to the underprivileged plebeians, allowing them access to the spectacular gladiatorial contests and chariot races at the coliseum and other vast stadiums.

Without the agreeable distractions and a full stomach, the masses might have grown discontented and started to wonder why they had little money, lived in inadequate accommodation and, unlike their rulers, could never afford life's luxuries. Immersing themselves in the excitement of the contests and cheering on their champions diverted their attention away from more mundane matters.

Juvenal was alluding to power, specifically the uneven distribution of it and how this imbalance was maintained. The sections of the populations that had little power and no real chance of gaining the advantages that go with it had to be placated somehow. If not, they might have grown restless and begun to ask searching questions that could destabilize power arrangements. Keeping them satisfied maximized the chances that they wouldn't notice. The entertainment might have been good wholesome fun – well, as wholesome as pitching humans against lions can be – but it also served an ideological purpose. It fostered a style of popular thinking that was compatible with a particular type of political and economic system.

We'll investigate how later scholars adapted Juvenal's explanation of the success of the gladiators to the analysis of contemporary sport in Chapter 5 Following

Juvenal, their arguments are essentially that sports and, by implication, other types of popular entertainment solidify the status quo.

THE RUSH OF THE SPECTACLE

Beside the civilizations of Egypt, Greece, and Rome, other cultures emerging in the pre-Christian era had activities resembling sport, though in this historical context we should observe Mandell's caveat that "the boundaries that we moderns use to separate 'sport' from other areas of human endeavor have been indistinct or not worth noticing in other cultures" (1984: 93).

So, we can't be certain that the swimming, diving, and combat, armed and unarmed, practiced by inhabitants of South Asia around 2,500 years ago approached what we would recognize as sport; they may have had a more specific traditional significance, possibly bound up in the caste system. Similarly, the equestrian pursuits of the Chinese, together with their competitive archery, may have been based less on recreation or amusement and more on military training. Yet, as with Greeks and Romans, the activities themselves have been adapted to suit changing circumstances. For example, the sport we call polo almost certainly started life as a Chinese method of target practice. Many of China's martial exercises, which could be used competitively, were functional and were used to maintain a high level of fitness amongst the working population. Japanese industries have successfully adopted this ancient policy, holding exercise sessions before work in today's factories.

The Chinese were probably the first to employ a ball effectively, though there is evidence that the Egyptians experimented. In northern China there was a primitive kicking game. The Chinese invented a projectile that was the forerunner of the shuttlecock and, presumably, propelled it by means of some sort of raquet or bat.

The military importance of the horse, especially fast and maneuverable breeds like the Hokkaido, is obvious and the Japanese perhaps more than any other population recognized this in their sporting traditions. Their competitive shows of speed and intricacy have clear counterparts in today's horse-oriented events, including dressage.

Japan's legacy of martial arts is large and well known; combat in the feudal age of the military caste samurai was based on several ancient disciplines and included the mastery of horses, weapons, and unarmed conflict. Samurai probably favored the now-extinct Nanbu breed of horses.

Many of the skills survive, though with modifications. The pattern that emerged in Japan as elsewhere is the use of sport as a military exercise as well as a pursuit to retain interest and capture enthusiasm while preparing its participants for the more practical discipline of defense. Wherever we find a cavalry, we almost invariably discover some form of competitive endeavor involving the horse. Typically, the competitors would be something of an elite, with resources and possibly patronage enough to compete and serve; they may well have been lionized as Greek heroes were. Certainly in medieval Europe, armed knights were the basis of the continent's supremacy and glory. The knights would be served by peasants and would enjoy status, though in material terms they may not have been much better off.

Practice fights between mounted knights gave rise to a form of combat known as jousting and, as modern fans are drawn by sparring sessions or exhibition games, spectators stood in line as the combatants galloped toward each other, lances extended. The object was to tilt the lance at the adversary in an attempt to unseat him. As the jousts gained popularity in the fifteenth century, they were surrounded by pomp, pageantry, and ritual, and formal tournaments were lavish affairs attended and heavily patronized by nobility. Jousting became an expensive pursuit quite beyond the reach of the peasantry, and indeed beyond all apart from the wealthy landowners whom the jousters served. Peasants would merely look on as the often huge and elaborate tournaments unfolded.

The combat was frequently along territorial lines, as in a 1520 tournament in northern France between King Henry VIII of England and King Francis I of France. A truly "international" event, it was spread over three weeks and attended by dozens of thousands. As well as the equestrian contests, tournaments might also have included sword fights and more theatrical displays of acrobatics and horsemanship – in the age of chivalry, women were strictly spectators.

Jousting, as with the many other forms of combat, had the military purpose of keeping knights in good fighting shape, but may have been transformed into an alternative to warring. Disputes could be settled less expensively and more enjoyably by tournaments than by costly internecine battles. From the twelfth to sixteenth centuries, tournaments became more organized and orderly, as did European society as a whole. Accommodation was made for spectators, scaffolds and stands being built as the jousts grew more popular and attracted large crowds in Italy, France, Germany and other parts of Europe. Jousters would be encased in about 400 lb of metal body armor, so the horses were bred for strength as well as the speed necessary for charging.

After the sixteenth century, the grand tournaments faded and rural events emerged, though tilts were often at targets, not humans. The tournaments gradually changed character from being hard-edged and competitive; "from sports to spectacle" is how Allen Guttmann describes the change in his book *Sports Spectators* (1986). The process is familiar: most sports today are presented as spectacles.

Hunting and archery coexisted with jousting and outlasted it, though never attracting comparable numbers of spectators. Archery survived virtually intact and is today an Olympic event; the old longbows have been considerably modified, of course. Civic festivals were organized around competitions and were grand occasions, drawing vast crowds to pageants all over Europe. The stag- and foxhunts were direct predecessors of the modern foxhunts, with the rich amusing themselves by setting free their hounds and giving pursuit; the poor would amuse themselves by pursuing them all.

Hunts and other "blood sports," including those described at the start of this chapter, continued to enjoy popularity among lower classes, whose penchant for watching tethered bears prodded with sticks and then set upon by fierce dogs is similar to that of the spectators who gathered at the Roman coliseum centuries before. Cockfights, which have almost universal appeal, were held in England from about the twelfth century and attracted audiences from the various classes. As we saw from the description at the beginning of this chapter, the activities frequently ended in dead, dying, or seriously hurt animals.

BOX 4.5 BLOOD SPORTS

Recreational pursuits that involved inflicting harm on animals were of four types, all very popular between 1780 and 1860 and modestly popular beyond. (1) *Baiting* involved chaining, tethering, or cornering an animal and setting trained dogs to torment or attack it: this was favored by the British and American plebeian, or working class. Typically, a bull or a bear would be brought by a butcher or farmer who would be paid to have it secured to a post while specially trained dogs were allowed to snap at and bite it. The bull, having been ripped by the dogs, would be slaughtered and its meat sold. Badger baiting involved releasing dogs down a badger's set to chase it out. Baiting animals as diverse as hyenas, ducks, and hogs, has been or even is currently being practiced. (2) *Fighting* consisted of goading trained dogs or cocks into fighting each other until one rendered the other unable to continue. This was a more commercialized activity followed by the English aristocracy, according to Holt, though, as with other blood sports, variations have been pursued elsewhere and fighting between scorpions, beetles, and spiders has been practiced in parts of Asia. (3) *Hunting* for amusement has been a popular pursuit over the ages, the quarry being ducks, cats, bullocks, among other animals. Some of these activities persist to the present day. (4) *Throwing* at animals or the animals themselves was popular in seventeenth-century England: for example, a rooster would be tied to a post, then pelted with sticks and stones until it died. Around the same time, in Germany and other parts of Europe, a popular pastime involved catapulting foxes, badgers, or chickens through the air.

Hugh Cunningham, in his *Leisure in the Industrial Revolution*, relates a Sunday morning meeting in London in 1816 at which several hundred people were assembled in a field adjoining a churchyard. In the field, "they fight dogs, hunt ducks, gamble, enter into subscriptions to fee drovers for a bullock." The Rector of the nearby church observed: "I have seen them drive the animal through the most populous parts of the parish, force sticks pointed with iron, up the body, put peas into the ears, and infuriate the beast" (1980: 23).

Although condemned systematically from the eighteenth century, blood sports persist to this day, most famously in the Spanish bullrings and in the streets of Pamplona. England's Bull Ring, in Birmingham takes its name from the city's market area where bulls were butchered. The actual bullring was an iron ring to which bulls were tethered and baited before going to slaughter. Bull sports ceased in England in 1825, a year after the founding of the Royal Society for the Prevention of Cruelty to Animals (RSPCA). The same organization brought pressure against dogfighting, which was banned by the Cruelty to Animals Act, 1835, only to go underground as an illicit, predominantly working-class pursuit.

The decline of cockfighting, bullbaiting and the like coincided with cultural changes that brought with them a range of alternative leisure pursuits. The whole spectrum of changes were part of what some writers have called the civilizing process – which we will cover in more detail in the next chapter.

But, before we are tempted into assuming that barbaric tastes and activities have completely disappeared, we should stay mindful of Richard Holt's caution: "The tendency by members of all social classes to maltreat animals for excitement or gain is by no means dead even today" (1990: 24). Dogfighting in particular persists in the West to this day and dogs are bred for the specific purpose of fighting. In the early 1990s, amid a panic over the number of ferocious breeds proliferating, the British banned the import of American pit bulls (such animals are required to be registered in Britain under the Dangerous Dogs Act, 1991; there are about 5,000 unregistered pit bulls trained for fighting rather than as pets).

For a while the law seemed to work, though dogfighting made a comeback in the early twenty-first century, especially in England. And, as if to remind us of our retrograde thirst for blood, a police operation in 2004 resulted in the seizure of 73 trained dogs, many of which had signs of fight injuries, and the confiscation of equipment used in dog-fighting. A year before, 19 roosters and more than $17,000 (£11,000) were seized in a raid on a cockfighting den in New York City. Seventy people were arrested. These episodes are still commonplace.

Blood sports in general and foxhunting in particular are seen as having central importance by Norbert Elias and Eric Dunning in their book *Quest for Excitement*. The "civilizing" of society demanded greater personal self-control and a stricter constraint on violence, but the process of hunting or just observing allowed "all the pleasures and the excitement of the chase, as it were, mimetically in the form of wild play"(1986). While the passion and exhilaration associated with hunting would be aroused, the actual risks would be absent in the imagined version (except for the animals, of course) and the effects of watching would be, according to Elias and Dunning, "liberating, cathartic."

The comments could be applied without any alteration to all of the activities considered so far. They are products of a human imagination ingenious enough to create artificial situations that human evolution has rendered irrelevant in practical terms. But, once created, they have seemed to exert a control and power of their own, eliciting in both participants and audience a pleasurable excitement that encapsulates the thrill or "rush" of a hunt, yet carries none of the attendant risks.

BOX 4.6 MIMETIC

From the Greek *mimesis* for imitation, this describes an activity that imitates or resembles another, and which is carried out especially for amusement. A child may mimetically play cowboys-and-indians or adult members of Round Table organizations may imitate battles, albeit in a mock way. In both cases, the deliberate imitation of the behavior of one group of people by another supplies the amusement.

History shows that activities, which at least resemble sports are rarely purely autotelic and can be augmented with other purposes. From ancient to medieval ages, the tendency was to imbue supposed sporting activities with a military purpose, often encouraging qualities within participants that were of obvious utility in serious combat. We also find a theme in sports history in which many of the main roles were occupied by privileged or elite groups who performed, while most of the supporting roles were played by peasantry or plebeians who watched. The public provision of entertainment by the powerful had a latent political function in diverting attention away from practical realities and material needs and animating sentiments and emotions that were not challenging to the established order of things.

Human relationships with other animals have been peculiarly ambivalent. Dogs, for instance, have been domesticated and cared for, and used to hunt other more vulnerable creatures and to retrieve birds which have been killed. Many other animals have simply been used as expendable prey, an observation that gives credence to the view that, while the hunt as a survival mechanism has receded, the violent impulses that it once fostered remain.

Animal abuses very gradually declined in the long period under review and, though they have been under pressure for over a hundred years, they certainly have not disappeared in the modern era. Animal uses, as opposed to abuses (though the distinction may not be acceptably clear-cut for everyone), are still very much with us, as dogracing and horseracing, remind us. The previously mentioned Iditarod in which packs of huskies pull a sled for eight days and nights in temperatures of −60 degrees is an organized competition in which the driver talks to, becomes as tough as, and even sleeps with his dogs, according to Gary Paulsen, in his *Winterdance* (1994).

This close relationship with animals suggests continuity in sports, which, if traced back, has its origins in the transition from hunter-gatherer to farmer. While the connecting thread appears at times to be only slender, we can infer that there is surely some human property that elicits a desire for a form of autotelic enterprise based on competition. The way in which it manifests itself differs from culture to culture, and so far in this chapter I have pulled out only fragments from history to illustrate the general argument. The impression is still clear enough to draw a plausible scenario and one in which a basic impulse continues to operate in widely different contexts. (A scenario is a postulated sequence of events.) In most of these contexts, some spectacle was made of violence.

Despite the ostensibly civilizing forces at work, physical cruelty and the infliction of damage on others continued to attract and entertain people. But, in the nineteenth century, very sharp and dramatic changes took place, particularly in Europe, that were to affect the sensitivity to, and public acceptance of, violence, and this was to have an impact on the entire shape and focus of sport. It was also to establish the framework of what would now legitimately pass for sports.

BOX 4.7 COCKFIGHTING

This probably has origins in ancient China and Persia. Greeks may have become aware of it after their victory over Persia at Salamis in 480 BCE and, in turn, introduced it to the Romans. For Greeks, the courage of fighting birds was regarded as exemplary: youths were encouraged to watch and emulate the birds' tenacity and valor in combat. Later, it became a mere source of entertainment, especially for gamblers. It first appeared in England in the twelfth century, though its popularity waxed and waned until the sixteenth century when Henry VIII built a royal cockpit at his palace. In the eighteenth and nineteenth centuries, cocks were bought and sold, bred and trained in a more organized way, one trainer, Joseph Gulliver, acquiring quite a reputation. Cockfighting was banned in 1835 but is known to persist in the United States and Britain.

TENOR OF LIFE, TEMPO OF WORK

One of the fashionable haunts of the nobility and upper classes in the early eighteenth century was James Figg's amphitheater in London. The round building with a central space for sporting events was surrounded by tiers of seats for spectators. Figg, himself a swordsman and prizefighter, opened the venue in 1719 and attracted large crowds to watch displays of animal baiting as well as human contests, featuring swords, fists, and staffs. Figg promoted contests between and among men and women.

Figg's reputation brought him appointments as a tutor to the gentry, instructing in the art of self-defense, which was regarded in those days as very much a gentleman's pursuit. There was very little gentlemanly restraint in the actual contests, which were bare-knuckle affairs without either a specified number of rounds or a points-scoring system. A match was won when one fighter was simply unable to continue. Three- and four-hour contests were commonplace, with wrestling throws, kicks, and punches all permissible.

Such types of combat were rife in England in Figg's time (he died in 1734) and drew on the ancient tradition of Greek combat sports. No doubt similar forms of combat took place in other parts of the world in the eighteenth century though, in England, fighting was to undergo a special transformation.

At about the same time as Figg's venture, another combat activity was gaining popularity, at least in parts of Britain. Ballgames were appearing: these were loosely organized according to local customs rather than central rules and were played with inflated animal bladders. Ancient Greeks and Romans also used pig or ox bladders, though they tended to fill them with hair and feathers, more suited to throwing than the fast kicking games that became popular much later. In the intervening centuries ballgames were always peripheral to activities such as combat, racing, or archery, but in the nineteenth century they seemed to take off.

I describe ballgames as different to "combat activity" although it seems that at least some variants of what was to evolve into football allowed participants to complement their delicate ball-playing skills with cudgels, clubs, and other instruments that Mr Figg and his associates would have been adept at using. Meetings would have resembled an all-out struggle much more than a practiced, rule-bound, timed, game with clearly defined goals and final results.

But violence was popular and the rough and wild folk games, as Eric Dunning and Kenneth Sheard call them in *Barbarians, Gentlemen and Players* were "closer to 'real' fighting than modern sports" (1979). The authors suggest that football's antecedents reflected the "violent tenor of life in society at large" and also the low threshold of repugnance "with regard to witnessing and engaging in violent acts." Sometimes, the distinction between witnessing and engaging became blurred and spectators would join in the action.

BOX 4.8 FOLK BALLGAMES

Ballgames were played all over England from the fifteenth century and possibly before. They were played on English national holidays, especially Easter Monday and Shrove Tuesday. The rules were variable, depending on where the games were played, though rules were more guidelines than formal laws. Villages would compete against each other, the object of most ballgames being to kick, throw, carry, or use some form of conveyance to transport a ball, probably made of animal skin or solid wood, from one point to another (such as a church or a clock tower). The custom was to start the game after a church service. Games would run to about three hours. Violence was a feature of most folk ballgames. Serious injuries always resulted from games and deaths were not uncommon. In fact, the flagrant violence was a factor in its eventual demise in the mid-nineteenth century. Revulsion at the violence combined with the popularity of organized ballgames such as rugby and association football led to their demise.

It's rather synthetic to link these pursuits of the eighteenth century with today's boxing, wrestling, or cage fighting, and types of football; first, because of the regional variations and, second, because of combinations of rules and characteristics that made any systematic differentiation of games impossible. Yet, somehow, the essentials of both activities have dropped into the stream of history and arrived in the twenty-first century as well ordered, highly structured, and elaborately organized sports. I use the two examples of fighting and football because they embody currents and changes that have affected the entire assortment of activities that have become contemporary sports. The decline in spontaneity and open brutality in sports mirrored trends in society generally.

The new rules of prizefighting, instituted in 1838, introduced some measure of regulation, including a "scratch" line which was a mark in the center of a 24-ft square ring which competitors had to reach unassisted at the start of each round, or else be judged the loser (that is, "not coming up to scratch"). It was a small but significant modification that removed the necessity of a beating into submission or a knockout to terminate a bout. In 1886, Queensberry Rules were devised to reduce the degree of bodily damage possible and to increase the importance of skill as a decisive factor in the "noble art."

Far away from Figg's boxing ring and the raucous folk ballgames, another set of forces were helping shape sports; they came from Britain's public (independent) schools, which were strictly for the children of the aristocracy or very affluent. Despite the popular beliefs that public schools in the nineteenth century were upholders of the virtues of sports, they actually echoed many of the sentiments of the Puritans, who disapproved utterly of any activity that seemed frivolous, including dancing, blood sports, and wagering (betting). Such entertainment was seen by Puritans as the mindless pleasure of flâneurs and, of course, such idlers were ripe for the devil's work. In the thirteenth and fourteenth centuries, Puritans suppressed any activity resembling a contest in their attempts to create an atmosphere of strict moral discipline. In the sixteenth century, the universities of Oxford and Cambridge banned ballgames.

Public school masters initially tried to prevent the development of soccer in particular, believing it to be disruptive of order and morally debilitating. There was also the feeling that it was demeaning for the sons of the upper classes to practice activities that were, as one headmaster of the day described them, "fit only for butcher boys . . . farm boys and laborers" (quoted in Dunning and Sheard 1979: 47). Gentlemen scholars became the new Corinthians in sharp contrast to the laboring commoners.

Intellectual trends in Germany and France were influenced by the philosopher Jean-Jacques Rousseau (1712–78) whose treatise *Émile* (first published in 1762) argued that physical training and competitive sport would yield positive results in the overall education of a child. Ideas drifted across to English public schools, so that, by the 1850s, two main revisions were made to the original ideas on sports. Expressed by Peter McIntosh in his *Fair Play*: "The first was that competitive sport, especially team games, had an ethical basis, and the second was that training in moral behavior on the playing field was transferable to the world beyond" (1980: 27).

The ideas fused in the form of "muscular Christianity," an influential creed that encouraged spirited physical activity. Unselfishness, justice, health: these were the type of ideals that were manifest in sport, but also in any proper Christian society.

Public schools, influenced by the doctrine, began to integrate a program of sport into their curricula. Team games were important in subordinating the individual to the collective unit and teaching the virtues of alliances. It was often thought that England's many military victories were attributable to the finely honed teamwork encouraged by public schools. Again, we glimpse the notion of sport as a preparation for military duty: the playing fields of public schools were equated with battlegrounds (Eton and Waterloo, for example). Thomas Hughes's classic, *Tom Brown's Schooldays* (1857) is full of allusions to the role of public schools in producing populations suited to rule over an empire.

BOX 4.9 MUSCULAR CHRISTIANITY

The term was first used in 1857 by a reviewer of *Tom Brown's Schooldays*. It became applied to a doctrine about the positive moral influence of physical exercise and sport, which had its intellectual roots in the philosophy of Rousseau in France and Johan Gutsmuths (1759–1839) in Germany, and which was approvingly adopted by the public schools of England in the late nineteenth century. Charles Kingsley (1819–75), the church minister and author of the classic children's story *The Water Babies* (1863), was a strong supporter of muscular Christianity. Tony Money's *Manly and Muscular Diversions: Public schools and the nineteenth-century sporting revival* (1997) is a scholarly account of its influence during the Victorian era.

The physically tough and toughening version of football, as practiced by Rugby School under the headship of Thomas Arnold and his assistant G. E. L. Cotton, gained acceptance in many public schools. Its toughness was useful in sorting out those fit enough to survive and perhaps later prosper in positions of power. The frail would either strengthen or perish. Its appeal to the prestigious public schools bent on turning out Great Men was soon apparent as the sport of rugby spread through the network and, in time, to a number of "open" clubs in the north of England (which admitted nouveaux riches and working-class members).

Exporting its sports has been a major trade for England over the decades. Versions of the football played at Rugby and other public schools were popular among college students at North America's principal universities in the 1880s. The throwing and passing, as opposed to kicking, game was played at a competitive level. As early as 1874 there is a record of a game between Cambridge's Harvard University and McGill University, Montreal. Interestingly, Wilbert Leonard documents a game of soccer between the two New Jersey universities, Rutgers and Princeton, as far back as 1869. Harvard refused to play soccer and Yale responded accordingly.

Muscular Christianity was also instrumental in carrying the other principal variant of football to the working class. Churches encouraged association football. A quarter of today's English clubs were founded and, for a while, sustained by churches; they include Aston Villa, Everton, Manchester City, and Tottenham Hotspur. The churches were eager to proselytize in urban centers, which by the 1880s were humming with the sound of heavy machinery and, given the rising popularity of football among the working class, it seemed a sensible method of promoting their interests.

Industry itself wasn't slow to realize the advantages of possessing a football team comprising members of its workforce. Places like West Ham, Stoke, and Scunthorpe can boast enduring soccer clubs that were originally works outfits. Arsenal was based at Woolwich Arsenal, a London munitions factory. Games, which were only played on designated holy days and other festive occasions became more and more regular, routine, and organized.

In a similar way, many North American pro football franchises started as factory teams. The Indian Packing Company, of Green Bay, Wisconsin, had its own team in the first decade of the twentieth century; as did the Staley Starch Company, of Decatur, Illinois. Players were paid about $50 per week and given time off to train. In 1920, both companies affiliated their teams to a new organization that also had teams from New York and Washington, DC. The teams evolved into the Packers, Bears, Giants, and Redskins respectively.

We might stretch the point and describe the early works teams as para-industrial: organized much as an industrial force and intended to supplement the strictly industrial. It was a very deliberate policy pursued by factory owners. In some ways, sport was a foil for industrial order; a potent instrument for instilling discipline in the workforce. But, if sport was an instrument, it had two cutting edges for as well as carving out new patterns of order it was also responsible for outbreaks of disorder. Work and leisure were cut in two by the imperatives of industry. The more fluid way of life in which the manner in which one earned a living blended imperceptibly with the rest of one's life disappeared as the factory system issued its demands, which were a workforce ready to labor for a set amount of time at a specific site.

During that time workers operated under virtual compulsion; outside that time they were free to pursue whatever they wished, or could afford. Sport was a way of filling leisure time with brief, but exhilarating, periods of uncertainty: the questions of who or which team would win a more-or-less equal competition was bound to prompt interest and speculation, as, it seems, it always has. The spell of physically competitive activity, far from being broken, was strengthened by the need for momentary release from a colorless world dominated by the monotonous thuds and grinds of machinery. Competitions, whether individual combat, ballgames, or animal baits, drew crowds; but public gatherings always carried the potential for disruption.

Public gatherings and festivals, and other staged events attracted a working class, which was in the process of becoming industrialized but which had not yet done so by the mid- to late nineteenth century. It was still adjusting to what John Hargreaves in *Sport, Power and Culture* calls the changes in "tempo and quality of industrial work" (1986).

Hargreaves argues that the English church's efforts in building football clubs had the effect of controlling the working class so that it would be more pliant for ruling groups. In fact, Hargreaves' entire thesis revolves around the intriguing idea that sport has helped integrate the working class into respectable "bourgeois culture" rather than struggle against it – and we'll return to this theme in Chapter 5.

But the integration was never smooth and police were regularly called to suppress riots and uprisings at football matches, prizefights, footraces, cockfights, and so on, as large groups spontaneously grew agitated and unruly. Boxing events to this day employ "whips" who are promoters' chargés d'affaires responsible for most of the minor business. But, as the etymology suggests, the original whips were employed to encircle the ring, cracking their whips or lashing at troublesome members of the audience (ancient Romans also employed whips to lash riotous crowds at their gladiatorial contests).

Local laws were enacted, prohibiting meetings in all but tightly policed sur-roundings, sometimes banning sports completely. The rise of the governing bodies within individual sports represents an attempt to absorb working-class energies within a formal structure, thereby containing what might otherwise have become disruptive tendencies.

The same forces affecting combat helped reshape football, taking out some of its ferocity and establishing sets of rules in what was previously a maelstrom. In 1863, the Football Association was formed to regulate the kicking form of the sport (the word soccer probably derives from "assoc," an abbreviation of Association). The version that stressed handling was brought under the control of the Rugby Union, which was created in 1871.

Rugby's Great Split, as Tony Collins (1999) calls it, into distinct amateur and professional organizations came in 1895, the latter being known as Rugby League, which remained confined to the northern counties of England where it was favored by the working class. The other major change in rugby came in North America, where in 1880, the addition of downs to replace the to-and-fro of rugby and a straight line of *scrimmage* instead of the less orderly *scrummage* gave American football a character all of its own (the forward pass rule was introduced in 1906; this was, of course, a major departure from rugby, which permits only lateral passing).

Baseball's governing body has its origins in the 1858 when the National Association of Base Ball Players was formed. The game was played for many years before, probably evolving out the English games, base ball (note: two words) and rounders, in which players struck a ball with a bat and ran through a series of bases arranged in a circle, or a "round." Baseball was the first fully professional sport in America, charging admissions to ballparks and attracting a predominantly blue-collar fandom.

The changes in the organization of sports were responses to demands for orderliness and standardization. England, and, later, North America, metamorphosed into an industrial societies where the valued qualities were discipline, precision, and control. Sports not only absorbed these qualities, but promoted them, gradually influencing perceptions and expectations in such a way as to deepen people's familiarity with the industrial regimen.

Industrialization drew populations to urban centers in search of work; not work quite as we know it today, but uncomfortable, energy-draining activities performed for long hours often in squalid and dangerous conditions. This type of work needed a new mentality. People were expected to arrive at work punctually and toil for measured periods of time. Their labors were planned for them and their efforts were often highly specialized according to the division of labor.

Behavior at work was subject to rules and conditions of service. Usually, all the work took place in a physically bounded space, the factory. There was also a need for absoluteness: tools and machines were made to fine tolerances. Underlying all this was the British class structure, or hierarchy, in which some strata had attributes suited to ruling and others to being ruled. The latter's shortcomings were so apparent that no detailed investigation of the causes was thought necessary: their poverty, or even destitution was their own fault.

All these had counterparts in the developing sports scene. Time periods for contests were established and measured accurately thanks to newer, sophisticated timepieces. Until the early nineteenth century, everywhere operated on its own local time, usually derived from sun dials and displayed on clocks on churches and other public buildings. Noon in Bristol, for instance, was about 10 minutes later than it was in London, only 106 miles away. This was of no importance when people traveled in horse-drawn vehicles, but trains and other public transport demanded standardization. In 1840, the Great Western Railway in Britain standardized its timetable to Greenwich Mean Time; in 1853 America's first union station – i.e. where tracks and facilities are shared by a number of rail companies – was opened in Indianapolis, Indiana. Timetables and reliable schedules brought the need for time to be consistent across the networks. This was reflected in sports.

Standardized rules, including time periods were introduced into competitions. Divisions of labor in team games yielded role-specific positions and particular, as opposed to general, skills. Constitutions were drawn up to instill more structure into activities and regulate events according to rules. They took place on pitches, in rings and halls – in finite spaces. Winners and losers were unambiguously clear, outright, and absolute. And hierarchies reflecting the class structure were integrated into many activities. Captains of teams, for example, were "gentlemen" from the upper echelons. The sense of order, discipline, location, and period which sport acquired helped it both complement and support working life.

As the form and pace of sport imitated that of industry, so it gained momentum amongst the emergent working class seeking some sporadic diversion from its toil, something more impulsive and daring than the routine labors that dominated industry. While sport was assuming symmetry with work, it still afforded the working class an outlet, or release from labor; it was pursued voluntarily during the time spent away from work.

As the nineteenth century drew to an end, most sports took on a much more orderly character: both participants and spectators came to recognize the legitimacy of governing organizations, the standards of conduct they laid down and the structures of rules they observed. The whole direction and rhythm of sport reflected the growing significance of industrial society. In his *Sport: A cultural history*, Richard Mandell writes: "Like concurrent movements in law and government, which led to codification, and rationalization, sport became codified, and civilized by written rules which were enforced by supervising officials (the equivalent of judges and jurors)" (1984: 151).

The reasons for concentrating on nineteenth-century England are: (1) it's here we find something like a factory's smelter shop where rationalized, organized sport appears as an extract from the molten historical trends; (2) the English experience radiated out amongst the imperial colonies and ex-colonies, including North America, with sports, as well as trade, "following the flag"; and (3) it's this period of history that has excited many writers sufficiently to produce theories of the rise of sports in modernity. In the next chapter, I'll consider five theoretical approaches that shed light on the reasons for the rapid growth of sports in the late nineteenth and early twentieth centuries and, indeed, for their persistence into the twenty-first.

Combat Sports in the Ancient World by Michael Poliakoff (Yale University Press, 1987) describes in fine detail the early forms of combat, such as the Greeks' pankration ("total fight") and Egyptian wrestling. "The will to win is a basic human instinct, but different societies give varying amounts of encouragement (or discouragement) to the individual's attempt to measure himself against others," observes Poliakoff in his chapter entitled "The nature and purpose of combat sport." Elliott J. Gorn's *The Manly Art: Bare-knuckle prize fighting in America* (Cornell University Press, 1986) updates the argument.

Sports in America: From wicked amusement to national obsession edited by David Wiggins (Human Kinetics, 1995) collects 19 essays organized into 5 parts: (1) Pre-1820; (2) 1820–70; (3) 1870–1915; (4) 1915–45; (5) 1945–Present. The third part, dealing with industrialization and urbanization is especially relevant; in this, various writers focus on the period 1870–1915.

History of Sport and Physical Activity in the United States, 4th edition, by Betty Spears and Richard A. Swanson (Brown & Benchmark, 1995) is one of the most respected and durable histories of North American sport and should be read in conjunction with *Sports Spectators* by Allen Guttmann (Columbia University Press, 1986) which is densely packed with historical detail on the emergence of sport. Guttmann's focus is far wider than that implied by the title and actually provides a basis for understanding sport. "We are what we watch," writes Guttmann toward the end of a book that captures how sports can be used as a barometer of historical change and one which should be read by any serious student of sport.

Richard Holt's books, *Sport and the Working Class in Modern Britain* (Manchester University Press, 1990) and *Sport and the British* (Oxford University Press, 1989), examine what now seem to be crude forms of sports and reveal the links between these and today's versions. Older activities gradually faded as industrialization encroached and cultural patterns changed, but Holt emphasizes the continuities and "survivals" from old to new. Complementing these is Hugh Cunningham's *Leisure in the Industrial Revolution* (Croom Helm, 1980).

Crossing Boundaries: An international anthology of women's experiences in sport edited by Susan Bandy and Anne Darden (Human Kinetics, 1999) is a collection of materials on the largely undisclosed history of women in sports.

Ancient Greek Athletics by Stephen G. Miller (Yale University Press, 2004) is a detailed account of the original Olympiad, right down to how competitors tied their foreskins. Nigel Spivey's *The Ancient Olympics* (Oxford University Press, 2004) complements this, while *The Eternal Olympics: The art and history of sport* edited by Nikolaos Yaloris (Caratzas Brothers, 1979) is a large format book, packed with pictures of artifacts and reproductions of artwork, many from the pre-Christian era.

Football: The first hundred years – the untold story by Adrian Harvey (Routledge, 2005) traces the origin and early development of what became the global game.

A Social History of Swimming in England, 1800–1918: Splashing in the Serpentine edited by Christopher Love (Routledge, 2009) is an interesting account of one of the most ancient yet most neglected sports. Love analyzes the development of organized swimming and diving (as well as synchronized swimming) against a background of cultural as well as technological change.

Sport History Review edited by Don Morrow (Human Kinetics) is a biannual journal that concerns itself with sports history.

ASSIGNMENT

Cockfighting and boxing: these are two sports that have deep historical roots, but which have aroused controversy. Cockfighting is illegal; and both American and British Medical Associations lobby for a ban on boxing. Despite its illegality, cockfighting persists underground. Defenders of boxing argue that, if banned, boxing would also go underground, making it more dangerous. But, one might contend that drug-taking is a widespread underground activity and that does not mean we should legalize it. Compare boxing and drug-taking, taking into account that both cost lives, yet both are engaged in by young people on a voluntary basis. If one is legal, should the other be?

HOW OLD ARE SPORTS?

Four thousand years, if you accept the theories of Nikolaos Yaloris, who detects evidence of what he calls "true athletic spirit" as long ago as the second millennium Before the Christian Era (BCE). There is evidence of activities resembling sports in the Aegean civilization that centered on Crete, as there is evidence of high standard art, work in copper and bronze, and linear script all around the same time.

Others date sports much more recently. Some say sports started during the revival of art and literature known as the Renaissance, beginning in the fourteenth century, while others maintain that sports as we understand them today started in nineteenth-century England. It depends on how you define "sports." Most historians tell us to guard against exaggerating the similarities between ancient and medieval contests and contemporary competitions. The actual activities may resemble what we now recognize as sports, but the cultural milieus were completely different and the meanings given to the activities quite unlike today's.

The boundaries we use to separate sports from other areas of life "have been indistinct and not worth noticing in other cultures," writes Mandell. Ancient Greeks, for example, believed winners of events were chosen by gods and the competitions they held were of profound religious importance; as such, athleticism was all-pervasive. Pre-Meiji (before 1868) Japan held archery and equestrian contests, but these were linked to military purposes rather than being purely athletic competitions.

The first Olympiad took place in 776 BCE and was animated by the same spirit that guided the intellectual inquiries of Pythagoras (580–500 BCE), Hippocrates (c. 460–377 BCE), and Socrates (469–399 BCE): to explore the boundaries of human possibilities. Evidence of this can be discerned in the dramas of Sophocles (496–406 BCE) and Aeschylus (c. 525–456 BCE) and the military conquests of Alexander the Great (356–323 BCE). They form disparate parts of a wider enterprise to control and subordinate nature to human requirements, using both physical and intellectual means.

By combining the efforts of various historical scholars, it is possible to construct a timeline that allows us to trace the existence of athletic activities. The dates are, of course, approximate, and indicate the time of the first appearance of the activities. The places are often vague, referring to regions rather than the countries as we define them nowadays.

BEFORE THE CHRISTIAN ERA (BCE)

4000	**Mycenae, Hellas (Greece)**. Horseracing.
3000	**Mesopotamia, Sumeria.** Chariot racing. Archery contests. Stick fighting. Paramilitary athletic training.
2300	**Indus Valley region (Pakistan, India)** Horse and chariot races. Combat contests in ancient city cultures, with irrigation schemes and organized system of government.
2000	**Crete, Hellas**. Athletic competition with rules. Bull-leaping, combat contests linked with religious festivals. Throughout Hellas (Greece). Gloved combat contests; footraces, chariot races. Athletic training. Emphasis on victory. **Egypt**. ballgames, staff and knife contests. Egyptians used irrigation in Nile Valley and applied mathematics to the construction of the pyramids at Gizeh.
2000	**Egypt**. Wrestling contests.
1600	**Minoa**. Combat sports using thonged fists.
1360	**Egypt**. Hunting on Nile. About this time, the Egyptian empire began its slow decline.
1200	**Olympia, Hellas**. Beginning of Hellenic Middle Ages. Jumping events, discus, spear throwing, foot and chariot racing, armed combat contests. Funeral games to honor the dead.
776	**Olympia, Hellas**. Inaugural Olympic Games. Footraces only.
708–680.	Pentathlon, wrestling, boxing, pankration, horse races added to Olympic program.
600	**Hellas**. Integration of athletics and education. Physical and moral courage intertwined. Healthy body, healthy mind. Rivalries valued in all cultural spheres, including musicians, poets, sculptors etc. Competition for excellence, fame and honor i.e. *agôn*.
576	**Sparta, Hellas**. Specialized physical training with specialized role of trainer. Athletics part of military education. Sparta was a powerful city-state in

Greece and defeated its rival Athens in the Peloponnesian War, 431–404 BCE, to become the leading city of its time.

| 400 | **Hellas**. Purpose-built athletic stadium. Professional athletes receive subsidies from cities to train full-time. |
| 146 | **Greece** subjugated by Romans. Athletics continue, but with increasing emphasis on killing sports e.g. gladiatorial contests (featuring slaves), pankration, archery. |

CHRISTIAN ERA (CE)

300	**China**. Equestrian sport, including polo. Competitions with military utility, including archery, boxing, wrestling and paramilitary gymnastics. First use of paper makes detailed record-keeping possible. Han dynasty is first to create a civil bureaucracy with codified rules run by the Mandarin class.
393	**Rome**. Christian Roman ban on all pagan festivals, including Olympic Games.
410	**Rome**. Fall of Rome. Beginning of dark ages – 10th/11th century.
500	**Middle East.** Horseracing.
646	**Japan**. Archery. Equestrian events, including dressage.
900	**Europe**. Equestrian sports. Jousting
1000	**Japan**. Ballgames, possibly adapted from Chinese versions. Sumo.
1100	**Rheinland Pfalz (Germany)** Tournament attended by 40,00 knights.
1150	**England**. Archery contests.
1400	**Europe** (especially Burgundy, Brabant). Tournaments with equestrian events (including jousting), fencing and sword duels.
1450	**Scotland**. Early forms of golf/hockey ("driving").
1500	**Europe**. The Renaissance is generally thought to have begun in Florence, in western central Italy, where an interest in music, the arts and culture flourishes, giving rise to an enthusiasm for activities that bring joy and which are pursued for recreation rather than serious or practical purpose. International tournaments featuring archery, swordfights, jousts and other contests continue, though more playful games emerge.
1555	**Europe**. Ballgames e.g. *calcio* in Italy, *Faustball* in Germany and elsewhere (earlier) among Aztecs, Inuit, Japanese, Maoris.
1570	**Japan**. Paramilitary sports. Equestrian events. Archery. Swordfighting. Spear-throwing. Shooting. Martial arts, principally competitive jujitsu.
1600	**England**. Rural hunting. Hounds, horses. Prey includes boars, wolves and red deer.

1600	**Europe**. Animal baiting: dog pits, bear pits, cock pits etc. Rise in gambling. Rural horseracing.
1603	**Japan**. Sumo becomes a professional sport. Other sports include cockfighting, fishing, falconry, and ballgames, including *demari* and *temari*. A badminton-like game called *hanestsuki* is among several recognizable physical games played, though board games are also popular during the Edo period, which ends in 1868.
1660	**Germany** and elsewhere in Europe. Formal competitive dueling.
1787	**England**. Marylebone Cricket Club (MCC) formed.
1836	**Japan**. Weightlifting.
1800	**England**. Horseracing in enclosures, early in century.
1851	**USA.** First America's Cup yacht race
1858	**USA.** National Association of Base Ball Players (NABP) formed. This was the first of many baseball organizations. The architecture of what we now know as Major League Baseball was designed in 1903.
1860	**Europe, North America, Japan**. Rationalization of sports begins: training and trainers appear, growth of organizations to codify and regulate activities and record results. The framework of modern sports is established over succeeding years.
1863	**England**. Football Association (FA) formed. Association football, or soccer, and rugby divide into distinct sports with own governing organizations.
1871	**England**. Rugby Football Union (RFU) formed. Divides into RFU and Northern Ruby Union, later to become the Rugby Football League, in 1893–5.
1876	**USA**. Walter Camp, of Yale University, publishes a reformulation of rugby's rules, introducing downs, scrimmage, and, later (in 1906), the forward pass. The rules change the character of rugby and produce a distinctly American form of football.
1880	**USA, Europe**. Cycling craze among women and men.
1880	**England**. Formation of Amateur Athletic Association (AAA), Amateur Boxing Association (ABA)
1886	**England.** Queensberry Rules instituted in boxing. Amateur Swimming Association (ASA) formed.
1888	**England**. Lawn Tennis Association (LTA) formed.
1891	**USA**. Basketball invented at YMCA training college in Springfield, Massachusetts. James Naismith credited with being originator. NBA founded in 1949. **England**. National Sporting Club, the precursor to British Boxing Board of Control (BBBC), formed to regulate professional boxing.

1896	**Greece.** Modern Olympics (amateur) created. Baron Pierre de Coubertin credited with being originator.
1904	**Global.** Formation of Fifa (association football) precedes founding of several international governing organizations, including: Fina (swimming), 1908; IAAF (athletics), 1912; ILTF (tennis), 1913; and FIBA (amateur boxing), 1920.
1906	**USA.** Intercollegiate Athletic Association formed. Later develops into NCAA (National Collegiate Athletic Association).

Sources:
Coombs (1978); Deal (2006);Kühnst (1996); Mandell (1984); Miller (2004); Poliakoff (1987); Polley (2007); Spivey (2004); Vandervell and Coles (1980); Yaloris (1979).

MORE QUESTIONS . . .

>> Why were Roman contests so different from Greek athletics?
>> Is it fair to describe ancient competition as "sports"?
>> What would happen if we stopped children under the age of 11 playing *competitive* sports?

READ ON. . .

Nikolaos Yaloris (ed.), *The Eternal Olympics: The art and history of sport*, Caratzas Brothers, 1979.
Richard D. Mandell, *Sport: A cultural history*, Columbia University Press, 1984.
Michael B. Poliakoff, *Combat Sports in the Ancient World: Competition, violence, and culture*, Yale University Press, 1987.
Peter Kühnst, *Sports: A cultural history in the mirror of art*, Verlag der Kunst, 1996.
Nigel Spivey, *The Ancient Olympics*, Oxford University Press, 2004.
William E. Deal, *Handbook to Life in Medieval and Modern Japan*, Oxford University Press, 2006.
Martin Polley "History and sport," in *Sport and Society*, Sage, 2007.

CHAPTER 5

KEY ISSUES

▌ How do theories help us understand sports?

▌ What is the Protestant ethic?

▌ When did the civilizing process begin?

▌ Where do ethologists find their evidence?

▌ Why is sport like religion?

▌ . . . and how can we tell if a theory is good or bad?

The Hunt for Reasons

THE FIGURATIONAL MODEL

Let's be clear at the outset: theories have a purpose – it's to help us understand. They should clarify, illuminate, make intelligible, assist comprehension. If they don't do any of these, then either they're not very effective or they're expressed in a way that bewilders us. Theories that are more likely to obfuscate people than enlighten them often have pretensions to greater knowledge. But if they don't succeed in communicating this, then we are left to wonder how valuable they are.

Norbert Elias (1897–1990) is often cited as the pre-eminent theorist of sport. His grand theory situates the rise, development and continuing attraction of sport in the wider context of what he called the civilizing process, which began in the middle ages, that is the period of European history from the fall of the Roman Empire in the West (fifth century) to the fall of Constantinople in 1453. In Elias's conception, the civilizing process started in the later part of the period, between 1100 and 1453, which was when separate kingdoms began to emerge and the growth of trade and urban life changed the social landscape utterly. Both the church and monarchies grew in power and, from the fifteenth century, there was an increase in interest in the arts, literature and scholarship.

Elias argues that the period is characterized by a lessening of violence as means of resolving conflicts and the rise of governing states that appropriated the rights to legitimate violence. As violence diminished, so the power of the state was legitimized: it was widely recognized as having the lawful right to use violence. Elias never uses the word "civilization" as this denotes an end state; he prefers to see civilizing processes constantly at work, always in perpetual motion. So, how does this explain sports?

Elias used the word "sportization," which might seem like a crime-against-grammar, but refers to the symmetry between the development of organized forms of competition and the civilizing process. In England, the raucous and rowdy folk games, which often resulted in death and serious injuries and which were played without any specific, codified – i.e. arranged into a systematic code – rules of play, were brought into a common fold through the application of precise and explicit rules governing competitions. Strict application of the rules ensured equal chances for rivals and supervision by officials guaranteed fairness. So a mixed bag of chaotic and often disordered activities developed into distinct, rule-bound contests, refereed according to strict standards and evaluated according to clearly defined criteria. This reflected what was happening in society generally.

Elias argues that both processes gathered pace in the nineteenth century and accompanied the English Industrial Revolution. Yet, he is wary of theories that explain one in terms of the other. "Both industrialization and sportization were symptomatic of a deeper-lying transformation of European societies which demanded of their individual members greater regularity and differentiation of conduct" (1986: 151).

The "transformation" so central to Elias' theory had roots as far back as the fifteenth century and involved the gradual introduction of rules and norms to govern

BOX 5.1 THEORY

From the Greek *theoros*, for contemplation, theory has three related meanings: (1) a series of linked concepts or ideas that purport to explain a set of known findings (e.g. figurational theory); (2) a set of principles that prescribes an activity (pedagogic theory, i.e. how teaching should be done); (3) an abstraction used to describe what should happened if certain conditions are met ("in theory, this should work").

The most common in sport and exercise is (1): theories are advanced to make sense of a phenomenon in terms of known principles, but in a way that clarifies or de-mystifies, rather than establishes truth. In his classic 1963 treatise the philosopher Karl Popper (1902–94) argued that knowledge proceeds through *Conjectures and Refutations*, theories being the incomplete information conjectured, and research being attempts to refute, or prove them wrong. If the theory is not refuted by the research, then it stands corroborated, though not proven.

While good theories, for Popper, are those that are amenable to empirical testing, the clarifying power of some theories is self-contained. For example, the theories of Sigmund Freud (1856–1939) and Charles Darwin (1809–82), while thorough, cogent, and illuminating, do not lend themselves to rigorous testing, yet they have transformed the manner in which we understand ourselves.

human behavior and designate what was appropriate conduct in a given situation; it also involved the rise of impersonal organizations to maintain rules. These reflected a general tendency in Europe toward interdependence: people began to orient their activities to each other, to rely less on their own subsistence efforts and more on those of others, whose tasks would be specialized and geared toward narrow objectives. In time, chains of interdependence were formed: a division of labor ensured that each individual, or group of individuals, was geared to the accomplishment of tasks that would be vital to countless others. They in turn would perform important activities, so that every member of a society depended on others, and no one was separate or completely independent.

The pattern of relationships that emerged is called a *figuration* and this is a key concept in Elias's theory: a figuration (or configuration, as it is sometimes called) is a social arrangement in which every part is interconnected and always in motion. Visualize a vast spider's web in which every filament is constantly changed, forming new connections, breaking others, inflating and contracting, but always moving. No actual spider's web would be intricate enough for an accurate resemblance, but the complex crisscrossing and its organic nature give some sense of what Elias has in mind. He prefers this kind of image to that of a society, which suggests something fixed as opposed to the ever-changing process he envisages as part of his theory. Within each configuration, there are relations of power and authority, giving a political as well as social complexion to the arrangement.

For the civilizing process to advance with reasonable efficiency, people would have to be discouraged from pursuing their own interests and whims in an unrestrained way. Earlier philosophers, Thomas Hobbes (1588–1679) being the most notable, had argued that human action is motivated entirely by selfish concerns, the greatest of which is fear of death. For Hobbes, the natural state of humanity was a "warre of every man against every man" ("warre" being an early spelling of "war," of course).

While Elias doesn't subscribe to this brutish conception and actually challenges the notion that there is such a phenomenon as a natural state of humanity, he certainly argues that the civilizing process depends on methods of control over emotions and behavior, particularly aggressive behavior. (In Elias's model, there simply can't be a

▌BOX 5.2 CONFIGURATION

Austin Harrington *et al.* provide a useful capsule definition of configuration: "Shifting networks of mutually oriented human beings with fluctuating asymmetrical power balances . . . patterns, regularities, directions of change, tendencies and counter-tendencies, in webs of human relationships developing over time." They invoke the metaphor of "dancers on a dance-floor as a mobile figuration of interdependent people [that] helps us to envisage nation-states, cities, families and even feudal, capitalist and communist societies as figurations. We can talk of recognizable patterns emerging from such shifting figurations, just as we might discern the 'tango', or the 'waltz', or simply 'dance in general'" (2006: 200).

natural state independent of the figuration: the configuration is a product of the actions of individuals, but those individuals are products of the configuration; each owes its existence to the other.)

The need for control grew more acute in eighteenth-century England, where, in the aftermath of civil strife, many people feared a recurrence, according to Elias and Dunning (1986: 171). The state was the central authority responsible for internal orderliness and overall organization and planning. With the formation of state control came what Elias calls a "civilizing spurt."

As with all Elias's arguments, there are links: sport just can't be unlinked from the changes that impelled human societies to control the use of violence and encourage an observance of manners (1982). Manners are used here in a wider sence than politeness (such as saying "please" and "thank you" etc.): Elias means social behavior oriented to the consideration of others. We became aware of the sensibilities of others and adjusted our conduct accordingly so we could respond without upsetting them. Table manners and etiquette were, in a sense, exaggerated reflections of this and Elias takes them seriously. Yet his focus is wider and he understands manners as integral to the civilizing process. We can add that acquiring manners implicated us in becoming more *cultured*.

Linked as they are, the control of violence and the rise of manners, are part of one general tendency. So, for example, the decline of dispute settlements through violence and the rise of social prohibitions on such things as spitting and breaking wind are not unconnected in Elias's scheme. They both represent new standards of conduct in changing configurations, or social arrangements. The level of acceptable violence drops as the emergent state takes over the settling of disputes and monopolizes the legitimate use of violence. As rules and conventions develop, they spread to all areas, so that standards are imposed, both externally and internally as well as being controlled by the state; individuals control themselves according to accepted or "correct" codes of conduct. And these features seep into sport, or, more accurately, the games and practices that preceded what we would now call sports.

Since the days of the Ancient Greeks, which is Elias's starting point, civilization has progressed with the state's power and therefore control over violence within the family and between neighbors, clans, and fiefdoms, increasing at a pace roughly equivalent to our internal controls over emotions and behavior; in other words, self-restraint. (The similarity to Freud's conception of society taming our more primitive urges through the super-ego is quite pronounced here.) In their essay on "Figurational sociology and sport," Patrick Murphy *et al.* point out that Greek combat sports "involved much higher levels of violence and open emotionality than those permitted today, and were less highly regulated"(2000: 95–6).

According to Elias, inhibitions about violence were also lower, so there would have been little queasiness or sense of guilt after either witnessing or engaging in actions that would today be deplored as savage, brutal – in other words, uncivilized. If we jumped on H. G. Wells' time machine and zipped back to watch a pankration in the ancient Greek games, we'd find it rebarbative, that is repellent and obnoxious. At least most of us would.

The civilizing process is a vast world trend, but not a completely linear one: there are phases in history when a figuration may "decivilize" and regress to barbarism, tolerating a higher level of violence and ungoverned behavior. Elias describes this as a reverse gear. Equally, there is allowance for sharp accelerated movements forward, such as in the civilizing spurt Elias believes is so crucial to our understanding of modern sport.

While it would caricature the civilizing process to equate it with changes in self-control, this particular aspect of the wider development acted as an agent in generating "stress-tensions" which, in turn, agitated the need for organized sport. How does Elias see this happening? First, an abstract observation from Elias's introduction to *Quest for Excitement* (co-edited with Eric Dunning): "In societies where fairly high civilizing standards all round are safeguarded and maintained by a highly effective state-internal control of physical violence, personal tensions of people resulting from conflicts of this kind, in a word, stress-tensions, are widespread" (1986: 41).

Next, most human societies develop some countermeasures against stress-tensions they themselves generate and, as Elias writes in the same introduction, "these activities must conform to the comparative sensitivity to physical violence which is characteristic of people's social habits (customs and dispositions) at the later stages of a civilizing process" 1986: 41–2).

So, the ways in which people "let off steam" mustn't violate the standards that have become accepted by society at large. Watching humans mauled by wild animals might have provided stimulating and enjoyable release for the ancient Romans, as might burning live cats or baiting bulls for the English in the nineteenth century. But, the civilizing process, according to Elias, changes our threshold of revulsion for enacting and witnessing violence, so that, nowadays, some cultures in the West find a sport like cage fighting – relatively mild in historical terms – intolerably violent (even boxing is banned in Sweden, for instance). The methods we choose to discharge tension closely reflect general standards and sensitivities.

Foxhunting is Elias's favorite example. In recent years, there have been fiery debates over whether or not foxhunting is a sport: in the nineteenth century there was no dispute: it was. In fact, sports included outdoor field events, such as fishing, archery, shooting and all forms of hunting. Organized foxhunting started in England in the sixteenth century and in North America in the mid-seventeenth century, though, of course, hunting is an immemorial practice. Once synonymous with the word "sport," foxhunting is now an anachronism and pressure against it would no doubt have prompted its demise were it not a pursuit practiced exclusively by the landowning elite.

This originally English custom was quite unlike the simpler, less regulated, and more spontaneous forms of hunting of other countries and earlier ages where people were the main hunters and foxes were one amongst many prey, boar, red deer, and wolves being others. Foxhunting became bound by a strict code of etiquette and peculiar rules, such as that which forbade killing other animals during the hunt. Hounds were trained to follow only the fox's scent, and only they could kill, while humans watched.

The fox itself had little utility apart from its pelt; its meat was not considered edible (not by its pursuers, anyway) and, while it was considered a pest, the fields and forests were full of others, which threatened farmers' livestock and crops. The chances of anyone's getting hurt in the hunt were minimized, but each course in the wall of security presented a problem of how to retain the immediacy and physical risk that were so important in early times. Elias believes that the elaboration of the rules of hunting were solutions. The rules served to postpone the outcome or finale of the hunt and so artificially prolong the process of hunting. "The excitement of the hunt itself had increasingly become the main source of enjoyment for the human participants," argue Elias and Dunning (1986: 166).

What had once been foreplay to the act of killing became the main pleasure. So the foxhunt was a virtual pure type of autotelic hunt: the thrill for participants came in the pace and exhilaration of the chasing and the pleasure of watching violence done without actually doing the killing. And, remember, this *was* sport: it lacked the competitive element so vital to contemporary definitions, but it was practiced to elicit the arousal of the hunters. Apart from that, it had no utility. In other words, the chasing itself was the purpose and, in this sense, it bore similarity to today's sports. After all, the thrill of sports is in trying to score as much as scoring.

The influence of the civilizing spurt is apparent in the restraint imposed and exercised by the participants in the foxhunts. The overall trend was to make violence more repugnant to people, which effectively encouraged them to control or restrain themselves. Elias stresses that this should be seen not as a repression but as a product of greater sensitivity. The foxhunters didn't secretly feel an urge to kill with their own hands; they genuinely found such an act disagreeable, but could still find pleasure in viewing it from their horses; what Elias calls killing by proxy (this bears some resemblance to Jacobson's argument covered in Chapter 1).

Despite all attempts to abolish them, hunts persist to this day, probably guided by appetites similar to those whetted by the sight of humans being masticated by raptors. Hundreds of millions of *Jurassic Park* fans can attest to the enjoyable tension provided by the latter, albeit through the medium of film. While Elias doesn't cover contemporary hunts, we should add that their longevity reveals something contradictory about the civilizing trend and the impulse to condone or even promote wanton cruelty.

To ensure a long and satisfying chase, and to be certain that foxes are found in the open, "earth stoppers" are employed to close up earths (fox holes) and badger sets in which foxes may take refuge. Many hunts maintain earths to ensure a sufficient supply of foxes through the season (foxes used to be imported from Continental Europe). The hunt doesn't start until after 11 a.m. to allow the fox time to digest its food and ensure that it's capable of a long run. During the course of a hunt, a fox may run to ground and will either survive or be dug out by the pursuant dogs, a virtual baiting from which even the dogs emerge with damage. New hounds are prepared by killing cubs before the new season, a practice observed and presumably enjoyed by members of the hunt and their guests.

In Elias's theory, foxhunting was a solution to the problems created by the accelerating trend toward civilization and the internal controls on violence it implied. The closing up of areas of arousal, which in former ages had been sources of pleasurable gratification (as well as immense suffering), set humans on a search for substitute activities and ones which didn't carry the risks, dangers, or outright disorder that society as a whole would find unacceptable – the quest for excitement.

The English form of foxhunting was only one example of a possible solution, but Elias feels it is an "empirical model," containing all the original distinguishing characteristics of today's sport. Other forms of sport, such as boxing, football, cricket, and rugby showed how the problem was solved without the use and abuse of animals; the first two of these were appropriated by the working class. All evolved in a relatively orderly manner, well matched to the needs of modern, bureaucratic society with its accent on organization and efficiency and ultimately in line with the general civilizing process.

The explanation of sport is but one facet of Elias's grand project, which is to understand the very nature and consequences of the civilizing process. It follows that critics who are not convinced by his general model are certainly not by his specific one. The actual idea of a civilizing process has the tinge of a theory of progress in which history is set to proceed through predetermined stages, which can't be altered. Elias's mention of the irregularity of the process and the reverse gear are marginal to the main thesis which suggests that, as Paul Hoggett puts it, "civilization seems to march onwards fairly straightforwardly without any collapsing back into barbarity" (1986: 36).

Many contemporary observers of sport might want to argue that collapses are quite commonplace and point fingers in the direction of soccer stadiums, once the sites of open, almost ritualistic, violence between rival fans. Elias and his devotees would recommend a more detailed examination of history to appreciate that violence has for long been related to soccer; only the media's amplification of it has changed. Presumably, the same could be said about foxhunting which continues, despite protests, today. But this response is only partially satisfactory, as many other sports have developed violent penumbra quite recently and it is hard to establish any historical connections with, say, boxing, cricket, and rugby, all of which have experienced major crowd disorder over the past few decades.

It's interesting that the nucleus of Elias's model has not been attacked. A basic proposition is that "pleasurable excitement . . . appears to be one of the most elementary needs of human beings," as Elias puts it in his "An essay on sport and violence" (1986a: 174). Yet, Elias never documents the sources of such needs and, considering that the entire project rests on them, one might expect some expansion. This is mysteriously absent. Is it a biological drive? Part of a survival instinct? A deep psychological trait? Elias's treatment seems to suggest that the need for "pleasurable excitement" is of a similar order to the need for food, shelter, sex, and other such basic needs, rather like ones in Abraham Maslow's theory of motivation (which we'll cover in Chapter 6). Certainly, it appears as basic as these, though social and ecological circumstances might change the way in which we interpret our needs as well as our wants. They might not be as static as Elias supposed.

This may seem a small quibble with what is after all a hugely ambitious attempt to illuminate the nature and purpose of modern sport by connecting its changing character to the civilizing transformation of the past several centuries. Far from being an autonomous realm separated from other institutions, sport is totally wrapped up with culture, psyche, and the state. Human "stress-tensions" are linked to large-scale social changes.

Elias's theory, like others, is a collection of ideas or suppositions that try to explain something – in this case, the existence of sport and continuing pull of sports. They're often based on general principles, not always with supporting evidence. The intention is that the theory can be converted into conjectures or propositions that can then be set against reality. Not that this always works in practice: some theories are hard to test and those that can be are often challenged. Rival theories criticize them for interpreting facts in a way that supports the original principles. So they become circular.

The problem is: we just can't get to grips with the reasons for something without theory. We have to have some sort of organizing framework in which we can arrange our facts in a way that makes them comprehensible. Whatever lawyers say, the facts *do not* speak for themselves. So, when Elias wrote about the sources, expansion, and direction of sports, his theory is not intended as a definitive statement, but, rather, as a possible answer to some of the more taxing questions about sports. His is but one theoretical approach; there are others that we'll move to next.

CRITICAL THEORY

Sport is a remarkably ironic thing, its chief characteristic being that it provides an entertaining relief from work while at the same time preparing people for more work. This is the central insight of a group of theorists who have, in one way or another, been influenced by the work of Karl Marx. Although Marx himself didn't write about sport, others have interpreted his theories in a way that provides insights into the political and economic utility of sports.

Marx wrote in the mid-nineteenth century and his focus was modern capitalism, an economic system based on a split of the ownership of the means of production (factories, land, equipment, etc.). Owners of the means of production are bosses, or bourgeoisie, in whose interests capitalism works and who are prepared to milk the system to its limits in order to stay in control. The working class, or proletariat, is forced to work for them in order to subsist. As the system doesn't work in their interests, they have to be persuaded that it could if only they were luckier, or had better breaks, or worked harder. In other words, the system itself is fine; it's actually the workers who need to change for the good. As long as workers are convinced of the legitimacy of economic arrangements, then capitalism is not under threat. So the system has evolved methods of ensuring its own survival. And this is where sport fits in.

Because Marx's own thought was subjected to so many different interpretations, it was inevitable that no single analysis would emerge that could claim to be "what Marx would have written about sport had he been alive today." When theories of sports bearing Marx's imprimatur began to surface in the early 1970s, they were far from uniform, their only linking characteristic being that sports were geared to the interests of the bourgeoisie, or middle class, had the effect of neutralizing any political potential in the working class and contributed in some way to the preservation of the status quo. Sports were, in other words, to be criticized, not just analyzed.

The principal scholars claiming to work with a Marxist approach were the American Paul Hoch, Jean-Marie Brohm, a French writer, and the German theorist, Bero Rigauer. Other commentators, such as Richard Gruneau, John Hargreaves, Mark Naison, Brian Stoddart, and William Morgan, later contributed toward what has now become a respectable body of Marxist literature on sports. The work of Hoch, Brohm, and Rigauer is informed by the spirit of the Frankfurt School, and which we can summarize as Critical Theory. The second group takes as its starting point the theories of the Italian Marxist, Antonio Gramsci, whose central concept of hegemony has provided a focus for studies of sport and which we will cover in the next subsection.

BOX 5.3 KARL MARX (1818–83)

The German philosopher and economic theorist is one of the most influential thinkers of recent times. He was the founder of modern communism and author of several seminal volumes, including *Das Kapital* and the *Communist Manifesto*, which he wrote with Friedrich Engels. After graduating from Berlin, Marx worked as a journalist; he moved to Paris in 1843, before going to England where he lived from 1849. While Marx's theory changed as he matured, there is a critical impulse that runs through everything he wrote: *de omnibus dubitandum est* ("be doubtful of everything") was Marx's motif. Marx's philosophical approach is materialism, which does not mean a tendency to consider material possession as important in this context, but refers to the belief that consciousness is the result of humans' interaction with their material environment. Marx's method for analyzing history is dialectical materialism, meaning that all social and political events result from conflicts over material needs, so we can best understand the world by examination of these conflicts or ever-changing contradictions. Marx held a grudging admiration for capitalism, though he felt its unequal and conflict-riven structure had an inbuilt time limit. Capitalism was based on a basic division of capital-owners, or the bourgeoisie, who dominate – and workers, or the proletariat. Workers have no choice but to produce more value than necessary to pay the costs and the surplus is appropriated by capitalists in the form of profit. The workers have little or no control over their own lives, while the capitalists grow richer. Marx's admiration, such as it was, stems from the elegance of this unbalanced arrangement. Capitalists devised an elegant method of convincing workers that the system was perfectly fair and just. But Marx predicted that eventually a crisis would disrupt the system and workers would unite in their opposition, leading to a revolution and clearing the way for a communist society.

Sports serve four main functions for capitalism, according to John Hargreaves. First, organized sport helps train a "docile labor force": it encourages in the working class an acceptance of the kind of work discipline demanded in modern production; hard work is urged in both sport and work. We've noted before how the organization and tempo of industry became reflected in sport and Hargreaves sees the congruence as almost perfect. In his *Sport, Culture and Ideology*, Hargreaves compares the features of sport and industry: "A high degree of specialisation and standardisation, bureaucratised and hierarchical administration, long-term planning, increased reliance on science and technology, a drive for maximum productivity, a quantification of performance and, above all, the alienation of both producer and consumer" (1982: 41).

Major events, like the Olympic Games and Super Bowl, are given as examples of the final point. Second, sport has become so thoroughly commercialized and dominated by market forces that events and performers are treated as – or perhaps just are – commodities that are used by capitalist enterprises: "Sport is produced, packaged and sold like any other commodity on the market for mass consumption at enormous profits" (1982: 41).

The trading or transfer of players typifies the commodification. The third area in which sport fits in is in "expressing the quintessential ideology in capitalist society." What Marxist theorists have proposed here is that sport works in subtle ways at indicating qualities or imperatives in people; all these qualities have counterparts in society at large. Aggressive individualism, ruthless competitiveness, equal opportunity, elitism, chauvinism, sexism, and nationalism: all these are regarded as admirable. Their desirability is not questioned in sports and the uncritical approach to them is carried over to society. Fourth, there is the area of the state: this bureaucratic administration represents capitalist interests. It follows that every intrusion into sport by the state must be seen as some sort of attempt to link sports participation with the requirements of the capitalist system.

Four areas, then, but hardly a theory; they are really only lowest common denominators for all those favoring a Marxist conception of sport. Beyond these, there are a variety of theories all taking their lead from Marx in the sense that they see the split over the means of production as central. In other words, sport has to be analyzed in terms of class relations. In 1972, Paul Hoch published his *Rip Off the Big Game: The exploitation of sports by the power elite*, in which he advanced one of the most acerbic Marxist critiques of sport, which he likened to the mainstream religions about which Marx himself wrote much. Religion was regarded as little more than a capitalist convenience, absorbing workers' energies and emotions and supplying a salve after the week's labors.

Sport has much the same significance. Both religion and sport work as an opiate that temporarily dulls pain and gives a false sense of well-being, but which is also a dangerous and debilitating narcotic that can reduce its users to a helpless state of dependence. The attraction of sport is as compelling as that of religion and its effects are comparable: it siphons off potential that might otherwise be put to political use in challenging the capitalist system.

Keen readers will have spotted a resemblance here: the Roman poet Juvenal, as we noted in Chapter 4 satirized the follies of Roman society, particularly its regular gladiatorial contests, which he mused was a massive distraction designed to take the plebeian classes' minds off their dreadful material lives. "Bread and circuses" were expedient ways of averting revolts and uprisings.

The title of Jean-Marie Brohm's book indicates his position on contemporary sport: *Sport: A prison of measured time* (1978). By this, Brohm means that the institutional, rule-governed, highly organized structure of modern sport has been shaped by capitalist interest groups in such a way as to represent a constraint rather than a freedom. Sport is in no sense an alternative to work, less still an escape from it "since it removes all bodily freedom, all creative spontaneity, every aesthetic dimension and every playful impulse" (1978: 175).

The competitor is merely a prisoner, whose performances are controlled, evaluated, and recorded, preferably in measurable terms. Capitalism as a system stifles the human imagination and compresses the human body into mindless production

BOX 5.4 CAPITALISM

An economic system in which most productive assets are held by private owners, and most decisions about production and distribution are dictated by the market rather than the political powers. In formal terms, owners of productive means (corporations, industries, commercial businesses, and so on) are sometimes called the capitalist class, whereas those who work for salary or wage, are once known as the working class, though change in the occupational sector has made the distinction redundant. Often executives work for salaries and are credited with stock options and profit or performance related bonuses. The classic capitalist economy is regulated by market imperatives and, in theory, thrives without the involvement of the state. After the economic downturn of 2008, however, most capitalist systems now incorporate some element of government involvement. This goes beyond the establishment of institutional rules, such as contract law and international trade policies: when markets collapse, government bailouts, such as injections of public funds (i.e. tax revenues) into private business, are required to assist the system. Mature capitalism, as it is sometimes known, effectively integrates free market economies with state regulation. In contrast to capitalism, the complete state control of economic and social affairs is known as *dirigisme*.

work; and as sport is but one part of that system, it can do little more than reproduce its effects. It just obeys the "logic" of the system. As Richard Gruneau writes in his *Class, Sports and Social Development*: "For Brohm, capitalism has shaped sport in its own image" (1983: 38).

Others, like Bero Rigauer, in his *Sport and Work*, agree with the basic assumptions and emphasize how corporations have penetrated, or completely taken over sport. It is as if sport has been appropriated by one class and used to bolster its already commanding position in the overall class structure (1981). For Rigauer, sport has aided the economic system by improving the health of workers and so minimizing the time lost at work through illness.

Like Brohm, he sees a "technocratic" takeover of sport, with performances being subject to rationalization and planning and training becoming more time absorbing and important than performance itself. Initiative and creativity are stifled, rendering the human performer as the "one-dimensional man," so called by the Marxist philosopher Herbert Marcuse (from whom Brohm and Rigauer draw inspiration). For Rigauer, sport is part of "the social processes of reproduction" in the sense that it contributes to the continuation of capitalism without our ever seeing it as such (2000: 44).

In all accounts, the human beings are depicted as passive dopes, pushed around by factors beyond their control. But are humans just like hockey pucks? Do they really respond so readily and easily? Those who think not find the work of Hoch and Brohm rather too deterministic – all thoughts and behavior are determined by outside forces emanating from the capitalist system. Sport is but one tool for maintaining the domination and exploitation of the working class.

In contrast, other writers prefer to see the working class playing a more active role. Certainly, there is reciprocity between the way in which modern sport is organized and the functions it fulfills on the one hand, and the requirements of capitalism on the other. But this doesn't deny that different groups (classes) are involved in different sports and at different levels at different stages in history. Sport is not, as Hargreaves puts it, "universally evil." Its meaning and significance have to be investigated more closely. Other Marxist writers, including Gruneau and Hargreaves himself, have attempted to do this. All would go along with the more orthodox Marxist approach, but only so far.

Sport is much more multifaceted than the others acknowledge. It may give substance to wider ideologies and exfoliate working-class energies, but it can also be useful as a builder of solidarity within working-class groups, which are brought together with a common purpose. "It is precisely this type of solidarity that historically has formed the basis for a trenchant opposition to employers," observes Hargreaves (1986: 110).

Public gatherings at sports events have always generated a potential for disorder and have attracted the state's agents of control. Some writers have even inferred a form of political resistance from the exploits of soccer hooligans. So, involvement in sport can actually facilitate or even encourage challenge rather than accommodation. Far from being a means of controlling the masses, sport, on occasion, has needed controlling itself. On the issue of sport as a preparation for work, Hargreaves reminds us that not all sports resemble the rhythms and rationality of work. Fishing and bowling provide relaxation and relief in very stark contrast to work.

Hargreaves (1986) argues against a firmly negative view of sport as providing only "surrogate satisfactions for an alienated mass order . . . perpetuating its alienation" and instead argues for a more flexible, spontaneous interpretation. Sport may perform many services in the interests of the status quo, amongst them a belief in the ultimate triumph of ability ("if you're good you'll make it" – in sport or life generally). It also helps fragment the working class by splintering loyalties into localities, regions, etc. But it can also provide a basis for unity and therefore resistance to dominant interest groups: "Part mass therapy, part resistance, part mirror image of the dominant political economy," as David Robins puts it (1982: 145).

BRITISH AND AMERICAN EMPIRES

Even those who stick valiantly to Marx's first principles are embarrassed by the literalism of the type favored by Hoch and others of his persuasion. Staying true to Marx and applying his class-based formula to virtually any phenomenon is like trying to vault with a pole made of timber: not only is it heavy, but it's rigid (actually, ancient Greeks did use wooden poles). Other writers have opted for more flexibility, taking basic Marxist ideas as they have been reinterpreted by later theorists, in particular Antonio Gramsci, whose central contribution was through the concept of hegemony. Those who followed Gramsci (1891–1937) wanted to restore role of the human being to that of an agent, someone who was active and could intervene in practical matters rather than just respond to the logic of capitalism.

According to hegemony theory, there is nothing intrinsic to sports that make them conservative or subversive: they have no essential qualities. Under capitalism, sports have been supportive to the existing order of things; but there's no necessary reason why, given different circumstances, they could not have a liberating effect.

▌BOX 5.5 HEGEMONY

From the Greek *hegemon*, meaning leader, this refers to leadership, supremacy, or rule, usually by one state over a confederacy, or one class over another. It has been used in a specifically Marxist way by Antonio Gramsci, who sought to understand how ruling, or leading groups in a capitalist society maintain their power by indirect rather than direct economic or military means. They do so by creating a culture that is shared by all but which favors one class over another, usually the most deprived. It is domination, but of intellect or thought rather than body, though ultimately there is a relation because the labor of subordinate groups is exploited. It is important to appreciate that hegemony is not some artificial contrivance: it is a genuinely felt set of beliefs, ideas, values, and principles, all of which work in a supportive way for the status quo and hence appear as common sense. According to Gramsci, an entire apparatus is responsible for diffusing ideas that complement and encourage consensus. These include the Church, education, the media, political institutions, and, if Stoddart, Naison, and others are to be accepted, sports.

For Richard Gruneau, as sports become more structured in their institutional forms, they constrain and regulate much more than liberate their participants. The kind of liberating features of sport he has in mind are spontaneity, freedom of expression, aesthetic beauty. Politically, sports can yield the kind of solidarity that contributes toward the women's movement, civil rights campaigns and other types of protests against injustice and inequality. In sports, there are opportunities to mobilize against the status quo, not just comply with it. Historically, this has not been the case and the enthusiasm for sports, particularly among the working class, has bolstered the social order.

Flocking to sports as amusement, the working class assimilates its values and principles, most of which dovetail perfectly with those of the wider society. Fair play and the opportunity to go as far as one's ability allows are sacrosanct in sports: meritocratic ideals are important in society too. One legitimates the other. Forgotten is the fact that, in any capitalist system, there are gross, structured inequalities in the distribution of income, wealth, and prestige and that these are replicated one generation after the next through an inheritance system that favors rich over poor. For hegemony theorists, it is important that those at the poorer end of the class structure regard this as commonsensical; that they are not constantly questioning the legitimacy of a system that consigns them to also-rans. Sports encourage this by promoting the good of meritocracy and the equality of life chances that seem to be available to everyone, but, in reality, are not.

Mark Naison and Brian Stoddart have offered studies of sports that draw on Gramsci's concept of hegemony and its role in supporting empires. Naison's early article, "Sports and the American empire" (1972) and Stoddart's analysis of the "Sport, cultural imperialism, and colonial response in the British empire" (1988) plus his more recent *Sport, Culture and History* (2008) advance our understanding of the economic and political utility of sports in stabilizing what might otherwise be disruptive colonial situations. Both writers acknowledge the work of C. L. R. James, whose historical analysis of cricket showed how the values supposedly embodied in the sport were disseminated throughout the Caribbean and how these were of enormous benefit to a colonial regime endlessly trying to manage the local populations.

Sport for both Naison and Stoddart is a means of cultural power, not direct political power as suggested by the others. "Athletic events have increasingly reflected the dynamics of an emergent American imperialism," writes Naison (1972: 96). "As the American political economy 'internationalized' in the post-war period, many of its most distinctive cultural values and patterns, from consumerism to military preparedness, have become integral parts of organized sports." And Stoddart: "Through sport were transferred dominant British beliefs as to social behavior, standards, relations, and conformity, all of which persisted beyond the end of formal empire" (1988: 651).

BOX 5.6 IMPERIALISM

From the Latin *imperium,* meaning absolute power or dominion over others, this refers to the political and economic domination of one or several countries by one other. The union of the different countries, known as colonies, is the empire. There is an unequal relationship between the ruling sovereign country, sometimes known as the metropolitan center, and the peripheral colonies, which are reduced to the status of dependants rather than partners. Technically, the United States' colonial dependencies have been few compared to, say Britain or those of other European powers in the nineteenth and early twentieth centuries. But its indirect political influence and its economic pre-eminence over a vast network of other countries have convinced many that there is North American imperialism.

By participating in sports, populations who came under American and British influences were taught teamwork, the value of obeying authority, courage in the face of adversity, loyalty to fellow team members (especially the captain) and, perhaps most importantly, respect for rules. Stoddart writes of cricket, though it could be applied to any sport: "To play cricket or play the game meant being honest and upright, and accepting conformity within the conventions as much as it meant actually taking part in a simple game" (1988: 653).

Ruling over colonies in far-flung parts of the globe could have been achieved by military force; indeed, it was initially. But coercion is not cost-effective, especially so when the geographical distance between the metropolitan centers and the peripheral colonies was as great as it was, particularly in the British case. But, if a population could be persuaded that the colonial rule was right and proper, then this made life easier for the masters. Sports provided a way of inculcating people with the kind of values and ideas that facilitated British rule and a "vehicle of adjustment to American imperialism, its popularity an index of America's success in transmitting adulation of its culture and values" (Naison 1972: 100).

None of this suggests a passive acceptance of the rule of America or Britain. As Thomas Sowell writes in his *Race and Culture: A world view*: "Conquest, whatever its benefits, has seldom been a condition relished by the conquered. The struggle for freedom has been as pervasive throughout history as conquest itself" (1994: 79).

By exporting institutions as strong as sport it was possible to create shared beliefs and attitudes between rulers and ruled, at the same time creating distance between them. Organized sports, remember, were products of the imperial powers, most of the rules being drawn up and governing bodies being established between the 1860s and 1890s, exactly the period when the imperialism was at its height. The rulers, having experience with sport, were obviously superior and this reinforced the general notion they tried to convey – that they were suited to rule, as if by divine appointment.

The rules of sports were codified at a central source, transferred to all parts of the vast imperial web, then adhered to by people of astonishingly diverse backgrounds. The colonial experience in general was not unlike this: ruling from a center and engineering a consensus among millions. Impoverished groups over whom Americans and British ruled were introduced to sports by their masters. When they grew proficient enough to beat them, that posed another problem. West Indian cricketers became adept at repeatedly bowling fast balls that were virtually unplayable.

New Zealand developed a style of rugby that made it almost invincible. Australia beat England regularly at cricket. The problem as it was seen on British soil was that such achievements might be "interpreted as symbolic of general parity," as Stoddart puts it (1988: 667). Baseball was "popularized by the increasing number of American corporate and military personnel" in Puerto Rico, the Dominican Republic, Venezuela, Mexico and elsewhere, writes Naison (1972). Now, many players from those countries play in U.S. leagues.

The concept of sport as a purveyor of imperial culture is a powerful one, especially when allied to a Marxist analysis of the role of ideas in maintaining social structures. Sport, in the eyes of critics like Naison and Stoddart, is not the blunt instrument many other Marxists take it to be. For them, its value to ruling groups is in drawing subordinate groups toward an acceptance of ideas that are fundamental to their control. This was appropriate in the empires of America and Britain, where orders and directives came from a central source; just like the rules of any sport.

For theorists influenced by Marxism, sports can never be seen as neutral. They can be enjoyed; indeed they must be enjoyable to be effective. If we spotted the surreptitious purposes of sports, they could hardly gratify us at all. For them to work, sports must be seen as totally disengaged from the political and economic processes. In the colonial situation, it was crucial that sports were enjoyed and transmitted from one generation to the next. Yet, according to Marxism, this should not deflect our attentions totally away from the valuable functions sports have served – and probably still serve – in the capitalist enterprise at home and abroad. This gives a different slant to the variety of Marxism that sees sports in a one-dimensional way: as politically safe channels, or outlets for energies that might otherwise be disruptive to capitalism. Yet, it clearly complements it in identifying the main beneficiary of sports as capitalism.

RATIONALIZATION AND THE PROTESTANT ETHIC

Max Weber's theories are typically seen as either a direct challenge to Marx's or an attempt to augment them with additional ideas. Unlike Marx and his followers who emphasized the role of material, economic, or productive factors in shaping all aspects of social life, Weber believed ideas and beliefs played a significant role; not in isolation, but in combination with the kind of material factors Marx had played up. In particular, Weber argued that the rise of modern capitalism is, in large part, a result of the diffusion of Protestant tenets throughout Europe and America. Protestantism did not cause capitalism, but its principles and values and those of early capitalism were so complementary that Weber detected an "elective affinity" between them. The attachment is what Weber, in the title of one of his major books, called *The Protestant Ethic and the Spirit of Capitalism* (1958).

The Protestant ethic that emerged in the sixteenth century and, over the next three hundred years spread through Europe and the United States, embraced values, attitudes, and behaviors; it encouraged rational asceticism (or austerity), goal-orientation (ambition), constancy (determination), thrift, individual achievement, a consciousness of time and work as a "calling." In other words, the ethic encouraged the very beliefs and action that were conducive to rise of business enterprises and, eventually, capitalist economies. While it was originally a religiously inspired protocol, the Protestant ethic transferred to everyday life, promoting human labor to a central position in the moral life of the individual and elevating the business entrepreneur to an exalted status. Laboring in one's chosen vocation was extolled in sermons and in popular literature (for example, the writings of Cotton Mather, Benjamin Franklin, and Thomas Carlyle) as both a duty and vehicle for personal fulfillment.

To understand how all this ties in with the growth of sports, we need to go back to the time before the Protestant ethic had risen. The Renaissance was a period beginning in the early fifteenth century, in which individuals seemed to find release. Starting in Italy, then spreading throughout Europe, creativity, self-expression and imaginative construction became watchwords. Europe underwent an extraordinarily fertile period of cultural rebirth in which many great masterworks in art, architecture, and engineering were produced.

One of the effects of this was a growth in play and recreation. As artists and scientists were released to exercise their imaginations on new, previously undreamed of projects, so others were released to express themselves in playful physical activities. Ballgames in particular enjoyed a surge in popularity. Elementary forms of tennis and handball emerged, known as *pallo della mona*, *rachetta* and *paletta*. A rough and often dangerous version of football called *calcio* was also played. These and other games had none of the organization or regulation of contemporary sports and they were played in a rather different spirit: the object was to take pleasure from the activities – not necessarily to win.

As playful games gained in popularity, they fostered occasions for spectators to watch. Not that this made them any more competitive. For example, fencing contests were closer to acrobatic exhibitions than outright conflicts: opportunities to express one's physical abilities in front of audiences. In this sense, they had some resemblance to the ancient Egyptian games of the second millennium BCE. Of the latter, J. Sakellarakis writes: "The sole purpose of such displays of athletic prowess was to entertain a spectacle-loving people rather than to serve an ideal similar to that expressed by the later Greek Olympic Games" (1979: 14).

In the Renaissance, no higher values of glory or honor were embodied in games: they were to be enjoyed and watched, plain and simple. Urban festivals and tournaments became popular throughout Europe in the fifteenth and sixteenth centuries. Inter-town rivalries were friendly, if raucous. The predominant Roman Catholic Church at first tried to outlaw the carnival-like activities; they had no obvious utility, either practically or spiritually. Faced with a gathering momentum of interest in games such as *calcio*, the church eventually conceded and actually recognized such pastimes by allowing them to be played on Holy Days, a tradition that has endured in one way or another.

Catholicism's influence waned as the belief that human beings could shape their own destinies gained currency. Among the most influential Protestant reformers was John Calvin, who lived between 1509 and 1564, and taught that humans, rather than remain subservient to papal dictates, could save their own souls and change the world around them in the process. Human conduct should be ordered according to divine ends, preached Calvin: discipline, abstinence and the avoidance of pleasures of the flesh were among the many principles he laid down. So, the playful activities about which the Catholic church had been reserved were quite definitely opposed. Those accepting the ethic of Protestantism were forbidden from taking part in anything so frivolous and cheerful as game playing.

The Catholic church's response to the challenge of the Reformation was to reinterpret tournaments, festivals and carnivals at which games were played as representations of the Catholic faith, performed for the greater glory of god and serving the added purpose of maintaining a healthy body. But, as Protestantism grew and the science it encouraged developed, magic, mysticism, and many theological doctrines were driven out in a process Weber called the "disenchantment" of the natural world. Catholicism came under attack, as did all activities that involved expressive human movement.

In his book *The Influence of the Protestant Ethic on Sport and Recreation* (1997), Steven J. Overman pays close attention to the consistency between the ethical principles and the impulses that led to the rise of what he calls "rationalized sport" which was "built on the prerequisite that sport was to be taken seriously" (1997: 161). Activities that were once regarded as useless and trivial were rationalized in a way that made them agreeable to Protestants. By this, Overman means that the casual, impromptu and hit-or-miss nature of games and sport-like activities were turned into pursuits that bore much closer resemblance to today's regulated sports.

Older cultures, including Spartan and Roman, had exploited the utilitarian potential of sport, linking training and competition to military purposes. The athletic field was perfect preparation for combat. In *Max Weber: From history to modernity*, Bryan S. Turner notes that, while never enthusiastic about athletic contests in themselves, nineteenth-century Protestants were prepared to interpret athletic activities as having a rational motive: they promoted healthy bodies, strengthened "character" and assisted the production of a hale and hearty population that was habituated to discipline and hard work (1992).

BOX 5.7 MAX WEBER (1864–1920)

The German theorist is regarded (with Karl Marx and Emile Durkheim) as one of the founding fathers of sociology. In his 1904 volume *The Protestant Ethic and the Spirit of Capitalism*, he argued that there was a relationship between the work ethic promoted by Protestantism and the development of early capitalism. Unlike Marx, who believed consciousness emanated from humans' engagement with the physical environment, Weber argued that ideas have an important role to play in social change. In fact, his entire body of work is inspired by this concept. Weber analyzed how societies in the twentieth century were becoming more rationalized: bureaucracy was dominating spheres of activity, administration was becoming overpowering in industry, and commerce and discipline were becoming more pronounced everywhere. Life in general was becoming predictable and the outcomes of human actions calculable. Weber called this an "iron cage" – one that we had built ourselves.

In other eras, athletic competition or games might have been pleasurable escapes from the grind of everyday life. But the Protestants preferred to stress their pragmatic value. The seriousness of purpose that directed action toward goals, the stress on calculable outcomes rather than sheer chance and the avoidance of pleasures of the flesh were features of the Protestant ethic; but they were also features of the newly rationalized athletic contests that emerged in the late eighteenth and nineteenth centuries.

The labor-intensive character of sports and recreation had been recognized years earlier. The late seventeenth-century scientist Robert Boyle observed that "tennis . . . is much more toilsome than what many others make work"; and the philosopher John Stuart Mill mused "many a day spent in killing game includes more muscular fatigue than a day's plowing." Such views chimed well with Protestants who championed hard work: they denounced monks as lazy parasites because their lifestyle did not count as work. Early settlers in North America were even suspicious about Indian males who hunted, while females did the real physical work – laboring in the fields, rearing children, and preparing food.

The conception of athletics as paid work goes way back before 1869 when the Cincinnati Red Stockings became the first salaried club, or 1864 when the English instituted the "gentlemen *vs.* players" distinction to ensure that the working-class players who were paid were not genuine "sportsmen." But, after the 1860s, professionalism began to change sports. For example, an old practice first used in fifth century BCE Sparta was revived: employing a specialist person to supervise training. The coach, or trainer, was given the responsibility of ensuring that athletes prepared adequately for their event; this meant taking sports seriously, using rational planning, systematic routines, and, perhaps most importantly, exercising self-discipline. All had analogous features in the Protestant ethic.

If the devil makes work for idle hands, there was no room for his enterprise in sports. Work and productivity replaced pleasure and recreation in several sports, a notable exception being the Olympic Games, which were re-introduced in a modern form in 1896. The Olympic movement strove to create a tenuous and largely artificial link with the ancient games that ceased in AD 393. As such, it prohibited professional competitors and allowed only those who participated in athletics for the honor and pride of competing. Early games were not the spectacles we have become used to in recent decades: programs of events were smaller and competitors were poorly prepared – training was frowned-on by amateurs.

Yet, by the 1924 Olympics, a more goal-directed approach had begun to appear. Hugh Hudson's 1981 film *Chariots of Fire* captures the emergent trend nicely. Leading up to the games, the two central athletes, Harold Abrahams and Eric Liddell, are steadfast in the training, Abrahams actually using a professional coach Sam Mussabini (who is not even allowed into the stadium because he has been paid) to oversee his regimen. Yet a third competitor, Lord Andrew Lindsay, presents an alternative portrait of the English gentleman competitor of the 1920s: he places champagne flutes on the edge of his hurdles during practice runs to deter him from clipping them and spilling his favorite tipple. After training (and, occasionally, before) he partakes in a few glasses of champagne. He is the complete gentleman-amateur, with no trace of the single-mindedness, less still the ruthlessness, that gradually takes hold of his fellow Oxford student Abrahams.

While amateurism – from the Latin *amorosus*, pertaining to love – was not sacrificed by the International Olympic Committee until much later, the elevation of winning over just competing became a more prominent feature. And winning required hard work, discipline in training, and efficiency in performance. A further point of symmetry between the Olympics and the ethic that guided society into industrial modernity was the exactitude of its record keeping. Quantification was absolutely vital for industrialism, of course. The Olympic Games, like their ancient predecessors, kept strict registers of results. With the technological benefit of accurate timepieces, the modern games were able to log times and distances, setting in motion a quest for record-breaking performances.

This is one of the characteristics Allen Guttmann believes marks out the traditional from the modern society, the others being secularism (decline of religion), equality, specialization, rationalism, and bureaucratic organization. In his book *From Ritual to Record: The nature of modern sports,* Guttmann argues that, while sports, or at least their progenitors, were originally intended as alternatives to work, they became reflections of it (1978). Overman goes even further: "The Protestant sport ethos succeeded in transforming sport into a regimen of goal-directed behaviors which are the antithesis of pure play" (2000: 338).

By the end of the 1920s, the meaning and purpose of sport had completely changed: they had become organized, regulated, and subject to rules. The rational planning that Weber had analyzed as a major feature of modernity had supplanted the spontaneity and freedom of earlier forms of play. The focus of sports narrowed: to coin a phrase, winning was the only thing. And this was consistent with a Protestant ethic that praised and honored the accomplishment that derives from exertion, perseverance, abstinence, and self-control. Rewards are not given; they are earned.

In presenting a model of the Protestant ethic and its pivotal role in the rise of capitalism, Weber did not intend to explain the mutation of sports into the rational activities we witness today. But his analysis offers a way of recognizing how the ethic that conferred on work a positive status, stressing its benefits and condemning idleness, made a considerable impact on reshaping sports.

BOX 5.8 CORINTHIANS

From the ancient Greek city of Corinth, site of the Isthmian games, which was known for its wealth, luxury, and licentiousness, Corinthians being its inhabitants. In the early nineteenth century, this took on sporting connotations when it was appropriated by wealthy gentlemen amateurs, who could afford to ride their own horses, sail their own yachts, and pursue sports for no financial gain – in contrast to the professional players. The self-styled Corinthians believed they embodied the true spirit of sport for its own sake. Today, we occasionally describe a figure or several figures who display the highest standards of sportsmanship as embodying the Corinthian spirit.

Pierre Bourdieu (1978) has examined the manner in which games and unorganized pursuits became rationalized and, like Weber, arrived at the conclusion that sport, in its acquisition of rules and institutions, began to reflect work. But Bourdieu interprets this process not as a corollary of a more general trend in western society, more as an expression of the moral ideals or ethos of society's most powerful groups – what Marx called the bourgeoisie. Bourdieu argues that it was the sons of the emerging affluent entrepreneurs and land-owning nobility who shaped sports to their own requirements. Mastering tennis or golf or knowing how to ride in a fast-paced hunt or shoot with accuracy conferred a valuable distinction. The industrial working class was much more enthusiastic about mass sports, such as football, which was cheap and placed few material demands on the participant or fan.

Unlike other theorists considered in this chapter, Bourdieu does not offer a fully rounded account of the origins, development, and purpose of sport, but he does suggest that there was practical utility in sport in distinguishing classes by means of what he calls habitus, this being a set of patterns of thinking, behavior and taste. The taste is internalized as we mature, so that it appears "natural," a kind of disposition.

Working-class people's interest in football, as opposed to, say, tennis, appears to be part of the natural order of things. As sports acquired different codes and standards of etiquette through rationalizing, so doors opened and closed, giving sports a class-structured character. Bourdieu's arguments are varied and we will return to them in later chapters, particularly in relation to exercise, the body, and violence. For now, we need only to note his supplement to the rationalization argument.

ETHOLOGY'S MAGIC MIXTURE

While he dismisses most of the Marxist approaches to sport as "political claptrap," Desmond Morris discerns a "small grain of truth" in the idea that events that fascinate, excite, and entertain people also distract them from "political terrorism and bloody rebellion." But, on examination, this aspect of sport "is not political after all, but rather has to do with human nature" (1981: 20). Morris, as a student of animal behavior and who affords humans pride of place in his perspective, has turned his sights to sport in his book *The Soccer Tribe*.

BOX 5.9 ETHOLOGY

This is the scientific study of animal behavior; its parameters were set by Austrian biologist Konrad Lorenz (1903–89) and Dutch zoologist Nikolaas Tinbergen (1907–88), joint winners of the 1973 Nobel Prize. The questions of how animals learn, how they communicate, and whether they experience emotions were explored through systematic observation and analysis. Lorenz, in particular, identified fixed patterns of behavior that were the product of both instinct and learned techniques. Among these learning methods were imprinting and imitation, though Lorenz accentuated the role played by innate – i.e. rather than learned – tendencies. Tinbergen focused on the ritualistic elements of animal behavior, the most notable of which was that of chickens which establish a hierarchy, often known as a "pecking order" without resort to open conflict. Tinbergen argued that a great degree of animal behavior is innate and stereotyped – which, in this context, means fixed and repetitive. Desmond Morris (b. 1928) built on the early research in an attempt to apply ethological methods to the study of human behavior. Best-selling books such as *The Naked Ape* (1967) and *Manwatching* (1977) popularized ethology.

Morris begins from an observation of the 1978 soccer World Cup Final between Argentina and Holland, an event comprising 22 brightly clad figures "kicking a ball about in a frenzy of effort and concentration" on a small patch of grass, and watched by something like one-quarter of the entire world's population. "If this occurrence was monitored by aliens on a cruising UFO, how would they explain it?" asks Morris. His book is a kind of answer.

Morris adopts the role of the puzzled, detached observer, recording notes in the ship's log in an effort to discover "the function of this strange activity" and, while his sights are fixed on soccer, his records have relevance for all sports. His rejection of the Marxist "social drug" approach is understandable, for Morris is an ethologist and prefers to find the answer to questions about human behavior in innate, or inborn, characteristics, not social or political realms – though it's important to recognize that Morris certainly acknowledges the *social functions* of sport, even if he argues its origins are natural.

Sport is truly a "safe" diversion from violent behavior. But were political systems to change, the aggression would still exist and would still need an outlet. Political frustrations may aggravate aggressive tendencies, but they do not cause them. This removes the need for any detailed social or psychological theory: sport in general and association football in particular are grand occasions for venting instinctively violent urges.

Morris goes on to expose several interesting facets, the first being the ritual hunt. Morris's initial premise is much the same as the one offered in this book: that the predecessors of sport were activities that "filled the gap left by the decline of the more obvious hunting activities." The activities passed through a series of phases, the final one being symbolic in which players represent hunters, the ball is their weapon and the goal the prey. Football players "attack" goals and "shoot" balls. Sport is a disguised hunt, a ritual enactment.

Morris calls today's athletes "pseudo-hunters" whose task of killing the inanimate prey is deliberately complicated by introducing opponents to obstruct them, making it a "reciprocal hunt." Goalkeepers of a soccer team resemble "claws" of a cornered prey "lashing out to protect its vulnerable surface." Its parallels with hunting have given soccer global appeal. Some sports, such as archery, darts, bowling, billiards, snooker, skeet, skittles, curling, croquet, and golf, all concentrate on the climax of a hunt in the sense that they all involve aiming at a target. They lack the physical risks and exertions of a headlong chase and the necessary cooperation between members of the hunting pack. Tennis and squash are more physical, but, unless played in doubles, lack teamwork. Some sports, especially motor racing, capture the chase aspect of hunting and also retain dangers.

Basketball, netball, volleyball, hockey, cricket, baseball, lacrosse, and rugby football have plenty of fast-flowing movement and a climactic aiming at targets. Yet the risk of physical injury isn't too high. Morris believes that, apart from soccer, only Australian rules football and ice hockey approach what he calls the "magic mixture." The former has been isolated geographically and the latter suffers because the small puck (the "weapon") makes it difficult for spectators to follow the play (while Morris does not mention it, attempts have been made to resolve this by experimenting with a luminous puck that is easier for television cameras to pick up). Soccer seems to capture all the right elements in its ritual and has the potential for involving spectators to an intense degree, which makes watching all the more satisfying.

For all its ritual, soccer – and for that matter many other sports – has a tendency to degenerate into what Morris calls a stylized battle. At the end of play there is usually a winner and loser, and this is not a feature of hunts. Soccer caricatures many other sports in arousing its spectators; fans seethe and fight, they are outraged at bad play or decisions, and euphoric at good results. Other sports engender similar reactions, but at a milder level. At least one piece of research has put this to the test, focusing on hooliganism at football grounds as "ritualized aggression" in that it is not typically violent in a destructive way, but conforms to an "order" with unwritten rules and codes of behavior. As befits an ethological approach, comparisons are made with nonhuman species, which use ritual displays of aggression for various purposes, but do so without transgressing boundaries. The stylized war for Peter Marsh and his co-writers, Elizabeth Prosser and Rom Harré is bounded by *The Rules of Disorder* (1978).

In a similar vein, Morris argues that sport serves as a safety valve through which people vent their spleen in a way that would be unacceptable in many other contexts. But attending an emotional event, as well as providing an outlet for anger and frustrations built up during the week's work, may add a new frustration if the result isn't satisfactory and so make the spectators and players feel worse than before. So, the fan (who happens to be male in Morris's example) "goes home feeling furious. Back at work on Monday, he sees his boss again and all the pent-up anger he felt against the soccer opponents wells up inside him" (1981: 20). So, every game is therapeutic and inflammatory "in roughly equal proportions."

Another ambiguous function of sport is its capacity to act as a status display. Again, Morris writes about soccer, but in terms that can be adapted to fit other sports: "If the home team wins a match, the victorious local supporters can boast an important psychological improvement, namely an increased sense of local status" (1981: 20). Soccer, like most other organized sports, developed in a period of industrialization; as we have noted, many British clubs began life as factory teams. A successful side conferred status not only on the team, but on the firm and even the area. Winning teams and individuals are still held in esteem locally because a victory for them means a victory for the community or region.

The conferment of status is quite independent of objective material positions. Since the publication of Morris's book, this aspect of his argument has become more relevant, as depressed areas in which local manufacturing industries have collapsed or in which communities have been destroyed have yearned for success through sport. The troubled West Midlands city of Coventry was boosted by the local football club's first-ever English Football Association (FA) cup win in 1987. Northern Ireland gained respite from destruction and bloodshed on fight nights when boxing occupied centerstage in the sports world. On a national level, staging a major sports event can have an uplifting effect economically and politically as well as culturally on a whole country, as Hugh Dauncey and Geoff Hare show in their collection of essays *France and the 1998 World Cup*. The 2004 Olympic Games were a vital part of the regeneration of Athens as a major capital city and an integral part of the European Union.

Morris's fourth function of sport as a religious ceremony is arguably the most underdeveloped in his assessment, but others before him have expanded on this concept. Like a religious gathering, a sporting event draws large groups of people together in a visible crowd; it temporarily unites them with a commonly and often fervently held belief not in a deity but in an individual sports performer, or a team. Sport is a great developer of social solidarity: it makes people feel they belong to a strong homogeneous collectivity, which has a presence far greater than any single person. Morris equates the rise of sport with secularization: "As the churches

. . . emptied with the weakening of religious faith, the communities of large towns and cities have lost an important social occasion" (1981: 23). The function has been taken over by sport.

This argument has been expressed by a number of writers, perhaps most famously by Michael Novak, whose book *The Joy of Sport* is a reverent acknowledgment of the ecstatic elements of sport (1976). Certainly, the general view that sport has assumed the position of a new religion is a persuasive one and is supported by the mass idolatry that abounds in modern sport. (For the most complete study of the relationship, see Shirl Hoffman's *Sport and Religion*, 1992.) We need look no further than the opening or closing ceremonies at the Olympic Games, or half-time at the Super Bowl, to see the most stupendous, elaborate displays of ritual and liturgy. These are precisely the types of rituals that have been integral to mass religious worship in the past.

The purposes they serve would be similar. In measurable terms, one could suggest that sport is more popular than religion: far more people watch sport than go to church; sport gets far more media attention than religion. Sports performers are better known than religious leaders. In all probability, people discuss sport more than they do religion. So, it seems feasible to say that sport occupies a bigger part of people's lives than does religion.

Despite the distance Morris puts between himself and social theorists, his argument veers close to that of Émile Durkheim (1858–1917), with Marx and Weber, one of the pioneers of sociology. Durkheim used the term collective effervescence to capture the effects of large numbers of people coming together to worship or celebrate a holy event: effervescence means fizzing, of course, and this is what Durkheim suggests can happen to people when they congregate. But it can only be created by people acting as a group, relating to each other, sharing their feelings or memories. It's a property of the whole, not the individual members.

But religion is intended to provide transcendental reference points beyond everyday experience; it gives moral guidelines; it instructs, informs, and enlightens. Some fanatics may believe sport does all these things. Realistically, it does not, though this is not the thrust of the argument. Do religious believers follow the guidelines or learn from the enlightenment? Some might respond that sports fans do. People follow sports with much the same zeal and commitment as active church-goers follow religion and, although it might seem insulting to religious adherents, sports fans do pursue a faith, albeit in their own way.

The comparison between sport and religion extends beyond superficial resemblances when we recognize that sport has become a functional substitute, supplying for the follower a meaningful cause, an emblematic focus, and a source of allegiance, even belonging. But there is still another way in which sport fills a vacuum left by religion and here we come back to the concept of sport as a social drug.

Morris, who is dismissive of Marxist theories of sport, fails to make the connection between the two functions. The "opiate thesis" we encountered earlier, when applied to sport, shows how sport can function to keep workers' minds off political revolt and so preserve the status quo – which is, according to Marx, what religion was supposed to do. Morris, in rebutting this, states the argument rather crudely, making sport seem a "bourgeois-capitalist plot," a conspiracy orchestrated by the bosses. As we saw in previous sections, this isn't quite the intention of Marxist writers.

There are two residual functions, both of which Morris concedes are exaggerations. As big business, sport is commercialized and run effectively as if making money was the sole organizing principle. This is partly true, but misses the reason for the involvement of the "vast majority" which is because they "love" sport. "Money is a secondary factor," according to Morris. As theatrical performance showbusiness influences are very evident in sport nowadays and the suggestion is that sport has become a mass entertainment. This is true for football, boxing, baseball, and other sports, but not for bowls, netball, judo, and many other minority sports. Even then, sport, by definition, can never be pure entertainment for as soon as the unpredictable element of competition is gone, it ceases. It then becomes pure theater.

Morris's treatment is not a formal theory, but a catalog of functions which soccer serves, as indeed do all sports at various levels, from the psychological to the political. There is no attempt to link the functions together, nor much evaluation of which functions are most effective. Its minor strengths lie in drawing our attention to the many ways in which sport has embedded itself in modern culture and the modern psyche. Try thinking of something that can simultaneously function as a stylized battle, a religious ceremony, and a status display. Morris offers what is really no more than a preamble to his "dissection" (as he calls it) of soccer, but even in this he dismantles the notion that sport is "only a game" and indicates that a match is "a symbolic event of some complexity."

Ethological arguments have a commonsense plausibility: if we study some animal behavior and draw conclusions, then it seems reasonable to generalize our conclusions to all animals. And, of course, human beings are living organisms that feed on organic matter, have specialized sense organs, a nervous system and respond to stimuli: they are animals. This is faulty reasoning. Human being are, for sure, animals. But, they have consciousness: they are aware of their surroundings and respond to them intentionally. When we act, we usually mean it. Yes, we might occasionally react to a stimulus as a reflex action, without conscious thought. But most of the time, thought guides action.

Morris has an argument and sticks to it: behavior is innate rather than learned and sport comes from our biological imperative to participate in behavior that is both thrilling and solidifying in the sense that it binds us together. The paradox is that, despite his rejection of social and political theories, his conclusions dovetail quite well with some of the classic social theories, especially of religion. But Morris's reasoning is dangerously near what's known as the deterministic fallacy: all events, including human action, are ultimately determined by causes external to free will, in this case instincts. Most animal behavior may well be impelled by instincts. Some human behavior may be too. But not all: the decisive actions we take are thought through, taking into consideration both the physical and cultural environments in which we live.

Morris doesn't have what might be called a multidimensional view of sport: his project is strictly limited. This doesn't restrict us, however: we can extrapolate to produce a decent account of the origins and social importance of sports.

So much for attempts to make sense of sport through grand theories, all of which have merits yet none of which is without problems. At least they provide frames of reference within which we can operate when investigating some of the more specific issues concerning sport. Remember: the value of theories lie in how much enlightenment they bring. All the theories surveyed in this chapter shed some light on the field of sport. Think of them as floodlights, each one illuminating an area of the field. Throw the switch on each one individually and you will see one area bathed in light and the others in shadow. Switch on all at once and we light up the entire field.

Table 5.1 Major theories of sport

Theory	Figurational	Marxist	Weberian	Ethological
What drives it?	Configuration	Class conflict	Rationization	Human nature
And the underlying trend is?	Civilizing process	Hegemonic control	Growth of capitalism	Instinct Suppression
The source of sport?	Control of violence	Economic power	Religious beliefs/ economic change	Innate aggression
What's the real reason for sport?	Quest for excitement	Distraction	Reflection of social organization	Symbolic hunt
And what are its effects?	Stress-tension release	Pacification of working class	Rationization of sports	Outlet for violent behavior

OF RELATED INTEREST

The Soccer Tribe by Desmond Morris (Jonathan Cape, 1981) describes the way an alien might descend to earth and try to get to grips with the strange customs and practices of soccer fans and players, which Morris likens to tribal behavior; while the author doesn't offer a theory to explain the behavior, he suggests an ingenious historical account of how soccer evolved.

Leftist Theories of Sport: A critique and reconstruction by William J. Morgan (University of Illinois Press, 1994) is a challenging evaluation of the major tendencies in critical theories of sports. After examining the varieties of Marxism, Morgan offers a "reconstructed critical theory." Morgan argues that the "mass commodification" of sports amounts to "the capitulation of the practice side of sport to its business side."

The Influence of the Protestant Ethic on Sport and Recreation by Steven J. Overman (Avebury, 1997) is a brilliant Weberian analysis of the development of contemporary sport in North America. As the title suggests, Overman is concerned with identifying the ways in which religious ideas impacted on the emergence of sports.

"Part one: major perspectives in the sociology of sport" in *Handbook of Sports Studies* edited by Jay Coakley and Eric Dunning (Sage, 2000) consists of seven chapters all devoted to theory; they include illuminating chapters on figurational and Marxist approaches. One of the book's editors, Eric Dunning has his own *Sport Matters: Sociological studies of sport, violence and civilization* (Routledge, 1999) which provides an elegant defense of figurational theory while remaining alive to the contributions of Weber, Marx, and several other theorists.

Sport, Culture and History: Region, nation and globe by Brian Stoddart (Routledge, 2008) is the historian's most complete work to date: he brings together insights from sociology, politics, and business to produce a theoretical analysis of sport that embraces cricket in the 1930s, golf in the present day, and the role of colonialism in sporting development.

Sociology of Sport and Social Theory edited by Earl Smith (Human Kinetics, 2009) is a collection of chapters, each focusing on a different aspect of sport, though, for our purposes, the first two chapters are most relevant: Rob Beamish's interpretation of Weber's theory and Eric Dunning's rendition of Elias's are both valuable.

ASSIGNMENT

On page xxxii of the introduction to their *Handbook of Sports Studies*, Jay Coakley and Eric Dunning write: "The viability of our field depends on our ability to develop collective agreement about rules for making 'truth' or, perhaps better, claims about the 'realty congruence' of our propositions and findings. In the absence of such an agreement, we cannot share and criticize each other's ideas and research in a manner that produces general understanding as well as a foundation of knowledge." Do you spot any possible ways in which the theoretical approaches covered in this chapter might lead to such an understanding or "foundation of knowledge"?

In the Mind

KEY ISSUES

▌ How can psychology enrich our understanding of sports?

▌ What makes winners win and losers lose?

▌ When are retirements from sport just career intervals?

▌ Where is the zone . . . and how can we get there?

▌ Why do some athletes thrive in the clutch while others choke?

▌ . . . and what separates Armstrong, Schumacher, and Federer from the rest?

THE BIGGEST CHOKE IN HISTORY?

It was the 128th British Open at Carnoustie, Scotland, in 1999. Jean Van de Velde had led for three days, having played some of the most sublime golf of his career. He'd been something of a prodigy, starting playing as a six-year-old in his native France. Having qualified for the PGA Tour in 1988 after a distinguished amateur career, he won the Roma Masters in 1993. But, as he approached the 72nd hole with a three-stroke lead, he knew that the biggest prize so far was within reach. There was nothing in his bearing or behavior to suggest he would play this hole with anything but the same adeptness and composure he had brought to the previous 71. Gathering momentum, Van de Velde looked set for a peak performance, all facets of his game gelling together at exactly the right time. Then, something extraordinary happened. There followed 15 of the most incomprehensible minutes in sports history.

Faced with a relatively innocuous hole and needing to make a double bogey (6 or better) on the par-4, 487-yard hole, an element of caution was all that was required to seal victory. There was no logical reason to suppose the Frenchman would play anything but conservatively. His decision-making had been flawless thus far. The voice of reason was surely whispering to him. Yet his behavior suggested that he just wasn't listening. Let's eavesdrop.

Voice of reason: OK, the title is there for the taking. The main thing is: don't get anxious about the prospect of your first major trophy. Just play conservative, risk-free golf, keeping composed and relaxed, but just sufficiently aroused to perform at maximal efficiency.

Response: VdV elects to hit a driver off the tee, sending it 20 yards to the right and almost drives into the notorious Barry Burn. The ball flies over the water and comes to rest on dry ground, sitting up on low rough.

Voice of reason: Not a good start, but far from disastrous. Now, let's make the rational choice by taking a wedge and chipping safely back into the fairway. This will pave the way for an easy approach shot onto the green. Then it's two putts for the championship.

Response: VdV pulls a 2-iron from his bag and strikes for the green. It's a wildly ambitious attempt and completely unnecessary in the circumstances. The shot screws to the right, hits the grandstand and ricochets back about 25 feet into knee-high heather.

Voice of reason: The title is still winnable. The sensible route is now to punch the ball sideward back into the fairway as a prelude to the green. No need for panic. Keep the poise. Don't even think about the shot itself. Just choose it and let your body go through the mechanics. Over to autopilot for the rest of the tournament. Let it guide us safely to the title.

Response: VdV goes straight for the green. It's a brave though heedless shot and the ball comes to rest in the water.

Voice of reason: Now, we have a little problem. Not an insurmountable one, but sound decision-making is called for. What are the options? (1) Take a penalty stroke and a drop. (2) Avoid the penalty stroke and play the ball from the water. With a big title on the line, this is something of a no-brainer. Go with (1).

Response: VdV kicks off his shoes and socks, hitches up his pants to his knees and wades into the water. As he does so, he notices the ball sink even further under the water so that it's submerged by two inches. This is a huge moment. If he fails to scoop the ball out of the burn, he remains stuck in the water and title hopes evaporate right there. He changes his mind and takes the drop.

Voice of reason: We're still alive, but we're now in the rough about 60 yards from the pin. The main thing is to avoid the bunker, so make a mental picture of the ball sailing comfortably to exactly where you want it to land. Don't rush this one. Pace yourself carefully, bring your heart rate down and, whatever you do, don't snatch at it.

Response: VdV clears the water, but his ball lands in the front greenside bunker.

Voice of reason: Now we have a little tension creeping in. If we don't make this shot, our rival, who seems to draw sustenance from every error we make, is going to win without even having to fight for it. Make a mess of this one and we don't even get to a playoff. Ah, what the hell, we've probably blown it anyway. Just get it over with.

Response: A nice bunker shot from about 25 feet rolls 6 feet past the hole. VdV smiles, as if he hasn't a care in the world. He looks relaxed and still confident.

Voice of reason: All's not lost: we're one shot away from a playoff. Remember: this cup has to be won and, if we manage it, we can dismiss the last few shots as a blip and get back to the kind of golf we were playing earlier.

Response: VdV looks loose and at ease as he makes the putt. The game goes to a playoff with Paul Lawrie and Justin Leonard, but VdV struggles to find his earlier form, while Lawrie, a Scot playing with strong home support, gathers impetus and triumphs.

It's often been said that the French would rather lose in style than win without it. But national stereotypes can't explain Van de Velde's almost inconceivable flop. His skill wasn't in doubt: he'd played efficiently, even masterfully up to the point where victory was in sight. The *Atlanta Constitution* echoed many, many others when it described Van de Velde's failure as "the biggest choke job in all the history of golf" (July 19, 1999). Van de Velde dismissed this: "I couldn't live with myself knowing that I tried to play for safety and that I blew it . . . So I made my choices . . . it's a game and I play at that game because I enjoy it, " he told the *Independent* (July 19, 1999). (Van de Velde's fortunes declined further in 2002 when he suffered a serious knee injury, which needed surgery.)

His account evoked thoughts of the Kevin Costner character in Ron Shelton's 1996 film *Tin Cup* who, when faced with the choice of playing safe for a win, opts for a series of ambitious, but ultimately self-destructive shots. Neither, it seems, were flexible enough to adapt their approach to suit conditions. There are few constants in sports and champions need to be able to adjust to changing circumstances. Many have the game, as they say; only a few have the mind.

Lawrie confessed that his "mind was racing" as he watched Van de Velde fold, leaving him the opportunity to pull off the unlikeliest win of his life (quoted in the *New York Times*, July 19). He meant that, while he must have started the hole believing he would just go through the motions, he experienced a state of alertness after witnessing Van de Velde's faltering. He began to anticipate a different outcome to the one everyone (including himself) had expected. His attention narrowed as he prepared to respond to the newly evolving situation. Glimpsing the possibility of the title, Lawrie's task would have been to maintain his form without becoming over-aroused and tightening-up.

BOX 6.1 MIND

This is a convenient term rather than a precise concept with empirical referents. It's used, often vaguely, in contrast to body to suggest mental properties and processes, such as consciousness, volition, and feeling. Some schools of thought, such as psychology's behaviorism or philosophy's physicalism (the doctrine that the real world consists only of physical things), find the term unhelpful and prefer to include only observable phenomena in their investigations. Others tend to employ the term cautiously, concentrating on specific features, such as memory, perception, or cognition – the action of knowing. While the investigation of the mind, or the soul, dates back to antiquity, systematic analysis began in earnest in the mid-eighteenth century. Two seminal publications appeared in 1855: Herbert Spencer's *The Principles of Psychology* and Alexander Bain's *The Senses and the Intellect*. Over the next several decades, scholars as diverse as Sigmund Freud (1856–1939) and Edward Thorndike (1874–1949) took the study away from the realms of philosophy and toward a more scientific examination.

In terms of skill, Van de Velde and Lawrie were evenly matched. Leonard was also arguably their equal. Analyze the physical profiles of the top hundred players of golf or any sport and there would probably be little difference in terms of visible skill, nor in their manifest capacity to endure the elements or withstand injury.

The phrase *primus inter pares* means first among equals and it's not a self-contradiction. Even when athletes of identical physical prowess meet, there's always a difference. There are still champions and runners-up. Advantages always exist. This raises questions. What are the sources of the advantages and how do some athletes

BOX 6.2 PROFILING

The process of selecting salient psychological characteristics of a person and integrating these into a coherent image that can guide inquiry and enable predictions. The person in question may be hypothetical: police profilers who construct representations of criminals from evidence of their crimes and behavioral traits to assist investigations are often featured in tv shows and films, though, as Angela Torres *et al.* point out, "the main goal of profiling in real investigations is to narrow the scope of a suspect pool rather than to identify a single guilty criminal."

The purpose of profiling in sports is less dramatic: it builds a metaphorical sketch of an athlete based on his or her physical, technical, tactical, and psychological competencies and moods, and applies this in several ways, all designed to enhance performance. Profiles have been used to interesting effect in the assessment of emotion. For example the profile of mood states (POMS) was used to build a representation of an athlete's emotional state just prior to competition. The participant would be asked to describe his or her state in terms of: tension, depression, anger, vigor, fatigue, and confusion.

In one of the more successful applications of personality assessment research, W. P. Morgan used POMS with Olympic wrestlers and found members typically exhibited an *iceberg profile:* they tended to score highly on vigor, lower on anger and fatigue, and much lower on tension, depression, and confusion. Expressed graphically, with the states defining a horizontal axis, an iceberg shape surfaces. Aspiring or less proficient athletes would probably show other variations, such as having too much tension or too little vigor. Profiles help establish a representation of an optimal set of states, moods, or properties. From this, deviation can be measured to assess how far individuals need to change before they approach the desired profile.

A different approach to profiling is to study the development of the key psychological characteristics shared by certain groups, for example Olympic champions. Daniel Gould *et al.* were interested in how profiles are nurtured, particularly by family and coaches: their effort was to study "a complex system made up of a variety of factors of influence," rather than a static picture. Identifying these factors is a retrospective study, reflecting back on experiences (2002).

acquire them, while others find them elusive? In answering these questions, we'll notice how the distinguishing features are rarely physical. The differences between athletes lie in, for instance, their motivation, commitment, discipline, self-confidence, emotional control, and a cluster of other features that constitute their psychological makeup.

In this chapter, we'll follow the example of those tv cop psychologists in building a *profile*, in our case, of the model athlete. We'll focus in particular on elite athletes – those who have become champions. By definition, that makes them a minority. But, they have characteristics that virtually every athlete of any level needs in order to progress. We'll also look at some of the reasons why other athletes don't progress.

MOTIVATION: THE SPUR TO ACTION

In the late nineteenth century, two minor experiments turned out to have major importance. Max Ringelmann was an engineer at the French Institute of Agronomy (that's the science of soil management and crop production) whose research focused on the relative work efficiency of oxen, horses, and men, and involved elementary tasks such as rope pulling, measuring the amount of force exerted per subject. With each new person added to the human group so the amount of force for each individual was diminished. Contrary to Ringelmann's expectations, there was a shortfall of effort as the size of the team increased. The suspicion was that mechanical problems were not the source of what became known as the Ringelmann effect: the cause was motivational loss.

A few years later, in the United States, Norman Triplett compared the performances of cyclists riding alone with those paced by the clock and those racing against each other. There was a pronounced improvement across the three situations, leading Triplett to conclude: (1) the presence of others aroused the "competitive instinct" which, in turn released hidden reserves of energy; (2) the sight of others' movements had the effect of making riders speed up.

Together, the experiments showed that the physical performance of humans is significantly influenced by factors that would today be described as psychological and these factors were themselves affected by different environmental conditions. Both experiments discovered that the presence of others affected the level of performance, in Ringelmann's case the reason being a change in motivation, or "social loafing" – slackening off when working toward a common goal with others. The idea that motivation, that is, an internal state or process that energizes, directs and maintains behavior, can have such an overwhelming effect on physical performance sounds obvious. Maybe it was obvious in the nineteenth century too, though no one seems to have been too inclined to test it, at least not until these two experiments.

The realization that internal states had a bearing on athletic performance, or indeed any kind of goal-directed physical activity, opened up the possibility that, if we could study them, we could probably change them. Pitch a motivated athlete against one who is unconcerned about the outcome of a contest and the chances are that the former will prevail. Not always, though; for reasons that we'll cover later. But, the message was clear: find the sources of motivation and that will provide the clues as to how performance can be modified.

During the first half of the twentieth century, a kind of architecture of the human mind was drawn up. Different schools offered their own designs on the structure of intellect, cognition, emotion and other human faculties associated with mental life. Motivation featured in most analyses. It referred to the mainspring of action: the force, drive or impetus that impels movement (the Latin source of motivation is *motus*, to move). It's what makes us tick, so to speak, and, as such, provides us with an entry point for the inspection of the mind of the athlete.

Motivation is what spurs us into action: it directs us toward certain objectives or in specific directions. The resulting behavior is always intentional, in the sense that we mean something to happen; though the outcomes don't always turn out the way we intended. Where there's no conspicuous link between behavior and an outcome, there's usually no motivation. So, for example, if you want to be a chess grand master, then you probably won't be motivated to train with free weights (unless for another, unrelated purpose). The anticipated outcomes, effects, or consequences of a motivated behavior are vital. This is why motivation is such a priceless commodity: physical skills are insufficient in themselves.

The big question is: what induces us to act? In other words, where does motivation come from? Abraham Maslow's answer in the 1950s was based on his celebrated hierarchy of needs, which was a structure based on human imperatives, the primary one of which was biological (hunger, thirst, temperature maintenance, and so on). Imagine these as the bottom tier of a pyramid. Above this are other layers of ever-more cultivated needs, including the need for affiliation with others, aesthetic needs and the need for self-actualization – to find fulfillment in realizing one's own potential. Motivation works upwards: once we satisfy basic needs, we ascend to the next tier. In Maslow's theory, motivation has origins in human needs, or drives.

Sigmund Freud (1856–1939) too believed humans are motivated by primal drives, in his case sex and aggression. In childhood, parents forbid the free expression of sex and aggression and these become repressed, remaining in the unconscious. For Freud, these unconscious motives manifest in later life, exercising an influence over conduct, though in disguised ways, such as in illness, accidents, mannerisms, or Freudian slips (of the tongue).

Neither account is of much use to sports analysts. Not unless they're intending to deprive an athlete of a basic need and make the satisfaction of that need contingent on an appropriate performance. Alternative theories of motivation center on cognition and are based on the view that we're motivated to action in areas where we experience positive feelings of competence and esteem. In other words, if I like ice dancing, but look about as graceful as donkey when I hit the ice, I'm unlikely to be motivated in this pursuit. But, I might casually pick up a basketball and throw it clean through the hoop every time, without even trying. The display draws the acclaim of my peers and I sense a contented afterglow as I walk away. Chances are that I'll be motivated to get back on the court and improve even more. Secretly, I might still harbor thoughts about ice dancing, but I'll be motivated to improve my ball skills in preference.

Self-based approaches, as they're called, explore the ways in which we become motivated and how we maintain that motivation. If someone desires to look like a supermodel but regards themselves as podgy, their motivation might be to exercise and eat less as a way of closing up the discrepancy between what they are currently like and how they want to be. The desire functions as motivation. Whether their original equation is accurate isn't relevant. The person might already look like Kate Moss. They just want to be even thinner. Subjective evaluations are all-important; there's no presumption of rationality. A middle-distance runner might think that by doubling his or her mileage in training, they will run faster in competition and they'll be motivated to do so; at least until they find themselves out of the medals (the British runner of the 1970s, David Bedford, thought and did exactly this. Although he started favorite to take gold in the 1972 Olympics, he failed).

If we feel we can demonstrate competence in an endeavor, we'll be attracted to it and will sense a locus of control in our attribution of success or failure: we're the ones who will determine how well we do in an event, not fate, nor the weather conditions, the referee, luck, god, or any other external factor. Believing that we control our own destinies is a powerful impulsion to succeed and, correspondingly, avoid defeat. It can work the other way too: if an athlete believes he or she is responsible for a sequence of disappointing performances, they may lower their sights, experience a drop in motivation and slide to further losses.

BOX 6.3 LOCUS OF CONTROL

This refers to the perceived location of the source of control over one's behavior (*locus* is Latin for place). So, if someone perceives that the forces that control what happens in his or her life lie outside them, perhaps with other people or with abstract forces over which they have little or no influence, then there is an *external* locus of control. Alternatively, the person might see themselves as an agent of his or her own destiny, believing in their own ability to control events. In this case, there is an *internal* locus of control.

Most athletes are motivated to achieve, but the level at which they strive to achieve is, of course, variable. They may just want to demonstrate their ability at playing golf at the club, for instance. Or they may seek the approval of peers. Or they may simply set themselves goals, such as to beat their fellow players at the club, or perhaps go all the way to major championships. These goals can either change as a player matures, or they may stay the same. A pro golfer who has never won a major may have a burning ambition to win one. Once he or she wins one, they may feel that they've accomplished their mission.

What seems clear is that successful athletes all hold what's called an achievement motivation: they personally seek success and, in their quest, will look for challenges, show persistence, remain unafraid of losing and blame themselves in a way that allows them to improve when attributing wins and losses. They'll also value *extrinsic* rewards. While some players are urged to perform at their best and derive feelings of satisfaction from turning in a competent display, the athletes we popularly regard as "winners" are the ones who measure their success against others. They'd prefer to perform poorly and win, rather than well and lose.

Clearly, we act because we want to achieve something, even if it's only getting out of bed in the morning. This in itself is motivated action. It strikes us as obvious that athletes have different motivations to the rest of us, but we should guard against regarding these as fixed. How many potentially good athletes do we know who seem suddenly and perhaps inexplicably to lose motivation? The world is full of people who had the skill, but not, as sports writers often say, the hunger. The metaphor is not such a bad one: it suggests an uneasy or discomforting state someone desires to avoid or escape.

Competitors at every level want to avoid failure. Coming eighth out of eight sprinters is not a failure if the last-placed runner records a personal-best time and has identified this as a goal. Being beaten on a points decision is not a failure if the loser was up against a vastly more experienced boxer and turned in a career-best performance. The ultimately successful athlete can assimilate reversals of fortune such as these and manage to maintain motivation for the next competition. It depends on the goal they set themselves: to master a skill or proficiency or to achieve a desired result regardless of the quality of performance.

Being motivated is clearly the most basic requirement of a competitor: action needs to be aimed at an end or goals, short or long term, or the individual never even gets near athletic competition. Of course, many sports careers have been brought to an

BOX 6.4 GOAL

An aim, objective, or end result that a person plans for, or intends to achieve is, of course, a goal. The concept should not be confused with a *dream*, which is a mental image, or *fantasy* that carries no necessary assumption that action will follow, or *purpose*, which is a purely internal target that guides behavior. A goal is external to the subject (though goals cannot, in practice, exist without an internal purpose). An aspiring player may say her dream is to win the U.S. Open, yet fail to practice enough to make necessary improvements. Another athlete may have a purpose that motivates her to train hard to improve, but may have no clear specific goal that will strengthen her commitment and narrow her attention. But, an athlete with a goal orientation will have a practical program designed to enable the attainment of tangible objectives. So, a goal is a level of performance proficiency that a person intends to reach within a timeframe.

To be effective, goals have to incorporate: (1) a clearly defined level of performance proficiency, which includes a minimum standard; (2) a timeframe inside which the level should be reached; and (3) a direction (for behavior). Goals allow an individual, or group to devote full attention to implementing intentions and, once they are achieved, supply the self-confidence to make key decisions.

Todd Thrash and Andrew Elliott make a distinction: "Mastery goals are focused on the development of competence or task mastery, whereas performance goals are focused on the attainment of competence relative to others."

abrupt halt: injury, distractions, setbacks, an aversion to training are a few of the countless reasons why people drop out almost as soon as they get into sports. The ones who stay adapt. They have to, if only to survive in such a competitive environment.

COMMITMENT – WHY SOME KEEP IT AND SOME LOSE IT

"You only get out of this game what you put in." How many times have we heard this adage? It refers to commitment. Committing yourself to something or someone means pledging or obligating yourself and implicating yourself in a course of action from which there are limited escape routes.

Clearly, progress in sports requires some level of commitment, whether it's in terms of time dedicated to training or abstinence from other satisfying endeavors. Yet, commitment isn't the same as monomania (an inflexible fixation on one thing), but an adaptable orientation that allows an athlete to pursue specific objectives, although not to the exclusion of other potentially fulfilling pursuits. At least that's what the manuals will tell you. Familiarity with some of the top athletes of recent eras suggests that their commitment was more demanding.

Gabriela Szabo, the pre-eminent female middle-distance runner of the early twenty-first century, slept 16 hours a day, waking at 7 a.m. and eating two slices of bread before going back to sleep again for another 90 minutes. She would then run the first of two sessions totaling 22 miles (35 kilometers) eating and sleeping between them. In other words, there was nothing else in her life apart from training and competing. She retired in 2005, aged 30.

A typical day of tennis pro Ana Ivanovic consisted of a training session before breakfast, then another after, then lunch, followed by another training session. A massage completed the day. Tiger Woods began practicing every day at 5 a.m. during his tenure as the world's number one golfer. Titles don't usually liberate competitors from their daily grind; if anything, they inspire them to greater levels of commitment.

The relationship between motivation and commitment is clear: an athlete who is motivated to achieve is more likely to submit him or herself and voluntarily impose restrictions on their freedom as long as they believe it will yield benefits. But, there's always change. A smallscale study of a swim school by Robert Rinehart captured the most irresistible change in sports. Young swimmers arrived committed and ready to accept the discipline necessary to become successful. The discipline was both "inscribed by others, including coaches and parents, and it is inscribed by itself," meaning that the athletes submitted their bodies to frequently rigorous demands necessary for cultivating skills.

The swimmers were initially attracted to the sport because of the "love of water" or the sheer joy of swimming, but they soon surrendered any notion of enjoyment and accepted that competitive success would only come through regular, predictable, systematic training. Drawing on the work of Michel Foucault, Rinehart shows how what he calls "the relative freedoms of swimming" were replaced by a "disciplinary system both insidious and tenacious." Movements were broken down into minute fragments, each analyzed and subject to electronic surveillance; attendance was checked, progress was monitored, goals were set. The study illustrates how the denial that's so important to discipline in competitive sports isn't simply imposed: it's internalized by the athletes themselves.

It's a minor study with a major point to make about how athletes, if they are to make progress, incorporate the rules and codes of training rather than just have them dictated to them. Again, we see the importance of motivation: without an achievement orientation, the required behavior can't be induced; it needs to be forced. Typically, as an athlete ascends in competition, the incentives that motivate become palpable. The intrinsic pleasure of competing might still exist, but the more powerful rewards are extrinsic – money, titles, records.

There are also disincentives at work: the monotony of repetitive exercise, the abstinence and, perhaps most importantly, the absence of tangible proof of potential are among the reasons why athletes drift away from the sport they once found so attractive. Some athletes regress or just withdraw from competition. Among the more obvious reasons for this are alternative career opportunities or new responsibilities (like parenthood) that leave insufficient time to devote to sports. But, then there is the sense of failure that sometimes results from repeated exposure to defeat. We've all been in unpleasant, negative situations. If we feel we can do something about them, we'll do it, and, if we don't, we get out.

If prospective athletes experience their failure to reach goals as the result of inevitable factors that lie beyond their control, then redoubling efforts, changing tactics, or modifying training are seen as futile. They see themselves as helpless. In 1980, Carol Dweck published an influential paper in which she drew on Martin Seligman's earlier book *Helplessness: On depression, development and death* (1975). Dweck argued that children who attributed failure under competitive conditions to such things as lack of ability, luck or other factors over which they had no control, showed a tendency to concede defeat and opt out of sports. They avoided challenges, believing that could do nothing to influence the course of events. Failure became certain, in their eyes. Dweck coined the term *learned helplessness*.

Failure in itself matters far less than how a young athlete interprets that failure. So, helplessness is linked to how they explain outcomes or results. We learn to think of ourselves as, in some way, lacking the power to change matters. Like dogs, which were systematically subjected to unpleasant treatment and refused to escape, even when presented with an opportunity to do so, humans become habituated to failure (the dog experiment provided one of the early insights into this condition).

Unforgiving coaches ("you're useless"), or indifferent peers ("you didn't deserve to win") are likely to promote learned helplessness. While assurance ("a slight change in your technique will yield a big improvement") will convey a sense of empowerment. The reason why many would-be athletes drop out is not so much because of their technical inability: even limited athletes can view their sheer participation as a success if it's a source of pleasure to them. It's the sense of helplessness that many find so disagreeable, if not obnoxious.

SWITCH TO AUTO

Contrary to what commentators occasionally say, skill is nothing to do with instinct: it's learned, developed, improved, and refined through practice. Skill comprises three types: motor skills, which are sequences of physical movement; perceptual skills, which involve receiving information about the environment; and cognitive skills, which relate to thinking, and depend on anticipation and decision-making. In all three types, extended practice reduces the need for conscious involvement: the performance of the skill becomes automatic.

Different sports demand different permutations of the three types of skill, of course. Few perceptual or cognitive skills are needed for weightlifting, for instance. Whereas success in golf depends on choosing and carrying out strokes that are appropriate to particular conditions, and so involves all three types. Both need gross motor ability, including short bursts of muscular effort and body coordination. Actually, many sports that ostensibly demand different skills share several perceptual and cognitive skills, if not motor skills.

Typically, improvements in skill acquisition are rapid at first, then slow down to a gradual pace and some athletes insist that, in maturity, decreases in one are compensated by increases in another (injury, loss of ambition or lack of physical condition rather than the erosion of skill ends sporting careers). Improvements in accuracy and coordination aren't achieved by repetition of the same skill, but by new, unrelated challenges, which means that highly skilled athletes rarely shirk different, possibly awkward, tasks.

It barely needs stating but skill alone means very little outside the competitive environment. There are several reasons why, the most obvious being that we're confronted by people who have much the same skills as us and often deploy them to nullify ours. In the fictional scenario cited earlier in which I can throw the ball unerringly through the hoop, I might still never be much good at basketball. I might outstrip everyone when allowed to stand and compose myself when preparing to take a free shot. But, confronted by lightning-fast rivals in open play, I'm slow, lose composure and become fazed. There's no necessary carry-over from a self-paced skill (when the player has complete control over the execution of the skill) and externally paced skills (when other players' movement affect if and how the skill can be realized).

The competitive environment also dictates whether an athlete can use *closed* skills: the exact conditions under which the skill is going to be performed is established in advance and incalculable factors are minimized, such as in ice dancing, gymnastics, or synchronized swimming. By contrast, *open* skills are needed in situations in which change and inconsistency are the norm. Any sport in which confrontation and collision are ingredients need open skills: athletes have to make quick decisions and react to movement, either of other athletes or of missiles, in order to perfect the skill.

Some individuals appear to have natural aptitude, but this is a potential to perform a task; it only means that the person can be trained to perform a skill. They may have ability, that is unlearned qualities that enable them to accomplish the task without much, or even any instruction or practice. Training enhances that ability, so that they can perform it with greater degrees of proficiency. But, we shouldn't make the error of assuming skills are natural or species-specific properties. In his 1972 study of feral children, *Wolf Children and the Problem of Human Nature*, Lucien Malson records how children deprived of human contact and reared in the wild by animals in their formative years, are usually mute quadrupeds who begin to stand erect only after painstaking tutoring. One boy could use his hands only for picking up objects between his thumb and index finger. Some eventually use language but not competently. Yet many were adept at tree climbing and other dexterous acts not usually associated with humans – skills that they presumably acquired through imitation and repetition.

Most, if not all aspiring athletes, set goals. Repeatedly, this is shown to be the most effective method of improving competence. Prescribing limited, realistic objectives yields results, though the range of results differs, depending on the athlete. Overall, goal setting is a superior technique to the "go out there and do your best" approach. Here we sense the importance of commitment again: failure to reach a goal can be disheartening, perhaps even humiliating and few athletes reach every single goal. Yet a success has several positive consequences, the most visible of which is a rise in self-efficacy. While self-efficacy is extremely changeable, some athletes have relatively stable levels. These are the kind of people who relish challenges, persevere at meeting them, show resolution and achieve at consistently high levels. When athletes are evenly matched in all other respect, self-efficacy can prove a crucial difference, especially over longer competitions (involving overtime, extra time, tiebreakers etc.)

BOX 6.5 SELF-EFFICACY

A person's or a team's belief in their capacity to produce a desired or intended result under specific conditions is self-efficacy. It is a cognitive mechanism that affects behavior. As conditions change, so might someone's belief in their competence to bring about the result change, as might the strength of their commitment. So, self-efficacy is specific to situations and changeable. Unlike self-confidence, which suggests trust and assurance in oneself across a range of endeavors, self-efficacy relates to particular tasks, which might include, for example, a particular physical activity, rehabilitation from injury, or recovering from alcoholism or another kind of dependence. It also relates to conditions. A recovering alcoholic might experience self-efficacy, but only if he steers clear of his old drinking friends; a marathon runner might believe she excels in most weathers, apart from when the temperature drops below 32°F (0°C).

We've all practiced a skill over and over without quite mastering it until we arrive a point when it suddenly clicks and we can do it. Then, every time we do it, we wonder why we struggled so much before. We assemble it in our repertoire of other skills and consign it to memory. This is the point where the automaticity to which I alluded previously takes over. Surrendering conscious effort to motor control involves a belief in one's own capacities; in other words, self-efficacy releases us to concentrate on other aspects of our game. This is how we build the repertoire.

Repeated success enhances self-efficacy to the point where occasional defeats are insignificant and have little impact on an athlete's self-confidence. Confident athletes enter contests certain in the knowledge that they'll achieve whatever goal they've set themselves. We all know what a valuable resource confidence is: trusting one's own ability and judgment, being self-reliant, assured and, on occasion, bold confers a sizeable advantage. Over-confidence, on the other hand, is a different matter: being preemptory, assuming that the desired outcome is already secure often leads to the kind of bombastic complacency that proves ruinous. The difference between self-efficacy and self-confidence is narrow and some scholars, such as Robin Vealey (1986), have drawn criticism for failing to distinguish the two (see Manzo's critique, for example). One way of understanding the two is by visualizing increments of self-efficacy as courses of bricks in a wall, which is eventually a solid – though not indestructible – structure of confidence.

An achievement oriented athlete who commits herself to a course of action, inscribing self-discipline and obedience to a regimen in the pursuit of a set of skills, typically sets goals in a steady, piecemeal acquisition. Those in search of overnight success are always disappointed: skills come in small degrees until most of them can be performed automatically. As skills are mastered, so self-efficacy builds and the type of confidence one often associates with competitors manifests prior to or even during competition. But, what actually is going on in the mind of an athlete when the competition is in process and how does this separate the winners and losers?

Often a victorious athlete is one who stays focused throughout a competition. Focused refers to a state of arousal in which concentration is unwavering. It means operating at the highest possible level of attention, so that a competitor is able to screen out all irrelevant stimuli in the environment and select only visual and audible information that's relevant to the immediate task. Some athletes can be focused in the lead-up to a competition, train steadfastly, perhaps for years (if their goal is an Olympic medal, for example), but lose focus in competition. Others can focus in both training and competition.

Even though the concept has become a little too elastic in recent years, it remains a valuable tool that can be used to ascertain what separates the champions from the also-rans. Lapses in concentration or distractions can be disastrous in competition; so the facility for gating out extraneous stimuli for long periods is crucial. Imagine the focus required of Formula One drivers: while their visual focus falls on the track ahead, they are constantly receiving instructions through their helmets from their pit crew and must respond alertly and accurately, not just for a few minutes, but for several hours.

Competitors in team sports, on the other hand, must focus in a different way: both visual and hearing foci must be wider to take account of movements and sounds of others. They can't afford to focus only on their own game: they have to listen to the instructions of others and take note of players in their peripheral vision. This is called "scanning" (see Van Schoyck and Grasha, 1981). A team player must stay alert to the behavior of colleagues and opponents, anticipate what will happen, and has little time to think about how he or she is going to execute a particular skill. There's a general point to be made: effective athletes tend to be those whose mastery of skills is so consummate that they can virtually perform them automatically. In other words, they think about what they're going to do, not how they're going to do it. Lance Armstrong, whom I will consider in more detail shortly, remembers how his cycling improved when he learned this lesson: "I was pushing too hard, not realizing it. I sat down, and focused on execution."

BOX 6.6 AUTOMATICITY

"Thinking that occurs without much awareness or effort is called automated," writes Michael Martinez. "When a skilled driver navigates a very familiar route, seemingly without effort, she is probably relying on automated thinking. In other words, she is exhibiting automaticity." In sport and exercise, people, having mastered a basic skill, can often execute it without concentration, focusing instead on other aspects of their performance, such as tactics, or their opponent's intentions. The process is associated with having an external focus of attention: rather than being aware of the position and movement of parts of the body, the performer typically focuses on external aspects, such as targets or goals. So, for instance, inexperienced golfers are gradually discouraged from thinking about their swing: once the basic technique is practiced, they should emulate proficient golfers and allow the swing to be automatic. The same injunction applies to skill acquisition generally: the arduous, conscious process of learning how to execute a move is eventually replaced by automatic operations: skilled performers can surrender the information on how to consign the skill to memory and think not about what they are doing, but why they are doing it, for what overall purpose and what they will do if it does not work? Too much reflection on the mechanical elements of a skill will actually interfere with its smooth functioning.

Like anything else in sports, focusing is worked at: athletes cultivate the facility for filtering out features of the environment that are not relevant to them. They either devise or are advised on methods of perfecting this. For instance, many athletes self-talk: they literally say out loud scripted sequences of words. In Sam Raimi's 1999 movie *For Love of the Game*, Kevin Costner plays a pitcher who is able to obliterate crowd noise by quietly uttering, "clear the mechanism." Another use for it came from Pat Rafter, who lost a Wimbledon final in 2000 to Pete Sampras, despite self-talking "Relax. Relax" throughout the match. He reached the final again the following year. "This time I'll be saying: 'Choke. Choke'," said Rafter. It was to no avail: he lost in five sets to Goran Ivanisevic.

Self-talk is one of a number of techniques athletes employ to key themselves to a peak performance. Sports history is full of one-off episodes in which athletes hit a career-peak, which they're never able to scale again (Buster Douglas' win over Mike Tyson in 1990; Bob Beamon's record-shattering long jump in 1968). Other athletes maintain peak performances year-after-year. People like Yelena Isinbaeva who, by 2009, had broken 27 world pole vault records and won 9 major championships. Roger Federer won 15 grand slam tennis titles up to 2010. Haile Gebrselassie started breaking world distance records at the age of 21 and was still breaking them at 35. Martina Navratilova won 167 single titles and remained as the world's number one tennis player for a total of 331 weeks (that's almost six-and-a-half years).

These athletes possess no essence of greatness. Extraordinary as they were and are, they have the same biomechanical features as their peers and, in objective terms, their skills were not of a qualitatively different order. The difference is that they were able to reproduce their best form consistently and in a variety of contexts. (Interestingly, Navratilova played until she was 49.) Lance Armstrong is another great athlete of recent history. He is, in many ways, exemplary: he clearly had an unerring capacity to reach a peak performance at precisely the right time, not just for a year or two, but consistently over a period long enough to constitute an epoch in sporting terms.

INTENSITY PERSONIFIED: ARMSTRONG

Armstrong finished 111th, dead last, in his first professional race, the Classico San Sebastian, a 1-day 120-mile event through Spain's Basque country. He was 27 minutes behind the winner. In 1992 – the year he came 14th in the Olympic road race – he was 20. Five years later, he had advanced testicular cancer, which had spread through his lungs and brain. Specialists told him that there was a 60 percent chance he was going to die. Yet, he underwent surgery and chemotherapy, survived and resumed his cycling career.

In 1999, Armstrong won the first of his seven straight Tours de France with a winning margin of almost seven minutes. There followed a period of total hegemony. His sixth victory in 2004 placed him in ahead of the sport's legends, Eddy Merckx, Jacques Anquetil, Bernard Hinault, and Miguel Indurain, all of whom won five titles. His coach, Chris Carmichael, reckons that to set Armstrong a goal of emulating any of these would "have been almost dooming him for failure." Armstrong himself admitted to having little appreciation of cycling history, innocence he put down to being a Texan, as opposed to a continental European.

When Armstrong retired in 2005, he was approaching his 34th birthday. His form hadn't deteriorated and he was physically hale. There were, it seemed, no more mountains to climb. He just ran out of challenges. But with Armstrong, nothing was predictable: in 2009, he came out of retirement to compete once more in the Tour de France, finishing third out of 199 riders. There are few clues to his seemingly inexhaustible motivational reserves. Nowhere in his autobiographies or interviews is there a convincing explanation of what – to coin an overused term, but a pertinent one – drives him. It's as if Armstrong was impelled in a specified direction by some sort of force. Plenty of athletes return after a retirement and some of them have continued to perform at near maximal capacity.

Michael Schumacher returned to the European Formula One Grand Prix in 2010 at the age of 41. With seven F1 titles, Schumacher had, like Armstrong, dominated his sport for a long, unbroken period. After a brief and modest spell in baseball's minor leagues, Michael Jordan went back to the basketball court following a 17-month spell away from the game between 1993 and 1995. The man many regard as the greatest ever to play the game led his former club, the Chicago Bulls to three more NBA titles. The aforementioned Navratilova retired 1994 at the age of 38 after winning 18 individual Grand Slam titles, but, after 6 years, made a successful return in doubles. Perhaps the nearest experience to Armstrong's is that of Mario Lemieux who suffered Hodgkin's lymphoma (cancer originating from white blood cells) a herniated spinal disc, tendinitis and chronic back pain and cardiac arrhythmia (abnormal heart rhythm). The lymphoma forced him to retire in 1997, aged 32; he returned to the National Hockey League in 2000 to produce some of his best ever form. There are many other successful and many, many more unsuccessful ones and each has its own reasons – though it doesn't feature in any of these cases, lack of money is a common one.

BOX 6.7 MOTIVATION

There is little agreement on the precise meaning of a concept that is absolutely central to sport and exercise studies. A sample of the various interpretations available includes: "the intensity and direction of behavior" (Silva and Weinberg, 1984); "processes involved in the initiation, direction, and energization of individual behavior" (Green, 1996); "the forces that initiate, direct, and sustain behavior" (Beaudoin, 2006); "an intervening process or an internal state of an organism that impels or drives it to action" (Reber, 1995); "the tendency for the direction and selectivity of behavior to be controlled by its connections to consequences, and the tendency of this behavior to persist until a goal is achieved" (Alderman, 1974); and "the desire to engage and persist in sport, often despite disappointments, sacrifice, and encouragement" (Hill, 2001). Distilling these, we are left with *an internal state or process that energizes, directs and maintains goal-directed behavior*.

After the inauspicious start to his professional career, Armstrong developed into a world-dominating athlete. His recovery from cancer makes him untypical, of course. Yet, in many other senses he presents an object lesson. On his own account, he went into hospital as one man and emerged another. In physical terms, he had lost about 15 lb (6.8 kg), but the real changes came in his mind: Armstrong remained ambitious, structuring his career around goals, though without ever envisioning a career of legendary proportions. But, even the step-by-step goals he'd set for himself must have look beyond him when he was diagnosed with cancer. Small incremental targets rather than great ambitions became the order of the day.

There is a sense of reclamation with anyone who has successfully fought a life-threatening illness: having got their lives back, they can approach any other achievement as a kind of bonus. After his recovery, Armstrong returned to the road a more relaxed rider. The benefits of relaxation have long been recognized in sports, either as part of an athlete's preparation for a contest, a winding-down technique after competition or, occasionally, a way of restoring composure during competition. Anxiety is one of the greatest impediments to effective performance, so an athlete, who enters a competition calmly, emotions under control, with breathing, heart rates, and muscular tension all within desirable limits is well poised. What was there to get anxious about after you'd just beaten cancer?

Armstrong's first Tour win was seen by many as an aberrant result. A rank outsider, he took the favorites by surprise with a plucky, carefree series in which he showed more adventure than in his previous career. He wasn't burdened either by his own or others' expectations. Nor, it seems, was he constrained by his previous form. "The only way to make advances is to try out new things and to work on new regimes and protocols," he told Carol Lin on the *CNN Saturday Night Show* in 2003 (Lin, 2003). He was talking about cancer treatment, but he could just as easily have been referring to cycling tactics.

Then, improbably, he repeated the win. It's often said that becoming a champion improves an athlete. Apart from the obvious upgrade in self-efficacy, there is self-esteem, that is, how worthy or valuable a person considers themselves. They're more likely to interpret failings or setbacks as attributable to others rather than their own deficiencies. This is a dangerous tendency and can lead to complacency or arrogance. But, it can also be a boon in reinforcing the all-important quality of confidence. After two successive wins, this is a quality Armstrong had in abundance. It must have been worth five minutes start every day of the tour.

There were other changes: Armstrong produced about 6 percent more muscular power than in previous years. Allied to a newfound openness to new tactics, this turned him into a top climber – something he'd previously never envisioned. The belligerence or tenacity evident in his cycling was no longer in evidence. The origins of this became clear in his own memoirs when he recounted how he regarded cancer as an opponent that had to be conquered. After this, rival cyclists must have seemed relatively compassionate. He also discovered – to his surprise – that he wasn't as efficient in one-day events any more, so his move to the classics was born of necessity.

Armstrong's astonishing comeback marks him off as a singular athlete. Yet, in many other ways, he personifies characteristics shared by a great many consistently successful performers. We've already noted the imperative property of motivation, the indispensability of commitment and the requirement for discipline. Armstrong allied these to an anxiety-free approach, openness to new ideas and a sheer doggedness. Success generated its own self-fulfilling dynamic. (Armstrong's detractors suspected that he used performance-enhancing dope, though he never returned a positive test. Even if he did, he would hardly have been alone.)

Once in the heat of competition, Armstrong, like other champions, was able to perform at a peak, in his case for 21 days at a stretch. Hitting a peak at precisely the right time and maintaining it for the appropriate period is arguably the most valuable asset of accomplished athletes. We hear talk of being in the *zone*, or in full *flow* when athletes reach a *peak* performance. Athletes sometimes groan that they've peaked too early or just couldn't get into the zone. There are no secret formulas for reaching a peak when it's required, though some researchers argue that practice enhances its likelihood. Others reckon that those periods of total congruity between objective excellence and subjective satisfaction are impromptu and occur fortuitously. For athletes who hit peaks every so often, maybe. But, for an athlete, such as the effortlessly fluent Brian Lara, who becomes completely absorbed at the crease and remains that way for hours on end, game after game, there is more than chance.

Some athletes practice autogenic relaxation prior to a game, others opt for Zen techniques. There are a variety of methods for trying to induce a level of awareness that facilitates peak performance. Myriad accounts of elite performers suggest no common routine, apart from a narrowing of attention and a visualizing of the immediate objective; for example, winning the next hole, batting the coming ball,

BOX 6.8 ZONE, PEAK, AND FLOW

The zone refers to a mental state in which athletes believe they can perform to peak levels. In this conceptual space, athletes acquire an enhanced capacity to focus and, in some cases, a level of consciousness that facilitates exceptional composure. They also report blissful feelings and an agreeable loss of their sense of time and space, complemented, on occasion, by almost otherworldly sensations that have been likened to a spiritual experience. When in the zone, athletes have related passages of *peak experience*, when they abandon all fear and inhibition and perform to the best of their ability, at the same time enjoying a sharpness of perception. This is a subjective experience and may or may not coincide with an objectively verifiable peak performance.

Reports of this altered state of consciousness or transcendence have led some writers, including A. Cooper, to suggest that being in the zone is akin to a spiritual experience, meaning that its effects go beyond material or physical changes. Kathleen Dillon and Jennifer Tait put this idea to the test, concluding that there was a relationship between spirituality and the zone, though without knowing its direction: "Spirituality may lead to more experiences in the zone, or experiences in the zone may lead to more experiences of spirituality, or a third variable like propensity to altered states of consciousness . . . may account for this relationship."

Whatever the source, the overall point is complemented by Kenneth Ravizza's research on *peak performance* which includes accounts of "focused awareness, complete control of self and the environment and transcendence of self": the individual has a *centered present focus*, meaning that "consciousness is channeled into the present moment" and outside distractions are eliminated. Concentration yields a *narrow focus of attention* exclusively on the object of the individual's perception. There is also *complete absorption* in the task at hand and, often, individuals lose track of time and space. Ravizza's participants reported feelings of *harmony and oneness* in which "total self is integrated physically and mentally" and fatigue and pain disappear.

The emphasis on awareness, automaticity, effortlessness, and bliss suggests strong comparisons with the concept of *flow*, a state in which athletes lose self-consciousness, self-judgment, and self-doubts and just allow themselves to be carried along by the performance – they just go with the flow. In these senses, getting in the flow shares characteristics with both the zone and peak performance. We can add one more shared characteristic: evanescence – they fade quickly. Being in zone may be a lustrous and vivid encounter; but it is a short-lived one. Whether or not it is possible to create conditions under which athletes can enter zones is an open question. Some believe relaxation, self-talk, and related strategies can maximize the chances of zone entry. Hypnosis has also been used as a route to the sought-after zone. Subjects in Susan Jackson's 1992 study of flow believed that, while the state was not available on demand, it could be approached through physical preparation and mental practice (reported in Jackson and Csikszentmihalyi, 1999).

leading the next stage, rather than winning the whole competition. Once into the flow, the various elements of skill come together, eliciting automaticity, which helps maintain the momentum.

Any event at all can effect a shift in momentum: a fielding error, a mis-hit, a flash knockdown – potentially anything. An event works as a catalyst, prompting a response from the athlete. Cognitive, physiological, and behavioral changes combine to produce a driving force that affects the athlete's behavior and, in turn, elevates or depresses his or her performance (Taylor and Demick, 1994). Change in perceptions (in particular, of self-efficacy) and arousal, translates into performance. Conversely, losing momentum, or experiencing negative momentum, can prove detrimental to performance, especially if a lead has been depleted and one's opponent is coming from behind. So even momentum-assisted athletes encounter interruptions during competition.

In his memoir *On and Off the Field,* the cricketer Ed Smith offers an insight into how better players are able to rescue the momentum. His view is predicated on the assumption that the best players aren't necessarily better than the norm: their technique is not necessarily superior and they're not gifted. What they do better than most is listen to one of two voices, weak and strong, which start to "battle" in the midst of competition. When the player lacks momentum, the weak voice provides a rationale for failure: "a teammate will get the runs," "you're tired," "this is just an off day," "your adversary is in exceptional form." So, there is a compelling reason for escape: embarrassment – "you can make it right another day." Even the best players succumb to the weak voice sometimes, but less often than more modest players. More usually, they'll listen to a stronger voice that's willing them to persevere until they recover the momentum. The so-called "clutch players" are those who thrive in adversity, and who, on this account, pay attention only to the stronger voice no matter how much momentum has been lost.

Listening to the strong voice works when striving to get back into a game, though, in the Van de Velde calamity, it seems the stronger voice urged the golfer to play exuberantly if irrationally with victory in sight. The voice of reason must have been drowned out.

BOX 6.9 CLUTCH

An emergency or critical moment in a contest. Some competitors thrive in such situations. Roger Federer was one. An example: in the 2009 French Open fourth round, he was two sets down to Tommy Haas, and faced a break point at 3–4 in the third. Eschewing panic, he won the point, the game, the set, and eventually the match. Mark Otten's research reveals that clutch players have high levels of "intuitive control," which is defined by Walter J. Perrig as "a form of control comes into play when goal-oriented actions, decisions, or interpretations have to be realized under conditions of uncertainty or lack of knowledge. This behavior is in relation to phenomenological qualities like hunches or feelings, rather than insights or identification, or recollection" (2000: 116).

Voices in the head might well be heard by some athletes, but they are best regarded as a convenient metaphor for the conflicting demands experienced by athletes in stressful situations. The more searching questions include why athletes hear the contrary voices at all and why they respond to them in sometimes starkly different ways.

Fear is common in sports: it goes some way toward understanding the rapid disintegration of some athletes' form at crucial stages in competitions they seem poised to win. Those who are unafraid either of losing or winning hold a significant advantage: they'll continue to trust their game, rather than switching their attention to it and, in the process, trying too hard. Their effort goes into completing the task rather than the execution of specific skills.

One of the perils of becoming a champion is satiation. Once the mission is accomplished, an inevitable period of self-satisfaction follows and the weaker voice becomes dominant. For some, complacency sets in and they retreat into mediocrity or perhaps retirement, safe in the knowledge that they achieved what they set to do. Others, like Armstrong – and Schumacher and Federer, of course – used the boost in confidence that accompanies a major triumph as fuel for the next mission. The difference is simple: some athletes are attracted to their sport. At least, this is a view offered by Laura Finch, who points out that if an athlete is drawn toward a sport, he or she is likely to exhibit high intensity in pursuing it (2001). By intensity, we mean the quality of eagerness, or passion an athlete brings to both training and competition.

Finch's point seems manifestly obvious: if we like doing something, we'll approach it with more enthusiasm than if we didn't. But, this isn't always the case. Changing coaches or switching to a different club, for example, can increase (or decrease) an athlete's intensity. For instance, in the early 2000s, Bolton Wanderers of England's Premier League became known, in the words of its manager, as a "refuge for battered footballers." Players of proven capabilities, who were seemingly past their best, typically found new leases once at the club. Manager Sam Allardyce believed the secret lay in providing a player with "an environment where he can feel happy again and enjoy his football again."

Professional athletes rarely enjoy their sports in the same way as children or youths. Think about it: by the time an athlete is 32, they've been repeating more or less the same routines for 16 years, possibly more. They may be well paid for their endeavors and content themselves with the thought that, if they weren't in sports, they'd be in a less lucrative and more tedious line of work. But, there are the injuries to consider too: training helps promote a healthy body, but competition involves damage, the long-term effects of which manifest themselves years later. The temptation to quit and find a new career path is countered by the possibility of earning more money from competing. Occasionally, they have no choice: Evander Holyfield, for example, earned about $100 million over 24 years in boxing, but faced bankruptcy when aged 45 and was obliged to fight on.

Sometimes, the challenges are more personal. Jerry Rice, wealthy and with every accolade his sport had to offer, continued to play in one of the meanest leagues in sport until aged 42. "I've pushed this body for 20 years," he reflected when he retired in 2005. That was probably close to an answer to the question "why?" The gratification came through testing his corporeal limits in the NFL.

Many more athletes show no signs of mellowing in their maturity and approach their game with a level of intensity others can match but rarely surpass. Maybe their motivation is money; maybe it is to test themselves. Or maybe it is just what Michael Novak called "the joy of sport." For athletes who compete for the intrinsic satisfactions of sport, there is invariably physical decline: loss of muscular power, speed, and flexibility can be minimized through training. Slowing reaction times can't. Yet, there is something satisfying about competing.

Perhaps the big compensation is decision-making: making choices in the conditions of uncertainty that prevail in sports, involves often complex deliberations, like predicting probable consequences and imagining the likely impact of a course of action on opponents' future decisions. Like any other skill, decision-making is learnt, though, in this case, slowly and painstakingly over years. Some young athletes are able to make decisions with a mastery that belies their youth. Most, however, acquire the skill through experience drawn through the years. The gratifications engendered by witnessing the outcome of the right choice at the right time must be hard to match.

EMOTIONS, IN AND OUT OF CONTROL

Despite the *Atlanta Constitution*'s verdict, Van de Velde's failure probably didn't deserve the dubious accolade of the biggest choke in history. That distinction is awarded, by common consent, to Jana Novotna who led Steffi Graf 4–1 in games and 40–0 in the third set of the 1993 Wimbledon women's final. Novotna, who had looked confident and in control, inexplicably crumbled and lost. It became known as "the choke." A technically able player, Novotna was left wanting again in the French Open of 1995, when leading 5–0 and 40–30 with serve against Chanda Rubin, who survived 9 match points.

Even in golf, Van de Velde is rivaled by Greg Norman who held a six-shot lead over his nearest rival with one round remaining of the 1996 Masters. On the ninth through twelfth holes, he relinquished his lead to Nick Faldo then went on to lose the trophy by 5 strokes. For collective chokes, the Houston Oilers have a claim: having ran up what seemed an unassailable 32-point third quarter lead over the Buffalo Bills in the 1992 NFL playoffs, they contrived to lose 41–38.

Sudden surges of severe anxiety at critical stages are common in sports. Typically, they are experienced by athletes who are approaching victory, but become tense and apprehensive at the prospect and abruptly lose form. They call it a choke because it bears resemblance to a temporary suffocation. The sufferer rarely has chance to recover composure before his or her rival capitalizes.

When winning becomes an active possibility, arousal levels increase to the point where physiological functions interfere with performance. Obviously, all athletes need to be aroused to some level. No one wants to go into a competition too mellow or chilled. They want their sweat glands open, blood vessels constricted, pupils dilated and respiratory volumes and metabolic rates elevated. But, there is an optimum level of arousal. The athlete needs to align these physical changes with the required level of composure, so that the appropriate level of arousal is maintained throughout a contest. If the levels are too low, the performance might be sluggish;

too high and it might be too frenetic to be effective. Think of the level of arousal defining an inverted U, with the arc at the top of the ∩ being the target area. Too little arousal (to the left of the ∩) or too much (to the right) and the performance is adversely affected.

This "inverted-U hypothesis" as it's called (by, among others, Fazey and Hardy, 1988) looks good on paper, but real examples from sports expose its limitations. How can it explain Novotna's abrupt descent from peak form to the abyss? Players are often stricken with anxiety and disintegrate as if falling from a cliff top. It's as if their arousal levels equip them well for most of the competition, then, faced with the likelihood of victory, the levels shoot up, prompting a catastrophe. Presented graphically, this "catastrophe" theory would suggest a kind of ⟩shape. High levels of arousal in themselves don't cause the downfall: only when combined with anxiety. So what brings about the anxiety in some competitors and not others?

Many competitors are able to coast into early leads, but become afraid when the prospect of a win looms. They become stricken by what they believe to be the heightened expectations of others. This translates into the sensation of pressure and they become temporarily disabled and choke. Large crowds tend to multiply the perceived expectations, which turns up the pressure.

Some of the famous chokes we have covered earlier involved athletes who played effectually in early stages of a competition, when little was anticipated of them. Then, as victory came into view, they seemed to become frantically aware that were actually expected to win and, instead of continuing to play as they had, began attending to what we might call the mechanical features of their game. Other athletes may be able to do this in some circumstances, yet not in others. When they experience the type of stress brought on by heightened expectations, they tend to focus more on what they're doing and lose the automaticity that guided their early play.

Frequently among the favorites to win major international competitions, the England national football team typically failed to live up to expectations. Considering the sport's first league originated in England in 1888 and the Premier League is the richest in the world, the national team has underachieved. Fear of failure has been diagnosed as the cause of the team's problems. This means that the players were stricken by the high expectations of others and rarely performed to their best.

In the 1970s, Matina Horner used a similar, though much-criticized, argument to explain why women didn't achieve at the highest levels (1972). She described "fear of success" as a kind of horror some women athletes experience when they approach victory in a realm traditionally dominated by men. Winning carries with it an implied lack of femininity (see A. W. Heaton and H. Sigall, 1989, for a formal exposition of the concept).

None of this helps us understand why some athletes choke and others seal wins with cool efficiency and some others excel when actually facing defeat – the clutch players. R. W. Grant's argument that background factors, such as upbringing, athletic history, personal experiences, and interactions with coaches, have a bearing doesn't help much either (1988). Maybe choking is more of a norm than we think. After all, tennis is a game that has to be won. In other sports, leads can be protected and choking players can disguise their conditions. A boxer with a points lead might choke over the final few rounds but still win, a football team might see its lead shrink yet

BOX 6.10 FEAR OF FAILURE

Athletes who are overwhelming favorites to win a competition are sometimes disabled by an unwelcome emotion prompted by the belief that they are likely to fail: stricken by the high expectations of others, they fail to perform to their best. As well as needing to achieve, they will be motivated to avoid failure and will behave in a way that reduces the likelihood of experiencing failure. This may take a passive form (feigning injury to remove themselves from being evaluated by others) or perhaps trying too hard to exhibit competence to others. Fear of failure has often been linked with the impostor (sometimes spelt "imposter") phenomenon, which refers to a condition in which people harbor doubts about their own capabilities, even when presented with evidence of these. High-achievers, not only in sport but in any sphere of activity, believe others overestimate them and will eventually expose them as phonies. Impostors' concerns are underpinned, justified, and preceded by fear of failure.

still end the game with a winning margin. If there is more choking about than we notice, perhaps the athletes who manage to stave off pressure and close out games are the ones worthy of analysis. These are often thought to be immune to *stress*.

There is a spectrum of interpretations of what stress actually means, from a pressure or force that causes significant and unwanted changes to almost any form of discomfort (the latter is probably truer to the original meaning of its root *destresser*, an Anglo-French word meaning to make unhappy). Athletes are usually under stress when expectations of them are, as they see them, too high or, less commonly, too low. The effects include anxiety, tension and a general apprehensiveness, particularly when approaching or during competition. It acts to the severe detriment of a sports performance – unless the athlete is able to accommodate it. Even top athletes, perhaps especially top athletes, experience the type of stress we read about so often. Yet, as they say, they don't let it get to them. They must be tough.

In contrast to physical toughness – which refers to durability and a high threshold of pain – mental toughness suggests qualities of mind or intellect. For example, Michael Schumacher presents an epitome of mental toughness, one incident in particular showcasing this. In 1996 at the Circuit de Catalunya near Barcelona, he won an astonishing race in treacherous hard rain that forced several of his rivals, including Damon Hill to retire. Hill said: "I'm happy to be in one piece. You could not see the track. You are putting your life on the line more than normal." Hill's response seemed rational. Schumacher, trailing in sixth place, defied the poor visibility and slick track by driving with a total disregard for his own safety. At one point, he lapped at five seconds faster than the rest of the field.

In achieving a ferocious victory at the Nürburgring Grand Prix of Europe, in 2001, Schumacher all but squeezed his younger brother Ralf into the pit wall to defend his pole position. While technically permissible, it was a potentially perilous maneuver and Ralf had to brake to avoid a collision. Schumacher's almost inhuman resolve, his capacity to remain unflustered in even the most hazardous conditions and his preparedness to take risks others wouldn't even contemplate separated him from his contemporaries.

How he came by these qualities, we can't be sure. But, there's at least a clue in his background. He was the German junior karting champion in 1984 and 1985 when 15/16. Competing at such a high level as a teenager must have required practically all the features we have covered so far in this chapter plus a capability for confronting physical danger without flinching or even allowing emotions to obstruct rational decision-making.

There is no consensus on what constitutes mental toughness. But, were we to search for living model, Schumacher would be a solid candidate; and, in some measure, all elite athletes need it. After all, very few sports careers are not punctuated with occasional setbacks: defeats, injuries, suspensions and so on. Defeats can be especially damaging for some; for others, they are temporary reversals; for still others, they are stimuli, evoking a new response. How a setback is accommodated is crucial. An athlete buoyed by confidence will draw from it lessons that will help him or her avoid another.

Attributing the setback to, for example, lack of preparation or poor officiating enables the athlete to interpret the setback as temporary. Less able athletes are more likely to attribute failure to their own deficiencies, prompting the likelihood of further setbacks. So, being able to take the occasional setback is another aspect that complements the mental toughness that contributes to success. Perverse as it sounds, suffering setbacks can be one of the most beneficial experiences in an athlete's career. To be specific, the setback itself is not the source of value: the athlete's response *is*.

BOX 6.11 MENTAL TOUGHNESS

"Mentally tough athletes respond positively to adversity and are able to persist in the face of disappointment and setbacks," states Ronald E. Smith. "They often exhibit peak performance in pressure situations, and they tend to more consistently perform in accordance with their skill level." Jean Côté adds: "Mentally tough athletes are able to keep their emotions in control and are calm and relaxed under pressure situations." Michael Sheard and Jim Golby's study concluded: "Individuals high in mental toughness are disciplined thinkers who respond to pressure in ways that enable them to remain relaxed, calm, and energized." In sum, mental toughness suggests an unusually high level of resolution, a refusal to be intimidated, an ability to stay focused in high pressure situations, a capacity for retaining an optimum level of arousal throughout a competition, an unflagging eagerness to compete when injured, an unyielding attitude when being beaten, a propensity to take risks when rivals show caution, and an inflexible, perhaps obstinate, insistence on finishing a contest rather than concede defeat.

We're now approaching a psychological profile of elite performers. Motivated strongly enough to commit themselves to a disciplined regimen and prepared to surrender themselves to a coach or advisor, they develop self-efficacy from early, modest success and assemble a self-confidence that will protect them from the occasional reversal of fortune. They'll attribute success and failure in a way that prompts them to strive rather than dwell. Instead of looking distantly into the future and dreaming of glory, they'll set themselves smaller, achievable goals, always remaining, or perhaps becoming receptive to new ideas and strategies. All the time, they'll be readily accepting new challenges that will assist them in acquiring skills. Once those skills are mastered, they'll consign them to memory, so that they'll have no need to attend to them once in competition. The execution will be automatic.

In the midst of competition, they'll be aroused, yet rarely so anxious that their performance will deteriorate. Getting into a rhythm or flow becomes an important feature, so they might practice methods of gating out distractions, or self-talking themselves into an effective state. Performing at a peak becomes a self-sustaining habit. The kind of fears that can paralyze athletes are conquered or controlled. This is one of the key attributes of achieving athletes: maintaining control over emotions that might otherwise destabilize or ruin a game is a quality even the most seemingly headstrong athletes possess. Those who genuinely do "lose it" – as opposed who artfully appear to do so just to interrupt their rival's momentum – are rarely consistent winners. And those who fall prey to anxiety, fear or some form of stress are always susceptible to choking.

Mentally tough athletes are not emotionless: they are just skilled in subordinating emotions to the greater requirements of winning competitions. Success in any sport typically requires making decisions and the best way to make them is by taking account of as much relevant information as possible and reacting to it in a rational way. Emotions are, in many ways, enemies of rational calculation. Sometimes an emotional choice pays off and, urged on by a loud crowd, an athlete attempts what might seem a suicidally ambitious move that wins a contest. It's hardly a prescription for long-term success, however.

Motivation ebbs away from many athletes once they have achieved their objective; though, for others, there is no loss. Success can function as a stimulant, firing the athlete to new levels of intensity. The longevity of some performers, though sometimes induced by avarice, is more probably the result of the pleasure of competition and the attendant benefits it brings.

Studying the psychology of athletes teaches us that there's no one-size-fits-all profile. Our distillation of the features that contribute either to success or failure over the short or long term provides us with an abstraction. The reason why the likes of Schumacher and Armstrong repeatedly won is as much to do with their adaptability as their psychology: they change to suit changing conditions of competition. In other words, we might say they're context-sensitive. Environmental conditions, opposition, the vicissitudes of competition: these and countless other factors contribute to the context in which they must perform. And context never stands still. This is where intelligence matters.

Intelligence is the capacity to comprehend and understand in a way that enables successful adaptations to changing environments. There are abundant rival definitions, though this seems to capture the thrust of what intelligence is about – learning and abstracting from actual experiences and adapting accordingly when new demands arrive. Successful athletes have it. This doesn't mean to say that they score high on IQ tests, though some do; it means that they have, what the psychologist

Robert Sternberg describes as "the ability to make sense of and function adaptively in the environments in which one finds oneself (1996).

"Adaptively" is the key here. A rookie learning a certain type of play in a football team, a boxer modifying his or her style to accommodate a cut that opens up during a fight, a basketball player traded from another club who tailors his or her game to fit in with new colleagues, a cricket captain who changes the field to discomfort batsmen, a baseball pitcher who alters every pitch to deceive different batters: these are examples of adaptive play that occur regularly in competition and the responses are instances of what we might call sporting intelligence. The evidence suggests Van de Velde didn't have it.

A particular type and quality of intelligence operates in sports and, though it hasn't been measured by conventional tests, evidence of it is right there to be seen in competitions where tactics and good sense are required – which is almost all sports.

For every Armstrong or Schumacher who seem to present us with a blueprint of the perfect sporting mind, there is a Diego Maradona, extravagantly skilled but prone to dependencies which eventually consigned him to ill-health, or a Colin Montgomerie, relaxed, confident, and technically superb but who couldn't win a major. In other words, there are elite athletes who achieve in spite of what a sport psychologist might identify as failings and other athletes who have no apparent failings, yet never win the big trophies. Identifying the features that are shared by achievers – and those shared by non-achievers – helps us understand the psychology of winners and losers, though never perfectly. One of the appealing qualities of sports is, as we've already noted, its incalculability. This applies as much to its competitors as anything else.

OF RELATED INTEREST

Bruce Ogilvie and Thomas Tutko's *Problem Athletes and How to Handle Them* (Pelham) was first published in 1966 and it was followed in 1967 by *The Madness in Sports* by Arnold Beisser (Appleton-Century-Crofts). Both books showed how psychological theories could be used to enhance athletic performance and are popularly credited with precipitating interest in what became sport psychology.

Psychological Dynamics of Sport and Exercise, 2nd edition, by Diane L. Gill (Human Kinetics, 2000; the 3rd edition is an ebook written with Lavon Williams, also Human Kinetics, 2009) is perhaps the best pound-for-pound textbook on sport psychology. Among the others are *Foundations of Sport and Exercise Psychology* by Robert S. Weinberg and Daniel Gould, 4th edition (Human Kinetics, 2009), *Psychological Foundations of Sport* edited by J. M. Silva and D. E. Stevens (Allyn & Bacon, 2002), and *Sport Psychology: Contemporary themes* by David Lavallee, John Kremer, Aidan Moran, and Mark Williams, (Palgrave, 2003).

Sport and Exercise Psychology: The key concepts, 2nd edition (Routledge, 2008), is my own A to Z and combines a dictionary-type approach with essay-style expositions, highlighting significant studies. *Fundamentals of Sport and Exercise Psychology* by Alan S. Kornspan (Human Kinetics, 2009) is a primer.

Pure Sport: Practical sport psychology by John Kremer and Aidan P. Moran (Routledge, 2008) is an unusual approach to sport psychology: it attempts to apply theoretical ideas in sporting experiences, highlighting the importance of, for example, motivation, self-efficacy and relaxation in actual performance.

Cultural Sport Psychology edited by Robert Schinke and Stephanie Hanrahan (Human Kinetics, 2009) strays from orthodox sports psychology by emphasizing the importance of nationality, ethnicity, and religion and other cultural factors in influencing the mentality of athletes.

ASSIGNMENT

You're a television critic for a newspaper; your main job is to write the television schedules. Due to the illness of a colleague, you're asked to write a psychological profile of an athlete of your choice. Your inclinations lead you to write the story in a style you're used to. So, choose your athlete and compile the profile, using the style of a tv schedule, like:

9.00 p.m.: The Apprentice. Candidates are given two projects. The first is to work with The Miss Universe Pageant, dealing with potential host cities and then organizing the event. The second project is to oversee the renovation of Palm Beach Mansion, a 68,000-square-ft oceanfront property in Florida.

10.00 p.m.: CHOICE *The Mentalist.* Hit U.S. drama series that's based on the work of Patrick Jane (Simon Baker), an independent consultant with the California Bureau of Investigation (CBI). A former celebrity psychic, Patrick readily admits that he was a fraud, but the razor-sharp observation skills he honed to successfully dupe his former clients prove perfect for helping the CBI to solve its most serious crimes.

11.00 p.m.: Big Brother. Another four housemates face eviction as the climax approaches.

12.00 p.m.: FILM *No Country for Old Men* (Joel & Ethan Coen, 2007). A good guy (Josh Brolin) who found some bad guy's money and took it is trailed across 1980s Texas by a chilling killer (Javier Barden) and a world-weary county sheriff (Tommy Lee Jones). An unhurried but very tense chase movie; meditative, but heavy with fatalism.

2.30 a.m.: Golf . Highlights of today's Open action.

3.30 a.m.: Law & Order: Criminal Intent. Goren suspects a woman's family was involved in her murder.

CHAPTER 7

The Pursuit of Perfection

KEY ISSUES

▌ How did Jane Fonda change us?

▌ What is the culture of narcissism?

▌ When did fitness become a culture industry?

▌ Where was the first exercise-oriented society?

▌ Why do we exercise (don't answer "to keep fit")?

▌ . . . and who was Charles Atlas?

AEROBICS: THE MAGIC BULLET

In the 1970s, no one could even spell it. Now, everyone knows that it means popular exercise, specifically a type of exercise that improves the body's cardiovascular system in absorbing and transporting oxygen.

Either directly or indirectly, aerobics has been responsible for countless tapes and DVDs, books, magazines, and dietary products, as well as an industry in apparel and footwear, another producing training aides, such as steps, swiss balls, and weights, and yet another in cross-training machines and treadmills. Not forgetting an employment sector for the gym instructors who teach the aerobics classes and the trainers who teach the instructors. When you consider these industries alongside the millions of people around the world who habitually engage in some form of aerobics, you realize that aerobics has become more than just an exercise: it's a culture.

To discover why and how a simple form of activity with an odd name that seemed straight out of biology lecture notes became such a phenomenon, we need to be self-reflexive. In other words, we have to reflect or imagine ourselves and ask questions: when did we start working-out, for what purpose or goal, and with what effects? Put another way: what is exercise for?

Anyone who answers, "to keep fit" is stuck in the wrong age. In the 1960s, the sight of someone pounding around the streets in shorts or a thick fleecy tracksuit (before polyester became popularly available) would occasion surprise or laughter. Onlookers might have offered mocking encouragement like, "Hup, two, three!" to the eccentric runner. And he or she *would* have been considered an eccentric in the sense that they were unconventional and slightly strange. This, remember, was a time before the word "jogger" existed, at least not to describe a regular roadrunner.

Gyms were either parts of schools or colleges or belonged to specialist sports organizations, such as football clubs or boxing camps. They would have been austere places too, having none of the comforts of well-upholstered contemporary gyms. Keeping fit for those who chose to do so involved doing a few press-ups and crunches before breakfast or maybe spending a few minutes with primitive devices, such as chest expanders, which were three springs joined by handles that the user gripped and stretched apart.

Today, joggers are moving parts of the landscape and we pay them little or no attention. Gyms, or fitness clubs as they became, are everywhere and accommodate a wide demography, including everybody *apart* from competitive athletes, who mostly favor specialist training. One of the staples of all gyms is, of course, the aerobics class. It's transmuted into boxercize, jazzercize, aquacize, and dozens, if not hundreds, of other variants of the basic cardiovascular workout; but the common matrix is aerobics (from the Greek *aerios*, meaning air + *bios*, life).

Joining a gym, jogging, or even walking regularly are often prescribed as ways of combating depression, eating disorders, obesity, smoking, and a host of other maladies of modern life. Exercise is one the nearest things we have to a magic bullet – an effective, all-purpose cure for physical and even psychological ailments. Whether it actually does have all the wonderful properties of a magic bullet isn't of direct interest to us in the present context, though I'll include later some references to research on effects of exercise. What *is* of interest are the reasons behind the dramatic change from an exercise-intolerant culture to one in which exercise and physical fitness are habitually prescribed and valued practically everywhere. As Barbara J. Phillips puts it: "Exercise permeates our culture" (2005: 525).

BOX 7.1 FAT/THIN

"Fat," writes Andrea Abbas, "is seen as indicative of moral lapse, ill health, physical incapacity and social worth." Abbas traces how body fat became an influential factor in promoting exercise generally and running in particular as health-promoting activities. In other words, if fat were understood differently and regarded, for example, as a sign of wealth and affluence, or beauty – as it has been in history – then exercise culture would not have taken the form it has.

Abbas' argument complements that of several other writers, who have taken their lead from Susie Orbach's 1970s polemic *Fat Is a Feminist Issue* (1978). It's easy to imagine body fat has always been a concern; actually, it only became a concern in the late twentieth century, and, even then, only for women. Exercise culture offered a solution of sorts. Together with a miscellany of fad diets and dietary aids, regular physical exercise promoted weight loss. But perhaps at a cost.

Abbas notes that, in the early 1980s, "developing muscle was not desirable for women." But, "running, along with other body cultures of the seventies, eighties and nineties, changed the shape of the ideal body for women . . . linking toned muscles with idealized femininity."

Maybe Abbas exaggerates: from the 1990s, a different type of female ideal emerged, far, far from the ideal immortalized in Peter Paul Rubens' seventeenth-century portraits of generously sized women, and not as close to the muscular ideal Abbas imagines. True, the complete absence of superfluous fat became equated with attractiveness, but where were the muscles? The lean body became an aspiration epitomized by Kate Moss, who first appeared in a Calvin Klein advertising campaign in 1993; "heroin chic" made the ultra-thin, size-zero body stylishly elegant. Moss appeared well nourished alongside the generation that followed her, creating, as Bruce Blaine and Jennifer McElroy put it, "the impression that weight is controllable and that anyone who is heavy, especially a woman, can lose weight if she makes the effort" (2002: 355).

The reality is, as Naomi Wolf's *The Beauty Myth* and other publications have pointed out, that the majority of women will never attain such thin bodies, no matter how much they exercise or diet. Another reality is that this will not stop women trying; at least not as long as "she's a size 10" remained a put-down. Anorexia nervosa and other eating disorders have been attributed to the rising number of women prepared to restrict their food intake severely, sometimes to life-threatening levels, in order to become and remain thin.

Black women are not prone to such problems. In a 2006 study, Laura Azzarito and Melinda A. Solmon found, in common with other research: "African-American girls resisted the slender, White ideal body, and instead accepted a larger and voluptuous ideal body shape." Voluptuous means ample, buxom, or full-figured and would be a good adjective to describe Rubens's women.

THE HISTORY OF EXERCISE

In Chapter 4 we saw how, in the Classical World, 4000 BCE to 476 CE, during the period when western culture is conventionally though to have taken shape, the ancient civilizations of Greek and Rome placed great value on the human body, both as an object of adornment and of practical purpose. The grace, beauty and performance of the human body were honored at the religious festivals that were forerunners of competitions. Preparation for events would have resembled what we now regard as training, though mostly without the intensity we associate with today's regimens.

The conspicuous exception was the Spartan experiment. Between 431 BCE and 404 BCE, the southern Greek city of Sparta was engaged in a war against Athens.

Spartans were fearsome warriors bred and reared for physical action in a military training camp from the age of seven. Children who were too frail or infirm to withstand the punishing regimes were abandoned and left to die.

The initiation to the camp was grueling: recruits were forced to run a gauntlet while older youths would flog them with whips. This was a taster of what was to come: years of arduous physical training in austere, disciplined conditions followed by mortal combat. Sparta defeated Athens in the Peloponnesian War to become the leading city of Greece. Its dominance was based on its extraordinary experiment in what we call today social engineering – applying cultural ideas and plans to meet specific problems.

The most famous Spartan was King Leonidas, who was killed along with his compatriots while defending against the Persian army at Thermopylae, a narrow pass between the mountains and sea in Greece in 480 BCE. The conflict was dramatized in Zack Snyder's 2006 film *300*, the title describing the number of Spartans who fought and died in the battle.

As warfare receded, the requirement for a toughened and physically fit population ready for military action waned. But, Sparta's emphasis on physical fitness was influential and spread to other Greek city-states, such as Athens, Corinth, and Thebes. The concept of testing the limits of human physical prowess was, of course, expressed most spectacularly in the games at Olympia, about 50 miles (80 km) to the northwest of Sparta, starting in 776 BCE and continuing till 393 BCE.

Spartans saw practical value in exercise and the physical fitness it produced: theirs was a warring culture and they needed successive generations of young men (women were not allowed in the camps, apart from when they were imported for the gratification of the men) who were conditioned for combat. So, their motives were instrumental: fitness was not an end in itself; it served as a means in pursuing a different aim – success on the battleground. Similarly, physical education, as it came to be called in the nineteenth century, was used to foster the development of more able and effective servicemen. As the title of Roberta J. Park's historical study "Muscles, symmetry and action: 'Do you measure up?' Defining masculinity in Britain and America from the 1860s to the early 1990s" suggests exercise was used as a test of manhood.

Historically, we can find other examples of cultures that valued and promoted exercise, fitness and physical health, but for extrinsic purposes, often relating to military functions. Today our motives are less extrinsic though, as we will see, not entirely *intrinsic*. We're still often motivated by goals or purposes far removed from physical fitness.

"Purposive exercise" is what Jan Todd calls physical activity that's "always rational; its regimens are undertaken to meet specific physiological and philosophical goals." In her historical study *Physical Culture and the Body Beautiful: Purposive exercise in the lives of American women, 1800–1875*, Todd distinguishes purposive exercise from physical activities that involve competition, relaxation, or any kind of "play element." By contrast, "purposive exercise is about change – about creating a new vision of the body [and involves] the implicit promise of improved appearance, the quest for better health, and the desire to feel stronger and more competent" (1998: 3).

While Todd is specifically concerned with the first three-quarters of the nineteenth century, her definition captures the essence of how and why women – and men – work out today. Exercise produces agreeable changes in us. Nobody believes their health will suffer, or they'll become ugly or weak as a result. Quite the opposite: we change for the better.

Todd credits Dioclesian Lewis as the most inspirational proponent of purposive exercise in the nineteenth century. Lewis had studied physical education in Europe and became something of an innovator, introducing exercise rings and dumbbells (then made of wood) into exercises.

Lewis's ideas and practices were compatible with radical feminists of the period in the sense that he wanted to make women bigger, stronger, more independent and ready for taking an active role in society. In contrast to prevailing ideas on women, Lewis saw them as capable of holding their own with men in all areas of life, including professional life.

The second half of the nineteenth century also saw the growth of what was known as the sanitation movement, this being a broad-based campaign to improve the physical conditions in which people lived and their personal well-being. A sanitarium was an establishment for people who were either suffering from a chronic illness, convalescing after illness or just wanted to improve their state of health (*sanitas* is Latin for health).

The most celebrated proprietor of a sanitarium was John Harvey Kellogg, a physician, who advocated vegetarianism and abstinence – from sex as well as alcohol. The name Kellogg will be familiar, of course: John Harvey's corn flakes – one of several foods using wheat, oats, and corn – were originally served to his clients at his sanitarium in Battle Creek, Michigan, but his brother went on to market the product that still sits on breakfast tables all over the world. By the start of the twentieth century, Battle Creek was like a goldrush town with rival cereal makers striving to dominate an increasingly diet-conscious market, a situation lampooned by Alan Parker in his 1994 film *The Road to Wellville*, in which Anthony Hopkins plays John Harvey.

As we'll see in Chapter 8 Bernarr Macfadden was a stalwart campaigner for health and fitness and lectured far and wide on the benefits of exercise. His magazines *Physical Fitness* and *Women's Physical Development* (later *Beauty and Health*) were, on reflection, parts of an embryonic fitness industry. By 1920, Macfadden had established himself as a visionary publisher and advocate of physical culture. Like Eugen Sandow before him, he exhibited human bodies as if specimens of perfection: strongmen flexed their muscles and performed deeds requiring strength, while women paraded their swimwear-clad bodies. So why is Macfadden relatively unknown?

Image is the main reason: who can put a face – or a body – to the name? But say "Charles Atlas" to anyone born before, say, 1960, and they'll immediately conjure up an image of a hulking white man in leopard-skin trunks, fists clenched readied for action. "Charles Atlas" was in fact Angelo Siciliano, an Italian who moved to New York in 1905 and was later described by Macfadden as the "world's most perfectly developed man."

THE PURSUIT OF PERFECTION

HOW JANE FONDA CHANGED THE WORLD

Siciliano's impressive body wasn't a freak of nature; nor, for that matter, a product of weight training. He practiced his own version of what later became known as "dynamic tension": this involves resistance training by pushing against walls or the floor and by opposing muscles against each other. Try clasping your hands in front of you and pushing one against the other for ten seconds: the strained state resulting from the forces was the key to Siciliano's technique. Macfadden spotted the commercial potential: if the method could be systematized and published as an exercise program, there was money to be made. But Siciliano wasn't a name that rolled off the tongue. How about "Atlas"? This was the name of the mythological Titan who rebelled against the Greek god Zeus and was punished by having to support the heavens – quite a feat of strength.

By 1940, when he was 42, Charles Atlas was synonymous with strong, muscular masculinity. His 12-step exercise plan was published in a booklet that was available via mail order. No gym membership or apparatus was necessary: you worked-out in your own bedroom, pushing against walls, pulling on doors, and using natural resources.

The program was advertised in comic books, newspapers, and magazines and, if ads can be said to be iconic, Charles Atlas's were truly that. They featured strip cartoons in which a young, wimpish-looking man is minding his own business on a beach with an attractive female when another, bigger guy embarrasses him by mocking his frail body and kicking sand in his face. The girl walks on and the wimp skulks away to invest in Atlas's program. His musculature transformed, the now not-so-wimpy protagonist returns to exact revenge and win back the girl, who swoons, "You are a real man after all." Even if the girl was shallow, she is, we assume, still worth the effort. The cartoon fable was recycled, the wimp enduring humiliation at dancehalls and fairgrounds before re-emerging as beefcake.

Atlas died in 1972, aged 80; by then, exercise was no longer the preserve of circus strongmen, professional athletes, or vindictive weaklings seeking to validate their masculinity. Nor was it the pervasive cultural pursuit we know today. Physical health and fitness were hardly considerations for devotees of Atlas's program: the purpose was to develop an attractive body. Attractive, that is, to women. By the time of Atlas's death, Joe Weider had inherited his position as the leading symbol of muscular manhood. Weider's ads were fired by the same spirit as Atlas's. "In every age, the women, they go for the guy with the muscles . . . never go for the studious guy," a 1980 advertisement advised (quoted by Alan M. Klein, 1986: 125).

Weider was a bodybuilder-turned-gym owner who, like Macfadden, found fame largely through his publications. *Muscle & Fitness* still circulates. In 1981, he aligned himself with a new form of exercise that was, in its own way, as vigorous, animated, and adrenalized as the disco music that accompanied it: aerobics.

Christine MacIntyre was an aerobics enthusiast, who sensed the commercial potential of combining dance and group exercise. The magazine she created with Weider was called *SHAPE* and, according to its former editor in chief Barbara Harris:

"*SHAPE* and group exercise in some ways seemed to grow up together. MacIntyre wanted to present credible, correct and safe information in a way that would inspire and motivate readers" (quoted in Alexandra Williams, 2007: 64).

The term aerobics as a description of exercise (as opposed to a concept from biology) had been introduced by Kenneth H. Cooper who, in 1968, published a book extolling the virtues of continuous exercise for 20 minutes or more designed to improve the efficiency of the body's cardiovascular system in absorbing and transporting oxygen.

Aerobics became much more than a form of exercise. In many ways, it defined a new culture. First, because it was exercise meant to be practiced in groups: people assembled and worked-out in unison, making aerobics an occasion for socializing; the context in which the exercising took place was crucial. Second, aerobics caught on among women and, by the 1980s, was associated mainly – though not exclusively – with vigorous females; this distinguished it from earlier exercises that were, as we've seen, aimed at men and were intended to authenticate their manhood.

BOX 7.2 EXERCISE DEPENDENCE

Also known as exercise addiction, and closely associated with – though not the same as – *anorexia athletica*, exercise dependence is "a craving for exercise that results in uncontrollable excessive physical activity and manifests in physiological symptoms, psychological symptoms, or both," according to Heather Hausenblas and Danielle Symons Downs, who differentiate between *primary* and *secondary* exercise dependence. The former physical activity is an end in itself, whereas, in secondary exercise dependence, control, and manipulation of the body shape and composition is the ultimate goal and exercise is a means of achieving this.

D. Smith and B. Hale's research on bodybuilders indicated that a low level of life satisfaction is a common antecedent condition: the typical dependant is "single, childless, of intermediate or low socio-economic status, and will have a relatively low level of subjective well-being." Trainers frequently take up bodybuilding to compensate for dissatisfaction elsewhere. But their resulting obsessive approach to training leaves them with a "psychologically dysfunctional and undesirable state of mind."

The strength of their attachment to bodybuilding means that they cannot easily cut down the amount of time spent at the gym. Exercise dependence, like other dependences, involves compulsive behavior, and exercisers feel that they are unable to control themselves: they feel they *have* to work out. The fact that this form of dependency can persist often for several years suggests that it does not necessarily lead directly to physical debilitation and the dependent person may operate quite functionally in society.

Because its accent was on rhythmicity, aerobics had affinities with dance. Aerobics classes – as group exercise sessions were called – were always conducted with music, typically soul-influenced sounds with a heavy, regular bass beat. And, as if to strengthen its links with club culture, participants subscribed to aerobics fashion codes: headbands, leotards, and legwarmers were de rigueur.

Aerobics was culturally in tune with the 1980s, a decade when obsessions with youth, affluence, glamour, money and celebrity dovetailed with the individualism encouraged by rightwing governments in the United States, led by Ronald Reagan, and in Britain, led by Margaret Thatcher, both proponents of enterprise and self-improvement. Aerobics promised exactly that – self-improvement. Aesthetically, films like Adrian Lyne's 1983 *Flashdance*, and John Badham's *Saturday Night Fever*, from 1977, complemented aerobics.

Outside the gyms and dance studios, the streets were pounded by runners, many inspired by the jogging proponent Jim Fixx, whose 1977 book *The Complete Book of Running* was a paean to both the physical and spiritual benefits of jogging. The prescriptions of Fixx and Cooper were persuasive, though their overall influence in shaping a generation's orientation to exercise were eclipsed not by a book, or even a film, but by a video.

No one can catch lightning in a bottle; but Jane Fonda came close. The lightning, in this instance, was the fervor for exercise that seemed to have flashed in from nowhere; the bottle was a video – not a movie, a DVD, or a download, but one of those rectangular plastic contrivances that brought consumers unprecedented flexibility in the way they viewed movies and tv programs. In 1982, Fonda, then a youthful-looking 45, had established her reputation in films such as Alan Pakula's *Klute* in 1971 and Colin Higgins's *Nine to Five* in 1980, though it was her earlier appearance in 1967 as *Barbarella* (director: Roger Vadim), the comic strip character from the year 40000, that defined her persona: a radiant, rebellious nymphet.

Fonda had identified herself as a feminist and campaigned for various social causes, including those of North American Indians and women's rights. Yet it was her 90-minute video, originally titled *Workout, Starring Jane Fonda,* and later better known as *Jane Fonda's Workout* (released by Karl Video, 1982) that captured the zeitgeist if not the lightning.

The video was based on Fonda's own book *Jane Fonda's Workout Book,* which had been published in 1981, the year in which MTV started transmission. While aerobics classes were filling up across the world, not everyone wanted to squeeze into clingy gear and cavort in the company of others. Fonda's video instructed beginners how to get fit without fear of embarrassment and without the expense of joining a gym: all you needed was a VCR and a room. Over the next several years, Fonda's original video sold 17 million copies – making it the best-selling video in history – and spawned 23 specialist tapes (exercise for pregnant women; working out with weights, etc.). As Jane Fonda the actor faded from view, Fonda the workout guru shone like a beacon, guiding a generation towards regular exercise.

Fonda's status was both as a glamorous Hollywood star and a hellion – her willingness to join forces with political and social movements earned her a reputation as a troublemaker. In another era, this would have been disastrous for a mainstream actor. In the 1970s, with the United States' unpopular involvement in the Vietnam

War and civil rights legislation proving less effective than expected, a high profile woman – and gender was a burning issue – who was prepared to engage publicly with these and other matters of wide concern was an exceptional being. She was believable. At least in the 1980s: in 2002, she was heckled during a trip to Jerusalem.

Maturity was also a factor: even on the cusp of middle age and, in Hollywood terms at least, a veteran – *Barbarella* had been 15 years before the video, remember – Fonda provided living evidence of the benefits of exercise for women, mature or adolescent.

Am I exaggerating Fonda's role in kicking-off exercise culture? Perhaps. After all, no single individual sets in motion a cultural change of such unprecedented productivity. She didn't singlehandedly launch fitness culture. If she hadn't done it, someone else would have emerged. In an era of big hair, rah-rah skirts, power shoulders and *Like a Virgin* (1984), Fonda became the symbol of a new femininity: strong, able, fit and still unambiguously female. The Victorian myth of frailty we will cover in Chapters 8 and 9 had long since been exposed, but, even so, exercise had still been seen as largely a man's domain, with the likes of Charles Atlas forging a link with virility.

If Fonda hadn't broken the link and created a new association, someone else would have. Someone like Jamie Lee Curtis, who played an aerobics instructor in the 1985 movie *Perfect* (director, James Bridges) or *Flashdance* star Jennifer Beals. Both would have made credible guarantors of the new culture. Actually, French dancer Marine Jahan, the uncredited body double for Beals, who performed the dance sequences in the film, released her own workout video series.

All these women, in their own way, testified to exercise's ability not only to make you feel good, but *look* good. In this sense, it assisted what Steve Hall *et al.* call the "democratisation of narcissism and its assimilation of everyday individuals into conspicuous consumption and the competitive individualist ethos (2008: 215). While Hall and his colleagues believe this process started much earlier in the twentieth century, it underwent a kind of spurt in the early 1980s: any woman could potentially look as sexy as Jane Fonda. They could buy the products, do the workouts and, later, with the greater accessibility of cosmetic surgery, change their appearance to meet the challenges of a competitive culture that valued both individual success and the *appearance* of success.

SPARTANS IN THE INDUSTRIAL AGE

In 1983, Michael Walsh, wrote an article for *Time* magazine, "Make way for the new Spartans," in which he described the re-awakening of the old ethic. "To the executive frustrated by the glacial pace of corporate decision-making or an attorney confounded by the delay of logjammed courts, a bout with the barbells or a tenmile run is, by contrast, a challenge almost Grecian in it one-on-one classicism," wrote Walsh (1983: 92).

Writing amid the enterprise culture of Reaganomics and Thatcherism, when individualism was praised and initiative encouraged and when, as the character

Gordon Gecko of the 1987 movie *Wall Street* put it, "greed is good" (and "lunch is for wimps"), Walsh found exercise rather than sport perfectly symmetrical with the times. "Self against self – the most difficult struggle of all," is how Walsh described the challenge of exercise.

Even when his respondents offered him reasons for exercising such as "clearer minds" and "better sex lives," Walsh had his own thoughts": "The appeal of exercise is more fundamental: no one can do it for you" (1983: 92).

In exercise, people found an affordable equivalent to individual striving in other spheres of life, whether in commerce, domesticity, or personal fulfillment. In this sense, workouts were like a parallel reality where exercisers put in their best efforts and earned their rewards in the form of wellbeing and good looks.

Occasional voices of dissent were heard from the scientific community. For example, Henry A. Solomon, in 1984, tried to expose what he called *The Exercise Myth* and decried strenuous exercise, such as that involved in aerobics and running, as a "a public health hazard." But exercise with purpose was gathering momentum and the preaching of Fonda and the many others who followed her was persuasive. It led to a heightening awareness of the value of physical activity, whether in exercise or sport, to health and well-being (the two concepts becoming practically synonymous).

Exercise became the lever not only of a cultural shift, but of an entire industry. It was packaged and marketed much like other products capable of being bought and sold: a commodity, conveyed to the market in the form of books, videos, health clubs, and aided by dietary supplements, vitamins, and wholefoods, not forgetting the specialist footwear and apparel and the magazines. Like any other commodity, its value was enhanced by the endorsement of celebrities, Fonda being the most influential. Alexandra Williams writes: "As group fitness evolved from 'no pain, no gain', 'feel the burn' [Fonda's mantra] to its current position as a legitimate, established part of a healthy lifestyle, the industry itself became more corporate and standardized" (2007: 65).

Aerobics championships added a competitive element, though much of aerobics' success was due to its adjustability: people exercised at their own level, with their own objectives and their own gratifications. Its group structure became an enduring arrangement for exercise. Basic aerobics led to more specialist classes in, for example, boxercize and aquarobics. Supplementary equipment, like steps and cycles were introduced. Pilates, qigong, and yoga were combined to bring a spiritual dimension to exercise. A cascade of DVDs soon replaced Fonda's early workout tapes.

In the 1980s, exercise classes were typically conducted to the sound of Cindy Lauper, Tina Turner, Duran Duran, or other artists who became beneficiaries of the licensing fees charged to gyms and instructors. This arrangement continues to the present day, effectively creating a subsidiary industry.

Like other industries, the health and fitness industry was also an occupational sector. Glenna G. Bower's 2008 study revealed how, after the 1970s, certifying bodies introduced qualifications for those who want to work in the industry as, for example, nutritionists, physical therapists, or personal trainers. Her analysis also revealed that the industry accounted for 16 of 30 fastest growing occupations in the United States. Of the 36 million health club members, 52 percent were women (compared to 50.8 percent of the total population).

BOX 7.3 EFFECTS OF EXERCISE #1: OBESITY

Obesity describes the condition of having an excess of body fat, not simply being overweight. It is possible for a 250 lb (114 kg) weightlifter or heavyweight boxer to be overweight, but, as this is probably due to muscle rather than fat, they would not be obese. Someone who scores 30 on body mass index (BMI), on the other hand, is obese. The BMI is calculated by dividing one's weight (in kilograms) by the square of one's height (in meters), to establish categories ranging from "normal" to "obese class III" (40+).

There are several different types of obesity. *Endogenous* obesity describes a condition in which the causes of the obesity originate internally, for example from an endocrinal imbalance or a metabolic abnormality. Ovarian obesity is identified mainly in females who have sex hormonal imbalances, particularly later in life. There is some dispute over whether there is a "fat gene," which instructs the body to develop fat cells and which would suggest a genetic form of obesity

Exogenous obesity, by contrast, is caused by external factors; for example, overeating, particularly high fat, high carbohydrate foods, and lack of exercise. This is responsible for what Andy Miah and Emma Rich have called an "obesity epidemic." According to Steven Joyal, the prevalence of obesity has increased dramatically since the late 1980s, doubling in the United States alone. There was a sharp rise of 20–30 percent in the 2002–6 period.

Exercise, while often hailed as the antidote to obesity, is not quite as effective as it appears. "Diet and exercise are ineffective in producing substantial long-term weight loss for a majority," concluded Wayne C. Miller in his review of the research in 1999. And, in July 2008, the *Harvard Health Letter* summarized the results of several studies in an article "Does fitness offset fatness?": "Exercise doesn't erase the health-related consequences of carrying too many pounds."

There are contradictory forces at work. "Every aspect of modern environment and sociocultural lifestyle is geared towards discouraging physical activity," observe the Swiss medical scholars P. M. Suter and N. Ruckstuhl (2006: 59). Children are brought up accustomed to "physical inactivity and the consumption of brand products." The writers use the term "obesigenic" to describe today's environment (*genic*, in this instance meaning well-suited to). On the other hand, as we have seen, we also have, to follow Suter and Ruckstuhl's phrasing, an exercisagenic culture, which, over the past several decades, has produced an entire industry catering for every known requirement.

Lee F. Monaghan argues that an "obesity industry" has developed in response to "the institutionalized war on fat," which is waged in the name of rational medicine. His critical approach to "healthism," a set of ideas that promotes slimness and equates this with well-being, highlights the role of organizations such as the World Health Organization (WHO) in spreading concern with body weight and panicking heavy people into thinking they are obese. Monaghan is especially critical of the crude BMI measure, which is "the most commonly used proxy for adiposity when authorities claim there is a public health crisis [and] serves as a basis for claiming most men in nations such as England, the USA and elsewhere are overweight or obese and therefore ill, diseased or at risk" (2007: 605). Adiposity is the condition of being or tendency to become fat.

While Monaghan focuses specifically on men, many other studies have examined the effects of healthism and its equation of weight with sickness on women. The preponderance of body dissatisfaction (see pages 167–8) among women can be attributed directly to concerns over weight.

Exercise and fitness were incorporated into a commercial activity concerned with a lifestyle and the manufacture of goods to accommodate that lifestyle. "Fitness becomes commodified," observe Peter Freund and George Martin, "and what in reality requires little equipment, technical knowledge or specialised space, becomes a complex, expensive and arcane enterprise" (2004: 280).

On this account, contemporary life is physically undemanding and, in many cases, sedentary. The fitness industry reintroduced physical demands in the form of commodities, for example, step machines for hills, treadmills for tracks, and cable machines for natural loads. The problem with this argument is that it gives the impression that exercise culture was a logical response to the absence of physical activity, whereas, as Lars-Magnus Engström points out: "Humans appear to have a genetic need to save energy and not to undergo unnecessary exertion" (2004: 112).

"Physical exercise must always be understood as a cultural manifestation, and cannot be understood from a biological point of view, even though such exercise, or lack of it, has biological and medical consequences," writes Engström (2004: 109).

This is quite a challenge, but let's attempt such an understanding.

MAKING OBJECTS OF OURSELVES

Pirkko Markula headed one of two key studies, both from the Antipodes and both critical of fitness culture. Markula argues the emancipatory promise of group exercise was an empty one. "Rather than being free, women are prisoners of more detailed regulations of beauty," concludes Markula, whose study in New Zealand revealed that most women exercisers pursue an ideal body even though they realize that their pursuit is futile. The result is an "antagonistic relationship with their bodies." Markula asks: "Why do women drive themselves for the image they find fallacious?" (1995: 446).

The answer is all around: "Cosmetic, beauty, fitness, and leisure industries have emerged to guide people in their quest for perfection . . . aerobics . . . is advertised to help women battle their aging, bulging, and sagging bodies in a manner similar to other body industry products" (1995: 443–4).

Ivanka Prichard and Marika Tiggeman proposed: "Exercise environments play a role in the development and maintenance of self-objectification" (2005: 26). Prichard and Tiggeman suggest, in Western culture, women are constantly looked-at and assessed. Self-objectification refers to a process in which women see themselves as objects "for others to view and evaluate on the basis of this appearance." Their research in Adelaide, Australia, revealed that a high number of woman who regularly attended a gym were motivated by the desire to lose weight and improve their appearance. Gyms, with mirrored walls, gaping men, and ads featuring lithe, tanned women with spray-on gym gear provide opportunities "for experiencing an objectified view of the self" (2005: 27).

Markula acknowledges that working-out regularly in the company of others can yield benefits, including providing a safe environment for being physically active and for meeting other women. But other benefits are equivocal: "Even the heightened self-esteem derived from a better body ultimately serves the purposes of the powerful to continue the oppression of women in society" (1995: 449).

The critical impetus that drives both studies is an interesting one, especially as the majority of research on exercise focuses on its positive effects. The Antipodean studies open out the context, disclosing how exercise culture grows as a response to an idealization of the female body as a product or an object that can be viewed and assessed.

A third study based on the experiences of a British athlete who spent time in Australia, was similarly disapproving of a culture that promoted "the idea of physical activity as a kind of medicine or tonic that we take to improve our moral or medical health."

The study's authors, Cathy Zanker and Michael Gard, found that their subject's engagement with physical activity was "destructive." The reason, they believe, is that, "fighting obesity has become the *raison d'être* for promoting physical activity." Zanker and Gard question the "moral certainty that physical activity makes you a better person" (2008: 62).

While none of these studies uses *aestheticize*, this is actually the process both are analyzing: it means to represent something or someone as being beautiful or artistically pleasing. The fitness industry's marketing strategy has deployed images of firm, toned, and lissome bodies both to embarrass and entice its potential consumers. "It is hard to think of a problem for which physical activity is not seen as a cure," write Zanker and Gard, alluding to the magic bullet (2008: 49).

What they and, for that matter, Prichard and Tiggeman, and Markula miss in their eagerness to disclose the problems exercise culture creates for a woman is that men's bodies have also been aestheticized. The beautiful male body has flared sporadically, as we've seen, through the agencies of Charles Atlas and movie stars like Steve Reeves in the 1960s and, in the 1980s, Arnold Schwarzenegger. But these were prohibitively colossal figures rather than people who could be emulated. Now, anonymous models in cologne ads or sports celebrities offer more attainable exemplars. What's striking about them is their ordinariness: they look as if they eat wholefoods, drink plenty of bottled water and, most evidently, work out regularly.

BOX 7.4 EFFECTS OF EXERCISE #2: MENTAL STATES

The beneficial effects of exercise on mood have been well established by several studies, including that of Cheryl Hansen *et al.*, in 2001, and William Russell *et al.*, whose 2003 work showed how moods could be enhanced by exercise, as long as the exercise is "self-selected" (that is, chosen by the exerciser rather than imposed).

Even in extreme cases of mental illness, exercise has been shown to have restorative effects. Case studies by David Carless and Kitrina Douglas revealed that participation in exercise and competition can contribute towards recovery, first, by becoming central to a participant's identity and "sense of self," and, second, by providing participants with an activity that represents a fresh start in their lives (2008).

More diffusely, Ken Green argues that participation in non-competitive exercise assists the "process of individualization during which young people learn to think of themselves as individuals and acquire self-identities" (2004: 82).

They also look as if they are unembarrassed about using moisturizer, hair preparations, or even the odd smear of eye shadow. One thing is for certain: they take care to maintain their bodies.

We might modify Markula's question and ask: "Why do men accept this controlling regime? Same reason as women, maybe. It would be naïve to suggest symmetry between women's and men's historical experience and, for reasons we will discuss in Chapter 9, social arrangements have reflected the interests of men, certainly during the nineteenth and most of the twentieth century. But it's equally naïve to assume only women have been aestheticized. As Aaron Taylor writes: "Women's bodies are not the only objectified physiques" (2007: 352). Men too have succumbed to the seductive forces of the body industry.

"Many men are not able to ignore the sociocultural image of the ideal masculine beauty," writes Nina Waaler Loland, who conducted research in gyms in Norway and concluded: "Aerobicizing men as well as women are in a process of 'becoming': they continually wish to improve their imperfect appearance" (2000: 119).

Loland also found that, at the gym, "women see themselves as others see them; they see themselves *as* another," and so "objectify themselves" (2000: 122). But, men do it too. Their motive for working-out is not strength, fitness or health, but "better bodily appearance." As Lee F. Monaghan puts it, the primary concern among male exercisers is "with bodily aesthetics rather than health" (2001: 338).

Barbara J. Phillips adds one more detail to complete the symmetry: "Both men and women compare men to an idealized body type" (2005: 534).

Why? The answer is not as obvious as it might seem. Exercise is supposed to be indivisibly linked with health. Yet, writing for the *Journal of the Philosophy of Sport* in 1985, Frans De Wachter noted: "An instrumental concept of health has been superseded by a representational one" (1985: 58).

Anthropologists have for years reminded us that concepts of health differ within and across cultures, though De Wachter was analyzing what he called the emergence of "somatic culture" (somatic, from the Greek *soma*, meaning relating to the body, as distinct from the mind). Basically, he argued that, in the 1980s, the body became "a system of differentiation" – a sign of recognition or difference. It became incorporated into a world of other signs, by which he means objects that indicate the presence of something else. Health wasn't just a state of being free from illness or injury: it could be exhibited.

De Wachter believes that it became possible for people to display their health through athletic bodies. The body became a social symbol of health and fitness, in much the same way as a Porsche expressed earnings power and Armani represented good taste. So, when Prichard and the other scholars covered earlier complain that women who go to the gym are "objectifying" themselves, they miss an important point: *everyone* who goes to the gym, buys a workout DVD, exercises at home, diets, takes supplements or in some way engages with exercise culture, is, whether they know it or not, willingly or unwillingly, implicating themselves in an exhibition of the body. In the 1980s and, it may be argued in the present, the imagery of health was what really mattered. "Enhancement of the outer body," as Barry Glassner wrote in 1989 was the prime purpose of exercise.

De Wachter was writing before exercise culture hit its stride, and his arguments grew more plausible over the following decades. He embedded health in an economy of signs, meaning it became an expression of other aspects of our identity, gender and social position and, as such, could be produced, consumed and have values attached to it. Consumer culture effectively meant that, to exhibit who we were, or at least how we wanted others to see us, we could buy cars, clothes and pretty much everything else, including a healthy-looking body.

Erving Goffman's ([1956] 1971) research into what he called *The Presentation of Self in Everyday Life*, in some ways, anticipated De Wachter's ideas: we have images of ourselves that we are constantly maintaining in the presence of others and these images serve as marks of social *distinction*. In the 1990s, Pierre Bourdieu extended this argument, explaining how the body is used to communicate a multitude of information about ourselves: in Bourdieu's terms, the body conveys a specific

BOX 7.5 EFFECTS OF EXERCISE #3: ACADEMIC ACHIEVEMENT

There are a few crumbs of comfort for those students who exercise regularly and like to think their physical workouts help their academic work. But only crumbs: over fifty years of investigation have demonstrated either no, or, at best, a weak relationship. Most of the research has admittedly focused on schoolchildren, rather than young adults, though the results appear to be generalizable to other levels of academic performance. Combining the historical results of research with those of their own study, LeaAnn Tyson Martin and Gordon R. Chalmers conclude that physical activity has only a "trivial positive effect on academic achievement."

"habitus." This refers to techniques and knowledge that enable us to navigate our way through different walks of life, while at the same times presenting a specific image appropriate to the context in which we find ourselves.

IF YOU CAN'T CHANGE THE WORLD, CHANGE YOUR SELF

While she doesn't reference any of these writers, Phillips, to whom we referred earlier, would almost certainly approve of their arguments. Her premise is complementary: "For every need, there is only one solution: consume something" (2005: 533). From this, she builds an explanation of exercise culture based on our ability to use our bodies to reflect other aspects of our self and, crucially, "cultural pressure."

"The fitness boom of the 1980s corresponds to a perceived *lack* of social control," she reasons. Global issues, such as famine and poverty and a context of rapid social change left people with feelings of powerlessness. "Consequently, individuals turn inwards."

The argument has echoes of *The Culture of Narcissism*, Christopher Lasch's book about the changes that began in the 1970s. Lasch describes "the apotheosis of individualism," in which self-centered feeling reached its highest state of development. After the turbulent 1960s in which young people all over the world challenged and subverted traditional ideals, values, and norms, people saw the same problems: war, nuclear proliferation, structured inequality, persisting racism, political corruption, and ideological divergence. Their rebellious efforts changed hearts and minds, but not the material facts. So, they "retreated to purely personal preoccupations," according to Lasch, "getting in touch with their feelings, eating health food, taking lessons in ballet or belly-dancing, immersing themselves in the wisdom of the East, jogging, learning how to 'relate,' overcoming the 'fear of pleasure'" (1979: 4).

Exercise was part of an entire program. Personal wellbeing, health, and psychic security became the motivating goals for the generation that had earlier wanted to change the world. Phillips sums up the mentality of young people in the 1980s: "If they cannot control and change their world, they will control and change their own bodies through exercise" (2005: 529).

Understood in this way, "exercise takes on moral overtones," as Phillips puts it. It was a solution, but not just to physical conditions: it offered a means of solving or at least dealing with a situation that appeared to be beyond the capabilities of people. They just couldn't change a world that seemed bent on self-destruction: the Vietnam War had ceased (in 1975), but, in 1983, President Ronald Reagan ordered the invasion of the Caribbean island of Grenada and, in 1987, the United States, still under Reagan's presidency, was revealed to have covertly sold arms to Iran. The proceeds of the sales were then used by officials to give arms to the Contras, a Nicaraguan guerilla force opposed to the leftwing Sandinista government.

Phillips doesn't specify these as factors, but they were part of a pattern of events that seemed out of anyone's control and contributed to the "turn inwards" that produced exercise culture. The fitness industry that developed around exercise added another turn. It offered the prospect that people could buy the results they desired

BOX 7.6 EFFECTS OF EXERCISE #4: SEXUAL DESIRABILITY

Can working-out make you more sexually desirable? The question must have at least crossed the minds of anybody who has ever been into a gym. So, here's the answer – yes. A German study by Johannes Hönekopp *et al.* suggested, "physical fitness . . . is indicated by facial attractiveness in women." Lurking in the research team's argument is Charles Darwin's concept of natural selection, the process whereby living organisms better adapted to their environment tend to survive and produce more offspring. So we select breeding partners who are also best adapted and one of the more reliable signals we look for is, as Hönekopp *et al.* point out, physical attractiveness. Good-looking people, we assume, are physically fit and will make good mates. The researchers are actually using an evolutionary conception of fitness, i.e. the ability to survive and reproduce, rather than the condition of being physically healthy, though the two are not totally separable. And the study is complemented with American research by Tina Penhollow *et al.*, which confirmed that keeping physically fit did improve the chances of having sex, especially among older gym goers.

even if they felt they were in some way deficient. "The elimination of the sense of lack through consumption is one of the most predominant cultural messages presented by advertising," writes Phillips, meaning that, for example, buying supplements, or hiring a personal instructor could function as a substitute for actually changing the body (2005: 536).

Joining up the dots between Lasch and Phillips, we get the outline of an exercise culture shaped not so much by a healthy awakening, but by (1) a focus on self-improvement nurtured by the narcissism of the 1970s and (2) an ethic of consumption assisted, encouraged and refined by the fitness industry that developed in the 1980s.

We now have an understanding of how physical exercise and fitness developed and changed through history and how the specific form of exercise culture we recognize today has origins in the cultural changes of the late twentieth century, particularly the rise of narcissism and consumerism. It's important to bear in mind that exercise culture promotes a conception of health as something we display through our bodies and that we use our bodies to convey a multitude of information about ourselves. As we've seen this has induced some scholars to criticize exercise culture for its objectifying effects. But what are its other effects?

CULTURAL THERAPY

Some scholars, like Alan M. Klein, detected the benefits of self-focused endeavor. "This study sees the narcissism institutionalized in bodybuilding as therapeutic," he concluded his research article "Pumping irony: Crisis and contradiction in bodybuilding" (1986: 129).

Many other studies affirmed the advantages of exercise, though Klein's emphasis is not so much on the physical aspects of exercise as the "cultural respectability," as he calls it, that was granted to weight training, powerlifting and bodybuilding in the 1980s. Klein reckons that, historically, the pursuits have been "stigmatized," though enthusiasts' attention to "diet, training, and routine" was a prescient preoccupation. Nowadays, anybody who is concerned with his or her health attends to these.

Perhaps Klein exaggerated the extent to which bodybuilders were shamed by their pursuits. As we've seen, Charles Atlas had built up a global mail order business by the 1940s, indicating that there were plenty of men who were prepared to enlist the help of a training program to improve their muscularity. Yet his overall point is a powerful one: in an era of representation, when bodies performed the actions of speaking or denoting, exercising and its results could be, as Klein concluded, therapeutic.

Exercise is a cultural as well as physical activity. Andrea Abbas, in her study of long distance running, describes the practice as "self-focused development" (2004: 170). But even the solitary runner is moving in a cultural space and, as such, is operating in an environment populated by others. The reason for going to a gym is ostensibly to push the body through a series of maneuvers designed to improve cardiovascular capacity, drop or gain a few pounds, replace fat with muscle, and so on. But it's also to mingle with other like-minded people, share stories, gossip, chat and, in myriad other ways, socialize. As well as the physical consequences of regular exercise, there are social consequences too, most of them positive.

Ruth Henry *et al.* studied the "Effects of aerobic and circuit training on fitness and body image among women" and discovered what they call "body cathexis," this being "the degree of satisfaction a person feels about various parts and processes of the body" (2006: 284). (Cathexis is a psychoanalytical term meaning the concentration of mental energy on one particular object.) "Exercise improves female body self-image," they concluded, "however, a woman's ideal body image continues to shift toward a thinner standard . . . she 'raises the standard' and may become less satisfied with her body again" (2006: 298).

The reasons for the perpetual standard-changing lie in what Bruce Blaine and Jennifer McElroy call, "the moral context of obesity and weight loss in our culture – where weight fat is self-indulgence and dieting is a kind of atonement that produces the 'thin' reward" (2002: 356).

But, unlike many researchers, Henry and co. don't rage against the fashion and advertising industries for using thin models and, wittingly or not, advancing thinness as an ideal standard to which women should aspire. In fact, "the pursuit of thinness is commonly perceived as action or goal in which young women can obtain favorable social responses thereby enhancing self-esteem" (2006: 283). They can demonstrate control over their own bodies, autonomy, and success. Problems arise only when exercisers start to pursue unattainable thinness.

Other studies pick up where Henry *et al.* leave off. For example, Renee Despres asked, "at what point does the quest for ultimate fitness turn into an unhealthy obsession?" (1997). Her answer though is not very enlightening: where someone is "trying to fill an emptiness." We have all experienced the feeling that what we do is unfulfilling or has little value or purpose. Or, if we haven't yet experienced it, we probably will at some stage. Not everybody develops an obsessive gym habit.

The men "questing for ultimate fitness" (to use Despres' phrase) in Michael Atkinson's study were responding to "fear, doubt, and anxiety about what constitutes masculinity" (2007: 184). They begin to suspect their bodies are seen by others as "socially nonmasculine" and their way of alleviating the discomfort is to join the gym and embark on a tough workout program supplemented by protein shakes, creatine, diuretics, growth hormones, and other substances that would get them disbarred from the Olympic Games.

Feelings of insecurity don't just pop into people's heads, of course, and Atkinson identifies a variety of social changes, including work practices and media influences that affect how we understand masculinity. Men are target consumers for a range of products, including supplements, which are supposed to enhance masculinity. This isn't quite such a recent development as Atkinson assumes, as the Charles Atlas ads remind us, though, since the 1980s, there has been a market bombardment of "men's products." The crisis is "sociogenic" in the sense that it is produced by social changes (*socio* relating to society, *genic* meaning produced by).

Exercisers who work out within limits enjoy the benefits of good health, physically and psychologically, though Atkinson detects what he calls "a slightly 'dangerous masculine' mindset" which leads exercisers to take "calculated risks with their bodies" in their effort to achieve "a desirable masculine body . . . which is lean, muscular, powerful, free from blemish yet rugged, and sexually attractive" (2007: 172).

The body, for these exercisers, is a site of social distinction: a way of expressing other features of the self, the most important being masculinity. Their "habitus" embraces not just modifying bodies, but wearing clothes of a certain style, eating specific foods, including supplements, and, according to Atkinson, "sexual displays."

The notion that people go to gyms to get fit is trite and misleading: the reality is that there might be a number of exercisers who think they are just maintaining good health, but even they, on closer inspection, are motivated by other concerns.

OF RELATED INTEREST

"The symbolism of the healthy body: A philosophical analysis of the sportive imagery of health" by Frans De Wachter (in *Journal of the Philosophy of Sport*, vol. 11, 1985) includes the provocative statement "Decades ago, women did not have a body." De Wachter's argument about how our awareness of our own bodies "as status symbols" links exercise with consumption. In many ways, it anticipates the more influential work of Pierre Bourdieu.

"Relationship among sex, imagery, and exercise dependence symptoms" by Heather A. Hausenblas and Danielle Symons Downs (in *Psychology of Addictive Behaviors*, vol.

16, 2002) is one of an increasing number of studies that investigate the causes and consequences of exercise dependency. Others include:

"Exercise-dependence in bodybuilders: Antecedents and reliability of measurement" by D. Smith and B. Hale (in *Journal of Sports Medicine and Physical Fitness*, vol. 45, 2005); "Exercising for the wrong reasons: Relationships among eating disorder beliefs, dysfunctional exercise beliefs and coping" by Konstantinos Loumidis and Adrian Wells (in *Clinical Psychology and Psychotherapy*, vol. 8, 2001); and "Physical activity as a source of psychological dysfunction" by A. Szabo (in *Physical activity and psychological well-being* edited by Stuart J. Biddle, K. R. Fox, and S. H. Boutcher (Routledge, 2000).

"Social change and physical activity" by Lars-Magnus Engström (in *Scandavian Journal of Nutrition*, vol. 48, no. 3, 2004) is a short, but valuable article based on a Swedish study. Engström reminds us: "Physical exercise must always be seen as a cultural manifestation, and cannot be understood from a biological point of view, even though such exercise or lack of it, has biological and medical consequences."

"Working out: Consumers and the culture of exercise" by Barbara J. Phillips (in *Journal of Popular Culture*, vol. 38, no. 3, 2005) begins from the premise "exercise permeates our culture" and tries to fathom out how we arrived at this situation, locating its beginnings to "the fitness boom of the 1980s" when individuals decided, "if they cannot control and change their world, they will control and change their own bodies through exercise." Roberta J. Parks goes deeper into history, discovering traces of a nascent exercise culture in the 1860s, as she reveals in "Muscles, symmetry and action: 'Do you measure up?' Defining masculinity in Britain and America from the 1860s to the early 1900s" (in *International Journal of the History of Sport*, vol. 22, no. 2, 2005).

"Women's motive to exercise" by C. Thogersen-Ntoumani, H. J. Lane, K. Biscomb, H. Jarrett, and A. M. Lane (in *Women in Sport and Physical Activity Journal,* vol. 16, no. 1, 2007) is based on research that found "women are not likely to exercise purely for fun and excitement . . . extrinsic motivates are not necessarily detrimental to exercise behavior in women." So, factors operating from outside, such as a medical instructions or a pressure to conform to social norms can be effective motivations for women.

ASSIGNMENT

You have been going to exercise classes at your gym for the past five years and, while you're not excessively concerned with your appearance, you take a certain pride in your overall look. A member of your classes struggles with the physical demands and disappears. Weeks after the disappearance, you see the person in a bar and ask why they dropped out. The person's answer disturbs you. He/she reckons other members of the class made fun of his/her lack of fitness and his/her fatness. You don't think the person is particularly fat, though, compared to you, they appear to be somewhat overweight. You personally know four other members of the class. So you confront each one individually. Record the responses of each, then explain what they said to the person affected by their apparent remarks. Here's the twist: If you are a female, imagine you are male; if you are male, imagine you are female. The person who dropped out is the same gender as you.

WHY DON'T MORE GAY ATHLETES COME OUT?

Two reasons: (1) they fear the reaction of others; (2) they don't want to risk losing money. "There are players out there in soccer, in American football, in baseball, in all the sports, that people love, admire, embrace and hero-worship who are gay. That is just a fact," discerned British-born ex-NBA player, John Amaechi, adding that, even in the twenty-first century, many athletes still have a "stereotypical view that there is such a thing as a gay predator that will hit on anything that moves."

Amaechi came out at the end of his pro career. Yet few admit their sexual orientation while still playing. Why? Esera Tuaolo declared in his first post-coming out press conference: "If I would've come out in my early career in the NFL, I don't think I would have had the opportunity to play for nine years. I think my career would have been cut short. And also, I think it would've been dangerous for me" (quoted in Steele, 2002).

The danger, as Tuaolo saw it, would have been from fans as well as fellow players. Like David Kopay before him, Tuaolo took the safer option. In the 1990s, when Tuaolo was playing, most gay players came out in the relative security of retirement. British football player Justin Fashanu was an exception.

Fashanu chose to come out via a news story (in a British newspaper *The Sun*, October 22, 1990). His club terminated his playing contract and he moved to several others clubs in Canada, Scotland, and the United States. He committed suicide in London in 1998 after fleeing the States where he allegedly assaulted a teenage male. Fashanu had earlier claimed he had slept with a Tory party politician, which may not have helped his case. The final years of his life were made unbearable by his admission, particularly as he was a born-again Christian and felt conflicted. Amaechi reckons some players claim religious backing for their antagonistic response to gay men.

Fashanu, like Tuaolo, operated in a sporting subculture steeped in homophobic and misogynistic mistrust, a place where manhood is in constant need of revalidation; and where "male athletes who appear to lack aggressiveness and "intestinal fortitude" may find themselves labeled a "pansy" or a "queer" by their coaches and teammates," as Bryan E. Denham points out. In other words, it's a dangerous place for homosexual men.

So when Australian ruby league player Ian Roberts declared himself to be gay through the publication *New Weekly*. there was a predictably hostile response. Roberts continued playing. That was 1995; there have been no further declarations in rugby league since.

Other less conspicuously macho sports have provided more accommodating though not welcoming environments for gay sportsmen. In 1998, two Canadian Olympians came out within months of each other. Stung by the cancelation of a contract as a motivational speaker on the grounds that he was "too openly gay," Mark Tewksbury, the gold medal-winning swimmer from the 1992 Olympics, who set seven world records in his athletic career, came out voluntarily in a television interview.

Brian Orser claimed his career would also be "irreparably harmed" if his homosexuality were made public. Involved in a palimony suit with his former partner, Orser requested to an Ontario Court Justice that records of the case be sealed. When the request was denied, Orser was effectively outed. One immediate consequence was that he lost his job as a television commentator, yet again underscoring the financially ruinous consequences of coming out. Tewksbury also suffered financially as a figure skater.

The potential loss of earnings that inevitably follows an outing is the second factor that weighs on the minds of gay athletes. Thoughts drift back to the experience of Billie Jean King, who suffered a sharp drop in earnings after she came out in 1981. At a time when the incipient women's movement was making demands for equal pay, reproductive rights, and an end to sexist discrimination, King was a vocal campaigner for women's rights in sports and equal pay for women.

When King's former hairdresser and secretary Marilyn Barnett took legal action against her to ascertain property rights, King at first denied that she had an intimate relationship with Barnett. Later she acknowledged it, becoming the first female sports star openly to declare her homosexuality. The case was thrown out after the judge heard that Barnett had threatened to publish letters that King had written her. Reflecting on her conflict-strewn career, King observed: "My sexuality has been my most difficult struggle."

Despite this and the fact that King was married (she divorced in 1987), King's sexual proclivities had become a matter of public record and her sponsors dissociated themselves from her, leaving her with the task of making a comeback to meet her legal costs.

In the 1930s and 1940s, Babe Didrikson, the track and field star and golfer, worked hard at presenting a feminine and heterosexual front in spite of suspicions – suspicions that were not actually confirmed until years later with the publication of her biography, which contained details of her friendship with Betty Dodd.

Martina Navratilova's relationship with writer and lesbian activist Rita Mae Brown was revealed in a 1981 *New York Post* article. Navratilova never concealed her lesbian relationship, though she probably missed out on the kind of commercial opportunities available to other, more conspicuously heterosexual, players. On her own estimates, she lost $12 million in endorsements.

By the time of Navratilova's era in the 1980s and 1990s, there had been a liberalizing of attitudes toward homosexuality, though the possibility of losing lucrative contracts remained an inhibiting prospect. In this sense, sports lagged behind showbusiness: numerous Hollywood stars from the 1940s to the 1990s, hid their sexuality and masqueraded as straight. Rock Hudson, who, for many symbolized wholesome masculinity, actually got married to perpetuate the subterfuge. He died from an Aids-related illness in 1985.

By the end of the 1990s, several entertainers had either come out, or been involuntarily exposed, and not suffered financially as a result. In 1997, the comic Ellen Degeneres, in an art-follows-life episode of her sitcom, declared herself a lesbian on air. The majority of advertisers pulled their commercials, leaving only Volkswagen, a lesbian tour operator, and advertisements for forthcoming films in the breaks. There is no conclusive evidence that advertising in the show would have had a negative impact on sales. Nor did Degeneres' career flop: quite the reverse in fact; she later got her own successful talk show and signed an endorsement deal with CoverGirl cosmetics. In 2008, she married Portia de Rossi.

The manner of George Michael's outing was quite different: he was arrested for committing "a lewd act" in a Beverly Hills restroom and pleaded "no contest." After the incident, Michael became open about his sexuality. He continued to tour and sell CDs (100 million to date). Like many other entertainers, his earning power was undiminished by the revelations. The suspicion remains that advertisers and promoters would be less forgiving if sports stars came out. Even if athletes are willing to come out, their advisors probably caution against it. "It is the fear of losing or not gaining new product endorsements that this billion-dollar sports agent cites as a major reason," writes Eric Anderson, summarizing one advisor's explanation of the athletes' reluctance (2005: 50).

A question remains: is it different for girls? In 1999, Amélie Mauresmo, of France, became famous not only for her worldclass tennis and muscular body, but for her candor about her lesbianism: at the age of 19, she talked freely to the media about her relationship with a woman. But, more typically, athletes come out either toward the end of their careers, or even in retirement, or after innuendo. It was something of an open secret for many years before golfer Muffin Spencer-Devlin's announcement that she was gay in 1996. She chose to do so through the pages of *Sports Illustrated*. In the aftermath of the magazine's revelation, other golfers and officials acknowledged that there were other lesbians on the women's tour.

Mauresmo and indeed several other female athletes who have come out since the mid-1990s have not appeared to have been subjected to undue distress, probably because popular attitudes are never uniform. It seems more permissible for a female athlete to be gay than her male equivalent. Mark T. Harris untangles this in his analysis of the relative calm that greeted the coming-out of Sheryl Swoopes: "Swoopes's gay status doesn't matter because who really cares about professional women's basketball anyway?' In other words, women's sport is considered less important than men's, so the sexuality of its stars is correspondingly less important.

MORE QUESTIONS . . .

>> Is coming out easier for gay sportsmen than for gay sportswomen?

>> Should the media out gay athletes without their permission? After all, you have to break eggs to make an omelet – the "omelet" in this instance being a more enlightened environment free of prejudice against gay people . . . and the broken eggs being the individuals whose lives are upset by the revelations.

>> In 2009, British PR advisor Max Clifford declared that he represented two high-profile gay football players whom he advised stay in the closet because "football remains in the dark ages, steeped in homophobia." Was his advice wise or cowardly?

READ ON . . .

Billie Jean King and Frank Deford, *Billie Jean*, Viking, 1982.

Mary Jo Festle, *Playing Nice: Politics and apologies in women's sport*, Columbia University Press, 1996.

Pat Griffin, *Strong Women, Deep Closets: Lesbians and homophobia in sport*, Human Kinetics, 1998.

Tyler Hoffman, "The umpire is out," *The Advocate*, no. 877, 2002.

Eric Anderson, *In the Game: Gay athletes and the cult of masculinity*, SUNY Press, 2005.

Mark T. Harris, "Women, gays, and basketball," *Z Magazine*, 2006, http://www.zmag.org/zmag/viewArticle/13801.

John Amaechi, *Man in the Middle*, ESPN Books, 2007.

David James "Will a gay footballer ever come out of the comfort zone?," *Observer*, April 15, 2007, http://www.guardian.co.uk/football/2007/apr/15/sport.comment2.

David Coad, *The Metrosexual: Gender, sexuality, and sport*, SUNY Press, 2008.

Control of the Body

KEY ISSUES

▮ Who was the first advocate of strong women's bodies?

▮ What is so natural about the body?

▮ When were sexual differences discovered?

▮ Where do we draw the line between natural and artificial?

▮ Why is the body cultural as well as physical?

▮ . . . and what difference do cyborgs make to sports?

▮ MORE LIKE THAT OF A MAN

Before the 2004 Olympic Games, the International Olympic Committee decided that athletes who had undergone sex reassignment surgery would be allowed to compete in all future Olympic competitions, provided they met certain criteria on the duration of hormonal treatment or timing of surgery. The Stockholm Consensus as it was known was a surprisingly bold decision to admit transsexual athletes. It was also ironic: decades before, it was thought that just competing in sport precipitated changes in sex.

"Too much activity in sports of a masculine character causes the female body to become more like that of a man." Biologists Lynda Birke and Gail Vines use this cautionary quotation from a 1939 book on women and sport to remind us of the risks female athletes thought they were taking (1987: 340).

Historically, sports, particularly those that involve strenuous competition have validated manhood: by providing the kind of unmediated athletic challenge rarely encountered in working days, sports made possible a strong and assertive proclamation of men's strength, valor and, above all, physical superiority over women. Industrial society brought with it, among other things, a less physical life, one in which manual labor, while still essential in many spheres of work, was less dangerous and taxing than in pre-industrial times.

The proliferation of organized sports toward the end of the nineteenth century is due in large part to the desire for an expression of canalized aggression to counteract what was becoming an increasingly sedentary lifestyle. Sports had the added benefit of providing a sense of traditional masculinity, which was being eroded as the seas of industrial and urban change swept against it. At the same time, a scientific discourse over the female body focused on two themes. Helen Lenskyj summarizes them: "Women's unique anatomy and physiology and their special moral obligations" (1986: 18).

Both, it seemed, derived from nature and were unchangeable. And both effectively disqualified women from sport. The perils of competing in sports for women lay not in the effects of exercise on women's bodies, but in the reaction of society to their achievements. Jennifer Hargreaves points to the wider relevance of this when she writes: "The struggle over the physical body was important for women because control over its use was the issue central to their subordination: the repression of women's bodies symbolized powerfully their repression in society" (1994: 85).

There's no such thing as a natural human body. Never has been: the body has changed physiologically over the years: improvements in nutrition, better sanitation, healthier living conditions, and better understandings of its structure and functions have made an impact on the body. These physical changes have cultural counterparts: changes in the popular comprehension of the body. Hence Hargreaves' reference to the "struggle over the physical body." It wasn't a physical struggle, but an effort to understand the potential and the limits of women's bodies.

Bernarr Macfadden was a key figure in this struggle and his story reminds us that the way we make sense of our and other people's bodies is open to sometimes quite considerable changes. His story offers a perfect case study.

Macfadden was, among other things, a publisher, an advocate of vigorous exercise and campaigner for the relaxation of censorship. In 1893, Macfadden watched a demonstration of strength by Eugen Sandow, in Chicago. Sandow pulled a few strongman stunts and posed in a way not unlike today's bodybuilders. Sandow (real name, Friedrich Müller) had built an international reputation, posing near-naked for rapt audiences, designing training programs for the British army and editing several publications on health and exercise. Macfadden was so inspired, he went away and invented an exercise machine consisting of cables and pulleys. He also wrote a manual on how to use "The Macfadden Exerciser," as it was called.

Macfadden toured the United States and Britain, exhibiting himself as evidence of the machine's efficacy. He lectured on the benefits of physical exercise and struck up poses, much as Sandow had done. Soon he became a rival to Sandow, who had made money from a mail order training program. Macfadden's manual changed into a freestanding magazine with articles on training and diet. In 1899, he published a second magazine, *Physical Culture* (retail 5¢). Later, he launched the first women's physique magazine *Women's Physical Development,* which was changed in 1903 to *Beauty and Health.*

One of the premises of Macfadden's philosophy of physical culture was that oneness with nature is absolutely vital to a healthy life. It followed that a natural act like sex should be practiced as often as possible. He encouraged sex in his publications – much to the annoyance of censors who objected particularly to the illustrations that accompanied his articles on sexual activity. According to Macfadden, a healthy sex life was highly conducive to physical fitness. What's more, he publicized this through his magazine.

The magazine was so successful that, in 1919, Macfadden expanded his business interests with another publication, this time a more tabloid-like venture specializing in confessions. Again the magazine was decried, especially by censorious church groups, which insisted that sexuality and the body were private issues and should be kept that way.

Macfadden published copious articles about physical beauty, how to achieve it and how to show it off to your best advantage. A sedentary life was the worst enemy of beauty: good looks came through exercise and plenty of sex. Macfadden was years ahead of his time, of course: the prevailing wisdom was that women were naturally fragile and ill equipped for the kinds of activities applauded by Macfadden. In fact, Macfadden's training prescriptions were seen as downright dangerous for women.

The popular view of the day was that women were naturally beautiful the way they were: the kinds of physical changes brought on by regular exercise were liable to make women unsightly. "To men and women in the first half of the nineteenth century, any sort of muscular development on women was seen as useless and unattractive," writes Jan Todd in her article "Bernarr Macfadden: Reformer of the feminine form" (1987: 70). "Strength was beautiful in men and ugly in women."

Todd traces how the ideal female form was in the throes of change. "Ethereal frailty," as she calls it, was on its way out in the 1870s and, by the turn of the century, the hourglass figure had evolved into an "S" shape, with more prominence given to women's busts. The prettiness associated with women during the Victorian era "had given way to height, grandeur and sturdiness." The emerging ideal woman was described as a "Titaness."

Macfadden set out to find his perfect woman in 1904, when he promoted a contest eventually won by Emma Newkirk, of Santa Monica. Run like a beauty pageant, but with quite different criteria, the contest was augmented with other competitions, all featuring women. Foot races, wrestling and, bizarrely, fasting competitions were held. As expected, in an age when the role of women at sports events was thought properly to be ornamental, Macfadden's project proved controversial.

One of Macfadden's particular dislikes was the Victorian corset, which was both a harmful and constricting article of underwear and a symbol of female captivity, confinement and downright servitude. Even when playing tennis, women were obliged to wear corsets under their full-length skirts, long-sleeved blouses and boater hats. And tennis was one of the few sports in which women were allowed to compete in the early years of the century.

Todd points out, that while Macfadden was campaigning, unprecedentedly high numbers of American women were going to work: "The number of women who entered the work force increased at a rate faster than the birth rate" (1987: 74). So, conceptions of women were changing. The time had not yet arrived when women could enter a full team at the Olympic Games. But, it was alright for a woman to work a full day in a factory.

Popular understanding of the purposes and limits of a woman's body was in the process of change and, while Macfadden may not appear in anybody's "Who's Who" of feminist reformers, Todd believes he made a "significant contribution" to the aesthetic shift that encouraged a more energetic, active role for women. By projecting images of strong, fit and vigorous females, he paved the way for a reconsideration of women. Specifically, he initiated new perspectives on women's bodies. For Macfadden, firm, healthy, and toned bodies were not simply for decorative purposes; they were active, agile, mobile, and could perform as athletically as men's.

We'll never know Macfadden's intentions. Maybe he was a shrewd entrepreneur with an eye for an opportunity; having witnessed Sandow's success, he set about improving on it. Courting controversy as he did served to improve his business position. But, even if his motives were tainted, the effect he had on provoking discussions on the female body is undoubted. Subsequent popularizers of what we might call the cult of the body beautiful borrowed from Macfadden's portfolio. Angelo Siciliano a.k.a. "Charles Atlas" made his fortune through his "dynamic tension" system of bodybuilding. A champion bodybuilder himself, Atlas' claim that "You too can have a body like mine" was featured in mail order advertisements the world over.

In the 1940s, Joe and Ben Weider tried to extend bodybuilding from its exhibition format to a fully fledged competitive sport. This was quite an innovation, as it carried no connotation of strength. Unlike, for example, weightlifting, bodybuilding focused solely on the look of the human body, its symmetry of shape, the sharpness of muscle separation, the tone of the skin, and so on. The brothers' intention was create bodybuilding the legitimate competitive sport it now is. (Atlas and the Weiders were instrumental in the development of fitness culture and we have considered their contribution in Chapter 7.)

The value of these case studies from the past is in their ability to tell us something about the present. Macfadden reminds us how the body has been like a moving tapestry: images or designs changing in a sequence of events in which he was centrally involved. Atlas's project changed perceptions about the fixity of the human body: it wasn't in a permanent, unchangeable state, but could be reshaped according to our own priorities. He provided instruments with which we could initiate that reshaping. The Weiders built on this, demonstrating the often breathtaking forms bodies can take once subjected to resistance training.

They might not have known it, but they were all making a point that has been made in different ways by many scholars: the body isn't so much a thing as a process.

MARKED OUT BY NATURE

Introducing their collection of essays *The Making of the Modern Body: Sexuality and society in the nineteenth century*, Catherine Gallagher and Thomas Laqueur observe of the human body:

> Not only has it been perceived, interpreted, and represented differently in different epochs, but it has also been lived differently, brought into being within widely dissimilar cultures, subjected to various technologies and means of control, and incorporated into different rhythms of production and consumption, pleasure and pain.
>
> (1987: i)

Their point is that there is no single understanding of human body that holds good for all cultures at all times. Of course, every body is made of flesh, blood, and bones and, nowadays, the odd piece of metal or plastic. But, the significance of the body and the purposes it serves change as our interest in it broadens, or narrows. The way we care for it, nourish it, adorn it, display it, represent important statements about our culture. The space it occupies, the curves it defines, the manner of its regulation, the methods of its restraint; its fertility and sexuality: these and other features make the body a potent instrument for understanding ourselves and our culture.

From today's standpoint, Macfadden's ventures appear to be ludicrously tame. After all, what was he saying? That beauty and fitness go together and that sex can be healthy. His infamous magazines featuring the partially clad female form that incurred the wrath of the censors were as innocuous as a DC comic and probably less exciting. Macfadden, though, was doing something more than peddling mags and exercise machines: he was pushing people to a new awareness of their own and others' bodies. He was urging women in particular to experience their bodies differently.

Macfadden flew in the face of popular wisdom when he maintained that women not only could, but *should* do vigorous physical exercise. This was in stark contrast to what most felt was appropriate to women, who were simply not naturally suited to such endeavors. It was a matter of scientific fact established by an intellectual tradition in which women's bodies were defined by scientists as objects of sexuality and reproduction.

Nelly Oudshoorn's extraordinary book *Beyond the Natural Body: An archeology of sex hormones* analyzes how this conception of the female body dominated medical discourse through the eighteenth and nineteenth centuries. In this period, intellectual curiosity centered on the dissimilarities between men and women: in what respects were they different? This may strike us as perfectly obvious; the fact that it does illustrates again just how dramatically understanding of the human body can change. Oudshoorn's work underlines that new knowledge does not just make the body more transparent: it actually alters its nature – nature being the order we impose on our physical environment to help us make sense of it.

Oudshoorn acknowledges that her account was influenced by the work of Thomas Laqueur and Londa Schiebinger. Laqueur's studies of medical texts indicate that the concept of a sharp division between male and female is a product of the past three hundred years and, for two thousand years before that, bodies were not visualized in terms of differences. Think about this: the division of the world into men and women based on sex is a relatively new convention. Previously, there were just people, some of whom could have children, others of whom could not. Hormones had not been discovered, sexual difference was not a concept, so it was impossible to conceive of a distinct bifurcation of types based on sexual characteristics. Even physical differences we now regard as obvious were not so obvious without a conceptual understanding of sexual differences. In some periods, a woman's clitoris was thought to be a minuscule protuberance, an underdeveloped version of the equivalent structure in men – the penis.

For most of human history, the stress was on similarities, the female body being just a "gradation," or nuance of one basic male type. "Medical theory taught that there was but one sex," writes Jeffrey Weeks in his book *Sexuality*, "with the female body simply an inverted version of the male" (2003: 43).

Needless to say this vision complemented and bolstered a male-centered worldview in which, as Laqueur puts it in his *Making Sex: Body and gender from the Greeks to Freud*, "man is the measure of all things, and women does not exist as an ontologically distinct category" (1990: 62).

The tradition of bodily similarities came under attack, particularly from anatomists who argued that sex was not restricted only to reproductive organs, but affected every part of the body. Anatomists' interest in this was fired by the idea that even the skeleton had sexual characteristics. Schiebinger's medical history *The Mind Has No Sex: Women in the origins of modern science* shows that anatomists in the nineteenth century searched for the sources of women's difference and apparent inferiority.

Depictions of the female skull were used to "prove" that women were naturally inferior to men in intellectual capacities. In the process, the concept of sexual differences was integrated into the discourse; so that, by the end of the nineteenth century, female and male bodies were understood in terms of opposites, each having different organs, functions and even feelings.

Oudshoorn's work picks up the story by identifying how the female body became conceptualized in terms of its unique sexual essence in the 1920s and 1930s. In these decades, sex endocrinology created a completely new understanding of sexual differences based on hormones. Eventually, hormonal differences became accepted natural facts. Knowledge, on this account, was not discovered but produced: research on hormones created a different model of the sexes, which was adopted universally and served to re-shape our most fundamental conceptions of human nature. Women were different to men in the most profound, categorical, and immovable way.

So, women were not only discouraged from participating in sports and exercise, but were warned against it. "Medical advice concerning exercise and physical activity came to reflect and perpetuate understandings about women's 'abiding sense of physical weakness' and the unchangeable nature of her physical inferiority," writes Patricia Vertinsky in her essay "Exercise, physical capability, and the eternally wounded woman in late nineteenth century North America" (1987: 8). In this and her later book *The Eternally Wounded Woman: Women, doctors and exercise in the late nineteenth century* Vertinsky explores how physicians' interpretation of biological theories of menstruation led them to discourage taxing physical exertion.

Menstruation – the eternal wound – was seen as a form of invalidity and its beginning meant that young women would need to be careful in conserving energy. Growing up had quite different meanings for young males and females, as Vertinsky observes: "Puberty for boys marked the onset of strength and enhanced vigor; for girls it marked the onset of the prolonged and periodic weaknesses of womanhood" (1987: 17). Remember, this was the popular view at a time (1880s) when the full ramifications of sexuality were the subject of great debate.

Disabled by menstruation women were less –than perfect when compared to men. Their physical inferiority prohibited them from competing against each other, let alone men. As in so many other instances of exclusion, the justification was based on patronage: it was for women's own sake. If they tried to emulate their physically superior male counterparts, they would be risking damaging themselves.

Scientific studies of how menstruation defined and delimited a woman's capacity for physical activity shaped popular thought, their credibility enhanced by their apparent symmetry with folk beliefs and taboos concerning impurity and contamination. Vertinsky notes that scientific and medical theories were "strongly colored by these traditional beliefs" (1987: 11).

Women were thought to be so handicapped during monthly periods that they were prone to accidents and hysteria, making sport and exercise unsuitable areas of activity. Another scientific view was that women possessed a finite amount of energy and, unlike men, were "taxed" biologically with special energy demands necessitated by menstruation and reproduction. Women could never aspire to the kind of intellectual and social development pursued by men because they were simply not built for that purpose: they were naturally mothers.

There were some schools of thought that held that the enfeebling effects of menstruation could be offset by cold baths, deep breathing, and mild exercising, such as beanbag-throwing, hoops, or golf. Especially appropriate, according to Alice Tweedy, writing in *Popular Science Monthly* in 1892, were "homely gymnastics" i.e. housework. Other physicians prescribed rest and energy-conservation. While these may sound like (if the reader will pardon the phrase) old wives' tales, they had the status of scientific fact in the period when organized sports were coming into being. Sports were intended for men only.

Vertinsky quotes a passage from influential physician Henry Maudsley who, in 1874, wrote that "women are marked out by Nature for very different offices in life from those of men . . . special functions renders it improbable she will succeed, and unwise for her to persevere in running over the same course at the same pace with him . . . women cannot rebel successfully against the tyranny of their organization" (1987: 25).

The same natural tyranny that dictated women's exclusion from sports and exercise restricted women's activities in all other areas of social life.

"Scientific definitions of human "nature" were thus used to justify the channeling of men and women . . . into vastly different social roles," writes Schiebinger in her article "Skeletons in the closet: The first illustrations of the female skeleton in eighteenth-century anatomy" (1989: 72). "It was thought 'natural' that men, by virtue of their "natural reason," should dominate public spheres of government and commerce, science and scholarship, while women, as creatures of feeling, fulfilled their natural destiny as mother, conservators of custom in the confined sphere of the home."

One can imagine why Macfadden's startling ideas caused such a stir. In proposing a more active capability for women, he was unwittingly undermining a whole set of roles that had been reserved for women and which supported an entire configuration of social institutions. Even the most tremulous suggestions about activities for women were likely to incense those whose interests were best served by passive women.

For example, toward the end of the nineteenth century, cycling was a popular pastime in North America and Europe. Both men and women cycled, though to mixed reactions from the medical community. While the advantages to men's health were acknowledged, there was suspicion about the uses of cycling to women. Peter Kühnst quotes a physician, who, in 1897, pointed out that cycling offered women the "opportunity for frequent and clandestine masturbation" (2004: 37).

Medical experts doubted whether women's bodies were up to the rigors of cycling. Many doctors believed that the pedaling motion when operating a sewing machine gave women sufficient exercise, according to Helen Lenskyj (1986: 30). One wonders what those doctors would have thought about the 6-day, 274-mile Hewlett-Packard International Women's Challenge pro biking race, or the women's Tour de France (and particularly about Canada's Linda Jackson, who competed regularly in and won some of these events when approaching her 40th birthday).

VIRILIZATION AND DE-FEMINIZATION

As we have seen, up till relatively recently, women's bodies were considered ill equipped to cope with the physical and mental demands of sports. An entire discourse devoted to the subject of the effect of exercise and competition on the body and minds of women threw up all manner of reason why women should not enter sports. The same discourse served to justify women's subservient position in society generally.

This did not stop women who wanted to get involved in sports and in her *Out of Bounds: Women, sport and sexuality*, Lenskyj provides examples of competitors in several sports and women's organizations that would cater for them. She also points out that sportswomen were generally seen as odd. Labeled as tomboys or hoydens, they were thought to lack "femininity" and even represent a moral degeneracy that was thought to be creeping into society. Macfadden, incidentally, had pointed out that almost all beautiful women had been tomboys in their youth.

"Although some doctors advocated exercise therapy in the early 1900s, a time when rest, not exercise, was the accepted medical treatment for virtually all diseases and injuries, they rarely made the connection between exercise therapy and women's full sporting participation," writes Lenskyj (1986: 30).

And then there was the little matter of *virilization*. It's not a word we hear a lot of, not nowadays, anyway. It refers to the development of secondary male physical characteristics, such as muscle mass, facial hair, broad shoulders, and deep voice in a woman (or precociously in a boy). Typically, the changes are induced by excess production of testosterone, the male sex hormone, which is found in both sexes, though significantly less in females' adrenal glands. In the 1930s, it was thought that prolonged exercise induced an imbalance in women's hormones, causing an overproduction of testosterone, virilization, and a resultant "de-feminization."

The assumption was that exercise and competition in themselves would cause female genital organs to decay and so pervert woman's true nature. Not only was a woman's body regarded as too weak and liable to serious hormonal dysfunction if she went into sports, "but the competitive mentality was antithetical to her true nature," reported the respected *Scientific American* journal as late as 1936, adding that women had an "innate tendency to shun competition." By this time, women were already showing competence in a variety of Olympic sports, including track and field, swimming and many team sports. Yet, fears about the long-term effects persisted and physical prohibitions were reinforced by social ones.

Lenskyj's study reveals how sneering comments about tomboys added to alarm over the masculinizing effects of sport grew into fully fledged condemnations of sporting females' alleged sexual proclivities. Women aiming to succeed in sports were freighted with scientific and popular beliefs and images about the rightful place of women. Any achievement of note was a subversion of established wisdom. Lenskyj's thesis is that, in all other social contexts, women's femininity served to validate male identity and male power at both individual and social levels. A woman who defied scientific orthodoxy and excelled in areas defined by and for men, was a threat.

Women who managed to negotiate a successful passage into sports, or any other traditionally male domain, for that matter, were snagged in a paradox, which, as we see in the next chapter, still persist. Lenskyj reports that male heterosexual standards were applied to sports and women who succeeded were immediately suspected of being lesbians. If they were not lesbians before they went into sports, they would be before long. Their achievements were undermined by the presumption that they were not natural women at all; or, as Lenskyj puts it, by "the equating of any sign of athletic or intellectual competence with masculinity, and by extension, with lesbianism" (1986: 74)

Those who failed escaped allegations, especially if they had conventionally good looks (as defined by heterosexual males, of course). "Thus, the unathletic or unintelligent woman suffered no handicap in men's estimation as long as she was attractive. Although beauty redeemed a lack of intellectual ability, the reverse was not true," writes Lenskyj. "Moreover, it seemed that athletic ability did not redeem any feminine inadequacies. Beating a man at golf was hardly conducive to a harmonious relationship" (1986: 74–5).

The association between athletic excellence and masculinity proved an almost unbreakable one and, even today, as Kerrie J. Kauer and Vikki Krane remind us: "A common stereotype is that female athletes are lesbians . . . negative stereotypes about female sportswomen keep all women in sport in subordinated positions" (2006: 43).

No culture that promotes masculinity could surrender one of its bastions of masculine pride to women. But, preaching conformity to male standards requires a transgressive influence as an example of otherness. It appeared that women athletes might fill that position; their transgressions being punished with the stigma of homosexuality, or the stain of virilization. All this would be grossly offensive today; but, as mid-century approached, it was nothing of the sort. In fact, it was common sense and rested on a scientific discourse that had been in progress for a couple of centuries.

The thought of female sports performers functioning within these kinds of restrictions was not a promising one. Yet, women showed that their talents were suppler than they may have appeared. Struggling through the fears and prejudices, women showed that their bodies were sturdier than they appeared and their minds as competitive as any man's. Besmirching sportswomen remained commonplace through the 1940s and 1950s. At the 1952 summer Olympics, the achievements of brawny Soviet field athletes and tenaciously competitive Japanese volleyball players were regarded with skepticism: were they women at all? Appeals for sex tests followed.

Actually, the calls for some standardized sex testing had been growing since 1946 when three female medal winners at the European Athletic championships declared themselves to be men. They had "male-like genitals" and facial hair as well as chromosomal indicators of maleness. In 1952, two French female medalists were later exposed as males. The cries for testing reached full pitch in 1955 when it was revealed that the German winner of the women's high jump at the 1936 Berlin Olympics was in fact a man who had been pressured into competing for the glory of the Third Reich.

BOX 8.1 GENDER VERIFICATION

The process of establishing the gender of a person, gender verification was previously known as *sex* testing and has been used in sports competitions since the 1966 European track and field championships. There had been demands for some form of test since 1946, when three female medal winners came under suspicion due to their facial hair and ambiguous genitalia. Chromosomal tests suggested they were men.

Certificates from the athletes' countries were accepted as proof, though innuendo and anecdotal evidence of similar irregularities became more commonplace in the years that followed, prompting the requirement for all female participants to parade naked before a panel of female doctors in order to validate their femininity at the 1966 games in Budapest. Shortly after, a chromosomal test was introduced. Eva Klobukowska, a Polish sprinter, who passed the physical inspection examination at the Budapest games, was found to have one chromosome too many to be declared a woman: she had a rare chromosomal condition that gave her no advantage (she had internal testicles) and was forced to return all her medals and retired prematurely from competition.

The summer Olympics of 1968 employed a histological test for the presence of a Barr body. This is a small, densely staining structure in the cell nuclei of female mammals, consisting of a condensed, inactive X chromosome and is thought to be diagnostic of femaleness. In 1977, the New York Supreme Court ruled that the United States Tennis Association's insistence that Renee Richards should take a Barr body test was "grossly unfair, discriminatory, and inequitable, and violative of her rights." Richards had earlier undergone sex reassignment surgery, having played as Richard Raskind on the men's circuit.

The Barr body test was replaced in 1992 by polymerase chain reaction (PCR) determination, which was intended to identify uniquely male DNA sequences. But, as J. C. Reeser points out: "The attempt to rely on genetic testing methods of sex determination had opened up a veritable Pandora's box of problems" (2005: 696).

Reeser means that athletes who were female in terms of their observable characteristics (i.e. phenotype), sometimes appeared be male in terms of their genetic constitution (i.e. genotype). "The most common of these 'intersex states' is the condition of androgen insensitivity," writes Reeser. Androgen insensitive syndrome is a congenital condition in which individuals are externally female but have the Y male-sex chromosome; it affects 1 in 60,000 males. Seven of the 8 athletes with non-negative PCR gender verification results at the 1996 Atlanta Olympics were ultimately permitted to compete, highlighting the ambiguity surrounding sex testing.

By 2000, the majority of international sports federations had dropped attempts at gender verification, though doubts remained about how to respond to trans-sexual athletes, who had undergone surgery and hormone treatment to acquire the physical characteristics of the opposite sex. *Note*: a person born with the physical characteristics of one sex but who aligns him- or herself psychologically with the opposite sex, without surgery is more usually known as transgendered, a term that also encompasses intersex persons, as outlined above, and others who do not conform to popular types.

Following the Richards controversy, a Canadian mountain bike racer, Michelle (formerly Michael) Dumaresq competed as a female for Canada at the World Championships, having undergone reassignment surgery in 1996. This sparked debate with the International Olympic Committee and, in 2003, its medical director Patrick Schamasch announced: "We will have no discrimination . . . the IOC will respect human rights . . . after certain conditions have been fulfilled, the athlete will be able to compete in his or her new sex" (the "conditions" related to length of hormone treatment and timing of surgery).

The admission of transsexuals to the Olympic competition of their "new sex" did not remove doubts over the fairness of this change in protocol. During the earlier-mentioned *Richards v. USTA* case, the World Tennis Association and the U.S. Open Committee opposed Richards' right to compete on the women's circuit because "there is a competitive advantage for a male who has undergone 'sex-change' surgery as a result of physical training and development as a male."

It remains possible that, as Reeser puts it, "residual testosterone induced attributes could influence performance capacity [for male-to-female athletes]." Of course, an athlete found with exogenous testosterone in his or her system would fail a drugs test and be liable to disqualification.

Finally, mention should be made of the case of Heidi Krieger, of the former German Democratic Republic, who won the shot gold medal at the 1986 European championships, when aged 20 and later revealed that she had been on a *doping* program that included anabolic steroids for the previous three years. In 1997, Krieger underwent surgery to have her female sex organs, including breasts, ovaries, and womb removed. Krieger legally changed her name to Andreas and became officially a man, though he did not continue his athletic career.

Other individual competitors, like Stella Walsh, the Polish-American track and field athlete, were the subject of widespread discussion in the 1930s and 1940s. It was not until her death in 1981 that it was discovered that she had male-like testicles. The innuendo about Walsh was mild compared to that about Irina and Tamara Press, of the former Soviet Union. Irina won the 100-meters gold and Tamara triumphed in the shot and discus. They both disappeared suddenly from active competition soon after the introduction of mandatory sex testing, or what we now call gender verification in 1966.

Prior to this, certificates from the country of origin were sufficient proof. But visual examinations from gynecologists replaced this at the European Athletic champion-ships in Budapest. Chromosomal testing was introduced in 1967, when Polish sprinter Eva Klobukowska was disqualified from competition after failing such a test. To her apparent surprise, she was found to have internal testicles (a condition that is not as uncommon as it sounds).

At the time, knowledge of the extensive performance-enhancing programs that were being pursued in Soviet bloc countries, especially the Soviet Union and East Germany, was obscure. The connection between taking anabolic steroids and the acquisition of male features was not widely known. In retrospect, it is probable that many of the female athletes who were suspected of being men had been inducted into steroid use, probably at an early age.

Lenskyj's comment that "it has served male interests to stress biological differences, and to ignore the more numerous and obvious biological similarities between the sexes" returns us to where we were before the emergent scientific discourse of the eighteenth century started kicking in (1986: 141). The implication of Lenskyj's statement is that women's experience in sport would have been radically different if they had not been the subjects of an intense yet tortuous debate on the precise nature of the female body.

Despite the fears, women were cautiously admitted to the more taxing track events of the Olympics, though the sight of exhausted females fighting for their breath as they crossed the line of the 800 meters in 1928 was so repugnant to Olympic organizers that they removed the event from women's schedules. Not until 1960 was the distance reinstated for women.

A new movement in the 1970s was driven by a quest for self-understanding or self-perfection; in other words, personal growth. Christopher Lasch, in *The Culture of Narcissism* (1979) argues that people became preoccupied with themselves: they admired themselves, pampered themselves, attended to themselves. Like Narcissus of the Greek myth who fell in love with his own reflection, people became emotionally and intellectually fixated with their own images. As we saw in Chapter 7 during the 1980s, the preoccupation with the body intensified, giving rise to an industry dedicated to the requirements of keeping in shape and attending to body maintenance.

The term body maintenance itself reveals how we came to regard the body as analogous to a machine, particularly a car that requires regular servicing and repairs to perform efficiently. The analogy works both ways: diagnostic checks are now advised for cars between major services. But, if the term itself is relatively new, the concept behind it is not. "In traditional societies, religious communities such as monasteries demanded ascetic routines with an emphasis upon exercise and dietary control," writes Mike Featherstone in his "The body in consumer culture" (1991: 182). Denying the body more earthly gratifications meant that higher, spiritual purposes could be pursued. The whole Christian tradition emphasized the primacy of the soul over the body, which needs to be repressed. It was, after all, the body not the soul that succumbed to temptation.

Perversely, one of the main intentions of body maintenance is to maximize the opportunities to succumb to such temptation. People restrain and care for their bodies in order to feel good about their appearance. In other words, they want to believe they look attractive to others. The often-unstated purpose of cultural imperatives to become fit, healthy, and toned is sexual. An athletic body is a sexy one; a dissipated one is definitely not.

We have now entered a stage that we might call the culture *beyond* narcissism. Lasch was writing of a period slightly before the body became such a focal point of people's lives; when we were less absorbed about the status and appearance of our bodies. Now, we have idealized forms to which we are supposed to aspire. Television commercials, magazines, movies, videos, and many other media heave with images of supermodels and hunks, who, three decades ago, would have been regarded as freaks of nature and muscle-bound monstrosities, respectively. Now many people want to mimic them.

Macfadden was hounded for publishing pictures of women and men who would be overdressed by today's magazine standards. Pick up any copy of a respectable publication like *GQ* or *FHM* and you'll find about a dozen pictures of women in swimwear or underclothes, the kind of shots that would have embarrassed Macfadden himself.

Today's culture has fostered a self-awareness of our own bodies that has produced its own corollary: we're interested in other people's bodies, not for licentious reasons, but just out of curiosity. This is part of the same mentality that allows us to declare often highly personal details about ourselves in the interests of security, but fires our interest in the lives of others – as the success of confessional tv programs suggests. We do not mind disclosing more of ourselves just as long as we can inspect more of everybody else. Their bodies included.

The hundred years or so after Macfadden first saw Eugen Sandow's act brought changes of such enormity in the way people related to and experienced their own and others' bodies that it is laughable to imagine how his projects caused offense. The fact that they did and that Macfadden was forced to operate like an early Larry Flynt reminds us of an important point: that when people thought and looked about bodies in Macfadden's day, they were thinking and looking very differently than we do today. So differently in fact that we might as well say they were thinking and looking about two different things.

How about the bodies of female sports performers? Today's women athletes are often indistinguishable from rock stars or fashion models and, in fact, some double as models. But, never mind their looks: they perform to standards and have capacities that are not far behind – and are, in some cases, ahead – of men's. Rarely, if ever, do we doubt their durability, resilience, or downright toughness. We're probably not sure why we ever wondered at these features. There are reasons.

MORE SELF-CREATION THAN IMPOSITION

In Chapter 3, I examined the body as a collection of about 60 billion cells, organized into substances like muscle and tissue, flesh and bone. In this chapter, I am presenting an alternative way of approaching the same thing: not as a physical entity, but as a subject of a discourse, the center of scientific debate and public discussion. Women's bodies in particular have fascinated scientists and philosophers for the past three hundred years: the search for the "true nature" of women led to the female body becoming something of a terrain on which competing versions contested their claims.

Overwhelmingly, favor swung toward a conception of the female body that was capable of certain types of function but either incapable or unsuited to others, usually those that were regarded as male undertakings. These included not only sports, but, to repeat Schiebinger, the "public spheres of government and commerce, science and scholarship." The symmetry was consummate.

Think for a moment about the ways in which men have sought to restrain women. The ancient Chinese practice of footbinding was ostensibly to prevent women developing large and therefore (in Chinese males' eyes) ugly feet: small feet were the epitome of beauty in Chinese culture. It also effectively confined them to the bedroom away from the gaze of men other than husbands. As feet were generally first bound when the woman was 7 years old, she would be hobbled The custom was abolished by imperial decree in 1902; it had lasted for more than a thousand years.

As cultures define physically appropriate shapes for women, so women have been obliged to conform. Witness the neck brace used by Ndebe women, or the plates that are wedged between the lower lips and the mandible of Ubangis in Equatorial Africa. Neither practice has the practical utility of footbinding, which restricted women's physical mobility so that it was virtually impossible to escape servitude. In these cases, women voluntarily mutilate their bodies for the pleasure of men.

Clitoridectomy is widely practiced in many parts of the Middle East and in the North and sub-Saharan desert. About 74 million women have currently undergone this procedure, which involves excising part or the entire clitoris. The catalog of infections, complications and long-term effects of this mutilation is immense. It reminds us of how far men will go to reaffirm the subjugation of women through the control not only of their reproductive functions, but of their ability to experience sexual pleasure (in one form of clitoridectomy, the clitoris is excised, as is the labia minor, before the sides of the vulva are sewn together with catgut, to be ritually opened with a dagger on the eve of the woman's wedding). The process is defended as an integral part of some sections of Islamic faith, but, as Linda Lindsey writes in her *Gender Roles: A sociological perspective*, "Regardless of how it is justified, it is a grim reminder of the subjugation of women" (1990: 104).

BOX 8.2 PREGNANCY AND MOTHERHOOD

While scientists once cautioned that exercise might damage women's reproductive functions, the potential benefits of the hormones produced in early pregnancy were realized in the 1950s. During the first three months of pregnancy, the mother's body generates a natural surplus of red corpuscles rich in hemoglobin. These assist cardiac and lung performance and improve muscle capacity by up to 30 percent. A pregnant woman also secretes increased amounts of progesterone to make muscles suppler and joints more flexible. Oxygen consumption, a measure of fitness also known as aerobic capacity, can rise by as much 30 percent during pregnancy. It has also been argued that childbirth can permanently raise pain barriers.

Olga Karasseva (now Kovalenko), a gymnastics gold medal winner at the 1968 summer Olympics, later revealed that she had become pregnant and had an abortion shortly before the games to prepare her body. She also claimed that, during the 1970s, females as young as 14 were ordered to have sex with their men friends or coaches in an effort to become pregnant (reported in the British *Sunday Times*, S1: 23, November 27, 1994). Suspicions that female athletes from the former Soviet Union planned abortions to coincide with competitions first surfaced in 1956 at the Melbourne summer Olympics, then eight years later at Tokyo. One estimate at the time suggested that as many as 10 out of 26 medal winners might have manipulated their pregnancies, though no conclusive proof ever came to light.

Yet, the fact that not all mothers return as better athletes weakens the physiological argument and suggests there may be psychological changes that follow childbirth. Having children changes athletes' perspectives, in some cases, precipitating a more relaxed attitude and less pre-competition anxiety. For some, this might improve performance, though for others it could be counter-productive, leading to a drop in motivation and a corresponding slackening-off in training. Sports history is full of females who have improved their performances after becoming mothers. Fanny Blankers-Koen, whom we cover in Chapter 9 is perhaps the most celebrated, but there are others, including:

Shirley Strickland De La Hunty (Australia) won 7 medals in 3 successive Olympics between 1948 and 1956, including 3 golds. At 31 and the mother of a 2-year-old, she won 2 golds at the 1956 Melbourne Games.

Wilma Rudolph (United States) was a bronze medal winner in the 4 × 100 meters relay at the 1956 Olympics when she was 16. She had a daughter then triumphed at the 1960 Olympics, winning 3 golds.

Irena Szewinska (Poland) competed at 5 Olympics, 1964–80. Her best form came after she gave birth to a son in 1970. Four years later, she broke the world 400 meters record, then broke it again 2 years later at the Montreal Olympics where she won gold.

Ingrid Kristiansen (Norway) was a formidable distance runner before becoming a mother and virtually invincible after setting world records for the 5,000 and 10,000 meters and the marathon, all within 2 years of giving birth.

Valerie Briscoe-Hooks (United States) won the 200 and 400 meters gold medals at the LA Olympics of 1984 two years after giving birth to her son.

Evelyn Ashford (USA) won 2 golds at the 1984 Olympics, then had a daughter and returned to the track to finish second in the 100 meters at the 1988 Olympics. She also won golds in the 4 × 100 meters relay at both the same and the subsequent Olympic Games.

Liz McColgan (Scotland) gave birth to a daughter in 1990, having won a silver at the Seoul Olympics 2 years before. Four months after giving birth she came third in the 1991 world cross-country championships and, later that year, won the 10,000 meters at the IAAF world championships in Tokyo.

Svetlana Masterkova (Russia) had a daughter in 1994, then won both the 800 and 1500 meters at the 1996 Olympics in Atlanta.

Derartu Tulu (Ethiopia) won Olympic gold for 10,000 meters in 1992, came fourth over the distance at the 1996 Olympics, then took a 3-year break, during which time she had a daughter. At the 2000 Olympics, she recorded a personal best time in winning gold in the 10 k.

With thanks to Quentin Webb, of Reuters.

What we must ask ourselves is: are these kinds of gory activities so different from the things women do to themselves even today? Victorian women and their daughters self-destructively squeezed themselves into whalebone-lined corsets that were so tight that they stopped blood circulation and distorted the spine. Now, women have swapped this contraption for liposuction (vacuuming fatty tissue from the epidermis), rhinoplasty (slicing open the nose and filing down gristle) and all sorts of cosmetic surgery designed to bring women's bodies into alignment with men's expectations (silicone breast implants being a supreme example; the American Federal Food and Drugs Administration severely restricted these after the damaging effects of them became known, though they are still widely available in Britain).

Then we still have to reckon with the less invasive, but no less disabling attempts women make to meet with men's approval. By defining ideal shapes in ways that please them, men incline women toward near-starvation diets or, worse still, chronic eating disorders like anorexia nervosa and bulimia. The continuing popularity of aerobic classes and their progeny, step classes, boxercise, etc., are related to changes in how men define the perfect shape. The 1950s Monroe model looks podgy by comparison with the lean supermodels of today. Women remain willing to connive with men: they are still prepared to risk their health to chase what Naomi Wolf calls *The Beauty Myth*. But, the myth is "not about women at all," argues Wolf. "It is about men's institutions and institutional power" (1991: 10, 13).

In her essay "Femininity as discourse," Dorothy E. Smith reminds us that: "We must not begin by conceiving of women as manipulated by mass media or subject passively to male power . . . when we speak of 'femininity'" (1988: 39). Femininity, she argues, is more a matter of self-creation, not just imposition. This allows for a conception of femininity, or, perhaps, more accurately femininities, that is not fixed but always in the process of redefinition. No one is suggesting that there is an equally weighted balance of power with men and women trading ideas on how the body should look. Men have had their own way in most areas of society and this is no exception. But, where the female body is concerned, they have had either to resort to coercion (footbinding, clitoridectomies) or secure the complicity of women themselves.

As we have seen, transgressive bodies have been liable to penalties, whether through the application of stigma, or disqualification. Rewards went to the soft and weak. The unwritten rules or codes of the discourse dictated that women whose bodies and exploits did not conform were not "real" women at all. The 1980s witnessed the emergence of a number of women athletes who defied the coded expectations and, in the process, began to re-write a different code.

BOX 8.3 ANOREXIA NERVOSA

Anorexia nervosa, often shortened to just anorexia, was first documented medically in 1874, entering the popular vocabulary from the 1980s onward when cultural evaluations of fatness changed significantly. The value placed on being slim was promoted and maintained in popular culture, particularly by a fashion industry that projected images of waif-like models as ideals. It was thought that an exaggerated sense of being fat impelled between 1 and 4 percent of the female population toward one of the two main eating disorders (with an increase in anorexia occurring primarily in white females between the ages of 15 and 24 years). Only a small minority of men had eating disorders – an estimated 10 percent of the total reported cases.

Research has revealed no hereditary basis for eating disorders and there appears to be no pattern in family background. Subjects with eating disorders commonly have disturbances of mood or emotional tone to the point where depression or inappropriate elation occurs; but no causal link between the two has been found; only an association. The disproportionately high number of women affected has invited an interpretation of anorexia as a striving for empowerment: women with such disorders are not usually high-achieving and financially independent professionals and, as such, have few resources apart from the ability to control their own bodies. But, in this respect, they have total sovereignty.

Rachel Bachner-Malman has introduced the idea of vicarious agency into the debate, suggesting that parents set out to compensate for their "own lack of success via their children" and the children's perception of their need to overachieve works as a predisposing factor.

Explanations of eating disorders in sports rely on similar cultural factors, but include additional sports-specific constituents. Monitoring weight is normal in most sports: in some, leanness is considered of paramount importance. Sports that are subject to judges' evaluation, like gymnastics, diving, and figure skating, encourage participants to take care of all aspects of their appearance. About 35 percent of competitors have eating disorders and half practice what researchers term "pathogenic weight control."

In some sports, looking young and slender is considered such an advantage that competitors actively try to stave off the onset of menstruation and the development of secondary sexual characteristics; or to counterbalance the weight gain that typically accompanies puberty. Menstrual dysfunction, such as amenorrhoea (abnormal absence of menstruation) and oligomenorrhoea (few and irregular periods), frequently result from anorexia. In endurance events, excess weight is generally believed to impair performance. Athletes reduce body fat to increase strength, speed, and endurance, though they risk bone mineral deficiencies, dehydration and a decrease in maximum oxygen uptake (VO^2_{max}).

CROSSING BOUNDARIES #1: MUSCULAR FEMININITY

Almost as newsworthy as Ben Johnson's expulsion from the 1988 Olympics, was the spectacular performance of U.S. sprinter Florence Griffith Joyner. "Flo-Jo," as the media dubbed her, had risen from relative obscurity of a so-so track athlete in a couple of years; her personal-best times for the short sprints tumbled and her physical appearance altered visibly. Not only was she bigger and more conspicuously muscular, but her outfits were more suited to a catwalk than a running track.

Had she not won a bagful of medals, detractors would no doubt have dismissed her, perhaps in the way they did Mary Pierce, the 1990s tennis player: as a bellwether of fashion who looked aesthetically pleasing, but could not compete consistently at the highest level. Or Anna Kournikova, whose tennis never matched her achievements in music videos and fashion shoots. If that had been the case, there would have been no violation of the popular image of female athletes: the ones that look like women have limited athletic ability.

Griffith Joyner's track presence challenged the media: would they concentrate on her record-breaking speed, or her flamboyant appearance? In the event, they escaped the double bind by integrating sexuality and athleticism. Anne Balsamo calls the media's treatment of Flo-Jo "the process of sexualization at work," and we will see in Chapter 9 how this process affected a generation of high achieving female athletes (1996: 44).

Of course, sports history is full of unconquerable females. Yet none had resisted type as much as Flo-Jo. Far from being a delicate-looking creature, she was chunky, strong and radiated power; *and* she still managed to conform to heterosexual standards of female attractiveness. It was as if she was stamping out the message that women can be big, good-looking, well dressed, and still produce in the competitive arena.

In her *Coming on Strong: Gender and sexuality in twentieth-century women's sport*, Susan Cahn argues that: "A reservoir of racist beliefs about black women as deficient in femininity buttressed the masculine connotation of track and field" (1994: 138). African-American achievers not only in track and field but other sports, were regarded as "mannish" and, as Cahn calls them, "liminal figures." (Liminal, in this sense, means occupying a position on both sides of a boundary.)

There was some ambivalence about Griffith Joyner even before the 1988 games. Linford Christie, the men's 100-meter winner at the 1992 Olympics, reacted to her win in the U.S. trials in which she took a barely comprehensible 0.27 seconds off the existing world record. "No woman can run 10.49 legit," he pronounced. "I know what it feels like to run 10.49 and it's hard" (quoted in the British *Sunday Mirror Magazine*, September 4, 1988). She further astonished the world by breaking the 200 meters world record twice at the games. Slurs faded when she retired with a lucrative portfolio of modeling contracts. Despite the gossip, she never failed a drugs test. Her world records remained intact, Marion Jones' 10.71 in 1998 being the closest time.

She retired with her "real woman" status intact, having changed some of the rules of the discourse irredeemably. Gone was the quality of otherness usually afforded big, strong women. Griffith Joyner herself may have elicited confusion by mixing the athletic with the erotic, but subsequent women in track and many other areas of sport, normalized the image of the powerful female body. Almost immediately after her death in 1998, journalists turned rumors into claims: Griffith Joyner's body and her track performances were almost certainly enhanced by drugs, many writers charged, presumably in the safe knowledge that they could not libel a dead person.

Four years before Flo-Jo's triumph, the film *Pumping Iron II: The women* was released. Directed by George Butler, who had co-directed the Schwarzenegger vehicle *Pumping Iron* (1976), the docudrama focused on the lead-up to the 1983 Caesar's Cup bodybuilding competition in Las Vegas. The film introduced the world to the astounding Bev Francis, an Australian woman whose body pullulated with "manly" characteristics. Tall, flat-chested and square-shouldered, Francis was so vasculated that snakes seemed to be crawling beneath her skin.

Female bodybuilding had been around for years before. As a sport, female bodybuilding began in 1979, a product largely of Doris Barrilleaux who was formerly a physique photography model. Barrilleaux started the Superior Physique Association, which set down competition rules for female bodybuilding contests. In 1980 she was asked to head a national American Federation of Women Body-builders. Butler's movie not only took the sport to a global audience, but it dramatized one of the questions that had tormented the sport since about 1980. The Francis model was clearly transgressive: she had a woman's body that for intents and purposes looked like a man's, not just any man's, but one of a latter-day Hercules.

In technical terms, Francis was an obvious winner: her body fulfilled all the criteria of muscle development, separation, symmetry, etc. She had also made it her avowed intention to take women's bodybuilding to its next level. The problem was: she just did not look like a woman. Neither were her nearest rivals, feminine in the traditional sense; but Carla Dunlap – an African American who was the ultimate winner – and Rachel McLish were recognizably women.

In terms of strict bodybuilding criteria as applied to men's competitions, neither Dunlap nor McLish came even close to the extraordinary, imposing Francis. But, the debate in women's bodybuilding was whether to reward someone who, while superior in terms of musculature and skin tone, would be seen widely as a steroid-pumped malformation or a raging dyke, or both.

In all probability, most female bodybuilders were seen in the same way. To date, they are the mightiest transgressors of the traditional feminine ideal. The fragility, vulnerability, and passivity of the eternally wounded woman are effaced. Instead, female bodybuilders present powerful signifiers of strength, resilience and activity.

Linda Hamilton famously prepared for her role in the movie *Terminator 2* (1992) with a specially designed training program that left her with a hard, yet lean physique, complete with the now *de rigueur* corrugated abdominals. Looking at the DVD now, Hamilton seems very ordinary; yet, in the early 1990s, her look was something of a breakthrough – an example of how a woman's body can be masculinized while still looking unmistakably female. Bodybuilders did not manage to do this.

When they first came to public attention, women bodybuilders were derided as freaks by men, who found them repulsive. Anne Bolin suggests why when she writes that bodybuilding "exaggerates Western notions of gender difference – muscles denoting masculinity and signifying 'biological' disparity between the genders" (1996: 126).

Women bodybuilders were stepping on the domain historically defined as male. Men are supposed to be the ones with the muscles. Putting their male colleagues to shame did them no favors: the typical male response was to reject them as "unnatural." And, in a sense, they were: after all, natural, as coded by a discourse that had been in operation for the previous three centuries, meant weak.

It's tempting to regard the women who paraded their striated bodies in the 1980s as *pre*-feminists For instance, in their paper "Pumping irony," Alan Mansfield and Barbara McGinn write: "Because muscularity has been coded as a fundamentally masculine attribute, its adoption by women has offered a threat and a challenge to notions of both the feminine AND the masculine" (1993: 65).

As head of a research project based in Tampa, Florida, and Birmingham, England, I, with my co-researcher Amy Shepper, interviewed competitive female bodybuilders. The pattern that emerged from the case studies was that most had taken up the sport after a personal trauma, such as the breakup of a relationship, a bereavement, or a serious accident. Changes in the body wrought by intense training and strict dieting occasioned a change in self-assurance. Their confidence up after competing, they immersed themselves more deeply into what might allowably be called a body-building subculture. Here the reactions of fellow bodybuilders were important and the often-hostile responses of outsiders were disregarded. Standing on line at a supermarket checkout, one woman heard the sarcastic question of a male behind her: "Is that a *woman*?" he asked his friend rhetorically. She turned, looked at him and asked no one in particular: "Is that an *asshole*?"

But, while their bodies may have been transgressively masculine, their behavior when not training was not. Away from the gym, most slid comfortably into traditional roles as carers and houseworkers. The majority was involved in heterosexual partnerships and cooked, laundered, cleaned, and performed the whole panoply of duties associated with the natural woman. Some of those who were not involved in heterosexual relationships functioned in traditional ways for their brothers. Gaining control over one's body, it seems, does not imply gaining control of one's life. This tells us something about the pervasiveness of male hegemony: a woman can release herself in one very important sphere, while at the same time retaining attachments, identifications, and dependencies in another.

Balsamo believes there are other ways in which female bodybuilders are domesticated. In her *Technologies of the Gendered Body: Reading cyborg women*, Balsamo reasons that, while their bodies transgress gender boundaries, they are not reconstructed according to an opposite gender identity. "They reveal, instead, how culture processes transgressive bodies in such a way as to keep each body in its place," she writes, suggesting that, for white women, their bodies are subjected to an idealized "strong" male body. "For black women, it is the white female body" (1996: 55).

Women who tread on the hallowed male turf of bodybuilding do not have their bodies "recoded according to an oppositional or empowered set of gendered connotations," Balsamo writes. In other words, they are seen less for what they are and more for what they are not. So, any threat they might appear to pose has been rehabilitated and the gender hierarchy remains intact.

Studies of female bodybuilding following Balsamo grappled with the contradiction of what B. Christine Shea called "resistance and compliance." For Shea bodybuilding is both empowering and disempowering in three distinct ways. First, although women used bodybuilding as a "site of resistance to traditional gender norms . . . by allowing women to build muscle and blur the lines between masculinity and femininity . . . society has normalized the muscular woman in such a manner as to render her 'non-threatening' and even 'sexy'" (2001: 46).

BOX 8.4 HETEROSEXISM, HETERONORMATIVITY, HOMOPHOBIA, HOMONEGATIVISM

The assumption that heterosexuality is the normal sexual orientation is known as *heterosexism* and leads, as Barber and Krane add, to "an omission or disregard for individuals who are not heterosexual." *Heteronormativity* refers to the state in which heterosexuality is prescribed as normal. It often elicits *homophobia*, meaning an extreme aversion to lesbians, gay men, and homosexuality in general. It derives from *homo* (for homosexual) and *phobia*, meaning an irrational fear or dislike of a specified thing or group (e.g. arachnophobia; hydrophobia). The related term *homonegativism* is defined by Heather Barber and Vikki Krane as "learned beliefs and behaviors towards nonheterosexuals. . .demonstrated through 'negative stereotypes, prejudice and discrimination.'" This employment of the prefix "non" in "nonheterosexuals" connotes a deviation from prevailing heterosexual ideas and practices.

Second, women experience boosts to their self-esteem when they first begin bodybuilding, but they can get depressed when their bodies don't live up to their own, perhaps unreasonably high expectations and further depressed when they suspect they are losing their sex appeal. Third, contests provide a showcase where women can display the results of their work in the gym, but the criteria used in judging often involves what some call "heteronormative" elements. In other words, even the most muscular women are expected to exhibit the softness and curvature conventionally associated with women.

Shea concludes that, far from being a transgressive force, female bodybuilding has been hijacked and now reinforces "hegemonic femininity" "by normalizing, objectifying, and sexualizing the female bodybuilder" (2001: 47).

Marcia Ian, herself a bodybuilder-turned-scholar, agrees with some of this, but points out that in male bodybuilding "the central activity is exposing to view the passive and objectified male physique" (2001: 77). So, the male bodybuilder makes himself available for public inspection rather than actually doing anything: he is engaging in something passive and feminine (Ian points out that the word passive derives from the same Latin root as passion, which means to suffer and be acted upon).

On this account, sport inscribes dominant narratives of gender identity on the material body by providing the means for exercising power relations on female flesh. Not only bodybuilding: in some measure, all sports operate to perpetuate gender divisions. They do so in two ways. (1) By intervening in the physiological functioning of female bodies: scientific theories and experiments on sexual differences had the effect of opening up women's bodies to surveillance, as we have seen. (2) By institutionalizing subordinate status for women's events and competitions: women's sport has been separated from men's in all but a very few contemporary events. Both confirm that while the female is more durable and capable of exertion than once thought, there is still a natural state, corporeal boundaries that cannot be crossed, at least not safely.

When they are crossed, there is often alarm, if not fright. "The horror of the hyperhuman body is particularly acute when female athletes threaten to exceed normative dimensions and begin to resemble the proportions of their male counterparts," writes Tara Magdalinski (2009: 115).

The reaction to French tennis player Amélie Mauresmo's rise to prominence at the 1999 could have been designed to hold up this argument. "*Sie ist ein halber Mann,*" said Martina Hingis of Mauresmo, her opponent in the final of the Australian Open: "She is half a man." Mauresmo had already been stung by Lindsay Davenport who reflected on her, "I thought I was playing a guy."

The then 19-year-old French player was tall and muscular but hardly ripped and she spoke freely about her relationship with another female. The old appellation "mannish" looked set for a return once the media got involved. "Oh Man She's Good," declared the Melbourne tabloid *Herald Sun* in its headline; the paper's story featured two photographs of Mauresmo, including one shot from the rear that showed off her musculature. According to Pamela J. Forman and Darcy C. Plymire's interpretations of the media treatment: "Mauresmo's body signaled the arrival of an era in which female players challenged traditional male terrain" (2005: 121).

Forman and Plymire's assessment of Mauresmo's impact includes the phrase "panic over her body," which seems to overstate the reaction. Mauresmo's strikingly unusual appearance on the tennis court wrongfooted many journalists as well as competitors. She wasn't the first lesbian to come out; but, in her case, she had never been "in" so there was no surprise about her sexuality. Not much shock, but plenty of awe. "Mauresmo's alleged masculinity," as Forman and Plymire call it, made her "ambiguous presence . . . an exotic form of glamour . . . thereby containing the threat of lesbian sexuality and identity" (2005: 126).

Mauresmo was, according to these scholars, exoticized – made to appear strikingly out of the ordinary. She was; though, ten years after her first major appearance, there were several other female athletes with comparably muscular bodies. And, while Forman and Plymire write of "the lesbian threat," there was no menace or trouble posed by Mauresmo's lifestyle preferences in the twenty-first century. The presence of homosexuality still disturbs some sports, of course; but surely not tennis. We'll return to this issue, though before we move on, we need consider another group engaged in "crossing the boundary" and that includes transsexual and transgendered athletes.

CROSSING NATURAL BOUNDARIES #2: LIMINAL SEXUALITY

Despite troublesome issues historically, sport now appears to recognize that there are few compelling reasons for tests to verify a competitor's sex, though as J. C. Reeser points out: "The issue of how best to integrate athletes who have undergone sex reassignment surgery into sex specific sports competition continues to be vigorously debated." According to Reeser, the arguments come down to one issue: "What it means to be female."

BOX 8.5 TRANSSEXUAL/TRANSGENDERED

A *transsexual* is someone who has undergone surgery and hormone treatment to acquire the physical characteristics of the opposite sex. A pre-operative transsexual who has not received hormonal treatment but has lived as the self-identified gender for a number of years can qualify as transsexual according to some policies. *Transgendered* is an adjective describing a person, who identifies with or feels emotionally they belong to the opposite sex.

Is someone whose observable characteristics are female and lives as a legal female, but has the XY male chromosomes rather than the female XX a woman? Eight athletes with similar conditions were allowed to compete as women in the 1996 Olympics. What of athletes preparing for sex reassignment surgery by undergoing hormone treatment – pre-operative transsexuals? The Gay Games permit such athletes as long as the athlete's identity documents match the self-identified gender; if not, the athlete needs to prove he or she has lived for at least two prior years as the self-identified gender (bank statements and personal letters count as proof). Despite the inclusion of transgender, transsexual, and intersex athletes, Heather Sykes believes the stipulations and reservations "make it necessary to examine the cultural anxieties that underpin the intransigent transphobia in sport" (2006: 10). (Transphobia is an aversion to people who are transsexual or transgender.)

Sykes argues that the approach of women's and gay advocacy groups toward trans-athletes has been "paradoxical." Some women's groups have objected to male-to-female (mtf) transsexuals who compete in women's events, while others have worked "to dispel transphobic myths about mtf muscular and genetic advantage."

BOX 8.6 INTERSEX

Otherwise known as androgen insensitivity, this state of being intermediate between male and female affects about 1 in 60,000 people who have a 46XY genotype, which is the typical male chromosomal makeup, but do not develop male sex character-istics because their cells do not respond to the male hormone testosterone. While chromosomally, intersex persons are male, they look like females (i.e. they are pheno-typically female) and are often raised as social females. In sport, they possess no competitive advantage.

Sykes is critical of the Stockholm Consensus which "uses the most conservative, medicalized criteria to determine access for transsexual athletes . . . and . . . continues to exclude many transgender and intersex competitors" (2006: 11). It also dis-criminates against trans-athletes who have limited access to medical facilities. And yet: "It is important to note that policy and scientific discourses rarely, if ever, refer to unfair situations created by female to male transsexual athletes competing in men's sports, indicating a belief in the superiority of hegemonic masculinity" (2006: 8).

Heteronormativity, in Sykes' interpretation, assumes men hold a natural advantage over women in competitive sport, an idea I will put to the test in the next chapter. Her conclusion is that the IOC's criteria for inclusion render its policies "highly conservative" and the gender policies of the Gay Games pay no respect to "lived realities." The implication of the argument is that any sport that imposes boundaries will discriminate against some "border dwellers and hybrid bodies." Instead, Sykes advocates "the most expansive" policies, by which we presume she means dissolving existing sex categories as admission criteria.

The body is both natural and unnatural. Sports show us that we are constantly redefining the limits of the body. Not only can we re-make our body in ways that we consciously control, but we can move it faster, higher and longer, lift heavier weights and propel objects farther. The whole project of sport is based on the assumption that their are no natural confines of the human body; and if there are, we have not yet approached them. When we remind ourselves of this, it makes Sykes' argument even more potent: a pursuit that exhibits the impossibility of imposing limits on the human body actually does precisely this, albeit in a manner that appeals to commonsense and implicit assumptions about masculinity. It is a paradox that has even more dimensions, as we will see in the final part of this chapter.

CROSSING NATURAL BOUNDARIES #3: CYBORGIZATION

Many of us are already cyborgs. Some of us will wear contact lenses. Others will have steel plates in their heads, plastic joints, and graphite replacements for cartilage. A friend of mine walks round with a plastic panel inside him after having an abdominal hernia fixed; he's also had his myopia done with laser surgery. Another friend's father has a pacemaker to regulate his heart. My own dad should wear a hearing aid, but could never get used to it. How many people do you know who have nose jobs, face lifts, Botox injections, lip augmentations, or breast enlargements? This is even before we get to amputees who have some form of prosthetic, or those people who have undergone transplant surgery and now have someone else's vital organs. Then there are people who have microchips inside them. The list goes on. If we really wanted to stretch a point and insist that a cyborg is any fusion of body and technology, we could round up recipients of drugs, including vaccines. Very few of us have not had our bodies modified in some way. Cyborgs are not half-human/half-machine creatures from science fiction: they're us.

Cyborgs are already in sports, of course. I'm not referring to athletes who enhance their performances with dope, licit or illicit. I mean people like Sean Elliott, who played for San Antonio Spurs after a kidney transplant and reconstructive surgery on both knees (his brother donated one of his kidneys). And Aron Ralston, who competed in Adventure Duluth, a six-discipline (kayak, canoe, run, swim, mountain-bike, and skate) race in Minnesota, with a prosthetic arm and hand. Or Neil Patton, who played on San Jose State University's football team with a prosthetic leg, becoming the first non-kicker ever to suit up for NCAA football.

Perhaps the most celebrated cyborg athlete was the 400-m runner Oscar Pistorius, who, at the age of one, had both legs amputated below the knee. Not content to compete in the Paralympics, Pistorius campaigned to race against fully abled athletes and, though he was able to in his native South Africa, he was barred from the IAAF World Championships and the Olympic Games. Reason? To enable him to walk and run Pistorius had two carbon fiber blade-like implements fitted to his limbs. Hence the obvious nickname "Blade Runner." The blades, known as Cheetahs (a homonym that might have been invented for newspaper headlines), were considered an unfair mechanical advantage over ordinarily-abled competitors, providing Pistorius with extra leverage and spring.

Pistorius's nickname came from Ridley Scott's 1982 movie *Blade Runner*, though the "replicants" of that film were not, technically speaking, cyborgs, but completely fabricated androids. A cyborg is, according to Chris Hables Gray, a "self regulating organism that combines the natural and artificial in one system" and "any organism that mixes the evolved and the made, the living and the inanimate" (2001: 2).

The key is the combination of the "natural and artificial." We are, it seems, in the throes of "cyborgization": there's a sort of co-evolution going on, human bodies adapting to a changing environment with the aid of technology. There's nothing terribly new about this: bifocals and false teeth were early instances and artificial limbs were, as any reader of *Treasure Island* knows, popular among pirates like Long John Silver in the eighteenth century. The Napoleonic Wars in Europe, 1803–15, and the American Civil War, 1861–5, left many combatants disabled, leading to a demand for replacement limbs. These were rudimentary when compared to the possibilities offered in the twentieth century. Again the supervening necessities of war played an important part.

The concept of fixing humans with spare parts was a far cry from the possibilities offered by science fiction, of course. While the idea of robots and hybrids had been entertained for years, the first film actually to use the term cyborg was Franklin Adreon's *Cyborg 2087*, released in 1966. The plot is familiar to fans of the later *Terminator* series: a cyborg, played by Michael Rennie, is sent back from the future to save civilization.

In the late twentieth century, the idea of a fusion between human and machine captured many imaginations, including that of the makers of the television series *The Six Million Dollar Man*, the 1973 pilot of which was entitled *Cyborg: The six million dollar man*. The premise of this was that an injured war hero is put back together using technology that enables him to perform extraordinary feats, like running as fast as a train. A glut of movies followed similar themes, the most celebrated being Paul Verhoeven's 1987 *Robocop*, which spawned two sequels.

Fascinating as the prospects are, humans were, for long, ambivalent about cyborgs. The Greek myth of Prometheus is a cautionary one. After stealing fire from Olympus and teaching mortals how to use it, Prometheus was punished by being chained to a rock and left to the vultures. "A little knowledge is a dangerous thing," is a slogan that has a similar meaning. The *Frankenstein* story too: the obsessed scientist creates

BOX 8.7 CYBORG

The term itself is from the Greek *kubernetes*, meaning one who steers vessels, which was anglicized to cyber, cybernetics being the science of systems of control in animals and machines; if a system is *cybernated*, it means it is controlled by machines. Added to this was "org," short for organic, as in parts of the body adapted for special functions, from the Greek for tool, *organon*. The word entered the popular vocabulary of the late twentieth century via science fiction. The growth of people who emerged from surgery with synthetic parts replacing their original organs suggested that the cyborg was not just a fictional creature. Bionic parts, were mechanical productions that performed like living organs and appendages. Appropriated by scholars, such as Donna Haraway and Chris Hables Gray, cyborg came to define a political reality, a way of challenging traditionally accepted divisions supposedly based on natural arrangements. Haraway is known for her credo: "I would rather be a cyborg than a goddess."

life from an assembly of human parts, only to lose control of his creation. Today, we seem less cautious. Perhaps, it's because we sense we're approaching the limits of human possibility. To go further, whether in sports or any other sphere of endeavor, we need not only to assist our efforts but to augment them – make them greater.

Some writers welcome the fusion of human and machine. Donna Haraway, in her *Simians, Cyborgs and Women*, argues that, in cyborgs, we have the nucleus of a society freed of stifling gender roles. In this and her earlier work, Haraway called for a recognition that we are all, in some respect, cyborgs and that we should take advantage of this. Why continue respecting the traditional divisions between animal/human/machine, asks Haraway? We should be transgressing them: using all available technologies to take control of our bodies in ways that give us satisfaction.

This wouldn't be music to the ears of drug-testers in sports, nor those who favor the continuation of separate events for men and women. As Brian Pronger points out in his essay "Post-sport: Transgressing boundaries in physical culture": "In sport this means encouraging people to experiment with the cybernetic boundaries of their bodies, thus resisting the boundary project of a sports system that requires athletes to technologize their bodies but punishes them if they are caught doing so" (1998: 286).

"Modern sport is a paradox," states Tara Magdalinski. "It seeks to surpass established records with astonishing performances that push the body its current limits. . .[yet] substances and techniques, applied directly to the athletic body or utilized within the conduct of sport for the sole purpose of enhancing performance, represent, for many, the most exigent crisis currently facing sport."

Doping aside, athletes are well engaged in cyborgization and the indications are that this will precipitate the crisis Magdalinski expects. The effects of injuries and disabilities are often overcome with technologies. It's a small step away from actively using similar technologies to go beyond maximal performance. Structural, bio-chemical alterations to the body may sound drastic, but, as we will see in the chapters ahead, genetic engineering is already on the agenda. We'll return to this in Chapter 11 and in the conclusion. For now, we recognize that the body is natural and artificial, physical, and cultural.

OF RELATED INTEREST

Out of Bounds: Women, sport and sexuality by Helen Lenskyj (Women's Press, 1986) traces the massively hindered progress of women into mainstream sports from the 1880s, paying special attention to the various ways women's achievements were discredited, typically by accusations of impropriety or unnatural status. It can profitably be read in conjunction with Patricia Vertinsky's excellent *The Eternally Wounded Woman: Women, doctors and exercise in the late nineteenth century* (Manchester University Press, 1990).

The Making of the Modern Body: Sexuality and society in the nineteenth century edited by Catherine Gallagher and Thomas Laqueur (University of California Press, 1987) is a collection of essays all devoted to exploring different aspects of the body's changing meanings. It is perfectly complemented by *Beyond the Natural Body: An archeology of sex hormones* by Nelly Oudshoorn (Routledge, 1994), a detailed exploration of how the "discovery" of sex hormones established as a scientific fact the precise natural differences between men and women.

Sexuality, 2nd edition, by Jeffrey Weeks (Routledge, 2003) has a chapter on "The meanings of sexual difference" in which the author discloses several perspectives including one that suggests that "heterosexuality and homosexuality are not emanations of the genes or hormones or anything else: they are regulative fictions and ideals through which conformities are generated, reinforced and 'normalized'. . .The norms are inscribed on the body in a variety of ways through the relations and rituals of power which prescribe and proscribe appearance, physicality, who and what is desirable and so on."

Genetically Modified Athletes: Biomedical ethics, gene doping and sport by Andy Miah (Routledge, 2004) and Robert Pepperell's 3rd edition of *The Posthuman Condition: Consciousness beyond the brain* (Intellect, 2004) examine how genetic modification, intelligent machines and synthetic creativity challenge traditional assumptions about humanity.

"Transsexual and transgender policies in sport" by Heather Sykes (in *Women in Sport and Physical Activity Journal* vol. 15, no. 1, 2006) is a challenging argument against sport's acceptance of traditional sex categories and its refusal to recognize "instability" in sexual identities. One might expect a more enlightened approach from the Gay Games, though this has not been the case. Useful in this context is Caroline Symons' *The Gay Games: A History* (Routledge, 2009).

"Able bodies and sport participation: Social constructions of physical ability for gendered and sexually identified bodies" by Ian Wellard (in *Sport, Education and Society*, vol. 11, no. 2, 2006) is based on an empirical study on how hegemonic masculinity is an embodied practice performed, displayed and reinforced through sport: "The ability to successfully take part in physical activities is determined by many factors, most notable are performances of gender, where traditional, hegemonic masculinity is favoured."

Sport, Technology and the Body by Tara Magdalinski (Routledge, 2009) challenges the conventional "nature/artifice construct" which limits the way we visualize humans' relationship with performance technologies. The author believes the construct is rooted in *Chariots of Fire*-like principles of amateurism and gentlemanliness: "To use any and all measures to enhance a performance is thought to privilege winning over participation and, potentially, cheating over morality" (see Chapter 18 for a discussion of this morality).

Renée Richards played on the women's tennis tour before it was discovered that she was formerly Richard Raskind. Hastily, the United States Tennis Association, and the Women's Tennis Association introduced a Barr bodies sex test, which Richards refused to take. S/he was excluded from competition. In 1977, the New York Supreme Court ruled that requiring Richards to take the Barr test was "grossly unfair, discriminatory and inequitable, and violative of her rights" (see Renee Richards' biography, *Second Serve* (with J. Ames) Stein & Day, 1983; and Susan Birrell and Cheryl Cole's "Double fault: Renee Richards and the construction and naturalization of difference" in *Sociology of Sport Journal* vol. 7, 1990). A decade later the U.S. Golf Association responded to the transsexual golfer, Charlotte Ann Woods, by introducing the requirement that only women who were "female at birth" were eligible for women's tournaments. In the 1990s, Canada's Michelle Dumaresq made news competing as a mountain-bike racer. Formerly Michael, Dumaresq had sex reassignment surgery in 1996 and competed for Canada at the World Championships in Austria. In 2003, the IOC's medical director Patrick Schamasch announced that, in regard to transsexuals, "We will have no discrimination . . . the IOC will respect human rights . . . after certain conditions have been fulfilled, the athlete will be able to compete in his or her new sex." Discrimination against transsexuals appears to be receding. But, has it disappeared?

Perhaps surprisingly, Richards criticizes the decision: "Sex-assignment is based on putting materials into your body." But, the IOC insists safeguards are in place to prevent an athlete reaping competitive benefits from a sex change. Hormone treatment should have ceased at least two years before competition.

Construct a narrative in which it is revealed that several members of the current tennis circuit, the national track and field team and some beach volleyball players have undergone similar surgery to Richards and produce such impressive competitive performances that rivals complain that they have an advantage. Each of the individuals concerned provide documents certifying they are legally male. But the protests persist. Take careful note of Balsamo's reminder that "gender is not simply an effect of the circulation of representations and discourse, but also the effect of specific social, economic, and institutional relations of power" (1996: 162).

KEY ISSUES

▌ How come even top sportswomen are still sex commodities?

▌ Why do men think their manhood is under threat?

▌ When did ladies stop being ladies and become women?

▌ Where is the proper place of women – the home or the playing field?

▌ What stopped women competing with men?

▌ . . . and who were the women that challenged sexism in sport?

CHAPTER 9

Sports Emasculated

▌ LADIES FIRST

To . . . e.cashmore@staffs.ac.uk
From . . . h.g.wells@timemachine.org
Subject: women

Professor Cashmore: If you've ever read any of my short stories, you may be familiar with "In the modern vein: An unsympathetic love story" (1894) in which case you'll know that, when I first encountered the facility for time-shuttling, I used to attend what we called tennis parties, these being gatherings of invited guests to friends' homes, where people could eat, drink and play tennis on the lawn. I was an admirer of the game of tennis, a practice that I understand you later called a sport. This was one of the few competitive activities women were believed to be capable of playing. Athletic competitions were the domains of men, who were more muscular and sufficiently robust to withstand the physical exertion required. In many ways, the position of women in competition reflected their position in the political arena. Women in Great Britain and the United States of America were campaigning for the right to vote.

Shortly after the publication of *The Time Machine* women became more militant in their attempts to secure political recognition. Emmeline Pankhurst's suffragettes, as they were called, suffered indignity and violence in their ultimately successful efforts, but their only excursion into sports was horrific: in 1913, Emily Davidson threw herself under a horse owned by King George V at the Derby race. It took until 1918 before the franchise was extended and the shackles of Victorian Britain were left behind. You can imagine my surprise when I paused in your time to review a game for which I have long held affection. The gentle game of to-and-fro in which women, clothed in full-length skirts and straw hats, transferred the ball from one side of the net to the other had been replaced by an altogether different type of activity.

The women, many taller and more muscular than men played with strange-looking rackets and hit the ball with a barely believable force. Unlike their predecessors, they ran about the court, not daintily, but like male sprinters. They also wear the most astonishing garb; and they grunt, sweat and behave in a manner that would have been considered quite unsuitable in my day. I also had chance to see athletic women run distances that were once thought to be harmful; play ballgames that leave their contestants bruised and pummeled; and even witnessed women engage in prize fighting with a fury one associates with men. Actually, I recall reading about female pugilists milling (as we used to call fighting) in the eighteenth century, though I didn't travel back to watch them. My question is this: how on earth did women become such fierce competitors, when they were once just decorative onlookers? Perhaps, when you write the next edition of your text, you might suggest an explanation.

Cordially
Herbert George

Imagine if H. G. Wells were to re-visit the late nineteenth century and advise the then fledgling organizations that were governing sports that, contrary to the wisdom of the day, women were eminently capable of competing with men. The organizations might have allowed women admission, but not in separate events. They might have stipulated that if women could compete in football, tennis, track, and all the other major sports, then they would have to take their chances against men. In one stroke women would have been transformed from spectators to competitors. Of course, they would have been beaten repeatedly, especially in events in which muscular strength counted. That much is certain. After all, training, diet, rehabilitation facilities and all the technologies that assist competitors today were just not available, nor even thought of at the end of the nineteenth century when Wells was writing

Still, it's interesting to conjecture what sports would be like now. One answer to this is: no difference. Women will always come second and, usually, a very poor second to men. An alternative is: they are able to hold their own in virtually every sporting matchup in which raw physical strength is not the decisive factor. That's most sports, of course. I have an answer to the question, but, to arrive at it, I need to explain the guiding logic.

Question: why are there so few women in sports and why they have so little success compared to men? Today's women enter sport in considerable numbers and their achievements are many. But sportswomen are still a numerical minority and, in measurable terms at least, their performances do not match those of men. In terms of earnings, those at the top end, like tennis and golf champions, count their income in millions, but they still don't earn as much as the highest earning male athletes.

Pressed to offer an immediate explanation we might take the simple, but misleading, natural ability argument, suggesting that women are just not equipped to handle sports and are always carrying a physical handicap. But the argument exaggerates physical factors and ignores historical, cultural and psychological processes that either facilitate entry into or halt progress within sport.

We saw in the previous chapter how a scientific discourse about the natural state of the female body gave rise to popular beliefs about the dangerous effects of vigorous exercise on women. For the moment, we should take note of three significant implications of this discourse: (1) women were not regarded as capable either intellectually or physically as men; (2) their natural predisposition was thought to be passive and not active; (3) their relationship to men was one of dependence. All three statements are sexist and have been strongly challenged since the late 1960s, of course, but their impact on the entire character of sport is still evident today.

BOX 9.1 SEXISM

Like racism, sexism is a set of beliefs or ideas about the purported inferiority of some members of the population, in this case, women. The inferiority is thought to be based on biological differences between the sexes: women are naturally equipped for specific types of activities and roles and these don't usually include ones that carry prestige and influence. Much of the scientific support for this type of belief derives from scientific and medical debates from the eighteenth and nineteenth centuries, though even today it manifests in the form of prejudice, discrimination, and stereotyping.

BREAKING THROUGH HISTORY

The first female sports champion was Cynisca, who won the *quadriga* (a chariot with four horses abreast) race in 396 BCE. In their book *Crossing Boundaries*, Susan Bandy and Anne Darden praise Cynisca for owning, training, and entering the horses, but note that "she was barred from attending and competing in any of the Panhellenic festivals of ancient Greece" (1999: 2). "Her victory, then was from a distance, from the outside." Cynisca was acknowledged as the winner of the event but, as Bandy and Darden put it, "Cynisca's experience as an outsider, not a participant, foreshadowed the role of spectator that women were to play for centuries in sport" (1999: 2).

Athletic contests were part of young women's education in ancient Sparta and Crete. In ancient Greek and Roman cultures, women would hunt, ride, swim, and run, but not (usually) engage in combat. Yet, they were not allowed to compete, nor, in Cynisca's case, even watch competitions. Women were assigned roles as spectators and outsiders.

In the medieval period, women were still seen not as active agents but as objects to be placed on a pedestal, protected, and revered and, if necessary, fought for. But, there were exceptions in the Age of Chivalry: some women, certainly noblewomen in parts of Europe, jousted. In his book *The Erotic in Sports*, Allen Guttmann gives examples of women, not only jousting, but fighting men with staffs. He also cites "a titillating contest between two naked women armed with distaffs, one upon a goat, the other on a ram" (1996: 41). And, apparently, footraces between women were common attractions in parts of Europe in the thirteenth century, the condition of entry being that the competitor must be a prostitute (1996: 43).

Typically, these races took place after men's archery contests. It is also probable that women competed in a forerunner of the modern game of darts that involved throwing 18-inch hand weapons at a barrel. Certainly, many women were adept archers and, by the eighteenth century, shot on level terms with men. Peter Kühnst's book *Sports: A cultural history in the mirror of art* includes a plate of a 1787 fencing match between a female and male (1996: 199). Returning to Guttmann, accounts from eighteenth-century England suggest that female pugilism, often of a brutal kind, existed and sometimes resulted in women with faces "covered with blood, bosoms bare, and the clothes nearly torn from their bodies" (1996: 53).

Activities before the nineteenth century, while resembling sports in content, were not strictly sports in the contemporary sense of the word. By the time of the emergence of organized, rule-bound activities we now recognize as sports, women were effectively pushed out of the picture. Frail of body and mind, women could not be expected to engage in any manner of physically exerting activity, save perhaps for dancing, horseriding, bowling, and the occasional game of lacrosse. Out of the discourse on sexual difference (examined in the previous chapter) came an image of the female as very distinct from the male, with totally different propensities and natural dispositions – a sexual bifurcation.

The Victorian ideal of the woman was gentle, delicate, and submissive. Women might let perspiration appear on their alabaster complexions, "glow" during exercise, but should never succeed in sport which was customarily associated with ruggedness, resilience, assertiveness, and a willingness to expend "blood, sweat, and tears." The occasional woman who would attempt to emulate men was risking harm to her body, particularly her reproductive organs.

Women, it was thought, were closer to nature than men: their duties should be confined to those nature conferred on them, like childbearing and rearing. Their role was to nurture. Far from being the product of a male conspiracy, this view was widely held and respected by men and women alike. Accepting that anything resembling strenuous exercise was detrimental to their well-being, women actually contributed, in a self-fulfilling way, to sexist beliefs about them. "The acceptance by women of their own incapacitation gave both a humane and moral weighting to the established scientific 'facts,'" writes Jennifer Hargreaves in her *Sporting Females* (1994: 47).

True, many women were campaigning forcefully and sacrificially in their quest for political suffrage, but their quest did not extend into sports. Women, particularly upper-middle-class women, sat ornamentally as they watched their menfolk participate in sports. But a closer inspection of women involved not so much in competitive sports but in active leisure pursuits, such as rock climbing or fell walking, would have revealed that women were as robust as men and their equals in endurance. Concordia Löfving, of Sweden, and her successor Martina Bergman Österberg, both dedicated themselves to training women in gymnastics during the late nineteenth century.

Pierre de Coubertin, who visualized the modern Olympics, embodied Victorian sentiments when he urged the prohibition of women's participation in sport. The sight of the "body of a woman being smashed" was, he declaimed, "indecent." "No matter how toughened a sportswoman may be, her organism is not cut out to sustain certain shocks" (quoted in Snyder and Spreitzer, 1983: 155–6).

The Olympics were to be dedicated to the "solemn and periodic exultation of male athleticism . . . with female applause as reward," said de Coubertin. Despite his reservations, women were included in the 1900 Olympics, four years after the inauguration, though in a restricted number of events and not in competition with men. (Even as recently as 1980, Kari Fasting notes how women were not allowed to run a 3,000-meter event [just under two miles], the reason being that "it was too strenuous for women" (1987: 362).)

A year after women's inclusion in the Olympics, there was a second, this time relatively unsung trailblazer for female sports. Wealthy Frenchwoman Camille du Gast was the first to challenge male supremacy behind the wheel. In 1901, she competed in the great 687-mile race from Paris to Berlin. Because her 20-horsepower Panhard was the smallest car in the race, she had to start last of the 127 entrants, but went on to finish ahead of many of the larger cars driven by some of Europe's top drivers.

Capital-to-capital races were popular in Europe in the early years of the twentieth century, but they often resulted in deaths and serious injuries and were discontinued, leaving Madame du Gast to pursue a different sport – motor boat racing – though not before she had inspired other women to take up competitive driving. Over the next 30 years, women made their presence felt at all the major European circuits. Gwenda Hawkes, of Britain, in the 1920s, and Australian Joan Richmond and Canadian Kay Petre, in the 1930s, were among the several women to campaign regularly on the racing circuits. Their involvement was curtailed by the cultural pressures on women to return to the home after the World War II effort (1939–45). Women were largely absent from motor racing until their re-emergence in the 1990s, when the social changes made it possible for women to assert themselves in areas, including sports, that had been dominated by men.

Golf was a sport considered appropriate for women, at least ladies (as opposed to working-class women): it made minimal physical demands and could be played in full dress. The languid elegance of swing made the sight of female players pleasing to men's eyes; women were not expected to strike the ball with any force. England's Cecilia Leitch changed all that: she brought to the sport a power and competitive spirit that had previously been associated with only men's golf. In 1910, she played a highly publicized game against Harold Hilton, a renowned amateur who had won two Open championships. Leitch, having practiced hitting balls into the wind, won, and was acclaimed by suffragettes. Although she went on to win many titles, her legacy was the style and sense of purpose she introduced to women's golf.

Style was also a hallmark of Suzanne Lenglen, the French tennis player; though it was the style of her outfits rather than her play that made most impact. Tennis was actually one of the few areas where women were allowed to compete, though only those of means could afford to. As well as full skirts, they wore tight corsets, high-necked, long-sleeved blouses, and boaters. It was a convention of Victorian society that women should appear decorative at all times, of course. Like golf, tennis was a seemly sport for women.

In the early 1920s, Wimbledon was the preserve of the elite, to whom even training was considered vulgar, if not outright cheating. Women were expected to be clothed head-to-foot. Lenglen, who dominated Wimbledon between 1919 and 1926, shocked traditionalists when she appeared in loose-fitting, pleated skirts that finished just below the knee. Defying custom, she swapped the blouse for a tee-shirt-style top that left her arms exposed. She also spurned the corsets and the hats, preferring a bandana not unlike those favored today. In 1931, Lili de Alvarez of Spain caused a rumpus when she appeared in shorts.

Tennis's related sport, table tennis, or ping-pong, was not thought befitting women: too much scurrying about and aggressive bursts of activity. The break-through player in this sport was Maria Mednyanszky, a Hungarian, who became the first women's world champion and went on to win 18 world titles. Her all-backhand style which saw her crowd the table was strikingly different in its day. In the 1920s, Mednyanszky elevated what was once a parlor game into a serious competitive sport for women.

Baseball has never been considered suitable sport for ladies. "Unladylike" is one of those words with a certain ring to it: the many activities to which it refers are to be avoided by any female who favors keeping her dignity. In the nineteenth century, the application of the term to behavior that involved some degree of physical exertion was commonplace, unless females out of necessity performed the behavior. Washing, cleaning, fetching coal, and emptying chambers were activities performed by working-class women, but they could have few pretensions to being ladies. These were typically the kind of women whose daily duties were so draining that they wouldn't have the inclination to add to their physical workload. Gentlewomen and the wives of the emergent bourgeoisie would have time for croquet, tennis, and perhaps archery, but were self-consciously "ladies."

But, as the nineteenth century passed and women were made to play a vigorous role in World War I (1914–18), the flimsy illusion of women as delicate creatures in need of men's protection was challenged. A vocal and effective suffragette movement was prying open new areas in politics and education for women. "Furthermore the 1920s was an era when men feared that the Industrial Age had 'feminized' American culture by sending men to offices and factories and leaving responsibility for socializing young males in the hands of women. Athletics became a way for men to prove their manhood, especially because it "allowed them to pursue 'manly' sporting activities in the company of other men," writes Heather Addison (2002: 31).

The World War II effort also drew women to factories, trucks, and areas of work traditionally reserved for men. The war periods also left a gap in sports that women filled. One famous example of this was the All-American Girls Baseball League, which was started in 1943. The brainchild of Philip K. Wrigley, of the chewing gum company and owner of the Chicago Cubs, the league was made up of women's teams. Major League Baseball's ranks were depleted by the number of male players who were drafted into the armed services in the war effort and it was feared that a substandard competition would drive away fans.

Women had been playing baseball and softball at a competitive level at colleges from at least the turn of the century and possibly before. The war demanded that many women leave their traditionally defined domestic duties and work in factories or other parts of industry; it seemed perfectly consistent for women sports performers to occupy positions previously held by men too. The league's popularity waned when men returned home from war and resumed playing, though attendances were poor in the postwar period. But, there was a legacy, as Susan Cahn points out in her *Coming on Strong: Gender and sexuality in twentieth-century women's sport*: "Women ballplayers offered the public an exciting and expanded sense of female capabilities" (1994: 163). The women's league was the subject of the Penny Marshall film *A League of Their Own* (1992).

While women were allowed to enter Olympic Games from 1900, their track and field competitions were regarded as a sideshow, lacking the intensity and vigor of men's. This perception persisted regardless of the quality of competition. The woman who more than any other was responsible for changing this was Fanny Blankers-Koen, of Holland, who collected four gold medals at the 1948 Olympics when aged 30 and a mother of two.

One of the typical strategies used to discredit female sports performers was to de-feminize them either through innuendo or allegations of homosexuality. In the 1930s and 1940s, Babe Didrikson, the American track and field star and golfer, worked hard at presenting a feminine and heterosexual front in spite of suspicions – suspicions that were not actually confirmed until years later with the publication of her biography, which contained details of her friendship with Betty Dodd. By contrast, Blankers-Koen's public persona was enhanced by her motherhood and, in this sense, she was an important harbinger: a heterosexual woman who could also break world records (and at several events).

Swimming prefigured a later fusion of sports and showbusiness. Johnny Weissmuller, who won a total of five gold medals at the 1924 and 1928 Olympics went on to a successful film career after landing the part of Tarzan in 1932. He played the role 12 times. The man who broke Weissmuller's 400-meter freestyle record at the 1932 Olympics, Buster Crabbe, also played Tarzan, though he became better known for his portrayals of Flash Gordon and Buck Rogers.

Hollywood repeated the success with swimmer Esther Williams who made her debut in the 1942 movie *Andy Hardy's Double Life* and went on to become a fully fledged star, though mostly in swim-related roles. Like Lenglen before her, Williams visibly embodied a popular, male-defined image of femininity. While they had their detractors, both helped change perceptions of women: freer, possessed of great exuberance, and unafraid to display their bodies. Yet, there were other women who were not interested in conforming to men's expectations.

In the 1930s, women from provincial badminton and tennis clubs in New Zealand got together and played rugby. It was planned to coincide with a men's matchup played on the same day and had no serious intentions: it was a sort of exhibition, almost a spoof of the men's game. Although women had played a version of rugby football in Wales in the nineteenth century, the NZ game was the first recorded competition played according to rugby union rules and, as such, was something of a breakthrough for women's sports.

Rugby had traditionally been a byword for macho sport, the type of game for which women were thought ill suited. After the Kiwi women had broken the taboo, women all over the world set about doing likewise. Organized matches in the United States and France started in the 1960s, leagues sprung up in Canada and all over Europe in the 1970s, and a Japanese women's league was established in 1983. The Women's Rugby Union was founded in 1983 in response to growing enthusiasm for rugby from women in Britain. It staged its first World Cup competition in 1991, Wales hosting a 12-nation tournament which was won by the U.S. "Eagles" who beat England in the final game.

BOX 9.2 FANNY BLANKERS-KOEN (1918–2004)

No woman track athlete has managed to match Blankers-Koen's four golds, won in the 100 and 200 meters, 80 meters hurdles, plus 4 × 100 meters relay, at a single Olympics. Yet, as the rules stood in 1948, she was barred from entering more than three individual events. She held world records in high jump and long jump at the time. Blankers-Koen was then 30 and a mother of 2. Her feats, including 20 world records, advanced the cause of women's sport appreciably in the twentieth century. Competing in an era when running 800 meters was considered unsafe for women, Blankers-Koen defied conventional expectations about combining family life with an athletic career. Track and field was an amateur sport in her day. After a promising start in which she appeared at the 1936 Olympics in Berlin, her athletic career was interrupted by World War II, in which her native Holland was occupied by the Nazis. It was not until the 1946 European championships that Blankers-Koen was allowed to compete internationally again; she won 2 golds. After her triumph of 1948, she continued to compete, winning 3 more European titles and setting her final world record, in the pentathlon, in 1951. In 1999, the IAAF honored her as the woman athlete of the twentieth century.

At various points over the past hundred years or more, there have been women or teams that have broken new ground in sport. Whether wittingly, or not, they became feminist emblems. We have surveyed just a few of the more conspicuously influential figures in women sport. But, as the 1960s drew to a close and a vital new form of feminism known as "Women's Liberation" surfaced, sportswomen who were prepared to challenge male traditions were immediately re-cast as political icons. This was not because of who they were, nor even what they did: but, because of the perfect synchronicity of their timing. Of the two most prominent feminist sports icons of the two decades from 1967, one was an averagely talented marathon runner who was never championship material; the other was one of the most consummate champions of her generation. We will examine them and their impact next.

DE-GENDERING BEGINS

On April 19, 1967, a 20-year-old Syracuse University student entered the Boston Marathon as "K. V. Switzer" and was given the number 261. About four miles into the race, a race official noticed that K. V. Switzer was a woman; as women were not allowed in the race, Jock Semple tried to remove her from the field. He was stymied and Switzer went on to complete a historic marathon. Her well-publicized run demonstrated to the world that women were capable of competing in an endurance event that had, up to that point, been officially men-only. Women, it was thought, were not physically able to withstand the rigors of over 26 miles of road running.

The International Olympic Committee did not even include a 1,500-meters event for women until the Munich Olympics of 1972 – the same year as the passing of Title IX. It was 1984, 17 years after Kathrine Switzer's historic run, before there was a women's Olympic marathon. Switzer maintained that she was unaware that women were not legally admitted to the event in the 1960s. She filled out her application form and signed her usual signature, enclosing this with a medical certificate. "I wasn't trying to get away with anything wrong," Switzer later insisted. "I wasn't trying to do it for women's rights." But, her impact on women's sports was immense. Her disingenuous use of initials, she claimed, was due to the fact that: "I dreamed of becoming a great writer and it seemed all the great writers signed their names with initials: T. S. Eliot, J. D Salinger, e.e. cummings, and W. B. Yeats."

Switzer became world famous for her run, which grew in symbolic terms over the next several years. The picture of Semple attempting to abort her run took an almost iconic status: a male vainly trying to thwart a determined woman trying to break into male territory. Switzer ran eight Boston Marathons in total and used her success as evidence in her campaign to have a women's marathon established as an Olympic event. She also approached the cosmetics company Avon, which sponsored a series of high-profile marathons for women in 1978–85.

There is often special providence in an event. Seven months after Switzer's run, the United States National Organization for Women (NOW) under the presidency of Betty Friedan held a conference, which drew publicity from all quarters in its attempt to create an agenda for women's issues. Although it was actually the second annual conference of NOW, the inaugural meeting had nowhere near the same impact. News of the conference reached Britain at a time when legislators were debating reforms and stimulated interest in the incipient women's movement.

Among the eight-point "Bill of Rights for Women" there were demands for the enforcement of laws banning sex discrimination in employment, more day-care centers, equal educational and training opportunities and the right of women to control their reproductive lives. This final demand effectively called for greater contraceptive facilities and for the repeal of laws limiting abortion – demands that were already satisfied, at least partially, in Britain.

The conference functioned as a clarion call for the feminist movement, which was to have resonance in every sphere of cultural life, including sports. Switzer may not have been self-consciously feminist, but, in practical terms, her contribution to the feminist cause was extremely valuable. As well as attracting media attention, she effectively undermined sexist myths about the fragility of women and their inability to complete marathons without incurring physical damage. Because of the circumstances in which she made her run, she was virtually forced into becoming a spokesperson for feminism, a position she filled with growing assurance.

The marathon is rather an instructive case study. Between Briton Dale Greig's first official run in 1964 and 2004, the world record for women improved by over 1 hour 12 minutes. In the same period, the men's record was reduced by 7 minutes 16 seconds. Women are nearly 92.25 percent as fast as men over the distance today, compared to 1925 when they were only 67.6 percent as fast as men.

The moral of this would seem to be that, when women are allowed legally to compete in an event, they can perform at least on comparable terms with men. One wonders how great or small the marathon time differential would be had a women's event been allowed in the Olympics at the time of Violet Percy's first recorded run. "The same as it is today," might be the skeptic's answer, marshaling the support of

BOX 9.3 THE PROGRESSION OF MARATHON RECORDS

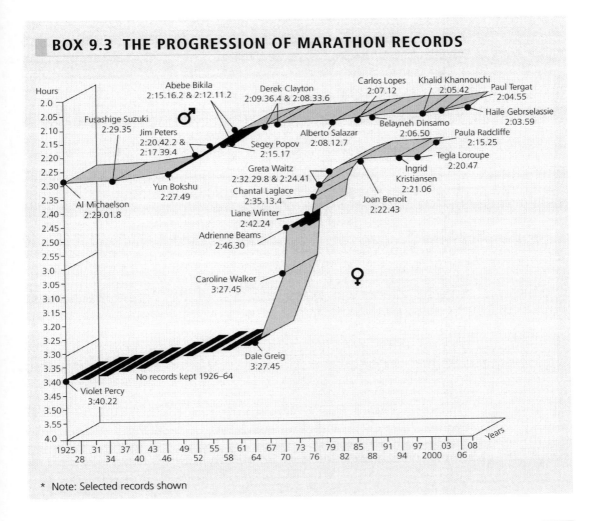

* Note: Selected records shown

significant differences in all women's and men's track records. But marathons, though separate events in major international meets, regularly pitch men and women together and, in this sense, they provide a meaningful guide. From the 1970s and the boom in popular marathons and fun runs, women have mixed with men, competed against them, and on many occasions beaten them. The gap shown in the marathon figure would surely have been narrower had television not intervened and insisted that women started their races prior to the men, thus removing the opportunity for females to test their mettle against the world's fastest males.

It's misleading comparing performances in male and female events, which have developed separately. Tennis has for long been open to at least those women of resources sufficient to afford it. Only in the most playful mixed doubles have they been allowed to confront male adversaries. One-off exhibitions between the likes of an aged Bobby Riggs and Billie-Jean King (and, before her, Margaret Court) owed more to theater than competitive sport, though "The Battle of the Sexes," as it was hailed by the media in 1973, was a victory of sorts for King. But, it was a minor struggle compared to the one she faced eight years later.

"My sexuality has been my most difficult struggle," King reflected on her conflict-strewn career. It had been known in tennis circles that many of the world's top female players engaged in lesbian relationships, though few had either come out voluntarily or been outed by others. In 1981, King's former hairdresser and secretary Marilyn Barnett took legal action against her to ascertain property rights; in other words "palimony." King at first denied that she had an intimate relationship with Barnett, then acknowledged it. The case was thrown out after the judge heard that Barnett had threatened to publish letters that King had written her.

King won her first Wimbledon title in 1966, when aged 22. Her prize was a £45 ($30) gift voucher for Harrods. She went on to win 39 Grand Slam titles. Echoing the remonstrations of "women's liberation," King began demanding prize moneys for women players. Professionalism was already under consideration in tennis. Although ostensibly an amateur (she worked as a playground director), King was "professional" in her approach to the sport. Her preparations were careful and disciplined and her on-court behavior was often belligerent. It was she rather than John McEnroe who introduced the histrionic protests against umpires' decisions. Admired for her ruthlessness in some quarters, crowds turned against her.

King's major professional initiative was to organize an exclusively women's tennis tour which began in 1968. Operating outside the auspices of "official" organizations, King's tour was openly professional in much the same way as pro men's tours such as the Kramer Pro Tour. BJK was able to recruit fellow player Rosie Casals, but few of the other top players. Interestingly, Wimbledon allowed professionals within three months of the start of the King/Casals tour; and the rest of the world's tournaments went open soon after.

Love her, or hate her, there was no denying King became the pulse of women's sport. In 1971, she became the first female athlete to win $100,000, an amount that established her in the top ten earners in sport. King aligned herself with the pro-abortion campaign that had grown in momentum and the Title IX legislation of 1972. And, as if to cement her position as a feminist champion, she negotiated a deal with the Philip Morris tobacco company to set up the women-only Virginia

BOX 9.4 TITLE IX

In 1972, the United States Congress passed Title IX of the Educational Amendments and so instituted a law that would seriously affect all educational institutions offering sports programs. The law specified that: "No person in the United States shall, on the basis of sex, be excluded from participation in, be denied the benefits of, or be subjected to discrimination under any educational program or activity receiving federal financial assistance." At first, this was unpopular among the male-dominated sports officials of schools, colleges, and universities. In 1979, three women athletes from the University of Alaska sued their state for failing to comply with Title IX in providing adequate funding, equipment, and publicity compared to the male basketball team. This set in train more actions, so that, by the end of 1979, 62 colleges and universities were under investigation by the Office for Civil Rights. The resistance to offering equal opportunity to women has continued to the present day.

Slims tour. Virginia Slims cigarettes were marketing in such a way as to appeal to newly independent women.

King had no compunction about accepting sponsorship money from a tobacco company, in fact very few people considered the combination of sports and tobacco sponsorship objectionable. The USTA set up a rival women's tournament, though it was clear that King's ascendancy during 1972–5, her most prodigious championship-winning period, and her sheer notoriety made the Virginia Slims the major attraction in women's tennis.

After BJK's sexual proclivities had become a matter of public record, her finances collapsed: heavy legal bills and the withdrawal of sponsorship money forced her into resuscitating her playing career. Actually, she made quite a fist of her comeback, progressing to a Wimbledon semi-final at the age of 40.

The zeal with which King levered tennis away from the control of men was almost matched by her initial reticence about her homosexuality. Her first ineffectual denials gave way to a reluctant admission of her affair, though she maintained she was not a lesbian. In the 1980s, outings were not yet in vogue. After King, they became commonplace, especially among female tennis players; though, less frequently among male sports performers. (See BURNING QUESTION: Why don't more gay athletes come out? (pp. 171–4))

King won 39 grand slam titles in women's singles, doubles, and mixed doubles, though her efforts off the court and perhaps her personal affairs established her as the most influential female athlete of the late twentieth century. She was also the best known, her status rivaled for a while only in 1976 when the Romanian Nadia Comaneci became the first gymnast to score a perfect 10.00 at the Olympics.

King's contribution not just to women's sport but sport in general is indisputable: she castigated a male dominated institution that had become too comfortable in its disregard of women as serious competitors and, in a sense, acted as a cultural lightning conductor, transmitting the electricity in the atmosphere during the

1970s. She also, perhaps unwittingly, contributed to a stereotype that had circulated since before the days of Didrikson and which would persist for the next several decades: that female athletes were lesbians. We'll return to this later in the chapter.

The question we asked of marathons stands with tennis: how would the world's number one female fare in a head-to-head with the top male had women been playing competitively against men since the 1950s? Again, the skeptic might argue that the results would be basically the same, the support this time coming from the copious amount of evidence on the physical differences between the sexes – that is, differences that do not refer to social or cultural influences.

We can gain some measure of the rate of women's progress in sports over the past couple of decades by glancing back at what was once a standard text, *Social Aspects of Sport*. In the 1983 edition of their book, Snyder and Spreitzer wrote about the types of sport women have been encouraged or discouraged from pursuing. "The 'appropriateness' of the type of sport continues to reflect the tenets of the Victorian ideal of femininity," they wrote (1983: 156). They went on to identify three types, all drawn from a 1965 essay written by Eleanor Metheny, "Symbolic forms of movement."

1   *The categorically unacceptable* includes combat sports, some field events, and sports that involve attempts to subdue physically opponents by body contact, direct application of force to a heavy object, and face-to-face opposition where body contact may occur.
2   *Generally not acceptable* forms of competition include most field events, sprints, and long jump; these strength-related events are acceptable, the authors believe, only for the "minority group" women, particularly, we presume, ethnic minorities.
3   *Generally acceptable* for all women are sports that involve the projection of the body through space in aesthetically pleasing patterns or the use of a light implement; no body contact is possible in sports such as swimming, gymnastics, figure skating, and tennis.

The division suggested continuity between Metheny's original arrangement of the 1960s and the way things stood almost two decades on. Basically, sports that emphasized aesthetics and grace as opposed to strength and speed were acceptable. The rougher pursuits involved head-on collisions were not. Now, the whole formulation seems about as fresh as disco music and mullets. Types (1) and (2) no longer exist. Women compete in every sport, even the ones that were once strictly "men only." Even the once-exclusive male preserve of combat sports has been breached. Professional women cage fighters appear regularly on major MMA bills; Taekwondo, an exhibition event at the 1988 Olympics, was featured as a competitive event in the 2000 games. Women are involved in virtually every form of combat sport.

The inclusion of marathons and 10,000-meter races in the Olympics indicates that women are now seen as capable of handling endurance and strength events as capably as men. Nor are these events dominated by black women. Leadership has circulated among Europeans, Africans and Asians. Of course, black women, especially, have achieved excellence, for reasons we will come to in Chapter 10.

Over the years, women have not achieved as much as men; yet the conclusion that women can't achieve the same levels doesn't follow logically from the original premise that they are biologically different. In fact, it could be argued that, if women had been regarded as equally capable as men physically, then they would perform at similar standards, and that the only reason they don't is because they've been regarded as biologically incapable for so long. In early editions of this book, I included a section on the physical differences between men and women and how these affect sporting performance. I highlighted the areas of skeletal and cardiovascular systems and body composition, comparing the typical women's body with the typical male's.

It would be ridiculous to deny that there are differences, though I now believe they are of significantly less importance than our conceptions about them. As we have discovered in this and the previous chapter, the body is a process, not a thing: it is constantly changing physically and culturally, as do our personal perceptions. Sporting performance promotes changes in terms of muscular strength and oxygen uptake; changes in diet and climactic conditions induce bodily changes too, of course. In our particular culture and this stage in history we understand women and their association with men in one way; in another place and at another time, this relationship may be understood quite differently. It is a matter of convention that we organize sports into women's and men's events, just as it's a convention to award Oscars for the "best actor," a man, and "best actress," a term that's still used to describe the best female actor.

It seems contradictory then to itemize the differences in adipose tissue, respiratory volumes, activity of sweat glands, etc. To do so would fall into the same trap as those who went to so much trouble to "prove" that women were simply not capable of sporting endeavor.

There can be no argument about the fact that the experience of women in sports virtually replicates their more general experience. They have been seen and treated as not only different to men, but also inferior in many respects. Historically, women's position has been subordinate to that of men. They have been systematically excluded from high-ranking, prestigious jobs, made to organize their lives around domestic or private priorities, while men have busied themselves in the public spheres of industry and commerce. Being the breadwinner, the male has occupied a central position in the family and has tended to use women for supplementary incomes only, or, more importantly, as unpaid homeworkers, making their contribution appear peripheral. Traditionally, females have been encouraged to seek work, but only in the short term: women's strivings should be toward getting married, bearing children, and raising a family.

Since the late 1960s and the advent of legal abortion and convenient female contraception, women in the West have been able to exercise much more choice in their own fertility and this has been accompanied by feminist critiques of male dominance. Empirical studies showed wide discrepancies in earning power and this prompted legislation on both sides of the Atlantic designed to ensure equality in incomes for comparable jobs.

One of the loudest cries of feminists was about the abuses of the female body: women, it was argued, have not had control over their own bodies; they have been appropriated by men, not only for working, but for display. "Sex objects" were how many women described themselves, ogled at by men and utilized, often dispassionately. Against this, they recoiled. Even a respectable magazine like *Sports Illustrated*, ostensibly interested in what women do as opposed to what they look like, devotes an annual issue to photographs of women posing in swimwear. And, at practically any tennis tournament, the press will almost certainly gravitate toward the best-looking rather than best player.

Women are underrepresented in politics compared to their total number in the population. They consistently earn less than their equivalent males and are increasingly asked to work part-time. Despite recent changes in the number of places in higher education occupied by women, they tend to opt for subjects (like sociology and art) that won't necessarily guarantee them jobs in science and industry. When they do penetrate the boundaries of the professions they find that having to compete in what is, to all intents and purposes, a man's world, has its hidden disadvantages – what many call the glass ceiling.

Some argue that this state of affairs has been brought about by a capitalist economy geared to maximizing profits and only too willing to exploit the relatively cheap labor of women who are willing to work for less than men, mainly because they've been taught to believe that their work is unimportant and subsidiary to that of men, and that their "real" work is domestic not industrial. Others insist that women's subordination has a larger resonance that transcends any political or economic system and is derived from patriarchy, a state in which men have continually sought to maintain the grip they have had on society and have found the deception that "a woman's place is in the home" a great convenience which they wish to perpetuate. Whatever the motivation behind the successful effort to keep women subordinate, its effects have been felt in sport, where women have for long been pushed into second place.

Women's experience has been one of denial: women simply have not been allowed to enter sports, again because of a mistaken belief in their natural predisposition. Because of this, the encouragement, facilities, and, importantly, competition available to males from an early age hasn't been extended to them. In the very few areas where the gates have been recently opened – the marathon being the obvious example – women's progress has been extraordinary. Given open competition, women could achieve parity with men in virtually all events, apart from those very few that require the rawest of muscle power. The vast majority of events need fineness of judgment, quickness of reaction, balance, and anticipation; women have no disadvantages in these respects. Their only disadvantage is what many people believe about them: in sports as in life, women will simply never catch up.

MEN'S 10 PERCENT ADVANTAGE

Imagine a man attempting to park a car. He looks at the space, then quickly uses mental imagery to assess whether his car will fit, pulls forward, then backs into the spot. A woman's approach to parallel parking is different: she mentally converts the picture into words, estimating the car's length, the size of the space available, then takes time to evaluate whether one will go into the other. At least that is one interpretation of what happens. According to Anne and Bill Moir, men can form a spatial image easily, while women cannot; they need to reduce the situation to a verbal form. And this constitutes a "fundamental" difference between the sexes. As the Moirs put it, "women are generally more verbal, men are more spatial" (1998: 116).

This has clear implications for sports. Able to assess spaces, judge distances and coordinate hand and eye, men are well-equipped to tackle the demands of athletic competition; they are, as the Moirs say, "good with things." Women, by contrast, are not: they are "good with words" – which is not a great deal of help in sports. In their book *Why Men Don't Iron: The real science of gender studies,* the Moirs pull together a number of studies, all of which purport in some way to confirm the view that the difference between males and females is not a matter of cultural convention, nurturing, stereotyping or, indeed, anything to do with the environment.

"The truth is that the brains of the two sexes are organized in different ways, and it is this difference which gives rise to the differences in ability," argue the Moirs (1998: 119). The sources of this structural and chemical difference are biological. A typical six-week-old embryo is exposed to a cascade of genes – a sort of hormonal soup – that affect later sexual characteristics. Many of these characteristics are obvious. Others are not. Marshaling support from researchers into brain functionality and morphology, the Moirs insist that we have neglected more fundamental, though less visible differences between men and women. Brain differences give rise to different abilities. "Real science" shows that permanent differences in brain capacity can never be removed. Men will always be better at some things than women and vice versa.

In itself, this sounds retro, though not especially threatening. After all, some science, as we discovered earlier, has found genes that predispose some individuals toward homosexuality and others that determine that the person will become an alcoholic. We'll also see in Chapter 10 how one theory explains the differences between blacks' and whites' athletic abilities as due to biological differences. These have been controversial because they imply that no amount of social change can do much to alter constant differences and the inequalities that turn on them.

For instance, the Moirs believe that the equal sports facilities mandated by Title IX is the "most ludicrous application" of the doctrine of "absolute equality between the sexes" (1998: 144). On their account, it is not surprising that young men are better at physical events: they are more aggressive, impatient and competitive than young women and they have brains suited to high-speed, high-pressure situations. These are traits likely to be of service in sports. And the reason why men typically have them is not because they are socialized into them; but because they have the right neurological equipment and ten times more testosterone than women. "For boys there should at least be more active and practical learning; more action and stress; a firmer structure and more competitive (virile) tests," they argue, as if confirming that men truly are from Mars (1998: 152).

On this account, the male is an adventure-seeker, attracted to "dangerous sports and physically risky activities involving speed or defying gravity (like parachuting or skiing)" (1998: 161). A woman's "instinct is to avoid risk" (1998: 163). Again differences in the engineering of the brain explain all, including why women underperform compared to men in, well, just about everything that matters, including sports. The Moirs directly answer the question I set at the outset. They cite two marathon times: that of Boston Marathon winners Moses Tanui, 2:7.44, and Fatima Roba, 2:23.21, who were 15.37 apart. "In track and field events, on the whole, males have a 10% advantage, and nature will keep it that way" (1998: 165). In addition to the physical advantages of greater lung capacity, faster metabolic rate and proportionately more hemoglobin, men have a brain with "triggers" that prompt their bodies to pump out more testosterone and "testosterone is to competition what oxygen is to fire" (1998: 166).

This type of argument has been used before, though the Moirs are careful to support their claims with evidence from studies by, among others, Roger Gorski whose studies demonstrated that male rats, if starved of testosterone in fetal stage, becomes female in later sexual orientation (1991). Other researchers who are cited approvingly include Munroe and Govier: their work on sex differences and brain organization indicates that females use both hemispheres of their brains to process language, while men involved in verbal tasks utilize only the left brain (1993). Ernie Govier, in particular, argues that males who are verbally gifted (one assumes he means professors, like himself) have female brain patterns (in his 1998 essay "Brainsex and occupation"). But, the crucial insight about boys doing better than girls in spatial tests comes from Gina Grimshaw who has worked with several co-researchers and discovered a correlation between exposure to testosterone in the womb and "male-typical brain patterns." Interviewed by the Moirs, Grimshaw confirms that male and female brains are neither the same, nor equal and this has consequences for the way boys and girls learn (1998: 125).

Any number of social scientists agree that there are significant learning differences between young males and females, though most would maintain that the differences are due, not to brain organization, but to cultural determinants. The learning process begins from the get-go: the way children are named, dressed, rewarded, punished, taught, in the most general sense, dealt-with – these are all influenced by the different expectations people have about males and females. This does not necessarily mean that the research used by the Moirs is misguided or invalid. It just means that it is less earth shattering than the authors suppose.

Say there are biologically driven differences in brain structure: a sophisticated social scientist will accept the possibility, at the same time adding that the biggest influences on our lives come not from within but from without. Our parents, peers and "significant others" bear heavily on us; the institutions that surround us and enter our consciousness induce us to think and behave in ways that strike us as perfectly natural, but which are, in all probability, social. Differences may appear so deep and distinct that they have sources in biology, but it is often the shaping effect of culture that makes us who we are. Culture has a habit of overpowering biology. And, as culture is constantly changing, so are we.

In other words it doesn't take a sledge-hammer to crack the Moirs' nut: while their argument exaggerates the effects of biological factors, we do not have to reject out of hand the evidence they gather to substantiate it in order to arrive at a different conclusion. Perhaps the reason why men and women are not equal is *not* because they are different biologically, but because they are treated differently. The parallel processes of exclusion that have operated in sports and in society generally should alert us to the possibility that, over time, cultural conventions have a tendency to be accepted as natural inevitabilities.

Women have underachieved in sports relative to men. We have seen how sports were originally intended exclusively for men and how, for most of their history, stayed exactly that. Women were warned off either forcibly or by medical scares and those who did have the temerity to venture toward the male domain were stigmatized as freaks. So, when they eventually broke onto men's turf, female athletes started from a position of weakness. Even then, they were, and are still, reminded by many that they occupy a secondary status. Paid less, with fewer representatives in senior administrative, coaching, media and academic positions, women are left in little doubt that they remain trespassers rather than tenants.

That's history, though. Women are now well ensconced in sports. They may not enjoy the same amount of media coverage as men, nor equitable prize money and they may even endure the sneers of those who continue to look at women's basketball, football, rugby, and so on as inferior versions of men's sports. But women have made their impact felt everywhere. Sports have been emasculated.

SEXUALIZATION

In 1995, the *New York Times* columnist Robert Lipsyte wrote a story on what he called "The emasculation of sports" (April 2, 1995). Lipsyte mourned the passing of "manly virtues of self-discipline, responsibility, altruism and dedication" (1995: 52). "Sports were promoted as the crucible of American manhood . . . after the closing of the Western frontier in 1890, there was no place left for American men to transform themselves into the stalwarts who would keep democracy alive and lead the country to global greatness." Sport effectively became the "new frontier"; an artificial one, perhaps, but one that could still function as a proving ground.

How did women fit into sports? "Not comfortably," answered Lipsyte. As we observed in the previous chapter, those sportswomen who didn't look aesthetically pleasing were assumed to be mannish, or full-on lesbians. Gradually at first, then more quickly from 1980, the role of women – and by implication men – in sports changed. No longer were they mere spectators, subordinates or underachieving versions of their male counterparts. In sports like tennis, golf and track and field, they copied the examples of men, training hard and competing unsparingly. Whether on court, track or anywhere sports were played, women started to "exhibit the same killer instincts that we thought were exclusive to men," as Lipsyte put it.

We might add to Lipsyte's account the impact of a number of gay male athletes who decided to declare their sexual preferences from the 1980s. Tom Waddell, the Olympic decathlete, was one of the first and, while he didn't start an avalanche of disclosures, his example seemed to embolden a few other high profile sportsmen. This further complicated the picture: as well as women who revealed features traditionally associated with manhood, there were male athletes who openly defied older conceptions of red-blooded masculinity.

Coinciding with the changes in gender roles was a change in the institution of sport itself. It became entertainment. Lipsyte believes that sports once had a "moral resonance" in the sense that its central figures were supposed to embody rightness, rectitude and decency. And while he conceded that there is a "rose-colored prism" through which sportswriters view the world, he lamented the disappearance of sports that conveyed key values, such as "honoring boundaries, playing by the rules, working together for a common goal, submitting to authority" (1995: 51).

As sports mutated into pure entertainment, Lipsyte believes that the moral lessons that sports once taught were squeezed out by the mandates of money. People watched sport for amusement, not instruction. They participated for money, not for honor.

Even allowing for the idealized view of sports, Lipsyte's point about the role-reversal, or role-disarrangement (as we might more properly call it) is a strong one. At a time when sport itself was undergoing something of a transformation to an overtly commercial entertainment and shedding whatever moral imperatives it once held, women were forcing their way into the mainstream. They were doing so by demonstrating their ability to compete just as well as their male equivalents. We will cover the process through which sports became a division of the entertainment industry later. For now, we should note the fortune of the timing.

While women were making their presence felt, so sports was becoming showbusiness-like. Women were welcome performers on the new stage. Perhaps they didn't command as much interest as male athletes, maybe interest in some of them centered on features other than their athletic prowess and certainly their achievements in many cases were seen as inferior to those of men. But, sports, to use Lipsyte's phrase, was emasculated: its days as a purveyor of all things fine about manhood were over. No longer the exclusive preserve of men, sports, reluctantly at first, became a gender-neutral arena. And despite all the criticisms that women continued to occupy a marginal status, there could be no denying that every step made by women advanced them toward the center. But, there is a backstory to the progression.

Even as late as 2001, Patricia Clasen was asking the question: "Why is it that women who compete in highly competitive physical activities need to express their femininity so overtly?" Her answer: "Western dualisms have created a paradox for women in athletics . . . women need to emphasize their femininity to the point of commodification" (2001: 36).

Even in the twenty-first century, Clasen believes, "the presence of women threatens definitions of masculinity." She argues that the traditional dualism, in which women are obliged to conform to certain expectations of what it means to be a woman, has created a paradox for women who want to be successful in sports. A paradox occurs when a person or thing conflicts with pre-conceived notions of what is reasonable or possible (the word comes from the Greek *para*, for beyond, and *doxa*, meaning opinion).

With Lipsyte, Clasen agrees that the commercialization of sports has introduced new opportunities and demands, but, where Lipsyte sees change, Clasen sees permanence, especially in "patriarchal discourse." Sports continue to constitute a masculine domain, she argues. As such, successful female athletes feel under pressure to reassert their femininity, aided and abetted by a media ablaze with words and images that accentuate the way an athlete looks rather than the way she performs. In other words, women have submitted to a kind of "commodity feminism" in which they have broken with older notions of womanhood, but surrendered to a new kind; one in which they allow their bodies to be objectified. (Question: don't all athletes allow their bodies to be objectified? After all, when we watch sports, we're admiring bodies in motion.)

Clasen's argument draws support from research, including that of Christeen George *et al.* in 2001: "The media is not necessarily the cause of this marginalization but plays a vital role in its maintenance." Michael Messner agrees that women are marginalized, sexualized, put down or just plain left out of sports coverage. What images of women escape into public discourse "come out of the masculinist cultural center of sports," writes Messner (2002: 93).

From this perspective, there have been two major effects of recent changes in sport: (1) a particular conception of manhood is preserved; (2) women have been sexualized.

BOX 9.5 SEXUALIZE

To make sexual by attributing a sexual role, meaning, or character to someone, or someone's image. Jean M. Grow observes of Anna Kournikova in the 1990s: "In her role as product and cultural endorser Kournikova prominently displays her highly sexualized femininity over her less competitive athletic abilities, allowing her to reap enormous financial benefits." In a related context, Christa Williams writes: "Increased exposure to over sexualized and underfed images in the media is correlated with increased dieting and body-image problems in girls." Sexualization is the act of sexualizing. According to Victoria Carty, its purposes are both cultural and political: "The sexualization of female athletes . . . is used to maintain patriarchal arrangements and serve the interests of male-dominated structures."

Critics line up to admonish the media, female athletes, or, more usually, both. Jennifer Knight and Traci Giuliano blast the media for "emphasizing their [women's] relationships with men" in the media's coverage of athletes (2003: 272). "This pattern is not frequently found in coverage of male athletes," comment the authors, presumably not intending the gay innuendo.

According to Knight and Giuliano, being a successful athlete contradicts a woman's prescribed gender role; women are required to "overcompensate for their masculine behavior on the field by acting in traditionally feminine ways off the field" (2003: 273).

Victoria Carty complains about women: "The willingness of athletes to display their bodies and accentuate feminine traits and heterosexuality takes away from their athletic achievement and status as athletes" (2005: 134).

The title of Carty's analysis carries her question: "Textual portrayals of female athletes: Liberation of nuanced forms of patriarchy?" She argues that women have made considerable advances in sport and the media, in which she includes the advertising industry, print media and tv. This is 'traditional male territory" and, as women encroach, "the issue of how gender is used to appeal to consumers becomes complex."

Carty explains that some sportswomen have been happy to "use their recognition as athletes for personal benefit, not for athletic skill but because men find them attractive." Others have tried to foreground their strength and athletic ability. The subtlety of Carty's argument is in showing how the media have responded by redefining the meaning of athletic prowess: "Muscles come to symbolize sexual attractiveness and beauty rather than power . . . female athleticism is redefined as sexy or romantic and intended for men's pleasure rather than for women's health, enjoyment, or empowerment" (2005: 146).

Rather than accusing women of caving in to men's salacious demands or blaming the media for exploiting helpless women, Carty suggests an adaptation in which "men have responded to changing notions of femininity by using institutional arrangements that they control to further feminize athletes" (2005: 145).

So men are still behind connivance though women sometimes "explicitly promote and play into the image of the glamorous sexy, and objectified female body to gain financial rewards and prestige" (2005: 140). She reminds readers that Venus Williams' contract with Reebok was worth $40 million. Does this mean women are accepted on athletic ability solely, exclusively, and entirely? Not quite. For a start, no woman has cracked the top 20 highest earners in sport. And besides: there is always Maria Sharapova, who won three tennis grand slams between 2004 and 2008, but then slipped out of the world's top 60. Even without tournament wins in years, Sharapova's looks secured her contracts with, among others, TAG Heuer, Tiffany & Co. and Sony Ericsson that earned her an annual income of $20 million, making her the top female earner in world sport.

Clearly, money and status have a certain empowering potential, but they're earned at a cost: high-achieving athletes, wittingly or not, become objects of the "male gaze," and perhaps fantasy figures: "Complicity reinforces the system of male domination through the objectification and exploitation of women" (2005: 134).

Carty's use of "complicity" tells us that she suspects female sports stars of being in cahoots with the media, ad agencies and the corporations that pay them big money. But there is one ad campaign in particular that convinces her that there is an alternative: it was run by Nike on U.S. television in 2000 and featured women in a variety of sports, all competing rather than posing. Carty's reading of its message is: "Women do not have to give up their feminine appearance or qualities to be fierce competitors. And femininity need not neutralize their athletic prowess" (2005: 151).

This is an interesting conclusion, especially when Carty adds: "This ad perhaps best expresses how women can take advantage of sport for their own personal benefit . . . women are reclaiming their own bodies" (2005: 151). It's interesting because another study, this time by Darin Arsenault and Tamer Fawzy in 2001, examined Nike's advertising and came to similar conclusions.

Nike is, of course, a corporation intent on retaining market leadership and maximizing its profits. Women present a sizeable and growing portion of its potential market; so advertising has to reflect this. Arsenault and Fawzy argue that: "Nike attempted to offer women the opportunity to throw off the chains of patriarchy through its provision of a vision of a woman as athletic and competitive, yet nurturing, capable of change, and cognizant of her role as a link between past and future" (2001: 74).

Remember, advertising is a key part of the media that many scholars insist is keeping women at the margins. In this study, representations of women break violently with the tradition that portrays women as "soft, effeminate, yielding, compliant and submissive to men" and show them instead in sex role-reversals. Women are authority figures. Yet the authors believe Nike was not bold enough: its use of symbols and images, such as flowers, plaid backgrounds and smiley faces, "are indicative of women's rather than men's experiences," argue Arsenault and Fawzy.

Jean M. Grow's study added insider detail to the story of Nike's advertising. She reports that, during the 1990s, an advertising team composed largely of women, "challenged social constructions of gender and sports" (2008: 312).

But there was resistance to the change. Even though Nike executives kept "wanting the women's ads to remain hegemonicly [sic] feminine" and accused their advertising team of "pinkifying the Nike parent brand," those responsible for advertising pushed ahead with a different brief. As Grow puts it: "The creatives persevered as a collective unit, reflecting the actions of a feminist organization" (2008: 337–38).

Nike is very much part of the transformation of sports since the 1980s. It has played no small part in bringing about many of the changes that has turned sports into popular entertainment. Women's encroachment on the inner circle of sports has not only been affected by this transformation: it has assisted it. As an influential organization, Nike has cultivated a market among women and then exploited that market. Its advertising has reflected this. Envisioning women as strong, vigorous, formidable and, in almost every way, the equals of male athletes suggests symmetry. The authors of all three studies criticize the advertising's construction of women, positive as it is in many respects, for failing to disconnect it from its patriarchal past, yet spot the changes initiated by Nike's advertising.

One odd aperçu in Carty's analysis is: "Stereotypes about female athletes being lesbians are pervasive in the world of sport" (2005: 143). How does Carty square this with her main argument that woman athletes are sexualized for the delectation of men? She maintains that the media have made efforts to mask homosexuality among female athletes and seize every opportunity to emphasize heterosexual qualities. Presumably, sexualizing women can be understood as part of this effort. But, if images of female athletes do, as Carty and several others stress, invoke sexual ideas and feelings, why should lesbian stereotypes be pervasive? Remember: the stereotype has circulated since the late nineteenth century and has been given periodic boosts, however unwillingly, by Billie-Jean King and, before here, Babe Didrikson.

The reason for the stereotyping is summed up by Jan Boxill, who recognizes the significant inroads made by women in sport over the past few decades and observes: "Men see this as threatening, as women wanting to be men" (2006: 123).

Even allowing for some exaggeration in Boxill's argument, there is empirical support for the impact of this kind of perception. Kerrie J. Kauer and Vikki Krane's 2006 study "'Scary dykes' and 'feminine queens'" highlights the contradictory effects of being involved in sports: feeling empowered, while constantly reminded of their "otherness" – that they didn't conform with popular expectations of what females should be. (The Other – usually with a capital "O" – is a term used in philosophy, sociology, cultural studies, and cognate disciplines to describe a group that is different from or opposite to oneself and so provides a kind of identity reference check for what one is *not*. Otherness is the overall quality attributed to the group.)

Kauer and Krane are unequivocal in their conclusion: "A common stereotype is that female athletes are lesbians . . . negative stereotypes about female sportswomen keep all women in sport in subordinated positions" (2006: 43). Not quite all: the sportswomen who consent to being sexualized in exchange for money would probably not see themselves as subordinated – though Kauer and Krane might respond by arguing they rank lower than their equivalent males, and generally occupy supporting roles.

So, where does this leave women in sport today? Are they sexualized, or stereotyped? There's empirical support for both, leading us to the conclusion that there is a coexistence of popular representations. Most conspicuously, there are apparently heterosexual women, muscular, athletic, and fit (in the sense of being in vigorously good health); less obviously, there are, according to the research, widely circulating images of female athletes as, to use Kauer and Krane's terminology, "scary dykes." There is one more indisputable fact we have to add: there is another group of female athletes who are seen as neither bootylicious nor butch – just brilliant.

In the twenty-first century, awareness of the likes of Michelle Wi and Sanya Richards ranked with that of Condoleezza Rice or J. K. Rowling. They were known for their accomplishments, not their appearance or sexual proclivities.

The media haven't quite managed to suppress their tendency to drool over model-lookalikes, with or without athletic ability. And the day when women's sports command equal coverage with men is still some way off. Yet, change is undeniable. Well, perhaps not undeniable. For instance, in the 2009 edition of his *Sports in Society: Issues and controversies*, Jay Coakley argues, "sports celebrate a form of masculinity that marginalizes women and many [gay] men" (2009: 272).

In 1978, when the first edition of Coakley's text was published, perhaps. But surely not in 2009? Sports has witnessed profound changes since the 1980s, driven by the conversion of competition into entertainment, the pressure of the women's movement and perhaps even the redundancy of sports as a way of authenticating manhood. Some female athletes are given the media treatment and addressed as if they were just models; some will even willingly play along with the sexualization, happy to reap the material rewards. Others may inspire age-old stereotypes about lesbians, though one wonders why, after the pioneering examples of Billie-Jean King in the 1970s and Martina Navratilova in the 1980s, why any lesbian sportswoman would want to hide behind a heterosexual pretense. Unless, of course, they wanted to endear themselves to the media and engage in what Carty calls "complicity."

Where did that leave masculinity? After all, if sport was originally conceived as a place where a man could prove himself, what should be made of the growing number of women who were proving themselves? If the incursions of women into sport disarranged conventional notions of femininity, then notions of masculinity were thrown into corresponding disarray.

CALLING MANHOOD INTO QUESTION

A practice predicated on manhood, patriarchy, and myths about women has a lot to answer for. Its only excuse is that it's given a lot of people an awful lot of pleasure. Sport never pretended to be an equal opportunities pursuit. It never needed to: for the largest part of its history, it was a realm populated by men, all eager to test their spirit against another's and, in the process, exhibit their manly fortitude. Up to the mid-1980s and perhaps beyond, it would have been unimaginable to allow women to compete at the same kind of level as men. Don't forget: there was no women's marathon event in the Olympics until 1984. Once the demon of women's frailty had been exorcised, sports began its own form of spiritual cleansing, starting with the problem of masculinity.

BOX 9.6 INTEGRATED SPORTS

While the physical advantage men are said to have over women has been exaggerated, differences in strength and power preclude women from competing head-to-head in some sports, such as weightlifting. In most sports, however, physical differences are less important than skill. How do women fare in integrated sports?

- *Equestrianism*: Women and men compete on equal terms in a completely integrated sport. Whether in show jumping, three-day eventing, dressage, enduring and driving disciplines, women regularly beat men.
- *Sailing*: There is integration in solo ocean racing, though, since 1988, women compete in a separate category in Olympic sailing events. These include Ellen MacArthur and Emma Richards
- *Motor racing*: Although there are no rules that prohibit mixed races, there are no female Formula One drivers. The Italian Lella Lombardi is the only woman to have scored points in an F1 race, the Spanish Grand Prix, of 1975.
- *Snooker*: In the early 2000s, the women's number one, Kelly Fisher, played on the men's Challenge Tour, which is one level below the main tour. Fisher was not ranked among the world's leading 100 men.

Several others sports allow integrated competition, though not at all levels. For example, Margaret Thompson Murdoch was the first woman to win an Olympic shooting medal in 1976, though most Olympic events are now segregated. There also separate Olympic events for women and men in bowls, though, at club level, the sport is completely integrated. Similarly, in darts, women compete with men at club level, but have their own major events.

Actually, there is no problem of masculinity as such: only when masculinity is asserted in distinction to femininity and assumes a superiority, often of an aggressive kind – as many considered it did in and through sports. The particular conception of masculinity propagated in sports was that of the macho male, red in tooth and claw, antagonistic toward gays, contemptuous of women, and robust in the defense of a rigid separation of gender roles. At least, that's one version of masculinity. There are many, many others. In his book *From Chivalry to Terrorism*, the historian Leo Braudy spends 550 pages detailing the various conceptions of what it is to be a man; he even names some of them, "the adventurer," "Don Quixote," the patriot," "the pirate" (one doubts if he had Johnny Depp's mascara'd Captain Jack Sparrow from the *Pirates of the Caribbean* movies in mind). There's no single type of masculinity: there are innumerable versions.

"The sports hero" is one of Braudy's types and this is the version that's typically wheeled out by critics like Mariah Burton Nelson, whose book *The Stronger Women Get, the More Men Love Football* proposed that sports are like incubators for misogyny, and Robert Connell, who, in his *Masculinities*, argued that sports is a leading definer of masculinity in western culture. Admittedly both books were published in 1994 and have self-obsolesced more quickly than their authors would have wished for. Yet, they epitomized a style of thinking that was popular in the 1990s, one that visualized sports as a monolith on which there hung a WOMEN NOT WELCOME sign.

Also written in 1994 was an essay by David Whitson in which a rather different vision emerged. According to Whitson, a variety of forms of masculinity and femininity coexisted in sports, especially in newer events, such as mountain bike racing, snowboarding and skateboarding. Older macho conceptions surfaced in more overtly physical sports, including collision sports, but even these were to change as the end of the millennium approached.

Forms of masculinity that "explicitly critiqued the more traditional form" became apparent in skateboarding, as Becky Beal explained in her "Alternative masculinity and its effects on gender relations in the subculture of skateboarding" (1996). This was complemented by the "ambivalent masculinity" discovered in windsurf culture by Belinda Wheaton in 2000.

"Masculinities as forged in boxing are contradictory, frail, vulnerable and fragmented, all of which suggest counter intuitive readings of the hegemonic traditional masculinity," writes Kath Woodward, whose research suggests: "At times it appears to be a transgressive masculinity . . . that demonstrates vulnerability and ambivalence" (2004: 16).

Even in men's hockey, a form of masculinity "predicated on a hard-hitting, physically aggressive game. . .for at least 50 years," Kristi A. Allain discovered change in 2008. The traditional masculinity has survived challenges to its hegemonic position in the past and, on Allain's account, "privileges particular expressions of hegemonic masculinity while simultaneously marginalizing alternative masculinities, which are considered feminine" (2008: 463).

But those alternative conceptions are at least present and will continue to challenge the form that dominates hockey culture, shaping how "players learn to think about the world" and, presumably, their own identities.

All these studies found incongruities, Beal especially noting the creation of different roles for men and women. This finding was echoed in a research review by Lee McGinnis *et al.* in 2003. "Gender significations are less limiting in some ways

BOX 9.7 CRISIS IN MASCULINITY

According to many writers, men have been in crisis since the late nineteenth century. As the factory system became more dominant, fewer men owned their own businesses or controlled their own labor. Women began to enter the job market in increasing numbers. Fears that culture was becoming "feminized" were stoked up when, following the end of World War II, women receded from the workplace, leaving them the responsibility for socializing their young. Participation in sports has been seen as one response to the crisis: it allowed men to prove their value in the company of other men. The newer crisis appeared in the wake of the women's movement, when displays of manhood considered appropriate in the post-war period were rendered inappropriate. Overtly aggressive, dominant, and emotionally repressed behavior was derided, if not stigmatized, reducing men to what Stephen Whitehead and Frank Barrett, in their *The Masculinities Reader*, describe as a "confused, dysfunctional and insecure state."

than they were in the past," concluded the research team; but, "gender still matters" (2003: 7).

True. And it should, argue some writers, including Susan Faludi, who, in 1999, wrote of an unseen war on men. Traditional codes of manhood are no longer honored, observed Faludi. Men have been, as the title of her book, *Stiffed*, suggests.

Faludi's argument, in a way, complements Lipsyte's statements about the emasculation of sports. Both writers agree that the arrival of an age when the media and entertainment industries predominated effectively ended the traditional gender division. There were other factors, of course; but the upshot was that "ornamental culture," as Faludi calls it, called for less doing and more showing. Men were once doers: those who were honored were astronauts, military heroes, even breadwinners. Now, "we are surrounded by a culture that encourages people to play almost no functional roles, only decorative or consumer ones." Culture has re-shaped our conception of manhood to the point where men are valued less on their "internal qualities." More on their appearances.

This has led to what we called role-disarrangement. Men are eagerly rushing into roles that were once designated as trivializing and humiliating – when women performed them. Think about sportsmen: they have no hesitation in appearing in photoshoots, on catwalks, in celebrity magazines, none of which has any interest in athletic ability. They flex their biceps, curl their lips, smile or sneer for the cameras. They affect a gangsta attitude or a glamour boy pose and purr "because I'm worth it" in L'Oreal commercials. In other words, they exhibit the same traits that used to be attributed to women. Far from resenting the idea of being objectified, men seem to love it. Women rebelled against what used to be the "feminine mystique"; men show no such insurgency. Perhaps it's because the women's movement had a clearly defined enemy in the form of men. If men have been destabilized and reduced to a state of confusion, they do not seem to mind. This seems to be a case of "Crisis? What crisis?"

So, how do we distil manhood in this era of ornamentation? Is it personified in Dwayne Johnson a.k.a. The Rock? Michael Urie ("Marc" from *Ugly Betty*), Seth Rogen? Sacha Baron Cohen? The question might once have been answerable; now it's hardly worth asking. Mainly because of the reasons we have covered earlier. Stephen Whitehead and Frank Barrett summarize them:

> A combination of, firstly, rampant, soulless consumerism; secondly, women's (feminism's) successful assault on male bastions of privilege; and, thirdly, more widespread social and cultural disapproval of traditional displays of masculinity.
>
> (2001: 6)

Sports may well have been emasculated, as Lipsyte suggested. Not castrated, nor sterilized, nor even weakened. Emasculated in the sense that the all-male preserve where misogynist values and sexist assumptions were allowed to go unchecked has been replaced. Not that gender divisions have been wiped away. But, there has been change and the likelihood is that change will continue, though perhaps not soon enough for women in sport.

OF RELATED INTEREST

Sport and the Physical Emancipation of English Women, 1870–1914 by Kathleen McCrone (Routledge, 1988) looks at the entry of women into sport during the Victorian period. It was a crucial time in the development of sport and also one in which myths about women abounded. At public schools, the new sports with rules and timescales were meant to instill character and decisiveness fitting for future purveyors of the Empire. Women were not seen as purveyors. There are several other histories of women in sports, including *Coming on Strong: Gender and sexuality in twentieth-century women's sport* by Susan K. Cahn (Free Press, 1994) and *Feminism and Sporting Bodies* by M. Ann Hall (Human Kinetics, 1996).

"The emasculation of sports" by Robert Lipsyte was published in the *New York Times* (April 2, 1995, section 6) and might profitably be read in conjunction with Susan Faludi's *Stiffed: The betrayal of the modern man* (Chatto & Windus, 1999). Together they advance an image of today's male, in and out of sports, under pressure. "Men aren't simply refusing to 'give up the reins of power,' as some feminists have argued," asserts Faludi. "The reins have already slipped from most of their hands."

The Masculinities Reader edited by Stephen Whitehead and Frank Barrett (Polity, 2001) is a collection of essays predicated on the view that masculinity and indeed gender are defined and sustained by culture, rather than biology. The book contains a short chapter on "how contemporary black males utilize sports as one means of masculine self-expression within an otherwise limited structure of opportunity"; it's complemented by Kenneth MacKinnon's *Representing Men: Maleness and masculinity in the media* (Hodder Arnold, 2003).

"Gender typing of sports: An investigation of Metheny's classification" by Brenda A. Riemer and Michelle E. Visio (in *Research Quarterly for Exercise and Sport*, vol. 74, no. 2, June, 2003) revisited Metheny's postulates nearly forty years after the original publication. The twist in this research was that they asked schoolchildren to assess Metheny's formulation. "Although we may see girls participating in what Metheny viewed as masculine sports, the opposite does not seem to be true for boys and feminine sports," the authors concluded, adding that "this does not mean that girls and women are socially accepted when they participate in masculine sports . . . but they see the opportunity to participate."

"Textual portrayals of female athletes: Liberation of nuanced forms of patriarchy?" by Victoria Carty (in *Frontiers*, vol. 26, no. 2, 2005) analyzes how female athletes have been turned into "the ideal image of male fantasy." Carty argues: "Women do not have to give up their feminine appearance or qualities to be fierce competitors. And femininity need not neutralize their athletic prowess."

"'We be killin' them": Hierarchies of black masculinity in urban basketball spaces" by Matthew Atencio and Jan Wright (in *Sociology of Sport Journal*, vol. 25, 2008) offers a contrast to the studies quoted earlier in the chapter. Unlike many sports in which "ambivalent" masculinities are created, this study examines local basketball and how engaging with it offers African Americans the opportunity to construct "a meaningful sense of self". In the study, young men create a traditional "black masculinity." In an aside, the authors remark: "There were, however, also instances in which these young men took up alternative masculinities," though they do not develop this point.

ASSIGNMENT

You are H. G. Wells and it's 1890. Your publishers have asked you to write about the future. In particular, they want you to turn your attention to the pursuits that are currently occupying the population: athletic competitions. You know from your time traveling that these are set to become immensely popular in the coming century. Your publishers believe that the suffragettes will go from strength to strength and one of their demands will be for open competition, with men and women going head-to-head in all the major sports. Write the story, plotting the progress of women and men to the present day. Remember: sports authorities do not recognize separate gender-based events. Extrapolate creatively from known evidence, which may be drawn from sports and social histories, using statistics where appropriate.

CHAPTER 10

Behind on Points

KEY ISSUES

▌ How come blacks' success in sports reflects failure in other parts of society?

▌ What is the difference between a black shoeshine boy and a black sprinter?

▌ When can we expect more black managers, coaches, and administrators?

▌ Where do black people turn for inspiration?

▌ Why are we still discussing the issue of race in sports?

▌ . . . and who was Tom Molineaux?

A MILLION DREAMS, ONE STAR

April 13, 1997, Augusta, Georgia. Tiger Woods, a 21-year-old golf prodigy becomes the youngest player to win the Masters. Woods is instantly and spectacularly transformed into a symbol of integrated America. Fifty years after Jackie Robinson's breakthrough into major league baseball, Woods breaches the final bastion. Golf, for long a stalwart institution of segregation, has finally found a champion who embodies the spirit of multiculturalism. The timing of Woods' valorization is especially pertinent: it follows a sequence of racially motivated incidents, the most infamous of which is the Rodney King beating in 1991, though the Ku Klux Klan's torching of a black church in South Carolina in 1995 is a less publicized though no less repellent episode.

June 7, 1998, Jasper, Texas. James Byrd Jr, a 49-year-old African American, is walking home from a niece's bridal shower. A pickup truck driven by a white male and carrying two other white men draws alongside him. Byrd accepts a ride and jumps inside the vehicle. But, instead of driving Byrd home, the men take him to a wooded area, beat him, chain him behind the truck and speed down a bumpy road, dragging his body. Byrd's severed head, neck and right arm are discovered about a mile from where his shredded torso is dumped. A trail of blood, body parts and personal effects stretches for two miles.

Two pieces of history, one remembered, the other forgotten. Tiger Woods went on to become one of the most celebrated and highest earning athletes ever. James Byrd Jr is virtually forgotten. But both in their own ways affect our understanding of racism. When the Byrd killing made news, it came toward the end of a torrid period in which the Rodney King beating and the riots following the acquittal of Los Angeles police officers charged with the offense and the torching of a black church in South Carolina by the Ku Klux Klan all served to remind the world that racism in America was very much alive. Following the Byrd murder, the innocent Haitian named Amadou Diallo was shot by New York police officers. It was an incident that had similarities to Britain's Stephen Lawrence case, which revealed the indifference of police to the killing of a young black man by racist whites.

Remembering Woods, the way he emerged, the manner in which he dominated golf, and the style with which he became one of the most visible men alive, almost made it possible to forget the unpleasant realities of race. Like Michael Jordan before him, he earned more money, more respect and as much if not more kudos than any athlete in history. He also inspired the dreams of countless others. But, are they realistic dreams, or just dangerous fantasies? The vast majority of those who try to emulate Woods will fall a long way short and may sacrifice what might otherwise have been serviceable ambitions in their quests.

In this chapter, I'll address not only this question, but, perhaps more importantly, why we should be asking it at all. After all, whose business is it if someone wants to channel all his or her energy into the pursuit of an ideal? Sports themselves thrive off the zeal and ambition of millions of "wannabes," the vast majority of whom never approach the level where they can make a living, let alone a fortune, out of sports. Tens of thousands of young African Americans and African Caribbeans who grew up in American and British inner cities in the final three decades of the twentieth century are now reflecting on a sports career that never was. They, like literally millions before them, had watched television, listened to radios and read newspapers and magazines and logged onto to internet. There was the evidence before their eyes: Kobe Bryant, Floyd Mayweather, Ashley Cole, black sports stars lauded all over the world, winning titles, medals, and making the kind of money that qualifies you for a place in *Fortune* magazine. These and other stars supplied evidence that sport was like Eldorado – a place abounding in gold. And unlike many other areas, it was easily accessible to black people.

Back in 1968, the American sports writer Jack Olsen speculated that the pursuit of a career in sport would be just as futile as searching for the city of gold and perhaps more destructive: "At most, sport has led a few thousand Negroes out of the ghetto. But for hundreds of thousands of other Negroes it has substituted a meaningless dream."

While the time and effort demanded in trying to become another Bryant or Cole is so great that it may ruin a young person's prospects of doing anything else, the actual chances of emulating them are infinitesimally small. Failed sports performers have quite frequently destroyed any other career possibilities they might have had. No sports performer can avoid making sacrifices; the black athletes' sacrifices are just greater than most.

But, the gains are greater too, the reader might argue. Even a so-so career in sports can be lucrative when compared to the yield of an everyday job. Twelve or fourteen years in professional sport and an athlete can look forward to a comfortable retirement free of the irksome financial details that bother most of us. And, during that dozen years, the celebrity status that comes as part of the package,

Professional sport is such a lucrative area, nowadays, that even modest success earns a lot of money. And, no matter how you interpret the evidence, many blacks achieve success relative to the number of blacks in the total population. African Americans account for little more than 13 percent of the total U.S. population; African Caribbeans are, by the largest estimate, only 4 percent of the British population. Yet, the NBA consistently has a 80–90 percent majority of black players, and about 1 in 5 professional soccer players in Britain is black. Fifty percent of world boxing champions at any one time are black. We could marshal other figures to support what is an obvious fact: black people overachieve in sports; far more leave sport in failure and disappointment. We need to uncover some of the processes at work beneath these facts.

The experience of women as we covered in Chapter 9 contrasts with that of black people: while women have been underrepresented in sport's top flight for most of the twentieth century, there has been a preponderance of black champions in certain sports. There are also comparisons: being minorities, both have marginal positions, meaning that they are largely excluded from many of the key areas of society. Neither features prominently in politics, the professions, or other areas of society where important decisions are made that affect people's lives. (I'm using "minority" here not in a statistical sense, but in terms of capacity to influence the course of social and political events.)

The exclusion of both minorities is usually the product of an "-ism": as blacks are discriminated against and their accomplishments diminished through racism, so women are prohibited from competing on equal terms with men through sexism. Both remain on the underside of a lopsided structure of inequality and this has affected the involvement of both in sport in quite different ways. We've already dealt with the ways in which women have been pushed to the margins of society and how they've responded to this, particularly in sports. The focus in this chapter is on the experience of black people.

ONCE A SLAVE . . .

There is quite a story to blacks' involvement with organized sport in the West. It begins in the late eighteenth century during the American War of Independence, when General Percy of the British forces captured the Virginian town of Richmond. Impressed by the fighting prowess of a slave who worked on the plantations there, Percy took Bill Richmond – as he named him – under his tutelage and groomed him for prizefighting. While it could not have been an easy life, prizefighting had its perks (like extensive travel in Europe) and must have seemed far preferable to plantation work. Richmond was something of a prototype, his modest success encouraging slave owners and merchants to scour for potential fighters whom they might patronize.

The celebrated Tom Molineaux was one such fighter. Once a slave he was taken to England and trained by Richmond, eventually winning his freedom. Molineaux built on his predecessor's success, rubbing shoulders with the nobility and generally mixing with the London beau monde. It was in his classic fight with all-England heavyweight champion Tom Cribb that he created his niche in sports history. Molineaux was beaten and died four years later. He is the subject of George MacDonald Fraser's historical novel *Black Ajax*, which takes the form of eyewitness "reports" of the epic fight in 1811.

Peter Jackson was born on the Caribbean island of St Croix and traveled to Sydney and San Francisco before settling in England in the late nineteenth century. He, more than any pugilist of his day, embraced fame, though world champion John L. Sullivan's refusal to fight him denied him the ultimate title. Yet his decline was abrupt and he became a habitual drinker and was made to play in a stage version of Harriet Beecher Stowe's antislavery classic *Uncle Tom's Cabin*.

Some slaves continued to leave America to campaign as prizefighters in Europe, but most were pitted against each other locally. In the years on either side of Emancipation in 1865, African American men tried their hands in sports besides pugilism; they were most successful at horseriding and baseball. In the latter, they weren't permitted to play with or against whites. Their response was to form their own competitions known as Negro Leagues. Players from Cuba, Puerto Rico, and the Dominican Republic joined Negro League teams, though many were allowed to play for the all-white leagues, the most powerful of which was Major League Baseball (MLB), the framework of which had been established in 1903.

Ninety-eight years after the first Molineaux–Cribb clash, a black man ascended to the apogee of sporting achievement. John Arthur Johnson in 1908 challenged and beat Tommy Burns, a white man, to become the heavyweight boxing champion of the world. Fighting as "Jack Johnson," he broke the "color line" which segregated blacks from whites in all areas, including sport. In fact, after Johnson eventually lost the title in 1916, the line was redrawn and no black man was allowed to fight for the world title until 1937 when Joe Louis became champion. From that point until the end of the century, only three white boxers interrupted a sequence of black heavyweight champions.

Johnson and, in an entirely different way, Louis, were black icons of their day, Johnson especially cultivating a reputation as a "bad nigger," a moral hard man who, as Lawrence Levine puts it in his *Black Culture and Black Consciousness*, "had the strength and courage and ability to flout the limitations imposed by white society" (1977: 420).

Johnson was something of a celebrity before his time: he dressed expensively, traveled in style and, to the anger of many whites, enjoyed the company of white women. He was champion when the Ku Klux Klan was in its ascendancy and blacks were lynched for far lesser deeds than consorting with white females.

BOX 10.1 JACK JOHNSON: THE FIRST SPORTS ICON

Johnson (b. Galveston, Texas, 1878–1946) was perhaps the first ever athlete to warrant the now overused appellation icon. Lawrence Levine observes that he was "not merely a fighter but a symbol," meaning that, for black Americans, he represented them. Whites, on the other hand, loathed Johnson for winning the world heavyweight title. Former champion James J. Jeffries was forced out of retirement in an unsuccessful bid to win back the world title. When Johnson beat him, there were riots in many parts of the United States. Johnson was a controversial champion. It was widely believed that Johnson had been refused passage on the British passenger liner *Titanic* that was supposedly unsinkable but which struck an iceberg in the North Atlantic on its maiden voyage in 1912. There were 1,490 deaths, but Johnson was spared and this enhanced his status even further. In 1913, Johnson was found guilty of transporting women across state lines for immoral purposes and was made to flee to Canada and, later, Europe, Mexico, and South America. After losing his title to Jess Willard in Havana in 1915, Johnson returned to the United States and served 10 months in jail. He fought the last of his 112 professional bouts in 1928.

Far from being "bad," Louis, by contrast, was obsequious, apolitical and exploitable – as his poverty, despite vast ring earnings, demonstrates. He was hailed as a "credit to his race," a backhanded compliment during the 1930s and 1940s. Yet, he too was a potent symbol for black Americans who were short of heroes or role models on whom to style their own lives. Both he and Johnson were anomalies: conspicuously successful black men in a society where success was virtually monopolized by whites.

The other outstanding black sportsman of this period was Jesse Owens, who won gold medals in 100 meters, 200 meters, long jump, and 4 × 100 meters relay at the 1936 Olympics in Berlin. His inclusion in the relay was the result of a late switch: two of the original quartet, Marty Glickman and Sam Stoller, the only Jewish members of the team, were unexpectedly dropped, presumably to avoid offending Nazi sensibilities.

Owens' triumph at the "Nazi Olympics" as they became known (covered in Chapter 19) is often recognized as an embarrassment for Hitler who had hijacked the tournament to promote his racist ideology and supply proof of Aryan superiority. The Führer famously walked out in disgust rather than witness Owens celebrate his victories. But, in spite of the shadow of Nazism cast across the Berlin games, Owens' experience must have been a pleasant contrast to his life in the United States, where segregation was legally enforced. In Berlin, he was allowed to travel with and stay in the same hotels as whites. Returning to the United States, he received no congratulatory telegram from President Franklin D. Roosevelt, less still an invitation to the White House, prompting Owens to reflect: "Hitler didn't snub me – it was [FDR] who snubbed me" (quoted in Schaap, 2007).

Owens' major problem in the 1930s depression was to keep body and soul together and, when, after the games, he was asked to travel with the U.S. team to a competition in Sweden, he refused, preferring to capitalize on his success by taking up commercial offers in the United States. For this, he had his amateur status withdrawn, effectively ending his competitive career.

Owens was eventually reduced to freak show racing against horses and motorcycles. "People say it was degrading for an Olympic champion to run against a horse," Owens later admitted. But, he was broke: "You can't eat four gold medals." Donald McRae's book, *In Black and White* (2003), assesses the experiences of Louis and Owens during the 1930s.

Other black sports performers were similarly brought to reduced circumstances. Johnson suffered the indignity of imprisonment, of fighting bulls in Barcelona, of performing stunts in circuses, of comically playing Othello, and of boxing all-comers in exhibitions at the age of 68. Louis ended his days ignominiously as a greeter, welcoming visitors at a Las Vegas hotel. The careers of all three followed a comet's elliptical path, radiating brilliance in their orbit, yet fading into invisibility. Plenty of other blacks have followed the same route. Sports history is full of dreams turning to nightmares. But black sportsmen seem particularly afflicted. Not even "The Greatest," Muhammad Ali, could maintain his dignity in later years.

While boxing was the first sport in which blacks were able to cross the color line and compete with whites, others followed the form. In 1947, when Joe Louis was at the end of his reign as heavyweight king (and the year after Jack Johnson died), Jackie Robinson became the first black person to play major league baseball. He was sent death threats and his teams, Montreal and the Brooklyn Dodgers, were sometimes boycotted by opponents.

The hostility of his reception may have initially daunted administrators from recruiting black players, but by the 1950s the numbers entering major league were multiplying. Remember: Robinson broke the "color bar," as it was called, seven years before the historic *Brown v. Board of Education of Topeka* case of 1954 in which the Supreme Court of the United States declared racial segregation in public schools to be unconstitutional and launched the movement to desegregate U.S. society.

Michael Jordan, Charles Barkley, Magic Johnson, Shaq O'Neal: in recent history, these and other African American players have dominated American basketball. The trend began in 1951 when Chuck Hooper signed for Boston Celtics. Within 16 years, over half of all NBA (National Basketball Association) players were black. The specter of freak show that had hung over Owens and the others visited basketball in the shape of the Harlem Globetrotters whose goals were more in making audiences laugh than scoring hoops.

The Civil Rights Act of 1964 ordered restaurants, hotels, and other businesses to serve all people without regard to race, color, religion, or national origin. It also barred discrimination by employers and unions, and established the Equal Employment Opportunity Commission to enforce fair employment practices. It was followed in 1965 by the Voting Rights Act, which ensured voting rights for African Americans. As the segregationist barriers in education tumbled down, so black youngsters began to mix and play competitively with whites. College football came within reach of more blacks and this, in turn, translated into more black professional players. By 1972, African American players comprised 40 percent of the NFL.

BOX 10.2 HARLEM GLOBETROTTERS

Originally known as the Savoy Big Five, the basketball team was formed in 1926, its name taken from the Savoy Ballroom in Chicago, where the players used to perform. When the ballroom was converted to a skating rink, Abe Saperstein, who managed the team, took the team on the road, like a traveling troupe of players, playing exhibitions for money. Basketball was popular among students and played under the auspices of the NCAA, though Saperstein's outfit was one of a number of touring professional teams that played outside a formal league. After several name changes, Saperstein settled on the Harlem Globetrotters, Harlem being a district in northeastern Manhattan with a large black population, noted, in the 1920s and 1930s for nightclubs, jazz, and a literary movement.

In the mid-1930s, the Globetrotters changed their emphasis from competitive basketball to a display of spectacular skills and, later, outright clowning. It proved a commercially successful move and the troupe toured internationally. Many black players who were denied the opportunity to play in white professional leagues turned to the Globetrotters, though, in 1949, the NBA provided a competitive alternative.

The comic Globetrotters' popularity with whites was probably because of the players' conformity to the image of blacks as physically adept, but too limited intellectually to harness skill to firm objectives. From the 1960s, when civil rights gained momentum and black radicalism grew, the Globetrotters began to draw criticism. James Michener in *Sports in America*, wrote of the Globetrotters: "They deepened the stereotype of 'the loveable, irresponsible Negro'" (1976: 145). Their popularity waned, though they continue to tour even today.

IN THE BLOOD?

The British were astonished by Molineaux who was probably the first black athlete they ever saw when he challenged the all-England champion Tom Cribb in 1810. An account of the day described Molineaux: "The Black stripp'd, and appeared of a giant-like strength, Large in bone, large in muscle and with arms a cruel length."

It's a resonant portrayal, recorded in Peter Fryer's *Staying Power: The history of Black people in Britain*, and one that reveals whites' curiosity in the physical characteristics of blacks (1984: 448). The curiosity went beyond sport: in their attempts to make the difference between themselves and those whom they conquered appear natural rather than cultural, the imperial British associated blacks with natural, instinctive ability rather than learned competence. The trope endured.

In the same year as the Molineaux–Cribb matchup, Saartje Baartman, a South African woman known as the "Hottentot Venus," was exhibited like a freak in England and France. Spectators would examine her body, feeling her ample buttocks should they wish. After her death in 1816, noted anatomist Georges Cuvier dissected her body and used its parts as evidence to support his theory of fixed racial types. Like other prominent blacks who displayed their bodies, she was an emblem of exoticism and Otherness.

The appearance of black prizefighters in the aftermath of the abolition of the slave trade (Emancipation in the new world came between 1863 and 1888) aroused further fascination in the sources of blacks' physical distinctness. As the search for a justification of slavery gained pace, black sportsmen (unlike today, there were no female pugilists), like Molineaux and the several other prizefighters who followed him, were seen as much as specimens as athletes.

Every time a black athlete stepped up to the scratch mark (the line from which the fighting commenced), he became an exhibit. Ex-slaves, like Bobby Dobbs, and sons of slaves, such as Bob Travers, toured England, attracting the praise of journalists and audiences alike. They were, of course, rarities and, as such, became curiosities rather than the objects of disdain blacks were to become in the twentieth century. Yet they were still exhibits, shown publicly for the amusement of others or as living proof of the animalism of black people. Perhaps the most dramatic instance of this was the caging of an African youth in a Belgian zoo in the mid-nineteenth century. (By animalism, I refer to behavior that's characteristic of animals, particularly in being physical and instinctive.)

Even by 1907, when South Africa-born Andrew Jeptha became the first black boxer to hold a British title, blacks remained objects of enthrallment. Two years before, in a spectacle reminiscent of the Hottentot Venus exhibition, six Mbutis from the territory we now know as the Democratic Republic of Congo appeared at the London Hippodrome. The "children of nature," as they were called by *The Times* (June 4, 1905) did not sing, dance, or perform in any way: they simply came out on stage to be peered at.

The moral horizons of the nineteenth century were set by religious and scientific discourses. The publication of Darwin's *Origin of the Species* in 1859 affected both. If evolution and natural selection were the principles of natural existence, the reason why the poor remained poor and blacks were in a position of servitude lay in their deficiencies rather than in social arrangements or historical circumstances. So, it seemed reasonable to suppose that the demonstrable prowess of black sportsmen was the result of a natural surfeit of physical capacities. The same fortitude that had allowed them to survive the rigors of slavery had equipped them to excel in competition (this type of argument was to reappear in another guise in the twentieth century, as we will see).

The sporting achievements of blacks, especially following Emancipation, would have been consistent with this worldview. So it was possible for itinerant prizefighter Peter Jackson to draw acclaim and enjoy what we would now call a celebrity lifestyle. "I knew him in the days of his greatness when sitting on top of the pugilistic world, fêted and lionized," recalled the Earl of Lonsdale (quoted in Henderson, 1949: 20). As Jackson's fame waned in the 1880s, Arthur Wharton appeared as a goalkeeper for Darlington Cricket and Football Club and distinguished himself as an exceptional all-round sportsman when he became the first man to run 100 yards in even time (10 seconds) at the AAA championships of 1886. In his *The First Black Footballer:*

Arthur Wharton, 1865–1930 (1998), Phil Vasili quotes from a speech given by a politician who alluded to Wharton's proficiency in Darwinian terms. The British Empire, he said, was composed of "representatives of almost every race of men, and every stage of human progress . . . It is far from easy to understand savages" (1998).

After Wharton, the next black footballer to play for a British club was Walter Tull who appeared in the Tottenham Hotspur team of 1909. Sprinters Harry Edward and Jack London, both from Guyana, were regulars on the athletics circuit in the 1920s. By this time, Jeptha, who lived in London, had retired. He held his title before the British Boxing Board of Control was established. In 1929, when the board took control of the sport, its secretary justified a new policy with a oblique acknowledgement of blacks' natural advantage: "It is only right that a small country such as ours should have championships restricted to boxers of white parents – otherwise we might be faced with a situation where all our British titles are held by coloured Empire boxers" (quoted in Henderson, 1949: 340).

Born in Trinidad, Macdonald Bailey served in the Royal Air Force then settled in Britain, accumulating a record 16 AAA titles and a bronze medal while representing Britain at the 1952 Olympic Games. His contemporary Arthur Wint also served in the RAF, though he competed for his native Jamaica at the Olympics, winning gold in 1948. He returned to Jamaica in 1955. Another Jamaican, Lloyd "Lindy" Delaphena, played football for Middlesborough immediately after the war and then for Portsmouth till 1958. His playing career was free of the kind of racist enmity that was to become commonplace in the 1980s.

Welcomed as athletes, they might inadvertently have concealed deeper antipathies that surfaced only occasionally. One such occasion was in 1943 when the celebrated Trinidadian cricketer Learie Constantine was refused accommodation at London's Imperial Hotel because the management "did not want niggers at this hotel." The former Test player, who was revealingly described by the cricket writer Neville Cardus as "a sort of elemental, instinctive force," was awarded damages. Lord Constantine (as he became in 1969) had been based in England since 1929.

Sport is part of what Pieterse called the "terrain on which Blacks have been permitted to manifest themselves" (the other part being entertainment) (1992, p. 148). Out of their appropriate context, they were exactly as the hotel's manager described them. Years later, the sociologist Harry Edwards wrote: "The only difference between the Black man shining shoes in the ghetto and the champion Black sprinter is that the shoe shine man is a nigger, while the sprinter is a fast nigger" (1970: 20).

Britain had no legal segregation, though, as we have seen, discrimination was present and boxing employed its own version of a color bar. This was lifted in 1948 (the year after Jackie Robinson joined the Brooklyn Dodgers) when a British-born boxer, Dick Turpin, who had been boxing professionally for 11 years, was allowed to challenge (successfully) for the British middleweight title. Turpin's father was from Guyana, his mother from Leamington Spa.

In the same year as Turpin's triumph, the Labour government introduced a Nationality Act that facilitated access to Britain from its former colonies. A labor shortage combined with a post-war economic expansion necessitated drastic measures. Even Enoch Powell, the politician who later prophesied racial conflict, traveled to the Caribbean to recruit nurses for the understaffed National Health

Service. (Powell was, at the time, Minister for Health: in 1968, he sparked a conflagration on British race relations with a speech in which he predicted, "in fifteen or twenty years' time, the black man will have the whip hand over the white man".)

In 1951, Randolph Turpin, brother of Dick, became an improbable world champion, albeit for a short period of time: he beat Ray Robinson, who had been unbeaten in his previous 91 fights. Turpin's life followed much the same elliptical path as Peter Jackson's and Arthur Wharton's, as well as those of several great African Americans, including the previously mentioned Jack Johnson and Jesse Owens and heavyweight champion Joe Louis, all of whom experienced hardship once their sporting careers were over. After ascending to a sporting peak, Turpin ran into financial difficulties and was forced to engage in humiliating boxer versus wrestler freak matches when way past his prime. Turpin's demise was tragic: in 1966, he committed suicide by shooting himself.

While the Turpin brothers were born in England, most British-based blacks in the post-war period were from either the Caribbean or Africa, their decision to domicile themselves in Britain being a pragmatic one. Migrants headed to manufacturing cities, such as London, Birmingham, and Manchester, where the jobs were abundant. Traditional textile areas in Yorkshire and Lancashire were also targeted. In a period of full employment, native white workers moved up the occupational hierarchies, leaving less desirable vacancies, which migrants filled.

Caribbeans frequently worked in low-status, often-unskilled positions, despite having qualifications and experience suitable for more prestigious jobs. They were also herded informally into certain parts of the cities, where rents were low and overcrowding tolerated. Before 1965, there was no law to prevent overt racial discrimination. A landlord wishing to prohibit black tenants could advertise with impunity for "whites only." And yet the combination of depression and chronic unemployment in the homelands and the plentiful job opportunities in Britain was a potent one and one that motivated significant population shifts from the Caribbean.

The first wave of migrants harbored a distinct ambition: to have a temporary, profitable stay in the Motherland, as many regarded Britain, before returning to the Caribbean. The fortifying belief helped migrants endure the often unduly harsh conditions they initially encountered, though it soon transmuted into what some called "the myth of return." Many black boxers would have used their purses (as boxing pay is known) to supplement their income. Others had their eyes on bigger prizes.

Hogan Bassey was, in many senses, a reluctant migrant: he left Nigeria for Liverpool in 1951 purely to pursue his boxing ambitions. By 1957, he had realized them, winning the world featherweight title. He retired at the relatively young age of 27 and returned to Nigeria to become a coach.

Turpin's biographer Jack Birtley made no mention of racism, or any other kind of bigotry or unfairness that must have habitually confronted black people when he wrote his account in 1976. During Turpin's heyday in the late 1940s/early 1950s, racism was not popularly understood as a social problem, though Fryer argued, "prejudice against Black people was widespread." At least half of Britain's white population had never met a black person. "They saw them as heathens who practised head-hunting, cannibalism, infanticide, polygamy, and 'Black magic'," wrote Fryer.

"They believed black men had stronger sexual urges than white men, were less inhibited, and could give greater satisfaction to their sexual partners" (1984: 374). While Fryer did not specify whether they were regarded as "natural athletes," we can extrapolate from his conclusions. The point is, however, that blacks lived in a kind of peaceful, if slightly discommodious, coexistence with whites. All this changed in 1958.

A Midlands town best known for Robin Hood and D. H. Lawrence was an unlikely site for Britain's first significant racially motivated unrest since the war. Nottingham's industry, especially in mining and bicycle manufacture was an enticement for migrants in the post-war period. In August 1958, a gang of whites stormed into the St Ann's Well district, where many blacks lived, prompting 24 arrests. In the same month, a similar disturbance in London's Notting Hill went on for several days. Elsewhere, the pattern repeated itself, signaling the end of the peaceful coexistence and the beginning of a period of hostility. There had been earlier inchoate remonstrations – in ports such as Cardiff and Liverpool – but nothing so clear and emphatically racist. Mindful of the civil rights movement in the United States, the British government drafted two pieces of legislation: a restrictive immigration act in 1962 and an antidiscrimination act in 1965.

The attraction to boxing is not hard to understand. Its equipment needs are minimal. Its tradition of black champions freed it of the restrictions of many other sports. Its individualism rewarded those willing to make sacrifices in the pursuit of success – as all migrants have to do. Yet there were other prominent sports performers, notably in athletics. Roy Hollingsworth, a discus thrower from Trinidad, and Clive Long, from Guyana, both gained international honors in the 1960s, though it was a Jamaican, Marilyn Fay Neufville, who was the outstanding athlete of her day. Neufville arrived in Britain in 1961 when she was eight and, in her teens, ran for Cambridge Harriers in southeast London. There was some controversy about her decision to represent Jamaica rather than Britain at the Commonwealth Games in 1970. She won the 400 metres, setting a world record of 51 seconds in the process. Her career fizzled out prematurely as she struggled against injuries.

Neufville was not jeered or beaten, though her preference for representing Jamaica while she was resident in London angered many, especially as many black boxers sought to fight for British titles but were prevented from doing so by a rule that specified that a title contestant "has been resident in the United Kingdom for a period of not less than ten years." It was 1970 before a migrant boxer won a British title; that was Jamaican born Bunny Stirling who had moved to England in 1954.

The issue of patriotic fidelity swirled in the air. South Africa born Basil D'Oliveira was selected to play cricket for England in 1968 and prompted an international incident when a tour of the then segregated South Africa was aborted. Clive Sullivan became the first black captain of a British national team in any sport, when he led the rugby league team to a World Cup win in 1972. It was another 32 years before rugby union appointed Jason Robinson as the first black captain of England. In football, Viv Anderson was the first black player to represent England in 1978. Two years later, Roland Butcher played cricket for England and eight years after that David Lawrence claimed the distinction of becoming the first British-born black cricketer to play for England.

There was no novelty at all in black sportsmen and women displaying pride and commitment in representing Britain or England. So it came as a surprise when, in 1995, Robert Henderson wrote an article for the venerable cricket publication *Wisden*, maintaining that the England cricket team should consist only of "unequivocal Englishmen." This specious category excluded black players and white players born outside England. Portentously entitled "Is it in the blood?" The article prompted legal action by black cricketers Devon Malcolm and Philip De Freitas, both of whom played for England and were presumably stung by the suggestion that they might not have possessed the requisite substance. Over 8 percent of all county cricket players were from African Caribbean backgrounds. What made the widely reported argument more staggering was its timing: a year after Linford Christie's Olympic 100 metres triumph, following which the Jamaican-born athlete wrapped himself in the Union flag.

"Black athletic achievement is still haunted by the Law of Compensation, which postulates an inverse relationship between mind and muscle," writes John Hoberman, whose argument we will consider later (1997: 225). The link between physical and intellectual capacity on the one hand and race on the other was not a subject that engaged the British until the 1980s. But the sudden, surprising emergence of so many black athletes at the higher echelons of the nation's most popular sports coupled with concern over the persistent underachievement of black children at school prompted serious reflection.

The early prognosis about black schoolchildren's poor educational performance was that it would improve over time as they assimilated. Research suggested that it had become too consistent to be so easily dismissed. In 1980, the National Association of Head Teachers reporting to the Rampton Committee on the education of ethnic minorities stated: "If there is a difficulty of cultural identity among second generation West Indians, there is also much to counter-balance that deficiency including their natural sense of rhythm, colour and athletic prowess."

Black footballers seemed to provide clear evidence. After Delaphena's disappearance in 1958, South African Albert Johanneson played for Leeds United in the 1960s, Bermudan Clyde Best for West Ham United in the 1970s, and St Kittian Cec Podd for Bradford City and other clubs in the 1970s and 1980s. These were isolated cases about which there was no disquiet. But, when in the early 1980s black players began to appear in numbers, the reaction was startling. The players themselves were made to endure the torment of racial chants, monkey noises, and pelting with bananas from incensed crowds. They were also the focus of a media that found headlines like "Black Magic" irresistible. The then manager of West Bromwich Albion, Ron Atkinson, patronizingly dubbed Cyrille Regis, Brendon Batson and Laurie Cunningham the "Three Degrees" (after the Philadelphia female pop-singing trio which enjoyed success in the 1970s – and still tours).

In a way, the incredulity is understandable. It seemed, every week a previously unknown black player would surface. Yet fans regarded black players as contaminants and players like John Barnes, Garth Crooks, and Garry Thompson became inured to the roar of "nigger, nigger, lick my boots." Football fans' racist response became one of Britain's least creditable exports: over the next several decades fans in Spain, Italy and East European countries systematically abused black players. The practice continued in Britain into the twenty-first century: in 2003, fans at Sunderland chanted racist epithets during an England–Turkey game. In reply, campaigns, such as "Let's kick racism out of football," were aimed at combating the development.

Even the more measured responses had racist undertones. Former track hero and, later, neurologist Roger Bannister, in 1995, offered his observation, "as a scientist," as he put it: "Black sprinters and Black athletes in general all seem to have certain anatomical advantages." It had been possible painlessly to neglect the overachievement of blacks in many sports, but football was Britain's perennially most popular sport and, in the 1990s, black players flowed into Britain from far and wide. These included Tony Yeboah, from Ghana, Ruud Gullit from the Netherlands and Patrick Vieira from Senegal. Several coaches, managers, and owners marveled at the brilliance of many black players and concluded it was because of natural ability rather than the painstaking skill acquisition, practice and sheer hard "graft" (labor) associated with white players. In a similar way, Ron Noades, in 1993, when chair of Crystal Palace, detected that, while black players were effective in temperate weather, in winter, "you need a few of the maybe hard white men to carry the artistic black players through."

Animalism manifests in different ways. Abusing black athletes with ape-like gestures expresses long-standing racist inclinations; explaining blacks' prowess as the result of natural talent has much the same effect. Almost two centuries after Molineaux had excited thoughts of animalistic abilities, blacks' sporting achievements continued to be devalued or reduced to primal impulses.

THE THEORY OF NATURAL ABILITY

By the 1970s, Americans had become accustomed to black people's pre-eminence in sports: since Robinson's historic major league baseball début, African Americans had graduated to the top levels of baseball, basketball and American football, encouraging some writers to offer explanations. Martin Kane's was the most influential. First published in 1971, "An assessment of Black is best" mixed physiological, psychological with historical material to produce an argument based on racial characteristics: black people were naturally equipped to do well in sport. At the time, Harry Edwards opposed the view, arguing the reason so many black people do well in sport was that alternative paths to success were obstructed by racist practices. Sport, on the other hand, seemed free of racism and attracted an extraordinary number of highly motivated young men and women.

But Kane's theory had a commonsense appeal and was widely accepted. At the center of Kane's argument is the view that blacks are endowed with a natural ability that gives them an advantage in certain sports. Around this spun a number of other related points, many taken from Kane's interviews with medical scientists, coaches, and sports performers. An important, though now oddly dated, point is that there are race-linked physical characteristics.

According to Kane, blacks as a "race" have proportionately longer legs to whites, narrower hips, wider calf bones, greater arm circumference, greater ratio of tendon to muscle, denser skeletal structure, and a more elongated body. Typically, they have power and an efficient body-heat dissipation system. Kane inferred these features from a small sample of successful black sportsmen – that is, a minority with proven excellence rather than a random sample from the total population. And he concludes that blacks are innately different and the differences, being genetic in origin, can be passed on from one generation to the next.

So, cold climates are said to affect all blacks badly, even ones who are born and brought up in places like Toronto. Weak ankle bones would account for the relative absence of black ice hockey players. The disadvantages are transmitted genetically, as are natural advantages, which equip blacks to do well in particular sports where speed and power are essential. Kane argues that blacks are not suited to endurance events. Since the publication of the article, hundreds of African distance runners have undermined this point, though Kane tries to cover himself by claiming Kenyans have black skin, but a number of white features.

The second aspect to Kane's argument concerns psychological difference: he believes black people share a set of personality traits that are, Kane suggests, determined by race. Blacks have the kind of yielding personality that puts them, as one coach told Kane, "far ahead of whites. . .[they have] relaxation under pressure" (1971: 76).

It's possible that Kane mistook the actuality of relaxation with the impression of coolness. He might have studied black athletes in the 1960s and early 1970s and noticed how they never got stressed out, or looked tense. But competitors themselves actually work at portraying this: they consciously try to convey an image that reflects what some writers call "cool pose." That is all it is – pose, or a particular way of behaving adopted in order to impress others. More likely, black performers were as tense and concerned as anyone else. Possibly more so: sport for many blacks was not a casual recreation (as it may be for white youths), but a career path and every failure represented a possible sinking to obscurity; especially in the immediate post-civil rights years.

Slavery is the key to the third part of Kane's argument. "Of all the physical and psychological theories about the American blacks' excellence in sport, none has proved more controversial than one of the least discussed: that slavery weeded out the weak" (1971: 80). Here Kane introduces a version of the theory of natural selection, his view being that, as only the fittest survived the rigors of slavery, those best suited to what must have been terribly harsh environments passed on their genes to successive populations, who used them to great effect in sport. There are two drawbacks to this. First, it is preposterous to suggest that blacks bred for generations in such a controlled way as to retain a gene pool in which specific genes related to, for instance, speed, strength, and agility, became dominant. Second, these properties were probably of less significance in matters of survival than intelligence, ingenuity, and anticipation and Kane considers none of these as essentially black features.

While Kane's views might have been controversial in the early 1970s, they were inadmissible by 1988. That's when a CBS pundit named Jimmy "The Greek" Snyder expressed similar observations during an NFL pregame show. He was fired after suggesting that slave owners had bred blacks for sporting endeavors. But the episode illustrated the continuing currency of Kane's theory.

While Roger Bannister's views seemed to complement the theory, it was Jon Entine's 2000 book *Taboo: Why Black athletes dominate and why we're afraid to talk about it* that lent it credibility. Being careful to avoid charges of racism when explaining blacks' sporting achievements, Entine stressed, "genes set parameters, but it is life experiences that 'express' biological capabilities." Still, in the last instance, nature has primacy: "Cultural conditions exaggerate the small but meaningful differences that led to the athletic edge" (2000: 279).

Those "small but meaningful differences" were the subject of research by Bengt Saltin, who observed how highly trained Swedish athletes could be easily beaten by Kenyan schoolchildren and concluded that environments contribute only 20–25 percent to an athlete's proficiency: the rest is all natural. With this kind of evidence, Entine asked, with a sideways glance at British football's pre-eminent black players: "Is it just cultural serendipity that Brazilians are time and again the best soccer players?"

While it was asked rhetorically, it actually invited answers. If we take "serendipity" to mean the practice of making useful, unexpected discoveries, a reasonable historical case might be made. Slaves and their offspring, finding themselves at an impasse in which they and their forebears had their progress in society impeded by institutional arrangements (formal or informal), learned that a "terrain on which Blacks have been permitted to manifest themselves is sport," to repeat Pieterse. Applying themselves with unparalleled motivation and a determination to overcome adversity, they found success attainable, not easily, but attainable nonetheless. Sport provided them with an area in which they could, as David K. Wiggins puts it, "realize a certain degree of dignity" (1997).

Buoyed by this, their sons and daughters followed the same path, all the time helping carve out a tradition of accomplishment that inspired successive generations. The specific cultural conditions for Brazilian footballers' brilliance lie in Portuguese imperialism, the remnants of the plantation economy and the corresponding enthusiasm for football, after its introduction by Englishman Charles Miller in the early twentieth century.

Recall the research project covered in the Introduction: two groups of chimpanzees from Ugandan rainforests, when presented with the problem of extracting honey from a hole in a log, responded differently, one group using sticks, the others using absorbent leaves. The behavioral differences reflected cultural influences, that is, behavior acquired through simulation, imitation, or other forms of social learning. They relied on cultural knowledge rather than instinct or some other unlearned drive.

This is the nurture side of an argument that has tended towards nature. There are echoes of the race–IQ debate, which resists every attempt to bury it and returns in new guises to explain the different patterns of educational achievement among blacks and their peers. Sport presents a different though not unrelated conundrum. Is Hoberman's "law of compensation" actually in force? If blacks' achievements in American and British sport are because of their natural advantages, is their relative lack of progress in formal education because of natural disadvantages? One possibility offers the other.

The idea of the animally endowed black athlete refuses to go down without a fight. It includes expressions and images that ostensibly celebrate black achievement, while obscuring the historical circumstances that have commissioned blacks' progress in sport – and obstructed their progress in other areas. Paradoxically, the appearance of blacks in sports once considered out of reach has lessened its force. As recently as 1990, those who considered blacks equipped only for events demanding muscularity and speed would not have countenanced the prospect of black golf and tennis champions. Now it's clear that the barriers blocking their progress were social rather than physical.

THE HUNGRY FIGHTER THEORY

History alone tells us that sport has been one of the two channels through which blacks have been able to escape the imprisonment of slavery and the impoverishment that followed its dissolution; the other being entertainment. In both spheres, blacks performed largely for the amusement of patrician whites. This holds true to this day: the season-ticket holder or cable television subscriber, no less than old-time slave masters, have decisive effects on the destinies of sports performers. For this reason, slaves were encouraged; the incentive might be freedom or at least a temporary respite from daily labors.

There is an adage that emerged during the 1930s depression in Yorkshire, England, a county famed for its cricket and its mining industry: "Shout down any coalpit and half a dozen fast bowlers will come out." The theme is similar: that material deprivation is an ideal starting-point for sporting prowess. "Hungry fighters" are invariably the most effective. As we have seen, many fight their way out, only to return to indigence; but they're not to know that as they're striving for improvement. Blacks' supposed predilection for sport is more a product of material circumstances than natural talent.

This is the gist of a theory first put forward by Harry Edwards in the 1970s and which seems to stand the test of time. He argued that black people in America faced limited opportunities of advancement. Suspecting they would face obstacles in the professions, politics, or business, they plowed their energies into one of the two areas where they knew black people could succeed.

Whether or not sport *actually is* a viable avenue from despair is not the issue: it has been seen as such by people who lacked alternatives. And the perception has stuck, and probably will continue to stick as long as obstacles to progress in other avenues remain and perhaps long after they've been removed. After the election of Barack Obama to the presidency, few could seriously believe age-old obstacles to black people were still in place. Equally, few would maintain that racism had been obliterated, either in the United States or Britain. Black people remain underrepresented in several key areas of society.

Extrapolating from Edwards' original argument, we might contend that slave prizefighters began a tradition by setting themselves up – quite unwittingly – as cultural icons, or images to be revered and copied; in today's parlance, role models. The stupendous success of blacks in such sports as basketball, boxing, track and field, and so on has clearly been inspirational to countless young blacks over the decades. Even the examples of Obama and the several other black politicians who have defied the odds and risen to power haven't quelled the enthusiasm for sports. The prospect of $15 million+ per year and a celebrity lifestyle is clearly tempting.

Evaporating into insignificance are the millions of other aspirants whose fortunes never materialized and whose careers end shabbily. No matter how remote the chances of success may be, the tiny number of elite black sports stars supply tangible and seemingly irrefutable evidence that it can be achieved.

BOX 10.3 RACISM

Originally, a set of beliefs or ideas based on the assumption that the world's population can be divided into different human biological groups designated "races." Following on from this is the proposition that the "races" are ordered hierarchically, so that some stand in a position of superiority, to others. This is a classic type of racism; nowadays, ideas of superiority are often veiled in arguments concerning culture, nationalism, and ethnic identity. Quite often, these contain connotations of racism that are not specific, but only inferred. The expression "coded racism" conveys this.

Somewhere between the prizefighting ex-slaves of the nineteenth century and today's football plutocrats, black people skipped a transition. Why, in the twenty-first century, after the election of a black U.S. President, countless black judges, prominent black professionals and business owners, are we still discussing the issue of race in sports? It seems a legitimate question. An alternative would be to consign the whole issue to history and move on. This would be a reasonable point were it not for the persistence of a pattern that is as old as sport itself: the absence of black people in management or administrative positions, what Americans call the front office. ("Study: Gender, race gap still exists in sports front offices, sidelines," a report in *Diverse*, November 17, 2005, provides some back-up statistics.)

In the United States, some blacks have moved into these kinds of positions, though, in Britain conspicuous gaps remain. Black athletes continue to perform and entertain and are well rewarded for their exhibitions. But the function of exhibitions is to entertain, amuse or edify. Blacks' disengagement from the decision-making centers of sport suggests that in celebrating their achievement-strewn history in sport, there is the risk of concealing an inglorious exclusion that closely reflects their experience in society generally. Why is that?

Here's one scenario. Encouraged or cajoled, by physical education teachers at high school who might subscribe to the popular if mistaken view that blacks have "natural talent," young black people might suspect their teachers are right – they *do* have talent. Zealous scouts pump up the youths with inflated claims when they attempt to woo them. Many youths understandably find comfort in the view that they do possess natural advantages. The fact that such views are based on stereotypes not realities doesn't enter into it: beliefs often have a self-fulfilling quality, so that if you believe in your own ability strongly enough, you eventually acquire that ability. Let me provide two illustrations.

(1) A few years ago, I received a call from a journalist from the British *Sunday Times*. He was writing a story on black overachievement in sports and wanted to

know why no one actually expressed what he felt was an evident truth: that there is a natural edge that blacks possess. The fact that a journalist, who happened to be black himself, writing for a prestigious newspaper was prepared to entertain the idea was testimony to its power.

(2) Colin Jackson, the former world record holder in 110-meter hurdles, when confronted with the evidence that his success was due to his dedication and capacity for hard work, was disappointed: he harbored suspicions that, for some reason, he was naturally gifted. It's not only whites that have bought the myth of black natural talent in sport: black people have accepted and, in some cases, even clung to a defective theory that has actually performed a disservice.

Seeing blacks as great sports performers might seem a compliment, but, stay mindful of Edwards' observation about the difference between a champion black athlete and a black shoeshine man: they're both "niggers," it's just that "the sprinter is a fast nigger" (1970: 20).

Historically, sport, along with entertainment, was one of the areas in which blacks were allowed to maximize their prowess, and circumstances haven't changed sufficiently to permit a significant departure. Blacks still approach sport with vigor and commitment at least partly because persistent racism effectively closes off other channels. Even if those other channels have become freer in recent years, black youths have become accustomed to anticipating obstacles to their progress. So that, by the time they prepare to make the transition from school to work, many have made sports as a career their first priority.

With sights set on a future filled with championships, black youths fight their way into sports determined that, slim though their chances may be, they will succeed. And they usually do, though mostly in an altogether more modest way than they envisaged. Few attain the heights they wanted to conquer and even fewer surpass them.

Blacks' success in sports may look impressive, but, compared to the numbers of youths entering sport, their interest primed, their success is not so great. Sheer weight of numbers dictates that a great many African Americans and African Caribbeans will rise to the top of certain sports.

Cultures on both sides of the Atlantic have fostered strains of racism that, while less virulent now than in the late 1980s, are still malignant enough to convince young black people that their future in mainstream society may be curtailed by popularly held stereotypes about their abilities. Weighing up the possibilities of a future career, many opt for a shot at sports, where it has been demonstrated time and again that black people can make it to the very top and command the respect of everyone, whites included. Respect is a sought-after commodity by people who have been denied it historically. Ideas of the "white men can't jump" variety are conveyed to young black people by possibly well-meaning, but mistaken, coaches and high-school teachers who enthuse over a career in sports. Then the story separates into two contrasting plots. Some tread the road to respectability, even stardom, making a living they can be proud of from professional sports. Others dissolve into oblivion, never to be heard of.

What this scenario doesn't seem to account for is the scarcity of black competitors, let alone winners, in certain sports. Their exclusion from more expensive pursuits like golf, tennis and motor racing and so on is obvious: you need money to get started. So far the pull of the few black champions in these sports has been resistible. Young blacks still find the cheaper and accessible sports attractive options.

HOBERMAN'S LAW OF COMPENSATION

Earlier I invoked John Hoberman's Law of Compensation, which states that there is "an inverse relationship between mind and muscle, between athletic and intellectual development" (1997: 225). America has perpetuated falsehoods about black people's biological propensities; and "black athleticism has served . . . as the most dramatic vehicle in which such ideas can ride in public consciousness" (1997: 225).

Prominent black sports performers have been used as living evidence of a not-so noble savagery: virtually every sports star embodies concepts of racial evolution that are enthusiastically accepted by both white and black populations as support for the view that blacks are naturally good athletes, but not much good at much else. Among Hoberman's examples are Joe Louis "who was granted messianic status by his fellow blacks [and] was also depicted as a savage brute to his white audience" (1997: 115–26) and Mike Tyson whose "well-publicized brutalities in and out of the ring have helped to preserve pseudo-evolutionary fantasies about black ferocity that are still of commercial value to fight promoters and their business partners in the media" (1997: 209).

BOX 10.4 TYSON'S CASES

On September 19, 1991, heavyweight boxer Mike Tyson was indicted by a Marion County grand jury of raping Desiree Washington, a contestant at a Miss Black America pageant, who claimed Tyson had forcibly had sex with her in an Indianapolis hotel room. Tyson had attended the pageant. On February 10, 1992, Tyson was convicted of rape and sentenced to six years in prison. Washington later alleged that Tyson had given her a venereal disease. During his imprisonment, the boxer converted to Islam. Tyson was released from prison in March 1995, and resumed his professional boxing career five months later under the guidance of Don King. Richard Hoffer believes: "He [Tyson] was the perfect man for King's purposes, though, smart enough to be actively complicit in the con, but emotionally disorganized enough to defer to King in its execution" (1998: 266). The "con" was a series of easy fights spread over two years which earned Tyson $135 million. By 1998, Tyson was back in prison again for assault, having served a suspension from boxing for the infamous ear-biting incident with Evander Holyfield. Another spell in prison after a road rage incident looked to be the end for Tyson, but, despite being banned in some states, he continued to fight and, even in an obvious state of decay, remained the biggest draw in heavyweight boxing. He cropped up in movies such as *The Hangover* (2009).

Black boxers are bit part players in a "Darwinian drama par excellence, in that portraying the black male as an undisciplined savage confirmed both his primitive nature and his inevitable failure in the competition with civilized whites in a modern society," according to Hoberman (1997: 209). They are joined by an all-star cast that includes all top black athletes and the millions more who want to follow in their footsteps.

Hoberman argues that black people in the United States and, to a similar degree in Britain, have been depicted in an unending series of images that have contributed toward a social pathology. Whites are society's stewards. The typical image of blacks in the media is that of a violent physical people, habitually involved in criminal activity, entertainment, or sports. In the late twentieth century, the slayings of black musicians and the vulgar misogynist material of rap artists contributed to a "merger of the athlete, the gangster rapper, and the criminal into a single black male persona" that the sports, entertainment and advertising industries have made into the dominant image of black masculinity – a single menacing figure. The high-profile sports figures who have courted ambitions in music and movies supports Hoberman's point.

The power of Hoberman's argument is not so much in its dismantling of the myth of athletic prowess, which has been done before, nor in discerning the racist implications of exalting black athletic accomplishments; but in analyzing the ways in which the cost of black success, whether in sports or entertainment, far outweighs its benefits. Back in 1997, I was spending a sabbatical at the University of Massachusetts, Boston, when Tiger Woods became the first black player to win the U.S. Masters. As a Fellow of the William Monroe Trotter Institute, I was in the company of several distinguished African American scholars, many of whom greeted Woods' success heartily. But, why? After all, how badly does black America need yet another sports champion? For Hoberman, this is not liberation, but entrapment.

Woods, no less than Joe Louis, Michael Jordan, Serena Williams, or Lewis Hamilton, was a symbol of black potential that has been continually adapted to changing circumstances. The media visibility of successful black sports stars discourages thinking about what blacks have accomplished in areas such as education, politics, the professions; perhaps, more pertinently, what they have *not* accomplished in these areas. As David J. Leonard point out: "M. J., Kobe, and Shaq overshadow the realities of segregated schools, police brutality, unemployment, and the White supremacist criminal justice system" (2004: 289).

Even if you don't accept every point made by Leonard, his overall thrust demands consideration: conspicuously successful black sports stars create the misleading impression that racism and the inequities its precipitates are buried in the past and that race is no longer relevant. We can supplement Leonard's argument with the observation that, while in actuality race remains relevant, young black people continue to pin their ambitions on sport.

There is a scene in the movie *Hoop Dreams*, in which a basketball coach addresses his protégés with some sobering statistics (directed by Steve James, Fred Marx, and Peter Gilbert, 1994). Each year, 500,000 boys play high school basketball, he tells them. Of the 14,000 who progress to intercollegiate basketball, fewer than 25 percent ever play one season in the NBA. Don't reach for your calculator: it works out at about 1:143. Some American writers, like Jack Olsen and Nathan Hare, have looked at the underside of this "shameful story" (as Olsen calls it) which begins with visions of wealth and glamor but frequently ends in poverty, crime and, sometimes, insanity. Their conclusions concur with those of Hoberman in the sense that they believe that young blacks are seduced into sport and, in the process, ignore their formal academic and vocational studies. They invest so much energy in sport that little is left for other pursuits. So, by the time dreams fade, they are left with few if any career alternatives and join the gallery of "also-rans."

Sports that attract blacks are always expensive in terms of people: wasteful, profligate even. If it takes 143 ambitious kids to make one NBA player for one season, how many to produce a Jordan, or a Woods, or a Hamilton? Entering sports is less a career choice, more a lottery. As I noted earlier, the idea of recruiting bowlers from Yorkshire coalpits might have proved workable in the 1930s. Now, young whites are told to enjoy their cricket, but, first, get a degree and qualify as a lawyer or a doctor. The same piece of advice doesn't reach as far as inner London, or South Central LA.

There are always a small number of outstanding performers with naturally endowed faculties, but there's no reason to suppose that the black population has a monopoly or even a majority of them. Success in sport is due much more to non-physical qualities such as drive, determination, and an ability to focus sharply. Given that blacks see the job market as a maze of culs-de-sac, they may well accrue more than their fair share of these qualities. Failure has potentially direr consequences for them than for their white, working-class counterparts who, while still having limited opportunities, at least escape racialism.

Returning to *Hoop Dreams*, we hear the familiar cliché from one of the school players: "Basketball is my ticket out of the ghetto." One can almost hear a chorus of others saying the same thing. It is explosive motivational fuel. Add the "push" of outsiders, the magnetizing influence of black icons and you have a heady mixture – one which sends young blacks into sport year after year. If and when this slows, it's been suggested that this would reflect a quickening of the rate at which opportunities arise in the job market. In other words, if racism disappeared completely there'd be only a few black sports stars. That is not the case at present and, while discrimination persists, sport is bound to prosper from the contributions of blacks.

Some scholars challenge Hoberman's interpretation of this state of events. Douglas Hartmann, for example, writes: "Sport has been a crucial and leading institutional site in the struggle for racial justice . . . [and] for the development of an African American identity and aesthetic" (2000: 240). Hartmann doesn't accept that blacks are more fixated on sport than other groups. If they continue to gravitate toward athletic endeavors, it's because: "Sport offers African Americans opportunities and freedoms found rarely in other institutions."

While Hartmann believes there is irony in sports: historically, the experience of racism has inclined black people toward competition; nowadays, sport provides a social space in which conspicuously successful competitors can challenge racism. Hartmann may be right and, while he doesn't refer to it directly, the one area where a serious challenge could be mounted is in, as we mentioned earlier, the front office, where black people have been glaringly absent.

THE REBECCA MYTH

This situation proved so embarrassing for the NFL that, in 1998, the governing organization hired a recruitment agency to stage and video interviews with other black coaches and aspiring coaches and distribute the tapes around the league. This was part of an effort to raise club owners' awareness of the abilities of black coaches and stimulate more enlightened hiring policies. Players like Doug Williams and, later, Warren Moon helped destroy the fiction that black football players did not have the intelligence to play quarterback, so needed to be "stacked" in other positions. The success of people like Denny Green, Tony Dungy, Ray Rhodes, and others, may have helped dispel the similar fiction that existed about black coaches.

We know about the "before" part of the black experience in sports, how and why athletes make it to the pros, or fail in the process. The "during" phase can be read about in the sports pages of any newspaper. But, what happens "after"? Green *et al.* are exceptions. More usual are rags-to-riches and back-to-rags stories. Boxers especially have a knack of earning and blowing fortunes: Donovan "Razor" Ruddock was one of many millionaires-cum-bankrupts when he was declared financially insolvent in 1995. Others, go on to become sportcasters, movie stars and all-round media personalities; the most successful of these combined all three and became the most famous black sports star ever – but for the wrong reasons, of course.

Considering the heavy investment of black people in the playing side of sport, one might expect many to stay in sport and serve in officiating or administrative capacities Here there is an unevenness. Although, there has been a steadily growing number of black game officials since 1965 (when Burt Tolar became the NFL's first black official), the number of black coaches and administrators has been few. Green was the first African American head football coach when he joined Northwestern University in 1981. Art Shell was the first black NFL coach when he joined Los Angeles Raiders in 1989.

In Britain, Viv Anderson successfully transited from playing to managing, first at Barnsley, then as assistant manager at Middlesbrough, though it wasn't until 2008 that Paul Ince became the first black manager of a Premier League club, though his tenure didn't last a single season. Black people are certainly appearing in the front offices, but not in the numbers one might expect from a glance at the number of active players.

Daniel Burdsey, in his study of the paucity of British Asian players at the top levels of football, observes: "The under-representation of British Asians as professional footballers is mirrored by their near absence in non-playing roles, as managers, coaches and talent scouts, as well as in administrative positions" (2008: 121). Despite the demographic changes of the past several decades and the transformation of major sport, the front desk in Britain remains resolutely white.

BOX 10.5 DON KING (1931–)

The world's leading sports promoter has summed up his own rise thus:

"I was an ex-numbers runner, ex-convict who received a full, unconditional pardon. I am, what they would say in America, what everyone's supposed to be – when coming from the wrong side of the track to the right side of the track" (quoted in Regen, 1990: 115). After serving a prison sentence for manslaughter, King's first promotional venture was in 1972 when he staged an exhibition by Muhammad Ali in an African Americans' hospital in Cleveland. His first major promotion in 1974 (when aged 43), also featured Ali, when he regained the heavyweight title from George Foreman in Zaire. After this, King kept an interest in the heavyweight championship, either by promoting bouts or managing the champions. Mike Tyson left his manager Bill Cayton and entered into a business relationship with King. Tyson refused to criticize King, even when many of his boxers, like ex-champion Tim Witherspoon, turned against him. King has also co-promoted rock stars, such as Michael Jackson, and began his own ppv tv system, KingVision. His biggest promotion never materialized: Tyson's conviction and imprisonment for rape meant that a fight with Evander Holyfield (originally scheduled for November 8, 1991) fell through. It was expected to gross more than $100 million (£62 million), with the ppv operation alone drawing $80 million, foreign sales $10 million, and the promotional fee from Caesar's Palace $11 million. Former heavyweight champion Larry Holmes once said of King: "He looks black, lives white and thinks green." See Jack Newfield's *Only in America: The life and crimes of Don King* (1995).

One of the main reasons why owners and general managers have failed to appoint more black people is highlighted by Douglas Putnam, in his book *Controversies of the Sports World*: "Team owners and general managers, as businesspeople, prefer to hire candidates who are similar to coaches who have already achieved success or are similar to coaches they have known personally and admired" (1999: 27). If so, they might think in terms of a Bill Parcells, or, in Britain, an Alex Ferguson. "Consequently," writes Putnam, they "often pass over qualified blacks and hire whites with whom they are familiar . . . and to conform to their long-held ideal about what a successful coach should be" (1999: 27).

This is sport's equivalent of what the sociologist Alvin Gouldner once called the "Rebecca Myth," after Daphne du Maurier's famous novel. In the book *Rebecca* and Alfred Hitchcock's 1940 film of the same name, a young woman marries an English aristocrat, but, after moving into his mansion, meets an unfriendly housekeeper, Mrs Danvers, who idolizes the late mistress of the mansion, Rebecca. Entranced by the thought of the dead Rebecca, Mrs Danvers makes her new mistress's life a misery.

In his *Wildcat Strike: A study in worker-management relations*, Gouldner transposes this theme to an industrial setting and shows how the succession of personnel in senior positions can be impeded by the expectations of colleagues. "The successor may fail to show the old lieutenants proper deference, willfully or through ignorance of their expectations, but in either event making them dissatisfied," writes Gouldner (1965: 158). They resist the new boss as a "legitimate heir" to the position once held by someone they knew and trusted and withhold legitimacy unless he conforms to their ideal (Gouldner's study was an all-male affair).

The Rebecca Myth has obvious applications to players' responses to a newly appointed coach or manager, but it also helps clarify why owners and chairs fail to hire more blacks in senior positions: because they have what Putnam calls a "sub-liminal perception." Consciously or unconsciously, they desire to appoint someone who resembles a past manager/coach, who has brought success to their organization. And the historical chances are that this person will be white. This creates special difficulties for aspiring managers/coaches from ethnic minorities who need to convince prospective employers of their capabilities, but may also need their approval as someone who resembles a successful predecessor.

In his *Offside Racism: Playing the white man*, Colin King uses a similar approach to explain the paucity of black managers, coaches, or administrators in British soccer. Black ex-players wishing to make the transition are forced to perform to standards, that is "play the white man," in order to gain admission (2004)

Interestingly, there are (literally) one or two African Americans who have bypassed the salaried positions and headed straight for the seats of power. Beginning as a boxing promoter in the 1970s, Don King became one of the most powerful figures in sport: a man at the center of an extensive web of business interests stretching over a range of sports and sports-related areas. Peter Bynoe and Bertram Lee aspired to King-like powers in 1989 when they bought the Denver Nuggets of the NBA for $50 million (£31 million); they were the first African American owners of a major sports club. The deal went sour when Lee had cashflow problems and was made to sell his share. Bynoe also sold out in 1992, leaving the sport without a black owner. It took until 2002 before an African American became the owner of major league franchise. Robert Johnson, the publishing billionaire, opened up the NBA expansion franchise, Charlotte Bobcats.

Vince Payne was the first African American president of a major league club when he took over at the Milwaukee Brewers. Bill Duffy is a bigtime sports agent in the United States. These are success stories and, while there are only a few of them, there will be more in the years to come. Is this good news or bad? Good news – blacks breaking ground by demonstrating intellectual abilities; bad news – they stay in sports.

Historically and perhaps to the present day, sport has provided a cultural context for black people to express a particular identity, loudly and effectively. It has also, as we've seen, been a context in which black people have met with racist barriers, most – though not all – of which have been surmounted. Yet, the association between black people and sport remains: laughing off "white men can't jump"-type of aphorisms doesn't erase vestigial assumptions either from the minds of black people or anyone else. Sport has been one of the few domains in which they have excelled consistently. Its impact on the collective identity of black people continues.

Darwin's Athletes: How sport has damaged black America and preserved the myth of race by John Hoberman, (Houghton Mifflin, 1997) includes the insight that both blacks and whites have bought into the "myth" and how identifying with black sporting success has made black professional achievement "as seldom-noticed sideshow to more dramatic media coverage of celebrities and deviants." Also worth reading in this context: Marek Kohn's "Can white men jump?" which is Chapter 4 of his book *The Race Gallery* (Vintage, 1996). And, for contrast, Jon Entine's *Taboo: Why black athletes dominate and why we're afraid to talk about it* (Public Affairs, 2000).

"Rethinking the relationships between sport and race in American culture: Golden ghettoes and contested terrain" by Douglas Hartmann (pp. 229–53 in *Sociology of Sport Journal,* vol. 17, 2000) is an interesting counterpoint to Hoberman's argument: "Sport has been a crucial and leading institutional site in the struggle for racial justice". David J. Leonard takes a different approach in "The next M.J. or the next O.J.? Kobe Bryant, race, and the absurdity of colorblind rhetoric" (in *Journal of Sport and Social Issues*, vol. 28, 2004): he refutes the adoration of Woods *et al.* as "evidence of racial progress and colorblindness."

In Black and White: The untold story of Joe Louis and Jesse Owens by Donald McRae (Scribner, 2003) is the book cited in the text and, as its title suggests, narrates the experiences of two prominent African-American champions in the midst of the segregated America. Complementing this is *Out of the Shadows: A biographical history of African American athletes* edited by David K. Wiggins (University of Arkansas Press, 2006).

Race, Culture, and the Revolt of the Black Athlete: The 1968 Olympic protests and their aftermath by Douglas Hartmann (University of Chicago Press, 2004) is, as its title suggests, a chronicle of the build-up to the Smith–Carlos gesture and an appraisal of its effects. It can be profitably read in conjunction with *Glory Bound: Black athletes in a white America* by David K. Wiggins (Syracuse University Press, 1997) which critically examines the achievements of black Americans in sport against a historical background of racism and segregation. *A Hard Road to Glory: A history of the African-American athlete 1619–1918 vol. 1; 1919–1945 vol. 2; since 1946 vol. 3* by Arthur R. Ashe (Amistad Warner 1993) is a three-volume history of the participation of African Americans in sports.

"Ritual disorder and the contractual morality of sport: A case study in race, class, and agreement" by Daniel A. Grano (in *Rhetoric and Public Affairs*, vol. 10, 2007) makes several interesting points about the NBA: "Public perceptions held that the league was 'a space of racial threat' (more than 70 percent of its players were African American) and 'criminal menace' [in the late 1970s]." In the 1980s, less menacing players like Michael Jordan and Magic Johnson entered and "subsequently became regarded as figures who saved it."

"Racism and cultural diversity in Australian sport" by Paul Oliver (in *Alternative Law Journal,* vol. 32, 2007) is a short but interesting essay predicated on the view: "Racism has been the ugly underbelly of Australian sport for over a century." Oliver's exhaustive *What's the Score? A survey of cultural diversity and racism in Australian sport* is published by the Human Rights and Equal Opportunities Commission (Sydney, 2001). Further studies of race and Australian sport include Colin Tatz's *Obstacle Race: Aborigines in sport (*University of New South Wales Press, 1995) and Lawrence McNamara's more analytical "Tackling racial hatred: Conciliation, reconciliation and football" (in *Australian Journal of Human Rights*, 2000).

ASSIGNMENT

In 1947, psychologists Kenneth and Mamie Clark conducted a famous experiment: they asked 253 black children to choose between four dolls, two black and two white. The result: two-thirds of the children preferred white dolls. Conclusion: that black children had internalized the hatred society directed at all black people and so suffered from poor self-esteem. But this was before the rise of so many African-American and African-Caribbean sports icons. Repeat the experiment using a smaller sample of children, but use dolls in the likeness of famous sports stars: two black and two white. Document the results and draw out the implications, taking note of major social changes since the 1950s.

IS CHEATING FAIR?

"The rules of fair play do not apply in love and war." This is not an answer: it's a quote from John Lily's *Euphues* (1578). A contemporary of Shakespeare, Lily could have had no clue how his phrase would become so widely used as a mitigation of cheating. Of the many modifications, one stands out: "All's fair in war, I believe," claims the central character of John Pendleton Kennedy's 1954 novel of the American Revolution, *Horse-shoe Robinson.* "But it don't signify a man is good."

This is hardly a definitive statement, but it does highlight how the rules of fair play might be acceptably broken in some circumstances, though without necessarily making the violation morally right, or exculpating the offender (i.e. signifying he or she "is good").

To cheat is to deceive, trick, swindle or flout the rules designed to maintain conditions of impartiality. So how can this be fair in *any* situation? After all, fairness suggests honesty. To answer this we need to establish the circumstances in which cheating takes place, and the conditions under which cheating is practiced – the context of cheating.

Prior to professionalism, the aim of sporting competition was to perform at the highest level our bodies and minds permitted. Rules were designed as guiding principles, directions regarding appropriate behavior. Participants played on their honor: they trusted each other to be fair and honest. In a sense, the rules were superfluous.

Later, when winning became the ultimate goal, rules became *limits* – boundaries of permissible behavior; they were supposed to govern conduct and specify what we could and couldn't do. Rules not players governed acceptable conduct.

It's impossible to be precise about the time of the change in ethos. Sports such as association football and baseball were both professional in the nineteenth century, whereas rugby union did not go open until 1995. The Olympics were amateur for much of the IOC's history; but, during 1986–92, it introduced amendments in its charter that effectively permitted professionals to compete. Even allowing for this unevenness, we can surmise that, while competitors in all sports were committed to doing their utmost to win, those who competed for money rather than glory alone had to deal with temptation. They had "no reason not to cheat," according to William Morgan.

Rules, on Morgan's account, became technical directives that enabled practitioners to acquire "external goods," money being the primary one: any moral power the rules of sports once had disappeared. In the process, the underpinnings of sport were destroyed, argues Morgan, replaced by "market norms."

Morgan believes that the institutional imperatives of professional sports "underwrite and legitimate such rule breaking." Released from the moral constraints of playing on one's honor, professional competitors break rules whenever they believe they can escape being penalized for their infraction, and comply with every rule when they can't. If a player gets caught, it is either through technical infraction or miscalculation.

The ethos of professional sports is affected by sayings like "Winning isn't everything; it's the only thing" and "Is football a matter of life or death? . . . It's more important than that." Competitors are encouraged to adopt a win-at-all-costs attitude. So, it could be argued that the athlete who is prepared to risk disqualification and the defeat, shame and sometimes humiliation in order to win embodies the very qualities that define competitive sports in the twenty-first century.

However one wishes to interpret cheating – as an undesirable but inevitable consequence of professionalism, as an admirable characteristic of determined competitors – there is little doubt that it is a feature of all sports today. It manifests in three main ways:

(1) *An intentional infraction designed and executed to gain an unfair advantage*. Perhaps the most notorious unpunished instance of disguised cheating was Diego Maradona's "Hand of God" goal, when he palmed the ball into the goal of the England football team in a 1986 World Cup game. Video evidence showed that the Argentinean player used his hand illegally and probably intentionally. The referee did not see it and awarded a goal amid much protest. Maradona didn't confess his sin to the referee. As his biographer Jimmy Burns wrote: "Neither in the immediate aftermath of the game nor in the years that followed did Maradona ever admit to his folly" (1996: 163). Nor did New York Jets players own up to referee Phil Luckett, whose crew allowed a touchdown call to stand on quarterback Vinny Testaverde's play which finished over a foot shy of the endzone in the Jets' crucial 1998 game against Seattle Seahawks.

As the last major sport to turn professional, rugby union may have been a late developer. If any event symbolized its full membership of the ranks of professional sports, it was "Bloodgate." In 2009, during a Heineken Cup game, Harlequin's winger Tom Williams, under orders from coaches, feigned injury by biting on a blood capsule so he could be substituted. A club doctor then cut his mouth to make the injury look genuine. The club tried to cover up the incident and four previous uses of fake blood were revealed. It's conceivable that cheating occurred while the sport was amateur, though the contrivance of using blood capsules was probably a symptom of the win-oriented mentality of all professional sports.

"Bloodgate" showed that cheating is not confined to competitors. Owners, managers and coaches want to win just as fiercely as those who play under their guidance do. Tall stories of cornermen slipping horseshoes into their boxers' gloves may be laughable, but the most notorious instance of tampering with gloves was the Resto–Collins case of 1983. The unbeaten Billy Collins, then 21, took a terrible pounding from the normally light-hitting Luis Resto, who was 20–7–2 at the time. Collins' injuries were so bad that he did not fight again and was killed in a car accident nine months later. It was found that padding had been removed from Resto's gloves.

Resto was banned from boxing and, later, convicted of assault, conspiracy and criminal possession of a deadly weapon (his fists). His cornerman, Panama Al Lewis was convicted of assault, conspiracy, tampering with a sports contest and criminal possession of a deadly weapon. They both served 2 years in prison.

A conspiracy of owners and competitors lay at the heart of an F1 race-fixing in 2008: Renault team box Flavio Briatore and engineering chief Pat Symonds resigned after the disclosure that driver Nelson Piquet Jr. staged a deliberate crash during the inaugural Singapore Grand Prix in order to bring about the deployment of the safety car, which gave teammate Fernando Alonso a crucial advantage. When the safety car came into play, some drivers, notably Lewis Hamilton, were not able to refuel until the pit lane – closed on deployment of the safety car – was reopened. As a result, Hamilton lost times and was stuck in traffic. Alonso, meanwhile, in 17th place, but having already refueled, was able to come through and win the race. Renault's F1 future hinged on victory: it had been speculated that anything less would have effectively brought an end to the team's involvement in F1.

(2) *An unintentional infraction that goes unnoticed by game officials and which the offending player fails to report.* It is difficult to imagine an instance when a coach would not condone cheating if there was a guarantee that it would go undetected and an advantage to be gained. In a 1997 game of football between two English teams, Liverpool player Robbie Fowler was awarded a penalty after the referee ruled that Arsenal's goalkeeper David Seaman had fouled him. Fowler informed the referee that Seaman had not fouled him, but the referee was adamant that the penalty stood and Fowler duly took it. While Fowler's spotkick was saved and driven home on the rebound, one wonders what might have happened had the player remained true to his original confession and deliberately sliced the ball wide of the goal.

It strains credibility to believe that Liverpool's head coach would have commended him on his uprightness. More likely, he would have been disciplined for failing to act in the best interests of his team. In the event, the player was congratulated by teammates and was hailed as triumphant.

This was a rare case when a player actually owned-up to an official but was overruled in such a way that he prospered. Players are discouraged from such making such disclosures, not only by teammates and coaches, but by game officials themselves, who often interpret a player's confession – rare as they are – as an attempt to undermine his or her authority. Even if the original intention of the athlete was not to cheat, the structure of the game actually inhibits him or her from doing much else.

(3) *When rules are observed, but the spirit of competition is compromised.* Intention is never clear in instances of gamesmanship. These maneuvers are right at the margins of

fair game: strictly speaking legal, but designed to gain a benefit or relieve pressure.

During her losing match against Steffi Graf in the French Open final of 1999, Martina Hingis (a) demanded that the umpire inspect a mark on the clay surface after her forehand landed adjacent to the baseline, (b) went for a 5-minute restroom break at the start of the third set and (c) served underarm when facing match point on two occasions. While the actions did contravene the rules, they prompted Graf to ask the umpire: "We play *tennis*, OK?"

A dramatic fall by Arsenal player Eduardo in 2009 was the subject of intense, yet ultimately inconclusive scrutiny. Playing against Celtic in the European Champions League, the player tumbled after what appeared to be minimal contact with an opponent, and was awarded a penalty, from which his team scored. A retrospective charge of diving, or "simulation," yielded a two-match ban from Uefa; this was subsequently overturned when the governing organization failed to prove its case. Whether the player deliberately deceived the referee remains a talking point, though the absence of sanction suggests that the official view was that Eduardo was fouled and simply exaggerated his fall. Soccer players are so notorious for this that Fifa introduced rules that forced all injured (or pseudo-injured) players to be stretchered off the field of play before they could resume playing. Boxers employ a comparable stratagem, exaggerating the effects of low blows to gain time to recover when under pressure.

Instrumental qualities, such as prudence and calculation, are now parts of the character of professional sport, though we should guard against assuming amateurs were pure and virtuous. In 1976, for example, when the Olympics were amateur, Boris Onischenko, in a desperate bid for gold in his last Olympics, wired a switch under his leather grip, which triggered a hit when pressed during the fencing event of the modern pentathlon. He was disqualified after officials noticed that hits were registering even though his foil wasn't even touching his opponent. Money is the primary variable in motivational mixture behind cheating, but prestige, distinction and the status winning brings to the victor are also ingredients.

MORE QUESTIONS . . .

>>Should we admire rather than reprimand the cheat who escapes penalties?
>> Is there any truth in the proverb "Cheats never prosper"?
>> Do coaches and managers influence players' approach to cheating?

READ ON . . .

Gunther Lüschen, "Cheating," in *Social Problems in America*, edited by D. Landers, University of Illinois Press, 1976.

Peter McIntosh, *Fair Play*, Heinemann Educational, 1980.

Oliver Leaman, "Cheating and fair play in sport," in *Philosophic Inquiry in Sport*, edited by William J. Morgan and Klaus Meier, Human Kinetics, 1988.

Scott Ostler, *How to Cheat in Sports: Professional tricks exposed!*, Chronicle Books, 2008.

Barbara Bell, "Philosophy and ethics in sport," Chapter 3 in her book, *Sport Studies*, Learning Matters, 2009.

Fran Zimniuch, *Crooked: A history of cheating in sports*, Taylor Trade, 2009.

Champs and Cheats

AS OLD AS SPORT ITSELF

The Olympic motto is *Citius, altius, longius*, or faster, higher, longer and, during the twentieth century, sport found all sorts of ways of fulfilling this. Improving performance was the unquestioned purpose of not just Olympic sports but all sports. There wasn't a single moment of revelation when sport suddenly realized that moral questions were being posed by this pursuit of excellence, but, in 1976, the East German women's swim team won 11 of 13 gold medals at the summer Olympics. In particular Kornelia Ender became the first swimmer to win 4 gold medals at 1 games, all in world record times, 3 of them in individual events and 2 of those within 27 minutes of each other. She and her team were enthusiastically acclaimed as among the greatest athletes in history.

After the fall of the Berlin Wall in 1989, several East German athletes disclosed secrets of their training methods. Several told how they were given frequent doses of pills and injections of unknown substances. Ender revealed she started receiving injections at the age of 13. She was 17 at the time of the 1976 games. How should we look back on Ender? An essentially good, if naïve athlete who was exploited by a ruthless system? Or an overachiever who would stop at nothing in her efforts to rewrite the record books?

All sports are characterized by a conflict between opposites. Even off the field, good fights evil. The good is abundant: medals, championships, triumph, and, above all, the prevailing spirit of fair play. The evil is represented by the spread of doping among athletes willing to risk chemical side-effects, or even direct effects, in the attempt to build muscle, steady the hand, flush out body fluids, speed up the metabolism, improve endurance, or spark more aggression. There are substances available that can assist in all these, but woe betide any athlete caught taking them. Before addressing the issues of today, let's trace the history of drug use in sports. It's a common mistake to assume that using drugs in sport is a recent innovation: it's been around for as long as sport itself.

Taking supplements as a way of improving physical or mental performance in sports is arguably as old as sports themselves. Competitors in the ancient Greco-Roman games were known to eat animals' parts, such as horns or the secretions of testes, which they thought would confer the strength of bulls, for example. It's probable that Greeks habitually used plants and mushrooms with chemically active derivatives either to aid performance or accelerate the healing process.

In the modern era, as sports became professionalized, evidence of the systematic use of stimulants arrived initially through the six-day cycle races in Europe. Riders in the late nineteenth century favored ether and caffeine to delay the onset of fatigue sensations. Sprint cyclists preferred nitroglycerine, a violently explosive chemical later used in conjunction with heroin, cocaine, strychnine, and others. In his *Journal of Sports History* article, "Anabolic steroids: The gremlins of sport," Terry Todd records "the first known drug related death of an athlete", in 1886, after a cyclist had taken a "speed ball" of heroin and cocaine (1987: 91). Another cyclist, Arthur Linton, collapsed and died in 1896, though it is disputed whether or not his death was due to drugs.

"The most famous early case of drug enhancement, however, occurred in the 1904 Olympic Games in St. Louis," writes Todd. Marathon winner Thomas Hicks, of the United States, collapsed after the race. "Hicks' handlers, who had been allowed to accompany him throughout the course of the race in a motor car, admitted they had given him repeated doses of strychnine and brandy to keep him on his feet" (1987: 91). Hicks was allowed to keep his medal. (While known principally as a poison, the vegetable alkaloid strychnine was also used as a stimulant.)

There's irony in the fact that sports medicine's role in contemporary sports was given impetus by the efforts of sports federations to eliminate the use of the very products that medicine gave to sports. This is the conclusion of Ivan Waddington, whose article "The development of sports medicine" shows clearly that medicine was originally invoked by sports to help improve performance (1996). It did so, of course. Medicine's largesse included pharmaceuticals, many to treat sports-related injuries, but many others to promote competitive performance. In the 1950s, colleges in Germany and the United States were established to exploit the applications of medicine to sports.

The Male Hormone, a book by American microbiologist, Paul de Kruiff (1890–1971), which was published in 1945, covered research into the impact of testosterone on the endurance of men involved in muscular work; and this alerted some coaches to the potential of what was supposed to be a medically prescribed treatment. After returning from the 1952 Olympics convinced that the successful Soviet weightlifting team had used "hormone stuff," U.S. coach Bob Hoffman sought something similar for his own squad. The product he obtained was Dianabol, an anabolic steroid first produced by the CIBA company in 1958 and intended for patients suffering from burns. The gains in weight and strength were impressive enough to convince him and observers of the value of medical science in sports. During the 1950s and 1960s, there were no rules forbidding the use of pharmaceuticals and, as news of Dianabol circulated in the sports world, strength-reliant competitors, like field-eventers and football players started using steroids. Other sports were not slow to realize the importance of testosterone and, through the 1960s, it was commonplace for cyclists, skiers and an assortment of other athletes to use the substance.

BOX 11.1 TESTOSTERONE

This is a steroid androgen formed mainly in the testes that stimulates the natural production of sperm cells which, in turn, affects the male's masculine appearance. A feedback control system is at work involving the hypothalamus; this secretes a hormone called LHR which stimulates the pituitary gland to secrete luteinizing hormone (LH) and this, in turn, stimulates the testes to produce the testosterone. A high concentration of testosterone inhibits the secretion of LHR by the hypothalamus, which causes a drop in the level of testosterone, triggering the hypothalamus to release more LHR, LH, and ultimately testosterone in a smoothly regulated system. The word is a composite: *testis + o + sterol + one* (for *ketone*).

If there was a turning point in attitudes toward the use of drugs in sport, it was on July 13, 1967, when Tommy Simpson, then 29, collapsed and died on the 13th stage of the three-week long Tour de France. Simpson, a British rider, was lying seventh overall when the race set off from Marseilles. The temperature was well over 40°C (104°F). Simpson fell and remounted twice before falling for the final time. Three tubes were found in his pocket, one full of amphetamines, and two empties. The British team's luggage was searched and more supplies of the pills were found. At the time, the drugs element did not cause the sensation that might be expected today: the death itself was of most concern. In continental Europe, there was substantial and open advocacy of the use of such pills to alleviate the strain of long-distance cycling. There is little doubt that many of the leading contenders in the 1967 and other Tours were taking amphetamines. Seven years before, in a less publicized tragedy, another cyclist, Knut Jensen collapsed during his race and later died in hospital where amphetamine was found in his system. (His was the second Olympic death after Portuguese marathon runner Francisco Lazaro died from heatstroke in 1912.)

An attempt in the previous year to introduce drug testing was opposed by leading cyclists, including the five-times Tour winner Jacques Anquetil, who told the newspaper *France-Dimanche*: "Yes, I dope myself. You would be a fool to imagine that a professional cyclist who rides 235 days a year in all temperatures and conditions can hold up without a stimulant." Interestingly, Simpson was not denounced as a cheat at the time; his death opened up a rather different discourse about the perils of drug-taking rather than the morality of it.

The IOC had actually set up a Medical Commission in 1950, mainly to investigate the medical effects of the use of stimulants, especially amphetamines, to increase endurance. Simpson's death prompted the introduction of testing, which came into being at the 1968 winter Olympics, though it was, as Barrie Houlihan calls it, a "modest effort" and largely for research purposes (1997: 180). Todd cites an American decathlete at the Mexico Olympic Games of 1968, who estimated a third of the U.S. track and field team used steroids at training camp (1987: 95). Writer Jack Scott reported that drugs were circulated quite freely at Mexico and conversations revolved not around the morality of taking them, but which ones were most effective (1971).

The games themselves were memorable, with some athletes collapsing with exhaustion in the rarified atmosphere and others producing extraordinary performances. In particular, Bob Beamon improved the world's long jump record by 21.75 inches with a leap of 29 ft 2.5 in (8.90 m). In the previous 33 years, the record had progressed by only 8.5 inches; it took a further 23 years before Mike Powell broke Beamon's record.

Beginning 1960, East Germany had operated a systematic program of inducting about 10,000 young people into sports academies where they were trained, conditioned, and supplied with pharmaceuticals intended to improve their athletic performance. State Program 1425, as it was known, was responsible for some of the world's outstanding track achievements, including Marita Koch's 47.60-second 400-meter record set in 1985 and rarely threatened ever since. After the end of the cold war, a special team of prosecutors began sifting through captured files of the Stasi secret police and uncovered details of often-abusive treatment accorded young athletes. Offenders were later prosecuted.

THE STRANGE CASE OF DR ASTAPHAN AND MR JOHNSON

Drug use in American sports was less systematic: stories of baseball and football players' use of amphetamines, narcotic analgesics and other substances were escaping via books such as Scott's *The Athletic Revolution* (1971) and Paul Hoch's *Rip Off the Big Game* which concluded "that the biggest drug dealers in the sports world are none other than team trainers" (1972: 122). Ted Kotcheff's 1979 film *North Dallas Forty*, which was based on Pete Gent's account of pro football, showed football players trotting onto the field as near-zombies after taking copious amounts of painkillers and sundry other drugs.

Coaches were doling out amphetamines to pep players up and analgesics to help them play without the sensation of pain while carrying injuries before a game. After a game the players were, as Hoch puts it, "tranquilized to get their eyeballs back in their head – to even get a night's sleep" (1972: 123). Hoch cites two players who filed lawsuits against their clubs for administering drugs "deceptively and without consent" and which eventually proved detrimental to their health. (1972: 123).

Estimates about the amount of drug use are so vague as to be useless, but it is at least suggestive that, in 1983, a *Sports Illustrated* article stated that between 40 and 90 percent of NFL players used anabolic steroids (May 13). Several deaths were attributed to steroids in the years that followed. In 1987, the International Olympic Committee (IOC) recorded 521 positive tests for steroid use; this was 16 years after the introduction of antidrug legislation by the International Amateur Athletics

Federation (IAAF). Anabolic steroids weren't added to the IAAF's banned list until 1976; the organization didn't have a reliable test until 1974, anyway.

Recreational drug use was also widespread among athletes. In his 1986 book *Fractured Focus*, Richard Lapchick referred to an "epidemic in American sport" and highlighted several athletes who were either in prison or fighting addictions. The NBA, in particular, was infamous for the number of cocaine-using players and, as we will see in Chapter 16, improved its marketability only after introducing drugs testing. A succession of boxers, football players, and other athletes were penalized for cocaine use. While cocaine use was probably recreational rather than performance enhancing, the term "drugs" was used indiscriminately. Using such an emotive word had the effect of heightening the feeling that sports were adrift in a moral sea with no *terra firma* in sight.

Unquestionably, the case that converted concern over drug-use in sports from concern to hysteria was the ejection of Canadian sprinter Ben Johnson from the 1988 Seoul Olympics after he had won the 100 meters in a world record 9.79 seconds. Stanozolol, an anabolic steroid, was detected in Johnson's urine sample; he was stripped of his gold medal and his time expunged from the records. Overnight, Johnson went from the "world's fastest man" to the "world's fastest cheat." While he was the 31st competitor to be disqualified for drug use since the IOC instituted its systematic testing in 1972, Johnson's stature in world sport ensured that his case would make news everywhere and that he as an individual would carry the sins of all. As well as his medal and record, he instantly lost (at the most conservative estimate) $2 million in performance-related product endorsement fees.

Fifteen years later, it was revealed that Carl Lewis, who was awarded the gold, had tested positive for three stimulants, including ephedrine, two months before the 1988 Olympics, but was allowed to compete after the United States Olympic Committee (USOC) accepted his appeal that he was unaware of the contents of a herbal supplement he'd used. Of the other sprinters in the fateful race, third-placed Linford Christie was banned for two years in 2000 after a positive drugs test, fifth-placed Dennis Mitchell was banned for two years after testing positive in 1999 and sixth-placed Desai Williams was implicated in the Dubin inquiry into the use of banned substances by Canadian athletes. In retrospect, Johnson appears a convenient scapegoat.

BOX 11.2 DUBIN INQUIRY

This was the official inquiry headed by Charles Dubin set up following Ben Johnson's ejection from the 1988 Olympics. Among the inquiry's conclusions was the fact that there was a conspiracy of silence among athletes, coaches, and physicians. Dr Jamie Astaphan, Johnson's physician, referred to "the brotherhood of the needle." Dr Robert Kerr, author of *The Practical Use of Anabolic Steroids with Athletes* (1982), testified that he had prescribed anabolic steroids to about 20 medalists at the 1984 summer Olympics. At the hearings, IOC vice-president Richard Pound famously answered the question why, with rumors abounding, he did not ask Johnson if he took drugs: "As a lawyer, I felt I was better off not knowing" (Houlihan, 1997: 194–5).

Following the Johnson case, the use of drugs to improve athletic performance was universally condemned by sporting authorities. Lists of prohibited substances lengthened so that many prescription drugs and perfectly legal products that could be purchased at drugstores were banned. Alexander Watson, an Australian pentathlete was disqualified from the same Olympics as Johnson, for having an excessive level of caffeine in his system; to have reached such a level he would have needed to have drunk 40 regular-sized cups of coffee.

The expulsion of Argentinean player Diego Maradona from the 1994 soccer World Cup was the biggest "bust" since Johnson. He'd tested positive before in 1991 (and, would again fail drug tests in 1997 and 2000). Maradona all but has his cleats exchanged for cloven hooves during a media demonization. Like Johnson, he was an exceptional athlete, a world-class competitor who had, in the eyes of the world, resorted to cheating. But, there was a suspicion that, in another sense, he was not exceptional at all; he was simply one of countless others who systematically used substances to enhance their performance. They probably escaped detection through a variety of methods, such as coming off the drugs early, taking masking agents, or catheterizing (replacing the contents of one's own bladder with someone else's drug-free urine).

The Tour de France of 1998 disintegrated into chaos after the disqualification of one team, police raids on the hotels of several teams and a go-slow protest by riders at the 17th stage. The expulsion of the entire Festina Watches team was unprecedented in the race's 95-year history. All nine Festina riders were taken into police custody, along with three more team directors. The specific charge against the masseur was for smuggling drugs, including anabolic steroids and erythropoietin (EPO). Four people connected with a second squad, TVM, were also questioned over a seizure of banned substances.

The Festina manager, Bruno Rousel, told a police inquiry of "the conditions under which a coordinated supply of doping products was made available to the riders, organized by the team management, the doctors, the masseurs and the riders. The aim was to maximize performance under strict medical control to avoid the riders obtaining drugs for themselves in circumstances which might have been seriously damaging to their health." Rousel reported that the drug war chest amounted to £40,000 ($65,000) per year, or 1 percent of the team's £4 million annual budget.

Rider Frederic Pontier confessed to the French sports daily newspaper *L'Equipe* that he had used EPO and knew that an "important number" of other cyclists were also using performance enhancers. Police sweeps resulted in a number of other riders and officials being held for questioning. The crisis deepened when competitors sensed they were being, as rider Jeroen Blijlevens put it, "treated like animals, like criminals." Their snail's pace demonstration forced organizers to annul the Albertville–Aix-les-Bains stage of the race.

By the time of the Tour de France scandal, drugs-testing procedures were in place in all major sports and each had policies, most derived from the IOC's. The list of proscribed substances had lengthened to the point where athletes needed to be careful about reading the labels on over-the-counter headache or cold remedies in case they contained a banned constituent.

But anyone who thought the scandalous Tour of 1998 would sound out a warning around the world and effectively put a stop to doping in sport was being naïve. The positive tests kept coming – and from all sources.

Paradoxically, one athlete who never returned a positive drugs test became the most notorious offender of the twenty-first century. Marion Jones, winner of five Olympic medals in the 2000 games alone, was imprisoned after admitting to having lied to U.S. federal government investigators about using steroids. Her initial defense against allegations was that she'd repeatedly taken doping tests and never once failed. Circumstantial evidence was assembled that suggested she had. Eventually, Jones's admission that she used steroids and lied about it might have become a *cause célèbre* on the same scale as Johnson's disgrace in the late 1980s, but the response was something like a shrug, "Another one bites the dust, eh?"

Justin Gatlin, the 2004 Olympic 100-meter winner gave a positive test in 2006 and his suspension broke on the heels of two memorable cases, those of Floyd Landis's case in the Tour de France and world 100-meter sprint record-holder Tim Montgomery. In the background was another name – Balco. It wasn't the name of an athlete, a racehorse, or a Latvian soccer club, but a company: it stands for Bay Area Laboratory Cooperative and it specialized in producing dietary supplements that, when taken as part of a nutrition program, helped athletes build muscle, enduring and speed and helped recovery. Why is the name so important? Because, according to its proprietors, it supplied its products to several of the world's leading athletes, including NFL and Major League Baseball players as well as track and field athletes – not just any old track and field athletes, but Olympic stars, including the much-garlanded Jones.

Balco, which had operated since 1984, claimed its formulations had been used extensively by clients from around the world. Some of the products were acceptable to governing organizations. Others were either on the banned list or were related closely to substances on the list. The implications were potentially immense: if many of the athletes we had admired and respected for their achievements were boosting their performances with supplements that had escaped detection, how many more were there out there? How many world records, Olympic golds, baseball championships, boxing titles, football trophies, or other major prizes were won with a little assistance from Victor Conte, the man who ran Balco?

BOX 11.3 BALCO

The company was started in 1994 by Victor Conte, a one-time musician turned entrepreneur, who developed a legal dietary supplement called ZMA (zinc, magnesium, aspartate) that purported to build muscle and accelerate recovery after exercise. The product was used by several athletes and approved of by coaches, including the Ukrainian veteran Remi Korchemny. Conte formed the ZMA Track Club. Among the athletes who used Balco products were Barry Bonds, Bill Romanowski, Marion Jones, and Dwain Chambers. In 2003, an informant anonymously sent a syringe with residual amounts of a substance known as "the clear" to the USADA in Colorado, naming Balco as the source. The substance was the hitherto unknown THG. Traces were discovered in one of Chambers' urine samples and he was subsequently banned. In the same year, a federal grand jury initiated investigations into Balco for tax evasion, money laundering, and illegal distribution of controlled substances. In February 2004, the U.S. Attorney General announced a 42-count indictment against Conte, Korchemny, Greg Anderson, a trainer, and James Valente, a Balco director. The USADA notified several U.S. athletes, who had not failed drug tests, that they were either being investigated or charged with drugs violations.

BANNED SUBSTANCES

The IOC's banned list includes over 4,000 substances, which are grouped into five categories. They are anabolic steroids, stimulants, narcotic analgesics, beta-blockers, and diuretics. I'll deal with them in that order, before moving to an examination of blood doping, peptide hormones and procedures for detecting substances in sports competitors.

Anabolic steroids

In 1889, Charles Brown-Sequard devised a rejuvenating therapy for body and mind: the 72-year-old French physiologist had claimed he had increased his physical strength, improved his intellectual energy, relieved his constipation, and even lengthened the arc of his urine by injecting himself with an extract derived from the testes of dogs and guinea-pigs. His discovery triggered a series of experiments that led to synthesis of testosterone, the primary male hormone produced in the testes, in 1935. The German military was impressed enough to feed it to soldiers in an effort to increase their strength and intensify their aggression. Since then, synthetic testosterone has been attributed with almost magical qualities and become the most controversial drug in sports. For this reason, it is worth reviewing its history.

There's nothing new about the concept of ingesting animals' sexual organs and secretions: Egyptians accorded medicinal powers to the testes; Johannes Mesue prescribed a kind of testicular extract as an aphrodisiac; the *Pharmacopoea Wirtenbergica*, a compendium of remedies published in 1754 in Germany, refers to horse testicles and the penises of amphibious mammals, like walruses and manatee. These and several other examples are given by John Hoberman and Charles Yesalis, whose *Scientific American* article on the subject is essential reading for students of the history of performance-enhancing drugs (1995).

In 1896, an Austrian physiologist and future Nobel Prize winner, Oskar Zoth, published a paper, which concluded that extracts from bulls' testes, when injected in athletes led to improvements in muscular strength and the "neuromuscular apparatus." Here was the first official recognition of the significance of hormonal substances for sports competitors. Zoth anticipated the objection that a placebo effect might have accounted for the change in his sample of athletes and denied it. Around the same time, other scientists were excited by the prospect of finding the active ingredient in the male sex organ and specifying its effects.

BOX 11.4 PLACEBO

From the Latin *placere*, to please, this is a pharmacologically inert substance given to patients usually to humor them rather than effect any cure. Yet the substance often works as effectively (if not more so) as an active substance because the patient believes it will. The substance is called a placebo and its result is known as the placebo effect. This has many applications outside the clinical setting. Weightlifters have been told they were receiving an anabolic steroid while, in fact, only some of them received it – the others were given a placebo. Both groups improved leg presses, the first group by 135 lb, the other (receiving the placebo) by 132 lb. The sheer expectation of benefit seems to have been the crucial factor. A similar process can work in reverse. For example, subjects might be given active drugs together with information that they will have no effect: consequently the drugs might not have any effect. In other words, the direct effect of drugs alone might not be any more powerful than the administrator's or experimenter's suggestions. More recently, research has shown that high doses of testosterone given to healthy young men can increased muscle size but not necessarily strength. Increases in strength might come about as a result of the extra hard training the subjects were encouraged to do by taking the substance.

Clinical applications were many. In 1916, two Philadelphia doctors transplanted a human testicle into a patient who was suffering from sexual dysfunctions, starting a spate of similar transplants, the most audacious being a mass removal of the testes of recently executed inmates for transplanting into patients suffering from impotence. Pharmaceutical corporations spotted the commercial potential and initiated research programs to isolate the active hormone and synthesize it. By 1939, clinical trials in humans were underway, employing injections of testosterone propionate. Early synthetic testosterone was used with some success by women suffering from a variety of complaints, the intention being to alter a female's hormonal balance. One of the problems was that the testosterone virilized the patients: they took on male secondary features, like facial hair and enlarged larynx.

From the 1940s male sex hormones (androgens) were used to treat wasting conditions associated with chronic debilitating illnesses and trauma, burns, surgery, and radiation therapy. Anabolic steroids' efficacy in accelerating red blood cell production made it first choice therapy for a variety of anemias (having too little hemoglobin) before bone marrow transplants and other treatments arrived. Between the 1930s and the mid-1980s, psychiatrists prescribed anabolic steroids for the treatment of depression and psychoses. Recently, steroids have been used to arrest the muscle wasting that occurs during the progression of HIV infection and Aids.

Testosterone treatment is currently in use for strengthening older bodies, rejuvenating an ailing libido, and improving a declining memory.

Steroids weren't considered a problem at all for sports until the late 1970s. After the 1988 Johnson case, they became high-priority. German sprinters Katrin Krabbe, Silke Möller and Grit Breuer submitted identical urine samples in out-of-competition tests prior to the 1992 Barcelona games, but escaped a ban on a technicality. The case served notice that the drugs issue would remain on the agenda at all future games.

Today, few people doubt the efficacy of anabolic steroids: they *do* work. Precisely what makes them work, we still don't know for sure. There is, for instance, a school of thought that argues that the critical component in the equation is our belief that they will enhance our performance. If, for some reason, we stopped believing in them, then maybe anabolic steroids wouldn't yield the results they apparently do. At present, so much money is spent on testing for drugs that there is little left for ascertaining exactly what they do to sports competitors. If self-belief is the single most important factor, it might be that a placebo is at work. (For a fuller discussion of the purported effects of anabolic steroids, see Yesalis, 1993.)

Not all products specifically developed to enhance athletic performance are condemned – at least not universally condemned. For example, creatine was sold legally and endorsed by sports competitors and became popular as a result of its supposed muscle-building properties. Androstenedione, another product available over the counter at any health food store was use used by Mark McGwire during his history-making 1998 season. "Andro," to use its more popular abbreviation, had effects that many swore were identical to those of steroids: it stimulated the increased production of testosterone, but didn't appear on Major League Baseball's banned list at the time. On the other hand, Randy Barnes, the 1966 Olympic shot-put champion, was suspended for two years after andro was found in his sample – his second drugs test in eight years. The rights and wrongs of andro were discussed, but technically it was recognized as a food rather than a drug and McGwire, while criticized by some, used it with impunity.

Tetrahydrogestrinone (THG), on the other hand, landed its users in serious trouble. Developed by the previously mentioned Balco, the "designer drug" was detected in the sample of British sprinter Dwain Chambers, who was suspended as a result. He was also banned from Olympic competition. The unusual aspect of

BOX 11.5 ANABOLIC STEROIDS

From the Greek *ana*, meaning "up" and *bole* "throw," anabolism is the constructive metabolism of complex substances for body tissues, i.e. bodybuilding. Steroids are compounds whose molecules contain rings of carbon and hydrogen atoms; they influence cells by causing special proteins to be synthesized. So, an anabolic steroid is a compound considered to be responsible for the particular synthesis that causes the construction of muscle mass. The idea of using an anabolic steroid is to mirror the chemical action of the testosterone in the body and facilitate muscle growth.

Chambers' ban was that it wasn't preceded by a regular test, but by an anonymous whistle-blower, who sent a syringe containing THG to the U.S. Anti-Doping Agency in June 2003. The drugs testers had never seen and probably not heard of THG, but they identified it as related to banned steroids and tested urine samples retrospectively. This started the events that reverberated through every sport and caused observers to ponder: if THG was only stumbled across by accident, how many other substances with performance enhancing properties have escaped detection over the years?

Stimulants

Evidence of the systematic application of stimulants arrived initially through the six-day cycle races in Europe. Riders in the late nineteenth century favored ether and caffeine to delay the onset of fatigue sensations. Sprint cyclists preferred nitroglycerine, a chemical later used in conjunction with heroin, cocaine, strychnine, and other substances.

The basic effect of stimulants is to get messages to a complex pathway of neurons in the brainstem called the arousal system, or reticular activating system (RAS). This system is ultimately responsible for maintaining consciousness and determining our state of awareness. So, if the RAS bombards the cerebral cortex with stimuli, we feel very alert and able to think clearly. Amphetamines are thought to cause chemical neurotransmitters, such as dopamine, to increase, so enhancing the flow of nervous impulses in the RAS and stimulating the entire CNS. The sympathetic nervous system is stimulated, speeding up heart rate, raising blood pressure, and dilating pupils. In sports terms, the competitor is fired up and resistant to the sensation of fatigue, particularly the muscular pain associated with lactic acid.

One problem facing users active in sport who need nutrition for the release of energy is that amphetamines depress appetites. They used to be prescribed to dieters, though less so nowadays because dieters became dependent on the drug. This came about because the body quickly develops a tolerance, probably through the readiness of the liver to break down the drug rapidly. An obvious temptation is to increase the dose to achieve the same effect. So with increased use of the drug, the user becomes dependent. Weight loss and dependence are the more obvious side-effects; others include irritability (probably due to irregular sleep) and even a tendency toward paranoia.

There is another class of stimulants called sympathomimetic amine drugs, such as ephedrine, or ephedra, which acts not on the brain but directly on the nerves affecting the organs. (This produces effects in the sympathetic part of the autonomic nervous system: it speeds up the action of the heart, constricts arteries and increases lung inflation.) Ephedra was once commonly found in decongestants as well as over-the-counter dietary supplements with names like Ripped Fuel or BiLean. The U.S. Food and Drug Administration accepted evidence that the ingredient raised blood pressure and could promote heart ailments and banned it from general use.

Narcotic analgesics

Painkillers are used in all walks of life, but especially in sports where injuries are commonplace and a tolerance to pain is essential. Soccer and American football are examples of games involving the "walking wounded." Derivatives of the opium poppy were probably used by ancient Mesopotamians around 2000 BCE; they left instructions for use on wax tablets.

There are now methods of producing such derivatives synthetically. Opium, heroin, codeine, and morphine, along with designer drugs, are all classified as narcotics, which relieve pain and depress the CNS, producing a state of stupor. Reflexes slow down, the skeleton is relaxed, and tension is reduced. The negative effects are much the same as those of amphetamines, with the additional one of specific neurons becoming dependent on the drug and so providing a basis for addiction. Brett Favre had such an addiction.

The immediate effects of stimulants or narcotic analgesics would be of little or no service to sports competitors who rely on fineness of judgment, sensitivity of touch, acuity of sight, and steadiness of hand. Success in sports like darts, archery, snooker, shooting, or show jumping is based on calmness and an imperviousness to "pressure." The Canadian snooker player Bill Werbeniuk was famed for his customary ten pints of beer to help him relax before a game. His CNS would become duller and tensions presumably disappeared. How he managed to coordinate hand and eye movements, stay awake, or even just stay upright is a mystery. Alcohol has serious drawbacks, which include nausea and impaired judgment, not to mention long-term liver damage, and a variety of dependency-related problems.

Beta-blockers

The Vancouver-based Werbeniuk switched to Inderal, a beta-blocker that helped counteract the effects of a hereditary nervous disorder. After criticism from the British Minister for Sport, the World Professional Billiards and Snooker Association (WPBSA) reviewed its drug policy and included Inderal on its list of banned substances. Unable to find an alternative, Werbeniuk admitted to the WPBSA that he intended to continue using the drug and was eventually banned from tournaments.

Originally used by patients with irregular heartbeats, beta-blockers relieve anxiety by controlling the release of adrenaline and by lowering the heart rate; they are used by edgy showbusiness competitors – and horses. In November 1994, a racehorse, Mobile Messenger, tested positive for propranolol, a beta-blocker, after winning a race at Southwell, England. The effect of the drug on the horse would have been similar to that on a human: to slow down the heart rate and thereby alleviate stress.

Diuretics

Weightlifters and other sports competitors who compete in categories based on body weight have to calibrate their diet and preparation carefully. A couple of pounds, even ounces, over the limit can destroy months of conditioning if the competitor is made to take off the excess at the weigh-in. Jumping rope, saunas, and other methods of instant weight reduction can be debilitating and might drain cerebral fluid that cushions the brain against the wall of the cranium. Competitors in weight-controlled sports always check-weigh during the days preceding an event and, should their weight seem excessive, might take diuretics. These substances – widely used therapeutically for reducing fluid levels – excite the kidneys to produce more urea and, basically, speed up a perfectly natural waste disposal process. A visit to the bathroom is usually necessary after drinking alcoholic drinks or coffee; this is because they both contain diuretics.

Diuretics inhibit the secretion of the antidiuretic hormone which serves as a chemical messenger, carrying information from the pituitary gland at the base of the brain to parts of the kidneys, making them more permeable and allowing water to be reabsorbed into the body (thus conserving fluid). Hormones, of course, are carried in the blood. If the messages don't get through, the kidneys move the water out of the body. Continued use of diuretics can damage the kidneys. In recent years, the suspicion has grown that competitors have not only been using diuretics to reduce weight but also to flush out other substances, in particular the above-mentioned drugs.

It follows that competitors found to have diuretics in their urine immediately have their motives questioned. Kerrith Brown of Great Britain lost his Olympic bronze medal for judo despite pleading that the diuretic furosemide, found in his urine, was introduced into his system by a medical officer who gave him an anti-inflammatory substance containing the chemical to reduce a knee swelling.

Peptide hormones

The values of altitude training are undoubted. In Chapter 3, we recognized the importance of the protein molecule hemoglobin, which is found in red blood cells. It has a remarkable ability to form loose associations with oxygen. As most oxygen in the blood is combined with hemoglobin rather than simply dissolved in plasma, the more hemoglobin present in a red blood cell, the more oxygen it can transport to the muscles. Obviously then, competitors can benefit from having a plentiful supply of oxygen to react with glucose and release energy stored in food. The advantage of training at altitude, where the oxygen in the atmosphere is scarce, is that the body naturally compensates by producing more hemoglobin.

When the athlete descends to sea level, he or she carries a plentiful supply of hemoglobin in the blood, which gradually readjusts. Each day spent at lower altitudes diminishes the benefit of altitude training: a proliferation of hemoglobin ceases in the presence of available atmospheric oxygen. One way to "capture" the benefits is to remove a quantity of highly oxygenated blood during intense altitude training, store it, and reintroduce it into the circulatory system immediately prior to competition via a transfusion. This is known as blood doping and the IOC banned it in 1986.

The "doping" in this process doesn't refer to the administration of drugs but to the more correct use of the term, pertaining to a thick liquid used as a food or lubricant. There is, however, a synthetic drug that can achieve much the same effect. Erythropoietin (EPO) facilitates the production of extra red blood cells, which absorb oxygen, and leaves the user with no telltale needle tracks. As well as being more convenient than a transfusion, EPO has the advantage of being extremely difficult to detect once it has been administered.

The biggest EPO case was uncovered when French police traced a delivery of EPO and some masking agents to a Paris address. Fifteen people including cyclists Frank Vandenbroucke and soccer player Jean-Christophe Devaux were arrested along with Lionel Virenque, brother of French cyclist Richard Virenque who was already under investigation for his alleged part in the Tour de France scandal of the previous year. In 2004, Philippe Gaumont admitted using and providing EPO to other riders, suggesting that this remained the drug of choice for professional cyclists. Cycling's governing organization *Union Cycliste Internationale* (UCI), employs a hemocrit test that measures the red blood cell ratio and is suggestive of the use of EPO. Riders who register a dangerously high ratio are suspended from racing for their own safety. Even a low count can be a problem if anomalies are discovered. For example, Gorka Gonzalez was declared unfit to ride shortly before the 2004 Tour: his hemocrit level was below the 50 percent set by the UCI, but the presence of reticulocytes – young blood cells – indicated doping.

In attempts to boost red cells, some athletes sleep in hypobaric chambers or use hypoxic machines that are designed to replicate high altitude atmospheres. Such devices are not prohibited by sports organizations, though the benefits accrued are much the same as if athletes had opted for illicit methods.

Blood doping and EPO, in a sense, copy the body's natural processes and, at the moment, their long-term effects seem to be broadly the same as those of living at high altitudes. Another method of mimicking nature is by extracting the naturally occurring human growth hormone, somatotropin (hGH), which is produced and released by the pituitary gland, as discussed in Chapter 3. hGH controls the human rate of growth by regulating the amount of nutrients taken into the body's cells and by stimulating protein synthesis. Overproduction of the hormone might cause a child to grow to giant proportions (a condition referred to as gigantism), whereas too little can lead to dwarfism. hGH also affects fat and carbohydrate metabolism in adults, promoting a mobilization of fat, which becomes available for use as fuel, and sparing the utilization of protein. The potential of this mechanism for promoting growth has not been lost on field athletes, weightlifters, bodybuilders, and others requiring muscle build.

Illicit markets in growth hormone extracted from fetuses have been uncovered, though a synthetically manufactured version, somatonorm, has nearly made this redundant. In 1997, customs officers at Sydney, Australia, found 13 vials of Norditropin, the brand name of somatotropin, in a bag belonging to Yuan Yuan, a member of China's team in the World Swimming Championships. Yuan Yuan, at 21, was the youngest member of the team and ranked 13 in the world for the breaststroke. It was speculated that, as a relatively lowly member of the team, she was a guinea-pig intended to ascertain whether hGH could be detected through conventional equipment.

This has led some to believe that drug users can always stay one step ahead of those wishing to identify them: the line between what is "natural" and "unnatural" for the human body is not so clear cut as testers would like and science finds ways of replicating nature. By the end of the 1990s, substances such as insulin growth hormone (IGH) and perfluorocarbon (PFC), a type of highly oxygenated plasma, were impossible to detect through conventional methods. Others believe that drug-testing methods are keeping pace and not even the elite can escape detection, given a vigilant team of toxicologists and a sophisticated laboratory. But doubts remain.

DOUBTS ABOUT TESTING

Although antidoping policies have their origins in the 1970s, comprehensive testing equipment wasn't introduced until 1988, when Hewlett-Packard set up a system of gas chromatography and mass spectroscopy at the Korean Advanced Institute of Science and Technology. The IOC commissioned the new system for the Seoul Olympics; according to its makers, it could detect concentrations [of banned substances] as low as one part per billion; roughly the equivalent to detecting traces from a teaspoonful of sugar after it has been dissolved in an Olympic swimming pool. A further claim was that it could check a compound found in urine against 70,000 held in a computer's database in "less than a minute." As new substances have been added to the banned list, so the equipment has been modified to detect them.

The entire testing process comprises four phases. (1) Within an hour of the finish of an event, two samples of a competitor's urine are taken, one is tested for acidity and specific gravity so that testers can get a broad indication of any illegal compounds. (2) The sample is then split into smaller batches to test for certain classes of drugs, such as anabolic steroids, stimulants, etc. Testers make the urine alkaline and mix it with solvents, like ether, causing any drugs to dissolve into the solvent layer, which is more easily analyzed than urine itself. (3) This solvent is then passed through a tube (up to 25 meters long) of gas (or liquid chromatogram) and the molecules of the solvent separate and pass through at different rates, depending on their size and other properties (such as whether they are more likely to adhere to the material of the tube itself). More than 200 drugs are searched for in this period, which lasts about 15 minutes. (4) Any drugs found are then analyzed with a mass spectrometer, which bombards them with high-energy ions, or electrons, creating unique chemical fingerprints, which can be rapidly checked against the database. Should any banned substances show up, the second sample is tested in the presence of the competitor. (Another method is radioimmunoassay, in which antibodies to known substances are used like keys that will only fit one lock; the lock is the banned substance which is found by the key that fits it.)

Encouraged by the global response to the Johnson case at Seoul, the IOC stated its intention to implement all-year-round testing and, national sports organizations followed its example, though not without problems. By 1999, a catalog of cases involving athletes challenging their test results had accumulated. Among the most discussed was that Harry "Butch" Reynolds who tested positive for the steroid nandrolone in 1991, and was suspended by USA Track and Field (USATF) with the support of the IAAF. Reynolds challenged the decision all the way to the Supreme

Court and was eventually awarded damages totaling, $26 million (£16 million) and allowed to compete in the U.S. Olympic trials.

Further doubts about the reliability of testing procedures were cast by the case of British runner Diane Modahl who was banned from competition for four years after failing a drug test at a meeting in Lisbon, Portugal, in 1994. The test was administered under the auspices of the Portuguese Athletics Federation. From the sample taken at the meet, Modahl's urine showed a testosterone to epitestosterone ratio (T–E ratio) reading of 42:1. Any ratio above 6:1 provides evidence of the presence of an excessive amount of testosterone and thus grounds for suspension. A reading of six times the permitted ratio suggested that Modahl had taken gross amounts of a prohibited substance – much more, in fact, than Ben Johnson had when he was banned after the Seoul Olympics in 1988.

After being banned, Modahl appealed to an independent panel constituted by the British Athletics Federation and an investigation opened up questions about the testing procedures followed. Lacking conclusive evidence, the panel determined that there was reasonable doubt over whether or not Modahl had taken proscribed substances. The British Athletics Federation (BAF) agreed, the International Amateur Athletics Federation decided not to refer the case to an arbitration panel and Modahl resumed her running career. Her ban lifted on appeal, Modahl sought up to $500,000 (£305,000) in damages from the BAF, which became bankrupt in 1997.

Further questions about the reliability of testing procedures were raised when German marathon runner Uta Pippig challenged the finding of her test by pointing out that she had recently stopped using oral birth control and this had affected her hormonal system; she also pointed out that each of her drug tests following her wins in the Boston Marathon from 1994 to 1996 came up clean. Mary Slaney used a similar defense, claiming that the abnormal T–E ratio in her sample might have been attributable to hormonal changes in women in their late thirties and early forties who were taking the pill. Slaney, who completed the 1,500 and 3,000 meters double at the 1983 World Championships, was 37 at the time of her test in 1996. After a 3-year process, the IAAF arbitration panel discounted the claim.

Petr Korda escaped a 1-year statutory ban from the International Tennis Federation (ITF) after testing positive for nandrolone by convincing an ITF independent appeals panel that he did not know how the substance found its way into his body. The ITF itself was not happy with the outcome, but was prevented by a London High Court ruling from appealing to the Court of Arbitration in Switzerland. Perhaps the most original appeal was that of American sprinter Dennis Mitchell, who claimed the high levels of testosterone found in his test sample in 1998 were the result of having multiple bouts of sex and five bottles of beer the night before. Mitchell was suspended by the IAAF, but later cleared by the USATF drugs panel.

Tennis players Bohdan Ulihrach and Greg Rusedski were both cleared of drugs charges in 2003 and 2004 respectively after it was found that the Association of Tennis Professionals (ATP) through its trainers might have inadvertently caused as many as 30 players to have produced a unique ion chromatography pattern that appeared to suggest a doping offense under the ATP's own antidoping rules. The Rusedski decision, coming so soon after the previously mentioned suspension of

Dwain Chambers, threw up several doubts about the principle of strict liability, which the World Anti-Doping Agency maintains is central to a universally recognized policy. The principle places the complete onus of responsibility on the individual for any illicit substances found in a sample; the circumstances in which they those substances were ingested (e.g., by accident; through a spiked drink) are irrelevant. The ATP decision destabilized this principle.

The most unusual absolution was granted in 2009 when Richard Gasquet explained that he inadvertently ingested cocaine by kissing a woman he met at a club in Miami. The International Tennis Federation accepted the explanation and cleared Gasquet to play after a short ban.

BOX 11.6 WADA (WORLD ANTI-DOPING AGENCY)

The 1998 Tour de France debacle underlined the inadequacy of governing organizations in controlling the use of drugs: uncoordinated testing methods and different lists of prohibited substances rendered their efforts ineffective. The IOC urged a common set of standards at a conference convened at Lausanne in 1999, highlighting the need for an independent international agency, which would set unified standards for anti-doping work and coordinate the efforts of sports organizations and public authorities. The IOC took the initiative and convened the World Conference on Doping in Sport held in Lausanne in February 1999. Following the proposal of the conference, the World Anti-Doping Agency (WADA) was established. It was composed equally of representatives from the Olympic Movement and governments and was divided into an 11-person Executive Committee and a 37-member Foundation Board. WADA received $25 million from the IOC for its first two years of operation. After 2001 when it moved its headquarters to Montreal, it was it joint funded by the Olympic movement and national governments from around the world. The use of "doping" rather than "drugs" in its name suggests WADA is concerned with all materials that may enhance performance, including enriched blood and genetic modification. (The word dope is from the Dutch *doop*, meaning a thick liquid.)

DISCIPLINE AND CONTROL

Prior to the Ben Johnson case, the attitude of sports governing organizations toward drugs was not exactly benevolent, but certainly nowhere as punitive as it is today. Bans on certain types of substances were designed to safeguard athletes; their welfare took priority. The deaths of Jensen and Simpson in the 1960s drew sympathetic responses quite unlike the treatment afforded Ben Johnson in 1988. After the Johnson discovery, competitors found guilty of doping violations incurred penalties, ranging from fines to life suspensions. Media opinion became unanimous: users were condemned as cheats.

From the late 1980s, there was little disagreement over the use of performance enhancing substances and recreational drugs in sports: it was wrong and should be eliminated. The position acquired the status of an axiom – a principle that's so fundamental that it's self-evidently true and beyond questioning. Statements such as "doping in sports is wrong" didn't invite argument; they seemed to state fact. Yet this did little to stem athletes' desire to gain a competitive edge through fair means or foul. Barely a week goes by without news of a positive dope test in some sport. To understand the censure that unerringly meets drug-using sports competitors, we need to examine how the modern world has cultivated a wish for us to control ourselves, mind and body.

The civilizing process, as Norbert Elias describes it, is a historical trend beginning in the middle ages (starting about 1100) that has drawn us away from barbarism by bringing social pressures on people to exercise self-control. The capture of Constantinople by Turks in 1453 is the conventional end of the middle ages; the growth of interest in art and scholarship in the late fourteenth century marks the beginning of the Renaissance (see pp. 112–13).

At one level, this meant increasing our conscience as a means of regulating our behavior toward others. At another, it meant becoming enmeshed in a network of often subtle, invisible, constraints that compelled us to lead ordered lives. One important result of this was the decrease in the use of direct force: violence was brought under control and the state became the only legitimate user of physical violence – outside of combat sports, of course, and these were subject to progressively strict regulation.

The civilizing process implicated humans in some form of control over their bodies. As we saw in Chapter 5, Elias focused mainly on the restraint in using physical violence, but notes the simultaneous trend for people to subdue bodily functions and control their physical being. The physical body became subordinated to the rational mind. While Elias did not discuss this, we might point to the literary fascination with the potential of science to complete this process. Mary Shelley's *Frankenstein, or the Modern Prometheus* (first published in 1818) tells of Baron Frankenstein, a scientist obsessed by the possibility of reconstructing a total, living human being (which eventually turns on him). In *The Strange Case of Dr. Jekyll and Mr. Hyde* (1886) Robert Louis Stevenson imagined another man of science experimenting in mind and body, this time his own: he discovers a drug that transforms him into Mr Hyde into whom his own sublimated evil impulses are channeled. These and other works of fiction suggest a fascination with trying to reshape the body in accordance with the imperatives of the mind.

Pharmacological advances in the twentieth century hastened the probability that the body could be brought under complete control. Not only could maladies be kept at bay, or even vanquished, but moods could be altered and physical well-being could be promoted. As we have seen, the early efforts of Brown-Sequard at the end of the nineteenth century were to find a rejuvenating therapy for body and mind; his research, which was not so different from fictive Dr Jekyll's, presaged the development of anabolic steroids. Any initial suspicions about introducing chemicals into the body faded with two world wars in which colossal and often horrific injuries were treated or palliated with medicaments.

The desire for good health that followed the end of the 1939–45 war was complemented by the availability of drugs for the treatment of practically every complaint. A visit to the doctor was incomplete without a prescription, if only for antibiotics. An expanding range of over-the-counter remedies often made the visit unnecessary. The impact of drugs on people's self-evaluations was that ill health, pain, or even mild discomfort became less and less tolerable. The good life, which seemed to beckon in the post-war period, offered both freedom from suffering and access to well-being. The latter became accessible through a variety of non-medicinal options, including supplements, dieting, and exercise – all of which combined in an enthusiasm for the self, surveyed in Chapter 7.

It was almost inevitable that athletes, themselves embracing aspirations to self-fulfillment through control of the body, would turn to dope. Many kinds of substances have been used historically to promote performance, though rarely so effectively as pharmaceutically produced drugs. One did not need to be a pharmacist to spot how the effects of, say, amphetamines or anabolic steroids, might be of use to a competitor specializing in endurance or power, wishing to delay the onset of fatigue or train for longer and with more intensity.

The unanticipated, often tragic consequences of pharmacological products were not confined to sports. Thalidomide was prescribed to pregnant women in Australia, Britain and Germany in the 1960s as treatment for morning sickness and caused thousands of deformities in their children. The Jensen and Simpson tragedies, also in the 1960s, alerted the world to the dangers of ingesting chemical substances to affect changes in the body's condition. Yet, ironically, the imposition of controls by the IOC in the 1970s probably enhanced the appeal of many substances. In his book *Becoming Deviant*, the criminologist David Matza (1969) reasoned that banning something immediately makes it more attractive than it would otherwise be (see Table 11.1).

BOX 11.7 HYPOXIC

Hypoxic air contains 12–15 percent oxygen as opposed to sea level air, which contains about 21 percent. Athletes tend to use hypoxic facilities in two ways: sleeping in a confined unit – a hypobaric chamber or tent – in an atmosphere that simulates that at about 9,000 feet above sea level; or using a portable device intermittently, say, an hour a day, while awake. The expectation is that the body will respond by generating the production of red blood cells. Hypobaric chambers are also used for, among other things, preparing aircrews: atmospheres can be adjusted to simulate altitudes in excess of 100,000 feet.

As the importance of victory became more pronounced and professionalization made the rewards more extravagant, the value placed on winning replaced that of just competing. A success ethic came to pervade sports, making cost–benefit calculations simpler: the benefits of winning seemed greater than the risk of being

Table 11.1 Seven cases that shook sports

Who?	At?	What?	The impact?	What followed?
Tommy Simpson	1967 Tour de France	Amphetamine	Concern for athletes' health after Simpson's death, which follows that of fellow cyclist Knut Jensen	Limited drug-testing introduced in 1968 to safeguard health of athletes. US swimmer Rick DeMont loses gold medal for 400m freestyle at 1972 Olympics after a positive test.
Ben Johnson	1988 Olympic Games South Korea	Anabolic steroid (stanozolol)	Johnson stigmatized and alarm over cheating rather than health and safety mounts	Gold medal taken, time expunged and suspended. 3 years later, East German coaches admit giving anabolic steroids to athletes in their charge.
Diego Maradona	1994 World Cup, USA	"Cocktail" including ephedrine	By far the biggest drugs case in the global game prompts a recognition that soccer has a drugs issue with which to deal	Argentina's captain sent home in disgrace, later suspended for 15 months. Stronger antidoping policies introduced by all major sports.
Yuan Yuan	1998 World Swimming championships, Australia	hGH (somatotropin)	Awareness that synthetic versions of naturally occurring substances in widespread systematic use	Fina, swimming's governing organization, sends China's 23-member team home. New tests for "undetectable" peptides pursued.
Festina Team	1998 Tour de France	EPO (erythropoietin)	Evidence of organized doping programs for entire teams as 400	In same year, Mark McGwire breaks single season home run record after admitting to

Name	Year / Location	Substance		
			vials discovered in possession of coach and Festina team is expelled from Tour	using a then-legal steroid precursor. 2 years later, Manfred Ewald, ex-president of East Germany's Olympic Committee, goes on trial in Berlin charged with 142 counts of being an accessory to causing bodily harm. World Conference on Doping sets up WADA.
Edgar Davids/ Fernando Couto	2001 Italy	Anabolic steroid (nandrolone)	Other soccer players Frank de Boer and Jaap Stam also test positive for nandrolone	Doubts over nandrolone persist, with several athletes claiming that ingestion of legal supplements leads to misleading test results. 2 years later, British soccer player Rio Ferdinand suspended for 8 months for failing to give test sample.
Dwain Chambers	2003 California	THG (tetrahydrog-estrinone)	Realization that dope specifically designed to evade detection in use. THG not on IAAF's proscribed list but declared "chemically or pharmacologically related" to banned substances.	2-year ban and lifetime Olympic ban. Documentary evidence used rather than positive dope test. Federal investigations into Balco, which cites several worldclass clients from the U.S. Several big names missing from the U.S. Olympic team the following year.

found out, for many. As Michael Messner writes in his study *Power at Play*: "Many [competitors], because of the 'win at all costs' values of the sportsworld and the instrumental relationships they have with their own bodies, tend to feel that the short-term efficiency or confidence that is gained through drug use will outweigh any possible problems that may ensue from the drug" (1992: 78).

As the stakes in sports have changed, so the orientations of competitors have changed too: winning supersedes all other considerations, including *how* one wins. Today's athletes approach their events with a single-mindedness that would have been alien to their counterparts of the 1950s. They are prepared to train harder, focus more sharply and risk more in the attempt to realize their ambitions. If pharmaceuticals can help, we can be sure many athletes will give only a sideways glance at moral warnings. The crucial edge that many drugs are thought to provide can be the difference between fortune and ignominy.

These then are the reasons why so many athletes are prepared to use banned substances: (1) advances in science; (2) the growth of a pervasive drug culture; (3) an intensification of competitiveness. We know from the number of positive tests in almost every sport that even the most draconian measures do not deter them. So, why do sports governing organizations insist on trying to stop drug use? The answer is not quite so obvious as it seems.

THE PRISONERS' DILEMMA

Let's begin with a statement of the obvious, made by Andrea Petróczi and Eugene Aidman: "Athletes today are expected and encouraged to seek every possible way to improve their performance, including specialized training, hi-tech design of equipment and apparel, scientific and medical support, including the use of nutritional supplements" (2008: 2).

Petróczi and Aidman's research moves beyond this, however. Among the reasons cited for taking performance-enhancing drugs (not recreational) are: perceived external pressure, suspicion that rivals are using something, painkilling, meeting the physical demands of training. Most competitors would prefer to compete drug-free; many are still prepared to use, provided the substance is undetectable. Some don't see drugs in sport as a problem and accept that drugs are part of their training regime.

Petróczi and Aidman introduce the prisoners' dilemma: this is a situation in which two players each have two options, the outcome of which depends crucially on the simultaneous choice made by the other. It's called the prisoners' dilemma because it's like one of those scenes from *Law and Order* in which two prisoners each separately agonizes over whether to do a deal and confess to a crime without knowing what their accomplice is going to do.

In his autobiography, the Olympic discus thrower Werner Reiterer reflects on how he found himself caught on the horns of the same dilemma: "The minority of athletes who are natural are at a *disadvantage*," Reiterer believes. "You must adapt to an environment as it is, not as you think it should be." His adaptation was to use.

The framework proposed by Petróczi and Aidman makes this type of adaptation intelligible. "Doping practices grow out of habitual engagement in a range of acceptable performance enhancement (PE) practices, such as physiotherapy, advanced nutrition, training techniques, specialised equipment and apparel" (2008: 3). They also happen in a particular kind of environment in which there are effective, pharmaceutically produced drugs that are easily available and in which people habitually use "drugs to assist with aspects of life." They presumably have in mind drugs that work on the body's neurotransmission system: the most widely prescribed antidepressant is fluoxetine, better known by its commercial name Prozac. The ethos of organized sport is also part of the environment and, when Petróczi and Aidman point out, "the aim is winning, being the best or setting/breaking a record," they might also add: making millions and becoming a celebrity.

Inside the wider environment, there is the specific environment in which a competitor prepares and which influences the manner in which he or she approaches an event; in other words, the motivational climate, which is "shaped by expectations from coaches, parents, peers and fans, as it is perceived by the athlete" (2008: 4).

A mastery climate is one in which an individual's personal progress is accentuated, while a performance climate elevates results, outcome, and winning. The latter is more likely to influence a competitor's decision to use drugs. Petróczi and Aidman also include individual differences. These include a disposition toward risk taking and sensation seeking, a certain attitude toward authority, vulnerability to peer pressure.

So Petróczi and Aidman's model has three spheres of influence – environment, situation, and personality – each of which affects the decision about whether to engage in "functional drug use," which "refers to a strategic use of substance to achieve a set goal (i.e. to improve a function or skill)" (2008: 6). As such, functional use shouldn't be confused with "experimental, recreational or dependent use (abuse/addiction)."

Petróczi and Aidman's approach highlights the "vulnerability" of athletes as they progress through a sports lifecycle: at various stages, they make key choices, commitments about goals, investments in training and comparisons, asking themselves questions such as, "have you got what you hoped for?," "has the plan worked?," and "what is next?" At every stage, influences from coaches, friends, fans, and perhaps the media shape decision-making. Remember the background: a highly competitive win-oriented culture in which supplements and pharmaceuticals are habitually used.

Research by psychologists Peter Strelan and Robert J. Boeckmann is also predicated on the assumption that competitors, like most humans, are "rational calculators who, with the benefit of time and reflection, make decisions designed to be of net benefit to themselves. Most athletes' decisions to use banned substances are presumably rational" (2006: 2912)

Strelan and Boeckmann found that half of athletes in their study indicated there was some likelihood that they would use a performance-enhancing drug "for rehabilitation purposes" (2006: 2923). Their commitment was so strong that they believed using a banned substance was a "viable response to a career-threatening situation." Viable is an interesting choice of word: it suggests that the response was regarded as workable, a feasible way out of a tough predicament. It's also consistent with the prisoners' dilemma in which all decisions are undesirable.

So what are athletes thinking when they make their decisions? Moral beliefs and health concerns, according to Strelan and Boeckmann. The deterrent effect of legal sanctions and the disgrace involved is not so effective as WADA and sports governing organizations assume. The proliferating number of undetectable substances means that laws against drugs are impossible to implement and "unenforceable laws are less able to convey the moral or social threats required to inhibit behavior" (2006: 2926).

But, if competitors are "most likely to be deterred by their moral beliefs," as Strelan and Boeckmann contend, where do those moral beliefs come from? As we'll discover in Chapter 18 conceptions of rightness and wrongness are variable: they change over time and through space. Strelan and Boeckmann answer: "The ban on performance-enhancing drugs in sport reflects society's view that performance-enhancing drug use in sport is both morally wrong and potentially harmful to the individual" (2006: 2925).

In other words, if the laws against drug use didn't exist, then athletes would know they could use performance-enhancers with impunity and wouldn't believe they were engaging in an act that violated morality. I will deal with the perception of health risks separately. Strelan and Boeckmann's more interesting point is that the moral beliefs that work to deter drug use have their source in "society's view."

This completes a circle: athletes obey their conscience and pay little regard for legal sanctions, yet their conscience is affected by their moral beliefs which are, in turn, reflections of social disapproval as expressed in laws against drug use in sport. In any case, are laws against drugs really "society's view"? Philosophers Michael D. Burke and Terence J. Roberts don't think so: "There appears to be no general consensus on the issue: Some have suggested that it is fair for all athletes if drugs are banned . . . and others have argued that it is fair for all athletes if drugs are allowed and equally accessible" (1997: 99–100).

Strelan and Boeckmann's other main conclusion that concern over health prevents more athletes from using drugs should be compared with the findings of research nine years before theirs, in which competitors were offered a scenario: "You are offered a banned performance-enhancing substance that comes with two guarantees: (1) You will not be caught. (2) You will win every competition you enter for the next five years, and then you will die from the side-effects of the substance. Would you take it?"

Michael Bamberger and Don Yaeger found: "More than half the athletes said yes." And, if they were reminded that the health risks associated with performance-enhancing drugs are less than those associated with, for example, tobacco, alcohol, paracetamol, fluoxetine, and several other popular substances in everyday use, then maybe even more than half would succumb. Put the two studies together and the conclusion is: half would use drugs if they guaranteed success; half wouldn't, either because of health or morality.

The advantages of considering the reasoning behind the decision to use performance-enhancing substances is that it avoids the automatic and unthinking explanation that the users are just cheats. They are cheats, of course; anyone who breaks rules, intentionally or not, is a cheat. But are they acting dishonestly or unfairly in order to gain an advantage? The research suggests they may be trying to cancel out the advantages rivals may hold, or adapting "to an environment as it is" not as they think it should be. This is what's known as a defensive rule violation.

"Defensive rule violations are ones in which an agent breaks rules so as not to be disadvantaged by the fact that practically everyone else is breaking them as well," explains William J. Morgan (2006a: 186), who suspects it leads to a situation "reminiscent of Hobbes's famous state of nature in which all moral bets are off because all moral obligations to others have been suspended." The reference is to English philosopher Thomas Hobbes (1588–1679) who believed that humans are not naturally social beings and their actions are motivated by only selfish concerns.

Morgan thinks "the practice of doping is intimately bound up with a professional conception of sport, one in which winning is both separated from the play of the game and valued above all else that takes place within it" (2006a: 192). The professional ethos, in his opinion, "subverts the basic character of sport itself." The view would probably draw approval from WADA and its affiliates, though the sports analyst should never accept declarations purporting to contain wisdom without some sort of interrogation. To this we turn.

Q: WHY BAN DRUGS FROM SPORT?

A #1: Using drugs is cheating

"Breaking the rules with intent to avoid the penalties" is how Peter McIntosh defines cheating (1980: 2, 182). Günther Lüschen believes the conditions agreed on for winning a competition "are changed in favor of one side" (1976: 67).

Drugs change the conditions for winning. So do many other things. Take the example of blood doping for which athletes might draw penalties, including bans. In a strict sense, this is cheating. But, how about athletes who are born in Kenya or Ethiopia, both several thousand feet above sea level? Such athletes might be fortunate enough to be brought up in an atmosphere that encourages hemoglobin production in the body and they might find the transition to sea level really quite comfortable as a result. Witness the dominance of Kenyan and Ethiopian middle- and long-distance runners since the 1980s: equipped with natural advantages, Kenyans capitalized on the track, road and cross-country circuits, leaving weary European and American athletes in their wake.

Another accident of birth meant that Tiger Woods was given every available coaching and equipment facility to help him develop his golf skills since he was old enough to grip a club. His parents could afford to indulge their child and, as things turned out, their money was a shrewd investment: by 2009, Woods was earning close on $100 million per year, making him comfortably the highest paid athlete in history. Imagine a ghetto child from Brooklyn, someone with a similar profile to Mike Tyson: single-parent background, multiple stopovers at correctional facilities, and made to live by his wits; he becomes a prodigious golfer.

Were this imaginary figure to play Woods, would it be a fair match? When they came face-to-face in matchup, the conditions might appear fair, but one would hardly say they were "fair" in a deeper sense. One player has benefited from social advantages in a similar way to Kenyan runners, who have benefited naturally from being born at high altitudes. It would be a naïve person indeed who believed all is fair in sport and that background, whether social or natural, is irrelevant to eventual success or failure.

Even drugs themselves are "unfair" in more than one sense. Affluent countries have more chemists and better laboratories, so athletes from developing countries suffer disproportionately. But, perhaps drugs and a working knowledge of how to take them are more transferable than the developed world's high-tech facilities, Olympic-size pools and college bursaries that enable full-time training. In other words, drugs, from this perspective, could have a balancing effect and create fairer conditions.

A #2: Drugs are taken by choice

There is a big difference between the advantages bestowed by place of birth or social background and those that are enjoyed by drug users. Sports competitors can, as the slogan goes, "say 'no' to drugs" in much the same way as many say "yes." Swallowing tablets or shooting a substance into your buttocks are voluntary activities over which individuals have a high degree of control. We presume – and only presume – that the user has done a cost–benefit calculation, as the research in the previous section suggests, and exercises freewill when doing or agreeing to the action. Obviously, the same competitors have no say in where they were born or the state of their parents' bank account. By contrast, using drugs involves procuring an advantage quite voluntarily.

Yet there is more to this: first, because there are many other forms of advantage that are actively sought out and, second, because some are better placed than others either to seek out or eschew them. Were you a Briton following home Kenenisa Bekele in a 5,000-meter race, you might wish you were born, like him, in Ethiopia, where he also trains at over 2,600 feet above sea level. Impossible, of course, so you might think about going to high altitudes and engaging in a spot of blood doping. Quite possible, but illegal. Or take erythropoietin (EPO), which has much the same effect. Again, not legal.

Another possibility is just to train in some part of the world high enough to give you some advantage, or at least to neutralize the advantage Bekele gets from preparing in Addis Ababa. Perfectly possible and legal. Or even, sleeping in a hypoxic tent, which is also OK. The probable result is an advantage quite legitimately obtained through voluntary effort. But an advantage is gained all the same.

Not that everyone is able to exercise choice in such matters: a dedication to competition, a determination to win, and an unflinching resolve to withstand pain are needed and these qualities are easier to come by if the alternative is a one-way ticket back to the ghetto. If your alternatives look unpromisingly bleak, then choices can be rather illusory. Ben Johnson was born in Jamaica and migrated to Canada in 1980 at the age of 19, his ambition being the same as any migrant – namely, to improve his material life. Lacking education, but possessing naturally quick reflexes (which couldn't be changed) and fast groundspeed (which could), he made the best of what he had, so that, within four years, he was in the Canadian Olympic team.

Sport is full of stories like Johnson's: bad news – poor origins, little education, few occupational prospects: good news – physical potential and the opportunity to realize it. Johnson's early promise attracted coaches and medical advisors whose counsel he trusted and whose guidance he followed – perhaps gullibly. Countless young people with some form of sporting prowess when faced with the once-and-for-all decision of whether or not to sink their entire efforts in the one area in which they just might achieve success don't want to contemplate the alternatives. Given the chance, they'll go for it. And this means maximizing every possible advantage in an intensely competitive world. It's doubtful whether any athlete with a similarly deprived childhood would have any compunction about gaining an edge by any means. The choices they have are often too stark to need much mulling over.

Asking whether choice was exercised in trying to determine whether cheating took place is inadequate. Even if we were to dismiss the claims of a competitor (who tested positive for a given drug) that his or her drink was spiked (or similar), the question of whether that person freely exercised choice remains. It is feasible to argue that the choices of the university-educated daughter of an affluent North American family are roughly the same as those of the Mexican migrant worker's daughter in California whose one chance for some material success is through sport? To complicate matters further, compare both cases with that of someone insinuated into State Program 1425 as an 11-year old.

All this is not intended to exonerate those from deprived backgrounds who have sought an advantage through "foul" means rather than "fair." It merely casts doubts on the hard-and-fast distinction between fair play and cheating. If we want to sustain the distinction, we have to ignore the manifold advantages or disadvantages that derive from a person's physical and social background and which are beyond his or her power to change. We can attempt to get round this by isolating the element of choice and defining cheating only when a person has consciously and deliberately taken some action to gain advantage. This works up to a point if we cast aside doubts about the circumstances in which the decision was made. Again, backgrounds are important in influencing the decision.

So the pedestal on which sport stands when it tries to display itself as a model of fair play is not quite as secure as it might at first seem. Not only are advantages dispensed virtually at birth, but they operate either to limit or liberate a person's ability to make choices.

A #3: Drugs are harmful to health

Picture this: a new drug is introduced. It has great recreational value, giving pleasure to the consumer. It's alleged that it relieves stress while boosting concentration and this is because of a similarity between one of its constituents and acetylcholine, a neurotransmitter that triggers the release of dopamine – the chemical messenger that controls pleasure and pain, among other things. As well as its calming effect, it's also believed to curb appetites, so it can assist dieting.

A wide range of athletes spy advantages: the drug steadies the nerves of those who wish to remain relaxed under pressure and helps others unwind after stressful competition. But there's a downside: it contains a chemical that's extremely addictive, another that's carcinogenic; it also causes heart disease, bronchial complaints and a number of related physical problems. It accounts for nearly 5 million deaths worldwide every year. About 1,400 people in Britain and the United States die from problems associated with its use every day. 65 percent of its habitual users live in the developing world.

The doses of the anabolic steroid taken by Ben Johnson in the 1988 Olympics were allegedly lower than what the World Health Organization (WHO) subsequently found safe to administer as a male contraceptive. Many of the substances banned from sport and condemned as harmful to health are condoned, and even prescribed in other circumstances, prompting the thought that the banned drugs might not be so dangerous as some of the legal ones.

Sport's central philosophical point seems to be that, whatever people's backgrounds, if they are given the chance to gain advantages over others, they might fairly do so as long as they stop short of knowingly using chemical substances (at least some chemical substances). Some might counter the argument that supports this by saying that acupuncture, hypnotism, psyching techniques, and – in the case of the England national football squad in 1998 – faith healing might yet prove to have long-term consequences. And there is a growing school of thought that supports the view that the quantity and intensity of training needed in today's highly competitive sports might depress natural immunity systems, exposing competitors to infection. Sports clubs themselves acknowledge that players in need of surgery will often postpone operations in order to compete in key games. They do so with the full consent if not encouragement—and perhaps, in some cases, at the request – of coaches or managers, who are surely aware of the probability of exacerbating a condition by delaying corrective treatment.

This has led some observers to believe that the use of drugs is no better or worse than some other aids to performance. They are certainly no worse than many of the drugs commonly available outside the world of sport. Most sports frown on smoking and drinking too, though some have been grateful for sponsorship from tobacco companies. Others, like English football, have openly embraced breweries, at the same time committing itself to clamping down on drugs, both performance enhancing and recreational. Alcohol kills about 100,000 people a year, probably more if alcohol-related road deaths are included. The positive effects of alcohol in oxidizing blood, making it less sticky, are outweighed by the physical and social consequences of its excessive use.

The dangers of paracetamol and fluoxetine I mentioned earlier. Even everyday non-prescription drugs such as aspirin and antihistamine, which we presume to be innocuous, are not completely without potentially harmful consequences. Caffeine found in coffee, tea, and soft drinks is mildly harmful, but who, apart from governing bodies in sports, would dream of banning its general use?

The world is full of harm. We don't reject every thing or practice because it's potentially harmful. In fact, sometimes our choices about what and what not to reject seem arbitrary. The same medical organizations that approve of legal prescription drugs, often advise against the use of others. They also disapprove of and mount campaigns against practices that are quite legal. For instance, the British and American Medical Associations have urged a ban on boxing. Prolonged involvement in boxing exposes the boxer to the risk of brain damage and many other less severe injuries, is the claim of the anti-boxing lobbyists. This we know. Medical associations maintain that boxers should be protected, if necessary from themselves, in much the same way as any other athletes contemplating actions that might result in harm to their health. The effect on health of many banned drugs is small compared to that of boxing.

But to make boxing illegal because of this presumes that all the young and physically healthy young men and women are oblivious to the hazards of the sport when they enter. It assumes they are not rational, deliberating agents with some grasp of the implications of boxing – a grasp sufficient for them to weigh up the probable rewards against the probable losses.

Were information about the long-term consequences of boxing concealed, then the medical associations would have a very strong case. But the results of scientific tests are available and to assume that competitors are so witless as to know nothing of this may seem insulting and patronizing. If young people with a chance to capitalize on their sporting potential are informed of the dangers involved in their decision to pursue a line of action, then it's difficult to support a case for prohibiting this, at least in societies not prone to totalitarianism. Boxers might well judge the brain damage they risk in their sport preferable to the different kind of "brain damage" they could sustain in a repetitive, unsatisfying job over a 40-year period, or in an unbearably long spell out of work. The judgment is theirs. The alternative is to present those judgments to guardian agents.

But, boxers and, for that matter, any other kind of athlete don't reach judgments unaided. We've noted previously that all manner of influences bear on an individual's decision and, quite apart from those deriving from background, we have to isolate coaches and trainers. Bearing in mind the case of American football in the 1960s when coaches were assuming virtual medical status in dispensing drugs, we should remind ourselves of the important roles still played by these people in all sports. We must also realize that sports are populated by many "Dr Feelgoods" who are only too happy to boost performance without necessarily informing the competitor of all the possible implications. It's quite probable that many competitors are doing things, taking things, even thinking things that might jeopardize their health. But do they know it? Perhaps sports organizations might attempt to satisfy themselves formally that all competitors in sports, which do hold dangers, are totally aware of them and comfortable about their involvement. This would remove the educational task from coaches and trainers and shift the onus onto governing organizations.

In an interesting essay first published in the 1980s, Clifton Perry argues the case for and against blood doping, which, as we've seen, facilitates sporting performance through the introduction of a natural material that is indigenous to the body – blood. He offers the distinction between "performance enhancers" that do not cause lasting changes to the body of the user and "capacity enhancers" that do have long-term effects.

This means that anabolic steroids are ruled out – not on the grounds that they are capacity enhancers but because they have deleterious effects (there is evidence that they elevate enzyme levels in the liver). But does this mean that blood doping should be allowed as it enhances capacities without harmful consequences? Perry says no. His reason is based on the body's response to coming off the enhancer. "There is a difference between the loss of performance output through the loss of a mere performance enhancer and the loss of a capacity through inactivity" (1983: 43).

This is a noteworthy argument, if only because it postulates distinctions that are difficult to sustain in the twenty-first century. Some banned substances do have long-term effects, others don't. Diuretics, for example, are drugs that induce the passing of urine, are banned, not because they cause short-term dehydration but because they are often used in conjunction with other active substances.

Some drugs certainly are harmful to health – as are many other things. Governing organizations quite properly communicate this, though the distinctions that are often made between harmful substances and activities and apparently innocuous ones are frequently arbitrary and difficult to support with compelling evidence.

What if athletes procured substances with a dubious provenance from unlicensed people and then administered them in a willy-nilly fashion without the benefit of medical advice? This would be dangerous. Yet this is exactly what's happening at present.

A #4: Athletes are role models for the young

It follows that, if athletes are known and seen to use drugs of any kind, then young people might be encouraged to follow. While the substances that competitors use to enhance performance are often different to the ones that cause long-term distress at street-level, the very act of using drugs might work as a powerful example. But the argument can't be confined to sports: many rock musicians as well as writers and artists use drugs for relief or stimulus. Rock stars arguably wield more influence over young acolytes than the sports elite. The shaming of an athlete found to have used drugs and the nullifying of his or her performance is a deterrent or a warning to the young: "Do this and you will suffer the same fate." But the Red Hot Chili Peppers are not disgraced and their albums would not be expunged from the charts if it were discovered that they recorded them while Flea was using heroin. No one considers asking Andrea Bocelli for a urine sample after one of his concerts. The music of Chet Baker, a heroin addict, the acting of Cary Grant, who used LSD, the writing of Dylan Thomas, an alcoholic: all have not been obliterated.

Athletes are different in the sense that they operate in and therefore symbolize a sphere where all is meant to be wholesome and pure. But this puts competitors under sometimes-intolerable pressure to keep their haloes straight and maintain the pretense of being saints. Clearly, they are not, nor, given the competitive nature of sport, will they ever be.

Gone are the days portrayed in *Chariots of Fire* when winners were heroes to be glorified and losers were good sports for competing. Hard cash spoiled all that. A yearning for money has introduced a limitless capacity for compromise and previously amateur or shamateur sports organizations, including the IOC, have led the way by embracing commercialism rather than spurning it. Competitors too are creatures of a competitive world and probably more preoccupied with struggling to win than with keeping a clean image. They too were once innocents with dreams of emulating their heroes. Ambition and money have ways of re-shaping values.

All the same, the inescapable reality is that young people look up to top sportsmen and women. Even if top football players and basketball stars don't want to be role models, they often are. So, when parents of promising athletes complain that drug users set a bad example, they have a point. The fact remains: if their son or daughter progresses in sport, he or she will eventually be disabused of all innocence and realize that the closer an athlete gets to the top, the more prevalent the win-at-all-cost ethos becomes. At this level, the subversion of sport's character that sickens Morgan is likely to take effect.

A #5: Drugs are not natural

"A substance or technology is within the spirit of sport if it merely facilitates the fruition of [natural] capacities," according to Doriane Lambelet Coleman and James E. Coleman (2008: 1761). Sports utilize any number of devices that certainly make it easier for athletes to realize their potential. Pole-vaulters, for example, are not better vaulters when they use a particular type of pole, but they achieve better performances with the best science has to offer. Archers achieve more accuracy when a bow is equipped with sights.

Drugs don't just facilitate the exploitation of the body: they supplement it for specific periods of time. We have accepted world record times without dismissing them as due in large part to the wearing of lightweight, air-inflated spikes on fast synthetic surfaces. Still, we would have to agree that the same times couldn't have been achieved in flats on cinders. Blood doping, one might argue, is actually only the reintroduction of our own blood into our systems, albeit by means of transfusion and, in this sense, is more natural than some of the other devices that are commonplace in sports.

We might anticipate that Clifton Perry's reply to this would be that blood doping and other banned methods of enhancing performance involve the ingestion of substances. This is true; but it doesn't make them any more or less natural than some of the other methods of enabling the realization of natural potential. No one accuses a 300-lb rugby player or an Olympic heavyweight weightlifter of being unnatural. Yet, they've achieved the bodies they have through a combination of resistance training and high carbohydrate diets. We silently commend their efforts, even though, as Lambelet Coleman and Coleman point out: "Doped athletes may work even harder than athletes who do not use steroids because these drugs allow for more and more difficult training than would otherwise be possible" (2008: 1770).

In the same way, it could be argued that students are able to study more intensely and for longer periods if they use drugs that promote the capacity for mental focus, such as methylphenidate, which is often prescribed for attention deficit hyperactivity disorder (ADHD). The drugs aren't actually adding new knowledge: they're assisting their efforts to read, research, and revise. So, is it reasonable to argue that drugs improve the students' natural capacities? Or do they, to use the earlier term, facilitate the fruition of natural capacities?

This aspect of the argument against drugs presupposes: (1) there is such a thing as a natural state of the human body: we saw in Chapter 8 that this is a naïve and inaccurate understanding of the body; (2) technologies administered from outside the body are fine: laser surgery to correct vision is legal, as is sleeping in a hypoxic environment and breathing oxygen deficient air and, as we saw previously, many of us have undergone medical procedures that have left us with replacement body parts.

A #6: Drugs are bad for business

None of the arguments presented is airtight enough to convince a skeptic. Yet sports governing organizations' pursuit of dopers has taken on the status of a crusade: all-year-round surveillance, invigilation, regulation, and punishment are now institutional features of sport and their maintenance is costly. Yet athletes continue to take dope and testers keep spending more time and money trying to catch them. Why? If none of the previous answers ring true, we might turn to the motives of the IOC, an infamously corrupt organization which was involved in bribery, cover-ups, and various other malfeasant activities under the presidency of Juan Antonio Samaranch.

After the financial débâcle of the 1976 summer Olympics at Montreal, the IOC became much more of a commercial organization. All subsequent games were heavily supported by the likes of Coca-Cola, McDonalds, Panasonic, and a host of other mainly American and Japanese companies. While the IOC continued to present itself as embodying the spirit originally revived by de Coubertin, its ideals became progressively diluted. Samaranch had made clear his intention to extricate the Olympic movement financially from governments and become economically independent. In doing so, he made pacts with companies and the mass media; these, in a sense, surrendered the Olympics' independence to other more overtly commercial organizations and, more generally, to market forces.

Increasingly, the IOC grew reliant on money from not only sponsors, but from television companies. NBC, for example, paid the IOC $3.7 billion (£2.64 billion) over 12 years from 2000. Commercial organizations do not donate their money out of the goodness of their hearts; they do so to attract further business for themselves. By encouraging their potential market to associate their products with a clean and wholesome activity that commands the respect and affection of billions, they hope to promote sales.

Now, think about the word "drugs." What image does it conjure in your mind? Crack-addicted moms selling their babies, low-life smackheads waiting at pharmacists for their methadone, all-night revelers off their heads on ecstasy, gun-carrying rock slingers hanging at street corners like the crews in *The Wire*? Probably not a well-toned swimmer surfacing from an Olympic pool or a baseball pitcher propelling a ball at near 100 mph. An inadequacy of our language left us with one word for two types of substances with entirely different applications and purposes. Any substance, other than food, that, when taken into the body, produces a change in it is a drug: the term suggests no distinction between illicit recreational substances and pharmacological products.

What, if, in 1967, following the death of Tommy Simpson, the Tour de France organizers or cycling's governing organization UCI had been able to take a cue from Lambelet Coleman and Coleman, and insisted on calling the amphetamines found on the stricken rider "capacity-facilitators"? History might not have been so different.

There again, sport's sponsors might have been more comfortable with a more anodyne term. As it was, the prospect of what we popularly regard as a healthy, wholesome and virtuous pursuit becoming contaminated by the same stuff that was polluting several other parts of society was horrifying.

No corporation would knowingly spend money sponsoring, partnering or advertising an activity that disregarded or, worse, condoned the use of drugs. It would have been ruinous. The IOC and, later the rest of the sports world, responded, cautiously at first, and, when corporate money became more essential in the 1980s, punitively. From this perspective, the Johnson case was heaven sent: the IOC was able to demonstrate its intolerance of drugs, expelling Johnson from the games and, for a while, from sport in dramatic fashion. Johnson himself lost several million in sponsorship deals voided after his disgrace.

Just one more speculation: what if the winner of the women's 100 meters had also been disqualified for drugs? It's likely the Olympic movement would have lost credibility with its sponsors: the Olympic Games themselves might have collapsed without sponsorship money. In actuality, Florence Griffith Joyner was declared clean, despite hearsay that she had used performance enhancers to achieve her prodigious 10.47 seconds 100-meter record. After her death in 1998, only ten years after the fateful games, writers around the world were emboldened to declare that she had probably used drugs habitually. Some wondered whether there had been some sort of cover-up.

Vyv Simson and Andrew Jennings exposed the lengths to which the IOC had gone to conceal wrongdoings: many positive dope tests at Olympic Games in the 1980s and 1990s had mysteriously failed to reach the light of day, leaving the image of a squeaky clean IOC that had eradicated drug-use. (1992; see also Jennings, 1996). It wasn't until April 2003 that Wade Exum, the United States Olympic Committee's director for drug control between 1991 and 2000, released documents suggesting that, between 1998 and 2000, 100 athletes, including 19 Olympic medalists, competed, despite failing dope tests.

Subsequent Olympics were scandal-free, but as John Andrews, of *The Economist*, put it: "It would have been commercially disastrous – for athletes, organisers, sponsors and broadcasters – to have them declared anything else" (1998: 14). It's this kind of perception that gives weight to the argument that there is a commercial motive behind anti-drugs policies in sport.

The IOC, for long, paved the way for other sports organizations. Its initiative in clinching lucrative sponsorships acted almost as a template for other sports; but, it also had to lead the way in doping policies. Most of the world's governing organizations adopt the IOC's banned list and accept the reliability of its methods of detection. While they'll never admit that their purposes in trying to eliminate drugs from their sports are anything but pure, the argument has a plausibility that is, as we've seen, conspicuously absent from all other explanations (see Table 11.2).

These then are the main reasons why governing bodies have sought to eliminate drugs from sports and discredit those found using them. The reasons are not as straightforward as they appear and all are open to objections. Whatever the argument, we need to recognize: (1) that drugs are part of contemporary sports; and (2) whatever

Table 11.2 Why does sport ban drugs?

Argument	Evidence	Counter
Drugs are not fair	Decent corroboration: drugs can supplement, assist or compensate in athletic performance. They may also facilitate the realization of potential.	a. Historically, other performance supplements have been regarded as unfair. b. Circumstances of birth might confer more significant advantages.
Drugs are taken by choice	Yes: often on advice and with support of peers, coaches and trainers.	Often, the only alternative is lack of success at highest level.
Drugs are harmful to health	Some have negative effects; others do not.	a. Some sports activities are also dangerous. b. Many legal drugs are more damaging than banned substances.
Drugs are not natural	Partial support: many drugs are synthetic versions of natural products.	There is no natural body state: training, diet, environment etc. elicit biochemical change.
Athletes are role models	Strong support: young people seek to emulate sports stars.	a. Rock stars, actors and fashion models are also emulated. b. Once they reach a certain level, young athletes will become aware of drug use in sports.
Drugs are bad for business	Decent support: sponsors avoid contracts with athletes who have used, or are suspected of using drugs.	WADA and governing organizations maintain commercial motives do not guide drugs policies.

attempts are made to extirpate them, ways and means will be found to continue to use them. In a decade's time, it's possible that there will be no way of preventing competitors from taking drugs which doesn't involve prison-like supervision all-year-round, in training as well as competition: inspection, invigilation, regulation, and punishment would become features of sport.

Debates about drugs and how to eliminate their use and their impact on sports will continue, at least for a few more years. Discussions about the obligations of athletes, especially celebrity athletes, the impoverishment of sporting ideals and the loss of simple pleasures will exercise the minds of all interested parties. Typically, the effects of business interests in sports on drug-use are set aside, though, as I've suggested in this chapter, they are germane to the debate.

HIJACKING GENE THERAPY

What of the future? When will drugs become obsolete? As we've seen in previous chapters, research in genetic science is proceeding apace. Consider also that the desire to engineer a body to order has been around at least since 1818, when Mary Shelley published her classic horror tale, *Frankenstein.* Combine the two and you have some idea of what's to come. "Athletes will try to alter their genes so that they don't need designer drugs," says Arlene Weintraub in *BusinessWeek Online.*

> What's especially frightening about the emergence of new doping methods is that athletes who use them may be putting their lives on the line. Underground manufacturers of designer steroids don't go through the normal US Food & Drug Administration testing rigmarole to prove the drugs are safe.
>
> (June 14, 2004: 1)

Frightening enough to persuade some writers to urge a rethink on sport's approach to drugs. In his *Genetically Modified Athletes*, Andy Miah points out that: "Perhaps the strongest argument against doping in sport . . . remains the concern for the health of athletes" (2004: 31). Yet, "harm often seems integral to the activity" in sports (2004: 10). Just training or competing involves the athlete in potentially harmful endeavors.

Somatic gene therapy aimed at improving sports performance has, in all likelihood, not been tried; not yet, anyway. It carries the same kind of practical problems as other gene therapies. But it is conceivable that the biological performance enhancing products, such as EPO, hGH, or IGF-1 (insulin growth factor) could be administered in the form of genes. There is no known, reliable test.

Richard Gallagher, of *The Scientist*, sees nothing too awful with using drugs in sport, but cautions against gene doping: (1) the lifelong health risks "far outstrips even the gamble of injection of drugs"; (2) to allow experimental therapies developed for serious diseases "to be hijacked for trivial pursuits" is untenable (2005: 6). Sport counts as a trivial pursuit.

Gallagher's second point is unlikely to draw objections from even die-hard sports fans. His first point is also credible, though competitors are typically not cautious. Risks are endemic in sports: anyone who can't live with uncertainty, unpredictability and an amount of precariousness will not succeed in sports. *Newsweek*'s Oliver Morton acknowledges that athletes take risks all the time and that taking dope is an extra risk. But: "Drugs taken voluntarily, openly and with professional advice will add to these risks far less than they do when taken in a culture of hearsay and secrecy" (July 12, 1999: 4).

Morton maintains that athletes will continue to use dope, possibly ill suited to their purposes and designed in ways to conceal them from drug testers. Referring to the 1998 Tour de France, Morton writes: "The Festina team's approach of systematic and supervised drug enhancement, though it broke the rules, at least tried to ensure a certain amount of safety for the cyclists" (1999: 4).

"In an Open Olympics [in which doping was allowed] . . . there would be a strong incentive for effective but comparatively safe dosing regimes to be found and promulgated," reasons Morton (1999: 4).

Miah's argument is compatible with this. He urges a recognition of athletes "as autonomous agents, capable of making their own life decisions, where such decisions do not harm other individuals or devalue the practices within which those choices take place" (2004: 164).

Objectors might contend that dope-taking does "devalue" sports, though Miah points out that: "Ethical discussions have focused solely on the drug issue, to the neglect of a vast number of other technologies that confer a similar kind of effect" (2004: 175). We will focus on some of these ethical issues in Chapter 18.

Like Morton, Miah believes that in sports, as in all other areas of life, we are continually reshaping human bodies, moving them farther and farther from "the imperfect state in which evolution left them," as Morton puts it. Both writers see anti-doping policy as inimical to the interests of athletes, forcing them – however inadvertently – to take dope in clandestine circumstances and so endangering their well-being. It also denies them the ability to make informed decisions about their own lives: as research on the efficacy and effects of dope is never commissioned, athletes are left in the dark and grope their way along almost by trial and error.

As arguments such as these grow, sports governing organizations will have to respond, either through re-defining what doping actually means, or adding evermore draconian measures to the already rigorous apparatus of control and punishment. If the latter option prevails, then companies like Balco will prosper. Even antidoping agents accept that theirs is an unwinnable fight. Weintraub advises that "drug testers assume that there are dozens of designer steroids for sale, or in the labs" and interprets their comments to her as meaning that tests are always destined to be behind the curve: it's simply too easy to design undetectable drugs. She concludes by likening testers to dogs chasing their own tails.

OF RELATED INTEREST

Mortal Engines: Human engineering and the transformation of sport by John Hoberman (Free Press, 1992) is a masterly thesis on the relationship between medicine, technology, and the human body and can be read in conjunction with *The Steroids Game: An expert's look at anabolic steroid use in sports* by Charles Yesalis and Virginia Cowart (Human Kinetics, 1998), which traces the history of drugs testing, examines educational programs designed to curb drug use, and presents some of the legal issues relating especially to steroid use.

Sport, Health and Drugs: A critical sociological perspective by Ivan Waddington (E & FN Spon, 2000) argues that doping is banned from sports because it offends our sense of right and wrong. But there is irony in the role played by sports medicine: "The development of performance-enhancing drugs and techniques is not something that is alien to, but something which as been an integral part of, the recent history of sports medicine."

Drugs in Sport, 3rd edition, by David Mottram (Routledge, 2003) is a serviceable introduction to the field and can be augmented with a collection of essays edited by Wade Wilson and Edward Derse, *Doping in Elite Sport: The politics of drugs in the Olympic movement* (Human Kinetics, 2001). Doriane Lambelet Coleman and James E. Coleman offer a legal perspective in "The problem of doping" (in *Duke Law Journal*, vol. 57, 2008).

Andy Miah's argument is presented in the overall discussion of *Genetically Modified Athletes: Biomedical ethics, gene doping, and sport* (Routledge, 2004) and may valuably be read with Oliver Morton's short but incisive *Newsweek* story "As the Tour de France begins, it's time to rethink the way we treat drugs in sports" (July 12, 1999).

"Why drug testing in elite sport does not work: Perceptual deterrence theory and the role of personal moral beliefs" by Peter Strelan, and Robert J. Boeckmann (in *Journal of Applied Social Psychology*, vol. 36, no. 12, 2006) and "Psychological drivers in doping: The lifecycle model of performance enhancement" by Andrea Petróczi and Eugene Aidman (in *Substance Abuse Treatment, Prevention, and Policy*, vol. 3, no. 7, 2008) are the two challenging articles cited earlier in this chapter; both offer ways of understanding a competitor's decision to use drugs.

ASSIGNMENT

You are asked to review Michael Bamberger and Don Yaeger's conclusions that indicates that 98 out of 100 young athletes interviewed in confidence would be prepared to take a banned substance that guaranteed them competitive success in sports. Even, when presented with the prospect that the substance would mean certain death within a couple of decades, over half still said they would take it (*Sports Illustrated*, vol. 86, no. 15, 1997). After the review, you decide to do your own research along similar lines. Anticipate your results and interpret them.

CHAPTER 12

KEY ISSUES

▮ How do sports actually encourage deviant behavior?

▮ What is the difference between hostile and instrumental aggression?

▮ When did England ban ballgames?

▮ Where do we draw the line between sports violence and "real violence"?

▮ Why do we like athletes who break the rules?

▮ . . . and who said aggression in sport is as old as sport itself?

Not for the Fainthearted

THE ATTRACTIONS OF RULE BREAKING

December 24, 2004: The Atlanta Falcons today announced that they have extended the contract of Pro Bowl QB Michael Vick for ten years. Terms of the contract were not disclosed, but it is believed to be worth in excess of $70 million. In 2001 Vick was the first African American quarterback to be selected as the number one draft pick. At 22, Vick was the second-youngest quarterback ever selected to play in the Pro Bowl. The honor came on the heels of a season in which Vick set four NFL records and five team records as a first-year starter.

December 11, 2007: Michael Vick was sentenced to prison for running a dogfighting operation and will stay there up to 23 months. The disgraced NFL star received a harsher sentence than the other defendants in the federal conspiracy case because of "less than truthful" statements about killing pit bulls.

Vick was 29-years-old when he left prison in July 2009. He reckoned his imprisonment cost him a total of $142 million, including $71 million in Falcons salary, $50 million in endorsement income and nearly $20 million in previously paid bonuses. As incarcerations go, this was one of the most expensive in history. It also cost Vick his credibility; though not his playing credentials. The NFL reinstated him, making it possible for him to resume his professional career.

Quarterbacks often play into their thirties and, occasionally, into their forties (Steve DeBerg, Vinny Testaverde, and Warren Moon all played in the NFL at 44). So Vick had a realistic chance of resuming his pro career. But ask yourself this question: why would someone worth over a quarter of a billion dollars get busted not for drugs, booze, sex crimes, or any of the offenses typically associated with rich, out-of-control young men, but dogfighting?

Actually, it was the nature of the crime combined with Vick's status that turned this case into a media spectacle: professional sportsmen and women regularly get involved in misdemeanors and, sometimes, more seriously deviant behavior. Just before Vick's imprisonment, NBA referee Tim Donaghy, in 2008, was sentenced to 15 months behind bars for his participation in a gambling scandal, which implicated him in shaving points (a form of match fixing). And in 2007, Barry Bonds, baseball's all-time home run leader (estimated career earnings: $188.25 million) was indicted on charges that he made false statements before a federal grand jury about his use of performance-enhancing drugs.

Meanwhile in Britain, Joey Barton, the Newcastle United football player, was, in 2008, sentenced to six months imprisonment for an attack on a man outside a McDonald's restaurant. Barton had drunk 12 pints of lager earlier in the evening. Former world champion boxer Scott Harrison was jailed in Scotland in 2008 after pleading guilty to drink driving, assault, and breaching his bail conditions. He'd already served five weeks in jail in Spain when he was originally arrested near Malaga. In 2009, he was given two and a half years imprisonment by a Spanish judge for another assault.

This tiny sample of the crimes and misdemeanors perpetrated by professional athletes who, one might naively suspect, had enough savvy and enough money to stay out of trouble, provides no more than an insight. A comprehensive catalog would occupy several volumes. Michael Atkinson and Kevin Young have a phrase to describe the prevalence of rule breaking among athletes, "the pathological as normal."

In their book *Deviance and Social Control in Sport* (2008), Atkinson and Young argue that behavior that violates accepted cultural standards is actually pleasurable in many contexts. Watching a fight break out during an NHL game, for example, is, from a fan's perspective, a thrilling part of the action. A fistfight in a game of rugby is often an entertaining interlude in a sport that is itself violent. The same incident in a game of association football would occasion disapproval and plenty of tut-tutting, though spectators are rarely offended. As Atkinson and Young point out: "The lines demarcating wanted and unwanted deviance in any sport are not universal" (2008: 7).

BOX 12.1 DEVIANCE

Conventionally defined as behavior that departs from culturally accepted norms or standards, deviance has also been approached as a social response to certain behaviors. In other words, there are few, if any, instances of behavior that are universally regarded as violations of some standard, norm, or law. So people, groups and their behavior become deviant because certain labels (thief, prostitute, pedophile) are attached to their behavior by authorities, such as the criminal justice system. The reaction defines what is and isn't deviance more powerfully than the behavior itself. The word is from the Latin *deviant*, meaning "turning out of the way."

Rules: can't live without them, but most of us can't live without breaking them. Before you rush to contradict me, ask yourself whether you've ever downloaded a track from a p2p site, or driven over the speed limit: this kind of rule breaking can be almost like life-affirming force: it reminds someone that, when rules threaten to exhaust us into inanition, all we have to do is break them.

But breaking rules can also result in trouble, and the above examples plunged the athletes in question into a maelstrom of mayhem. Atkinson and Young argue that this is because they are "villainized" in the media (they mean portrayed as bad or menacing – demonized is probably a better word). Celebrity culture guarantees a sensationalistic treatment for even the mildest kinds of rule breaking when committed by sports stars. Often the athlete becomes better known for the misdemeanor than for sport. Ask the next 20 people you meet, "What was the boxer Mike Tyson famous for?" and more than half will say "ear-biting" – a reference to his disqualification against Evander Holyfield in 1997. Latrell Sprewell? The attack on his coach in 1999 is sure to figure. Kobe Bryant? Ben Johnson? You can anticipate the responses.

Whatever their appreciable achievements in the field of play, these athletes will forever be known for deviant behavior, whether actual or alleged (Bryant was, of course, cleared of sexual assault in 2004). Even Zinedine Zidane, widely acknowledged as one of the finest football players in history, will be remembered for the last action he performed in a competitive game: in the 2006 World Cup final: he headbutted Italian player Marco Materazzi and was immediately shown a red card.

Tony Blackshaw and Tim Crabbe argue "to be hated makes celebrities feel [to us] more 'real', authentic; that they have made their presence felt . . . to be 'deviant' is to be unforgettable" (2004: 75). The authors suggest that rule breaking and the violation of norms in sports has been "subsumed by consumer culture" (2004: 65).

They mean that, as sport has been commodified, so the very actions that were once condemned and censured are now sources of our fascination. Hearing about, reading about or actually witnessing "sex, perversity, sickness, filth and violence of a 'consumer' kind" makes our pulse race. In other words, the performance of deviant behaviour replete with danger and unpredictability is not so much well-suited but absolutely perfect for consumption via the media.

The spectacle of sport might once have been in the actual competition. In celebrity culture, the competition is but one facet of the entertainment. "The aspirational qualities associated with the endless possibilities of a consumer society" might remain wishful thinking, but sport is "a powerful seductive force" in drawing individuals beyond their immediate circumstances. We share vicariously with supposedly out-of-control athletes in just the same way as we might live through a game of Russian roulette or a car crash without actually putting a gun to our own heads or sitting in the front seat of the car (to borrow Umberto Eco's illustration). Our fascination with deviant celebrity athletes is "an expression of all our desires for a bit of the 'deviant' other and the self-expression it implies" (p.114).

I'll move to a fuller analysis of the overall impact of celebrity culture on sport in Chapter 17 but, for the moment, want to stay with Blackshaw and Crabbe, who conclude "there is no need to go beyond the surface representation of such celebrities . . . since they are constituted and consumed through their contingent performativity"

(p. 183). They offer their own versions of creative analytic practice in the attempt to reveal "something of the verisimilitude of the performativity of the 'deviance.' "

The concept performativity is taken from linguistics, but, in this instance, it means that deviance is something that's carried out visibly: in other words, there is nothing more than expression. Sport itself is a form of theater and its actors act out parts; but theirs is no mere performance. There are no subjects behind, beyond, and apart from the actual appearance. What matters, for Blackshaw and Crabbe is our consumption of deviance, not the 'deviance' itself (they are careful to use inverted commas throughout). Sport produces the very things it regulates and constrains.

Blackshaw and Crabbe provide an interesting and unusual scope on deviance in sport: far from being something that's forbidden, taboo, or rendered unmentionable by governing organizations, it's actually an integral part of the whole spectacular performance of sport. The more extravagant, exaggerated, and pantomimed the performance, the more consumers are gratified. Gratification, remember, arrives in different guises: it's possible to indulge or satisfy a desire by decrying it.

BOX 12.2 COMMODIFICATION

Treating something or someone as an article of trade that can be bought and sold on the market like a piece of merchandise is known as commodification, or commoditization. In a sense, professional sports trade in commodities. Economic value is assigned to people: they are valued according to the work they are able to do, i.e. their consumer use-value. The human body is frequently commodified in order to sell products, whether the performance of sport or the items of merchandise associated with it. The related term *commodity fetishism* usually refers to our (and this means all of us) worshipful adoration of animate objects, such as shoes, cars, jewelry, or, of course, people, whom we know only via their representations in the media. Fetishism implicates consumers in excessive and irrational commitments to objects that have no purpose or meaning outside a particular culture, but which provide gratification in a culture that places value on commodities.

Blackshaw and Crabbe's approach steers us away from the orthodoxy of trying to explain deviance in sport as aberrant, transgressive behavior, and invites us to mark the occasion of rule-breaking with a public performance . You could say: we *celebrate* deviant behavior. We may not praise athletes who are discovered *in flagrante delicto* with a prostitute, or who are photographed snorting cocaine by a prying paparazzo, or who shove lighted cigars into the faces of teammates (as the above-mentioned Barton did during a fracas in 2004). But there is satisfaction to be gained from making denunciations.

Denunciations have been among sport's favorite activities, from the condemnation of the Chicago White Sox players who took bribes to throw the 1919 World Series to the vilification of Zinedine Zidane for headbutting rival Marco Materazzi in the 2006 World Cup Final. Perhaps the greatest censure of all was reserved for Tiger

Woods, whose "transgression" as he called it, occasioned a global damnation. Woods' impropriety, as befits the richest sportsman ever to walk the planet, was a series of casual romantic or sexual relationships with women other than his wife. It formed the basis of a scandal of heroic proportions, and a whirlwind tour through the multiple women Woods bedded, actually or allegedly. At first a near-comical event in which Woods ran his car into a fire hydrant, then denied rumors of his infidelity, the scandal took on new proportions as Woods issued a statement in December 2009: "I regret those transgressions with all of my heart. I have not been true to my values . . . I am dealing with my behavior and personal failings behind closed doors with my family. Those feelings should be shared by us alone."

Maybe they should have, but a celebrity of Woods' stature was afforded no such privacy and his misdemeanor became arguably the most engrossing piece of wrongdoing of the century, emphasizing the voyeuristic pleasures we take from poring over others' foul play. The transgression was a spectacular reminder that the appeal of sport lies as much in rule breaking as rule abiding.

VIOLENCE

The orthodox approach to deviance in sport is to treat it as aberrant, or pathological, then try to explain it. Behavior that departs from accepted standards and functions like a disease is usually unwelcome and sports' governing organizations do their best to curb it. The alternative I've outlined so far is to understand deviance as so persistent that it is a regular feature of sport. If it's a disease, it's an endemic disease. The two least wanted strains are drugs and violence. My approach suggests there is nothing unusual about dope-taking in sport and Chapter 11 spelled out the reasons for this. Violence is another one of those phenomena that is widely condemned but also often condoned and frequently encouraged.

Sports governing organizations and media alike are sensitive to and intolerant of violence, probably because: (1) so much of sports competition is in itself very violent; and (2) it elicits such strong feelings among fans. There are plenty of people and groups who have no interest or empathy with sports who are only too willing to rail against sports for their excessive emphasis on aggression. Detractors blame sports for bringing out those nasty, brutish impulses that we manage to keep under control in other walks of life. Sports seem to license us to let rip.

Take boxing for example. It has been singled out by the American and British Medical Associations for its alleged barbarism. Writers who are, in many respects, thoughtful observers on sport, can understand why. "Boxing is not an expression of ghetto criminality or primitive aggression or some innate human propensity for violence," insisted Mike Marqusee in his *Redemption Song: Muhammad Ali and the spirit of the sixties*. "Though when a Mike Tyson comes along, it is all too easy to paint it in those colors" (1999:15).

This was written in 1999; since then Mixed Martial Arts have made boxing look like schmoozing. If you find yourself staring at an octagonal cage with one man standing over another pulverizing him, the best advice is keep reminding yourself of Marqusee's statement: there is no "innate human propensity for violence." Other possibilities – some explored previously – are to wonder why, despite, or perhaps in the light of, Elias's theories about the civilizing process, we are still intrigued by violence, or why several other sports that call for aggression (like football, or rugby) prompt criticisms, especially when they result in serious injury to competitors.

Parties with an interest in sports – like governing organizations and the media – are usually quick to point out that serious injuries occur in a minority of cases and that cases like Zidane's and Tyson's are extremely rare. Actually, that's not quite true. Comparable episodes occur regularly in several sports. In hockey, violence erupts, mostly between players, but occasionally involving officials (Andre Roy, of Tampa Bay Lightning, physically abused an official in 2002). In European and Central and South American football, red cards are commonplace, usually following outright violence or overly rough play. Practically every sport that features contact or collision either tolerates or promotes violence. Even non-contact sports: in 2004, during a Cambridgeshire village cricket match, batsman Michael Butt became incensed after he was bowled out and attacked his bowler with his bat; he admitted the assault and was sentenced to 175 hours community work and ordered to pay £200.

BOX 12.3 VIOLENCE

Behavior involving the exercise of physical force intended to hurt, injure, or disrespect another human, or property, is violence – from the Latin *violentia*, which has essentially the same meaning. In sports, as in many other areas, violence is equated with the unlawful use of force or intimidation, though many sports either tacitly condone or exhibit violence. Hockey is an example of the former and boxing the latter, of course. In both sports, however, the transgression of boundaries is still punishable, as this constitutes a rule-*violation* (from the same Latin root).

Violence should be distinguished from aggression, which is behavior, or a readiness to behave in a way, that is either intended or carries with it the possibility that a living being will be harmed, though no action or harm *necessarily* materializes – see below.

Sports provide a context for the sanctioned expression of violence. That much is clear. But that same context frequently encourages the *unsanctioned* expression of violence too. The line between them is a fine one. The context, in this instance, refers to both history and the surrounding environment in which fans view, cheer, boo and experience vicariously the same adrenaline rush competitors get when the competition is in progress. Let's deal with them separately before moving to the competitive situation itself. After this, we'll move to a consideration of "quasi-criminal violence" and then to collective violence among fans, particularly soccer fans.

History

We saw in Chapter 1 how the early folk games of England were raucous and perilous affairs, frequently ending with several casualties. Blood sports such as cock-fighting and bear-baiting were nothing if not violent, spectators jostling to get a view of animals, which would either be killed or mutilated. The prize fights that crowds flocked to see bore little resemblance to the boxing we see today: pugilists would try to pound opponents into either submission or unconsciousness (padded gloves were introduced not to minimize the damage, but to protect the hands of the fighters, enabling them to land harder punches without hurting their fists).

From the late nineteenth century, when governing federations began to impose formal structure and control on what were loose assemblies of competitive activities, restrictions on the outright use of violence were introduced. The brutal content of many sports decreased systematically as governing organizations moved with the times: as society's threshold of acceptable violence changed, so did sport's. Late football hits, overly savage beatings in the ring, unlimited head-high balls in cricket: these once-acceptable practices were reviewed and modified during the twentieth century. Even sports that weren't ostensibly violent were assessed: whip abuse in horse racing was banned, as was racket abuse in tennis.

Mindful of changing attitudes, sports federations adjusted their limits of tolerable violence, penalizing violators with fines and suspensions. This quasi-legal function of sports organizations became a more prominent feature of their operations. Sports defended their right to police themselves and to safeguard their own standards. Their administration of justice served to insulate them from the attentions of the wider judicial system. In other words, sports involved action that would almost certainly be punishable by law if it took place outside the sports arenas – and removed from the auspices of the official governing organization. Can you imagine what would happen if a tackle that's commonplace on the football field took place in a crowded department store?

Turn back the pages and reacquaint yourselves with the civilizing process that, Elias argued, affected every facet of social and personal experience. We and our forebears have been witnesses to a vast, all-encompassing trend that has transformed not just our behavior but our minds, the relationships we have with one another, the way we conduct our working lives, the manner in which we pursue leisure, the habits we acquire and break, the manners we observe and ignore, the rules we frame and how we manage their violation. All this is evident in the sports we play and watch and the pleasures we take from them.

Those who assumed authority for bringing what were once a haphazard mis-cellaneous bunch of raggedy games into structured, codified sports were obviously aware of the violence inherent in many competitive activities and the potential violence in practically all of them. To keep in sync with the rest of society's standards, they had to regulate them and penalize infractions, harmonizing sport with the civilizing tendencies in society.

Even then, it didn't keep away the legal eagles who were poised to swoop on behavior that appeared to violate not only sports' rules, but the rules that lay beyond. This type of behavior has been called quasi-criminal violence. The point is that, sports didn't evolve as a kind of separate species: they were constituent parts of a developing culture and, as such, were parts of the civilizing process. While we often state that sport *reflects* the surrounding culture or the wider society, this can be misleading: sport is actually an integral element of society and constitutive of culture. It shouldn't be understood as a reflection of either. So, when people make trite remarks like, "violence in sport reflects violence in wider society," they reveal a fundamental misunderstanding of sport, society and culture.

Environment

No fan wants to attend a game of football, hockey, soccer, or any other sport, and sit quietly for the duration, as they would, for example, at an opera or a symphony concert. The whole buzz about being there is to get wrapped up in the atmosphere of the occasion; to feel the elation, the depression and all the emotions in between. The fan can get all the thrills and still get home without stitches.

Being a fan is a relatively safe experience. Only relatively: as the example of British association football reminds us. In some situations, there is more violence off the field of play than there is on it, much more. The pitched battles in the streets of many Portuguese towns during the European Championship tournament of 2004 was no blip: soccer's fandom has a well-deserved reputation for violence. Soccer the world over seems to elicit peculiarly intense passions among its fans and violence has become a staple feature of the sport. While there's always the possibility of getting hurt in any large gathering, especially of rival groups of fans, injuries among fans of sports other than soccer are less common.

This doesn't negate the central point: sports are conducive to violent behavior and aggressive conduct. We want them to be. After all, whoever praised an athlete or a team for passivity? We don't expect tranquil attitudes or good-natured approaches: in fact, we demand aggressiveness, which is not the same thing as aggression or flat-out violence, but is never far away from them.

BOX 12.4 AGGRESSION

While aggression has been used as an inclusive term to capture diverse behavior containing hostility, harm, and violation, there is so little common ground among scholars that we might profitably start by establishing what it is *not*: "An attitude, emotion or motive . . . Wanting to hurt someone is not aggression. Anger and thoughts might play a role in aggressive behavior, but they are not necessary or defining characteristics . . . Accidental harm is not aggression . . . kicking a bench is not . . . sadomasochistic and suicidal acts [are not]," according to Diane Gill.

Yet, Barry Husman and John Silva contend that aggression is "an overt verbal or physical act that can psychologically or physically injure another person or oneself," meaning that sadomasochistic and suicidal acts would be, contrary to Gill, instances of aggression. In this definition, abusive email that can "psychologically" injure its recipient counts as aggression. But, Richard Cox emphasizes that the aggressive "behavior must be aimed at another human being with the goal of inflicting physical harm. . .there must be a reasonable expectation that the attempt to inflict bodily harm will be successful."

A consistent feature appears to be *intention*. The 1996 position statement of the International Society of Sport Psychology stipulated: "Aggression . . . is reflected in acts committed with the intent to injure" (Tenenbaum *et al.*, 1996). Yet even the inclusion of intention does not elicit complete agreement among scholars. Leif Isberg exchanges this for "the concept of *awareness* that an act will or could injure someone." Even, if a person did not intend to harm another, the fact that he or she was aware that it might make their behavior aggressive. Isberg deviates from most definitions when he suggests that aggression is not behavior, but rather "an unobservable starting point for potentially aggressive behavior."

An incident in which Reading player Steve Hunt collided with Chelsea goalkeeper Petr Cech, in October 2006, illustrates this: Cech suffered a depressed fracture of the skull, though the Football Association took no disciplinary action against Hunt because of the difficulty in establishing intent. While Hunt claimed he didn't intend to injure Cech, he would surely have been *aware* that his challenge could cause injury and so, under Isberg's definition, it would be an act of aggression.

There are other, deeper disagreements, but, for present purposes, we might propose that *aggression is behavior, or a propensity to behave in a way, that is either intended or carries with it a recognizable possibility, that a living being will be harmed, physically or psychologically.* In this sense, aggression is quite different from what nowadays we call aggressiveness, or assertiveness, and conceptually distinct from violence.

FRUSTRATION

Let's expand the argument to discover what theorists of aggression tell us about its causes. Ethologists (who study humans in the same way as they would any other animal and whose approach to sports we covered in Chapter 1) contend that we are born with an aggressive instinct that has been quite serviceable in our survival as a species. So, we defend our "natural" territory when it is under threat. Konrad Lorenz wrote that human aggression is like other forms of animal aggression, only we have learned to route it into safe outlets, sports being an obvious one (1966).

Sigmund Freud too viewed sport as a way of discharging aggression. In his theory, we all have a *death* instinct that builds up inside us to the point where it must be discharged, either inwardly (self-destructive acts), or outwardly (1963). Because we don't always have socially acceptable opportunities for turning our aggression outward, we displace it into acceptable channels. Sports are perfect: we can get all our aggression out of our system either by participating or just watching; either way, we rid ourselves of the aggression.

Without denying that aggression has its source in a biological drive, other accounts focused on the context in which aggression materializes, noticing that some environments seem to have more potential for eliciting aggressive behavior than others. Sports, of course, are designed to frustrate: individuals pursue aims, while others try to stop them. Several theorists have argued that frustration creates a readiness for aggressive behavior.

The frustration-aggression hypothesis, as it's called, states that, when goal-oriented behavior is blocked, an aggressive drive is induced. Further frustrations increase the drive. On this account, all aggressive behavior is produced by frustration. The hypothesis was introduced as an alternative to theories of aggression based on innate characteristics. Scholars such as John Dollard and his colleagues rejected the notion of human behavior as programmed by nature and argued instead that the way we act is the product of stimuli in the world about us – frustration being the stimulus that produces aggressive behavior (1939). Unlike Lorenz, Freud and others who portrayed sports competition as a cathartic experience, allowing all the aggressive energies to blow out, frustration-aggression theorists interpreted sports as heightening the possibility of aggression. Frustration of some order is inevitable in any competition. But, while this might help explain why aggression of some kind is likely to appear in sports, it leaves the issue of why some sports seem to have developed a tradition of violence, raising the possibility that there's a cultural element to violence too.

Albert Bandura's famous experiment with Bobo dolls involved asking groups of children to watch an aggressive model beating up a toy Bobo doll or treating it kindly (1973). The tendency of the children was to copy the model they observed, especially when they witnessed the aggressive model being rewarded for the assault. Bandura concluded from this and other studies that we *learn* aggression and in this sense, it's a cultural rather than natural phenomenon. Clearly, this finding is totally at odds with the view of many coaches and players who believe (presumably, with Lorenz) that sports are a good way of letting off steam, or getting our aggression out of our system. The aggression has never been in there, according to social learning theorists: we acquire it during our interactions with others. Crudely summarized, sport is an outlet for aggression in biologically based approaches, a mediating factor in the frustration-aggression hypothesis and an environment in which aggression is acquired in social learning theory.

This doesn't exclude frustration from the social learning account: frustration is one of several experiences that lead to an emotional arousal. But there may be others, including physical discomfort, or even pleasant circumstances, such as dancing in a club. Aroused by the physical exertion of dancing and a feeling of well-being, a person may be aggressive toward someone who accidentally bumps into them and makes them spill a drink. It may well be that the aggressor has learned this response through observing others at the same club, whose behavior was rewarded. Even if the person had been thrown out, his or her peers may have been suitably impressed. Several studies indicate that emotional arousal, regardless of the source, can increase aggression when the requisite stimuli are present. The consequences of the reaction to the aggression can have decisive effects in shaping future behavior.

The lesson is that much aggression is preceded, if not caused, by frustration and frustration arises from not being able to get one's own way. Isn't that what sports are all about? One person or group trying to get their way, while another tries to stop them. Whether viewed from a historical or contemporary perspective, sports are either violent or carry the potential for violence. Basic logic tells us that this will always be the case. The primary goal of sporting competition is to do one's utmost to win in the face of opposition. The opposition's primary aim is exactly the same. Each party is continuously trying to achieve the goal, while preventing the opposition from achieving theirs. It means that the competitive environment is alive with cues for aggression. And that can often tip over into violence – but not just any old violence.

Instrumental violence is used with a specific purpose beyond the violence itself. Its counterpart is *hostile* violence, which is designed to cause harm to another, plain and simple (see Husman and Silva, 1984). A football player might believe he or she has been hit by another player in an unfair way, which goes unnoticed by the referee. Incensed, the player chases the offender and lunges feet-first at his ankles with the sole intention of causing him harm. This is hostile.

The same player, later in the game, might jump to meet the ball in the air, at the same time, deliberately elbowing an opponent in the face. His aim in this instance is primarily to get to the ball first and his elbow action is a way of deterring another player who might otherwise obstruct him. In both cases, aggressive behavior inflicts harm, but, in the latter case, it's a means to an end and the end is defined by the purpose of the competition. The aggression serves as an instrument. The distinction in sports is not always so clear-cut. Even an enraged athlete who intentionally bites an opponent's ear does so in the context of competition in which he or she has the overarching aim of victory.

BOX 12.5 HOSTILE/INSTRUMENTAL

Conventionally, two types of aggression are specified: *hostile* (or reactive) and *instrumental*. The primary goal of hostile aggression is to cause harm to another: a football player might believe he or she has been unfairly tackled and retaliate by chasing and striking feet-first at the opponent's ankles with no intention of retrieving the ball. With instrumental aggression, there is a specific purpose beyond the aggression itself and the intention to harm, or awareness that the action might cause harm to another is incidental: the same player, later in the game, might jump for the ball, at the same time deliberately elbowing an opponent in the face – the goal is to reach the ball and the aggression is a way of deterring another player who might otherwise obstruct his path to the goal. In both cases, aggressive behavior inflicts harm.

Now that we've examined how sports have thrummed with aggression and violence through the ages and how the context of sports encourages the kind of frustration that leads to aggression, we arrive at an interesting question. Not why is there so much violence in and around sport? But, why isn't there more?

PIANISTS AND HUMPERS

Given the amount of money at stake in professional sports, it's hardly surprising that many competitors are prepared to do what it takes by fair means or foul to get the desired results. A win can mean an awful lot to competitors. Winning or losing a title fight can be the difference between boxing for several million dollars or a dozen or so thousand in the next fight (though it didn't for Tyson: in his first fight after the Holyfield débâcle, he earned $10 million).

Most ball players have bonus agreements built into their contracts. So playing a role in a major championship victory can make a big impression on your bank statement, especially when you have a clause like Pedro Martinez, of Philadelphia Phillies, whose basic contract was for what was in baseball terms a relatively modest $1m, but who stood to earn another $1.275m in incentives in 2009. In contrast, members of the Osasuna football team were offered ten suckling pigs by a local farmer if they beat rivals Espanyol in 2009. The incentive worked and they won.

The growth of commercialism brought about by television especially from the 1960s, as we have seen, introduced to sports more money than could have been dreamt of some twenty-five years earlier. In Chapter 11 I argued that the increase in the use of performance-enhancing drugs by performers is one result of this. Coaches over the years have driven competitors as hard as they could, pushing and prodding them to their peak performances. But the carrot is mightier than the stick. There's no better way to get the ultimate effort out of a performer than to offer irresistible incentives, usually money, rather than swine.

The results of this are obvious: perfectly conditioned, highly motivated, tunnel-visioned, win-oriented performers, who continually frustrate critics and some-times governing authorities with the excellence of their play and the tenacity of their approach. The "give-it-your-best-shot" approach gave way to a "must-win" orientation as athletes were encouraged to achieve, rather than just strive.

In many sports where competitors are physically separated, the changes in orientation manifested only surreptitiously. In tennis and billiards, for example, competitors exhibit their prowess in relative isolation. They don't, for example, break tackles, knock opponents out or dribble pucks around opposing players. In sports where contact or collision is inevitable, either by design or default, the effort to win by any means necessary takes on a different complexion. Physical encounters are less restrained than they might have been where only pride was once at stake. Serious injuries are accepted as part-and-parcel of today's sports. Illegal play is seen as permissible as long as it goes unnoticed by officials. When the price of failure is measured in terms of what might have been gained, success is pursued with a fury.

In other words, the efforts of sports to curb overly aggressive play hasn't been accompanied by a corresponding change in players' motivations or behavior. They're more motivated to win than ever and are prepared to bend if not break the rules to do so. This isn't to say that competitors from past eras didn't have ferocity, single-mindedness or callous disregard for others. These were qualities that might have been permissible, or even lauded. Today, sports governors realize that they're qualities that have to be kept in check. They don't want to neuter the competition, but they know that the bar has been raised: consumers want aggressiveness without being repulsed by unjustifiable and obnoxious violence.

Again, let's pause to reflect on Elias: he wrote of "the gradual transformation of behavior and the emotions, the expanding threshold of repugnance (1982: 71). A threshold is often used to describe a lower limit, as in "threshold of pain" – if it goes above this level, we can't tolerate it. In the middle ages, there was a level at which we wouldn't tolerate the sight of violence; as we moved to industrial society, this level changed and we were repulsed by violence that our predecessors tolerated. Today, most of us would find bloodsports involving animals cruel and abhorrent though our distant relatives permitted and even enjoyed them. So the threshold of repugnance has changed: we are far less tolerant of violence and brutality. This doesn't mean we've lost our facility for enjoying violence altogether.

The National Hockey League provides a fitting case study. In the 1970s, the NHL re-set its own threshold – and with interesting results. Watch the hockey played at Olympic Games, where there is a high degree of technical competence but none of the almost theatrical fighting that punctuates a typical NHL game. The experience is quite different and, I dare say, not as entertaining for an NHL fan. The George Roy Hill film *Slap Shot* (1977) is a satire on commercialism and violence in hockey. Manager Paul Newman tries to revive his club's fortunes by drafting-in three goons with limited skill, but a penchant for roughness. The team's principles are sacrificed; but the results improve and the crowd loves the boisterous tactics.

The film was made in the mid-1970s, when the Philadelphia Flyers dominated the sport, winning two straight Stanley Cups, with a ferocious brand of physical hockey in which the "hit" was a central weapon (the NHL defines a "hit" as contact that "significantly impedes" a player's progress). The Flyers' expert use of the bodychecking changed the character of the game: the crushing hits they put on opponents were calculated to intimidate; though, as with all forms of intimidation, once opponents started to hit back with interest, Philadelphia's superiority was broken.

Hockey at the time was a perilous sport: sticks were wielded like axes, fists flew furiously and players got slammed with bone-rattling hits. In their *Hockey Night in Canada*, Richard Gruneau and David Whitson wrote "hockey actually seems to celebrate fighting outside the rules as a normal part of the game" (1994: 189). Not so, said Ted Green, of Boston Bruins, who almost died as a result of a stick blow to the head that fractured his skull. The game in which it happened took place in 1969. In the following year, both Green and his attacker, Wayne Maki, of St Louis, appeared in separate trials in Ottawa, charged with assault causing bodily harm. It was alleged that Green provoked Maki. Both were acquitted on grounds of self-defense.

Within months of the Green–Maki case, a Canada-wide poll conducted by *Maclean's* magazine indicated that almost 40 percent of the respondents, male and female, liked to see physical violence in hockey. They were not disappointed over the next several years as the amount and intensity of what Michael Smith calls "quasi-criminal violence" increased – as, incidentally, did the popularity of hockey. The

NHL's attendances grew by about 40 percent over the 15 years from the mid-1970s; tv revenue increased about 12-fold.

"The belief that violence sells and that eliminating fighting would undercut the game's appeal as spectacle has been the official thinking among the NHL's most influential governors and officers," detect Gruneau and Whitson (1994: 185). Yet, in 1976, the Attorney-General of Ontario ordered a crackdown on violence in sports after a year that had seen 67 assault charges relating to hockey. In the same year, a particularly wild bust-up occurred during a World Hockey Association playoff game between Quebec Nordiques and Calgary Cowboys, whose player Rick Jodzio was eventually fined C$3,000 (U.S.$2,200, or £1,360) after pleading guilty to a lesser charge than the original causing bodily harm with intent to wound. There were also convictions arising from a Philadelphia–Toronto game in 1976: the interesting aspect of this one was that, in legal terms, a hockey stick was designated a dangerous weapon.

Despite the commercial success of the NHL after the mid-1970s and the rise of the Philadelphia Flyers, the league remained mindful that too much on-ice brawling could easily turn television away. Big-hit players threatened to overrun the game, making more skillful players less likely to survive. The NHL's crackdown on violence did not eliminate fights, but between the 1987/88 season to 1998/99 the average number of altercations dropped from 2.1 to 1.2.

Concern over the violence prompted the NHL to rethink its policies and clamp down. By the early twenty-first century, it had slipped from its position as North America's fourth major league sport and tv viewing figures collapsed, leaving it without the gargantuan contracts to which it had become accustomed. Maybe NHL without the big hits and the fist fights was just not the same.

Basketball is another sport that has benefited from more physical aspects. At the start of the 1980s, the sport lagged way behind hockey in terms of popularity in the United States. It now vies with baseball and football as the most-watched sport in the United States and has a large tv following around the world. Much of its success has been based on marketing strategies that have worked like a charm and a format that suits television perfectly. But, again, compare your experiences: watch a game of basketball from any Olympics before 1992, when an all-professional American "dream team" dominated. The action is fast, nimble and precise; yet there is something lacking; and I don't mean the climactic slam-dunks. The physical contact is almost polite alongside the bumps, knocks, shoves, and jostling we are used to seeing. Players don't get sent splaying after running into a colossus like Shaq O'Neal. None of the players has the mien of a pro boxer, as do any number of NBA all-stars.

The NBA purveys a different game from the basketball played by the rest of the world ten years ago. It's harsher, more physical and brings with it an undertow of violence that has made it commercially attractive. Small wonder that tv networks have clamored to throw money at the NBA, which has in turn plowed it through the clubs which have been able to pay players salaries to rival those of the best-paid boxers and baseball players. This has pumped up the stakes even higher, reinforcing the intensity of competition that characterizes the NBA.

The phrase "only in America" springs to mind when we come to comparing this trend with sports elsewhere in the world. Or, perhaps, only North America, because efforts south of the Rio Grande and throughout the rest of the world have been aimed at eliminating the violence that has been allegedly escalating in soccer. The sport has always been tough, of course; but soccer's world governing organization Fifa (Fédération Internationale de Football Associations) in the 1980s, became concerned that the pre-eminent teams were those that employed particularly physical players, whose specialty was intimidation. This had commercial implications, though they were never spelled out: if the finesse players were succumbing to the "cloggers" as they were known ("clog" meaning to impede or hamper), then the shape of the sport would change fundamentally, skill being replaced by a more robust style of play in which only the strong would survive.

"The game is for artists and artisans," observed Ferenc Puskas, the esteemed Hungarian football player of the 1950s. "The artists are like piano players, the artisans carry the piano." At a time when Fifa was expanding into Africa and Asia to make the sport genuinely universal and needed television monies to fund its mission, it could ill-afford to lose its virtuosos or allow them to be kicked around.

Over a period of years, Fifa issued a series of directives to soccer referees to control not only violent play, but disagreements with referees' calls (classed as "dissent"), time-wasting (the clock runs continuously apart from half-time in soccer), and "professional fouls." The penalties for these and other violations were severe: without the hockey-style sin bins, soccer players were ejected from games for the duration and faced further suspensions as a result as well as heavy fines. Despite attempts to contain aggressive behavior in many sports there remains a paradox.

For many sports to be effective as competitive spectacles, some element of aggression has to be present. "Within-their-rules aggression is not only tolerated but encouraged, especially in sports such as football and hockey and, to a lesser extent basketball and baseball," writes Donald F. Staffo in his prescriptive article "Strategies for reducing criminal violence among athletes" (2001: 40).

Staffo adds: "It should not be surprising, then, that reports of sports-related violence are as old as athletic competition itself." One only needs to see coaches before a game; they are never caught gazing reflectively out of a locker room window, whispering gently to their players, "Take a chill pill: we'll win if it's meant to be. Haven't you guys ever heard of karma?" More likely, they'll be roaring with passion, using every device they know to whip their players to an aggressive peak.

Sport, as I pointed out earlier, produces the very thing it tries to contain: it creates a milieu that sometimes endorses or encourages aggression, or at least creates conditions under which the possibility of violence is maximized. It then covers that milieu with a sheltering canopy as if to prevent outsiders interfering with internal affairs. Every sports governing organization condemns aggression and violence, though there is extreme variability is the punishments handed out to violators. In a way, the organizations are acknowledging the inherent potential for violence in a context in which frustration is inevitable. They're constantly trying to suppress it. Every so often, they simply can't contain the violence.

ILLEGAL MEANS

The Green–Maki case cited earlier wasn't the first famous instance of quasi-criminal violence. In a 1965 Giants–Dodgers game, the San Francisco hitter Juan Marichal whacked LA catcher John Roseborough with his bat. Marichal was fined by the league and suspended, but Roseborough sought retribution through a civil suit that was eventually settled out of court. In basketball, a huge case in 1979 involved not only the fining and suspension of the Lakers' Kermit Washington, but an accusation leveled against his club for failing to train and supervise the player adequately. He was ordered to pay damages. The player whom he attacked, Rudy Tomjanovich, was effectively forced into premature retirement as a result of his injuries.

Boxer Billy Ray Collins was also made to retire as a result of injuries incurred during his fight with Luis Resto. Going into the 1983 fight a hot favorite with a 14–0 record, Collins was surprisingly beaten and finished with his eyes so swollen that he was temporarily blinded. He did not box again and was killed in an auto wreck the following year. In the aftermath of the fight, Resto's gloves were confiscated by the chief inspector of the New York State Athletic Commission (NYSAC), who had them inspected by the manufacturers, Everlast, and a state police laboratory. Each glove was meant to weigh 7.95 ounces, but Resto's right glove was 6.92 ounces and the left 6.96 ounces. The Commission announced that unauthorized changes had been made to the gloves and permanently revoked the licences of Resto's trainer, Panama Al Lewis and Pedro Alvarado, who also worked his corner. Resto was suspended for a year. The fight was declared "No contest."

In October 1986, Resto and Lewis were brought to criminal court by the state of New York and convicted of assault, conspiracy and criminal posession of a deadly weapon – Resto's fists. Additionally, Lewis was convicted of tampering with a sports contest. Resto was sentenced to a maximum of three years and Lewis a maximum of six; both served 2½ years. There was, as Jeff Pearlman of *Sports Illustrated* put it, "overwhelming evidence that the boxing career of Billy Ray Collins Jr was ended by illegal means" (1998: 120).

Collins' estate filed a $65 million lawsuit against the NYSAC, arguing that the inspectors had an obligation not only to look at the gloves but also to feel them on Resto's hands, to look inside them—to do everything to ensure they had not been tampered with. The NYSAC contested that the term "inspection" was broad and added that the responsibility lay not with the Commission, but with the promoters, Bob Arum's Top Rank Boxing, which hired the inspectors. A further action by lawyers acting for Collins' estate was directed at Pasquale Giovanelli, an inspector provided by Top Rank. The case ended in a hung jury.

Another significant case of this kind occurred in an NFL game during the 1975 season. The plaintiff, Dale Hackbart of the Denver Broncos, suffered a career-ending fracture of the spine following a big hit from Charles Clark of the Cincinnati Bengals. Taking his case to the District Court, Hackbart was told that, by the very fact of playing an NFL game, he was taking an implied risk and that anything happening to him between the sidelines was part of that risk. An appeals court disagreed and ruled that, while Clark may not have specifically intended to injure his opponent, he had engaged in "reckless misconduct." This paved the way for his employer, the Bengals, to be held accountable.

This case was to have echoes almost two decades later in England, when a Chelsea soccer player, Paul Elliott, pursued a case against Dean Saunders, then playing for Liverpool. Following a tackle from Saunders, Elliott sustained injuries that prevented him from playing again. The court found that the context of soccer mitigated the offense and that Saunders was not guilty of reckless or dangerous play. Elliott's case was weakened by the fact that the play was not penalized by the referee during the game and so the judge was effectively asked to use a video and other evidence to overturn the referee's decision.

John Fashanu was taken to court twice for play that seriously injured fellow soccer players: one was settled out of court and he was cleared of the other, underscoring the point that guilt in a law court and guilt on the playing field are two different things. It could be argued that a player who directs his or her aggression against another in a wild and reckless way is doing so out of a desire to win rather than malice. The relevant principle was originally stated in English law in the *Condon v. Basi* case of 1985, when it was decided that, even in a competitive sport whose rules indicate that physical contact will occur, a person owes a duty to an opponent to exercise a reasonable degree of care. In *Condon*, the court accepted the evidence of the referee in an amateur football game that the defendant had broken the plaintiff's leg by a reckless and dangerous tackle and damages were awarded.

Despite the experiences of Saunders and Fashanu, professional athletes in Britain were dealt an ominous warning in 1998 when Gordon Watson, a player for Bradford City soccer club, won an unprecedented negligence action in the High Court. He became the first player to win damages in spite of returning to soccer after recovering from a double fracture eighteen months before. Bradford's chair insisted that he attempted to settle the matter without going to court, but found no satisfaction with soccer's authorities. The club also brought an action for recklessness against Kevin Gray, the player whose sliding tackle did the damage to Watson, but this was rejected.

In Elliott's case, the referee decided that Saunders attempted to play the ball and accidentally injured Elliott, which was how the game officials called it. In Watson's, the referee punished the violent tackle. This might suggest that officials' decisions are respected, though there are exceptions, the most remarkable coming in the aftermath of the European middleweight title fight between Alan Minter and Angelo Jacopucci in 1978.

A few hours after being knocked out, Jacopucci collapsed and ultimately died. In 1983, after a protracted and complicated series of legal actions, a court in Bologna, Italy, acquitted the referee and Jacopucci's manager of second degree manslaughter on the basis that they should have stopped the fight before the twelfth and last round. The ringside doctor, however, was convicted, ordered to pay Jacopucci's widow the equivalent of $15,000 (£10,000) damages and given a suspended eight-month prison sentence.

The courts have been wary of intervening in Britain, though the incidents involving Duncan Ferguson, Eric Cantona, and Paul Ince were exceptions that may prove to be the rule in future. Before examining this, let's retreat to 1975 and the case of Henry Boucha who played for the Minnesota North Stars of the NHL. During a home game against the Boston Bruins, Boucha got into a fight with Dave Forbes, for which they were both sent off for a period in the penalty box. On their way back to the game, Forbes lashed out with his stick, dropping Boucha to the ice. Concussed and bleeding, Boucha was helpless as Forbes leapt on him and, grabbing his hair, slammed his head onto the ice repeatedly.

Forbes escaped with a relatively light suspension of ten games from the NHL, but a Minnesota grand jury charged him with the crime of aggravated assault by use of a dangerous weapon. Forbes pleaded not guilty and the jury was unable to reach a unanimous verdict after 18 hours of deliberations. The court declared a mistrial and the case was dismissed. Boucha meanwhile needed surgery and never played again. Remember: *State v. Forbes* was a criminal case and its lack of a definite verdict left several pertinent questions unresolved. Smith believes the main ones revolve around whether Forbes was culpable or whether the club for which he played and the league in which he performed were in some way responsible for establishing a context for his action (1983: 20).

It's also relevant that the actual violent event took place as the players were re-entering the playing area rather than in the flow of the game itself, which is why it bears resemblance to the Eric Cantona affair. At first Cantona committed a foul during his team's game with Crystal Palace; for this, his second serious offense, he was dismissed from play. While walking from the field he was provoked verbally by a fan who had made his way to the edge of the playing area. Cantona turned toward the fan, lurched at him feet first and started to fire punches. Seeing the commotion, Cantona's team-mate Paul Ince ran to the scene and engaged with another fan.

While only Cantona was singled out for punishment by his club and the FA, both players were charged with common assault, Cantona being sentenced to two weeks' imprisonment. More severe was the three-month prison sentence imposed on Duncan Ferguson for head-butting a fellow professional soccer player in a game between his club, Rangers and Raith Rovers in Glasgow in 1994.

These were high-profile cases featuring top athletes. In contrast, Jesse Boulerice was a 19-year-old player for the Plymouth Whalers, an Ontario Hockey League (OHL) outfit from Michigan, when he found himself charged by the Wayne County (Michigan) Prosecutor's Office with a felony: assault with intent to do great bodily harm less than murder – a crime that carries a $5,000 fine and 10 years maximum imprisonment. In a 1998 game, Boulerice had swung his stick into the face of Andrew Long, also 19, a player with the Guelph Storm, who sustained multiple facial fractures, a broken nose, concussion accompanied by seizure, a brain contusion, and a cut across his upper lip. The OHL decided that Boulerice had "used his stick in a most alarming and unacceptable fashion" and suspended him for one year. The incident itself was captured on videotape and observers estimated that Boulerice's stick was traveling between 50 and 75 mph when it made contact with Long. Boulerice denied that he meant to hurt Long.

The questions raised by the Boulerice–Long case are germane to all sports in which violence of some kind is integral. Was there any criminal intent in Boulerice's conduct, or was it simply part of the ebb-and-flow of a sport that trades on aggression? In strictly behavioral terms, was the action any different from the hundreds of other instances in the same game that either went unnoticed or did not result in such serious injuries? Should we consider other factors, such as a chanting crowd, an excitable coach, or even the cash incentives? Jeff MacGregor's point is similar to the one made earlier in this chapter: "What is most surprising about the Jesse Boulerice–Andrew Long matter is not that it happened, but that it doesn't happen more often" (1999: 114)

One of the usual protections afforded sports performers in similar circumstances is the context: players frequently behave in ways that would be alien to them outside of the sporting arena; they forge rivalries that have no meaning apart from in their sport; they consciously psych themselves to an aggressive level in order to maximize their effectiveness. In other words, their disposition toward violent action is specific to the sport itself.

In the light of our earlier analysis of the history of sport and the frustration-steeped environment it creates, this seems reasonable. It's quite possible that the person might have violent tendencies that are only activated by competition. Or it could be that the player's "normal" character is at odds with the violent persona he or she feels bound to assume during a game. Or, it could just be that the player is aggressive in and out of sports. In a sense, none of this is relevant because the behavior itself is meshed into the context of the sport. Forbes, we presume, held nothing personal against Boucha and, if they met at, say, a party, they may well have got along together. Cantona would almost certainly have never met the man he assaulted had they not been player and fan respectively.

Sports are violent, but, as Michael Smith in his 1983 study *Violence and Sport* points out: "The fact is, sports violence has never been viewed as 'real' violence" and the public "give standing ovations to performers for acts that in other contexts would be instantly condemned as criminal" (1983: 9). Yet, in the years since the publication of Smith's book, many of those acts are being condemned as criminal and the impression is that governing organizations of sport have lost their ability to police themselves.

▌BOX 12.6 QUASI-CRIMINAL VIOLENCE

Michael Smith defines this as: "that which violates not only the formal rules of a given sport (and the law of the land), but to a significant degree the informal norms of player conduct" (in his 1983 book *Violence and Sport*). Typically, it will result in some form of injury that brings it to the attention of officials, and, later, tends to generate public outrage when the mass media report it. Sometimes, civil legal proceeding follows, though, according to Smith, who it must be remembered was writing in 1983, "less often than thought." Nowadays, court cases are more prevalent. *Quasi* is Latin for "almost."

It would be thrilling if it were not also horrendous. The truth is: we love watching violence; we just don't like the after-effects. No sports fan is going to put up his or her hands and say they like to see the likes of a concussed Petr Cech stretchered-off with a fractured skull, any more than they enjoy the sight of a teenager like Andrew Long, his face fractured, also concussed, in his case with his brain bruised. Our thresholds of repugnance are set at a level where we can't tolerate such damage to humans. And yet we habitually witness competitive events in which rivals spare no sympathy and play with a zeal that could be misinterpreted in a slightly different context as malicious. It would be tragic if it were not thrilling.

BEASTLIE FURIE

There are two versions of the source of the word fan. One traces it to the adjective fanatic, from the Latin *fanaticus*, meaning "of a temple"; so the fan is someone who is excessively enthusiastic or filled with the kind of zeal usually associated with religious fervor. The term crept into baseball in the late 1880s, but as a replacement for the more pejorative "crank," according to Tom Sullivan, writing for the *Sporting Life* of November 23, 1887.

The alternative is even older: the "fancy" was the collective name given to patrons of prize fighting in the early nineteenth century. There are references in Pierce Egan's 1812 classic *Boxiana*. "Prize fighters such as [Jem] Belcher, later Jack Randall, were revered by the 'Fancy,'" write Iain McCalman and Maureen Perkins in *An Oxford Companion to the Romantic Age: British culture, 1776–1832*. The fancy was "a wide social range of male gamblers, drinkers and sports fanciers" (2001: 218). Whatever its etymology, fan lost its religious and patrician connotations and became a description of followers, or admirers of virtually anybody or anything in popular culture.

Excessively enthusiastic people sometimes get aggressive, particularly if their passion is fueled by religious zeal. Sports fans often appear to be similarly motivated. The obsessive properties of fans are inspected in the Tony Scott film *The Fan* (1996) in which a fan, played by Robert De Niro, gets his spiritual nourishment only by following baseball: his job as a knife salesman holds no interest for him and he is prepared to sacrifice it in order to pursue his real love. When he discovers that his team's recently-signed superstar is interested primarily in money, he turns viciously against him.

The story has some basis in fact: in 1949, Philadelphia Phillies player Eddie Waitkus was shot by a fan. More recently, figure skater Katarina Witt and tennis player Steffi Graf were harassed by stalkers. In 1993, Graf's rival Monica Seles was stabbed. The attacker kept a shrine to Graf in his aunt's attic. Less well-known is the case of multiple world snooker champion Stephen Hendry: a female fan became fixated on the Scottish player and wrote him a series of letters which grew progressively abusive. In 1991, she threatened to shoot him, later claiming that her threat afforded her "power over people's lives . . . to know that you can cause such harm to people by doing something as simple as writing a letter" (quoted in *The Sunday Times*, September 29, 1996).

Creepy as these cases are, more disturbing stalkers follow singers and movie actors. For instance, Björk was sent a letter bomb filled with hydrochloric acid by her fan Ricardo López in 1996. Later, it was discovered that López had videoed himself making the bomb then shooting himself dead in a kind of sacrifice to Björk. Presumably the ability to take one's life and threaten another's confers a kind of power.

Cheryl Harris describes fandom "as a phenomenon in which members of sub-ordinated groups try to align themselves with meanings embodied in stars or other texts that best express their own sense of social identity" (1998: 49–50).

Following the exploits of others and perhaps displacing one's own perceived inadequacies in the process, fans can negate their feelings of powerlessness. If we begin from this premise that fans try to align themselves with others as a way of expressing some part of their selves and that this can be experienced as empowering, especially for those who have little material power, then we can move toward an understanding of collective fan violence.

Even if we acknowledge that extreme fans such as these are exceptional, we still have to contend with the intensity of emotion and fervor that fans – whether sports fans, or rock fans – experience. The curious aspect of fans is that they are so well behaved. They buy tickets, present them at the entrance, drink a few beers, scream and shout for a few hours and then exit the building usually in an orderly fashion. They never quite determine if they are strictly observers or fantasizing participants imagining what it must be like to be in the thick of the action. A little of both, perhaps, if the premise of Ken Loach's 2009 film *Looking for Eric* is to be accepted. In this film, a twice-divorced postal worker whose life is in disarray has a fantasy friendship with footballer Eric Cantona, who becomes his mentor and spouts equivoques such as "He that sows thorns shall reap prickles."

Fans don't want their idols to be goody two-shoes. There's gratification in discovering failings, quirks, and improprieties; Cantona had plenty. In fact, fans don't even have to respect, admire, or even like players, to be interested in them. Cases like Michael Vick's stand out because of their unusualness; but rule breaking among sports performers, whether in or out outside the context of competition, is unexceptional and fans are enthralled by the exploits of deviant characters. The wonder is that fans themselves are not incited to unruliness. They were once.

The first documented account of violent rivalry among sports fans dates back to the year 532 CE when a staggering 30,000 deaths resulted from conflict between chariot racing fans in Constantinople; the uprising was known as the Nika riots. Fifteen hundred miles away, and almost 800 years later in 1314, King Edward II of England banned large ballgames: "Forasmuch as there is great noise in the city caused by hustling over large balls, from which many evils may arise, which God forbid, we command and forbid, on behalf of the King, on pain of imprisonment, such a game to be used in the city in future."

Frequent laws banning ballgames followed the English types of football through the centuries, partly because of the violence that often erupted among its fans and partly because it was thought to distract young men from sports such as archery and boxing which, as we saw in Chapter 4 were useful for military duty. In 1514, the first published thesis on education in the English language described football, or at least its primitive equivalent, as "nothing but beastlie furie and extreme violence."

Football, along with other forms of recreation, was banned under the Puritan regime of Oliver Cromwell in the seventeenth century, only to resurface again at the Restoration of the monarchy in 1660.

As we've already seen, the folk games were insuppressible and were typically loud and rowdy affairs that left participants maimed or sometimes dead. Even when football, like other sports, became an organized competition in the late nineteenth century, it was still a rough, physical game that took few prisoners. Fans became more manageable when they were forced only to watch rather than participate and gradually their disorderliness very nearly vanished. But not quite: British fans regularly invaded the field of play, sometimes just to whoop and celebrate, but other times to attack the referees.

BOX 12.7 FOOTBALL

Football is a generic term covering the world's most popular team game, known variously as soccer, *voetbal*, *fussball*, and other derivations; American football, sometimes called gridiron; rugby, which is divided into Rugby League and Rugby Union; and Gaelic football and Australian rules football, which differ only slightly in terms of rules. Accounts of its origins usually include primitive kicking games using the inflated or stuffed bladder of an animal. In the middle ages, adjacent English villages would incorporate a version of this into their festivals celebrating holy days. These were, as David Canter and his colleagues call them, mêlées rather than games with no rules: the object being to move the bladder by any available means to the boundaries of one of the villages. The inhabitants of villages in Chester in the north of England became so fierce in their efforts to move the bladder that the event had to be abandoned (Canter *et al.*, 1989). Lack of transportation and mobility meant that the games remained localized until the mid-nineteenth century when common sets of rules emerged and standards created. An unlikely but popular story that purports to explain the division into throwing and kicking games involves a certain William Webb Ellis, a pupil at Rugby school, who in 1823, became confused and picked up a ball in what was intended to be a kicking game. Legend has it that rugby was born that day and it was this game that had offspring in the form of American football, Australian rules, and Gaelic football.

No sport has elicited fan disorder, disturbance, aggression and outright violence to the same extent as association football. Apart from the period between the two world wars, 1918–39, and for twenty years after World War II, English football in particular has been characterized by an unruly and fractious spectatorship. The sport's history reveals that violence has been a feature of games since long before its official designation as association football in 1863. Soccer is the most popular sport in the world and, while the specific form of disorder known as hooliganism originated in Britain in the 1960s, it quickly spread all over Europe and South America. The title of Janet Lever's book on the South American game captures the manic enthusiasm of fans, *Soccer Madness*.

The term "hooligan" is thought to be a corruption of Houlihan, this being the name of an Irishman, who migrated to south-east London in the late nineteenth century and enforced a reign of terror on the local pubs, many of which employed him as a bouncer. There's little evidence that Patrick Houlihan was even vaguely interested in ball sports, though ample to suggest he was a mean streetfighter. An undistinguished and disagreeable character, Houlihan had the questionable honor of giving his name to a social problem that was to endure for the best part a century after his death.

In 1921, a stadium in Bradford, Yorkshire, had to be closed for persistent violence. In the 1920s, fans of Arsenal and Tottenham Hotspur met in the streets of North London with knives and iron bars. Police baton charges on crowds were commonplace. One club took the view that a match should not be stopped unless the bottles being thrown were full rather than empty. In the 1930s, fans regularly spilled onto the field of play during or after games, sometimes attacking officials, occasionally striking players.

Many of the early eruptions of violence were at meetings between local teams, "derby games," such as Rangers vs. Celtic in Glasgow, and Everton vs. Liverpool. The rivalry between fans in these cities was intensified by a Catholic vs. Protestant edge, Celtic and Everton having Catholic ancestry. At a time when sectarian conflict in Northern Ireland was raging, the soccer "wars" seemed a logical, if perverse, counterpart. Anti-Semitism was thought to be behind the age-old conflict between North London fans of Arsenal and Tottenham Hotspur, the latter being traditionally a Jewish-owned club. But, then the violence, or "aggro" as it was called (short for aggravation), became, in the tabloid vernacular, mindless. Every weekend, local stores boarded up their windows, pubs were demolished and hospitals filled up with casualties from the games. Every game of soccer carried with it the threat of open violence between fans, wherever it was played.

A new turn in the 1980s signaled a paramilitary tendency among many fans, who gave themselves names, organized their troops into divisions and orchestrated their attacks on rival fans. Among the more notorious was West Ham's Inter City Firm (ICF), which is credited with the innovation of leaving behind specially printed business cards at sites of their fights. Other firms were Arsenal's Gooners, Burnley's Suicide Squad, and Chelsea's Headhunters. Soccer hooliganism reached its peak in the early 1980s.

The government, in response, adopted a number of measures which led to decline in violence at games throughout Britain: it was not reluctant to step into the sports arena and implement what might seem draconian legal measures to halt a problem that many felt had roots far beyond the sports stadium. Alcohol was banned from all stadiums in 1985. The 1986 Public Order Act made provision for the exclusion from games of those convicted of offenses against the public order. The 1991 Football Offences Act and the introduction of surveillance cameras also reduced the incidence of violent behavior at games.

None of these legal measures had too much impact on the behavior of fans traveling abroad, specifically to major European cities. Courts of law were empowered to prevent those convicted of hooliganism from traveling to games in countries outside England. But, this type of power was helpless to prevent the free travel of violence-seeking fans who had escaped prosecution.

In some ways, the English did the world a favor by creating, developing and refining a sport, then taking it to the rest of the world, from Lima to Lahore. Years after it had exported the sport, it exported a grimmer cargo. During the 1980s, hooliganism was rife throughout Europe. British passions were hard to rival; but Italians came very close. So, when the top clubs of each country met on neutral territory to decide which was the top team in Europe, some form of fan conflict seemed inevitable. Few could have anticipated the scale of the disaster at the 1985 European Cup Final game between Liverpool and Juventus, of Turin, Italy, at the Heysel Stadium in Brussels, Belgium: 95 fans were crushed to death and 200 others injured in the worst tragedy in soccer's history. After blame was apportioned, English clubs were suspended from European-wide competition for 5 years and Liverpool for 7. Juventus and its fans were exonerated.

So, why are fans of other sports so well behaved? This sounds like a perverse question, but, given the violent history not only of football but of other sports we now regard as mainstream, one might expect hooligan-style behavior to be more widespread. True, most sports have experienced episodes of near-hooliganism, but, for the most part, fan violence is incongruous at other kinds of football games, basketball, or even boxing. Or is it?

ACCUMULATING SOCIAL CAPITAL

". . . and we have some breaking news from Foxboro. We're getting accounts of crowd disturbances at the Patriots game. Our reporters there are telling us that rival groups of fans are fighting. We're going over live to see if we can pick up some of the action there. But, this is looking more and more like a scene from a British soccer game . . ." The local tv station in Massachusetts gets a scoop.

Next morning the *Boston Globe* carries the story, along with the question: "Is this the first evidence that the kind of mindless violence that has afflicted soccer for decades is creeping into US sports?"

The tempting and thoroughly exploitable possibility has scholars rushing out of their offices, journalists calling frantically for soundbites, church leaders tut-tutting about the collapse of morality, politicians scrambling for the highest moral plateau and, of course, the police chiefs promising that every football game will be subject to more stringent controls than ever.

The "serious crowd disturbances" might actually have been an old-fashioned fight between two sets of fans, whose inhibitions had been lowered by a few Budweisers and who were incensed by a couple of referee's calls that went against their team. But the images of their scuffle have been dramatically edited as if they had been plucked from a John Woo movie.

All this is very exciting for at least a segment of the football-following population who could use a little more action off-field and would welcome the chance to experience the same kind of thrill their European cousins have been enjoying for years. Next Sunday they go to their games ready for action, prepared for the kind of behavior the mass media have been focusing on for the past seven days. And, sure enough, the violence breaks out. The "prophecy," as sagely foretold by the media and an assembly of others, has duly been fulfilled.

An improbable scenario perhaps; but one that illustrates the self-fulfilling potential held by the media. Events can be created as well as shaped or influenced by the way the media covers them. Those who swear the media is behind all the hooliganism in Europe and Central and South America have a tall order. The copycat effect has been invoked to account for a number of violent episodes over the years. Riots have been a stock favorite.

The uprisings in English cities in the early 1980s and the Rodney King incidents of 1992 were thought to have been perpetuated by the mass media which, in transmitting images of rioters, virtually invited people to duplicate them. Cho Seung-Hui's killing of 32 people on the campus of Virginia Polytechnic Institute and State University, better known as Virginia Tech, in 2007, was thought to have been influenced by Chan-wook Park's 2003 film *Oldboy*, which the killer had viewed prior to his rampage.

The theory holds that once the mass media get hold of a newsworthy topic their tendency is to amplify or exaggerate it, presenting the impression that the event, or events, are larger, more important, more serious or more widespread than they actually are. But here the self-fulfilling prophecy kicks in: in creating distorted images, the media are actually establishing precisely the kind of conditions under which those images are likely to become a reality. And once they do, a perpetual motion mechanism starts. For example, the Columbine massacre of 1999 was followed by similar, if less dramatic, episodes around the world, not just North America.

This doesn't explain why the first events occurred, or how they ever stop. Critics of this type of explanation complain that it reduces the actual incident to an almost motiveless reaction to an image or sound. It heaps blame on a movie or the media for initially showing the image and, in so doing, deters investigation into the more complex issues surrounding the incident.

A 1987 study by Robert Arms *et al.*, "Effects on the hostility of spectators of viewing aggressive sports," concluded that "the observation of aggression on the field of play leads to an increase in hostility on the part of the spectators." Why? If we are exposed to models who are rewarded for aggressive behavior as opposed to models who are punished, we are likely to imitate them. Recall the Bandura research of the 1960s: it revealed the powerful part played by imitation in shaping our behavior. Simply observing aggressive behavior can affect our own behavior, if that aggression was positively sanctioned in some way, or, we should add, if the person interpreted the aggression as being positively sanctioned.

The kind of relationship Arms *et al.* has in mind came to life in May 1999 when a game between the two Glasgow soccer teams, Rangers and Celtic turned into a fearsome battle both on and off the field. A total of three players were ejected from the game and nine others were cautioned. The referee was hit by a missile during the game—and, later, had the windows of his house smashed. Violence on the field sparked violence among spectators. The crowd invaded the field and joined in a free-for-all. As evidence for the argument that violent play encourages, perhaps even causes violent behavior among spectators, this is solid.

The copycat effect is acknowledged to figure in the bewildering equation that results in collective violence, though other accounts have focused on the conditions under which the violence breaks out. Let's review some of the main accounts.

The sociologist's account

Far from being a recent phenomenon, violence related to soccer has a history as long as the game itself. The origins of violent behavior lay in the neighborhoods, where status was often the reward for being the hardest, toughest, and meanest – the baddest – character around. Not having the money to acquire prestige through conventional resources, like cars, clothes, and other material possessions, inhabitants of the 'hood would fight their way to the top of the pecking order. Inspired by Gerald Suttles' American analysis of *The Social Order of the Slum* (1968), Eric Dunning and his colleagues discerned a status hierarchy and fighting was the way to climb it. Habituated to fighting, the slum dwellers, or the "rough" working class as they called them, were the same people likely to go to watch a soccer game.

Simon Jenkins, a writer for the London *Times*, complements this account with his own version of "risk displacement theory" (*Times*, February 18, 1995). "This states that most people need a certain amount of 'risk' and will find it where they can," writes Jenkins. "Every visit to a soccer game embraces an element of risk, including the danger of crowd trouble." English soccer's authorities thought they had virtually eliminated the possibility of violence in the early 1990s when they ordered all Premiership and Football League clubs to improve their stadia by installing seats instead of the old-style terraces on which fans used to stand.

This worked to an extent: but the violence transferred from the grounds to the streets and the pubs, creating what one writer called "landscapes of fear." The risk element is present in a number of sports and its complete elimination would probably detract from the enduring fascination we seem to have with danger and uncertainty. Jenkins' point is that spectators are clearly aware of the risks they take and, presumably, make a kind of cost–benefit analysis, concluding that the thrill is worth the risk. The "quest for excitement" that's so important to the figurational perspective remains.

The psychologist's account

"Understanding" is the key word in psychologist John Kerr's theory: it's based on the individual's interpretation of the meaning or purpose of his or her own action (1994). Basically, Kerr argues that young people who get involved in fan violence are satisfying their need for stimulation through forms of behavior that involve risk and novel or varied situations. One of the attempts behind this approach is to get away from theories that offer the impression that we are consistent. Kerr believes that human behavior is completely inconsistent. "This means that a soccer hooligan who on one occasion smashes a shop window may on another occasion do something completely different." This depends on our "metamotivational state": we can "reverse" between them as easily as a traffic light changes from red to green; it all depends on the situation, or contingent circumstances.

"The soccer environment provides a rich source of varied pleasure for those who wish to pursue and enjoy the feelings of pleasant high arousal," writes Kerr (1994: 47). Most regular fans reach a satisfactory level of arousal; others do not and develop their own extreme variation in their quest for excitement. Accordingly, there is destructive behavior, which can, given the right motivational state and a conducive situation, be as gratifying as watching a good movie or poring over a work of art. Kerr detects that one way of achieving a high arousal is through "empathy with the team."

The ethologist's account

Focusing on the ritualistic elements of the violence, Peter Marsh and his associates viewed it as part of a huge dramatic performance in which youths acted out their parts without risking life and limb. Examining the sometimes quite elaborate hierarchies around which clubs' fans were organized (into troops, divisions, etc.), the researchers concluded that, while the belligerent behavior witnessed at football grounds appeared to be chaotic and unplanned, there were, on closer inspection "rules of disorder." Anybody who has been to a big game at a British stadium and witnessed first hand, or worse been on the receiving end of, crowd violence will be aware of the limitations of Marsh's approach. Nice idea when you're sitting in your ivory tower in the quiet university town of Oxford, where Marsh *et al.* did their research; ridiculous when you're in the thick of a brawl in London or Glasgow.

The Marxist's account

1970s-style Marxists, like Ian Taylor, argued that the behavior was a working-class reflex: as British soccer became more commercialized and removed from the old communities where it had originated, it left behind a body of fans who felt the clubs were somehow theirs. The violence was seen as a symbolic attempt to confirm their control over the clubs. Not only hooliganism, but industrial sabotage, vandalism, gangs and a variety of subcultural exotica were explained with reference to the breakup of the traditional working class in the post-war period. The argument may have appeared reasonable in the 1970s and 1980s, but has not worn well and is clearly inadequate to explain the continuing violence and its virtual universality.

The historian's account

Like other major sports, soccer is played in an atmosphere charged with competitive intensity in which rationality is rendered vulnerable to emotion and self-control is put to the most stringent physical tests. But, attachments in soccer are unlike other sporting ties: they often have a lineage dating further back than the nineteenth century. Affiliations are inherited like family wealth, except in this case the families, being mostly working class, have no wealth to speak of.

Soccer fandom was once about rank, domain, a collective way of marking one's territory. And, while those features might have been modified over the decades, their essence remains: soccer fans call themselves supporters; they see themselves as representatives of their clubs, defenders of their names, bearers of their traditions.

Feeling part of a unit capable of winning national and perhaps international honors, or at least challenging for them, has acted in a compensatory way for millions of soccer fans the world over. Once drawn from the industrial poor and deprived, the sport has never lost its base of support and continues to attract its most passionate following mostly from working-class people whose occupations are comparatively dull and unrewarding and offer little or no personal or professional gratification. By contrast, soccer does.

In this context, we might view approval given to soccer hardmen as a type of reward.

In *Code of the Street*, a study of a district in Philadelphia, Elijah Anderson writes: "In the inner-city environment respect on the street may be viewed as a form of social capital that is very valuable" (1999: 66). It becomes especially valuable "when other forms of capital have been denied or are unavailable." For many working-class soccer fans, fighting for their team may be one of the few resources they have for gaining respect of their peers. That is itself "social capital."

Inadvertently, Anderson suggests a way of understanding how aggression and violence were hardwired into soccer culture from the beginning. Association football, to give it its correct name (the abbreviation "assoc" apparently led to the shorthand soccer), was never just a sport. It was a method through which entire communities could test their mettle. Way before the formation of the English Football Association in 1863, the forerunners of the sport had attracted players and spectators (there was no clear distinction) from local areas who challenged each other, for what we'd today call bragging rights; that is, civic pride, collective respect and all-round esteem. Often the games would revolve around churches, adding another dimension to the competition. Later, factories started clubs, again with reputations on the line.

John Field argues that it isn't only violence that helps maintain social capital: "At least as important is the role of fear, sustained by folk tales of particularly memorable acts of violence," he writes in his 2003 book *Social Capital*. While he's discussing Colombian drugs gangs rather than soccer fans, Field's comments about the benefits are on the money: "As well as self-efficacy and a sense of identity, the members were having fun . . . In a turbulent and risky environment, young men in particular found a survival mechanism . . . Violent gangs are the only network where they encounter people that they like and who in turn like them" (2003: 85). (We discussed *self-efficacy* in Chapter 6.)

Some scholars suggest that football's deep roots among Britain's industrial working class gives the sport a unique quality. Gary Armstrong argues that the values, rituals, and codes of honor or shame that are intrinsic to football are indispensable items that have helped shape young men's identities over the decades and centuries. Fans, like birds of a feather, flock together and move about the country with a mixture of vague but macho purpose and extravagant menace, eager to prove their credentials.

This much is indisputable: fans don't just watch sports, they vicariously participate in it; they are part of the overall culture of which the actual period of play is but one part. In other words, there is a relationship between the actual competition and the fans' experience, but it is mediated by a cultural change that has affected the context in which the link between players and fans exists. Several facets of the relationship are captured in Nick Hornby's *Fever Pitch*, which charts the passage into adulthood of a fan of Arsenal, the North London soccer club. As a child, the first-person author is possessed of the kind of fanaticism that might be expected to dissolve in maturity. Not for Hornby: the ardor, fervor and passion stay with him, often overwhelming more practical concerns: "Football is a context in which watching *becomes* doing . . . I am a part of the club, just as the club is a part of me," he writes. The players are merely "our representatives," as Hornby puts it. The "organic connection" he feels with Arsenal is both stronger and more durable than anything players can ever feel.

The organic connection is one that links today's fans with their predecessors. It helps explain the singular emotions aroused by soccer anywhere in the world. Like a contagion, the organic relationship is infectious. To watch soccer and, for that matter, any sport in a detached, analytical manner, misses the point of the experience. For the fans, watching, to repeat Hornby, becomes doing – it's living activity, not observation. This is a crucial point and one that establishes a clear demarcation between the observer of cinema, the arts, concerts, and other forms of popular entertainment and the sports fan: the latter isn't observing so much as participating.

Atkinson and Young list fan aggression, violence (human and animal), and other kinds of behavior that have been identified as unwanted: "Each of these behaviors, in its own way, has been problematized in sport and has resulted in varying amounts of deviance labeling, stigma, disrepute, or punishment" (2008: 226). By "problematize," they mean turned into or regarded as a problem requiring a solution. Solutions in sport are usually abundant; effective solutions are scarce. That's because the very character of sport elicits behavior that may be officially condemned but is simply germane to the experience of either watching or participating in sport.

Even Vick's involvement in dogfighting, while initially shocking, is actually comprehensible in terms of the competitive, gambling culture in which he developed, the friends with whom he hung, the disposable money he had available, the sense of invulnerability that elite athletes seem to acquire as they progress. As Douglas Hartmann and Michael Massoglia point out: "The social status of athletes . . . may create in some young athletes a sense of entitlement and belief that they are above the law" (2007: 499)

This is the Apollonian face of sports: it cultivates the rational, ordered, and self-disciplined aspects of human nature. Athletes are not supposed to go out of control, of course. On the contrary: as they mature, they are expected to become more ordered and restrained. But Hartmann and Massoglia's research indicates that "more problematic or exaggerated aspects of sporting culture are ascendant for some behaviors and not for others."

These are what Eric Dunning calls the Dionysian and Epicurean faces of sport. He means that competitive activities are often spontaneous and emotional and appeal to sensual enjoyment. (Apollo, Dionysus, both gods, and Epicurus, the philosopher, are all Greek mythological figures who personify certain characteristics.)

Sport, as we know, is a culture in which aggression is valued. Combined with what Hartmann and Massoglia call the "thrill-seeking, hyperphysical nature" of sport, aggression produces behavior that is instantly decried and punished. Punishment or its threat seems to have little or no effect. Sport itself is the source of the behavior, which is why performers, whether competitors or fans repeatedly violate rules, norms and the standards of behavior typically expected of them.

OF RELATED INTEREST

Fever Pitch by Nick Hornby (Indigo, 1996) is a fictional account of life as an Arsenal fan. It was later made into two movies, one set in London, which stays close to the original story (director: David Evans, 1997); the other in Boston, where the central characters are turned into Red Sox fans (directors: Bobby and Peter Farrelly, 2005).

Sport Matters: Sociological studies of sport, violence and civilization by Eric Dunning (Routledge, 1999) contrasts patterns of sports-related violence in North America with those in Europe, though they have a feature in common: "A hedonistic quest for enjoyable excitement is often expressed in social deviance."

Code of the Street: Decency, violence, and the moral life of the inner city by Elijah Anderson (Norton, 1999) is not about sports at all, but is full of insights that can be readily applied to the culture of sports fans, the rules by which many of them live, and the way their world confers reward and exacts punishment. This is complemented by John Field's more general discussion of *Social Capital* (Routledge, 2003), and Gary Armstrong's *Football Hooligans: Knowing the score* (Berg, 2003), which focuses, as its title suggests, on British fans.

New Perspectives on Sport and 'Deviance': Consumption, performativity and social control by Tony Blackshaw and Tim Crabbe (Routledge, 2004) offers an original and innovative approach to our understanding of deviance in sports.

Deviance and Social Control in Sport by Michael Atkinson and Kevin Young (Human Kinetics, 2008) provides an overview of the many different types of deviance in sport. It begins with conceptual questions as to what is and isn't deviance and moves to an explanation of the processes that drive rule and norm violation. Young's earlier "Sport and violence" in *Handbook of Sports Studies* edited by Jay Coakley and Eric Dunning (Sage, 2000), is also useful in this context. John Kerr's *Rethinking Aggression and Violence in Sport* (Routledge, 2004) suggests an alternative approach to Young's.

ASSIGNMENT

1 A bitter rivalry between two NHL teams has been given an extra edge by a facial injury suffered by Kris Crawley, a player for the Saskatchewan Scorpions after an aggressive encounter with Friedrich Gaea of the Tacoma Terminators. The injured Crawley vows revenge and is reprimanded by his club for inflammatory remarks made to the media. The buildup to the next meeting of the teams is marked by the media's attention to the two players concerned and the "revenge" comments. In

the game itself, Crawley is sent cartwheeling by a hard tackle from Gaea. His flailing skate catches Gaea across the throat. Gaea bleeds to death on his way to hospital. While it is a freak incident, there are strong reactions. (The players and clubs in this example are fictitious, though the incident is based on the death of Sweden's Bengt Åkerblöm who died after an accidental collision with a fellow hockey player in a 1995 practice game.)

2 Max Strength, a professional football player, who is regarded as one of the league's best players and commands a salary in excess of $20 million per year, leads a celebrity lifestyle and is a regular on television talk shows. He is seen regularly in the company of female actors, models, and rock singers. He is spotted, while on vacation in Rio de Janeiro, coming out of a gay bar at 3 a.m. A fan captures the scene on a camera phone.

3 Johnny Knucklehead, a swimmer, returns from a successful Olympic Games to a rapturous reception. He exhibits his six medals on several television programs and becomes a widely known and liked figure. Questioned by a female reporter as he leaves a tv studio, he loses his temper and slaps the reporter across the face in full view of a throng of autograph hunters.

4 Lorne Clover, the manager of a baseball club is seemingly happily married with three children and popular with fans. He enjoys good rapport with the media and is known for his personable, accessible demeanor. A small group of journalists, with whom he is especially friendly, are privy to his personal cell phone number. One journalist becomes suspicious when he calls Clover and finds him mysteriously hesitant about his whereabouts. He investigates further and his enquiries suggest that Clover is having an affair with one of his player's wives.

Examine the fall-out of two of these incidents.

Representing the Challenge

MAKING SPORTS VISIBLE

Every so often, you see a movie or a photograph that's so rich and complex yet so authentic and believable that you learn something about sports that you just can't pick up watching the competitive action, reading the biographies or studying the stats. Sometimes you just think to yourself: "Now, I get it."

Taking delight or pleasure in art means being prepared to learn from it. In the preface to his *The Picture of Dorian Gray*, Oscar Wilde wrote: "All art is at once surface and symbol. Those who go beneath the surface do so at their peril." He meant that we can merely observe works of art, whether paintings, sculpture or literature, or we can imperil ourselves by trying to understand what it represents or stands for, and what it implies. He finished off by concluding: "All art is quite useless."

Sports are also useless – if by useless we mean having no practical purpose beyond their own specified area. That doesn't detract from our enjoyment. In this chapter I'm going to show how art provides us with a history of sport somewhat different from the history we have disclosed so far. This is a history as revealed through the eyes of painters, sculptors and filmmakers, many of whom were not interested in the significance of sport as a cultural institution; their interests were with images created in the movement excited by sports competition.

They leave us with images quite different from those typically provided by electronic media, especially television, the function of which is principally to report rather than interpret sports. I'll examine how these visual media have reflected and sometimes inspired changes in sport in the next chapter. For now, my aim is to disclose how artists over the years have interpreted sports and how their work reflects and advances popular understanding. As in other chapters, I'll be zapped back in time in my effort to discover a kind of alternative history of sport, which I'll find in several artistic expression modes, including film.

A related aim of this chapter is to recognize continuity amid the change. Over the centuries, countless artists' impressions of athletic competition are testimony to the centrality of sports in human culture. The organization and content of the compositions have changed dramatically within and between periods. But, the effort to visualize facets of sports has remained strong.

A third design of this chapter is to suggest how representations of sport resonate with values and standards specific to times and places. We will see how cultural approaches to, for instance, violence, gender and the cruelty, have been apparent in the work of artists focusing on sports. None of this suggests that art provides us with a straightforward document of sports or the cultures of which they were part. As painter Paul Klee once pronounced: "Art doesn't mirror the visible . . . It makes visible."

Klee, who worked in the 1920s using sports images as expressions of modernity, believed that art does not simply reflect reality. For him and, we can be sure, every other artist, art is an exposition, a way of witnessing the world, though not necessarily in a way we find comfortable or obvious. Art provokes and challenges as much as it pleases and reassures. This is not usually the purpose of illustrators, photographers, and camera operators. According to Guy Hubbard: "They are journalists and their purpose is to visually explain to people what happened as clearly as possible." In his article "Sports action," Hubbard distinguishes between this group and "Artists who express themselves through sports events [and who] are likely to be interested in portraying physical action and urge to compete and win." They feel no obligation to report what they see, argues Hubbard: "They are free to use their imaginations when interpreting sports action" (1998: 29–30).

Three aims, then: (1) to relate an alternative history of sport as told through the expressions, imaginations, interpretations of painters, sculptors, filmmakers, and other artists who have focused on sports as their subject; (2) to understand how something resembling what Nikolaos Yaloris, in his *The Eternal Olympics: The art and history of sport*, calls the "athletic spirit" has stirred artists' imaginations, albeit in quite different ways, for perhaps four thousand years and to highlight consistency across the ages; (3) to appreciate how art that focuses on sport can, indeed must, contain a record of the particular social milieux in which they were produced.

Faced with a cornucopia of materials, I have been extremely selective in my treatment. But, at the end of the chapter, there are recommended sources where the reader will find detailed accounts of the development of arts specializing in sports in specific periods. Peter Kühnst's *Sports: A cultural history in the mirror of art*, which covers the period from about 1450 to 1986, is a particularly solid collection of (mostly) paintings, graphics and photography accompanied by an analytical text. While Kühnst does not include film in his analysis, there is strength in his thesis that: "By following the evolution of sports and sports-like physical activities, one can see the degree to which they have been the expression of changes in thinking and feeling. They can be understood as an index of individual and social historical transformation" (1996: 9).

IMPRESSIONS OF COMPETITION

No genre has an official starting point, though it's tempting to identify 1766 as the year in which a warrantable artform called sporting art emerged, primarily through the work of the British painter George Stubbs whose landmark portfolio *Anatomy of a Horse* was published in that year and whose work is generally considered to have defined a new direction for artists. While Stubbs – to whom we shall return shortly – lent new shape and clarity to sporting art, he was by no means the first artist to have focused on sports. Indeed, artistic impressions of sporting events and competitors are as ancient as athletic competitions themselves.

BOX 13.1 GEORGE STUBBS (1724–1806)

Born in 1724 in Liverpool, Stubbs is generally regarded as one of the most influential artists of his period. Passionately interested in the study of anatomy in his youth, he was commissioned to illustrate medical textbooks with his engravings. In 1754, Stubbs visited Rome and, on his return, he was commissioned by several members of the English nobility to produce paintings of hunts and studies of horses. So exacting was Stubbs that he spent 18 months dissecting horses in a Lincolnshire barn, producing his *Anatomy of a Horse* collection in 1766. Coombs describes Stubbs' *The Grosvenor Hunt*, 1762, as: "Arguably, the greatest of all sporting pictures." The scene depicts a dying stag surrounded by hounds and hunters on horseback. Stubbs died in 1806.

Wall paintings and reliefs of men wrestling and lifting weights have been discovered in Egypt and dated to the second millennium BCE. There is evidence of other images showing figures seeming to play ballgames and fighting with staffs. In later Cretan and Greek cultures there were engravings and frescos that suggested the presence of an athletic spirit: depictions of bull-leaping and combative activities on seals and walls indicate an interest in dangerous competitions. These tell us that the activities actually occurred, but little of their significance. In his essay "Athletics in Crete and Mycenae," J. Sakellarakis points out that, while there is evidence of combat and other athletic activity in ancient Egypt, "these and other similar sports practiced in the East had essentially nothing in common with the Greek athletic contests except for the natural inclination to exercise a strong healthy body" (1979: 13–14). The purpose of the activities engraved on seal stones and rings or painted in frescos was to display athletic prowess and entertain spectators rather than convey ideals found in later Greek games.

The object of the earlier games was to exhibit a well-trained and skilled human body in contests against other humans and against animals. The games were performed at festivals in Minoan Crete in the second millennium BCE and had an almost ceremonial function, which Nikolaos Yaloris likens to acrobatic display. Representations of bull-leaping – in which the leaper stands in front of an onrushing bull and grabs its horns so that the bull's momentum tosses him (women do not appear in the pictures) in the air – are found in ancient monuments. Scenes from the combat events, also popular in the Minoan period, are found on vases, especially *kraters* which were vases placed in the tombs of the dead, suggesting that the activities held some religious significance.

The lack of written evidence forced scholars to rely on bric-a-brac and artifacts as well as the stylized artforms that survived. Apart from combat sports, which seem to have endured through several different cultures and epochs, racing of some sort is found in the decoration of ceramics; this includes footracing, horseracing and chariot racing, all of which in some way continue to the present.

Sculptures were characteristic of Greek art and, in this form, there is a pantheon of heroes, the most celebrated of which is Myron's *Discus Thrower (Discobolus)* in bronze from the fifth century BCE. The model for this work could well have been drawn from one of today's gyms. His body is lithe and cut, a flat midsection and prominent ribs giving him a very contemporary look. The position he takes in readiness of his discus throw is much the same as that of today's discus throwers, discus-holding arm outstretched behind him, other arm across his opposing knee, feet poised to rotate and thrust. It's a genuinely timeless piece.

For Greeks, sport, education, and culture were indistinct: they were all involved in the cultivation of the whole being; the mental and the physical were not dualities as the modern western conceptions, but part of the same unity. So, sport, at least in the way we understand it, did not exist: it was not a separate sphere of activities sectioned off from many other parts of life. Once this is understood, it becomes clear why so many athletic images adorn Greek art and artifacts. Sport was revered in ancient Greece and found its fullest expression in the Olympic Games.

By contrast the Romans, who subjugated the Greeks in 146 BCE, were indifferent to sport and, indeed, to art; though their contributions to architecture and literature were immense. The only sporting endeavors encouraged by Romans were those that contributed to the preparation for war. Whereas Greeks had idealized athletic pursuits and endowed them with spiritual purpose, Romans saw them as a kind of military training and undeserving of the cultural attention Greeks had afforded them in their art.

The Romans' lust for gladiatorial conflict is famous: trained, armed men fought in mortal combat against each other, or against animals. At Naples' National Archeological Museum, there is a fresco from Pompeii showing a Roman amphitheater and a number of other activities, some of which appear to be gladiator fights. While the Romans did not leave largesse of art, contemporary reconstructions of gladiatorial contests have been memorable. Jean Léon Gérôme's 1874 oil on canvas *Pollice Verso* is a frightening, dramatic depiction of the climax of a duel in which the triumphant gladiator, wearing a helmet and arm mail, stands over the fallen *netarius* (net-thrower), his foot on his throat. The viewer sees from the floor of the coliseum and witnesses the imposing crowd baying for blood. As was the custom, the gladiator looks to the emperor seated in his box; to his left are six vestal virgins, all signaling their wishes as to the fate of the victim – thumbs down.

It's probable that director Stanley Kubrick consulted Gérôme's work when he re-created a gladiatorial contest for his 1960 film *Spartacus*. Gérôme was painstaking in his research, obtaining casts of antique armor and weapons in his quest for authentic detail. In *Spartacus*, the similarities are pronounced, though Kirk Douglas did not wear the formidable headgear of the Gérôme victor. Ridley Scott's 1999 film *Gladiator* also recreates the visceral excitement of the Roman combat sports.

The Roman fascination with gory death manifested again in chariot racing. The floor of the huge Circus Maximus was often strewn with bodies as races progressed. Without doubt the most memorable reconstruction of such a chariot race is in William Wyler's 1959 epic *Ben-Hur* in which Charlton Heston and Stephen Boyd lead a field of racers, most of whom come to a bloody end. The race stands the test of time as one of the most exhilarating pieces of dramatized sport ever.

The fall of the Roman Empire in the fifth century ushered in a period of a thousand years that became known as the dark ages and then the middle ages. Artistic evidence of *les tournements* were preserved in the forms of great medieval tapestries that held narratives of the chivalric conflicts in which honor, glory and reputation were at stake. More durable were the woodcuts that proliferated particularly in what is now Germany in the sixteenth century. Albrecht Dürer was one of the foremost artists of his time.

Dürer was well-versed in fighting sports, including wrestling and swordsmanship. He illustrated the *Wallerstein Codex*, which was a manual of fighting, first published about 1470. Like some later artists of boxing, he believed that he needed to train with competitors in order to gain the insights necessary to produce his art. Germany led Europe in printing and woodcuts were used to illustrate manuscripts which could then be duplicated and disseminated. Jost Amman's 1565 *Emperor Maximilian's Tournament at Vienna* produced a celebrated vista that reveals much of the organization of tournaments. Eight jousts take place simultaneously in an enclosed courtyard outside of which are thronged spectators, some on horseback. Overlooking the courtyard are balconies from which the nobility watch in comfort. Guards patrol the area to keep order. In the competition, some of the knights have been unseated and have progressed to a ground battle with swords. The atmosphere of the scene is part sporting and part carnival, suggesting that tournaments were occasions for festivities as well as stark competition.

This type of mixture of activities gains full expression in Matthias Gerung's oil on wood *Melancholia*, of 1558, which features a vortex of activities, some of which resemble sports, others of which seem more like pure entertainment, still others of which appear to be celebrations. Knights in combat are also visible in Gerung's work, as are archers and bowlers, but there is no clear differentiation between the clearly ordered sport of Amman's work and other forms of recreation.

Contemporary visualizations of tournaments are commonplace thanks to the popularity of films, such as Jerry Zucker's *First Knight* (1994), in which Richard Gere plays the medieval knight Lancelot, and *The Adventures of Robin Hood* (1938, directed by Michael Curtiz and William Keighley), which featured the Nottingham outlaw of yore in a legendary archery contest (though neither Kevin Reynolds' 1991 *Robin Hood: Prince of Thieves* or Ridley Scott's 2010 *Robin Hood* included the competition).

ORDER AND TRANSFORMATION

Europe was in the midst of the Renaissance in the sixteenth century. The profound changes that transfigured the cultural and, eventually, scientific landscape mobilized the desire for creative self-expression which in turn led to new ways of explaining, understanding, and appreciating the world. Some of the activities that we now distinguish as sports had links, however tenuous, with games that were played in Europe in this period. Kühnst detects an early visual representation of ballgame in a Venice ceiling fresco produced in the 1550s: the players wear gauntlets and exchange a leather ball in what appears to be an early type of handball.

At the same time, the rough game *calcio*, which has some similarities with latter-day soccer, rugby, and its derivatives, like American football, was played by the working class. In northern Europe, woodcuts produced around 1520 feature ballgames that appear to be have been played for amusement. These types of games gradually gained in popularity, superseding the chivalric combat characteristic of the tournaments. Some of the tournament events, such as horseriding, running, and spear (later, javelin) throwing, mutated and survived; others, like jousting and vaulting did not, at least not in competitive forms.

But, the tournaments rapidly became anachronisms as the Renaissance spirit diffused throughout Europe, stimulating the progress, discovery, and a new sense of wonder with the natural world. This inevitably led to changes both in sports and in the way those sports were represented. In art, we find competitive sports signifying the desire for order, the rationalization of society and the mastery of the self. The Baroque style epitomized this: competitors define geometrical patterns, suggesting an order and control of space. The work of Johann Christioph Neyffer and Willem Swanenburgh in the early 1600s are works of art constructed like architectural plans, so that fencers and riflemen appear as lifeless points rather than active human beings. Their conduct is not spontaneous, but ordered.

Order was even brought to the chaotic and often violent *calcio*: a 1689 copperplate by Alessandro Cecchini shows a game being played: the field of play is clearly demarcated by perimeter fencing and guards are stationed strategically; even the players occupy set positions, much like they do in contemporary ballgames. Sports, like every other aspect of European society, was affected by the new model of knowledge known as science. Far from being mysterious if not unfathomable, nature was becoming comprehensible: theories about the world could be tested empirically, that is by appealing to human senses of observation: touch, taste, and sound.

Sports are often thought of as diversions from the rational planning and scientific rationality of other areas of life. This is only partly true: in the eighteenth century, as it became clear that the natural world was governed by laws, sports too underwent a revision. Luck, randomness and a certain ineffability have always been vital ingredients in sports, of course. But some of these could be subordinated or controlled using scientific understanding.

From 1800, sports began to devour the fruits of science. The same technologies that served industry aided sports. Races took place over prescribed distances, times were measured, results were recorded; sports acquired the same rationality as industry.

The importance of the stopwatch, which was first used in 1731, can scarcely be exaggerated. We find the scientific impulses to analyze, quantify, and record in the art of the period, art which became known as "sporting art."

All three impulses come together in the art of George Stubbs, who specialized in commissioned portraits of racehorses. As we have noted Stubbs' *Anatomy of a Horse* was published in 1766: it was not only work of great aesthetic beauty, but of scientific precision. As its title suggests, Stubbs' art lay at the borders of medical knowledge: he brought to his subject a surgeon's skill and a thoroughness that few of his peers could match. Stubbs seemed to have investigated the minutest of detail in his quest for the perfection of objective accuracy and his masterwork has been likened to da Vinci's studies of human cadavers two hundred years earlier.

Stubbs' work chronicles some of the racehorses of the day, reflecting a desire to record sporting achievements rather than just enjoy them and let them pass. There was also an element of exhibitionism, as Martin Vincent detects in his article "Painters and punters": "This kind of art had the triple advantage of showing off the patron's land, his horses and his sporting prowess" (1995: 32)

In his *Sport and the Countryside*, David Coombs refers to Stubbs and his fascination with horses: "His art sprang naturally from its environment, a prosperous, country-based economy in which the horse was the prime means of transport and a major source of motive power" (1978: 56). The horse was central to eighteenth- and early nineteenth-century life and commanded the attention of many artists. Their work provides a documentary of Britain's changing society between 1700 and 1900, when agriculture was emerging as the primary industry and sporting customs responded to the changes.

The horse was arguably of even greater importance in America, though it was not until 1822 that it became as embodied in art as it had been in England. Charles Hall, an agriculturist and breeder, commissioned paintings of thoroughbreds by, among others, Alvan Fisher, whose *Eclipse, with Race Track* is displayed at the National Art Museum of Sport at Indianapolis.

"At the end of the eighteenth century the countryside was becoming softer and more orderly as wild areas were conquered and cultivated," writes Anthony Vandervell and Charles Coles in their *Game and the English Landscape* (1980: 61). British sporting art bore a close relationship to the changing context, depicting races and hunts against a landscape that was being prepared for the coming of industry.

Other changes were delineated in sporting art. For example, William Powell Thomas' oil *Derby-Day* was created in 1858 and captures the atmosphere of the race track, members of different social classes segregated from each other: sports events were attended by all social classes, though they could not always mix. One area where they were free to mingle was the animal pit. William Hogarth's intimidating *Pit Ticket*, of 1759, shows male patrons, from aristocrats to thieves, huddled together around a cockpit, their devilish zeal for the fight apparent in their grotesquely drawn faces. *The Rat Pit*, by an unknown artist around 1860 (after the prohibition of cockfighting in 1849) shows members of different social classes stratified as if according to rank from the top of the canvas The picture bears a striking resemblance to Peter Blake's artwork for the cover of the Beatles' album, *Sgt. Pepper's Lonely Hearts Club Band*, the motley characters looking like lifeless cut-outs congregating around a central attraction, in this case a pit filled with fifty-odd rats and a tenacious terrier (reproduced by Coombs, 1978: 186).

Théodore Géricaux's *The Derby at Epsom*, painted in 1821, on the other hand, focuses on the thrill of a horserace in progress, the horses speeding toward the finishing line; and this too gives some indication of the changes afoot in society. Kühnst argues that this and other works that communicate speed, tension and the excitement of competition "show the transformation of physical exercises from static exhibitions of skill to lively achievement-oriented contests" (1996: 140).

This achievement orientation spread across the whole sporting spectrum from the beginning of the nineteenth century and the stylized poses of earlier art gave way to scenes of action in which competitors strove, not just to compete, but to win. Gustave Coubert's oil *The Wrestlers* painted in 1853, for example, shows two men clearly struggling for all they are worth. Frederic Remington's *Touchdown, Yale vs. Princeton, Thanksgiving Day, November 27, 1890, Yale 32, Princeton 0* suggests a less-than-friendly rivalry between the two teams as the players strain for supremacy. In these and in countless other works of the time, competitors are no longer statuesque, but dynamic and goal-directed. In a sense, the change mirrored the transition in art from Romanticism to Impressionism, which animated its subjects with a variety of techniques.

Impressionism originated in and refracted a world agitated by the twin forces of industrialization and urbanization. Advances in the natural sciences, especially chemistry, propelled a move toward mechanization and other technological processes. The same processes that revolutionized economies all over Europe made their presence felt in sports – and art. In 1896, when Coubertin launched the modern Olympic Games, the factory system was in full swing and populations were herding together in cities. European societies were at pains to restore stability in the face of fundamental economic and cultural shifts. Industry demanded order.

Rational progress, uniformity and standardization were the hallmarks of industrialism. It is no coincidence that they were also key features of Coubertin's vision: a comprehensive program of sports events carefully organized, each performance being quantified, ranked and rewarded according to standards of excellence. The effects of modernity, industrialism, and the technology they fostered were felt in sports; they were also felt in the modes through which sports were represented.

In the early 1880s, two artists, one American, one British, both of whom shared an interest in technology, came together at the University of Pennsylvania, their purpose being to apply science to art and produce objectively accurate representations of sports. Thomas Eakins was a celebrated oils painter who created some of the most evocative images of boxing and wrestling of the nineteenth century. His nude and near-nude studies of prize fighters formed part of a tradition of homoerotic sports art that found later expression in the sculptures of Eakins' student Charles Grafly and, later, in the art of John De Andrea, David Rohn, and Bruce Weber, the director of the film *Broken Noses*.

Eakin's collaboration with Eadweard Muybridge, a British photographer who emigrated to the United States in 1852, yielded work that changed artists', indeed everyone's conceptions of sports. Exploiting the potential of the relatively new technology of photography, Eakins and Muybridge sought to create the most physiologically precise record of sports action using the most technically efficient methods. *Studies of Human Movements* included over 100,000 stroboscopic photographs, each capturing a moment of sporting action.

Photography was arguably the most influential of all media in sports history. Prior to the pioneering work of Louis Daguerre, it had been difficult to capture a moving image without blurring, mainly because of the lengthy exposure time required. Also, the amount of equipment involved made it impracticable for sports events and images faded with age, anyway. But improvements in photographic paper reduced the exposure time and sharpened the images. Poses of people such as Bernarr Mcfadden and Eugen Sandow, whom we covered in Chapters 7 and 8, were widely circulated, adding to the reputations of both. We'll return to photography in Chapter 17 when we consider the importance of image diffusion in the rise of celebrities. For now, we should recognize the crucial role played by photography, not only in spreading interest in sports, but in advancing our understanding of athletic movement.

Let's take an obvious example. To the naked eye, a great deal of sports action is indistinct and uncertain. Artists had no way of knowing whether their work faithfully represented what actually happened. Stubbs and his peers, who were fascinated by horses, always imagined and represented them galloping in what's called the "rocking horse" position, all four hooves planted on the ground. Photography exposed the absurdity of this. Muybridge's work showed how all four feet sometimes left the ground at the same time. Though it seems obvious to those of us who have grown up with the benefit of slow-motion tv, it was astounding to people who depended on their eyesight alone. Next time you watch a sports event, try imagining what it would be like if you were relying only on what you see as your guide.

The art of Eakins and Muybridge had aesthetic beauty, but it also had practical application, enabling an understanding of the mechanics of motion and so establishing a base point for later studies. Their techniques were adopted and refined by photographer Étienne-Jules Marey who used time exposure experiments to disclose the minutiae of athletic actions. Among his more notable studies were *Fencing*, 1890, and *Mounting a Bicycle*, 1891, which were both educative and picturesque. Similar techniques were used by Harold Edgerton who produced stop-motion studies of, among others sports, pole vaulting and tennis in the mid-twentieth century. These artists brought to sports a punctiliousness and fidelity that was to resurface in later film documentaries, such as *Visions of Eight*, 1973, and *Hoop Dreams*, 1994.

Photography became popular in the twentieth century and artists of sport were adventurous in their use of the medium to portray sports in entirely new ways. Painters made use of photography to achieve a new level of naturalism and photographers innovated with new techniques to steer clear of naturalism. The photo-collages of John Heartfield in the 1920s extended earlier work, but introduced satire. For example, his *A Specter is Haunting Europe* features a runner made up of industrial parts, the head a stopwatch, pistons for limbs and what seems to be a clock card in place of a chest. The work satirizes both the preoccupation with industrial production and its effects on sports, which were becoming joyless affairs, interested in records and measurable achievements. The changes in organization and focus in sports is also a theme in the photo-collages of Laszlo Moholy-Nagy, Irene Hoffmann and Willi Baumeister. In all their work, there is a concern with the apparent mechanization of the modern athlete and the dehumanizing possibilities it entailed. A similar pitiless angular drive toward geometric perfection informs the work of William Roberts, particularly his 1967 "Goal" in which football players appear compressed into unison, their limbs bent like levers. We find the same concerns at the core of Jean-Marie Brohm's 1978 critique, the title of which sums up the author's thrust, *Sport: A prison of measured time*.

Modernity and the trends it ushered in continued to have salience with other artists, many either intrigued with or disgusted by its impact on sports. The reduction of what was once a playful, expressive activity to flat-out competition was a popular subject for many members of the avant-garde. Paul Klee, whose insight opened this chapter, produced his *Runner-Hooker-Boxer* in 1920: this aquarelle is structured like geological layers, its figure seeming to run through the strata; the sprinting figure wears a boxing glove on one hand and has an arrow jutting from the other. Robert Delaunay's oil, *The Runners*, 1926, visualizes its characters similarly: the faceless athletes run in unison. Even celebrated athletes can do little to distinguish themselves in a post-war culture that renders everyone anonymous, the artists seem to say.

THE GAZE OF HIS LADY

Among the vestiges from fifth-century BCE Sparta is a vase decorated with a scene from a woman's footrace. The barefoot runners wear long skirts and short-sleeved tops. Yaloris records that: "Women's sport was a feature of the education of girls in Sparta and Crete" (1979: 59). The same author also reproduces a mosaic depicting women training with dumbbells, practicing discus throwing and sprinting. "Women's sport was quite widespread in the Roman period," observes Yaloris (1979: 279).

Even in the medieval period when it is generally assumed women's presence at sporting events was purely decorative, there are artworks that show women in active roles. There are several illuminated manuscripts depicting women competing in jousts. As Allen Guttmann writes, in his *The Erotic in Sports*: "Robert de Borron's *Histoire du Graal* and the anonymous *Lancelot de Lac* are ornamented with pictures of mounted women wielding distaffs and spindles and charging at obviously disconcerted knights and monks" (1996: 41).

Kühnst includes in his impressive text a reproduction of Nicolas Arnoult's 1698 *Le Jeu du Volant* with three figures, two female, playing "featherball," which was a precursor of badminton. He also has a plate of Jean-Baptiste's oil *Girl with a Shuttlecock and Battledore* from 1741. In both works, the women appear to be middle class. A copperplate by Victor Marie Picot features, as its title suggests, *The Assault or Fencing Match which took place between Mademoiselle La Chevalière d'Eon de Beaumont and Monsieur de Saint Georges on the 9th of April 1787*. The female contestant is seen thrusting decisively at her male opponent.

In the late eighteenth century archery became popular with affluent English women who competed on level terms with men. The etching *A Meeting of the Society of Royal British Archers in Gwersyllt Park, Denbighshire* by Robert Smirke and John Emes, which is now in the British Museum, shows women archers in competition. In the sense that it allowed head-to-head contests between males and females, archery was unusual and a more telling picture from the same century is James Seymour's *A Coursing Scene* in which a woman sits sidesaddle on her horse while a male inspects a dead hare presented to him by his servant. "This is not a painting for feminists," remarks Coombs. "There is no doubt who is the master, as much from the nature of his expression as the gaze of his lady and stance of his huntsman" (1978: 20).

Hunting scenes in nineteenth-century works continued to depict women riding sidesaddle to protect their modesty. Sir Francis Grant's opulent canvas *Lady Riding Side-Saddle with her Dog, circa* 1840, is an example. The idea of women opening their legs to ride in the same way as men was an outrage to Victorians. But, in 1861, Pierre Micheaux and his son Ernest invented a machine they called a *vélocipède*, a riding machine that offered a cheaper, simpler, and more efficient mode of transport than the horse. The mass production of the *vélocipèdes* in France in the 1860s was quickly followed by what became known as the "cycling craze." Curiously, given the time in history, cycling was seen as a safe pastime for women.

Sir John Lavery's *The Tennis Party*, 1885, and Winslow Homer's *Croquet Scene*, 1866, chronicle the more typical sporting endeavors of women in the period and, even then, tennis and croquet were sports of the affluent. Cycling was relatively inexpensive and available to all classes. By the turn of the century, women all over Europe and America were taking to the road on bicycles. Spurning the reserve associated with sidesaddle riding, women made a hugely symbolic gesture by cycling – they opened their legs. Kühnst believes that of all the developments in sports, the bicycle "contributed the most to the emancipation of women by increasing their physical independence and personal freedom" (1996: 208).

Jean Béraud's 1900 canvas *The Cyclists' Café in the Bois de Bologne* shows women and men sharing drinks and inspecting each other's cycles during a break from their recreations. Bruno Paul's lithograph *Die Frau vor dem Rad: Hinter dem Rad: und aus dem Rad* ("The Woman in Front of the Wheel, Behind the Wheel, and on Wheels") cleverly essayed women's relationship with technology by displaying the same women cycling, working a sewing machine, and pulling an agricultural appliance.

BOX 13.2 CYCLING AND ART

Cycling has held a special appeal for several significant artists, including Henri Toulouse-Lautrec. The coming together of human and machine in competitive racing seemed to offer unique possibilities at the end of the nineteenth century when races spread across Europe and the United States. Toulouse-Lautrec was drawn to the cycling milieu: he regularly attended velodromes and race tracks and stood at the roadside in an effort to absorb some of the atmosphere that he then translated into his art, much of it commissioned by bicycle manufacturers, like Simpsons. Other significant artists of cycling include Jean Metzinger, Natalia Gontscharova, and the Futurist, Umberto Boccioni, in the early twentieth century, Fernand Léger in the mid-twentieth century, and more recently, Alex Colville. A great many other prominent artists have pictures of cycling in their portfolios.

Kühnst includes in his collection an anonymous photograph from 1910 that anticipates the later trend to mix sexual and sporting imagery: the female stands besides her bicycle, her skirt and petticoat caught on the handlebars and saddle so that her bare genitalia is revealed. While usually not as risqué as this study, many later works ventured toward the lewd, showing athletic women more as models than as active performers and often wearing skimpy clothes.

Picasso's gouache *The Race*, 1922, features two running women, each of whom displays a breast, their tops having slipped from their shoulders. Anton Räderscheidt's several studies of naked female sports performers in the 1920s typically incorporated a fully dressed male voyeur in the background. In the same period, Willi Baumeister depicted naked women running on tracks and diving from rocks, not perhaps, for prurient purposes, but with the effect of sexualizing the image of the female athlete. Even the celebrated Canadian artist Alex Colville's paintings of sports performers, include *Skater*, 1964, which invites the viewer to inspect the rear of a gliding skater, her arms clasped at her back, right leg raised perpendicular to her left and lycra-clad buttocks conspicuously displayed. There is a minor tradition in art that depicts women athletes engaging in competition but positioned, dressed, or undressed in a way that tempts salacity.

Robert Towne's 1982 film *Personal Best*, in which Mariel Hemingway and Patrice Donnelly play two pentathletes involved in a lesbian relationship, does not entirely escape this convention. As Guttmann remarks: "Although the film does justice to sports as physical *contests*, Towne never hesitates to underscore the erotic element" (1996: 119). Guttmann has in mind slow-motion studies of bare thighs and midriffs of female high-jumpers in mid-air, a bench-press session in which the spotter stands invitingly astride her prostrate training partner, and a bout of arm-wrestling that turns into a bout of sex.

LITE AND DARK

Hailed by some, denounced by others, the film *Olympia* (or *Olympisch Spiele*) was undeniably a monumental work of art. Ostensibly, a chronicle of the 1936 Olympic Games held at Berlin, Leni Riefenstahl's film was a propagandist disquisition that attempted to immortalize Nazi visions of Aryan supremacy. Commissioned to make a film of the games, Riefenstahl, perhaps naïvely produced a stylistic masterwork with cinematographic innovations to rival those of *Citizen Kane*. Despite its seminal artistry, the film is still an ideological frame to showcase Aryanism: so glaring is the Nazi iconography that the viewer can almost sense Hitler himself at Riefenstahl's shoulder.

The IOC had encouraged art and, at Coubertin's urging, integrated a program of artistic competition into the games with medals awarded for different artforms. So, a visual record of the Games was welcomed. Jacob Lawrence's gouache for the poster commemorating the 1972 Games at Munich was one of a series that have been acknowledged as stand-alone works of art. But it is another Olympic-themed work, Claus Mattyes' collage *Olympia*, 1978, that Kühnst singles out as the most revelational piece of contemporary sporting art. In it, a Magritte-style figure, bowler-hatted and wearing an IOC lapel pin, stands in front of a faux Greek statue which

BOX 13.3 LENI RIEFENSTAHL (1902–2003)

Famed German director of *Olympia*, which is hailed by many as the greatest-ever sports documentary and reviled by many others as a glorification of Nazism. Born in 1902, Riefenstahl was a dancer and actor who turned to directing in 1932 when she made *The Blue Light*. Influenced by Fanck's 1926 silent film *Mountain of Destiny*, she used specially imported lenses and film stock to further her experiments with lighting and composition. Having seen Riefenstahl's work, Hitler commissioned her to film the 1933 National Socialist Party Congress, a film that was released as *Victory of Faith*. Dissatisfied with the results, Riefenstahl filmed the following year's Congress at Nuremberg; this time, the end product was a visually stunning documentary, *Triumph of the Will*. Riefenstahl's *Olympia*, which was ostensibly the filmic record of the 1936 Berlin Olympics, was another work of brilliance, though its exaltation of Aryan manhood ultimately marred its critical reception. Wagnerian in atmosphere, the film's majesty is in its narrative construction, each scene building toward the thunderous climax. After World War II, Riefenstahl was boycotted. She died, aged 101, in 2003.

someone has defaced with a drawn-on beard and mustache. In the background, there is a bunting, but the flags are not just those of nations – they bear the logos of Coca-Cola, IBM, and the Playboy Club. There is even a dollar bill dangling from the bunting. The significance of these needs no explanation. And, as if to connect his work with that of Baumeister, Hoffmann and, indeed, the writer Brohm, Matttyes positions a clock centrally between the two figures.

Such cynicism informs much of the art since the 1930s. The age of innocence, when art glorified sport, had been drawing to a close for several years before Riefenstahl's film. Shortly after its release, the second world war occasioned a re-evaluation of sport's merits. It was not long before virtually every Olympic Games became political as well as sporting events. Coupled with this came the realization that more and more sports were becoming professionalized and the Corinthian ideals that had once motivated competitors were extinct.

The darker side of sports was explored exquisitely by George Bellows in the first two decades of the twentieth century. His usually grim images, often of boxing matches, feature faces in the crowds that seem to have spilled straight from a Hogarth canvas. Fighters collide viciously, blood spattering their bodies as fans frantically make wagers. A fighter's left hook sends a hapless opponent crashing through the ropes. The dim and dingy atmosphere of boxing halls is a fitting backdrop to a sport that enthralled Bellows in much the same manner as pedestrians are enthralled by car wrecks. For Bellows, boxing simultaneously repels and attracts.

It was probably only logical that, as film became a more established art form, directors would try to adapt features of Bellows' work for the screen. In the late 1930s and 1940s, films such as *Kid Galahad*, directed by Michael Curtiz and released in 1937, probed the dirtier aspects of the fight game. Robert Wise's *The Set-Up*, 1948,

BOX 13.4 GEORGE BELLOWS (1882–1925)

Born in 1882, in Columbus, Ohio, Bellows moved to New York in 1904 where he studied art under Robert Henri, a radical artist of his time. Bellows became associated with what was known as the Ash Can School because of his choice of subjects: in contrast to many studies that emphasized the dignity of competition, Bellows stuck to the sordid, often shameful side of sports. His characters were often rough, common people battling savagely in what often looked like a war zone. He inherited the mantle of art's greatest interpreter of boxing with works such as *Both Members of this Club (A Nigger and a White Man)*, an oil painted in 1918 which pictured a black and white fighter locked in combat, both literally and metaphorically. His *Dempsey and Firpo*, 1924, remains one of the most stirring works of sports art. Bellows died of a ruptured appendix aged 42, in 1925.

examined how a fixed fight goes wrong when no one tells the fighter he is supposed to take a dive. The short (72-minute) film, shot in black and white, casts shadows across virtually every scene to evoke the gloomy atmosphere of bleakness and moral uncertainty; a radio commentary punctuates the soundtrack as if to remind the viewer that the media has made its malevolent presence felt on a once-noble sport. Mark Robson's 1949 *Champion* was another portrait of a sport callously corrupted by avaricious businessmen. The familiarly dire portrait of boxing continued with films such as *Somebody Up There Likes Me* and *The Harder They Fall*, both 1956, and *Requiem for a Heavyweight* (in Britain, *Blood Money*), 1962.

In these and other films, romanticism was jettisoned and a savage realism was brought to the subject. Like the bronzes of Mahonri Mackintosh Young and Richmond Barthé, boxers are disfigured by the strains of competing in a sport that has long forgotten the principles of fairness and "sportsmanship."

This misanthropic approach was by no means confined to boxing. Paul Cadmus' oil and tempera work *Aspects of Suburban Life: Golf*, 1936, was one of four panels created during the Depression. Here golf is a putrid metaphor for the social inequalities of America: a well-heeled, cigar-smoking golfer sits while his supine caddy holds his clubs. The caddy is poverty personified; his shoes have holes in their soles, his jeans, which are a few sizes too big for his undernourished body, are tied with string. He tends to the needs of the conspicuously rich, all overweight and either ignoring completely or peering down their noses at the caddy.

Other disagreeable aspects of sports are dealt with by A. Paul Weber's *The False Penalty Shoot*. Weber envisions a game of soccer as disintegrating into a horrifying riot with the bodies of hundreds of spectators strewn about the field and thousands more pouring forward. The lithograph was produced in 1964 and bears an eerie similarity with the scenes evidenced at the Hillsborough stadium in 1989 when 96 fans died after the worst tragedy in British sports history.

Sports fans have not escaped the critical attentions of film directors. *The Fan*, 1996, featured Robert De Niro as a knife salesman turning on a baseball star who seems to have sacrificed sporting values for money. Tony Scott's film was a study in how contemporary sports are able to destroy the very things they build: devotion, loyalty, and hero-worship. A playful pitching competition between fan and player is shot like a gunfight in a 1950s western, the duel escalating as the fan vents his wrath. Fanaticism is also the focus of Philip Davis' undervalued account of a British police officer who goes undercover to penetrate a gang of hooligans. *i.d.*, 1994, communicated the dubious attractions of gang affiliation and organized violence. Particularly powerful are scenes in a British pub used as headquarters by the gang: here the *espirit de corps* that fuels the fanaticism is dramatically realized and the viewer is made privy to the attractions of fandom. Nick Love revisited London's hooligan pubs in 2004: his *The Football Factory* makes us onlookers to the violent subculture of soccer fans.

A Manchester United fan shares the focus in Ken Loach's *Looking for Eric* (2009), Eric Cantona, playing an apparition of himself, who visits the fan and dispenses valuable advice. The film's exploration of the depth of the fan's devotion to his hero is an interesting facet of an otherwise whimsical story.

The photographer Tom Stoddart used a close-up of the blistered, calloused and cut palms of a female gymnast's hands to convey the punishing effects of training regimes. Regarded by most as a beautiful and edifying sport, gymnastics was exposed by Joan Ryan's book *Little Girls in Pretty Boxes: The making and breaking of élite gymnasts and figure skaters* (1998) as hideously cruel. Stoddart's *Hands of a Seven-Year-Old Gymnast*, 1994, presents this ugly side of the sport and, like most quality sports photography, is capable of prodding viewers to regard sports in new ways.

Film, more than any other medium, has been able to expose the darker side of sports graphically and in often disturbing detail. In the fight films mentioned earlier, the decay of the sport was almost palpable; and, in later works, boxing served as an ungodly background against which to paint a larger human drama. John Huston's *Fat City*, 1972, is a piercingly miserable exploration of two losers and the exploitation of one by the other. *Raging Bull*, 1980, is Martin Scorsese's harrowing, monochrome biography of the middleweight champion, Jake LaMotta.

The very nature of the artform permits much more indulgence in the circumstances surrounding sports: the event itself is often filmed in a way that deliberately avoids *reportage*. Scorsese, for example, shot some fight scenes from the perspective of a boxer rather than a spectator, often dwelling on small effects like blood dripping from a ring rope. Scorsese hurls naturalism away, using LaMotta's fights as parts of a narrative that maps out his personal conflicts, especially with his belittled wife Vicky.

Perhaps the most earnest portrayal of the degradation of sports was John Sayles' film of the scandalous 1919 World Series, *Eight Men Out*, 1988. In it, the poorly paid and virtually indentured Chicago White Sox players are depicted as fodder for greedy owners and corrupt gamblers. Baseball action is shown sparingly, most of the plot centering on the bars and boardrooms where the real "action" is played out.

Venality is at the heart of several other films on sports, one of the most celebrated of which is Robert Rossen's 1961 *The Hustler*, which moves in and out of the grimy poolhalls of the 1960s; as its title suggests, gambling provides the mainspring of the plot. Most of the film is shot indoors and the black and white cinematography accentuates the grubbiness of both the sport and its milieu. Scorsese's sequel, like the original based on a novel by Walter Tevis (1959, 1984), finds the eponymous pool shark in middle age but still itching to test his mettle on the green baize. *The Color of Money* features his young tutee, who, though talented, is wont to "dump" the occasional game – lose deliberately – to make money gambling.

Gambling and the opportunities for corruption it offers are themes in Norman Jewison's *The Cincinnati Kid*, 1965, in which Steve McQueen plays a hotshot poker player in the 1930s, and in Stephen Frears' *The Grifters*, 1979, which involves a horse racetrack scam. A similar scam forms the nucleus of Stanley Kubrick's *The Killing*, 1956. In these films, the camera dwells on images of dollar bills, being bet, exchanged or, in *The Killing*, being swirled around, the black and white photography making them appear like leaves in a gale.

▌ BOX 13.5 MARTIN SCORSESE (1942–)

Regarded by many as the finest living filmmaker, Scorsese has directed two films with sports themes: *Raging Bull*, based on the memoirs of middleweight champion boxer Jake LaMotta, and *The Color of Money*, a fictional account of the late career of pool hustler Eddie Felson. *Raging Bull* is inarguably one of the best sports films ever: LaMotta is portrayed as a bombastic, intimidating, misogynist, who is endlessly trying to affirm his manhood in and out of the ring. The film provides, "One of the best records we have of white male masculinity," according to Judith Halberstam, author of *Female Masculinity*. LaMotta, who cooperated in the making of the film, beats up his wife Vicky as comprehensively as he does his ring rivals. He also takes a dive to appease the mob. She eventually walks out on him, leaving him to pursue a career on the fringes of showbusiness when his fighting career is over.

Pool, like boxing, is a sport in which the skullduggery is as – if not more – interesting than the competition. *The Color of Money* is a sequel to the *The Hustler* in which a young Felson loses his innocence and becomes a "winner." When he returns, he is still possessed of the same mentality, though, at 61 (Paul Newman's age when he played Felson for the second time; he was a youthful-looking 36 in *The Hustler*), he has forsaken the cue and spends his days selling liquor. Inspired by a cocky young player Vincent Lauria, a mirror image of himself 25 years before, he grooms him for a major championship. Lauria though learns his hustling lessons too well and sacrifices a game in favor of taking advantage of long betting odds – he bets money on his rival. Lauria is interested only in money, which, in his eyes, makes him a winner.

One of the most underrated attempts to uncloak the malignancy of contemporary sport is *Blue Chips*, a 1994 film by William Friedkin, in which an NCAA basketball coach played by Nick Nolte is pulled into offering money to secure college players. The movie's plot was uncomfortably similar to several real-life incidents involving illegal payments and points shaving. The film is an almost natural partner of the epic, 2 hour 50 minute documentary *Hoop Dreams*, 1994, in which directors Steve

James, Fred Marx, and Peter Gilbert track the progress of two African American youths who aspire to be pro basketball players: they are but two of countless young black men who single-mindedly pursue what is for most only, as the title implies, a dream. The *in situ* scenes at the home of the aspirants make the viewer feel like an eavesdropper on a private conversation.

Often neglected is *The Club*, 1980, an Australian film directed by Bruce Beresford that tells of the travails of an Australian Rules football club owner who trades in a star player only to find his man has undergone a conversion and despises the competitive machismo of contemporary sports. A comparable conversion is the plot device of *Jerry Maguire*, 1997, director Chris Columbus' tale of an avaricious sports agent who discovers a conscience and tries to mend his ways.

The best sports films edify by unsettling commonsense assumptions about sport: they leave us with qualms, even pangs of conscience. Clint Eastwood's Oscar winning *Million Dollar Baby* (2004) follows a hopeful novice female boxer as she dreams of becoming a champion. Then the film disorients its audience. An illegal punch results in brain damage and the dream mutates. Her coach, played by Eastwood, is forced to decide whether to leave her in a near-vegetative state or assist her in dying. Eastwood returned to sport again with his *Invictus* (2009), which revealed how Nelson Mandela harnessed South Africa's rugby World Cup triumph in 1995 to his own political strategies.

These are but a sample of the ways cinema has ripped away the sentimentality and honor traditionally associated with sports to disclose the grimmer, unethical aspects that are integral to professional sports. They find a kindred spirit in Armand Arman's dissection of football helmets, produced in 1972. Twenty-four helmets split in half are mounted on Plexiglas. Gone is the sheen, the insignia, and smooth curves that athletes are meant to wear with honor; instead, Arman presents a jumbled mess of dismembered metal, plastic and rubber parts. By literally deconstructing the helmets, Arman is exposing the innards of American sports.

It is tempting to add the silkscreens of Andy Warhol to this myth-shattering tradition in sports art. In 1978, Warhol produced portraits of Muhammad Ali, Chris Evert, Pelé, O. J. Simpson, and several other distinguished sports performers. The work has an ambiguity in the sense that each of the portraits is daubed over and modified, some might say defaced. Much of Warhol's work was intended to distort as a way of revealing hitherto unknown truths that lurk behind the images or façades we habitually confront. The Warhol symbols consecrate and condemn simultaneously.

Several films have used sports as metaphors for other areas of social life. There is a vital British tradition that starts with Lindsay Anderson's 1963 *This Sporting Life* set in the North of England, where Richard Harris' mud-spattered struggle on the rugby field parallels the rest of his life and, in many senses, that of the northern working class in the 1960s. In 1962's *The Loneliness of the Long Distance Runner*, directed by Tony Richardson, cross-country running is a simile for a young working-class offender's gutsy clamber out of a correctional facility. There is a resemblance between this and Robert Aldrich's 1974 film *The Longest Yard*, also known as *The Mean Machine* which features Burt Reynolds as a pro football player who winds up in prison and leads a team of inmates against a team of guards.

In all three, images of sport are coarse and unpleasant. Anderson's film, like Aldrich's, makes great use of shots that are unavailable to the spectator: inside scrums and scrimmages, where players spit and trade sly punches. (Barry Skolnick's 2001 remake of Aldrich's film, this time titled *Mean Machine*, was an out-and-out comedy.)

Oliver Stone's 1999 movie *Any Given Sunday* used an allegorical NFL franchise to illustrate the manner in which corporate interests overpower all others and, in the process, threaten the integrity, principles, and ideals that once lay at the heart of honest competition.

Professional wrestling couldn't be described as honest competition and, probably not even sport, though in *The Wrestler* (directed by Darren Aronofksy, 2008), Mickey Rourke's portrayal of a washed-up, bleach-blond, middle-aged pro, battered of body and heavy of heart, evokes thoughts of any sports star in steep decline yet unable to wrench themselves away from fading limelight. "The only place I get hurt is out there," he says, pointing to the world outside the ring. Rourke's pathetic wrestler is forced to work in a supermarket to make ends meet between each bout.

A big part of our enchantment with sports is their ability to evoke extremes and for every work of art that exposes dim and recondite areas, there is at least another that illuminates the glorious, heroic, and even spiritually uplifting qualities of honest competition. The choice is vast, though some films all but select themselves if only because they correspond so perfectly to what David Rowe describes as a "source of mythologies, allegories and narratives" (2004: 200).

The six *Rocky* films (the first and fifth directed by John G. Avildsen, 1976, 1990; the others by Sylvester Stallone, 1979, 1982, 1985, and *Rocky Balboa*, 2006) were collectively an epic saga of a down-at-heel fighter who is plucked from obscurity to challenge for the world heavyweight title. The fable follows Rocky Balboa, "The Italian Stallion," through his ascent, descent, and beyond. The fight action scenes are outrageously choreographed so that they have a comic book quality: ablaze with color and gravity-defying action, the fights that made the series so successful bore little resemblance to boxing. They are counterpointed by Rocky's delicate relationship with his lover and, later, wife. Boxing's dark corners are never fully explored and the film suggests that human courage and perseverance are the qualities needed to triumph. There are just deserts for those with the will to win; merit never goes unrewarded.

Rocky won the Academy Award for the Best Picture in 1976 and it is no accident that the Oscar winner of 1981 embodied similar ideals about the ethic of competition and the glory of victory. Hugh Hudson's *Chariots of Fire*, 1981, is set in the twilight of the British Empire and has no plot to speak of: it simply traces the build-up to the 1924 summer Olympics through the experiences of two real British track athletes. Harold Abrahams was a Jewish university student at Cambridge. Eric Liddell was a Scottish working-class Christian who ran because he believed it was for the greater glory of god. In a sense, both were outsiders and film rejoices in their achievements, employing slo-mo running sequences and a stirring Vangelis soundtrack to amplify all that is good about clean athletic competition. The famous scene of a joyous training group running along a beach, hair swept by the breeze, ocean waves lapping against their ankles, captures the wholesomeness of sport purveyed by *Chariots of Fire*.

If there is a painter whose work embodies the sentiments of these two films it is LeRoy Neiman. His work, particularly in the 1970s, was straightforward fast-moving narrative action. Neiman's characters seem to scorch the canvas: boxers' punches whizz toward their opponent, horses gallop almost into the viewer, tennis players throw themselves across the court. Compositions appear to occur so rapidly that there is no time for thought, less still criticism. Neiman's art is pure, glorious competitive energy.

Baseball films – and there have been dozens – typically gorge on narrative action. But not so Phil Alden's gently fantastic *Field of Dreams*, 1989. Hearing the mandate "if you build it they will come," farmer Kevin Costner clears a section of his plot in Iowa and constructs a baseball diamond. Sure enough, "they," the ghosts of great baseball players, appear from beyond the grave. Every frame is bathed in autumnal tones of greens and browns appropriate to a film that pines for a bygone age. Costner established himself in part through his sports roles. He also featured in two Ron Shelton films: *Bull Durham*, 1988, another baseball film, and *Tin Cup*, 1996, which was about golf. Other notable Shelton efforts include *White Men Can't Jump* and *Cobb*, the latter of which used an interview between a writer and the old baseball player, Ty Cobb, as a framing device; the narrative proceeds in a series of flashbacks.

No sport embodies the American Dream as consummately as baseball and, in their ways, every film featuring the sport has included the grand aspiration. None more so that than the Spanish language drama *Sugar* (directed by Ann Boden and Ryan Fleck, 2009), which follows a hopeful player from the Dominican Republic as he goes to spring training with the minor leagues in Arizona, then Iowa. His dream finally vaporizes and he flees to the New York, where he finds something resembling a normal life working in a store and playing baseball for fun.

Sports have often supplied raw material for the subgenre of fantasy-comedy, the most influential of which was *Here Comes Mr. Jordan*, 1941, directed by Alexander Hall and featuring Robert Montgomery as a boxer prematurely called to heaven due to a clerical error; returned to earth as an angel, the boxer seeks out his incredulous manager and seeks to resume his career. The plot was updated in 1978 and a football player replaced the boxer for Buck Henry's *Heaven Can Wait*, with Warren Beatty playing the deceased athlete. The cinematic conceit was to show the audience the returned player even though he was supposed to be invisible to the cast of the film. Much the same story was reprised again in 1997 with *The Sixth Man,* this time the departed-and-returned being a basketball player.

Slightly less whimsical were two comedies directed by David S. Ward, *Major League*, 1989, and *Major League II*, 1994, which followed the adventures of a baseball team of misfits who somehow contrived to win the occasional game. Another pair of baseball films was based on the real All American Girls' Professional Baseball League, which was formed in 1943 to fill the void left by male baseball players who were involved in the war effort. Penny Marshall's *A League of Their Own*, 1992, led to a less successful sequel. The baseball sequences were colorful and exaggerated, lending the films their phantasmagoric quality.

Goal! was Danny Cannon's 2005 fantasy about a Mexican migrant in LA, who is offered a trial with Newcastle United and a shot at playing in the English Premier League. Real game footage intercuts the drama.

Light comedy became outright farce in Harold Ramis' *Caddyshack*, 1980, Dennis Dugan's *Happy Gilmore*, 1996, and Frank Coraci's *The Waterboy*, 1999, all of which treated sports as a burlesque show. A similar playful mischief is evident in the work of pop artist Red Grooms. His *Fran Tarkenton*, 1979, is described by Louis A. Zona: "Grooms chooses to create a 'schtick' right out of vaudeville, as the greatest quarterback of his time tiptoes through a flower patch in search of a receiver . . . giving American pictorial art that sense of humor and humanity which has been missing" (1990: 122).

While Riefenstahl's *Olympia* had its ideological shortcomings, there was no doubt about its aesthetic triumph and it is still arguably the benchmark against which sports documentary features are measured. The previously mentioned *Hoop Dreams* was acclaimed as one of the finest documentaries in recent times: young black males become beasts of burden, laden with their failed parents' vanquished ambitions, as they strive to make it in pro basketball. In Leon Gast's *When We Were Kings*, 1997, Muhammad Ali's upset win over George Foreman in 1974 is embellished in a way that enriches the viewer's appreciation of the wider issues surrounding the fight, which took place in Zaire. Edited in such a way that observers of the fight function like a Greek chorus, the film intercuts footage of the boxers in training with clips of them in unguarded moments and scenes from the James Brown concert that preceded the boxing promotion.

Less inventive but still insightful was George Butler's *Pumping Iron II: The women*, 1984, which was a follow-up to the same director's 1976 *Pumping Iron* (which he made with Robert Fiore), but which is altogether more challenging, as it observed women competing in a ruthless yet sisterly way for the 1983 Caesar's Cup. The viewer seems to be secluded in hotel and locker rooms and made privy to personal conversations; the tight camera shots serve to convey competitor Bev Francis' torture and her trainer puts her through Procrustean schedules.

But, in terms of lineage, perhaps the rightful heir to *Olympia* is *Visions of Eight*, 1973, which brought together eight noted directors from around the world, each concentrating on a particular event or athlete at the Munich Olympics of 1972. Only John Schlesinger's segment incorporated the Palestinian terrorist hostage deaths into a sports story, this one about British marathon runner, Ron Hill. Others directors included Arthur Penn (of *Bonnie and Clyde* fame) who examined the pole vault, Mai Zetterling, who dwelled on weightlifting, and Kon Ichikawa, who scrutinized the men's 100-meter sprint. This sports documentary, like some others, shares many aims with the photography of Muybridge and his followers: by scrupulously attending to particularities the artist invites viewers to build their own vista. As in all art, it is the person attending to the work that is actually doing the work: making connections, filling in blanks, comprehending the meanings of the image. And so it has been with all art based on sport.

Were it not for our preoccupation with sports, then the art we have covered in this chapter would have less meaning, less value, and less significance culturally. The fact that the art I have referred to here is only a fraction of a much more formidable corpus of work bears witness to the seemingly perpetual interest in both sport and the art it has in some way inspired. Our fascination is not only with the activities themselves, but with the minute moments of a contest and the larger dynamics of the context in which it takes place. Art has enlarged our appreciation of both.

Motion Studies: Time, space and Eadweard Muybridge by Rebecca Solnit (Bloomsbury, 2004) makes a good case for the Muybridge as "a bullet shot through a book. His trajectory ripped through all the stories of his time . . . He is the man who split the second, as dramatic and far-reaching as the splitting of the atom."

The Eternal Olympics: The art and history of sport edited by Nikolaos Yaloris (Caratzas Brothers, 1979) alerts us to the vital importance of athletic competition to the culture and civic life of ancient civilizations by examining the evolution of sports and sports-related art from the second millennium BCE to the end of the ancient Olympic Games in AD 510.

Sport and the Countryside by David Coombs (Phaidon Press, 1978) concentrates on the period from the seventeenth century to the middle of the nineteenth, when hunting was virtually synonymous with "sports" and supplied the inspiration for a great many artists, especially painters. This may profitably be read in conjunction with *Game and the English Landscape: The influence of the chase on sporting art and scenery* by Anthony Vandervell and Charles Coles (Debrett's Peerage, 1980).

Sports: A cultural history in the mirror of art by Peter Kühnst (Verlag der Kunst, 1996) is a marvelous narrative exposition of the story of sports from the Renaissance onwards as told through art. "The artist's vision is a unique clue to historical change," argues Kühnst. The same author has compiled another revealing collection, *Physique: Classic photographs of naked athletes* (Thames & Hudson, 2004).

Sport in Art from American Museums edited by Reilly Rhodes (Universe, 1990) reproduces exhibits from the National Art Museum of Sport, Indianapolis; most of the art is from the nineteenth and twentieth centuries and includes the work of Stubbs, Eakins, and Bellows.

Sport on Film and Video: The North American Society for Sport History guide edited by Judith Davidson and compiled by Daryl Adler (Scarecrow Press, 1993) is one of a number of reference books on the subject; others include *Sports in the Movies* by Ronald Bergan (Proteus Books, 1982) and *Sports Films: A complete reference* by Harvey M. Zucker and Lawrence J. Babich (HM & M Publishers, 1976); there is an entry on "Films" in my own *Sports Culture: An A-Z guide* (Routledge, 2003).

"Screening the action" is a chapter in the 2nd edition of David Rowe's *Sport, Culture and the Media* (Open University, 2004) and the author sees the various ways in which tv, radio, film, and other media have depicted sports as evidence of "sport's amoeba-like cultural capacity to divide and re-form."

"Film on sport" is Chapter 2 of *Sport, Media and Society* by Eileen Kennedy and Laura Hill (Berg, 2009) and examines the codes and conventions of sports film. "For a sport film to succeed, it must contain the elements that make other films successful, relating a story that can appeal to a broad audience," write Kennedy and Hill. It could be argued that *Raging Bull*, *Million Dollar Baby*, *Hoop Dreams*, and other films that have disclosed new perspectives on sport have *avoided* the elements that might have given them mass appeal.

"You throw like a girl: Sport and misogyny on the silver screen" by Danya B. Daniels (pp. 29–38 in *Film and History*, vol. 35, no. 1, 2005) argues that "two different, but related themes have plagued women athletes as they have attempted to take their rightful place on the playing fields: masculinization and lesbianism." Daniels goes on: "The language and innuendo used and implied in sport films about women in general and woman athletes in particular support these two stereotypes."

"Million Dollar Baby" by Alan A. Stone (in *Psychiatric Times*, 2005) is an interesting discussion of Eastwood's Oscar-winning film by a professor of law and psychiatry, who concludes: "This is a fable, not with a happy ending, but with a moral lesson to convey. [The boxer] is all he [the manager] has in the world, and he wants to hang onto her, but she tells him she has had her moments of glory and asks him to put her out of her misery. If autonomy is the ultimate value in our secular world, then *Million Dollar Baby* is a persuasive argument for voluntary euthanasia." Edward Gallafent's "Violence, actions and words in *Million Dollar Baby*" (in *Cineaction*, vol. 68, 2006) is another analysis of the same film that situates it in the boxing films genre.

ASSIGNMENT

As the curator of a museum, you are charged with the responsibility of organizing an exhibition: *Sports: The heroes and the villains*. You may commission glass displays of artifacts, waxwork models, performance art, installations, and other forms of contemporary art (à la Damien Hirst, Tracey Emin, or Gillian Wearing), as well as more traditional artforms. Imagine the works you would include; these can include anything you consider suitable. Then write an account justifying the inclusion of your pieces.

WHY DO WE LIKE TO BET ON SPORTS?

Three reasons. (1) The obvious one: its adds to the thrill; watching, or listening to, sports events is exciting in itself and it becomes even more exciting if we have money riding on their outcome. (2) Competition lends itself to gambling; it lacks the randomness of games of chance such as roulette and cards, and invites the bettor to measure his or her own judgment against those of another person or firm. (3) Historically, sports and gambling have been intertwined; the entire development of sports features a coupling with betting. Many sports would not exist at all were it not for gambling and it could be argued that many others would not be so popular if we could not bet on them, whether legally or illegally. In fact, anthropologist Kendall Blanchard argues that to gamble is one of three prime objectives of sports, the others being to compete and to win prizes (1995: 122).

In all but five American states, sports betting is illegal. Yet Douglas Putnam estimates that as much as $120 billion is unlawfully wagered on sports every year. He reckons that: "the Super Bowl alone generates about $4 billion in illegal bets each January" (1999: 134). In other parts of the world, where sports betting is legal, particularly East Asia, the figures are much higher. The internet has opened up gambling on a global scale: a credit card, online facilities, and an awareness of sports events are all that are needed. Clearly, the betting is a powerful component of the commercial world of sport. A first step to understanding its appeal is to trace its origins.

Betting's underlying motive probably dates back to antiquity. Two great minds of the seventeenth century, Isaac Newton (1642–1727) and Gottfried Wilhelm Leibniz (1646–1716) inadvertently and improbably contributed to our understanding of this motive. Like Albert Einstein (1879–1955) who followed them, Newton and Leibniz were committed to a view of the world as ordered mechanically and moving according to definable principles with potentially predictable outcomes. As with all Enlightenment thinkers, reason and rationality lay behind all affairs, natural and social. As Galileo (1564–1642) had shown in his *Starry Messenger*, first published in 1610, forces that work to render the sky predictable were also at work on earth.

Chance had no place in this ordered universe. Ignorance was merely imperfect knowledge. Everything is potentially knowable; Newton and Leibniz were both prominent in the advancement of both theoretical and practical science. Given greater knowledge, we could apply the "infinitesimal calculus," a method of calculating or reasoning about the changing world. The seeming mysteries of nature could be comprehended and subordinated to the rational, calculating mind.

Gambling is guided by such reasoning: admittedly, the conscious thought that lies behind rolling a dice or drawing lots is hardly likely to resemble any kind of calculus, infinitesimal or otherwise; these are games of chance, played with the intention of winning money (though many claim to have discovered systems or formulae for winning). But, the motive behind betting on sports is very much influenced by a more rational style of thinking – that it is possible to predict the outcome of an event by the employment of a calculus of probability. No one wagers money on a sporting event without at least some inkling that they are privy to a special knowledge about how a competition will end. A hunch, a fancy, a "feel"; all these add to the calculus at work in the mind of even the most casual of gamblers when he or she stakes money on a competition.

Orientations of gamblers differ widely: some always feel a tingle or adrenaline rush, whether it is in watching a horse romp home or a dice roll across a baize; others observe from a position of detachment, their interest resting on only the result. The sports gambler bets with head as well as heart; the reward is both in the winning and in the satisfaction that he or she has divined a correct result from the unmanageable flux of a competitive event.

The seventeenth-century philosophers' concerns were not with gambling, though, in fact, they may well have observed the surge in popularity in games of chance in the pre-Enlightenment period. The philosopher Nicholas Rescher locates this popularity in wagering on contests of skill and chance during the English Civil War, 1641–5 (between Charles I and his Royalists or Cavaliers, and Roundheads, who emerged victorious), and the Thirty Years War in continental Europe, 1618–48 (the conflict between the Catholic Holy Roman Emperor and some of his German Protestant states).

Starved of entertainment, soldiers and sailors killed time by wagering on virtually any activity. Rescher cites a seventeenth-century soldier's remembrance of betting on a race between insects, such as lice. Returning to civilian society, the militia brought with them their habits and the enthusiasm for gambling diffused, aligning itself quite naturally with the games of skill that were growing in popularity in England.

Engaging in competitive contests simply for the satisfaction they afforded the competitor and observer was exactly the kind of wasteful and sinful behavior despised by Puritans, after their arrival in the New World in 1620, when they passed an anti-gambling law. England under Cromwell's command prohibited many sports and types of gambling.

After the Restoration of the monarchy in 1660, the renewed license for play fed an upsurge in gambling so great that laws were passed, principally to restrict the debts that were being incurred as a result of the growing stakes.

Some activities had attracted gambling for decades, perhaps centuries. Swordplay, for example, was a pursuit that was viscerally thrilling to watch and stimulated the human passion for prediction. As the military use of swords declined, so the contests continued simply for recreation and entertainment.

Gambling was actually the basis of many early sports, especially blood sports, in which a wager enhanced the amusements of watching animals fight or be ravaged. This was by no means confined to the West. Clifford Geertz's classic study of cockfighting in Bali emphasizes the significance of betting to the meaning of the event (1972). All forms of animal sports were fair game for gaming. Western-style dog racing which has its origins in eighteenth-century coursing (and involved highly bred and trained dogs which chased and – usually – killed a fleeing hare) became an organized sport, complete with its own organization in 1858, when a National Coursing Club was established in the United States. The betting norm became *pari-mutuel*, from the French, meaning mutual stake. In the 1930s, this also took off in on-track British horseracing, though it was known as the totalizer, or just "tote" – betting, in which winners divide the losers' stakes, less an administrative charge.

Appealing as it may be to link the rise of gambling with modern capitalism and the ethos it both embodies and encourages, sports betting is not confined to cultures characterized by materialism and acquisitiveness. Blanchard's work documents the centrality of betting, in some cases as an obligation, to sports in several cultures, many in the underdeveloped world. Yet western influences brought different aspects.

Blanchard gives the example of a Mississippi Choctaw sport to which betting was integral. In the 1890s, "local whites frequented the 'Indian ballgames' and with the whites came a new type of betting, whiskey, and a threat to the safety of Choctaw women" (1995: 175). After appeals from missionaries, the state of Mississippi outlawed gambling at all the ballgames. The sport faded away. While there were other factors, it is believed the elimination of betting from the sport was responsible for the demise. This suggests that the very existence of some sports is predicated on betting. Horse and dog racing are contemporary instances.

In Britain, a form of gambling on association football came to life in the early 1930s and captured the British public's imagination almost immediately. Newspapers had been publishing their own versions of "pools," as the bets were known, for many years, but the practice was declared illegal in 1928. Dennis Brailsford notes how the £20 million staked in the 1934/5 season doubled within two years. The outlay was usually no more than a few pence and the bets were typically collected from one's home. The aim of pools was to select a requisite number of drawn games, so it was not classified as a game of chance, but one of skill, thus escaping the regulation of gaming legislation. By the outbreak of war in 1939, there were ten million players of the pools. The popularity the pools enjoyed with working-class bettors stayed intact until the introduction of the national lottery (modeled on the U.S. state lotteries) in 1994.

Nowadays, betting on the spread is one of the most popular gambling forms. Originally spread betting was a form of gambling on the stock exchange. In sports, the spread is two values, an upper and lower limit, and the gambler typically stakes money on the outcome of an event being within or outside these values. The bettor can wager not only on the result of a contest but on any facet of it, such as the time of the first score, the identity of the scorer, the score at a certain time etc. Betting on sports, legally and illegally, was facilitated by the spread of the internet in the late 1990s. Because of the difficulty in regulating it, online betting became attractive where local laws prohibited or restricted most forms of betting, such as in the United States, or where gaming taxes were high, as in Britain.

MORE QUESTIONS . . .

>> Should the United States acknowledge that betting is an integral part of sports' attraction and legalize it?

>> Does televising sports make it more possible that people want to bet on them?

>> Why are some sports, like Jai Alai or horseracing, less interesting, if not meaningless without betting?

READ ON . . .

Howard J. Shaffer (ed.) , *Journal of Gambling Studies*, Human Sciences Press, since 1984.

Kendall Blanchard, *The Anthropology of Sports: An introduction*, Bergin & Garvey, 1995.

Nicholas Rescher, *Luck: The brilliant randomness of everyday life*, Farrar Straus Giroux, 1995.

Dennis Brailsford, *British Sport: A social history*, Lutterworth Press, 1997.

Gerda Reith, *The Age of Chance: Gambling in western culture*, Prometheus Books, 1999.

Mikal Aasved, *The Sociology of Gambling*, Charles C. Thomas, 2003.

Mike Huggins, *Horseracing and the British, 1919–39*, Manchester University Press, 2003.

Ellis Cashmore, "Gambling and sport," in *The Blackwell Encyclopedia of Sociology*, edited by George Ritzer, Blackwell Reference Online, 2007.

A Match Made in Heaven

▌ A GOOD THING

To . . .   e.e. cashmore@staffs.edu
From . . .   h.g.wells@timemachine.org
Subject: the wonders of the media

Professor Cashmore: It's 2021 and I'm in the USA. Today is a huge day over here: Global Bowl Sunday. This year the rival teams are Tokyo Samurai, appearing in their first Global Bowl and the Las Vegas Fortune. Vegas is going for its second championship this century, having won three years ago under their old name Las Vegas Bengals. The old Cincinnati Bengals' owner sold out in 2018 and the new owners, a consortium in which a Saudi Arabian prince has a 36 percent stake, and News Corp. a 20 percent interest, moved the franchise to Nevada. Now, the city of Cincinnati has been promised an expansion team and has been granted permission to reclaim its original name. So, the Vegas outfit changed to the Fortune – quite an appropriate name in several ways, including the investment that went into building the franchise an 85,000-seater stadium which has 70 percent of its capacity taken up by luxury boxes.

Still the investment has paid off handsomely and the club has been estimated as worth $8 billion – almost as much as Real Madrid, now owned by an oil-rich family from the sheikdom Qatar on the coast of the Persian Gulf. There are several sports clubs based in that region now. Bahrain and Riyadh were both awarded NFL franchises as part of the global expansion program. The whole deal was backed by a number of media corporations, which broadcast the games around the world. The global popularity of American football has risen, though association football is still the biggest draw. Big games can attract 40 billion+ viewers on ppv. The Global Bowl is beamed around the world and brings in near three billion.

I'll watch the game on the RayZ, a recent invention based on the old hologram principal in which a pattern is produced by interference between light beams and light broken up into a series of colored spectra (diffracted is the technical term for this). The result is a moving full-color three-dimensional holographic image of the game. The RayZ sits in the middle of the room and viewers can sit anywhere around it, as the images are formed in the beams of light that shoot upwards from the appliance. It's a tremendous improvement on the old 4 x 3 foot plasma screens. When you think of it, what took them so long? The first domestic television sets were available in the late 1940s and we had to suffer flat 2D images for nearly sixty years before 3D took over. Now, program makers use technology that allows 360° views. The viewer can freeze the action at any time and take a close look from whatever angle they choose.

The old *Matrix* movies from the 1990s used a primitive form of this, but, back then, they used to watch on flat screens, so the ability to move around the image was illusory. Now, people just walk around the beams of light. Although the technology behind it is quite old, it's only in recent years that it's become available as a domestic appliance. At least, that's what they tell us. You suspect there are powerful economic forces too. Think about television: they reckon we could have it in our homes twenty years before we did, but the big business interests that had invested heavily in radio feared that radio would be wiped out by tv. Radio clung on, though television is already beginning to look redundant.

They used to say that watching sports on tv was better than being there: slow-mos and action replays, together with the so-called expert analysis made televised sports a superior all-round package. But, nobody was convinced and people still flocked to the "live" occasions. But, this new technology is something different. It really is like being there. With the atmospheric audio, it's easy to imagine yourself actually at the event, except you can inspect the game from any angle instead of being confined

Cordially
H.G

If ever there was a marriage made in heaven it was that of television and sport. The commercial success of each was almost directly attributable to the other. From the 1940s to the present sports have grown in proportion to tv. Not only have they grown in scale and popularity, but they have become modified into virtual theater. And television's efforts at dragging sports toward the popular entertainment end of the market have paid off in terms of record-breaking viewing ratings. High-profile sports events draw audiences comparable with televisual phenomena, like the moon landing, the funeral of Princess Diana, or the finale of *Friends* which drew 52.5 million viewers in 2004 (advertisers were charged $2 million per 30 seconds).

Ever since we began watching rather than actually participating, we've been consumers of sport. I mean consumers in the sense that we purchase and use services and, increasingly, goods produced by the sports industry. We buy them for our personal use and gratification. The word consumption is from the Latin *consumptionem*, for using up or wasting, so its meaning has traveled quite well: after all, we don't spend our money on sports for investment purposes or for edification – we just waste it.

The way we consume sport has changed over the decades: in the late nineteenth and early twentieth centuries, spectators would sit or stand in physical proximity to the event and observe the competition as it happened. As interest grew, publications began featuring results and reports and this introduced another form of consumption. Readers could enact competitions in their imaginations. In the 1920s, radio offered a kind of aural firsthand witness to many sporting occasions. It could be argued that, with radio, emotion took precedence over physicality: it was no longer necessary to be physically present at a contest to experience the excitement that often accompanies a sporting competition. The imperative of radio was to convey as much of the atmosphere of a big fight, or baseball game as possible; of course, it was able to do this, not days or even hours after an event, but in real time.

Images came with television, at first communicated through airwaves, then cables, then via satellites. Television, as I will argue shortly, changed not only the manner in which we consumed sport, but the way it was produced. In fact, television changed sport utterly and completely by means of two instruments. According to Ping Wu, "saturation coverage and drama remain the essence of the media's success in shaping sport in the twenty-first century" (2008: 148).

Television chiefs must have been listening to George Benson's track in the 1970s, "Never give up on a good thing." They just kept filling the schedules with sport until it seemed consumers couldn't absorb any more. And then they kept going. The evidence of Wu's other point is right there on the screens every day: sport is presented theatrically as an exciting, emotional series of events with personalities, crises and all the stagecraft of a dramatic production.

Television's relationship with sport became an unexpectedly prosperous one: both entities grew rich and influential as a result of the fruitful partnership. In the process, they transformed each other, television validating its place as the premier communications channel, sports mutating into an entertainment medium that can properly be called showbusiness. The beginnings of this alliance lie in the 1950s, but its sources go back further; to the early nineteenth century, which is where I'll pick up.

THE COMING OF THE GOLDEN AGE: PRESS, RADIO, AND NEWSREEL

Founded in 1822, the British newssheet *Bell's Life in London* found its circulation rising as it included sports reports. Printed on pink paper, the weekly publication owned by Robert Bell, specialized in reports of prizefights, cricket, foxhunting and especially horseracing. Sports were hardly news, at least not in the hardest sense of the word, but reports of them had the desired effect and sales continued to rise. The paper held a monopoly until 1865 when another publication *The Sporting Life* issued what was to be a potent challenge. The success of *The Sporting Life* with its quick and detailed reporting and varied advertising prompted other publications to dedicate sections to sports coverage.

The North American equivalent of *The Sporting Life* was *Spirit of the Times: A chronicle of the turf, agriculture, field sports, literature and the stage*, a weekly journal that first appeared in New York City in 1831 and became the premier news sheet for horseracing news. Like its British counterpart, it also carried news of prizefights and hunting, though it also covered baseball, a sport that was growing in popularity and which would, in 1858, organize its first league, the National Association of Base Ball Players. By the mid-nineteenth century, consumers of sports were in the habit of buying a medium – a means for communicating information – for sports news.

Unlike many of the amateur sports participants, newspaper proprietors were interested in making money. There is no evidence that any of the early publishers held particular interests in competition; if sports news sold papers, they featured more sports. The effect of this was to prime further interest, as the British scholar Tony Mason points out: "It was the press who first elevated a minority of sportsmen and women into national celebrities, whose names and faces were recognized by people uninterested in sport; performers whose mere presence on the pitch would tempt people to the event; the exceptional performer" (1988: 50).

Mason's observation reminds us that the sources of what we now call the sports celebrity, whose fame relies as much on the media as on athletic performance are buried quite deeply in the nineteenth century. We'll investigate this in Chapter 17. For now, we need to take note of a clear symmetry of interests between those with an interest in exploiting the mass spectatorship potential of sports and those who could sell newspapers with stories about sports. Reporting in the press had the useful consequence of raising public awareness, so enlarging the mass spectator market – and it was a market: spectators were charged admission to watch baseball, cricket, association football, pugilism, and the other popular activities of the mid-to-late nineteenth century.

The value of newspapers that carried reports and results from sports to the organizers and promoters was obvious. Reading about, discussing, and arguing in the pubs, coffee houses, theaters, exhibitions, spectacles, pleasure gardens, or just on the streets, all served to create a culture in which sports were valued resources. The broadsheets were vital: of that there was no doubt. But there was uncertainty about radio, which came to the fore in the 1920s, when organized sport was available on a regular basis and warrantable mass market for sports had begun to take shape.

Radio could relay information on any event, but any advantage it held in terms of boosting interest was outweighed by its immediacy: instead of attending an actual event, fans may have opted for listening to "live" commentary on the radio. Radio's capacity to excite was enhanced by the social atmosphere it generated, listeners huddled together whooping and yelling as the commentator's voice crackled through the airwaves, the crowd's roar in the background.

Newspapers' positive influence on sport meant that journalists were welcome at all sports events. It would have been unthinkable to ask a newspaper's owner to pay an admission price like the rest of the audience. Radio company heads though were almost in competition with the promoters or leagues: their aim was to keep listeners completely fascinated by what they heard coming through the holes of wooden cabinets containing radio values. These valve radios would retail in the 1920s for between $35–100 in the United States and £25–100 in Britain, where consumers were obliged to pay a BBC license fee too (as they are still today). James Woods likens the prestige attached to radios in the 1920s to that of cars today: "The possession of a radio set did not merely signify a social status; it was an important symbol of personal prestige to the working man" (2001: 32).

The popularity of radios among all classes grew through the 1920s. By 1930, the Golden Age of Radio, as it is called, had arrived. While BBC radio's sole source of revenue was the license fee (commercial radio did not start until 1973), American radios relied on advertising and sponsorship. This gave them the revenue to bargain with sports organizers. For instance, in 1935, the radio rights to the Joe Louis–Max Baer world heavyweight fight were sold for a record $27,500 (then about £9,000), a staggering amount in the 1930s, but testament to the growing commercial power of the electronic media. Fears that radio commentary would hurt the gate were unfounded as 88,000 spectators attended the event.

By this time, radio coverage of sports was commonplace and, as this involved issues of proprietorship and copyright, it gave rise to an economic relationship between the media and sports organizers. Newspapers were regarded as good publicity; radio's effect was still ambiguous: it did pump up interest, but it could also keep people away. Radio still saw a profit in sports: it could attract large listening audiences for its sports programs. This meant that advertisers and sponsors were tempted to pay more to have their products associated with the event and so reach a large potential market. Sponsors of radio shows were among the first commercial companies to realize the financial benefits of linking their commodities with sports. The BBC, as a public service provider, had no need to seek the patronage of commercial advertisers when it began radio sports broadcasts in 1927.

Newsreels were short documentary films consisting of clips from news events. In the early twentieth century, they became a valuable source of information on world events. Filmed news of sports events occupied a segment of newsreels shown in movie theaters even before radio transmissions, but the films were at least a week after the event and could not compare with the thrill of a "live" radio broadcast. Even then, the newsreels featured only brief excerpts, what we would now call highlights. Cinemas showing only newsreels were known as news theaters; a typical program would last about an hour; this included cartoons as well as newsreels.

In the United States, a 1912 ban on showing fight films was relaxed in 1939 when Senate passed a bill to permit the transfer of boxing films from state to state. But, by this time, a new medium had crept into the homes of a select few.

░ LET THERE BE TELEVISION . . .

In 1937, a few hundred Londoners were the first to see the first outside broadcast coverage of British sport, when 25 minutes of a men's singles match was televised from Wimbledon. It was strictly an experimental service from the BBC, which had improved on an earlier, unsatisfactory, attempt by CBS to broadcast a fight by "sight and sound."

The main technical shortcoming of televising events was that cameras were fixed and were fitted with lenses that made the performers appear as tiny figures. Boxing, whose action takes part in a small, finite territory seemed reasonably suitable for the new medium and, in 1939, the BBC and NBC both broadcast fights, the BBC being fortunate enough to capture the British lightweight title fight between Eric Boon and Arthur Danahar, which is regarded as amongst the best-ever fights on British soil. In the same year, the BBC, still in its infancy, showed its first FA Cup Final and NBC telecast baseball, at first with one camera and, later, with two, which was a significant innovation as it permitted close-ups not even visible to audiences watching the game live.

Television was still only a futuristic luxury of the rich, with just 5,000 sets being sold in the United States in 1946. Within ten dramatic years, 75 percent of the country's households had a tv set. John Goldlust argues that: "The significance of sports for this phenomenal rate of penetration should not be underestimated," and that the televising of major sports events was "a key element in launching the television industry" (1987: 8).

This was early evidence of mutual beneficence that was to assist the rise and rise of both television and sports. Goldlust identifies in particular the transmission of the Melbourne Olympics in 1956 as a key event that greatly boosted the sale of television receivers. After this, the television industry of continental Europe and Latin America developed within the framework of either the BBC, which considered the televising of sport one of its statutory obligations in order to provide as many aspects as possible of the "national culture," or the American companies, which geared their schedules so as to maximize demand from advertisers.

Like the BBC, the U.S. broadcasters were previously radio-only broadcasters. They learned that, if manufacturers had products to sell and wanted exposure for their products, then placing commercials in the "natural breaks" (as the commercial spots were called) of a high-profile event was a rational and effective form of advertising. Even with a minute percentage of its potential audience watching, televised sports were attractive: as early as 1947, Ford and Gillette paid $65,000 (then about £20,000) for the rights to sponsor baseball's World Series on television, despite the fact that less than 12 percent of U.S. households could receive it. This was before the days of cable, of course.

Initially, major sports governing organizations were wary of television, assuming its impact could only be detrimental. As if to illustrate the point, between 1948 and 1956, the Cleveland Indians baseball team won a World Series and a pennant, yet suffered a 67 percent drop in attendance. The Boston Braves' crowds plunged by 81 percent following their National League victory in 1948, immediately after which they signed a tv deal for the next three years. The situation needed drastic remedial action, so the owner Lou Perini moved the franchise to Milwaukee and banned television cameras, apart from at the World Series winning games of 1957 and 1958.

The gates stayed healthy, prompting Perini to announce smugly: "We have come to believe that tv can saturate the minds of the fans with baseball. We would very much like to guard against this." Perini relaxed his strictures after 1962 and eventually sold out to a group that wholeheartedly embraced television by relocating the club in Atlanta where a tv–radio guarantee of $1.25 million (then over £600,000) per year awaited.

Another sport whose gates were hit severely was college football. Between 1949 and 1953, attendance declined by almost 3 million. The National Collegiate Athletic Association (NCAA) formed a special television committee and instituted rigid rules for limiting the number of telecasts. Even then, it took years before gates rose to their 1949 levels.

North American television feasted on boxing, which it left as a carcass in 1964 after 18 years of the kind of coverage Perini had feared for baseball. In some areas of the United States, boxing was on every night of the week, with promoters eagerly accepting television monies to augment profits. Gradually, the tv fees became the profits: live audiences dwindled, leaving the promoters utterly reliant on television for their revenue.

As tv was interested only in "name" fighters, the bigger promoters who had the champions under contract were able to capitalize, while the smaller promoters went to the wall. In the period 1952–9 alone, 85 percent of the country's small boxing clubs shut down. At the height of its power in 1955, boxing was watched by 8.5 million homes, about one-third of the available viewing audience in those days. By 1959, boxing commanded only a 10.6 percent audience share – which sounds much, much more impressive now than it did then when the market was uncluttered by cable channels. NBC was the first to cut boxing from its regular schedules in 1960. The other networks followed suit. Only the big fights got airtime. Not until 1980 when ESPN launched did boxing find a regular tv slot.

Unlike today, when every sport needs television for both revenue and promotion, there was uncertainty about the effects of tv on sport. This was the 1950s, of course: it seems absurd that sports governing organizations would actually contemplate an existence without television. But the fear was that attendances would tumble: who would want to pay hard cash for a ticket, then travel to an event, when they could switch on their television set and watch from the comfort of their own homes? The money the media offered was tempting, but the longterm consequences could have been ruinous.

In the 1950s, television was technically primitive and focused on the relatively simple sports. There were two main American networks, CBS and NBC and they would probably have used fixed cameras with a vacuum tube called an image orthicon developed in the 1940s; it was replaced in the 1960s by the vidicon tube. Indoor events, such as boxing were more television-friendly than baseball or football, though roller derby, a sport that dated back to the 1920s, was given a fresh lease on life by television in the late 1940s and 1950s.

CBS and NBC enjoyed a relatively peaceful coexistence, carving up the major sporting events between them. Similarly in Britain, the BBC had a perfect monopoly until 1955 when Britain's first commercial station ITV (Independent Television) started broadcasting. American readers will be interested to learn that British tv viewers hadn't seen a commercial before 1955 when they witnessed the first-ever ad shown on British tv – it was for Gibbs SR toothpaste (Elida Gibbs, now a subsidiary of Unilever, is still operating; check the online quiz if you want to watch it).

One third of the United States' major television stations was ABC, which began broadcasting in 1948, but was very much a minority channel without the resources to challenge the big two. ABC's Saturday afternoon show *Wide World of Sports* debuted April 29, 1961. It provided further evidence to support Goldlust's earlier point: in fact, the show was responsible for turning ABC into a legitimate network and a serious rival for the big two.

Not having access to the big sports, ABC decided to feature minority sports and activities that were barely sports at all and treat them in such dramatic ways that even those with no interest in sports would be converted. Rodeos, demolition derbies, and even the bizarre fireman's bucket-filling championships were all fair game for ABC's cameras, which wouldn't just document what happened but would take the viewer to where it happened. Cameras would venture to the tops of cliffs, peer over the edge, then draw back to view a diver hurtling into the seas below, where another camera joined him or her in the water. Sports were drama. Recall Wu's point about the media's shaping influence on sport: with ABC, there was the first attempt at dramatizing sports.

Inspired by the iconoclastic philosophies of Roone Arledge, ABC vandalized the established traditions and made an overt appeal to younger audiences, which were not bound by the fidelities of their parents. Women viewers were wooed, as they were demographically attractive to advertisers: research showed that women made decisions about household purchases.

BOX 14.1 ROONE ARLEDGE (1931–2002)

As ABC television's producer of network sports, Forest Hills-born Arledge mapped out a direction for television in the 1960s and, at the same time, established his tv network as a rival to the United States' then duopoly, comprising CBS and NBC. Instead of following sports events, Arledge believed television should take the initiative. Rather than accepting that sporting occasions had a "natural" appeal that should be reflected in television coverage, Arledge created interest across the widest possible range of the population. He recognized no barriers set by class, gender, or age. His premise was much the same as that of the advertisers on whose patronage ABC ultimately depended: if the demand is not there to begin with, build it. The way Arledge built it was by taking obscure sports and adding something to them, something that only television could provide. Among Arledge's ideas were the weekly *Wide World of Sports* and *Monday Night Football*, both of which were instrumental in drawing the hitherto neglected female sports fan to television screens. Arledge died in 2002.

ABC's approach was unashamedly populist, projecting personalities, highlighting unusual characteristics about them and reducing almost any competitive activity to its most basic elements. Frog jumping contests were not out of place in ABC's sports panoply. Gillette, one of television's biggest sports sponsors, hooked up with ABC with a Friday night boxing series and, encouraged by the response, fed in more money, which enabled ABC to capture NCAA football in the 1960–1 season. This was the first of many coups, the biggest being the American Football League (AFL), a second-rate rival to the NFL, but one which, given the ABC treatment, rose in popularity. In 1960, ABC signed a five-year television contract with the fledgling league, worth what seems today the trifling sum of just over $2m. But, then it was a huge risk: the National Football League (not then the NFL as we know it) had established itself largely due to the tv coverage of CBS and NBC. It had also made a clever concession to television, allowing "television time-outs," which were stoppages designed to permit the networks to screen advertisements.

ABC's alliance with the AFL changed the status quo. The United States in the 1960 was in the throes of upheaval as civil rights protesters campaigned to remove the barriers of racial segregation that divided American society. Whether the motivation was idealistic or pragmatic, the AFL recruited many of its players from small African American colleges. When the 1964 civil rights law was passed, the AFL was already a racially integrated league.

Gerald Scully suggests: "One could argue that the survival of the AFL as a league was made possible by access to national television, which helped financially in its own right and brought recognition and fan interest" (1995: 27). This is surely an understatement: the AFL wouldn't have existed in the first place without ABC television.

During its first five years of operation, the AFL solidified its credibility. So much so that, in 1966, the National Football League felt the need to broker peace. The two leagues merged to produce the NFL as we know it today. One significant innovation in the AFL–ABC deal was the pooling of broadcast rights. By dealing with the television as a league, the AFL eliminated the kind of interclub competition that occurs when individual clubs sell local and national broadcast rights, as some clubs are allowed to do in Europe.

In the same year as the NFL–AFL merger, BBC television in Britain screened the Fifa World Cup competition, staged in England. It was a prestigious tournament and the BBC beamed its pictures all over the world. The advantage of the camera over the naked eye had been appreciated since the 1877, when Eadweard Muybridge published his serial photographs of human bodies in motion from different perspectives, using shutter speeds of less than $\frac{1}{2000}$th of a second. The series disclosed new ways of understanding the movement of bodies (as we saw in Chapter 13). Television offered even further possibilities.

In the final championship game, the English team's third goal arrived giftwrapped for television. The ball thundered against the underside of the West German team's crossbar, appearing momentarily to bounce over the goal line before rebounding into the field of play. If the whole ball had crossed (not just broken as in American football) the plane of the goal line, then it was a goal. The German players said "no." But, the referee said "yes," and the goal stood. This was a cue for television to go to work:

BBC slowed down the action, freeze-framed it, reversed the angle; and it could still not prove conclusively whether or not the ball had crossed the line. The arguments raged and the footage rolled and rolled. Even today, the debate continues. Were it not for television, spectators would have caught only a glimpse of the goal and the game would have been consigned to history.

BOX 14.2 MONDAY NIGHT FOOTBALL

This has become something of an institution since its inception in 1970. ABC's innovation was an attempt to broaden the appeal of football by incorporating elements of drama and popular entertainment into its coverage. Unusual camera angles, personality close-ups, half-time interviews: these were all used to distinguish ABC's football from that of the other networks. It quickly commanded a one-third share of the viewing audience. ABC paid the NFL $8.5 million per year for 13 games and claimed this back by charging advertisers $65,000 per minute during the game. By the end of 1979, it was regularly the eighth most watched program in the United States, enabling ABC to charge $110,000 for a 30-second commercial slot. ESPN – like ABC, part of Disney – took over *Monday Night Football* in 2006. A British soccer version of this was inaugurated in the 1993 after BSkyB's deal with the Football Association. This later transferred to the now-defunct Setanta and, in 2009, to ESPN.

CONTROLLING THE CONSUMER

Unlike early British television which was once intended to become a "theater of the airwaves," American television has always been a business, like any other: whether they derive income from sponsorship or advertising, from cable subscriptions, from production or from station ownership, for-profit corporations have always dominated the industry in the United States. The logic of the marketplace has always dictated the course of action. During television's formative years, it followed the successful formula of radio stations, selling space in its programs to advertisers. Ford, General Electric, Singer, and other giants of the expanding industries of peacetime seized the chance of reaching a genuinely mass market of potential consumers.

British television originally took a rather snooty attitude, attracting funding not through advertising, but through licenses, which viewers were obliged to buy in order to receive tv signals legally (the original cost of the tv/radio license in 1946 was £2; the radio-only license was set in 1923 at 10 shillings – then about $1.25). BBC television even today resolutely refuses to screen commercials, even though its rivals operate on much the same lines as their American counterparts, which have always operated on a simple, but effective idea. Television offers to deliver to advertisers an audience of several million consumers, many of whom will be influenced enough by the "commercial messages" (as they were once politely called) to spend their money on the advertised product, whether it be soap, cars, financial services, or whatever.

Advertisers pay their money to the tv company, which in turn pays the cost of the production and distribution of its programs. The difference is, of course, what keeps the tv company in business.

The additional beauty of the arrangement is that viewers consume twice over: ostensibly, they are consuming the action, but advertising is gently convincing them they should buy iPods, shaving gel, coffee, and so on. This is why the real customers of television are not the people looking at the screens, but the advertising agencies who handle the affairs of product manufacturers and do business with the networks. The viewers are actually part of the deal: the more viewers I can promise an advertising agency, the more money I can charge for a commercial spot.

If the program draws only small viewing audiences, then advertisers are less inclined to part with serious money. If, as is sometimes the case nowadays, commercial time is sold on the supposition that x-million viewers will be watching a big football game, and, in the event, less than that number view the program, the television network may offer a rebate.

A complicating factor in this concerns demographics: some television shows attract high audience ratings (the measurement of viewers), but not of the right type. In the 1950s when television was building its following, content didn't discriminate too much between audiences and advertisers were eager to have their messages seen by as many potential customers as possible. A show such as *I Love Lucy*, which drew as many as 44 million viewers, was priceless to advertisers. Well, not quite priceless: its stars, Lucille Ball and Desi Arnez signed a contract worth $8 million with CBS and the show's sponsors Philip Morris, the tobacco company. It was, by far, the largest contract written for a tv show, but then again, it was, as the Philip Morris president put it, "the all-time phenomenon of the entertainment business" (quoted in Landay, 1999: 30).

As market research techniques developed, it became possible to identify which demographic segments of the market watched which programs. General Foods, for example, might have wished to target young people with a new cereal; advertising in slots during a show that draws an audience typically aged between 55–70 wouldn't be too attractive to the advertising agency handling the account for the product. Instead, the ad agency would analyze the kind of programs watched by their target consumers. Reality shows, or *X-Factor*-type contests would be more likely to draw younger viewers, as would all of MTV's output. So, healthy viewing figures are no guarantee of success: advertisers may opt for smaller audiences of the right type. All of which brings us to sport.

"Sports programming is extremely valued by the television networks," writes Scully. "The demographic profile of viewers is attractive to a certain class of advertisers, whose willingness to pay some of the highest advertising fees in the industry has propelled the growth of network television revenues to the major leagues" (1995: 28). *Note*: "demographic" is nowadays used as shorthand for demographic profile of a market segment which typically includes age, gender and socio-economic group; so advertisers may say they intend their commercial to hit the *Wired*-demographic, meaning they are targeting young men interested in multimedia gadgets and games, who probably like Mont Blanc pens (but can't afford them) and those key rings with Ferrari or Lamborghini logos that are used for carrying the keys to the Nissan.

It's no accident that early sponsors of television and radio sports programs were manufacturers of shaving products and brewers. Followers of sport were predominantly male and working-class: they shaved with soap and razors and drank draft beer. Sports audiences are now more variegated, but the essential point remains: they are likely consumers for a wide range of goods and services. Within the wide category of sports, there are variations. Golf and cricket, for example, tend to draw more affluent consumers to their screens, while football and baseball cross socio-economic boundaries.

Some events draw spectacularly huge viewing audiences. For instance, 175 million households regularly watch at least some part of the Super Bowl. This allows the television company to charge about $1.5 million per 30 second advertising slot, anticipating 56 units that yield a total of $84 million, a figure reduced to $74 million after advertising agency commissions. The commercials reach an immense number of people, but can they be worth $3 million per minute? An answer of sorts comes from Macintosh history: in 1989, Mac launched its new computer with a series of spots during the Super Bowl.

The very next day, $3.5 million-worth of said computer went over the counter and the sales figure grew to $155 million over the next 90 days. This is impressive, though Jib Fowles doesn't think it's typical. In his *Advertising and Popular Culture*, Fowles is skeptical about the supposed power of tv advertising (1996). He quotes another Super Bowl commercial, this time from 1991. A healthy 70 percent of the television audience recognized that Joe Montana had appeared in the commercial, but only 18 percent remembered what the ad was for. It was Diet Pepsi. (See also Rick Burton's "Sports advertising and the Super Bowl," 1999.)

All the same, we have to consider why so many corporations are willing to shell out over a million dollars for a commercial that's over in less time than it takes to make popcorn in the microwave. If their impact is so negligible, why don't all the big companies that squander their advertising budget on television commercials go out of business? The fact that they don't suggests that tv does influence our spending habits.

Even if the jury is still out, advertisers and tv execs alike seem convinced that commercials shown during sports events move goods off shelves. This means that, from television's point of view, the fan is a resource; an article used in a trade with advertisers. So, for example, an ABC executive in negotiation with an advertising agent is not going to discuss somebody's fabulous 40-yard touchdown pass in last Monday night's game, or that wondrous free kick that almost burst the back of the net: more likely the conversation will converge on how many people watched it, what were their class backgrounds, sex composition, ages, ethnic identities, incomes, and zip codes? It's as if television companies sell the fans to the advertisers.

Scully observes of the value of broadcasting rights in the United States: "A fourteenfold increase in baseball, a 16-fold increase in football, and a seventeenfold increase in basketball since the mid-1970s" (1995: 3). In Britain, Premier League football's £1.62 billion for the rights to screen live games from 2010 to 2013 reflects a thousandfold increase since the 1980s (and three-thousandfold since the first contract for live games in 1960). This tells us something about how much the tv companies holding the contracts expected to earn from advertising or subscriptions. But expectations do not always square with reality.

The current collective value of U.S. tv's contracts with major sports is $28.9 billion. After the advertising slump that followed the 2008 financial downturn, televising sports became a money-hemorrhaging venture. Advertising revenue simply didn't cover the costs of televising sports. This is why major networks featured many games on their cable channels. For example, ABC-owned ESPN (part of Disney) carries Monday Night Football, at least until 2013 and pays $1.1 billion a year. In total, the NFL receives $3.8 billion per year from television companies.

TNT, another cable station, with ESPN televises NBA games until 2016. Disney and Turner Broadcasting shelled out a total of $7.4 billion for the whole package through 2015. In Europe, the Italian Serie A football league rights are worth $1.3 billion (£7.8 million) over 6 years, a figure that pales besides the $3.13 billion (£1.9 billion) England's Premier League brings in every year (for domestic and global rights). One-off events have become increasingly dependent on television revenue: the fee for televising the World Cup of 2014, staged in Brazil, is $2.2 billion, which is just $2 million less than the cost of the 2012 Olympics.

Only the National Hockey League has occasioned caution among broadcasters. A combination of falling viewer numbers and labor disputes (in 2004–5, the NHL was canceled after a lockout) made the NHL less attractive to television. In 2006, the league signed a revenue sharing deal with Disney and NBC. There was no front-end NBC money for the NHL: only the promise of a share of advertising revenues when the figures went into the black. In other words, the television company had grown so wary of the harsh costs of overspending on sports, it decided to divide the risk with the sports league involved. The league had guaranteed income from Disney, however: $60 million for a year's coverage, to be followed by $70 million for each subsequent year, this being the equivalent of half of the value of the previous NHL contract with ABC/ESPN.

While the NHL is regarded as the fourth major league in the United States, it was in no position to argue with the tv companies. Sliding in television popularity, it had been passed by golf, NASCAR and college football, among others. So the drop in its tv revenues was hardly surprising. All the same, the deal should have prompted nervousness among sports leagues. The apparent disappearance of television's munificence after so many years might have been a sign of change.

Why then do broadcasters seem to covet sports so much? Three reasons: (1) *prestige*: Murdoch demonstrated this, with both Fox and BSkyB (as we will see below); (2) *other programs*: tv companies always used the advertising spots in sports shows to publicize forthcoming shows that will be shown at peak viewing hours and will attract plenty of advertisers; (3) *a long-term payoff*: one big event, like the Super Bowl, or a championship decider can recoup revenue lost in the preceding season. The *New York Times* writer Richard Sandomir once wrote that the payoff game is "like a luscious *crème brûlée* after a long dyspeptic dinner" (January 26, 1993). Take away the desert and all you have left is the kind of bellyache that may make certain sports less attractive.

▮ BOX 14.3 PREMIER LEAGUE

England's Premier League was created by the Football Association (FA) in 1992: 22 top clubs splintered from the established Football League to create a new league that did not have to share its television revenues with clubs from outside the league. Under previous arrangements the Football League's 92 member clubs distributed media income. Broadcasting rights were assigned to Rupert Murdoch's BSkyB subscription television channel. Manchester United won the first Premier League title in 1993 and remained the dominant force for the next several years. The Premier League brand became globally popular, prompting a further international tv deal valued at £800 million per year. The Premier League's £569 million a year compares favorably with Europe's other leading football leagues' domestic tv contracts, the yearly values of which are: France, *Ligue 1*: £412 million per year; Italy, *Serie A*: £348 million; Germany, *Bundesliga*: £288 million; Spain, *La Liga*: £206 million.

In the midst of financially uncertain times, BSkyB's £1.78 billion four-year deal with England's Football Association for the rights to screen Premier League games, seemed almost reckless. Of course, BSkyB's owner Rupert Murdoch, whose operations are more fully covered in Chapter 15 was something of a master risk-taker. In 1992, he carved open what had previously been a relatively cozy rivalry between BBC television and ITV (then, the only fully commercial terrestrial network in Britain). Eager to sell subscriptions to his recently launched BSkyB satellite network, Murdoch negotiated a £304 million ($575 million) deal for exclusive "live" coverage of English Premiership soccer. The BBC had to settle for a late-night highlights package, while ITV got nothing. It was the first time English viewers had been charged subscriptions to watch sport.

Nobody saw it coming, but it turned around the fortunes of both the previously faltering satellite station and the sport that had been rocked in the previous decade by tragedies. The European Commission (which is the executive division of the European Community), in the early twentieth century, grew uncomfortable with the exclusivity Murdoch has acquired and instructed the Football Association to distribute Premier League games among more than one television company. In the United States, legislation prevents collusive arrangements between the leagues and television. Most major leagues are obliged to distribute their product among various television companies. For example, the NFL allocates its games to the major networks and one or two cable companies and draws revenues from Fox, CBS, and Disney.

The original soccer deal worked well for BSkyB in Britain: subscriptions soared immediately, then leveled off at about 10 million, or about 16 percent of the total population. Major advertisers like Ford and Carling beer sponsored segments of the soccer coverage. On the other hand, the Murdoch-owned Fox dropped $350 million on its first four-year contract with the NFL.

BOX 14.4 SUBSCRIPTION TELEVISION

Unlike terrestrial television and basic cable, subscription television operates on the principle that viewers will pay extra monthly fees for the privilege of watching movies and events that are unavailable on other tv stations. Home Box Office (HBO) is the leading subscription service in the world. It was founded in November 1972 when it broadcast a hockey game from Madison Square Garden, New York, to 365 subscribers. It now has more than 16 million subscribers across 50 American states and screens 24 hours a day (this is still a relatively small number compared to terrestrial network tv which reaches 90.4 million viewers). Besides being a major screener of international sports events, HBO (which is owned by Time Warner) has become actively involved in the promotion of events, particularly world title fights. In France, Canal+ fulfills a similar function. In Britain, BSkyB is the foremost subscription channel.

Andrew Zimbalist, like Scully, predicted that a prudent sports executive should not expect as much television revenue in the future (1992: 160). But, Fox's deals seemed to defy commercial wisdom. Even with fierce competition from the internet, advertising remains attractive to television and there are few safer bets than sports when it comes to pulling in viewers. Even shows like *Sex and the City* and *Friends* lost popularity over time. Only unscripted shows like the *X-Factor* can compete, and these are a great deal cheaper to produce.

The U.S. networks' combined loss between 2001 and 2006 is probably near $6 billion ($400 million or so of those losses due to the ABC/ESPN/ESPN2 deal with the NHL). In Britain, two channels (ITV Digital and Setanta) have collapsed under the strain of football contracts, leaving dozens of clubs without tv income and many of them facing bankruptcy. The sports marketing agency ISL went belly-up after paying €2.3 billion for the tv rights to two soccer World Cups, 2002 and 2006, and discovering that its clients, the European networks, wouldn't pay its asking price.

Perhaps the most spectacular flat-out miscalculation was that of Dick Berol, who was head of sports at the tv-rights holding NBC, when he paid a jaw-dropping $3.7 billion (£2.64 billion) for the 27th, 28th, and 29th summer Olympics. In 2000, viewing figures were nearly a quarter down on the previous Olympics, which were held in Atlanta. His network drew more than $900 million worth of advertising, which translated into a $200 million profit on the $700 million outlay for the Sydney segment of the 12-year deal with the IOC. Disappointing viewing figures obliged NBC to calculate rebates for the aggrieved advertisers. Berol, it seems, believed he could redefine the demographics of televised sports in the way that Packer had: by packaging the Olympics like just another primetime tv show.

At Atlanta, U.S. tv focused so much on American competitors that actual winners of events, if they came from outside the United States, were sometimes effaced. Cameras opted for close-up examination of homegrown athletes. But, this was only part of the problem: the huge American tv market was interested in baseball, but not

Olympic baseball; basketball, but not Olympic basketball. Why watch so-called "dream teams" when organized leagues offered what fans considered more authentic competition? Sports that are integral to the Olympic movement, such as archery or weightlifting, were of no significance at all to North American viewers. The historic defeat of the U.S. 4×100 meters men's swimming relay by the Australian team was the final nail in NBC's coffin.

Sports were once cheap production numbers that drew viewers to their screens in millions. Those days have long since gone. While negotiating various deals with television, major sports governing organizations must have been taking notes. They quickly learnt that the same principles that applied to marketing beer or shaving foam, also applied to sports. Marketing, as Mark Gottdiener states, "has gone from a rather straightforward affair involving the *distribution* of goods to potential customers that existed as a generic mass, otherwise known as 'sales,' to a knowledge-based, purposeful effort at controlling consumer buying" (1997: 70).

From the 1980s, sports began marketing themselves, turning themselves into commodities; not commodities with use-values, but ones with symbolic values. Consumers were sold images they could blend with their personal histories or their identities: sports became a means of self-expression, a statement of lifestyle. While Gottdiener does not refer to sports, his observations about how consumers pursue particular kinds of lifestyles through their consumption patterns has obvious application. The NBA, more than any other sport, used television not only to re-brand itself, but to offer its followers a lifestyle option. Other sports on both sides of the Atlantic followed suit.

Licensed baseball caps became ubiquitous, replica shirts became staples of leisure-wear, endorsed products became mandatory for clued-up youth. It seemed almost serendipity when Nike came on the scene at exactly the right time in history; but as we will see in Chapter 16 the sports goods firm was actually a factor in the whole process through which sports became commodities. None of this was possible without the exposure provided by television. Sports used the same techniques as car makers, soft drink manufacturers and computer companies, attempting to manipulate consumer "needs," using art and design to create agreeable images and packaging their products to make them appealing. Today, it is virtually impossible to find a major sport that does not have a logo.

The evidence of many sports' marketing successes is abundant in the form of players' status and salaries, colossally expensive stadiums, stock exchange listings (for many British clubs), not forgetting the high-priced tv deals of the late 1990s and early twenty-first century. Even if the profit-sharing NHL deal prefigures less lavishness from tv corporations, there's still likely to be keen competition for the premier sports, even if it involves taking losses. As David Rowe writes in his *Sport, Culture and the Media*:

> The struggle for television sport can be seen to be more than a fight for profit: it reveals the cultural power of sport, particularly in the higher ranks of large corporate enterprises, where aggressive, competitive masculinity is as evident in the boardroom as in the locker rooms.

(2004: 78)

BOX 14.5 ESPN (ENTERTAINMENT SPORTS PROGRAMMING NETWORK)

This all-sports cable tv channel was the creation of Bill Rasmussen, who, in the 1970s, dreamt up an original idea for a regional network of radio stations to broadcast the University of Massachusetts' football games. Cable broadcasting was then in its infancy and Rasmussen was able to buy time on a communications satellite (transponder) inexpensively. He filled the time with small-scale sports commentary, interviews, and analysis. The Entertainment Sports Programming Network operated out of Plainville, Connecticut, and gained permission from the FCC (Federal Communications Commission) to begin broadcasting in September 1979.

Getty Oil sensed the potential of the enterprise and invested heavily; in fact, it assumed effective control and sold out to Texaco, which, in turn sold out to ABC television. ABC's interest transformed ESPN from a local operation to a national network, reaching 34 million homes by 1984. This was the year David Stern became the NBA commissioner and Michael Jordan made his debut for Chicago Bulls. ESPN had held a contract with the NBA for the previous two years and had shown NCAA games from the start in 1979 – which had the effect of familiarizing tv fans with the players before they transferred to the pro game. Perhaps inadvertently, ESPN had hitched its wagon to the NBA star, which went into orbit over the next several years. In 1984, the ABC network bought out ESPN, though two years later the network itself was acquired by Capital Cities Communications, which, in turn, was absorbed into the Disney corporation in 1995. Hence ESPN became part of Disney.

By 1998, ESPN was taken by about 70 percent of all U.S. television-owning households; of the total televised sports, ESPN carried 23 percent. In addition, the network's reach extended to 160 different countries around the world; it provided services in 19 languages. In 1996, it set up a second ESPN channel specializing in news items; and, to complement its extensive tv coverage, started ESPN Radio. Since 2003, it has had an internet presence. In 2009, ESPN took advantage of the collapse of Setanta television, which held the rights to a number of English Premier League games, and acquired rights to screen live games, though not exclusively (BSkyB maintained its dominant position as the provider of the majority of games).

Credibility is always on the line when tv companies bid for sports. Such is the cultural power of sports that few major networks would dare risk cutting them from their schedules. And sports have prospered extravagantly as the tv money has flowed in. In fact, sports must look back at the 1950s and wonder what they were ever worried about. Even if crowds dwindled, there is enough media money to make it viable to play behind locked doors, in a purpose-built studio perhaps. The idea behind a sport designed by and for television must have been in the thoughts of ABC executives when they helped launch the AFL in 1960. But it took an Australian to turn this into actuality: a sport custom-built exclusively for a tv channel.

▇ MADE-FOR-TELEVISION

In 1976, Kerry Packer, the head of an Australian television company, offered the Australian Cricket Board (ACB) a contract for the exclusive rights to screen Australian cricket for five years. The offer was refused. Determined to push ahead and feature cricket on his tv channel, known as Nine Network (now "9"), Packer signed up 35 international class players and organized his own "rebel" tournament outside the auspices of any of the traditional governing organizations of cricket.

Few sports respect their own history as much as cricket: it is one of the oldest and most traditional games and, for most of its existence, worked carefully to retain links with its past. The Marylebone Cricket Club, or MCC, was established in London in 1787 and remains the guardian of one the oldest and most conservative games. It didn't allow women members until 1998.

Packer was not especially interested in an organization created in the same year the English started sending convicts to their new penal colony in Australia (they'd previously sent them to North America, but, after the American Revolution, 1775–83, this was no longer an option). Packer was a television man; he was interested in programs that drew audiences.

Horrified traditionalists watched as Packer dressed his players in brightly colored uniforms, scheduled evening games under floodlights, and introduced yellow cricket balls. He used eight cameras, some trained on players' faces, and several microphones strategically positioned to pick up the players' often-blasphemous comments. The games were played in a single day, using limited overs, its format being, as John Goldlust puts it, "unabashedly spectator oriented, geared towards providing entertainment, tight finishes, big hitting and aggressive play . . . ideally suited for television" (1987: 163).

The dramatic cricket Packer promoted was barely recognizable as the age-old pursuit of English gentlemen, but television fans watched it. After a nervous first season, viewing figures and attendances both rose, enabling Nine Network to attract more advertisers. Established governing organizations, including the MCC, opposed the wanton commercialism, but eventually capitulated in the face of the tournament's rising popularity.

In 1979, Packer's marketing subsidiary secured a 10-year contract to organize the sponsorship of official cricket. Packer's attempt to capture exclusive broadcasting rights succeeded and, by the mid-1980s, he had virtually taken control of Australian cricket.

Crowds continued to flock to the stadiums and, more importantly for Packer, tv audience ratings stayed healthy. The players earned more money, the governing organizations took substantial fees for broadcasting rights and the Nine Network increased its advertising revenue by selling more commercial time during the ordinarily quiet summer months. Those who still thought cricket should be played with a straight bat and a stiff upper lip were offended by the changes Packer had instigated, but there was no going back.

Packer acted as a catalyst, instigating changes that were to transform cricket from a sport that might be described as television-hostile (played over a maximum five days, often at a ponderous pace and frequently ending as draws) to a shorter and frequently explosive game that provided nail-biting finishes. One-day cricket did not replace the more conventional format: it coexisted with it. By the end of the century World Cup cricket was a well-established part of cricket's calendar. It was played over a day, with a white ball, with players dressed in various colors and was watched by television viewers all over the world. It was, as David Rowe puts it, "moulded well to the demands of television in terms of its structure and guaranteed result" (2004: 183).

The Packer case gave early evidence of how television could change a sport radically. Cricket was a game that had remained largely unchanged since 1787. Yet it could not resist the challenge of a tv magnate intent on fashioning the sport to his own broadcasting requirements. Today, the imperatives of television have pushed cricket to another dramatic variation, Twenty20, which is played, typically, over three hours. T20, as it's known, was better tailored to television than any previous version of the sport and managed to make even Packer's cricket staid by comparison. Paul Starick, of Adelaide's *Sunday Mail* described the opening of the Indian Premier League in April 2008: "A Bollywood carnival of jangling music, dazzling light shows and extravagantly clad performers . . . Amid the razzamatazz and glitz of a cricketing revolution, it was easy to lose sight of the circus in the middle" (April 20, 2008).

Rugby League's change was, in its own way, revolutionary: the terms of its 1996 television deal obliged the sport to dismantle a 100-year structure and switch to a summer schedule to comply with Rupert Murdoch's plans for a Rugby Super League. The new league was to include European and Australasian teams and culminate in play-offs that could be broadcast around the globe by Murdoch's many media networks. Rugby League agreed, underlining how commercial considerations can supersede those intrinsic to the sport itself.

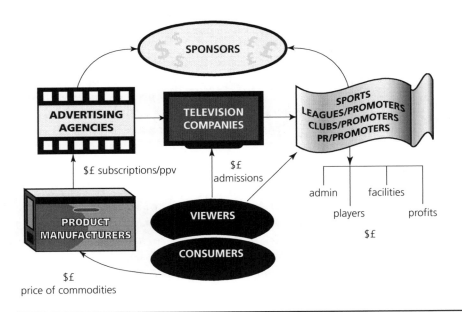

Figure 14.1 How we pay for televised sports

BOX 14.6 INDIAN PREMIER LEAGUE BY NUMBERS

$1.95bn: Cost to team owners to set up IPL.

$1bn: Sony Television and World Sport Group's contract for a 10-year television deal.

$122m: Cost of Mumbai Indians franchise, the most expensive team.

$54m: Sponsorship fee (over 5 years) paid by DLF, India's largest real estate developer.

$13.5m: Pepsi deal to be official IPL drink.

$1.55m: Bangalore Royal Challengers paid for Kevin Petersen at player auction (draft).

Lesser, but still significant changes have been instigated by television in other sports. For instance, the length of the NFL season was extended from 1990 after the signing of a $3.6 billion (£2.2 billion) contract. The reasoning behind it is spelled-out by Jerry Gorman and Kirk Calhoun in their *The Name of the Game: The business of sports*: "The plan for extension was to sell more advertising over a longer period, that space filled not by more games but by more televised games" (1994: 242).

The additional games, which were broadcast by the ESPN and TNT channels earned the NFL about $900 million. In the same year, the playoff format was changed to accommodate ABC television. The net effect was to double the tv network's payments to $225 million, according to Gorman and Calhoun; but "it all amounted to a serious strain on the trust and devotion of the fans" (1994: 242). Then again, fans take low priority when it comes to major issues such as these. As we have seen, the networks are sports' real customers – and advertisers their's.

Television's influence has not always been so obvious. Boxing's scaling down of championship fights from 15 to 12 rounds was motivated ostensibly by safety considerations, though there was little conclusive evidence that the serious injuries associated with boxing occurred in the final three rounds. A more probable explanation was that boxing changed to suit tv requirements. In its traditional form, a boxing match involved 15 3-minute rounds, 14 1-minute intervals, plus preamble and postfight interviews, yielding an awkward 70–75 minutes. Twelve rounds gave 47 minutes and, say, 13 minutes for padding, which fitted neatly into a 1-hour slot.

The Association of Tennis Professionals (ATP) implemented changes in 1994 that were even more clearly motivated by television's needs. It reduced the time allowed in preparing to serve by 5 seconds to 20 seconds, so speeding up the game. This followed the introduction of the tiebreak, which reduced the chances of protracted games that were difficult for tv to schedule. A repetition of the epic 5-hour, 12-minute, 112-game match between Pancho Gonzales and Charlie Pasarell in 1969 was rendered almost impossible. Though not quite: while it consisted of only 71 games, Fabrice Santoro's win over Arnaud Clément at the 2004 French Open took 6 hours, 33 minutes.

The ATP also loosened-up on it strictures concerning spectators: they could react freely and spontaneously and wander about during play, instead of sitting still and gasping "oohs" and "aahs" as at Wimbledon. Perhaps the biggest concession was that in allowing broadcasters to place microphones on the umpire's side of the court so that conversations between players and officials could be heard by a television audience.

The commercial imperatives of television have led to a proliferation of time-outs, which George Ritzer believes, "alter the nature of some sports, and [may] affect the outcome of a game." For Ritzer, this is just one instance of "the attempts to McDonaldize sports" (1998). Like fast-food chains, television emphasizes speed and quantity over quality. "In basketball this has taken the form of the 24-second clock for professionals and the 45-second clock for college athletes," writes Ritzer about initiatives designed to maximize points scoring. Ritzer notes other changes in sports, such as baseball's introduction of livelier balls, artificial turf that makes ground balls travel faster, outfield fences that are closer to the home plate and the AL's (American League's) designated hitter; all moves that make bigger scores probable.

BOX 14.7 THE CROWN JEWELS

These are sports events identified by the British government in 1998 as being of "national importance" and protected for live free-to-air transmission. The events were placed on two lists. A list: Football's World Cup and European Championship finals matches, the FA Cup final and Scottish Cup final; horseracing's Grand National, and Derby; Wimbledon finals; the Challenge Cup final and the Rugby Union World Cup final. The B list was partially protected: edited highlights had to be available free-to-air. In addition to Wimbledon highlights, the list included Rugby World Cup finals preliminary matches, Six Nations games involving the home countries, the Commonwealth Games, the IAAF World Athletics Championships, the Cricket World Cup final, semis and home country games, the Ryder Cup, and the Open Championship. After the events were protected, digital and satellite media and the internet transformed the landscape of television.

Television's influence can extend beyond the competition itself and into the ambience. Darts started life as a late nineteenth-century pub pastime. It took place in a confined space, allowed tight shots of the players' faces and generated plenty of alcohol-fueled passion. Potential sponsors and advertisers became uncomfortable about the habitual smoking and drinking in the crowd and made their concerns known to the British television company, which in turn approached the British Darts Organization (BDO). Spectators and players alike were instructed by the BDO to refrain from their normal activities in front of the cameras. Considering that the sport's origins lie in pubs, the change must have been tantamount to sacrilege to die-hard fans.

With very few exceptions, televised sports have changed as a result of their relations with tv companies. There are critics for whom "television is a corrupting parasite that latches onto the host body, sport, and draws life support from it while giving nothing back in return," as Michael R. Real characterizes their view (1998: 16). The "parasitism" of sports involves the various changes of rules, schedules and formats instigated by television. It must sadden those who mourn the days when sports were real "sports." There again, as Sut Jhally points out: "This seems to imply that before the influence of the media there was something that was pure sports" (1989: 80).

It's worth expanding on Jhally's remark. After all, there is no such thing as natural, unadulterated, pure sports. Roone Arledge, who inspired ABC's sports coverage, often defended his network's use of synthetic sports by reminding critics that sports were not delivered by god with rules inscribed on tablets of stone. All sports, even those in Ancient Greece, are in some way artificial. Teams of firefighters competing over how many buckets of water they can carry from point A to point Z is no more or less of a pure sport than 11 men trying to move an inflated ball in the opposite direction to another 11 men, or 8 women running hell-for-leather along a strip of track. The comparison reminds us that television has not so much corrupted or even transformed sports as extended and reshaped them.

The change is not always so dramatic as many writers seem to think: since the 1940s there has been a drip-by-drip transition, some sports gradually changing from one state to another. Grand, sprawling, majestic sports, like cricket and golf, no less than the cramped, frenetic basketball, have been changed through their commerce with television, but also just to stay popular with new generations of fans who demand instant gratification. As previous chapters have shown us, all sports are evolving entities, anyway – with or without tv. Rules, durations, start times, methods of evaluation, and so on have been changing for decades, centuries even. Sports never stand still. Television has imposed change rather than wait for it to happen. And audiences have responded (see Table 14.1).

IS WATCHING TELEVISION A CREATIVE ACT?

Sport, as we now know, is a way of ensuring audience ratings stay healthy and of keeping the advertisers' money rolling in. From the point of view of the television executive, that is. From the point of view of the consumer, televised sports is something very different. It's a form of entertainment that allows the fan to satisfy personal desires, pursue a type of fulfillment and even reach a form of self-actualization, if writers like Mark Gottdiener are to be believed. In his book *The Theming of America: Dreams, visions and commercial spaces*, Gottdiener argues that, far from being passive consumers conditioned by advertising into behaving as producers wish, television viewers are engaged in "the creative act of consumption" (1997: 158).

So far, I have looked at the industrial processes of production and distribution, the demands of advertisers and the money involved in connecting the people who

Table 14.1 Big fight-earners

In	$m	Out	$m
TELEVISION COMPANY	1 million worldwide ppv units @ $45 each =	45	Promoter's fee	20
			Other staff costs	5
			Administration	4
			Production costs including communications network, plant and equipment	4
			Advertising and marketing	3
			Commissions	2.5
			Overseas partner services	2
EARNINGS BEFORE TAX $5.4 million	TOTAL	45	TOTAL	40.5
PROMOTER	Fee from television	15	Boxers' purses	28
	Ticket sales	13	Publicity	2
	Site fee	6	Legal fees	2.5
	Sponsorship	2.5	Sanctioning fee to WBA or other governing organization	1.5
	Merchandise	2.5	Insurance	0.5
EARNINGS BEFORE TAX $4.5 million	TOTAL	39	TOTAL	34.5
BOXER	Champion's purse ($9m for challenger)	16	Manager's commission @33% of gross income	5.9
	4% of ppv gross	1.4	Trainer's commission @10 % of purse	1.79
	33% of merchandise sales	0.5	Training expenses	2.5
			Other operating expenses, including insurance cover	0.5
EARNINGS BEFORE TAX $7.21 million	TOTAL	17.9	TOTAL	10.69

Notes:
- The site fee is paid to the promoter for staging the fight at, for example, the MGM Grand in Las Vegas, the casino owners estimating that the interest generated by a big promotion will draw gamblers, who will collectively lose more than the site fee.
- A manager may take up to 33 percent commission from a boxer's gross purse (25 percent in Britain) and a trainer usually 10 percent; payments to other aides are included in the training expenses in the above example. A big promoter, such as Don King, may also manage one of the main boxers, so that his make is even greater than represented here.
- Financially, the risk is taken by the tv company: if the promotion fails to sell through the ppv agency, the promoter and boxers are still guaranteed fixed fees (though some boxers occasionally prefer to negotiate a commission-only deal).
- The figures represent a typical world title promotion rather than a megabuck heavyweight extravaganza in which the main boxers might split anything up to $80 million.

want to sell commodities with the people they want to buy them. Now, I want to turn to the consumers' perspectives. They too have changed over the years, perhaps most dramatically with the onset of television.

For decades, tv fans were led to believe that they received televised sports for free. All they had to do was buy a tv set (and a license if they lived in Britain), switch on and sit back. It seemed as if it didn't cost them a penny. In fact, they have always had to pay one way or another, even before the days of subscription television. It was usually by a few more pennies on, for example, the retail price of a bar of soap, the manufacturers of which advertise their products in the breaks of sports programs. Or, a few more dollars or pounds on the sticker price of a car. But they still had to pay. The cost of buying the broadcasting rights are built into the price the customer pays for all sorts of products. But, fans surely get something back in return. Would the typical armchair fan really get annoyed when reminded 0.5 percent of the cost of a car went towards the car firm's advertising budget, part of which was spent on placing commercials in the spots at halftime in big football games?

Maybe not; but they would demand something special in return. Sport in the raw is insufficient for the tv viewer: he or she wants it packaged and presented, just like any other commodity. After all, when viewers are asked to pay for the product, as increasingly seems to be the case, they want more than roving-eye-style presentation. In sports, the action doesn't speak for itself: it needs the direction and narration that produce drama. If you disagree, try hitting the mute button on your remote control next time you watch sports and see how long you can take it.

There is now a mature second generation of people reared on televised sports, the kind of people who prefer waiting for DVDs instead of going to the movies and playing computer games at home instead of playing ball in the park. Attendance at sports events must seem pretty one-dimensional to them. Some will insist the tension in the atmosphere of a packed stadium or arena can never be even remotely approximated by watching at home. Yet you can almost hear the groans: "Where are the captions and statistics?" "I missed that piece of action; how about a replay?" "I'd like to see that from a different angle, or slowed-down, or explained to me by an informed commentator."

Expectations and perceptions of sports have changed, as have patterns of viewing. Television has gently encouraged us to *read* sports differently: we may be watching the same piece of action as our grandparents, but we won't necessarily interpret it in the same way. We're also likely to watch more of it, if only because of the volume on the air, or through the cables. Television's facilities for replays allow us to relax our concentration. Missing a touchdown, a goal, a knockdown, a homer, or a hole-in-one is not a disaster when we can see it reviewed repeatedly from different vantage points. This, plus the comments, summaries and statistics that accompany the action, encourages a certain detachment and predilection for analysis.

Wu interprets this as what she, following Pierre Bourdieu, calls "a sports media 'habitus'" – that is, the unconscious patterning of everyday behaviour" (2008: 157). She means that we receive so much information, regularly and cyclically through the media that we have become completely habituated to it. We treat it as normal, predictable, almost second nature. Watching competitions on television has coagulated into a set of dispositions, practices, and, crucially, perceptions

Today's sports-watcher sits like an Argus, assimilating all manner of information, audio as well as video. One hesitates before suggesting it, but the pre- and post-event features have all but supplanted the actual competition. Perceiving and analyzing have become integral parts of the practice of watching televised sports and the better-informed viewer can cast a clinical eye on proceedings. The irony is: they can do so with less play-by-play concentration on the activity itself.

Perhaps I generalize too much: a 1998 study by Lawrence Wenner and Walter Ganz found that: "Many sports viewers are active, discerning, engaged and passionate." Yet: "Because sports spectators come to the viewing situation with different levels of sporting interest, knowledge and experience, they look for and receive different benefits from the experience" (1998: 250).

Beyond the "engaged" viewer, there are those who value the social dimensions of watching sports, those who use it as an emotionally cathartic blowout and those who just "use sports viewing to kill time." While Wenner and Ganz report on "The television sports viewing experience," they actually discern a series of different perceptions and experiences and for different sports.

For all the different orientations, there are basic competencies that viewers bring to sports shows and rewards they take from them. Whether or not this fulfillment measures up to Gottdiener's self-actualization is not clear, but what *is* clear is that we shouldn't underestimate the amount of critical intellectual work that gets done when watching televised sports, nor the appreciable gratification derived from the experience. All this suggests that, when we're asked to pay more for sport to be delivered to our home, we'll grimace, complain, and then pay up. And, it's certain that we'll have to pay more directly for our sports.

In the salad days between the 1960s and 1980s, sports were as valuable a commodity as television executives could have imagined: relatively inexpensive (no salaries or heavy production costs) and very watchable, as the ratings bore out. Some sports were elevated to international stature as a result of television. It was a match made in heaven. Now, the relationship is much more conflict-torn and the possibility of a divorce looms.

Established television networks have sought a bigger interest in the cable/satellite systems, giving rise to a complex multi-tiered mesh of alliances, often between rival media corporations. In the United States, all the networks have not only cable interests, but pay per view (ppv) links. As major sports find tv money harder to come by, they may buy into cable/satellite themselves or extend the kind of shared risk relationships. Whatever the future, we can anticipate much more interlocking between governing bodies and media groups in sports, rather than straightforward buying and selling of rights. The big leagues and big clubs will want more say in their own destinies. And this means we, the consumers, the fans, the television-watching public, are going to have to pay more for our sports.

Since the 1940s, tv viewers have expected sports for no more than the nominal charge of a few pennies on the price of an advertised product, or the cost of a license in the British case. Sports have been as much a part of television's stock-in-trade as

▮ BOX 14.8 PAY PER VIEW (PPV)

The first ppv event was in 1980 when the Sugar Ray Leonard–Roberto Duran fight drew 170,000 customers who paid $15 (£10) each. Rock concerts and operas followed sporadically, until the advent of TVKO, an agency owned by Time Warner, which also owned HBO. TVKO struggled to establish itself as an alternative, more selective, way of viewing until 1991 when it sold the Evander Holyfield–George Foreman fight to 1.45 million homes at $34.93 (£22). The Mike Tyson–Peter McNeeley fight in 1995 was an even greater success, going into 1.52 million households and grossing $63 million (£42 million) in the United States alone ($96 million worldwide). By comparison, less than a tenth of this number chose to buy a Guns 'n Roses concert for $24.95 (£15.60) in 1992 and just 34,000 homes took a Pavarotti concert in 1991. NBC's 1992 "Olympic Triplecast," a 15-day event was the biggest disaster to date: out of a potential 20 million homes equipped with the receiving equipment only 165,000 took the whole deal, with 35,000 taking single days. By contrast, the 2007 Oscar De La Hoya–Floyd Mayweather Jr fight broke ppv records with receipts of $120 million. De La Hoya was something of a ppv phenomenon, generating a total of $610.6 million on 12.6 million buys for 18 fights, the last of which was in 2008. While boxing continues to be a ppv staple, other events are important, particularly WWE's "Wrestlemania" and UFC, which generates about $200m per year through ppv.

soaps, news, and cop shows. But we have already seen some of the grander sports events either being lured away from the terrestrial networks by competing cable/satellite companies or passed over to the ppv services of the media giants themselves. The ppv route has already been explored by boxing and English soccer, with promoters and clubs sharing some of the risks. It's likely that other major sports will pursue similar packages with media giants rather than just selling rights in bundles.

Digital, or DIRECTV, signal ways ahead, with viewers exercising more individual choice in the market: they can select not only camera angles, replays and so on, but also actual events. And, of course, the investments several television groups have made in the internet suggest that the day may not be far off when we can download programs as swiftly and efficiently as we open our email. If this is so, it will be convenient for the consumer, but profitable for the program providers: viewers will pay for their chosen sports directly. There again, in sports, nothing is for nothing. It never has been.

Playing for Keeps: Sport, the media and society by John Goldlust is still an intriguing historical document, analyzing, among other things, Kerry Packer's revolutionary contract with cricket, which Goldlust argues changed the entire complexion of sports (Longman, 1987). For other historical accounts, see: *Games and Sets: The changing face of sport on television* by Steven Barnett (British Film Institute, 1990); *Sports for Sale: Television, money and the fans* by David Klatell and Norman Marcus (Oxford University Press, 1988); *Television and National Sport: The United States and Britain* by Joan Chandler (University of Illinois Press, 1988); *In its Own Image: How television has transformed sport* by Benjamin Rader (Collier-Macmillan, 1984).

The Theming of America: Dreams, visions and commercial spaces by Mark Gottdiener (Westview Press, 1997), while not specifically about sports, makes several interesting points about "the powerful compulsions of the consumer society that pressure people to make certain choices in the marketplace"; twenty-first-century sports would qualify as one such compulsion.

Representing Sport by Rod Brookes (Arnold, 2002) is a short examination of "the cultural and social significance of the increasingly important role of sport within a global media industry" and can profitably be read in conjunction with "Sport and the media" by Garry Whannel in *Handbook of Sports Studies* edited by Jay Coakley and Eric Dunning (Sage, 2000). The dated, but still valuable *MediaSport* edited by Lawrence Wenner (Routledge, 1998) contains the studies by Whitson and Wenner/Ganz referenced earlier in this chapter.

Sport, Culture and the Media: The unruly trinity, 2nd edition, by David Rowe (Open University Press, 2004) is the most comprehensive treatment of "the sport–media nexus," examining the production and content of mainstream media sport; the same writer has edited a companion volume, *Critical Readings: Sport, culture and the media* (Open University Press, 2004).

"Global and local influences on English Rugby League" by David Denham (in *Sociology of Sport Journal*, vol. 21, 2004) discusses how Rugby League was globalized largely by News Corporation, Rupert Murdoch's media conglomerate: "Media-led commercialization was seen as a globalizing force that offered the game more income, marketing expertise, and television exposure."

"Sport and the media" by Ping Wu in *Sport Sociology* edited by Peter Craig and Paul Beedie (Learning Matters, 2008) argues that we have cut a Faustian bargain with the media: "the price we pay for watching live sports broadcasting on television or online in the comfort of our homes (or the camaraderie of the pub) is that we give up our own authority of observing to a considerable degree and only see what the media allow us to see."

ASSIGNMENT

Imagine the kind of futuristic scenario depicted at the start of this chapter – but with a difference. Major sports have come under the total control of the mass media. So much so that there is no need for "live" audiences and events are viewed only via the screen. When people refer to the spectators, they mean the people watching at home. What were once mass open-air sports, like football and baseball, are now played behind locked doors. Indoor sports are performed in studios. How realistic is this? Support your argument with evidence from current trends.

Planet Murdoch

KEY ISSUES

▌ How come the most powerful man in sport isn't interested in sport?

▌ What is vertical integration?

▌ When did the professionalization of sports begin?

▌ Where can you go to escape televised sport?

▌ Why does sport follow the logic of the marketplace?

▌ . . . and how did UFC become a billion dollar sport?

LEVERAGE

The media mogul Paul Desmond likened him to Darth Vader, the fearsome cyborg from the *Star Wars* saga. Political journalist Alexander Cockburn described him as a "global tyrant." The usually sober *Columbia Journalism Review* portrayed him as a scorpion – the fabled one who stung the frog who did him a good turn. Not much love in these sobriquets, is there?

Rupert Murdoch started the twenty-first century as the most powerful person in sports. There were contenders, such as Robert Iger, the chief executive of Disney (of which ESPN is part), and Jeff Zucker, the president of NBC Universal (which holds television rights to many major sports events). But no one came close to Murdoch; his worldwide influence in almost every facet of sports was unique. No single person had ever exercised such power over sports.

The irony is that Murdoch had no particular passion for sports. A glance at his career reveals that he only took an active interest in sport in the 1990s, when he realized that he could use it, as he put it as a "battering ram" to smash down people's doors and install his television services. It was a dark ages sort of metaphor (when was the last time anybody used a battering ram?) but it revealed Murdoch's purposes: sport was strictly a means of selling tv subscriptions.

Over a 35-year period, Murdoch assembled the most formidable combination of sports clubs, production operations, and media outlets the world had ever known.

Through his media empire, he had the kind of leverage "undreamed of by bush-leaguers like William Randolph Hearst," as Thomas Frank puts it in his "The new gilded age" (1997a: 25). The meshing of media and sports into a combined network was either the masterstroke of a genius or the work of a megalomaniac—probably a bit of both.

It is, of course, no accident that Murdoch conquered both domains of sports and television. At the cusp of the twenty-first century, the two had become so organically attached that virtually any media entrepreneur had interests in sports, almost by default. Sports and the media became convergent fields: Murdoch's ability to unite them into a single business established him as the single most important player in the entire sports business – and I use the term to embrace the whole province of sports.

But, how was it possible for a person such as Murdoch to rise to a position of virtually unrivaled power in sports? What were the conditions under which he rose? And what would sports be like if Murdoch didn't exist? Would someone else have taken his place?

To answer these questions, we need to backtrack to a time when sports were exactly that – sports, not businesses. The introduction of money into pursuits or pastimes that were once played for enjoyment only set in motion a series of processes that changed sports irreversibly and, some would say, abominably. Money corrupts; that much we know. Some misty-eyed romantics will always complain that the filthy stuff has corrupted the ideals that were once integral to sports. Others will point out that the commercialization of sports is only part of an inexorable movement that has affected every aspect of contemporary culture. If people enjoy watching and appreciating something and, in some circumstances, are willing to pay to do so, then there will always be others eager to profit from their willingness.

Murdoch is but one of countless entrepreneurs, competitors, managers, and other personnel associated with sports who have profited handsomely. Where there has been a demand and a raw supply, there has been no shortage of enterprising people with ideas on how to connect the two and appropriate the surplus. This is a business approach to sports and one that conflicts with the cardinal rules of sport as they were originally laid out.

THE RISE OF THE PROFESSIONALS

All sports that are watchable have potential for commercial exploitation. An after-dinner game of snooker played in private without even a side-bet would not have this potential. Nor would a one-on-one basketball matchup in the privacy of a high-school gym. Take the snooker players John Higgins and Ronnie O'Sullivan and transport them to Sheffield's Crucible, or the ball players Kobe Bryant and Lebron James and pitch them together at LA's Staples Center and they become spectator sports. If contests can draw crowds, they qualify as spectator sports. And, if they are spectator sports, then people are usually prepared to pay for the privilege of watching.

It's perfectly possible to have mass spectator sports without the taint of money that many argue pollutes the central values of competition. The NCAA is strictly amateur and celebrates this fact, as does AIBA – International Boxing Association. Both organizations invoke a conception of sport as an activity that's performed not for money but for, as the name implies, love (from the Latin *amatorious,* "pertaining to love*")*. Fondness for the activity itself or the satisfaction drawn from winning fairly and squarely are the motivating principles, though, strictly speaking, participation should be regarded as more important than achievement.

Nowadays, "amateur" is almost a pejorative term, implying a lack of refinement or clumsiness – the opposite of professional. In the eighteenth and nineteenth centuries, the reverse was the case and the amateur symbolized all that was good in sport; while the professional was despised as a vulgarian who competed just for money. "Sports had as their ideal aim the production of pleasure," write Eric Dunning and Ken Sheard, "an immediate emotional state rather than some ulterior end, whether of a material or other kind" (1979: 153–4).

It was regarded as "unsportsmanlike" and "ungentlemanly" to show elation in victory and disappointment in defeat. Compare that with today's response to a touchdown or a goal. British public schools and universities were the wellsprings of the amateur ethos and there was concern at the prospect of the dignified ballgames practiced at Rugby, Harrow, and other upper-class schools, being copied by the lower classes, whose desire to win rather than just compete amounted to a defilement.

"Subsidized" players who were reimbursed for work time lost while playing, or who accepted straight cash for their services were a threatening presence in some sports, especially rugby. Amateurs could not devote so much of their time to their game as professionals and would be hard-pressed to maintain their superiority. There was also the suspicion that dangling a carrot in front of players would encourage them not only to play harder and forget the joy of it all, but to raise their ability levels through training. In the eyes of the nineteenth-century amateur, this was unfair: it produced a competitive advantage for those who committed themselves to self-improvement. Sports were meant to be about enjoyment, whereas "to train for sport and take it too seriously was," as Dunning and Sheard observe, "tantamount to transforming it into work and, hence to destroying its essence" (1979: 148).

Of course, sports did eventually become like work: by the second half of the nineteenth century, cricket and other ballgames, prizefighting and pedestrianism (the equivalent of competitive walking) paid contestants. Sports that were played by affluent classes, like golf, were rich enough to employ coaches; while other sports could pay expenses simply because they were popular enough to attract paying spectators. This caused the amateur gentlemen to confound the trend toward professionalism with greater fervor. Mass gatherings of working-class spectators, some of them partisan, posed what was seen as a threat to public order. So much so that such assemblies were outlawed in some circumstances.

Spectators didn't benefit from sports in the same way as participants. Quite the contrary: they suffered by degenerating into an excitable, amoral mass. At least, that is what the affluent classes thought. The gentlemen amateurs' reaction to spectator sports presents a type of metaphor for the changes that were occurring in society generally. The industrial working class was getting organized and showing signs of cohesion and solidarity in the face of employers who were worried by the prospect of having their authority challenged from below. Class antagonism, or sheer prejudice, manifested itself in several notable incidents, all designed to cocoon the exclusive elite of gentlemen from others. As well as the landowning English aristocracy, gentlemen would have included *nouveaux riches*, merchants, physicians, lawyers, politicians, and others with newfound prestige rather than inherited wealth.

Let's segue to an actual incident that illustrates the class tension of the period. In 1846 at Lancaster, in the northwest of England, there was a dispute following a Manchester crew's victory in the Borough Cup rowing competition. It was alleged that two of the crew, a cabinetmaker and a bricklayer, were not acceptable entrants because "they were not known as men of property." The debate continued until, in 1853, when the category of "gentlemen amateur" was distinguished from just plain amateur, for the Lancaster Rowing Club's purposes. Other clubs followed suit, stipulating that those who worked as mechanics, artisans, or laborers would not be eligible for competition as their employment, being physical in nature, equipped them with advantages.

This may have seemed a subterfuge to members of the working class, but it was perpetuated by the Amateur Athletic Association which, in 1866, officially defined an amateur as a person who had either never competed (1) in open competition, (2) for prize money, (3) for admission money, (4) with professionals, (5) never taught or assisted in the pursuit of athletic exercises, or (6) was not a mechanic, artisan, or laborer. Condition (6) was removed in 1880, but the intent of this typical pronouncement was clear: to exclude working-class competitors and so stave off the evils of professionalism. This applied only to track and field; in several other sports professionalism looked unstoppable.

By the 1880s, rugby and soccer became so popular, especially in the English north and midland areas, that spectators were prepared to pay hard cash to watch organized games between the best players. The money made it possible to pay those players. The Rugby Union was intractable in its opposition to this and, by 1895, had effectively forced the formation of a professional organization, which became the Rugby League in 1922. Soccer prevaricated, but, by 1885, had agreed to a controlled professionalism, with a maximum wage limit (what we'd call a cap today) and stipulations about the movement of players between clubs.

This was a similar restriction to baseball's "reserve clause" which prevented out-of-contract players moving on and depressed salaries overall. Baseball itself had much the same matrix as cricket and rugby, but, as Peter Levine points out, in his *A. G. Spalding and the Rise of Baseball*: "Almost from the outset, however, this amateur gentlemen's game was transformed" and baseball became one of the first professional spectator sports (1985). In 1858, fans were charged 50¢ admission to watch a three game championship series between local New York teams. In 1862, enclosures were specially built to accommodate paying fans and exclude those who wanted to watch games for free. As gate fees went up, so players began to reap some benefits, though their salaries were to prove a source of dispute for many years.

The subject of Levine's book, A. G. Spalding, was instrumental in the early development of baseball. Spalding, an American, had no respect for the English gentlemen's customs and approached baseball as if it were an industry – and he a captain of that industry. Spalding was puzzled by the amateur ethos: "I was not able to understand how it could be right to pay an actor, or a singer, or an instrumentalist for entertaining the public, and wrong to pay a ball player for doing the same thing in his way" (quoted in Levine).

BOX 15.1 A. G. SPALDING (1876–1915)

Born in Byron, Illinois, Spalding was the man who started the first sports goods manufacturing and retail industry. In 1876, Spalding opened what was then a unique store specializing in sports goods. Spalding's Baseball and Sporting-goods Emporium was based in Chicago and stocked baseball uniforms and equipment. The firm also manufactured baseball bats, croquet equipment, ice skates, and fishing tackle. Capitalizing on the cycling craze, Spalding published an *Official Cycling Guide* featuring pictures of bicycles, sweaters, and shoes, which he also sold. He anticipated later trends to sign players to endorsement deals and signed three pro cyclists to a contract that required them to use his cycles. Spalding, who had played professional baseball, had several other business interests, though his name is forever linked with recognizing and exploiting the demand for sporting goods and apparel.

While there's no evidence to suggest he studied the life of P. T. Barnum (1810–91), Spalding seems to have adopted much of the showbusiness pioneer's philosophy, especially about how people were always prepared to pay to witness entertaining spectacles.

By 1910 – five years before Spalding's death – attendance had soared to 7.25 million, though players' salaries were still kept artificially low, averaging under $2,500. In Britain, spectators were flocking to sports and stadiums were built to accommodate them. Professionalism was well established and organizers and promoters openly exploited the business opportunities offered by sports. Boxing, for long a pursuit of professionals at some level, whether in fairground shows or streetfighting, evolved into two coexisting organizations, amateur and professional, with boxers transferring from the former to the latter. Other sports refused to condone professionalism. Remember: this was a time before television, or even radio – the first commercial radio station in the United States started broadcasting in 1920s, from Pittsburgh.

Prosperous gentlemen of New York, concerned over professionalism, helped organize the National Association of Amateur Athletes of America in 1868. This became the Amateur Athletic Association in 1888. Intercollegiate sports, which gained in currency during the 1880s, were very much amateur affairs and kept a safe distance from the dishonorable baseball leagues. As association football had emerged as primarily an upper-class sport, which was appropriated by the English working class, so American football began life as a derivative of rugby played in the main by sons of the wealthy during their university years. The Intercollegiate Athletic Association (IAA) was formed in 1906 in response to an early-century crisis in college football: players were "moonlighting," playing for money under assumed names. The IAA was a precursor of the NCAA (National Collegiate Athletic Association) which was formed to protect amateurism and regulate college sports.

American football's career was not unlike soccer's, early professional outfits growing out of factory teams and cultivating a working-class following. The Indian Packing Company, of Green Bay, Wisconsin, had its own team in the first decade of the twentieth century; as did the Staley Starch Company, of Decatur, Illinois. Players were paid about $50 per week and given time off to train. In 1920, both companies affiliated their teams to a new organization that also harbored teams from New York and Washington. The teams evolved into the Packers, Bears, Giants, and Redskins respectively. Quite soon it was possible for the teams to divorce themselves from their industrial backgrounds and become independent employers: players who had learnt their skills at colleges could earn a decent living once their years of study were over. This seamless transition from university to pro club has been a feature of American football ever since, the draft being brought into play in 1936 (there is no equivalent in European sports).

Some sports were slower than others to accept the inevitability of professionalism. Tennis, for instance, adamantly refused to allow professionals into its prestigious competitions until 1968 when it went "open." From that point, players like Rod Laver, who had previously turned pro and been barred, reintegrated with amateurs whom they dominated so overwhelmingly that amateurism vanished from top levels over the next several years. Track and field for long assumed the ostrich position, burying its head in the sand despite widespread knowledge of "shamateurism" with athletes accepting generous gifts and exaggerated expenses for their services. In 1983, the International Amateur Athletics Federation (IAAF) accepted reality but insisted that payments should go via a subvention into a trust fund and be dispensed later to the athlete. By the end of the century, there were millions to be earned in both sports. Rugby was the last of the major international sports to allow professionalism when it went open in 1995. There are no longer any major sports that remain totally amateur.

SPORTS ENTREPRENEURS: FROM FIGG TO TURNER

In some dark and distant age, an enterprising witness to a contest noticed a crowd react excitedly to the sight of competition and thought: "Lo and behold! The gathered masses act as if 'twas them joined in battle!"

Inspired by this, the first sports entrepreneur would have brought the same contestants together again, but this time charging a fee for watching – the assumption being that the pleasure taken in just observing was worth a small amount. So, the sports business was started.

No one is officially credited with being the first person to spot the potential for earning money from sports. James Figg was one of the first to establish an organization to exploit the potential when he opened his Amphitheatre in London, in 1743. Figg attracted large crowds to watch his combat events, which were arranged on a regular basis and supplied him with a successful business, as we noted in Chapter 4 His concept was adopted from that of the ancient Romans, except that his motive was merely to take a profit rather than entertain plebeians with gory extravaganza. Figg's customers had mixed motives: to identify with and cheer on their favorite, to extract vicarious pleasure from watching, to wager, or just to meet other members of the "fancy," as patrons of prizefighting were collectively known (possibly an early form of the word "fan"). This reflects much the same mixture of impulses of fans today.

The correlation between high-caliber athletes and large crowds would not have been lost on early promoters. Figg's natural successors were the prizefight organizers of America in the 1800s. Some states, such as Massachusetts, outlawed prizefighting and this prompted organizers to stage illicit contests behind locked doors with a small, invited crowd. In his history of boxing *Beyond the Ring*, Jeffrey Sammons discovers that the first unofficial world heavyweight championship between Paddy Ryan and Joe Goss, in 1880, was "fought in virtual secrecy at Colliers, West Virginia." Sammons explains: "Organizers chose the tiny Brooks County town for its proximity to the Ohio and Pennsylvania state lines: if raided by hostile law officers, participants and followers could scatter across the border to escape arrest" (1988: 6).

In the same period, Richard Kyle Fox, an Irish migrant who was scratching a living by writing about events such as oyster-opening and one-legged dancing competitions, ventured into promoting events that he could then write about for local newspapers. In 1881, he had a chance encounter with John L. Sullivan, a prizefighter, who, so folklore had it, spurned Fox's offer to promote him. Sullivan went on to become the most famous athlete of his day and Fox's determination to secure his services or ruin him drove him to the position of American sports' first major promoter, offering either purses (fixed payments) or percentages of gate receipts to fighters. By the mid-1890s, top pugilists fought for what were then enormous purses of thousands of dollars. Sullivan is known to have charged in the region of $25,000 per championship fight (more than £9,000 in the 1890s) – remember, pro baseball players averaged only a tenth of this amount per year by 1910.

The legalization of prizefighting in New York in 1920 opened up new commercial possibilities for sports entrepreneurs. Sammons notes that, in 1922 alone, gate receipts in New York state totaled $5 million (in those days, about £1.8 million), a sum that made some conclude presciently that boxing was "an industry, financed by banks, and licensed and supervised by state laws and officials just as banking and insurance" (quoted in Sammons, 1988: 66).

If this was so, then boxing was a prototype for other sports. Opportunistic entrepreneurs were key agents in the process of establishing sports along business lines. Unquestionably, the most visionary was George "Tex" Rickard who promoted all but one heavyweight title fight that resulted in a new champion from the reign of Jack Johnson to that of Gene Tunney and whose elaborate publicity stunts and gargantuan promotions (regularly attracting 100,000+ spectators, with receipts of nearly $1.9 million for one show alone in 1926) established him as *the* sports promoter of his era.

Allegations that many of Rickard's contests were not only run as but actually *were* showbusiness events complete with scripts and stage directions were commonplace and drew comparisons with the above-mentioned master showman and his contemporary P. T. Barnum. But, the controversy only added to Rickard's notoriety and he was able to exploit the growing enthusiasm for sports, which featured not only combatants but a sense of occasion – an atmosphere that drew together the blue-collar and the plutocracy, the anonymous and the famous.

Rickard's promotions were huge but occasional extravaganzas. The market for everyday pro sports was also buoyant. Baseball's National League (NL) was having to stave off the challenges of several rival leagues which were prepared to undercut it with lower admission prices. The most formidable of these was the Western League, which later became the American League (AL). In 1902, the AL attracted 2.2 million fans to its games, compared to the 1.7 million who attended NL games. A truce was signed in January 1903, and this agreement established the framework of what became Major League Baseball (MLB). By the 1930s, baseball had become America's most popular sport, regularly attracting five-figure crowds. In the midst of economic depression, star players, like Babe Ruth, were able to command staggering salaries of $80,000.

▊ BOX 15.2 TEX RICKARD (1870–1929)

Born in Kansas City, Missouri, 1870, died January 6, 1929, Miami Beach, Florida, George Lewis "Tex" Rickard was one of the most important figures in the commercialization of sport. He promoted Jack Dempsey, world heavyweight champion from 1919 to 1926, and attracted the first $1 million gate (i.e. the total receipts from ticket sales). He also owned a National Hockey League franchise, the New York Americans, which started in 1926, but later folded. Rickard's business partner in many of his ventures was Jess McMahon, grandfather of Vince McMahon, of World Wrestling Entertainment (WWE).

The big-earning athletes were able to command such money not simply because they had more talent than their colleagues, but because (1) they had market appeal; and (2) they were surrounded by entrepreneurs who knew how to capitalize on that appeal. Promoters and owners of ball clubs were about as philanthropic in the 1930s as they are today. In the mid-1970s, Jonathan Brower's research into the subject concluded that they are "neither accustomed to nor comfortable with losing money in business ventures" (1976: 15).

They were – and are – in sports to make money; to them competition was – and is – business. Not surprisingly, promoters and owners have run sports organizations as if they were any other business, the only problem being that many ventures fail to make money. Ball clubs in particular are not typically great investments, though, of course there is great prestige and a certain celebrity status that attaches to owners. Ask Wayne Huizinga or George Steinbrenner; or Victor Kiam, owner of Remington, who apparently liked the New York Patriots so much that, in 1988, he bought the club. "He saw the acquisition as a good way to draw attention himself and to Remington," suggest Jerry Gorman and Kirk Calhoun, who quote Kiam: "I felt that with any exposure I got, there would be some falloff benefit for Remington" (1994: 30).

English football clubs continue to exert an irresistible pull on the rich. Witness Roman Abramovich's purchase of Chelsea FC in 2003. *Forbes* ranked him as the 15th-richest person in the world, estimating the Russian's wealth in 2009 to be $8.5 billion, or £5.3 billion, meaning that the club's yearly losses would not be a major headache. Think of someone with £53,000 in his savings account, who gives £1 per year to his favorite charity. Dr Sulaiman Al-Fahim, an Abu Dhabi entrepreneur representing a member of that state's royal family, paid £210 million for Manchester City FC in 2008, without any pretense of profit motive. He acquired the club, presumably, for similar reasons to those of the mysterious connoisseur who paid $160,000 (£100,000) for a bottle of 1787 vintage Chateau Lafite, or the art collector who forked out $106.5 million (£70 million) for Pablo Picasso's 1932 masterpiece *Nude, Green Leaves and Bust,* or the aficionado who, in 2010, paid $1 million (£646,000) for a copy of the launch edition of *Action Comics,* dated June 1938, cover price 10 cents, which has the distinction of being the first publication to feature Superman.

Whatever the motives of promoters, owners or any other entrepreneur in sports, their impact has been to transform sports into a unique collective enterprise. Why unique? Because sports might have veered toward but never became pure entertainment. Its packaging and merchandising may be indistinguishable, but sports' abiding appeal lies in their essential unpredictability. The outcome of a competition is never known, at least nearly never. During the 1950s, organized crime had such a stranglehold on North American boxing that the results of a great many title fights were prescribed. Promoters of sports events and owners or chairs of clubs are integral parts of a landscape filled with sponsors, agents, and hard-boiled marketing executives, all seeking to manipulate competitive sports to their own requirements. Yet, they are not simple conveyers of public demand: they originate the demand, shape it, manage it and, occasionally, destroy it.

Market forces being what they are, it's unlikely that sports would have grown into the massive business it now is without the assistance of the media. As things transpired, sports entrepreneurs did enjoy such assistance. Newspapers, radio and, later, television, were not slow in realizing that they too could turn a penny by extensively covering sports. This both responded to demand and stimulated further interest. As we saw in Chapter 14 television seized the commercial opportunities offered by sports and quickly extended its interest and influence in ways that would have been considered pure fantasy to any one of the 120,757 people who watched the Jack Dempsey–Gene Tunney fight in 1926.

The complementary nature of interests between sports entrepreneurs and media companies was too obvious to miss. If sports were popular, people wanted to watch them, if not in the flesh, then on the screen. Media magnates were never willing to part with the kind of money demanded by promoters and league commissioners (who represented the interests of clubs), but they usually did. Ever-grudgingly, they paid more and more for every new contract. Then Ted Turner, the head of a media corporation, hit on the novel idea: buy the clubs.

In 1972, the owner of Turner Communications agreed to pay the Atlanta Braves baseball club $2.5 million for the rights to games for five years. A year before the end of the arrangement, Turner offered the club's owners $9.65 million for the whole shebang. The new owner was called the Atlanta National League Baseball Club, which was a subsidiary of Turner Communications. The same company acquired a 75 percent interest in the Atlanta Hawks NBA franchise, in 1977; and, the following year, it bought a partnership in the Atlanta Chiefs soccer club.

An obvious advantage of owning the Braves was that their games had high ratings and gave Turner's tv station a strong presence in the local market. Perhaps more significantly, Turner was able to avoid the hard-fought negotiations that typically accompany a tv-ball club deal. The reciprocity was enhanced by the boost television exposure gave to home game attendance. Eventually, this gave the Braves more money

▌BOX 15.3 SPONSORSHIP

"Sponsorship is the support of sport, sports events, sports organizations or competitors by an outside body or person for the mutual benefit of both parties." This was how former British Minister for Sports, Denis Howell, once serviceably described sponsorship (quoted in Neil Wilson's *The Sport Business*). What exactly is *mutual* benefit? Athletes, clubs, and governing organization receive money. What do the sponsors get? Advertising, or exposure to a target audience is the answer: the company avoids the crassness often associated with straightforward advertising, escapes the resistance of cynical customers, and positions itself as a benefactor of sports.

Sponsorship of sports is not a new phenomenon: there are examples of commercial companies financing events, especially cycling tours in the late nineteenth century. The original Tour de France was sponsored by the publication *L'Auto*. But, the significant possibilities of mass exposure through the television opened up new relations between sports and corporations. Breweries were among the first and most enduring sponsors of sports to recognize the potential of televised sports. Pabst Riband, in the United States, and Whitbread's, in Britain, sponsored competitions in the 1950s.

Gillette has maintained an interest in sports on both sides of the Atlantic since the early twentieth century when it sponsored radio coverage of baseball. In the early twenty-first century, it signed the prolific endorser, David Beckham, to a deal worth up to $70 million.

The majority of leagues and major world competitions have sponsors, sometimes several. Some athletes have portfolios of sponsorship contracts, most with companies that have no obvious connection with sports, but wish their products to be associated with a popular and ostensibly wholesome pursuit or person. Sponsors seek athletes with images that signify something about their product.

to attract better players and so contributed to the playing performance. Improving performances brought more viewers to their tv screens and enabled Turner to crank up his advertising rates. As the team's W-L record improved, so tv and radio broadcast rights rose, becoming the single biggest source of revenue; in the 1990s, this regularly exceeded $22 million per annum.

The Hawks were a poor team when Turner took over. Its owners were prepared to move the franchise out of Atlanta. As in baseball, clubs received a pro rata distribution of television revenues from telecasts by the national networks, but unlike baseball clubs they received none of the gate receipts from away games. It took only till 1979/80 before the Hawks began averaging 10,000+ for home games and, although this subsequently slipped, attendance picked up again after 1988/9. This was the period when the NBA generally gained widespread popularity. Encouraged by this, NBC paid the NBA $600 million for four years' broadcast rights, 1990–4.

The Hawks's share of this was $22 million. TNT (Turner Television Network) retained broadcast rights for the 50-game regular season and, if appropriate, 30 playoff games; for this it paid the NBA $275 million, of which the Hawks saw about $10 million.

BOX 15.4 TED TURNER (1938–)

Born in the industrial city of Cincinnati, Ohio, in 1938, Robert Edward Turner, at the age of 24, inherited his father's billboard business and, with it, $6 million worth of debt. After turning the business around, Turner bought two radio stations in Chattanooga, Tennessee, and retitled the business the Turner Communications Corporation. He floated the company on the local stock exchange in 1970 to finance the acquisition of Channel 17 television station in Atlanta, Georgia. At first, he filled its schedules with old movies and tv show re-runs, but, in 1972, he bought the rights to the Atlanta Braves games. In 1976, he bought the ailing club and turned round its fortunes. The Major League Baseball authorities despised Turner's flamboyant conduct. In 1976, he was suspended from all baseball activities for a year. But, Turner was undaunted and continued to spend more money in the ultimately successful attempt to bring the World Series to Atlanta. Turner's flagship television network CNN started life in 1979: it was a highly innovative 24-hour all-news cable station. He augmented this with a movie tv cable TNT and, in 1992, split the Turner Broadcasting System (TBS) into five divisions, one of which concentrated on sports activities. In 1996, CNN/*SI* was launched: this was an all-sports news cable in competition with ESPN'S second channel. Turner's mega-deal with media giant Time Warner was one of a number of a series of mergers and transactions in the late 1990s. Turner continued to handle Time Warner's cable networks, including HBO, and ran the Braves, Hawks, and Thrashers.

Turner's strategy could not be faulted: it was a no-lose situation. And one which other media owners were observing carefully. So that, by the time Turner stepped up to plate with his bid for Los Angeles Dodgers, in 1996, several other media corporations had taken active financial interests in sports clubs and Turner found himself in competition with News Corporation owner Rupert Murdoch. Turner bitterly opposed Murdoch's ultimately successful attempt to buy the Dodgers, though he was outvoted when the 16 National League franchises took the decision in 1998. Turner's enmity was apparent when he promised: "I'll squish Murdoch like a bug." He must have had "P. T. Flea" of *A Bug's Life* in mind (directed by John Lasseter and Andrew Stanton, 1998).

VERTICAL INTEGRATION

Murdoch's purchase of the 20th Century Fox film and television studio signaled his arrival as a key player in the North American media. But, for many years before, he had been steadily building his interests. He had already assembled a bundle of British newspapers to add to his collection of Australian titles. But, a successful television company escaped him. Having been thwarted in an attempt to buy London Weekend Television, he turned to the United States where he had been impressed by the ascent of cable channels, especially ESPN and MTV. In 1983, he bought a struggling satellite operator, Inter-American, which he turned into Skyband. The purchase proved a disaster and Murdoch lost $20 million within six months. In the same year, he tried unsuccessfully to buy Warner, the Hollywood studio.

Fox was then struggling and, in 1985, Murdoch took advantage to buy at first a 50 percent stake and, later, full control from its owner, Marvin Davis. Fox was insignificant in the tv market, but Murdoch grew it into the fourth major network. One of the reasons he was able to do this was by outbidding the established trio of ABC, CBS, and NBC for the rights to screen the plum NFL games. The 1993 deal cost Murdoch what many thought an absurdly high $1.6 billion; Fox lost an estimated $100 million in broadcasts in the 1994/95 season alone. Undeterred, Murdoch also signed contracts with Major League Baseball and the National Hockey League.

Murdoch's logic? By wresting the popular Sunday afternoon games from CBS, he had established Fox as a major network. Many local television stations changed their affiliations as a direct result of the coup and, of course, advertising revenue soared. Solid audience ratings helped Fox advertise its other shows in the commercial spots, thus increasing viewer awareness of the station's menu.

Then, Murdoch changed the formula: he beat off Turner's challenge to buy the Los Angeles Dodgers, admittedly one of sport's astral franchises, but not worth $350 million (£217 million) in the estimation of most market analysts. On the heels of this deal, Murdoch, through his 50:50 joint venture with Liberty Media, bought a 40 percent interest in Los Angeles' Staples Center, the only arena in the United States to house four major franchises: Lakers, Clipper, Sparks, and Kings, of the NHL. The deal included an option on 40 percent of the LA Kings. As the Kings announced their intention to exercise their own option on just under 10 percent of the Los Angeles Lakers, Murdoch became a minority owner in an NBA franchise too.

Over on the other coast, Murdoch's Fox Entertainment Group's 40 percent ownership of Rainbow Media Holdings Inc., a subsidiary of Cablevision – which held a majority interest in Madison Square Garden, the New York Knicks, of the NBA, and the New York Rangers hockey club – meant that Murdoch had his fingers deeply in the pies of the NBA and the NHL on both coasts. Like Turner's strategy, Murdoch's was to control the media distribution networks *and* the content of the programs to run through them.

His attempt to repeat the strategy in Britain was stymied when a £600 million ($1 billion) bid for Manchester United, though accepted by the owners, was blocked by the Monopolies and Mergers Commission, an official body set up to guard against antitrust arrangements. Murdoch's BSkyB subscription network had earlier bought the exclusive rights to screen English Premiership games "live" and was, at the time, experimenting with pay-per-view transmissions. As Turner had earlier discovered, owning a ball club simplified broadcasting negotiations.

As we have seen, Murdoch was not the only media owner to have sensed the advantages in owning clubs: in the late 1990s, media companies owned at least 20 top clubs in baseball, football, basketball, and hockey. The process was known as *vertical integration*. Time Warner (later AOL Time Warner) acquired baseball's Atlanta Braves and the Atlanta Hawks basketball club after its takeover of Turner's holdings, which included his several cable channels; it also became owners of the Atlanta Thrashers hockey team. Disney owned the NHL's Mighty Ducks and the Anaheim Angels baseball club; it also owned ABC and ESPN. Wayne Huizinga, former owner of Blockbuster Video, owned baseball's Florida Marlins and the Florida Panthers hockey club. *The Chicago Tribune* owned the Chicago Cubs; Cablevision owned the New York Knicks and the New York Rangers (and tried to buy the Yankees); Ascent Entertainments owned the Denver Nuggets and Comcast owned the Philadelphia 76ers. Italian media magnate Silvio Berlusconi owned the AC Milan soccer club of *Serie A*. The French cable television company Canal+ owned the Paris St Germain club. These are but a few illustrations of the media-sports cross-ownership patterns in North America and Europe. But, on a global scale, Murdoch's operations had no counterpart.

BOX 15.5 VERTICAL INTEGRATION

The combination in a single organization of several stages of production and distribution of products or services, which would ordinarily be operated by separate organizations. The single organization's power in the marketplace is enhanced. So, for instance, a gym chain may manufacture its own equipment, operate its own juice bars, and handle its own advertising rather than contract out these operations to other companies. If the juice bar makes losses, the organization can subsidize it with the profits made in other divisions. There are obvious advantages in this for a service provider, but even greater ones for media organizations, as Amy C. Cosper points out: "There's tremendous synergy between content and distribution if you're a programmer." Contrast this with *horizontal integration*, which refers to an organization's expansion into different products, or services that are similar to existing lines, either by diversifying its own products and services or acquiring other companies. The gym chain may purchase a series of cinemas or theaters, or start producing grooming products.

In addition to Fox in the States and BSkyB in Europe, Murdoch had Star TV that stretched from Saudi Arabia to Australia and included the gigantic Chinese market, as well as Japan (24 countries in total). Think of all the sports Murdoch had access to through his American and British set-ups, then contemplate the size of the sports diet he could offer to markets in the rest of the world. It is estimated by Kevin Maney that, at any one time, Murdoch could "reach more than two-thirds of the world's television households and touch yet more people through movies and newspapers"

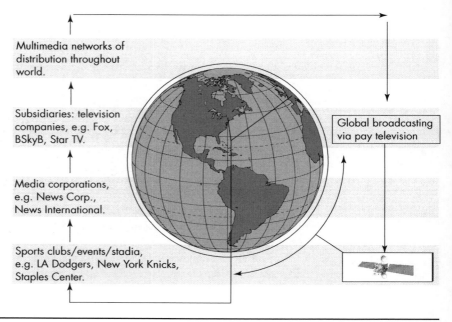

Multimedia networks of
distribution throughout
world.

Subsidiaries: television
companies, e.g. Fox,
BSkyB, Star TV.

Media corporations,
e.g. News Corp.,
News International.

Sports clubs/events/stadia,
e.g. LA Dodgers, New York Knicks,
Staples Center.

Global broadcasting
via pay television

Figure 15.1 Vertical integration

(1995: 173). Maney characterizes Murdoch's "awesome basket of assets" as: "The intertwining of the two trends of megamedia and globalization" (1995: 173).

Apart from the scale of Murdoch's empire, which frightened many, his methods of construction were also alarming. With his cross-ownership of several media, Murdoch would typically sacrifice profits from one medium and underwrite costs from another. An example was *The Times* of London, one of four quality national newspapers in a somewhat congested British market. Murdoch also owned the *New York Post*-ish *Sun,* which he had bought cheaply in 1969 and, within nine years, turned into the nation's best-selling daily. He did so by featuring bare-bosomed models, a bingo game, and sensationalist stories, many about the Royal Family. Profits from the *Sun* allowed Murdoch to use *The Times* as a sort of loss leader by dropping its cover price to about two-thirds of its rivals'.

Could the same tactic be applied to sports? Consider: Florida Marlins' owner Wayne Huizinga split up his 1997 World Series-winning team because the salary demands were too great. Faced with a similar situation, might a Murdoch-owned team underwrite salary costs with money from other ventures just to ensure the team stays ahead of the field and draws more television viewers? (As the Marlin's fragmented, the LA Dodgers' payroll totaled a league high of $90 million. In 2009, it was over $201 million.)

Any club owned by Murdoch was eligible for *The Times'* treatment. In other words, it could become the beneficiary of cash from other outposts of the empire. Even with salary caps, the consequence of this would be to weaken rival clubs and media groups by driving up wages. Such possibilities gave rise to the suspicion that Murdoch's goal was not ownership of clubs or media companies, but of sport and the communications industry. His track record suggested that, if he wanted something, he was prepared to pay over the odds for it. This is why *Big League, Big Time* author Len Sherman, writing before Murdoch clinched the Dodgers, trembled at the prospect: "Murdoch could, if he gained control of the Dodgers, deploy his newspapers and TV networks to forcefully thrust baseball into the international arena, forever upsetting the power structure of Major League Baseball, remaking the industry and the sport from top to bottom" (1998: 35).

BOX 15.6 KEITH RUPERT MURDOCH (1931–)

Born in Melbourne, Australia, in 1931. Attended Oxford University, then spent two years in London as a sub-editor with the *Daily Express* (1950–52). Murdoch inherited his father's newspaper holdings in 1952, and returned to Australia to run *The Adelaide News* and *Sunday Mail*. Having acquired more Australian newspapers he expanded to England in 1969, buying the *News of the World* and *Sun* newspapers. His U.S. operations began in 1973, with the purchase of the *San Antonio Express-News*, and, three years later, the *New York Post*, 1976. Murdoch's rubric organization, News Corporation, subsequently bought the *New York Magazine*, the *Star*, *The Times* of London and its sister paper *The Sunday Times*, the *Boston Herald*, the *Chicago Sun-Times*, several television stations, publishing companies, and airline, oil, and gas operations. Perhaps the most crucial acquisition came in 1985, when Murdoch bought 20th Century-Fox and some independent U.S. television stations from Metromedia: he reorganized them into the Fox Broadcasting Network. In the same year, he took U.S. citizenship. At this point, Murdoch "started uncoiling his tentacles into television, film, book publishing, and cable, where he found his true success," writes Lauren Janis (2001).

Murdoch sold *New York Post* to conform to Federal Communications Commission regulations in 1988 (he repurchased it in 1993 when it was on the brink of bankruptcy) and after that acquired Triangle Publications, including *TV Guide*. Murdoch's British tv interests center on the Sky satellite network, which began in 1989. Sky absorbed rival British Satellite Broadcasting to become British Sky Broadcasting (BSkyB) in 1990, then bought a controlling interest in Asia's Star-TV in 1993. Murdoch's rivalry with Ted Turner intensified in 1996 when he launched the Fox News Channel. Thus the architecture of a global media empire was in place. In 2003, Murdoch acquired a controlling 34 percent stake in Hughes Electronics (for $6.6 billion, or £4.3 billion), which operated the largest American satellite tv system DIRECTV, and, two years, later bought Intermix Media, the owner of MySpace, as well as two other web-based media properties.

Despite initial resistance the *Wall Street Journal* succumbed to Murdoch in 2007. According to *Forbes*, Murdoch was, in 2009, the 132nd-richest person in the world, with a net personal worth of $4 billion. His worldwide assets are valued at over $60 billion (Disney's market value is about $31.1 billion; it is the world's largest media corporation with assets of $65 billion).

In 2003, Murdoch vastly consolidated his command over the distribution of tv programming in the United States with the acquisition of a controlling interest in Hughes Electronics, whose DIRECTV had 11.3 million subscribers in the United States, making it the biggest distributor of programming.

Murdoch revolutionized sports' marketplace by investing for long-term value rather than short-term profits and building globally rather than nationally. If he had begun his campaign 10 years, or perhaps even 5 years before he did, his grand project may have quickly disintegrated and you would not be reading this much about him in *Making Sense of Sports*. He may still over-reach himself, of course. But, for him to have risen even as far as he did tells us something about the social changes since the late 1980s.

BETTER THAN SEX

Addressing the 1996 AGM of News Corp. Murdoch announced that sports "absolutely overpowers film and all other forms of entertainment in drawing viewers to television." Comforting stockholders with the news that the company held long-term rights to major sports events in most countries, he revealed future strategy: "We will be doing in Asia what we intend to do elsewhere in the world – that is, use sports as a battering ram and a lead offering in all our pay television operations."

It was a widely quoted remark and, as it turned out, an honest one. It was also the kind of remark that encouraged critics, as Johnnie L. Roberts observes, "to paint Murdoch as a Machiavellian barbarian bent on world domination" (2008: 41). Yet, for all the brickbats, as Roberts points out, "he revolutionized media markets from Australia to North America."

Murdoch's acquisitive quest for leadership, if not control of the global sports market, reflects both sports' crucial role in generating television ratings and television's equally crucial role in the healthy cashflow of sports. But was it a Machiavellian quest? Cunning? Certainly. Scheming? Yes. Unscrupulous? Well, Murdoch was thorough in his attention to detail and avoided wrongdoing, though his possessive tendencies were sometimes checked. For example, he was ordered by British regulators to reduce his stake in the commercial ITV network. The European Commission (EC) broke up BSkyB's exclusive right to screen live Premier League games.

As we noted before, during the 1980s, Murdoch was impressed by the ways in which dedicated cable channels, such as ESPN and MTV, were able to isolate specific demographic portions of the population. This was an agreeable development for advertisers; and the enduring commercial success of both of these confirms this. While he had no intrinsic interest in sports, Murdoch realized how effective these were in attracting a particular group of consumers, which he could, in turn, deliver to potential advertisers. At Fox and at BSkyB, Murdoch was prepared to bear brutal initial losses in anticipation that sports would ultimately woo demographically desirable viewers – the kind that drink alcohol, drive cars, and have private pension plans, for example.

The concept of using sports to sell products, possibly products only tangentially connected to sports (like beer, cars, and pension plans) seems patently obvious today;

but, in the 1960s, it was a daring innovation. Even in the 1970s, the possibilities were never totally explored. Only in the late 1980s and through the 1990s was sport's marketing potential fully realized. In retrospect, the linking of consumerism with sports may be the single most influential development since the advent of professional sport itself in the late nineteenth century.

The link was strengthened by the emergence of a new cultural equation in which sports' stock soared. In the early 1990s, "Sports had arguably surpassed popular music as the captivating medium most essential to being perceived as 'young and alive,'" according to Donald Katz, author of *Just Do It: The Nike spirit in the corporate world*. "Sports, as never before, had so completely permeated the logic of the marketplace in consumer goods that by 1992 the psychological content of selling was often more sports-oriented than it was sexual" (1994: 25–6).

Companies such as Nike, Coca-Cola, and McDonald's hitched their wagons to sports' star; and profited enormously as a result. While Nike was not the only company to have exploited the new status of sports performers, it did more than any other to enhance their status (as we'll see in Chapter 16). The new cultural equation

BOX 15.7 OLYMPICS AND MONEY

In 1976, Montreal spent C$2 billion (then about £1.3 billion) on staging the summer Olympics. It was left with a debt that took 30 years to repay. Mindful of this, few cities were prepared to risk holding the games. The 1980 Moscow games, which were boycotted by 61 countries, including the United States, were also a debacle. The organizers of the Los Angeles games scheduled for 1984 approached commercial sponsors to provide money and, in return, permitted them to use the Olympic symbol as a logo. The games demonstrated how the Olympics could be commercially viable: they accrued a "surplus" (Olympics do not make "profits") of $200 million+. The Olympic Partner (TOP) program, as it was called, raised $96 million in 1985–8; by 2005–8, the total had climbed to $866 million and included sponsors Coca-Cola, General Electric, and McDonalds. Sponsorship is now one of the four main sources of IOC money, the others being ticketing, merchandising, and, most importantly, broadcasting rights, which accounts for almost half the IOC's revenue. During 2005–8, media income was $2.57 billion. The IOC is able to command such money because it guarantees a global live average of 593 million television viewers and a total audience of near 1 billion for the summer Olympics. Historically, outside the United States, rights were sold in regional blocs. For example, the Asian-Pacific Broadcasting Union, a collection of broadcasting companies from Japan, Australia, New Zealand, and elsewhere, paid $18.1 million for the tv rights to the 2008 Beijing games. After this, the IOC negotiated separately and directly with broadcasters, thus building competition between broadcasters and driving up revenues. The IOC has also accommodated subscription tv channels by limiting the amount of live free-to-air coverage to a minimum of only 200 hours.

encouraged the interest of all manner of companies in sports, especially televised sports. Car firms, clothes makers, food manufacturers, and other organizations with no particular interest in sports apart from the ability to sell their products began to express interest. This took the form of both signing athletes to endorse products and advertising in the commercial spots that punctuated sports competitions.

The zest with which Murdoch bought television rights, often for sums that other major networks believed to be ruinous, attests to his confidence in the cultural power of sports to deliver its followers to his programs and, by implication, his customers – the advertisers. His ability to deliver grew out of his belief in thinking globally. Murdoch's master plan was never confined to one country, nor indeed one continent. Early in his career, he realized that Australia was simply not big enough for his ambitions. Moving to Britain, then to the United States, he recognized that markets had no natural boundaries: unlike nations, corporations, especially media corporations, were not confined by government and the limitations of any single polity.

The post-colonial world was one in which old empires had disappeared and new forms of interdependency had grown: nations relied on each other's support, not only militarily, but politically and, of course, commercially. Advances in tele-communications, particularly in satellite and fiber-optic technologies, enhanced the capacity and flexibility of media networks to carry services (data, video, or voice) around the world. No other phenomenon possessed this unique capability.

While no entity could actually *own* a nation's political system or economy, it was perfectly possible to own a telecommunications network that encircled the earth. The power this conferred on the potential owner was unequaled. Owners of the means of communications could exert influences in any number of countries. By the end of the twentieth century: the technologies that could make this theoretically possible were well advanced. They included: digital methods of encoding, transmitting, and decoding; multimedia cable and satellite networks to carry and disseminate information; and a single international collection of computer networks from which users could access information from computers anywhere in the world – the internet. Murdoch's various organizations had invested in all these and more.

One of the many consequences of the global expansion of the mass and multimedia has been the sharpening of awareness in other cultures. "Awareness" probably understates the case, because there has been a convergence of tastes, consumption patterns, and enthusiasm for lifestyles, many of which have origins in the United States. Witness the eagerness of young people all over the world to follow the NBA, wear replica clothes, and devour any artifact connected with basketball. Yet it is soccer, a sport largely ignored in the United States, that has become the first truly global game, capturing the interest of every continent, especially at the time of its World Cup championship. Neither of these sports would have occupied their current status without television.

The global convergence manifests itself in several other areas, of course. Like: the proliferation of fast-food restaurants, the ubiquity of Hollywood movies and the prevalence of American-English as a language that serves as a medium between different nations – indeed, many of the phrases in the new lingua franca derive from

BOX 15.8 UFC (ULTIMATE FIGHTING CHAMPIONSHIP)

In 1992, the Semaphore Entertainment Group promoted an eight-man all-in fighting tournament in Denver, Colorado, featuring contestants from Muay Thai, boxing, karate, jujitsu, sumo, shootfighting (a Japanese form of wrestling), and savate (a French kickfighting), who fought in an octagonal cage. Only eye gouging was illegal. The combat was styled after the *Vale Tudo* fights in Brazil, though the hybrid combat sport K-1 was also an influence. While popular in Japan and Europe, K-1 had not taken off in the United States.

Lacking both the legitimacy of a sport and commercial appeal, the Ultimate Fighting Championship (UFC), as it was known, looked set to be a strictly minority pursuit. Most U.S. state athletic commissions refused to sanction it, forcing events to remote locales. Television companies were not interested. Then, in 2001, casino-owner Lorenzo Fertitta and his brother Frank bought the brand (for $2 million), codified the competition's rules and established a regulatory organization. Opting for regulation was a sound business decision: the fighting was still violent with knee and elbow strikes, choke holds and hits on a floored opponent still permitted, but no head butts or groin shots. The competition was administered like a traditional sport with medical checks mandated for all fighters. The Fertittas changed the marketing focus, positioning itself as the combat sport for young people; boxing was dismissed as "your father's combat sport." They ran ads in celebrity magazines like *Maxim*.

The World Wrestling Federation (WWF) provided a business model in the sense that it had, since the early 1990s, opted to screen its promotions via cable tv, offering its big Wrestlemania shows only on pay per view. But, by 2000, its fake theatrics were losing appeal and its enforced change of name to World Wrestling Entertainment symbolized the severance of its already tenuous ties to genuine sport. UFC established complete control over its commercial activities, renting arenas, selling its own tickets and broadcasting its own promotions rather than doing deals with television networks.

By contrast, boxing promoters typically work with both the arena owners and the television companies, which effectively control the sport. For example, HBO will put up most of the money for a big boxing promotion, then hope to make a profit through ppv sales.

Unlike in boxing, owners of UFC took all the risks. In 2004, they ventured $10 million to produce a series called "The Ultimate Fighter," which was shown on Spike tv in the United States: this series followed 16 fighters trying to win a six-figure contract deal with Spike tv. In 2005, ppv sales rarely exceeded 10,000, UFC generating about $40 million in revenues. By 2008, revenues rose to $270 million. A typical ppv sub would be $45 (£28) and a big promotion would yield 100 million buys. UFC's average admission price was $276 (£173) with front row seats $1,000. *Forbes* estimated UFC to be worth $1 billion in 2009. Rival MMA groups have nibbled at UFC market dominance, but the organization televises in 76 countries and has promotional operations in Britain and Germany. UFC may be the first sport fully to exploit the potential of broadband expansion. This effectively means that it can use its own web-based platform to broadcast ppv events everywhere. UFC is still privately owned by the Fertitta brothers, and Dana White, its president, who owns 10 percent of the organization.

a sports idiom ("step up to the plate" is used in countries that don't even have baseball). Telstar, the first communications satellite, went into orbit in 1962; since then a miscellany of different transponders have been launched, offering a daily bill of fare of news, sports, and entertainment to a planetary audience. This has been interpreted as part of a generic pattern in which western powers have sought to conquer and control developing countries and maintain their dominance in a non-economic, non-military way: through the imposition of cultures.

Sport, no less than religion, television, and movies, has played a vital part in this process, occasionally called "Coca-colonization." The meaning of this is that, after the old western colonial powers ceded their control, multinational corporations took over and introduced a different form of control, this one based on the culture their products carry with them. Coca-Cola is the supreme example: an American product that became arguably the best-known brand in the world. It sourced materials, set up plants, employed labor and exported its products all over the world. It was also the most prodigious sponsors of sports and one of the biggest beneficiaries of sports' worldwide appeal.

These then are the conditions under which Rupert Murdoch was able to rise to his unique position. His influence developed out of an extraordinary combination of changing global conditions and a corporate set-up flexible enough to be able both to respond to the changes and push them in the direction Murdoch desired. All of which leads us back to the question: were Murdoch not around, would sports be as they are?

The answer is a tentative one: probably. There have been transformations under-lying Murdoch's rise, including a technological revolution in the communications field, corporate realignments in the media industry, an expansion of world commerce, a confluence of culture, and a new-found marketability of sports. All of these have established circumstances conducive to the growth of media-sports empires. Vertical integration, as we have seen, was by no means the sole preserve of Murdoch. Turner had turned around his television stations by incorporating sports clubs into his complex. Several other media giants also employed the strategy of gathering clubs and other sources of program content in their efforts to control the entire supply–demand chain. Ultimate Fighting Championship (UFC), the most recent sport to become globally popular, has also integrated its operations vertically, promoting shows and producing its owns broadcasts so that all operations are combined in a single organization (see Box 15.8).

Murdoch's strategy was on a grander scale and perhaps with a higher purpose; there were those who suspected his efforts to produce, transmit and sell events were part of a plan to control all sports. Yet, the strategy was not unique. Coming from a relatively isolated country with a small market, probably gave Murdoch a more global perspective than contemporaries, like Disney's Michael Eisner or James L. Dolan of Cablevision, both Americans who had little experience or interest beyond the United States.

Murdoch was also well versed in other media beside television. His father was a newspaper proprietor and his first few enterprises were in the Australian and British print media. The advantages of cross-ownership were not lost on Murdoch: profits from a lucrative medium could be used to underwrite short-term losses in another. Additionally, newspapers were useful as a way of publicizing other media. So, Murdoch held a competitive advantage when the predacious pursuit began. Were he not around, the other corporate predators would surely have extended their interests though perhaps not at the hellfire pace they did in late 1990s. The power in sports would still be distributed between about four or five media execs though no individual would reign as supremely as Murdoch.

What we once called spectators or audiences are now markets; what were once measured in thousands are now measured in dozens of billions. The global technological and commercial developments at the end of the twentieth century ensured that the shape and character of sports would be changed more radically than at any stage in organized sports' history. It is possible that entrepreneurs were slow in realizing the genuine commercial potential of sports. If so, they made up for it. They did so by opening out the potential market of those who wanted to sell products with sports and by turning sports themselves into products that could be transported around the world like articles of trade.

OF RELATED INTEREST

Big League, Big Time: The birth of the Arizona Diamondbacks, the billion-dollar business of sports, and the power of the media in America by Len Sherman (Pocket Books, 1998) is a fascinating case study of the MLB expansion franchise; as its subtitle suggests, the influence of corporate business and media conglomerates is apparent throughout.

The Economics of Sport and Recreation: An economic analysis by Chris Gratton and Peter Taylor (Routledge, 2004) is an introduction to the sports industry and *The Business of Sports* edited by Scott Rosner and Kenneth L. Shropshire (Jones & Bartlett, 2004) is a series of previously published extracts usefully collected in one volume.

The Bottom Line: Observations and arguments on the sports business by Andrew Zimbalist (Temple University Press, 2006) asks why owners buy sports clubs and whether lavishly paid and expensively traded players are actually value for money.

The Man Who Owns the News: Inside the secret world of Rupert Murdoch by Michael Wolff (Bodley Head, 2008) is based on 50 hours of interviews, though for more detail on Murdoch's business operations, *Virtual Murdoch: Reality wars on the information highway* by Neil Chenoweth (Secker & Warburg, 2001) and *SkyHigh: The inside story of BSkyB* by Mathew Horsman (Orion Business, 1997) are more valuable. Early accounts of his life: *Rupert Murdoch* by William Shawcross (Chatto & Windus, 1992), *Rupert Murdoch: A paper prince* by Georg Muster (Penguin, 1985), and *Arrogant Aussie: The Rupert Murdoch story* by Michael Leapman (Carol Publishing, 1985).

The man, the sport, the money" by Sean Hyson (in *Men's Fitness,* June–July, 2008: http://findarticles.com/p/articles/mi_m1608/is_5_24/ai_n25469447/) provides a financial breakdown of the UFC. "Caged violence rises from the canvas to land fistful of dollars" by Matthew Garrahan and Kenneth Li (in *Financial Times*, July 16, 2009) cover similar ground.

ASSIGNMENT

You are appointed head of marketing services at a worldwide credit card company, not unlike American Express. For years, your brand has marketed itself on class and privilege. Despite competition from other credit cards, the cachet your company has enjoyed has kept it among the market leaders. Recently, however, your exclusivity has become dated. Even your advertising slogans, such as "never be without it," and "that will do adequately" have become the target of comedians' jokes. Market share has declined sharply. After studying the spending and lifestyle habits of each of your 1 million cardholders your research department has concluded that there is a growing interest in sports among them. Design a series of initiatives that will exploit the sports connection and report the result.

The ✔ That Conquered the World

There was once a sea anemone, one of those invertebrates with a body like a thin column. It was called Adamsia palliata. Being a plant with a ring of stinging tentacles around his mouth, he could trap food but couldn't travel far to get it. One day, he met a hermit crab named Pagouros who lived in a castoff mollusk shell for protection. "How about if I live on your back and let you carry me around?" the sea anemone asked Pagouros. "That way, I can get to all the scraps of food I need." "And?" answered the crab. "Well, this seabed is a dangerous place for crabs," said the Adamsia, "but, with me on your back, you'd be well-camouflaged." The crab thought for a second, then agreed: "Deal." The two species lived together in a mutually beneficial partnership until the day when they got scooped up in a trawler's net. Resourcefully, Pagouros extricated himself, but only after the trawler had dragged the two way, way off their turf. "Actually, that wasn't so bad, was it?" said Adamsia after pulling himself together. "And look around you," Pagouros responded. "We're in new territory. This is all pretty exciting. Let's check this place out and, when we get bored, I'll snap onto a net with one of my claws and we'll let it carry us somewhere else." And so the symbiotic pair became world travelers, clinging onto trawlers' nets but without ever getting snared up. The moral of this story is: if there's reciprocal advantage in working together, do it, and never pass up the opportunity of a free ride around the world.

GLOBAL DIFFUSION

"Nike product has become synonymous with slave wages, forced overtime, and arbitrary abuse." Who said this? A protester at a G20 summit? Someone from the North Korea Confederation of Trade Unions? Unicef? Actually, it was Phil Knight, the founder of Nike. In 1998, faced with the uncomfortable reality that Nike, despite its position in the market and its reputation as a global brand, was being embarrassed by constant revelations about its treatment of workers across the world. Nike employs nearly 800,000 workers in 52 countries. Ninety-eight percent of its shoes were, at the time, produced in four countries: China, Indonesia, Thailand, and Vietnam.

In the late 1980s, the ✔ was everywhere. It was impossible to find a major sports event anywhere in the world that didn't bear the Nike imprimatur, either as a competition sponsor, or the supplier of footwear and apparel, or as an advertiser at the competition venue. It was equally impossible to visit a major city anywhere in the world where there weren't dozens of stores full of Nike products. Most cities had mini-department stores called Nike Towns that carried nothing but Nike. The millions of people that wore or carried Nike products presumably thought this was a good thing. Others didn't

As we'll see later in this chapter, a chorus of Nike critics has grown louder and louder after the early 1990s. Nike wasn't alone, of course. The Gap and Blockbuster were a couple of the several other corporations that came under attack for their (for some, dubious) role in re-shaping the world economy over the past few decades. Shell and BP too came under fire. Yet Nike had more cultural power than most. It managed to withstand the most severe criticisms, the boycotts, the traffic-stopping rallies, the anti-Nike movement, the hundreds of thousands of letters of protest, the dozens of hypercritical websites, and still stay at the forefront. How?

Two main reasons. First, Nike put its hands up: as Knight's admission indicates, Nike was prepared to concede that its early efforts of setting codes of conduct and monitoring compliance didn't end the abuses across its factories that produced its goods. It needed more comprehensive action. Perhaps more importantly, people believed Knight when he said he was going to pursue this kind of action, augmenting efforts to improve labor conditions with environmental programs. This leads to the second reason: Nike's credibility. The sources of this are in the Nike brand, of course. And the brand was built on figures who were known, respected, trusted, and believed in.

If you had a reputation as a stand-up guy, clean living, wholesome, and honorable and you not only approved of, but loaned your name to and unreservedly endorsed Nike, then consumers would pay attention. And, of course, they didn't come any more clean living, wholesome and honorable than Michael Jordan.

From the mid-1980s, Nike and Jordan lived in symbiosis in the manner of two different organisms attached to each other to their mutual advantage. Just like the hermit crab and the sea anemone (the first part of the fable is based on aquatic fact; the part about the trawler net is made up). Jordan was an exceptional athlete; with Nike he became a global icon. Nike made decent sportswear; with Jordan it too became a global icon.

The story of Nike's rise can be read as a version of how the production, distribution and marketing of goods was dispersed around the world and how the connections that made this possible introduced cultural changes that we are still experiencing. The process is, of course, globalization.

BOX 16.1 GLOBALIZATION

This has been used to refer to the emergence of an integrated global economy, cosmopolitan cultures, the expansion of world media, and, more generally, as the interdependence of societies around the world. Malcolm Waters provides a useful definition in his *Globalization*: "A social process in which the constraints of geography on economic, political, social and cultural arrangements recede, in which people become increasingly aware that they are receding and in which people act accordingly."

In this sense, globalization describes the trend toward increasing economic, cultural, and social interpenetration of governments and corporations, including banks, media groups, and manufacturing companies, as well as consumers. Critics interpret this as a post-Cold War (1945–90) form of capitalist exploitation of the developing world where labor and materials are used for the production of commodities that are sold with enormous markups everywhere. Two of the least desirable effects of globalization, from this perspective, are: the manner in which local cultures are homogenized into a single, featureless, anodyne blend; and local consumers are persuaded into buying products that have little relevance to their own cultures. Corporations like Nike are held accountable for this: Nike relies on international transactions, the relaxation of international trade restrictions, and the worldwide communications industry.

Nike presents a case study in globalization: starting as a small outfit selling Japan-produced shoes, it became a global brand employing labor and materials from the developing world, using the media to build recognition and forming commercial alliances with other organizations, including leagues and clubs. Nike didn't start globalization, though, in many ways, it presents an allegory and even an emblem. Few corporations have globalized so effectively. It could be argued that, as a brand, Nike is more valuable than many of the sports clubs and characters it sponsors, and these include the likes of Manchester United and FC Barcelona, two of the most valuable sporting brands.

Some scholars, like Barry Smart, argue that sport was ahead of the globalization curve: "From the late nineteenth century, the global diffusion of modern sport gathered momentum. The period 1870s to the 1920s represented a 'take-off' phase" (2007: 115).

Smart has a point: the first modern Olympic Games were held in 1896. It wasn't the spectacular tournament we know today, but it was an early sign that sport had a captivating quality that transcended national differences. The Olympics was actually the blueprint for the first World Cup competition in 1930.

The English originally didn't see the point of playing sports against foreigners: they assumed that, as creators of most of the world's major sports (including baseball, as we've noted in Chapter 4), and the formulators of the rules, they didn't need to prove their superiority against any Johnny-come-lately. So the French leapt in: Pierre de Coubertin engineered the Olympics and the World Cup was the brainchild of Jules Rimet and Henri Delauney. No one had even heard the word globalization at the time. Without the benefit of television, the only way of relaying footage around the world was newsreel, an audiovisual compendium of news stories shown in cinemas before the feature movie.

While Americans participated in the Olympic Games, they had, by the 1930s, converted rugby into American football (the American Professional Football Association was founded in 1920) and Major League Baseball was well established. While baseball was played in some parts of the Caribbean and South America, neither sport was played far afield. In any case, a territory of 3.79 million square miles with a population of 122,775,046 (in 1930) probably felt no need to enlarge its sporting boundaries. In fact, of all American sports, the NBA has been most effective in globalizing itself, largely due to its alignment with the entertainment industry.

Although John S. Hill and John Vincent argue, "In the field of sport, globalization has added impetus to international rivalries that date in the modern era from the 1896 Olympics," it could also be argued that its greater impact has been on cooperation, collaboration, and international partnerships (2006: 215). And, while U.S. sports were slow to globalize, American businessmen were not: several clubs in England's Premier League, including Manchester United, are owned by Americans. Far from adding impetus to rivalries, globalization has brought joint action.

The process Smart, Hill, and Vincent refer to is actually *internationalization*: bringing different nations and their representatives together in a single organization for a common purpose, such as a World Cup championship; in other words, making sports international. Globalization in the way Malcolm Waters understands it (as an integration of geography on economic, political, social, and cultural arrangements recede – see Box 16.1), began in earnest only after television opened up vectors of communication that would have been unimaginable as recently as 1960. But, in July 1969, 500 million people around the world watched live tv images of the son of a Ohio state auditor as he became the first man to set foot on the moon.

The Telstar communication satellite had been launched in 1962 and had been beaming programs across the Atlantic. But, of course, a transmission from the earth's own satellite was an extraordinary event and one that heralded the arrival of genuinely global media. I've dealt with the media in Chapter 14 For now, I want to recognize that television was indispensable to the globalization of sports, as it was, of course, to Phil Knight: without tv, he might still be selling out of his car – which was how he started.

THE SEDUCTION OF SNOW WHITE

Knight was neither a sprinter, nor a marathon runner. Authors of *Swoosh: The unauthorized story of Nike and the men who played there*, J. B. Strasser and Laurie Becklund, believe this is significant: when he started his business, Knight was not seeking instant gratification, but nor did he want to wait an eternity for success. He wanted to distribute his energies evenly, pace himself and exercise strategy – all elements of middle-distance running. Knight himself was no more than an able middle-distance runner on the track; but his application of the elements to industry was devastating.

After working with Bill Bowerman, who became head coach of the U.S. Olympic team at the 1972 summer games (and who, incidentally, was played by Donald Sutherland in Robert Towne's 1999 film *Without Limits*), Knight moved on from the University of Oregon and enrolled at Harvard Business School, where he studied to be an accountant. Here, Knight designed a class project in which he headed a hypothetical company that specialized in sports footwear imported from Japan. His premise was that labor costs in East Asia were far less than those in Europe and the United States.

During the early 1960s, the sports footwear and apparel market was dominated by a sibling rivalry between Adi Dassler, at adidas, and his brother Rudi, of Puma. The Dassler brothers grew evermore competitive in their attempts to establish leadership of the field. American and British manufacturers lagged way behind, specializing in flat-soled sneaker-type shoes, as opposed to the sturdy leather purpose-built jobs with arch and ankle supports that were being produced by the German brothers. But the German shoes were expensive.

Knight was an admirer not only of adidas' product, but the style in which it promoted its goods. But, he thought he could produce something as good, yet cheaper. His first forays into the industry were tentative: he asked Tiger (now known as Asics), a Japanese sports goods manufacturer to copy adidas' design and send him shipments; he would then sell for them in the United States. He consulted his ex-coach Bowerman who suggested improvements, particularly in terms of material.

Bowerman was a great believer in lightened shoes, his theory being that, if you count the number of paces a runner uses, say 880 strides over 1500 meters and multiply by the number of ounces you can save by making his or her shoes lighter, then the runner carries less weight and can travel faster. Take an ounce off the weight of the shoes and the runner is unburdened by 54 pounds. Bowerman's philosophy of running is expanded in his 1967 book *Jogging: A physical fitness program for all ages,* which he co-wrote with Waldo E. Harris.

Japan, in the postwar period, had made significant progress in developing nylon and leather substitute materials, this being made necessary by the lack of land suitable for cattle breeding – and hence no leather. This proved rather beneficial for Knight, who, in 1964, entered into a partnership with Bowerman, creating Blue Ribbon Sports (BRS) with capital of just $1,000. Knight and Bowerman intended to import Japanese-made Tiger footwear fashioned to their own specifications, though modeled on adidas, and sell in 13 western states.

Selling out of a car and taking phone orders from his father's basement, Knight built his reputation for selling shoes designed by athletes for athletes. He kept his day job as an accountant, leaving the design to Bowerman, while he concentrated on finance.

It was suspected that adidas was actually giving away its footwear simply to enhance its brand recognition: the distinctive three stripes on either side of the shoe was world-renowned. As Olympic and world championships were becoming global media events, thanks to the interest of television, so the athletic footwear market was expanding. Puma responded by taking the unheard of step of paying athletes to wear its products. While this is commonplace today, it was a breakthrough idea in the 1960s, when track and field was ostensibly amateur.

In Chapter 7 we analyzed the cultural changes of the 1970s: culture industries grew to prominence. Some industries, particularly the music and Hollywood film industries, seemed to have risen out of a cultural vacuum. They both sold essentially the same product – entertainment. Fitness was a different kind of product. The narcissistic interest in self-improvement, the growth of the exercise industry and the rise of the ethic of consumption all combined to produce an interest in fitness. An industry staffed by paid, trained fitness workers was a logical development.

Knight saw the potential of a commodity that zeroed in on the growing interest in fitness, while exploiting the fascination with entertainment. In 1972, he paid tennis star Ilie Nastase $3,000 to use his shoes. Nastase was an interesting choice: an exciting and excitable player, he seemed to personify an attitude that Nike shared: always prepared to challenge decisions, often belligerent, and frequently preferring to lose with style rather than win without it. Nastase, while fondly remembered as a baroque character, was never a tennis great; but everything he did, he did with flamboyance. In other words, he was more of an entertainer than a competitor – and this made him perfect for Nike. As with many seemingly inspired decisions, its motive was much baser than one might imagine. Both Nastase and the then promising teenager but relatively unknown Jimmy Connors had the same agent. Knight was offered both in a sort of package deal. Knight, needing to save a few dollars, signed only Nastase.

After the Amateur Sports Act of 1978, Nike was able to subsidize athletes: with most major sports abandoning their amateur status, track and field went open, though it had been known for years that under-the-counter payments had sustained the sport and that, in Soviet bloc countries, athletes were practically full-time professionals, anyway. Nike set up its own track club called Athletics West in Eugene, Oregon, and gave athletes enough support to pursue their sports without having to take part-time jobs. Knight resisted the temptation to include Nike in the name of the club, preferring to allow the worst-kept secret about Nike's financial involvement to circulate. Still, it was a crucial move in Nike's development because it was able both to subsidize and sponsor – which is tantamount to owning – a sport without violating any codes.

The beginning of Athletics West was also the beginning of Nike's transition from a private company worth $28 million to a global public corporation that capitalized, in 1980, at $240 million. In 1978, having disentangled itself from its original Japanese supplier, Knight set up manufacturing sources around Asia. He'd earlier paid a graphic designer $35 to create the ✔ and came up with the name Nike – taken from the Greek mythological goddess of victory. He dropped the BRS completely.

Fitness culture was most evident in the number of runners appearing on the streets and in the parks, but also in the growth of city marathons. London, Chicago, and Stockholm were among the cities that hosted major marathons, though New York was a touchstone. Strasser and Becklund note that, in 1970, there were just 156 entrants in the annual New York Marathon. By 1977, this had increased 32+ fold to 5,000 (now, 20,0000 people regularly start). And, to indicate Nike's presence in this boom, Strasser and Becklund point out that 11 of the first 20 finishers in 1977 were wearing Nike shoes. Even then, it would have been impossible to predict the scale of Nike's project over the next several years. Its products had earned a reputation for being runner-friendly: light mesh uppers and the characteristic waffle sole had found favor among joggers and pro athletes alike. But the sportswear market had limits.

Knight's biggest signing in 1978 was John McEnroe whom he paid $25,000. McEnroe was an even better fit for Nike than Nastase: his temperament ensured that even meaningless early round matches of tennis tournaments were likely to become explosive. McEnroe's histrionics gained him the kind of reputation that Knight wanted for his products: insubordinate, brassy, and defiant. With adidas still leading the market, it was Knight's ambition to position Nike as its most audacious contender. In one memorably tasteless sales meeting address in 1978, Knight likened adidas to Snow White. "This year, we became the biggest dwarf," he told his sales team. "And next year, we're going to get into her pants" (quoted in Strasser and Becklund, 1993: 271).

A central thrust of Knight's assault was the Tailwind, at $50 the most expensive running shoe to date and a technological innovation, incorporating a sealed module of air in its sole. Launched in 1978, it was a disaster initially, tiny particles of metal in its silver dye rubbing against the shoe's fibers and cutting the uppers. But Knight was undeterred and opened a sports research laboratory with the brief to its staff to come up with concepts like the air module every six months. It won't have escaped any reader's attention that the original idea behind the Tailwind later became the basis for the gargantuan Air Jordan line.

The link with Michael Jordan was forged amid concern about the future of Nike. In 1985, after eight years of market growth and increasing profits, Nike reported two consecutive losing quarters. The market had expanded and new players had entered the fray. While the supremacy of adidas and Puma had been ended, Reebok, a company started in England in the late nineteenth century, had come to the fore. In 1979, Paul Fireman bought the rights to the Reebok name and began a U.S. operation. Within two years, sales were up to $1.5 million and, by 1984, $65 million. Its sudden rise had caught Nike and indeed the whole sector unaware.

Nike's brand credibility was based on celebrity endorsement. Strasser and Becklund reckon that: "Even in 1980, most consumers were still not aware that many pro athletes were paid to wear shoes" (1993: 258). They probably learnt very quickly over the next few years; but, by then, it didn't make much difference, anyway.

Reebok's strategy was different: rather than aim at sports followers, it targeted the apostles of aerobics. Aerobics, as we learned in Chapter 7 was a new subsector of the sports market and one that Nike and the others had failed to exploit. For Reebok, the great outdoors did not beckon: its stomping ground was the sprung timber floors of health clubs.

After a shaky start to his enterprise, Fireman did a trading deal with Stephen Rubin, of Liverpool, and took advantage of Nike's apparent apathy. By 1983, Nike was leading the athletic footwear market, but was not producing any lines designed specifically for women's aerobics. The policy of signing high-profile sports personalities had stood Nike in good stead, but there were suspicions that it had outlived its usefulness. Reebok's campaign included giving away its products to aerobics instructors, whose pupils would take notice. Nike's U.S. revenues dropped 6 percent between 1983 and 1985.

With profits taking a pounding, Nike needed to cut back its endorsement budget: it opted to go after a few key athletes and offer them money, while just giving away free gear to others. In 1984, the NBA was making gains in the television viewer ratings. It only boasted a small number of stars – Larry Bird, Magic Johnson, Isiah Thomas – and they were under contract to the sports goods maker, Converse. Nike wanted to isolate a name player and tie its colors to him. At one point, it actually released many members of its roster, allowing them to find new sponsors.

By the time he signed his endorsement deal in 1985, Michael Jordan was already an Olympic gold medalist (in the days when the United States sent amateur basketball players, not "dream teams") and had left the University of North Carolina in his junior (third) year to sign for Chicago Bulls in a deal worth $3 million. Both adidas and Converse were interested in doing business, though Jordan eventually signed with Nike in what was then a ground-breaking arrangement.

BOX 16.2 LOGO

An abbreviation of logotype (from the Greek *logo* for word), this was largely advertising jargon in the 1980s, but has come into popular use in recent years. It describes an unbroken strip of type, lettering, badge or insignia used by organizations to promote their corporate identities in advertising and publicity material. Today, it is difficult to find an athlete or team that does not bear at least one, and, more usually many logos. Pro cyclists, tennis players, and racing drivers will have several logos on their uniforms, signifying their sponsors. Logos have been especially important in licensing sports-related products. Sports governing federations strictly control the use of logos by manufacturers and will seek redress from any company using, for instance, the "W" of Wimbledon or the silhouette of the basketball player of the NBA without permission. The growth of the sports logo is, in many ways, a symbol of the corporate character of sports.

MEANT TO FLY?

Like the majority of other players in the league, Michael Jordan was an African American. So, he didn't have the same credentials of other American sports icons: Babe Ruth, Jack Dempsey, Joe Namath, *et al.* The reverence in which many now hold Muhammad Ali disguises the fact that, in the 1960s he was regarded with contempt and described by once sports writer as: "a vicious propagandist for a spiteful mob that works the religious underworld" (Jimmy Cannon, quoted by Thomas Hauser in his *Muhammad Ali: His life and times*, 1997).

After Jordan left his university without graduating, David Falk, of the ProServ agency, secured him a five-year deal with the Bulls and opened negotiations with all the main sportswear manufacturers. The emergence of athletes as product endorsers – a process hastened by Nike, of course – meant that pro athletes regarded their salary as only one and not necessarily the biggest component of their income. Falk demanded that Nike paid Jordan in excess of his salary.

Nike's reply was to offer Jordan a guaranteed minimum of $500,000 plus a royalty. In other words, Jordan would receive a percentage of every piece of apparel or footwear sold. Not just items bearing his name, but all those in the Air range. That clinched it for Falk: adidas and Converse failed to match the terms and Jordan began the most remunerative commercial relationship with a sports good manufacturer in history.

BOX 16.3 DAVID FALK (1950–)

Born in Long Island, New York, Falk was the agent for a fleet of leading sports performers, including many of the best-known NBA players. Because of his influence over so many stars, he has often been portrayed as a puppeteer, pulling the strings of professional basketball. Falk joined the ProServ agency in 1975 and began specializing in negotiating contracts for pro athletes. His major coup was in signing Michael Jordan. Falk was something of an architect, designing a complex structure of corporate links for Jordan: endorsements for the likes of McDonald's, Gatorade, Wheaties, etc., positoned Jordan at the fore of every television viewer's mind. Falk masterminded what might be called the commodification of Jordan, the crucial phase of the process being Jordan's association with Phil Knight's Nike. Falk's own agency, Falk Associates Management Enterprises (FAME), is based in Washington, DC. Beside Jordan, Falk represented several other high-profile basketball players, including Charles Barkley, Patrick Ewing, and Allen Iverson.

With sales rising, Knight embarked on his most aggressive advertising campaign. In the year following his signing of Jordan, Nike's advertising budget leapt from $231 million to $281 million (almost 22 percent). It seemed like manic extravagance. But, the first year's sales of Nike's Air Jordan range, complete with a Jordan-silhouette logo, hit $130 million. And, as if to underline the importance of Jordan's tv presence, sales dropped off in the second year when Jordan missed 62 games through injury. Knight knew how to take risks: even Nike's first toe in British waters was more of a triple pike: in 1992, Knight signed a £4 million deal to supply Arsenal with training and competition wear.

Jordan himself said nothing in the first Nike advertising campaign featuring him. "Who said man wasn't meant to fly?" was the question strapped across the screen after a slo-mo clip of him in mid-air. Another famous campaign featured Jordan with the fictional character Mars Blackmon, who was drawn from Spike Lee's 1986 film *She's Gotta Have It*. Lee also directed the commercial, which was steeped in signifiers of urban street culture, including rap music. The triumph of this campaign was not only in sales, but in its projection of an African American as wholesome and unthreatening and yet still irreverent enough to hold his own on the streets.

In 1989, Reebok introduced "The Pump," a $170 training shoe with an inflatable insole that cushioned the wearer's foot perfectly. It was another fusillade in what had become known as the Sneaker Wars, in which sports goods manufacturers battled for the disposable income of young consumers. At the time, Nike had just slipped behind Reebok in the global trade war.

Four years later, Nike had regained the lead and forced Reebok into one of its most embarrassing moves. Recognizing the value of Jordan to Nike, Reebok tried to repeat the trick for itself, signing Shaq O'Neal for $15 million over five years. It was an expensive lesson. Not only did it pass on a renewal of O'Neal's contract after it expired in 1998, but Reebok cut Emmitt Smith for a $1 million buyout fee. In the three years leading to 1998, sales of sports shoes dropped and Reebok trimmed its roster from 130 endorsers to just 20. Incorporating players into the brand was no guarantee of cachet, nor of sales. The choice of player, the style of promotion and the social conditions under which the promotion takes place were all-important factors that Nike managed to judge to perfection. By mid-1997 Nike had cornered 40 percent of the U.S. footwear market.

The twenty-first century brought a broadening awareness of climate change and an opposition to the West's relationship with the developing world. Famine relief and foreign aid became prime concerns, as did the exploitation of labor, especially child labor. Nike was singled out as a culprit, as we will see shortly.

"No company enriched Michael Jordan more than Nike or benefited more from his career. Jordan had made around $130 million from Nike over his career by 1998," writes David Halberstam in his *Playing for Keeps: Michael Jordan and the world he made.* "Not all of Nike's growth was attributable to Jordan's presence, of course, but in 1984 the company had revenues of $919 million and a net income of about $40 million, and by the end of 1997, Nike's revenues were over $9 billion, with a net of around $800 million" (1999: 412–13).

What these bare figures conceal is the work Jordan's agent, David Falk, and Nike put into projecting Jordan and the role played by David Stern in turning

BOX 16.4 NIKE THROUGH THE DECADES

1960s: Knight trades under BRS, selling Japan-made footwear from the trunk of his car. Bill Bowerman designs a lightweight running shoe.

1970s: Knight builds Nike ✔ brand using McEnroe as principal endorser.

1980s: Knight's progress halted when Reebok captures growing aerobics market and responds by introducing the Air Jordan line.

1990s: Knight signs Woods, but Nike's market leadership slips. Knight leaves and returns to central role in running the company.

2000s: Criticisms of Nike's labor policies mount. Knight buys out Converse (for $305 million) and Starter (for $47 million).

the NBA from an unfashionable collection of forlorn clubs into one of the United States' major leagues. As the trawl net dragged the crab and sea anemone around the world, so television made the NBA and, by implication, Nike/Jordan globally famous.

STERN: THE MAN WHO SOLD THE NBA

1984 was a key year in the globalization of sports, though it wouldn't have seemed so at the time. David Stern took over as the Commissioner of the floundering NBA, Jordan entered the professional league and the then fledgling cable television network ESPN decided to sell out to the ABC network for $237 million. Two years previously, ESPN had broadcast its first NBA game as part of a two-year contract; it had been featuring NCAA games since 1979 and, because it reached (by 1984) 34 million homes, could fairly claim to have primed interest in college and pro basketball. The draft arrangement made it possible for viewers to map the progress of young, aspiring amateurs before they transferred to the pros and grow familiar with the style and personalities of the players.

Since the 1970s, America's (not just North America's) televisual landscape had become a lattice of cables, some underground, some on poles, all connected to stations, which received signals from satellites. Cable viewers all over the continent were able to pick up television shows that originated in the United States. ESPN had exploited America's penchant for sports, serving up competitive action all day, every day.

Stern realized the infrastructure was in place to transmit NBA everywhere, but was also aware that his league lacked the legitimacy of the NFL or Major League Baseball, mainly because it lacked the backing of mainstream corporations. And the reason it lacked it was that, as one advertising agency put it to Stern, "the pro game is too black" (quoted in Halberstam, 1999: 118).

The NBA, it was thought, was a sport played by black men and watched by black men. As the United States' black population was overrepresented in poorer socio-economic groups and had less disposable income than most, it was not a demographic sector much sought-after by advertisers. Stern's first attempts to persuade ad agencies that the NBA's audiences were not predominantly black, but were as mixed as audiences for the college game, cut no ice.

Halberstam argues that the enthusiasm for NCAA basketball was because: "The college game was perceived, perhaps unconsciously, as still operating within a white hierarchy, under powerful white supervision, a world where no matter who the foot soldiers were, the generals were still white" (1999: 118).

As professionals, black athletes were well-paid culture industry workers; con-tractually, they were as powerful as their coaches and able to dictate their own destinies. And this was troubling to white America, especially when coupled with the stories of drug abuse among professional sports performers, many of whom were African American. Overpaid young black males and cocaine seemed to go together in the consciousness of many Americans. Major corporations steered clear and the NBA's few backers were those interested in selling their products primarily to black consumers. Stern addressed this problem by introducing a league drugs policy: he struck an agreement with the Players' Association that allowed players with drug habits to own up without penalty. If they persisted in using illicit drugs, they could get expelled from the NBA. It helped clean up the image of the league.

A second major innovation of Stern's was the salary cap, which was introduced in 1984. The NBA cap was set at 51.8 percent of the league's "defined gross revenues." While salaries were comparatively meager in early years, by 1998, this translated as $26.9 million (£16.5 million) per 12-man team; or an average of over $2 million per player per year. Rather than let franchises operate independently (as, for example, Major League Baseball and, to a lesser extent, the NFL did), the NBA subordinated its members to the central organization and demanded compliance.

His new structure in place, Stern secured the sponsorship of the Miller Brewing Company and went after other corporations eager to tap into the youth market. The NBA was sold as a fast, exciting game with points racked up at a pace never approached by most other sports. It was also blessedly easy for the uninitiated to understand. Quite unlike the statistically laden baseball and the intricately ruled football, basketball was a straightforward game with a playing area that could have been designed as a stage for the more extravagant characters.

Two of the most famous players of the period were Earvin "Magic" Johnson and Larry Bird, whose frequent clashes became a staple feature of the NBA. Both high-class players, Johnson, of the LA Lakers and Bird, from the Boston Celtics on the opposite coast, had a rivalry that helped the credibility of pro basketball in much the same way as Ali–Frazier and Navratilova–Evert had helped their respective sports. Johnson and Bird first met in the 1984 Finals; three years later when they again met in the Finals, the television-viewing share more than doubled to 16 (i.e. 16 percent of the total viewing population). Johnson was an African American and Bird a white player; they were both intensely competitive and vied for the mantle of the league's best player.

Stern oversaw the early globalization of basketball: a total of 75 different countries received NBA telecasts in 1988. But, by 1989, when Stern was ready to renegotiate a new domestic television deal, the Johnson–Bird rivalry had lost its old potency. CBS had held the broadcasting rights since 1972 and was coming to the end of its four-year $188 million contract. NBC poured out a staggering $600 million to secure rights to the NBA for four years starting 1991. It seemed profligate; but NBC's head Dick Ebersol believed the demographics augured well.

Young people of all ethnic backgrounds followed the NBA avidly. NBC could offer its advertisers a direct route to the youth market at a time in history when young people were becoming the most sought-after consumers (sought-after, that is, by ad agencies and their clients). One of the most revealing acknowledgments of this is an ad for MTV that ran in the business sections of newspapers and was quoted by Thomas Frank: "Buy this 24-year-old and get all his friends for absolutely free," its headline read (1997b: 150).

Ebersol may also have sensed the potential selling power of a player who seemed well-equipped to replace any interest lost by the disappearance of Johnson–Bird and whose mannerisms and style were being emulated by young people. Today, the NBA is televised to 212 countries in 42 languages. It also started up the Woman's National Basketball Association (WNBA), its first big star being signed up, almost inevitably, by Nike.

Under Stern, professional basketball changed from a sport to an entertainment portal: watching a game was just entrance to countless other forms of merchandise, movies, music, games, and media, all of which were purchasable. David L. Andrews calls the whole enterprise an "emotive autocracy," meaning that "its various cultural offerings seek to direct the consuming public toward an uncritical engagement with, and thereby perpetuation of, its own virtuosity" (2006: 100). (An autocracy is a political system ruled by one person with absolute power.)

BOX 16.5 SHERYL SWOOPES (1971–)

Born in Brownfield, Texas, Swoopes was the WNBA's best known player and one of Nike's most prominent female endorsers. As part of the U.S. basketball team, Swoopes won a gold medal at the 1996 Olympics and, in the following year, joined the Houston Comets in the inaugural season of the WNBA. The Comets won four consecutive championships and Swoopes was consistently the club's, if not the league's best player. Nike tried to turn Swoopes into a "female Jordan," designing a range of shoes and apparel called Air Swoopes. Nike had earlier used volleyball star and model Gabrielle Reece in an advertising campaign, but her image was used in poses rather than action shots. Unlike Reece, Swoopes was better known for her play than her looks. In 2005, Swoopes announced that she was gay.

Nike, Jordan, the NBA. Take any one of these figures out of the equation and Jordan would probably be regarded as a good player; but certainly not as a globally recognizable icon. Take away Jordan and there would be no NBA, at least not a universally popular entertainment complex that boasts more celebrity players than any other sport. And Nike?

AIRBRUSHED ICONS

At the time of signing Jordan, Nike had around 20 percent of the world market in sports shoes and apparel that was led by Reebok. It's possible that Reebok, having ridden the crest of the health wave, would have suffered as the aerobics wave broke; it's also possible that another brand might have stolen its way into the hearts, minds, and pockets of young people. Nike picked the perfect intersection of history and personality. At a time when America was still mortified by its never-ending racial problems, it was comforting to know that blacks, however humble their origins, could soar to the top.

Jordan's play could mesmerize audiences, his persuasive advertising could enchant markets. He didn't talk politics and his comments about the condition of black people were platitudinous. His followers stayed spellbound as long as he didn't grow up: while he continued to play the game everyone played in their childhood or youth and acted as a role model of sorts for children, appearing in commercials with young people who sang that they wanted to "be like Mike," his supporters were happy. Were he to have chosen "adult" subjects to talk about in public, or criticized Nike's employment practices or got involved in the kinds of activities typically attributed to black males, then he would have been dropped. Jordan's success was conditional on his remaining a well-behaved man-child in the promised land: a black American who resisted every conceivable negative quality and remained virtuous in the eyes of whites. And the collective forces of Nike, the NBA and his agent were involved in this process; so too was NBC, which, as *Sports Illustrated* writer Rick Reilly put it, "airbrushed every Jordan zit into a dimple for 10 years" (vol. 90, no 2, 1999).

So different was Jordan from the image of the black male that stalks the popular consciousness, that it was almost possible to forget he was black at all. The dread engendered by a virile young black man did not apply to Jordan: he was a symbolic eunuch when it came to women: happily married and strictly unavailable. The goody-two-shoes image took a few knocks when details of Jordan's gambling habit were disclosed, but, if anything, the revelations helped in reassuring the world that this all-too-perfect being had all-too-human failings.

Jordan came to prominence as a black man with no axe to grind, someone who had risen to the top on merit. In a way, he was proof that the civil rights of the 1960s and days of what was once called an American dilemma were gone forever. Not all black people, he seemed to suggest, were preoccupied with racism and the obstacles it strewed in their paths. White America was in a kind of racial torment in the mid-1980s. The vigilante-style shooting by Bernhard Goetz of black assailants in 1984; the Howard Beach incident of 1986 when white youths assaulted three black men, chasing one to his death on a busy parkway. These had stretched racial tensions. A year later black teenager Tawana Brawley reported that she had been kidnapped and raped by a gang of white men; her story turned out to be a hoax but it added to the mounting psychodrama. The image of Jordan brought comfort amid an atmosphere of challenge and confrontation.

Jordan's didn't so much exit as recede into the background. He remained contracted to Nike through his ill-judged retirement and his comeback with the Washington Wizards. Nike's quest for a replacement was never going to be easy, though, in 2003, Knight closed arguably his most ambitious and audacious deal ever, signing a high-school basketball player to a $90 million endorsement contract. LeBron James had never thrown a professional basketball; in fact, he'd never thrown a hoop in college either. Nike fended off adidas, which, industry rumors suggested, had offered James an even larger sum. It was the kind of jaw-dropping deal that made Nike *Nike*. Within months, it launched the Air Zoom range of footwear and apparel, which it saw as the natural successor to the all-conquering Air Jordan range. Nike had bigger contracts – it paid Tiger Woods $100 million (£70 million) – but the James deal had symbolic importance: it demonstrated that, unlike other global corporations, it still had the same risk-taking tendency that lay behind its early success.

BOX 16.6 RIVALS

adidas: Formed in 1949 after a dispute between two Bavarian brothers, Adi and Rudi Dassler, who had been making sports shoes since the 1920s. Adi turned adidas into the leader of the sports goods market until the rise of Nike. In 2006, it took over *Reebok* for $3.8 billion.

Puma: Rudi Dassler's company boasted Pelé as its most famous endorser: he wore Puma in the 1970 World Cup. In the 1990s, after its efforts to break the Nike–adidas market leadership, Puma began to emphasize the aesthetics rather than performance features of their products.

Asics: Originally, Onitsuka, the basketball shoe maker started in 1949. After several mergers and takeovers, it became, in 1977, Asics. In the 1960s, Onitsuka Tiger (as the company then was) supplied Phil Knight's BRS company with footwear.

Fila: Originally an Italian clothes company started in 1911, Fila became known largely in the 1970s, when it signed tennis player Bjorn Borg as its principal endorser. In 2007, it was taken over by a South Korean company.

Lacoste: Started in 1933 by tennis player Jean René Lacoste, whose nickname was the Crocodile. Hence the logo. Son Bernard took over the company in 1963 and diversified from clothing into bags and sailing products.

Though often seen as a rival brand, Converse, *which started in Boston in the early years of the twentieth century and specialized in shoes with rubber soles and canvas uppers, was acquired by Nike in 2003.*

SHAPING AND SHAPED BY THE TIMES

In Chapter 15 we took note of Donald Katz's insight about sports' surpassing pop music as a vehicle for selling and how it even eclipsed sex as an orienting consumer theme in the early 1990s (1994: 25–6). In more recent years, the demarcation line between sports and sex has become less distinct, especially in the marketplace where sports and sex permeate, well, everything. The market is not confined to palpable goods and services: it peddles ideas and beliefs, including what Katz and indeed the people at Beavertown called "the Nike spirit."

In the 1990s, sports became "sexy" in more than one sense. Quite apart from the more overt pandering to male libidos by using female athlete models in erotic poses, sport sold itself as inescapably chic: wearing the right label on clothes was a virtual requirement. Sports clothing became leisurewear. No one was seriously going to spend $200+ on a pair of shoes decorated with all the right appliqués and then wear them for football practice. In the 1970s, people would have balked at the idea of becoming a mobile advertisement for a sportswear company; in the 1990s, they had to pay extra to have the name and logo plastered across their tops. And not just any name and logo: Lacoste might have been cool last year, but 12 months on, it could be passé.

Adidas was quicker to notice the potential of melding sports and entertainment, but slower to capitalize fully on it. In 1985, the then aspirant rap music entrepreneur Russell Simmons invited adidas representatives to a hip-hop concert featuring his band Run DMC. Unimpressed, the adidas people wondered what Simmons' point was until the impresario turned their attention to the crowd. One of the band members urged the audience to throw their adidases in the air. The result was a volcanic eruption of sports shoes, all bearing the trademark three stripes. adidas realized how their shoes, far from being just sportswear, were now fashion accessories; it signed a deal to sponsor the next Run DMC tour. The band itself responded by releasing its track "My adidas."

Whether Knight himself had prescience and knew sports were going to acquire a new status, or whether he contrived to make this happen, we may never know. Maybe he just happened to have the right product and the right moment in history. One thing we can be sure of: he understood the ephemera of taste. Never content to let a line succeed, he constantly replaced them with new lines of the same brand, forcing the brand to migrate and mutate. The changes came with head-spinning speed. No doubt, he learnt this tactic from fashion houses which organized output in terms of seasons. The label may have been a signifier of quality, but the collection from which it came was also material.

▌ BOX 16.7 BRAND

Brand comes from a pre-twelfth-century English word *brant*, meaning burn; it came to mean a burned-in mark on, for example, slaves or cattle. Later, it referred to goods of a particular make, though today it has a wider resonance. It's still a mark or distinguishing characteristic and it has its origins in goods, or commodities, made by or for a particular company. But, the brand is now an identity and one portable enough to migrate across products. The value of a brand is in its ability to elicit recognition across several sectors and add value to virtually any product that bears it. For example, Giorgio Armani is known essentially for high-quality clothes. Affix the Armani label to wristwatches and value is added. Attaching adidas to men's skincare products makes them recognizable: adidas is a name associated with sportswear, but its brand value is strong enough to migrate to sectors away from sports. ESPN is another powerful brand that has its sources in television, but has transferred to magazines and restaurants, all themed around sports. Evidence all around us suggests that consumers respond positively to brands: they dress in clothes bearing the names of fizzy drinks, football teams, universities, construction equipment, or anything with which they feel an affiliation.

This meant that Nikes became collectible: they could be dated, even cataloged. Connoisseurs – and they still exist – were able to date and value Nike items by just looking at them. A pair of first issue 1987 Air Max's, for example, was eminently collectible; these were the first model to make the air pocket in the sole of the shoe visible. On reflection, they were the shoes that kickstarted Nike's resurgence. With Reebok owning a 30 percent market share and Nike 21 percent, Knight gambled with the Air Max, paying Bo Jackson, who played both football and baseball, $100,000 to endorse them. The ad agency Wieden & Kennedy created the celebrated "Bo knows. . ." campaign to push the product, which was instrumental in Nike's return to market leadership. Hence, the historical significance of the Air Max.

In some senses, the ascent of Nike is attributable to the gnomic wisdom of Phil Knight, a man who seemed to know more about the mysteries of changes in youth culture and how to exploit them than any other entrepreneur. In another sense, Knight was just part of a new cultural equation that transformed the relationship between supply and demand.

Cultural tastes and fashions may not be totally controllable; but they can be heavily influenced. To take an uncomplicated example from Malcolm Waters: "The British taste for tea . . . could not have been cultivated in that damp little island had it not been possible to export its cheap textiles to Southern Asia, albeit to sell them in captive colonial markets, along with common law, cricket and railways" (1995: 66–7).

Nike couldn't have cultivated the global taste for its products if it hadn't been possible to make, advertise, and sell them everywhere, of course: it extended, expanded and even exaggerated cultural tastes in accordance with his own priorities. But, there also had to be a more diffuse enthusiasm for sport, especially basketball, and, in this sense, Nike was a catalyst.

Sports drew alongside the entertainment industry as one of the most longed-for means through which young, predominantly working-class people imagine becoming successful. Television, movies and even educational institutions were all parts of changing cultural configuration in which sports became more glamorous than at any stage in its history. All sorts of products could be sold merely by associating them with sports; which is why endorsement contracts became so lucrative.

Nike emerged after a rude awakening. America had learned that its hitherto unquestioned military and economic supremacy could be questioned after all. American forces finally left Vietnam in 1973 after 16 years. It was the longest war in which the nation had ever been involved. In defeat, America reflected on itself and saw a nation that had gone flabby, a citizenry that ate too much, exercised too little, and accepted freedom from pain or constraint as if by divine right. Nike's invocation "just do it" might have been intended for every American who had ever comforted him- or herself in the thought that they were a citizen of the richest, most unassailably powerful nation in history – and had been exposed.

In a sense, the rise of that other colossus of brands, Coca-Cola, might also be seen in the context of the United States' upheaval. In his *For God, Country and Coca-Cola*, Mark Prendergrast writes: "Coca-Cola grew up in a country, shaping and shaped by the times. The drink not only helped to alter consumption patterns, but attitudes toward leisure, work, advertising, sex, family life, and patriotism" (1993: 11).

Similar claims could be made for Nike in the last three decades of the twentieth century.

In fact, the parallels between Coca-Cola and Nike are inescapable. Both emerged from turbulent periods of change in American society and both became globally recognizable brands (Coca-Cola's enlarged its market during the 1930s Depression). Coke, like Nike, seized highprofile stars, in its case from Hollywood, to endorse its products: Joan Crawford, Clark Gable, and Greta Garbo were among Coke's panoply. Coca-Cola's links with sport are well-known: it provided soft drinks for athletes in the 1936 Olympics and continued to align itself with a health, vigor, robustness, and fitness, even when it became widely known that the drink itself did not promote any of these.

Jesse Jackson had famous conflicts with both Nike and Coca-Cola, in 1981 threatening a boycott of Coke if the demands of African American bottling plant owners were not met. Jackson reminded Coca-Cola that it had no blacks on its board of directors. It was the second major boycott threatened: in the early 1960s, Jackson's mentor Martin Luther King accused Coca-Cola of using black models in only subservient roles in its advertising and of having no black sales personnel. African Americans formed about 11 percent of the total U.S. population at the time, yet they consumed 17 percent of Coca-Cola.

In a similar way, Nike found itself at the center of an equal opportunities embarrassment when Jackson's Push organization revealed what some felt to be an irony – others, an outrage: Nike employed precious few black senior managers at a time when virtually every black urban male under 30 appeared to be wearing Nikes. (I'll deal with this in more detail below.) Both Coca-Cola and Nike were able to schmooze their ways out of embarrassing situations and maintain their popular appeal with markets that were predominantly white.

Racial issues have beset the United States and sport has mirrored many of them. Nike's adeptness in defusing potentially explosive situations was a factor in its ascent. The NBA too faced a problem. As we have noticed, Nike's destiny was tied to that of the NBA and its star player, Michael Jordan. Each, in its own way, was able to negotiate predicaments with racial implications to their own advantage.

THE MYTH

Nike became brand leader thanks to Jordan. But Jordan took from Nike much more than money. "It was Nike's commercials that made Jordan a global superstar," writes Naomi Klein (2001: 52). There had been other gifted athletes before Jordan, but none reached what Klein calls "Jordan's other-worldly level of fame." Pre-Nike, sports stars, no matter how great, were athletes who happened to do commercials. They weren't synonymous with a brand, as Jordan was. Nike changed all that, creating lavish tv commercials that became the measure by which others were to be judged. Nike embarked on what Klein calls "mythmaking," establishing an aura around Jordan. "Who said man wasn't meant to fly?" one of the ads asked, showing the gravity-defying Jordan in mid-air. It was almost possible to believe Jordan was actually capable of the unbelievable feats he performed in the commercials. No one's suggesting that Jordan wasn't great, perhaps the best basketball player ever. But, he wouldn't have been a global icon without Nike.

Then again, Nike wouldn't be the market leader without Jordan. In the June 1998 issue of *Fortune* magazine, Roy Johnson analyzed what he called "The Jordan effect" which described MJ's impact on the overall economy of the United States. Nike developed the Air Jordan line of footwear and apparel and, over the 1990s, it was worth, in terms of sales, $5.2 billion. Read that again: $5.2 billion; that's over £3 billion. For that you could buy Manchester United, New York Jets, and the Orlando Magic and still have change.

Money like this wouldn't have passed over the counter if Jordan had been playing to half-empty stadiums with his games shown on a modest cable network. Without the National Basketball Association and its global television exposure, Jordan would have had less visibility and a less visible Jordan would have been of only limited value to Nike. Put the three together and they formed a perfect triangle; take any side away and all you have is an angle. Each owes its global success to the global success of the other two.

Nike's success, like that of the other global brands, including McDonald's and Disney, was based on an apparent understanding of cultural changes, the main one being the shift to consumerism. While others envisaged a market waiting to be exploited, Knight saw new markets waiting to be created; products that were to be displayed rather than just worn; commodities whose value lay less in what they were, more in who was wearing them.

Knight's market was simple: the planet. He wanted – and got – Nike in every corner of the world. He outsourced his materials, meaning he obtained his goods from foreign rather than American suppliers. He had his shoes and clothes manufactured on low-skill, low-cost assembly lines in East Asia, but sold them literally everywhere. The outsourcing model turned Nike into a genuinely global operation.

While its production costs were low, Nike's prices were high: the first $100 sports shoes, in 1986, may have been a flop, but they cleared the way for more extravagant ventures. Knight himself always denied that his company produced anything other than sportswear, but Nike was a fashion item. Nike was worn at the gym, on the track, and in any sports arena; but it was also worn in the clubs and bars, on the streets, and, for a while, in the early 1990s in some boardrooms.

Its slogan "Just do it" had an odd resonance that seemed to appeal cross-culturally. Presumably prefixed by an unspoken "Don't think about it . . ." the phrase was a pragmatic appeal for action. Like other aspects of Nike's corporate persona, it was ideally suited to an age when theory was out-of-vogue, earning money was virtuous and lunch was for wimps, as the stockbroker Gordon Gecko famously put it in the Oliver Stone movie *Wall Street* (1987).

Right-wing governments under Ronald Reagan in the United States and Margaret Thatcher in Britain in the 1980s promoted a culture in which individualism and the ethic of personal achievement were paramount. Competition was not only healthy, but essential to the well-being of the individual; and this had ramifications at all levels. Cutbacks in welfare payments, affirmative action programs and other areas of public spending were designed to decrease what many saw as a dependency culture.

Nike embodied much of this spirit. Its messages were in sharp contrast to early sporting morals that emphasized the importance of competing over winning. Nike mocked second-placers. Even winning was only one stop on a quest to fulfillment. "There is no finish line," one of Nike's ads reminded its potential customers.

BOX 16.8 GROBAL AND GLOCAL

These are two hybrid terms used to distinguish different patterns of globalization. Nike, according to Andrews and Ritzer, "is positioned as being unequivocally grobal" (2007). The authors quote Phil Knight: "We want the brand to stand for the same thing all over the world." Grobal defines the attempt to impose a cultural product on many different territories, regardless of local culture. Glocal, on the other hand, refers to the integration of the local and global cultures. The term was introduced by Roland Robertson to highlight how global and local cultures fuse to produce unique new syncretism (1995). Despite Knight's boast, Nike's marketing is often fine-tuned to meet local requirements. When it hasn't met them, there have been mishaps, as Grainger and Jackson's New Zealand study indicates (2000, see below). While there are unchanging brand characteristics, Nike's advertising is what Andrews and Ritzer call "a multi-accented vision of the Nike brand." They give the example of an ad campaign in Japan that would have little relevance or even meaning outside that territory.

Nike couldn't have succeeded globally without Jordan, or the NBA and the tv deals it brokered. The whole phenomenon was made possible by video. I use the term here in its generic sense, referring to the transmission of images via communications technology. Obviously, television has been the most effective and most encompassing form of video technology. By the end of the twentieth century, few, if any, parts of the globe did not have access to television. Since the 1960s, sport and television have existed in a synergetic relationship, each depending on the other to create bigger revenues. The interest of sponsors, advertisers, and manufacturers seeking endorsements from sports performers is strongly linked to gaining the widest possible exposure to consumers.

As we have seen in Chapter 14 sports were appealing to television companies, principally because they were a lot cheaper than drama; when the viewing figures started climbing, the sports organizations began to hike their prices. Television responded by paying the asking prices, but needed to guarantee viewer ratings to make sports a viable proposition. One way was to make televised sports as, if not more, attractive than actually being there.

To state that Jordan would not exist were it not for television sounds frivolous; Jordan the player would; but not Jordan the icon – the image that has been relayed around the world countless times, plastered across billboards and buildings, stamped onto millions of food packets and even digitally mixed into cartoons. This is a Jordan that exists independently of Jordan the flesh-and-blood man; it is a phenomenon about which followers are prepared to believe almost anything, including the ability to fly.

Halberstam writes of Jordan's "other incarnation" borne of Nike ads: "The commercials were brief, but there were so many of them and they were done with such talent and charm that they formed an ongoing story. Their cumulative effect was to create a figure who had the power and force and charisma of a major movie star" (1999: 183–4). Of course, in contrast to movie stars, Jordan's deeds were not artificial.

So many pieces of information about the world reach our senses via electronic media that we might say we live in a videated culture in which entertainment and life have become not inseparable but the same. Images devour life so that our experiences are shaped by tv characters and tv coverage of news events.

The image of Michael Jordan was bigger, immeasurably bigger than the man. Jordan would simply not have been possible without the cultural and technological transmutations that turned society into one vast network of coaxial cables, every home in the world connected to all others via some kind of link. And if this incarnation of Jordan was not possible without tv, then the same must be said of the NBA, whose big contract with NBC guaranteed it the kind of exposure it needed to compete with other major league sports, and Nike which exploited the cultural and commercial possibilities of television in a way no other company had contemplated.

"Circuits of promotion" is David Whitson's term to describe the endless loop-like way in which various forms of "recursive and mutually reinforcing" streams of communications "generate more visibility and more business for all concerned" and in which "cultural commodities, including celebrities, can become vehicles for the promotion of more than one producer's product at once" (1998: 67). The case of Nike, the NBA, Jordan and, indeed, his club illustrate Whitson's point perfectly. He writes: "Nike . . . attached its corporate persona to images of Michael Jordan, but when Jordan appeared in Nike advertisements in the early 1990s, he was adding to the global visibility of the Chicago Bulls, the NBA, and the game of basketball, as well as promoting Nike shoes" (1998: 67).

BOX 16.9 THE DALLAS DEAL

In 1995, Dallas Cowboys signed a deal with Nike worth an estimated $20 million that appeared to contravene the NFL's revenue sharing policy. Reebok were the league's official sponsors. The Cowboy's owner Jerry Jones said he was conferring stadium, not team, rights on Nike. The ✔ was painted on Texas Stadium and a Nike-Cowboys theme park at Irving, Texas. American leagues typically negotiate sponsorship deals on behalf of all clubs. By contrast, European sports clubs are free to make their own arrangements. Manchester United, for example, clinched a £302 million ($500 million) deal with Nike to run from 2002 for 13 years.

There is no distinct effect to speak of; only another cycle, or circuit, popular culture feeding back into an international "economy of signs" in which the symbolic values of products and images replaces their use values and a pair of Nikes can fetch ten times more than another pair made of the same materials and under the same factory roof. This was and is the global economy that Nike both helped create and dominate.

ANTICORPORATE BACKLASH

You don't get to be a brand like Nike without a backlash. For critics, Nike has become shorthand for exploiting populations in the developing world, creating internecine violence in city streets and turning sports into a gigantic showcase for its high-priced wares. We'll deal with these reactions separately.

Operation Push

The civil rights activist and politician Jesse Jackson headed an organization called Operation Push (People United to Save Humanity), which was dedicated to securing equal opportunity for ethnic minority people in the United States. It became clear to Jackson that, in the late 1980s, Nikes were the footwear of choice for young African Americans. This wasn't a problem in itself. But with the prices of footwear rising, young people found themselves struggling to find the money. One response was to rob others of their valuable merchandise, precipitating what were called "sneaker wars" on the streets of America's cities.

In 1990, Jackson became uneasy with Nike's cultural pre-eminence among young black people. He realized that Nike's deployment of popular black athletes, especially Jordan, had helped corner the young African-American market. Jackson claimed, though without evidence, that Nike sold up to 45 percent of its products to inner-city youths, many of whom were African Americans, though Nike itself estimated only 13 percent of sales were made to ethnic minorities.

There was no doubt, however, that the management structure of Nike consisted mostly of whites. Jackson warned of a boycott of Nike products if Knight did not promise more contracts with minority businesses and jobs for black people, especially management positions. Knight was able to call Jackson's bluff, though he promised to re-evaluate Nike's equal opportunity program.

Anti-corporatism

Along with other multinational companies, international banks, and other agents in the global market economy, Nike was vilified by critics of capitalism, labor unions, farming lobbies, Friends of the Earth, and a variety of other organizations, as well as writers such as Naomi Klein whose 2001 book *No Logo* captured the heartbeat of the "anticorporate attitude," and filmmaker Michael Moore, whose *The Big One* subjected Nike to the same kind of scrutiny afforded George W. Bush in *Fahrenheit 9/11* and the National Riflemen's Association in *Bowling for Columbine*. Few corporations have aroused passions like Nike. Those that love the brand make their ardor visible by wearing its products and carrying its accessories. Those that hate it either just don't buy anything emblazoned with the signature ✔ or organize themselves in protest.

Klein describes one of Knight's first encounters with his detractors. Invited by Stanford University Business School to deliver a guest speech in May 1997, Knight was greeted by pickets who screamed at him to "pay your workers a living wage" (2001: 366). Public notice was served that an international anti-Nike movement was gathering momentum. Later in the year, a day of action resulted in protesters zeroing in on Nike Towns and Foot Locker outlets in 13 countries.

In Australia, anti-Nike demonstrators once wore plain cloth sacks with "Rather Wear a Bag than Nike" daubed across them. Students at the University of Colorado held a fundraising run, the admission price of which was the equivalent of a day's wages for a Nike worker in Vietnam, $1.60; the winner received a prize of $2.10, the cost of three square meals in Vietnam.

Nike's damage limitation included sponsoring community schemes, gifting equipment to schools and colleges, and invited human rights groups to inspect its factories anywhere in the world. The "No sweat" label appended to its stock was Nike's own way of retaliating to its critics. It argued, though not to everyone's satisfaction, that, while its wages were low compared to those in western economies, they were actually higher than local rates. It also cleaned up its factories to create better working conditions for its labor. Its boss, Phil Knight, insisted that his company had been unfairly made the "poster boy for the global economy."

Over the next several years, Nike was criticized for other forms of exploitation. Investigators exposed the menial wages Nike paid to workers in developing countries and compared these to the retail prices of its products in the West. The *New York Times* was unrelenting in its attacks on Nike's labor practices. Nike was one of several sportsgoods manufacturers which made use of poorly paid Asian labor; in fact, it was revealed that its some of its products were actually made under the same roof as its competitors', often by the same personnel. Nike's response was to get together with other sports goods manufacturers and draw up a code of practice. Self-satisfied, Nike attached "No sweat" tags to its garments, an allusion to the Asian "sweatshops" it once operated.

As if to underline its social conscience, Nike formed NEAT (Nike Environmental Action Team) in 1993. This project encouraged the recycling of worn shoes and created inner-city playgrounds and sports areas and worked as a sop to environmentalists. PLAY (Participate in the Lives of American Youth) was launched in 1994 with Jordan and Jackie Joyner-Kersee as figureheads: this was aimed at reclaiming public spaces for youth. A skeptic might interpret these initiatives as part of Nike's strategy to offset the harm done to its reputation by reports of its labor exploitation in emerging economies.

BOX 16.10 ATHLETIC LABOR MIGRATION

Global migration of athletes to compete in different parts of the world is a feature of the more general globalization of sport. Athletes, particularly elite level performers, migrate across nations and often across continents, their motivation usually being money. Hence migration is typically from developing areas to North America and Europe. The flow has been called the "brawn drain" that results in what Elliott and Maguire describe as "the deskilling of the donor country" (2009). The 2009 film *Sugar* (directed by Anna Boden and Ryan Fleck) follows the migration of a baseball pitcher from his native Dominican Republic to the United States. The Caribbean nation is a fertile land for Major League Baseball recruiters. Similarly, West African nations around the Gulf of Guinea have provided European football leagues with a rich source of players. Brazil, for long the world's premier international team, has, since the 1980s, experienced an outflow of players, leading to a debilitating cycle, as Alvito explains: "Structural factors weaken clubs, which are then obliged to sell [trade] players, reducing the quality of the games, as well as the identification and emotions of the fans, which aggravates the crisis and makes the sale of our stars inevitable."

Anticorporatist sentiments gained momentum in the twenty-first century, particularly after the 2008 financial meltdown and the recession that followed. Protests against global capitalism, consumerism, and the companies responsible for both proliferated. Nike's reply was, as Eugenia Levenson reports, to develop its commission to improve labor conditions into "a broader mandate . . . weaving environmental awareness into its design process" (2008: 165). In 2005, Nike started to release the names and locations of its factories. Its factory audits were passed to independent assessors for scrutiny. It was an ingenious adaptation and one that maintained Nike's position in the market that continued to thrive. Let me explain why.

The corporation grew amid a culture of ostentation, when clothes, jewelry, cars, and other commodities acquired value as identity cues: how you looked defined who you were. And Nike, as we suggested earlier, were the shoes of choice for African Americans and a great many more groups besides. Hence Nike's market leadership. It would be tempting to think that the whole industry would collapse in the post-meltdown period. If this were the case, this chapter would be examining the leftovers of a once-great corporation that was both part of and a catalyst of the globalization of the late twentieth century. Not so: Nike remained a key player. So how was Nike able to survive, if not prosper?

Young people born during early phases of the credit boom of the 1990s were "programmed to buy, buy, buy and it seems the credit crunch may not be enough to break the habit," observed the *Financial Times'* Samantha Pearson in 2009 (July 9: 14).

The reason, Pearson argued, is that consumerism and anticonsumerism coexist side by side. Those who pelted world leaders with eggs and marched through the streets at every G8 summit (i.e. meetings of United States, Japan, Germany, United Kingdom, France, Italy, Canada, and Russia) were representative of a section of young people. But other sections maintained the sense of entitlement cultivated during the credit boom: they believed it was their right to have Wiis, portable gadgets, music downloads and, above all, clothes. This was Nike's core market: 18–29-year-olds, who refused to cut back on their clothes expenditure regardless of their financial state.

Think of the best-known brand in the world. Did ✔ pop into your mind? More likely a multicolored six-letter logo beginning with a capital "G." Or the timeless cursive script of *Coca-Cola*, or even ▶You. According to Millward Brown Optimor's "100 most valuable global brands" report, Nike wasn't even the top clothing brand in 2010: it had been displaced by the style-savvy Swedish firm H & M, though remaining in the top 60. The remarkable thing is that Nike has been able to withstand the kind of PR hammering that would have finished many other corporations. As I argued earlier, its ability to do so was based on its credibility and its preparedness to own up to its own sins and meet the challenge set by the consumer market.

OF RELATED INTEREST

Two solid, if dated accounts of Nike and the changing social conditions that facilitated its growth are: *Swoosh: The unauthorized story of Nike and the men who played there* by J. B. Strasser and Laurie Becklund (HarperBusiness, 1993) and *Just Do It: The Nike spirit in the corporate world* (Random House, 1994) by Donald Katz, who has also written "Triumph of the swoosh," in *Sports Illustrated* (August 16, 1993).

"Nike's communication with black audiences" by Ketra L. Armstrong (*Journal of Sport & Social Issues* vol. 23, no. 3, August, 1999; reprinted in David Rowe's *Critical Readings: Sport, culture and the media*, Open University Press, 2004) examines the way in which Nike targeted black consumers. Also worth reading in this context: *Nike Culture: The sign of the swoosh* by Robert Goldman and Stephen Papson (Sage, 1999) which also looks at Nike's advertising and marketing.

"Sports marketing and the challenges of globalization: A case study of cultural resistance in New Zealand" by Andrew Grainger and Steven J. Jackson (in *International Journal of Sports Marketing and Sponsorship*, vol. 2, no. 2, 2000) records how Nike's global marketing strategy backfired: "Despite the common equation of globalization with homogenization. . .in any local context, domestic traditions, language and regulation still play key, often predominant, roles in determining culture and identity."

"Global games: Culture, political economy and sport in the globalised world of the 21st century" by John Nauright (in *Third World Quarterly*, vol. 25, no. 7, 2004) provides a sobering reminder of some of the new inequalities brought about by globalization: "For example, the combined annual income of Tiger Woods for 2003 was U.S.$76.6 million, while [the South Asian state] Bhutan's Gross Domestic Product amounted to

$68 million . . . The value of leading sport franchises such as Real Madrid, Manchester United or the New York Yankees exceeds the GDP of many developing nations such as Paraguay, Honduras or Zambia."

"Concerning the effect of athlete endorsements on brand and team-related intentions" by Brad D. Carlston and D. Todd Donavan (in *Sport Marketing Quarterly*, vol. 17, 2008) reports on a study that concludes: "As fans identify more strongly with an athlete, the more they intend to purchase the endorsed products." This may seem patently obvious, though the authors take account of mediating variables, such as whether the endorser plays for a team and whether the fans' like or dislike of the team affects purchasing decisions. Tiger Woods does not play for a team, of course: "Since Tiger Woods signed with Nike, annual sales for Nike Golf have grown to nearly $500 million with an estimated 24 percent per year growth in the first five years of the agreement."

ASSIGNMENT

You are a sports reporter for a local television station in Tulsa which has had an NBA franchise for ten years, yet has won nothing and reached the playoffs only twice. One of the league's most colorful players has recently become a free agent and has expressed strong interest in joining the Tulsa Tempest, as the club is called. The player is a controversial character who has been the NBA's leading rebounder for the past five years, but who has had several brushes with the law, is in the middle of a stormy marriage with a supermodel, and stars in action movies. Many doubt he will fit in with the conservative suburban style of Tulsa. The team holds a press conference at which the owner announces that the player has signed. The player shows up wearing a glittering ankle-length evening gown which, he boasts, is a Donna Karan creation. You have five questions. What are they and how does the player answer them?

IS BEING LEFT-HANDED AN ADVANTAGE IN SPORTS?

In some sports, yes. Considering that, in any given population and at any time, between 8 and 10 percent of people use their left hand more naturally than their right, the number of athletes cropping up in lists of all-time "greats" is disproportionately high – Babe Ruth, Brian Lara, Kenny Stabler, Martina Navratilova, Marvin Hagler, and Rod Laver – to name but a few.

Marshaling data about athletes, including both amateurs and world class professionals, Violaine Llaurens *et al.* concluded that, compared to their total size in the population, lefties are overrepresented in sports and actually have an edge in some. "Left-handedness frequencies in interactive sports (such as fencing, boxing, tennis, baseball, cricket), offering a strategic advantage to the rarer left-hander, appear to be very high, when compared with non-interactive sports (gymnastics, swimming, bowling), where the frequencies are no different from those of the general population," (2009: 889; frequencies refers to the rates at which something occurs over a period of time).

Left-handers have an advantage in interactive sports – those sports in which an opponent is directly confronted, as opposed to competing alongside – as in track, golf, swimming etc., where there is no overrepresentation. Not only are lefties over-represented in interactive sports, they achieve more than their numbers would suggest. Proximity is also a factor: the closer the interaction between opponents, the greater the prevalence of left-handers. So, we would expect more southpaw boxers than lefty baseball hitters or pitchers and even fewer left-handed rugby players.

Yet even in sports like tennis and cricket where competitors face each other at several yards distance, there is more than the expected number of lefties. Michel Raymond *et al.*'s research indicated that, over a 6-year period, about 16 percent of top tennis players were left-handed and between 15–27 percent of bowlers in international cricket and pitchers in Major League Baseball. For close-quarter sports, the difference was more pronounced: 33 percent of competitors in the men's world foils championships, increasing to 50 percent by the quarter-final stage of the competition. Remember: this is a group that represents 10 percent of the total male population at most. The pattern was less marked for women, though there was still overrepresentation at the fencing championships.

So, the stats confirm that left-handed competitors over-achieve in relation to their numbers in the total population But why? There may be a compensatory mechanism at work: left-handed people are disadvantaged in many areas, and so seek to compensate by becoming highly competent in others, if only as a matter of survival. Hand-to-eye coordination, quick reflexes, astute judgment, tactical awareness, or just raw strength could compensate for disadvantages elsewhere.

Alternatively, favoring one's left arm in a context geared to right-hand biases could confer a strategic advantage on competitors who favor their left hands. Because of the frequency of right-handers in any given population, sports performers are habituated in training and in competition to facing other righties. So, left-handers, because of their relative scarcity, have an edge of sorts: they hit, run and move in unexpected ways. This seems the more plausible explanation. Let's expand.

A study by Robert Brooks *et al.* of the 2003 cricket world cup discovered that: "Left-handed batsmen have a strategic advantage over bowlers. . .this advantage is greatest over bowlers that are unaccustomed to bowling to left-handers."

This complements the innumerable demotic accounts of orthodox (left leg forward) boxers who detest fighting southpaws because of the special problems they pose. These include having to jab along the same path as the opponent's jab and constantly having one's front foot trodden on. Similarly, baseball hitters swing at the ball in such a way that their momentum carries their bodies in the direction they want to move to get to first base; saving fractions of a second can be vital in a game where fielding is crisp and accurate. Pitchers, like cricket bowlers can deliver at unfamiliar angles. Returning serve against left-handed tennis players is known to be difficult for a right-hander, especially defending the advantage court; left-handed servers use slice to make the ball swerve diagonally across the body of the receiver or into the receiver's body. In basketball, a portsider typically tries to pass opponents on the side they least expect; there is barely time to determine whether the opponent is left-handed or not.

The strategic advantage of playing against opponents who are accustomed to anomalous patterns of play seems to be the answer to the preponderance of left-handed winners in some sports. In others, where being left-handed counts for little, their prevalence is about the same as in the general population. According to Raymond *et al.*, 9.6 percent of goalkeepers in soccer are lefties; and left-handed field-eventers account for 10.7 percent of all competitors. Yet, at the top levels of darts, snooker, bowling, and gymnastics, lefties are actually under-represented. Somehow, they gravitate toward the sports in which they possess a natural advantage. There are, of course, notable exceptions: golfer Phil Mickelson, pole-vaulter Stacy Dragila, MotoGP rider Valentino Rossi, for example.

As we noted in Chapter 2, natural selection favors the best physically equipped (strongest) species, which survive and are able to pass on their genes to their offspring. This would account, albeit in a crude way, for the persistence of left-handed people in an environment built largely by and for right-handers and in which social pressures might reasonably have been expected to persuade lefties to change their biases. The reason for this lies in history.

The correct word for left-handedness is *sinistrality,* deriving from the Latin for "left," *sinister*, which also means an evil omen (as in a sinister-looking person), or something malignant (sinister motive). Historically, there was little difference: left-handed people were associated with malevolence. As that myth receded, it was replaced by more enlightened empirical research, much of which still suggested some sort of undesirable characteristic. Most explanations were based on the lateralization of the brain, that is the degree to which the right and left cerebral hemispheres of the brain differ in specific functions. The human brain is divided into two hemispheres, the left side often being described as the dominant half because that's where the centers of language and speech and of spatial perception are located in most people. Nerves on the two sides of the body cross each other as they enter the brain, so that the left hemisphere is associated with the right-hand side of the body. In most right-handed people the left hemisphere directs speech, reading and writing, while the right half is responsible for emotions.

For years, it was thought that left-handedness was the result of a kind of reversal of the more usual pattern, with the main functions of the brain being on the right. But, in 1976, research by J. Levy and M. Reid showed that, in fact, most left-handers are still left-brain dominant and have their centers of language, speech, and spatial perception in the same place as right-handers. But was this unfavorable? Norman Geschwind and Albert Galaburda discovered an association between left-handedness and immune or immune-related disorders, this stemming from birth-related problems. Left-handedness was also related to disabilities, such as stammering and dyslexia. Later studies cast doubt on these conclusions.

Stanley Coren and Diane F. Halpern added to the woes of left-handers when they found that the mean age of death for lefties was 66 compared with 75 for righties. Again birth problems were cited as a cause: exposure to high fetal testosterone at birth may lead to developmental problems for left-handed people. And research by Warren O. Eaton *et al.* indicated that left-handers have "maturational lag" (a type of learning difficulty).

Coren and Halpern included the possibility that there were cultural factors involved. We live in a world that has been designed and built with right-handed people in mind. Door handles, telephones, cars: the construction of these and countless other technological features reflects right-handedness. So, when left-handed people perform even the simplest of functions, they find them slightly more awkward and so have a higher risk of accidents (and accident-related injuries). Several subsequent studies confirmed that lefties were more prone to accidents. The research supporting or refuting the relationship between left-handedness and early death, accident-proneness, maturational lag, and other pathologies continues.

Whatever the developmental problems associated with left-handedness and their consequences, sport remains one of the areas in which being sinister is a beneficial trait, others being music and mathematics, according to Llaurens *et al.* This may help explain why so many left-handers gravitate toward sport, though their disproportionate success seems to be related to anomalousness rather than innate superiority. By deviating from what is standard, or expected, left-handed competitors present unusual and unfamiliar challenges.

MORE QUESTIONS . . .

>> Is left-handedness still an advantage in sports that involve less use of the arms, like association football or diving?

>> How might you set about changing a naturally left-handed child into a right-hander?

>> Do left-handers pose particular problems for coaches and managers?

READ ON . . .

Stanley Coren and Diane F Halpern, "Left-handedness: A marker for decreased survival fitness," *Psychological Bulletin*, 1991.

Stanley Coren, *Left Hander: Everything you need to know about left-handedness*, John Murray, 1992.

Lauren J. Harris, "Do left-handers die sooner than right-handers? Commentary on Coren and Halpern's (1991) 'Left-handedness: A marker for decreased survival fitness'," *Psychological Bulletin*, 1993.

K. Pass, H. Freeman, J. Bautista, and C. Johnson, "Handedness and accidents with injury," *Perceptual and Motor Skills*, 1993.

P. Muris, W. J. Kop, and H. Merckelbach, "Handedness, symptom resorting and accident susceptibility," *Journal of Clinical Psychology*, 1994.

Robert Brooks, Luc F Bussière, Michael D. Jennions, and John Hunt, "Sinister strategies succeed at the cricket World Cup," *Proceedings of the Royal Society, Biological Sciences: B*, 2004.

Violaine Llaurens, Michel Raymond, and Charlotte Faurie, "Why are some people left-handed? An evolutionary perspective," *Philosophical Transactions of the Royal Society, B: Biological Sciences*, 2009.

CHAPTER 17

KEY ISSUES

▌ How do celebrities make us buy . . . practically anything?

▌ What makes sports so appealing to advertisers?

▌ When did the first celebrity sportsman appear?

▌ Where did celebrity culture come from?

▌ Why are we so fascinated by people who make no material impact on our lives?

▌ . . . and was David Beckham really "David Beckham"?

Buying into Celebrity Culture

▌ KNOWN FOR BEING . . . WELL, KNOWN

"People are recognizable as much because of who they're not as who they are," writes Tom Payne in his *Fame: From the Bronze Age to Britney* (2009: 203). Rodney Marsh was *not* George Best. He was around at the same time, and, like Best, he played professional football in a way that drew comparison. He was also a wayward type, a virtuoso on the field, but headstrong and obstinate and, in every way, "his own man." But he wasn't Best, the singular Irishman who consorted with beauty queens and movie stars, who looked like one of the Beatles, and who lived the kind of pleasure-seeking, philandering, womanizing life that kept the media rapt.

Marsh was born in 1944, Best in 1946. Both played professional football in the 1960s, and, while Best is acknowledged as the finest player of his generation, Marsh offered a thrilling rivalry. Marsh moved to Florida to play for Tampa Bay Rowdies of the North American Soccer League (NASL) in 1976. He stayed in the United States, managing the Rowdies and two other clubs in the 1980s. After his glorious years in Manchester, Best also went to play in the United States in 1976, playing for NASL clubs in LA, Fort Lauderdale, and San Jose.

Best seldom set out to court the media. He was pursued and eventually haunted by them. When he died in 2005, he concluded a strange career: a celebrity player he grew up in an age when sports stars were few. Muhammad Ali was a colossal figure and Joe Namath, of the New York Jets, was starrily known as "Broadway Joe" in the United States. Best never seemed comfortable with the extraordinary attention he generated. Marsh, on the other hand, embraced it. He worked for Sky Sports television until 2005 when he was fired after making an off-color remark about the tsunami disaster. In 2007, Marsh – then a spry 63-year old – submitted himself to the Australian rain forests in *I'm a Celebrity . . . Get Me Out of Here!* Again his misfiring remarks occasioned outrage before a ligament injury forced him out of the show.

Best was never a celebrity, at least not in the way we understand celebrities today. The bad news for him was that the media could not quite figure him out: should they cover him as an athlete, or a pop star? Nowadays, it doesn't make any difference: football players are treated in the same way as rock stars, movie actors, fashion models, or practically any other kind of figure that arouses attention. Best was an athlete who clearly liked the hedonistic lifestyle his peculiar status afforded him. He bought a nightclub and a boutique, as designer clothes stores were called in the 1960s. He was caught regularly drinking with showbusiness types. In his retirement, he, like Marsh, worked in the media. But the prospect of his agreeing to participate in a reality television show is unthinkable. Marsh, on the other hand, chimed with the times: he was willing to be a celebrity.

BOX 17.1 CELEBRITY

The status of being well known, praised, exalted, or attributed with importance is also used to describe persons, or things, endowed with such status. So, someone can *have* celebrity, and also *be* a celebrity. The provenance of the word is revealing: from the French *célébrité*, which derives from the Latin *celebritas*, meaning honored or renowned, the term has strayed into English language dissociated from references to accomplishments or great deeds.

The age of celebrity is well and truly upon us. We live in times when the famous are like new gods. We – and I mean all of us, fans, analysts, and journalists – don't just admire the famous. We adore, adulate, and, in some cases, worship a class of people that have become known as celebs.

Celebrities haven't just emerged: we've created them. We, the idolatrous audience, have, as the definition suggests, invested them with great importance. In some cases, we attribute almost supernatural qualities to them. Of course, they're flesh-and-blood mortals like the rest of us. Yet, at times, they seem to exist in a different world.

We seem to like the division between Them and Us. They, the celebs, seem to live in a world so richly large, so showily opulent, so untouchably distant that we can never hope to get near, less still join it. Up till quite recently, celebrities were locked away in the Them camp: the celebrities themselves were remote, glamorous figures and being a fan was based on mystery and ignorance. In recent years, the media have not so much reported on the stars as demystified them: secrets are shared with magazines, close-up interviews are featured on television, biographies spare no detail of personal lives, exposés embarrass the high-and-mighty. Videos have made it possible for fans to capture moments of an individual's or a team's life for their own delectation. There is now an entire industry geared to selling proximity to celebrities. This is a relatively recent development, traceable to no earlier than the 1980s.

Where there were once sports stars, or even superstars, there are now celebrity athletes. In fact, they're just celebrities: their fame might have had its sources in sport, but, when they appear in *Heat* or *People* or on the Jay Leno, or Jonathan Ross tv shows, or on the TMZ.com, or PerezHilton.com, they're indistinguishable from other celebrities.

Marsh rose to prominence at a time when fame was a byproduct of ability; it was incidental to his sporting prowess. In the 1960s and 1970s and well into the 1980s, athletes were judged as athletes: we evaluated them on their prowess on the field, their feats in the arena, not on whom they were sleeping with or what kind of designer underwear they favored, or what razors they endorsed. There might have been extra-sporting intrigue created by marriages featuring prominent athletes and showbusiness stars, such as the New York Yankee's Joe DiMaggio and Marilyn Monroe in 1954, or England's football captain Billy Wright and singer Joy Beverley in 1958. But these were exceptional unions. Ordinarily, athletes, even stars like DiMaggio and Wright, were confined to the sports pages.

But, remember the hoo-ha when Lance Armstrong and Sheryl Crow called off their wedding in 2006? Nowadays, athletes vie with showbiz types for the front pages and the gossip columns, let alone the celebrity magazines that have sprung up over the past decade or so. Top baseball and soccer players are every bit as newsworthy as actors or musicians – as are Tour de France winners. To be a celebrity means that you are *known*; for what doesn't matter. In fact, when you ascend to the A-list, being known supplies its own momentum and you become what known for what Daniel Boorstin, back in 1961, tautologically called "well-knownness" (1961: 57). Well, it seemed a tautology – saying the same thing twice – when it was published; now it seems a reasonable assertion. Well-knownness has become an independent variable. It doesn't rely on anything else for its validity.

Athletes aren't *just* known for their well-knownness, of course. At least, not initially. The source of their renown is their sporting prowess. Once that's noticed, they can garner recognition by their appearance, their partners, their presence at events, and practically anything that interests their audience, including exhibitions in porn videos. Even when their athletic performance declines, they can still draw attention. Falls from grace are eminently newsworthy, especially if they are spectacular falls. Witness Mike Tyson, Hansie Cronje, Marion Jones, Tonya Harding, or Paul Gascoigne. Even as they were brought to their knees, they retained the power to fascinate. The fact remains: we wouldn't have been interested in them in the first place if they weren't overachieving athletes. In this sense, sports celebrities differ from many others. Their public recognition is contingent on their performance, which means that they have to accomplish something that's widely accepted as having merit. That isn't necessarily the case with other celebs.

Unlike nature, celebrity culture *adores* a vacuum. Out of nowhere, it seems, came a plethora of tv channels, movies, DVDs, magazines, and websites, all dedicated to the exaltation of celebrities, many of whom had little to distinguish themselves – apart from their well-knownness, of course. Celebrities suddenly seemed to be everywhere; it was a space devoid of matter of any consequence, The word celebrity became prefixed to "ordinary" occupations, so that we were bequeathed with celebrity chefs, lawyers, and hairdressers. Then there were the ubiquitous "tv presenters," people with no conspicuous talent besides being amiable and, of course, well known.

Censured by critics for being crass, superficial, meretricious, fraudulent, vulgar, simple-minded, and containing no human verity, among other things, celebrity culture became nonetheless pervasive. No area of society escaped the effects of celebrification: not politics (e.g. Arnold Schwarzenegger), not education (e.g. Stephen Hawking) and certainly not the church (e.g. Luis Palau). While our specific interest is with sports, we can't separate this sphere from all the others that have been absorbed into celebrity culture. It might have appeared to pop out of a vacuum, but, on analysis, there were specific conditions under which the age of the celebrity came into being. A clue to the first one is in the idea of the hero.

In the past, heroes came from the ranks of great political figures, military leaders, explorers, scientists, and even philosophers. Sporting heroes were the ones who could not just play, but who embodied values we held dear. They were fearless individuals who would prevail in the most unpromising circumstances, never flinching from pain, nor accepting defeat, always prepared to give up personal glory in the interests of a higher entity, whether the team, the nation or even humanity.

BOX 17.2 HERO

A person admired for achievements and noble qualities (*heroine* for women is now regarded as gendered and a bit passé). The Greek origins of the word expose its meaning: an illustrious warrior, who had earned the grace and favor of the gods. Competitors at the ancient Olympiad were striving for divine benediction and one of the rewards of victory was heroic status. In its more contemporary form, heroes are considered to be figures who have distinguished themselves for their courage and accomplishments, especially in war. In sports, heroes are largely historical characters recognized in retrospect. For example, Babe Ruth (1895–1948) and Jack Dempsey (1895–1983) in the United States; Stanley Matthews (1915–2000), and Freddie Trueman (1931–2006) in Britain; Muhammad Ali (b. 1942) everywhere. There are many, many more – their reputations were based on what they did in the diamond, the ring, or on the pitch. They commanded respect as well as attention. We can name heroes from virtually any decade of the twentieth century, but few from today. Heroic status is conferred on athletes typically some years after they've ceased competing.

Ask yourself this question: would any sports star today be able to keep his or her private life "private"? In fact, there's a second question: is it meaningful to talk of a private life for celebrities? It's almost part of the definition of a celeb that you have to surrender all remnants of a private life to the media, which then make it available for public consumption. A sports celeb differs very little from any other kind of celebrity, whether from the domains of music, movies or fashion. They are all there to entertain us.

Professional sports today are constituents of the entertainment industry. The changes wrought in that industry by the twentieth-century revolution of media of communications are all about us: the coming of television, the proliferation of film, the advent of digital technologies, the creation of cyberspace: these are some of the key developments that have changed the way we get our entertainment, the way we consume it and the lifestyle patterns we make out of it.

BOX 17.3 HISTORY OF CELEBRITY

The condition of being well known is immemorial: dramatists and philosophers earned reputations for their wisdom and political and military leaders for notable achievements since the growth of city-states in the Aegean from 900 BCE Homer, Pythagoras, and Plato remain canonical figures. Alexander the Great commemorated victories over the Persian Empire by naming cities in his honor: the Egyptian port Alexandria was founded in 332 BCE. Alexander has been identified by Leo Braudy, in his *The Frenzy of Renown: Fame and its history*, as the first figure to foment his own fame.

Certainly, famous people appear throughout history; indeed, the way we study history is principally through the decisions and deeds of the famous. But celebrities index a particular type of historical context, one in which fame and accomplishments are decoupled. Some scholars argue that this is not unique to the late twentieth and early twenty-first centuries. "In the first half of the eighteenth century a process occurred by which a nascent culture of celebrity began to form side by side with an existing culture of fame," observes Stella Tillyard, who specifies three specific sets of circumstances: a weak English monarchy with limited moral authority, the lapsing of legislation controlling the numbers of printing presses, and to some extent printing itself, "and a public interested in new ways of thinking about other people and themselves."

Combined with limited prohibition on libel and the proliferation of places of entertainment, these led to a culture in which the casual and unconstrained conversation we now know as gossip about others' lives, public and private, became a kind of right of citizenship.

We now consume sports in much the same way as we consume drama, music, and other forms of amusement: by exchanging money for commodities. Purists once abhorred the way film and, later, television corrupted live theater; connoisseurs deplored the phonographic cylinders that were used to reproduce music. Traditionalists were more ambivalent over the conversion of sports into packaged goods, though many probably lamented the passing of times when being a sports fan involved more than buying a baseball cap and sitting at home with a six-pack and a bigscreen tv. It meant actually going to see competitive action; and, no matter how you analyze the statistics, younger people have tended to go to events less and watch tv more.

No matter what romantics tell us, sports are bigger than they ever were. Bigger, that is, in terms of worldwide popularity, awareness and, importantly, turnover. Never in history, have we spent more time watching sports, mostly on television. We have never been exposed to so many sports images in advertising and marketing. And we now spend much more money not only watching sports, but also buying the merchandise related to sports. Every year, Major League Baseball merchandise sales exceed $3 billion (£1.83 billion), which is more than the GDP of the South American country, Surinam.

Our desire to compete and our even greater desire to watch others compete burns as brightly as ever. The difference is that, in the twenty-first century, sports with international appeal are competing among themselves for the attention and loyalty of fans. With the deluge of sports on our televisions, we might expect an imminent saturation. Yet, there is no sign: sports are poised to maintain their universal popularity for two reasons. On the demand side, we want as much sports as we can get; on the supply side, the sports industry is responding with ever-more sophisticated ways of delivering the goods.

In other words, sports celebrities are delivered to us through exactly the same channels as other kinds of celebs: through the media. What's more we consume them in the same way as we consume the other celebs: by watching them perform on tv, buying the merchandise, logging on to websites devoted to them. We even still go to the actual events in which they appear.

All of which leaves us with an obvious though essential question: how did celebrity culture start? The answer is: with the time–space compression. Go with this for a moment; I'll return to it in the next section.

WATCHED, ADMIRED, PRIVILEGED, AND IMITATED

They're described by Len Sherman as "the most watched, admired, privileged, and imitated people" (1998: 189). Once celebrities were just famous, but, in the twenty-first century, they have acquired a kind of exemplary authority, an influence that they use not usually to facilitate social change or promote good causes, but to sell commodities. A cynical public, having given up and been given up by old institutions, "gladly seizes upon this substitute, a substitute that might not provide a lot of benefits, but doesn't require a lot in return either" (1998: 189). Apart from money, we should add.

Sherman offers a reason for the rise of celebrities to the position of moral authority. In times of national crisis, we're forced to place our faith in traditional leaders; what other choice do we have? Engaged in war or under siege, people look to their politicians, generals, and church leaders. These are active people, who base their reputations on what they say and do, the brave decisions they make, the steadfastness of their resolve, and the steeliness of their will. Like old sporting heroes, they are known for what they do.

In the absence of crises, our commitment becomes less secure and we have no need to trust them anymore. So, on Sherman's account, we look to alternatives. Celebrities may not be obvious replacements, but they are functional equivalents of leaders: people, who represent, influence, perhaps inspire, and command our attention, if not respect.

Daniel Harris agrees: "Celebrities are rapidly filling the roles that priests, politicians, and wealthy philanthropists once served . . . We are transferring moral authority to the only public servants that remain: pop singers, Hollywood stars, and the casts of our favorite sitcoms" (2008: 138).

And evacuees from reality tv shows, we should add. As traditional leaders once guided opinion on how to prosecute the good life, celebrities later instructed by example, consuming conspicuously and inexhaustibly. This then is the first condition under which celebrity culture came into existence: a loss of faith, trust, and confidence in established leaders. Now, we come to the time–space compression.

BOX 17.4 FAME

From the Latin *fama*, meaning reputation or renown, this is the condition of being recognized publicly, spoken of, and having one's actions reported. While it is often contrasted with infamy (notoriety or known for abominations), fame encompasses public recognition for all deeds, good and bad. Fame can be localized, in which case the subject is known by repute only within particular vicinities, or global, and in which case knowledge of the subject is pervasive. Global fame was rare before the twentieth century. The growth of the mass media and, later, multimedia, commissioned the development of genuine international renown. Television especially, from the 1950s, helped create a common culture in which figures from literally anywhere in the world could become recognizable everywhere. Psychologist David Giles emphasizes that today fame is frequently the result of attention from the media, i.e. rather than anything the famous person actually does: "The ultimate modern celebrity is the member of the public who becomes famous solely through media involvement." This in itself is a distinction, as Tom Payne points out: "To be famous is to be different, and even if you're famous for something quite ordinary, you're still distinguished by the property of fame itself."

As we saw in the previous chapter, one of the many consequences of globalization has been a common culture, tastes, labels, languages, being blended into a uniform whole. Not that we've all become submissive conformists: if anything, we have a greater range of choice than at any time in history. It's just that those choices come in neat packages and are mostly offered by global corporations, Nike being one of the principal ones, of course.

Globalization would not have been possible without a media capable of transmitting large volumes of information around the world, not just quickly, but instantly. By information, I mean news, entertainment and advertising. "Advertising, in particular, seeks to sell products by depicting idealized Western lifestyles, often under the universalizing themes of sex, status and the siblinghood of humanity," writes Malcolm Waters in his *Globalization* (2001: 203).

Satellites, or transponders, were the instruments of the media's global expansion. By wrapping the world in an invisible network of communications, satellite broadcasters were able to bounce information off satellites and send them literally anywhere. Satellite television companies recognized no national boundaries. This effectively meant that virtually everyone on earth was part of one huge market.

In Chapter 15 we saw how Rupert Murdoch, perhaps more than any other media figure, exploited the opportunities offered by the satellite technology pioneered in the 1960s, and the deregulation and privatization of the television industry in the 1980s and early 1990s. In February 1989, Murdoch's European satellite started beaming programs via satellite through his Sky network. By the end of the 1990s, his various channels reached 66 percent of the world's population (Stotlar, 2000).

The problem with having so many channels is content: what do you fill them with? MTV supplied a clue. To keep so much of the world glued to the screen, you need a formula. Sports, as we saw previously, was part of the formula designed to maintain people's interest. Televised programming detached itself from fixed content and began firing off in the direction of entertainment, by which I mean amusement – something that occupies us agreeably, diverting our minds from matters that might prompt introspection, analysis, or reflection. I'm not arguing that drama that provokes contemplation and critical examination can't be entertaining too, nor even that the narratives of soaps or cartoons aren't open to critical interrogation. And I'm certainly not underestimating the viewers' speedy acquisition of skills for screening and skimming information. But, for the most part, entertainment doesn't prompt us to modify ourselves in any way.

Light entertainment, to use a more indicative term, became a staple of a formula that demanded only a modest level of attention from viewers. Music+movies+sport. Asked to respond to this in 1990s, an informed person might have said: people will soon get sick of it; they'll feel bombarded, under siege, overwhelmed by too much entertainment. Yet here we are in the twenty-first century and, far from being overwhelmed, we can't seem to get enough.

Of course, the communications revolution didn't end with television and the proliferation of multimedia brought a further layer of information conduits. In a way, the internet worked as a kind of antidote to the potentially pacifying effects of too much televised entertainment. Lying on a couch for six hours a day watching undemanding programs is quite a different experience to sitting at a desk researching in an electronic database or following an online political debate. There are times when they complement each other too. Fans can watch a game on tv, then log on to analyze the game in a fans' chatroom, or even talk to players in "real time."

Let's remind ourselves of Sherman's plausible account of why we are now so devoted to sports. We've lost faith and confidence in established leaders, the central social institutions of state and government and rescinded our memberships of other organizations that were once regarded as valuable, such as unions, political parties, and volunteer groups. This occurred at around the same time as the proliferation of global networks of communication and the increase in entertainment-themed programs to fill those networks. As the media grew in importance, so traditional leaders lost their former status.

A coincidence? Perhaps. Or maybe one hastened the other. In times of national emergency, what alternative is there to having confidence in political leaders, placing trust in military leaders and having faith in religious leaders? In times of stability, skepticism turns either to cynicism or maybe to downright indifference.

Those baby boomers born in the immediate post-war period matured without the sense of crisis and foreboding that war instills. But they had their expectations tempered by parents whose experience of war served to remind them of the deprivations as well as abundance. The offspring of that generation had no such brake on their expectations. In other words, a generation cooled on their leaders and turned their attention to a new class of people who seemed to embody everything they craved.

All of this looks a little too opportune. At that precise time when people were cooling, the new media turned up right on cue and started delivering light, or more appropriately, lite entertainment to everyone's living rooms. We quickly succumbed, dropping existing allegiances and devoting our energies to following and aping the new privileged class that was populating our screens. Too neat. Something else must have happened. Or perhaps *someone*.

MADONNA: LIKE AN ANSWER TO A PRAYER

After the success of her fourth album *Like a Prayer* in 1989 Madonna appears to have seen the future: it was a world in which a new type of celebrity would dominate as consummately as dinosaurs dominated the Jurassic world. The days when people got to be famous and stayed that way through just making movies, hit records, or writing best-sellers were approaching an end. The most important feature of the coming age was visibility: doing was less important than, well, just being right there in the public gaze. With so many channels of communication being filled up with all manner of entertainment, there was bound to be an overflow of entertainers, most of whom would make little impression on the public consciousness. The ones who did were those who would not just make themselves visible, but transparent – there was no contradiction.

Madonna not only epitomized this, but helped it materialize. She seems to have struck a bargain with the media. It was something like this: I will tell you more, show you more about me than any other rock or movie star in history; I will disclose my personal secrets, share my fears, joys, sorrows, what makes me happy or sad, angry or gratified; I will be more candid and unrestricted in my interviews than any other entertainer. In other words, I'll be completely see-through. In return, I want coverage like no other: I want to be inescapable – I want to be everywhere, all the time. It was a delicious *quid pro quo*. The media went for it; and the age of celebrity was upon us.

As the 1980s turned to the 1990s, Madonna was, as she wanted to be, everywhere. This was surely the meaning of Blonde Ambition, the title of her 1991 tour. The following year, she bared herself in her book *Sex*, accompanied by the album *Erotica*. Being famous was no longer sufficient: to be a celebrity, you had to strip yourself, make consumers privy to as many aspects of your life as you dare. And, no one did it better than La Ciccone.

The beauty of the age of celebrity, though, was that the consumers weren't hapless chumps: they were educated in the arts of celeb-production by the very channels that presented them. Put another way, they didn't just look at the pictures: they were able readers. They did most of the work. All the celebs did was make themselves available. Madonna was the first celebrity to render her manufacture completely transparent. Unabashed about revealing to her fandom evidence of the elaborate and monstrously expensive publicity and marketing that went into her videos, CDs, stage acts, and, indeed, herself, Madonna laid open her promotional props, at the same exposing her utterly contrived persona changes.

From Material Girl to Monroe manqué to vamp to cowgirl, she made no attempt to conceal the artfulness of her constructions. Her 1991 movie called *Truth or Dare* in the United States and *In Bed with Madonna* in Britain, while ostensibly, a fly-on-the-wall documentary of the Blonde Ambition tour, was a study of a maternally warm, generous, though impulsive, woman, prone to the occasional but understand-able bouts of bitchiness, yet with wit and charm enough to win over her doubters. In other words, a study in celebrity management. The risk wasn't that fans might not be taken in with the film; they obviously wouldn't be. It was that they might feel cheated: learning only what they already knew.

Today, fans may be in awe of celebrities, but they understand that there's an entire industry at work and that they have been coopted by that industry. The deal is that the fans will stay awed and curious, while the industry will disclose more and more about the celebrities.

Transparency is also apparent in movies, especially ones that employ special fx. Often, television documentaries on "The making of . . ." exposing the technologies that helped create fantastical illusions in the films, are shown either prior or just after the theater release of the main item. A blatant promotional device, maybe; but part of the new bargain: let the consumers in on the trick. As recently as the late 1970s, fans would be astonished by movies such as *Close Encounters of the Third Kind* or *Alien*, leaving theaters asking, "How did they *do* that?" Such wonderment wouldn't be tolerated today. Savvy fans are up to speed on the powers of digitalization and pixels. They want to know exactly how particular fx were achieved and with what consequences.

Madonna wasn't single-handedly responsible for moving the tectonic plates of popular culture. But there is a sense in which she was an archetype: others who aspired to become celebs were going to have to follow her example. Conspicuousness was everything. Someone like the fiercely reclusive Greta Garbo, who carved a career from her inaccessibility, wouldn't have survived as a celebrity in the 1990s. The media would just move on to someone more approachable. Fans would quickly tire of someone who wanted to maintain a private life. In the age of celebrity, the private life was merely another realm for inspection, a point taken up by Joshua Gamson, who argues that we – the fans – became "simultaneous voyeurs of and performers in commercial culture" (1994: 137).

Gamson's research into the fans' experiences indicates that, while they are popularly regarded as witless dummies, fans are in fact aware of their own roles in creating, shaping, and perhaps destroying celebrities.

Accustomed to adventure, humor, sex, and violence in drama, fans developed an appetite for these in real life too. If they didn't find them in their own, they could at least experience them vicariously through the lives of the people they followed. Magazines like *Heat*, *People*, and *Hello* obliged, featuring tales of the celebs at play, which they spun into intriguing narratives for their readers.

Let's recap before we go on. I've identified three changes, two of which occurred around about the same time, the other of which had been in motion for several years before — this being the steady erosion of trust, confidence, and faith in traditional leaders. Of the other two, the proliferation of media, their encircling of the world and their resolution to the problem of "what can we fill all these new channels with?" was utterly crucial. Without the global apparatus, there would have been no effective means to communicate instantly and ubiquitously. And without the overabundance of entertainment programs, there would have been fewer opportunities for anyone, talented or talentless, to become famous.

BOX 17.5 CELEBRITY CULTURE

This is characterized by a pervasive preoccupation with famous persons and extravagant values attached to the lives of public figures whose actual accomplishments may be limited, but whose visibility is extensive. It became a feature of social life, especially in the developed world, during the late 1980s/early 1990s, and extended into the twenty-first century, assisted by a global media that promoted, lauded, sometimes abominated, and occasionally annihilated figures, principally from entertainment and sports. Celebrity culture defined thought and conduct, style and manner. It affected and was affected by not just fans but by entire populations whose lives had been shaped by the shift from manufacturing to service societies and the corresponding shift from consumer to aspirational consumer.

Madonna did have talent and not only singing talent: she also had the cunning to hatch a plan that would change the very nature of the media's relationship with performers. Alright, that's sounds more like a conspiracy than it actually was. But more than any other artist, Madonna uncovered herself to the media, making it less possible for others to engage the media without baring their all, so to speak. Not only this: Madonna also took the adventurous step of actually making her dealings with the media clear, as if she was involving fans in her manufacture. Actually, not "as if": she *was* involving the fans in her manufacture.

Years later, we witnessed the effects of this when legions of young people of massively varying degrees of ability performed in front of tv cameras in often embarrassing attempts to win contests like *Pop Idol*, or *American Idol*. And when people volunteered to open their lives up to public inspection in reality tv shows like

Big Brother. And when "ordinary people" would happily appear on shows like *Jerry Springer*, to disclose the most excruciatingly humiliating details of their personal lives and with no apparent embarrassment (presumably fortified by the knowledge that most of the audience would do the same if their positions were exchanged). And when once famous figures whose power to entrance had either faded or disappeared could leap back into the public imaginations simply by inviting television cameras to trail them around while doing nothing in particular. Ozzy Osbourne and Katie "Jordan" Price can testify.

SHOPPING AS A WAY OF LIFE

Walk around any shopping precinct in Britain and it won't be long before you run into someone wearing a replica shirt bearing the name of a football player. Replica shirts are less prevalent in the United States, though there are usually plenty of NBA tops to be seen. Of course, baseball caps are everywhere. It might seem perfectly obvious, but ask yourself why advertisers spend such fantastic amounts of money to persuade not only athletes but any celebrity, however minor, to endorse their products. The answer seems to be: because they help sell them. The tougher question is: how? What is it about seeing a celeb wear or use something, or even reading about them using it that makes us want to do the same?

The old purpose of shopping was to buy goods and services that we needed. It wasn't meant as an enjoyable experience: just something that had to be done to get through the week. We were consumers, but not in the sense that we are today. Maybe aspirational consumers would be more apposite: we consume because we yearn to be something, or even someone.

This sounds faintly pathetic, but that's just the way contemporary consumer society works: not by supplying goods that we need, but by promoting desires, wishes, and passions that can never be satisfied, only temporarily satiated until the craving

BOX 17.6 CONSUMERISM

Cultures preoccupied with the acquisition of consumer goods are characterized by consumerism and are sometimes known as consumer cultures. The impact of consumerism is total rather than segmental, as Steven Miles captures it in his *Consumerism as a Way of Life*: "Consumerism has an increasingly important role to play as a framework within which people conduct their lives . . . [it] offers the individual an arena within which he or she can seek out an individual biography, that biography is inevitably tempered by the fact that the individual can never be entirely unique within this realm." Consumerism promotes a kind of democracy in which people can express their individuality through purchases and display of commodities.

returns. That's why shopping is a joy. Retail therapy is the way to happiness, success, and even identity.

The cosmetics industry was something of a pioneer in this respect. As early as the 1930s, it marketed its products not according to their functional values, but according the benefit they were supposed to purvey. So, when you bought, say, Revlon products, you weren't buying foundation cream or lipstick, but glamor and attractiveness. Even as late as the 1960s, many advertisers hadn't caught on and were still marketing shampoo as stuff that cleans hair or cars as vehicles that go from A to B.

By the 1990s, shampoo provided shine, silkiness, protection from UV rays, and, above all, radiance. And cars were to be experienced rather than driven. Today, every advertisement tries to sell something other than the actual product: a lifestyle, an image, or a solution to a problem with which it has no obvious association.

We know what the advertisers want: to move products off the shelves or out of the showrooms. What do consumers want – products? Obviously, but not just for their use-value. In his book *Celebrity*, Chris Rojek argues that fans "seek validation in imaginary relationships with the celebrity to whom they are attached in order to compensate for feelings of invalidation and incompleteness elsewhere in their lives" (2001: 52).

We don't have to agree with all of this: it's possible that fans (and we'll assume Rojek means all consumers who have even a fleeting interest in celebrities) are not all searching for compensation for the emptiness of their own lives, but maintain "attachments," perhaps as a way of associating with people they admire, respect, or are just fond of. That probably applies to all the readers and the writer of this book. Whether we admit it or not, we all buy things that celebrities promote.

Even if they don't have lucrative endorsement contracts, celebrities are promoting. They're like walking, talking, advertisements for the good life. I mean by this that their sheer presence advertises a version of the kind of life we should all aspire to. We can approach, though never reach, that good life through buying the kinds of products they conspicuously consume, all of which, when bought, can take us that little bit nearer to people who rarely acknowledges our existence.

Lee Barron invoked Pierre Bourdieu's concept of *habitus* to understand how consumers are invited to engage and share with fashionable celebrities endorsing products, in particular clothes, cosmetics, and personal products: "To purchase such items may, symbolically at least, enable the consumer to share in the glamour of such celebrities" (2007: 457).

In this sense, celebrities not only advertise commodities, but the culture in which those commodities acquire value. Celebrities promote what some call "consumption as a way of life": their sheer presence persuades consumers to buy goods for which there is no obvious need. To extend Barron's point, the "need" is developed in the *habitus*, the way in which experience is constituted. Celebrities are both fabricators of and ambulant advertisements for consumer culture.

Consumer culture was originally built on the materialism, envy and possessiveness that flourished in the post-war years. Desire drove us towards appropriation: we wanted to have the things we saw dangled in front of us by advertising. The advertising industry had sensed that people didn't buy products just because they needed them: the needs had to be encouraged. Desire worked much better. If you desire something, the second you have it, the desire is gone. So, the trick was to keep pumping up new desires: as soon as you upgrade the fridge, you start thinking about a new car. As soon as you get the car, you start thinking about a new house. "The accelerator of consumer demand," as Zygmunt Bauman calls it, is pressed hard down as new offers keep appearing on the road ahead.

Bauman argues that one of the triumphs of consumer culture is in changing the principle behind buying from need to want and, then, to desire – turning shoppers into pleasure seekers. "Consumer society has achieved a previously unimaginable feat: it reconciled the reality and pleasure principles by putting, so to speak, the thief in charge of the treasure box", Bauman concludes (2001: 16). What we used to think of as irrational now strikes us as perfectly normal. Max'ing out our credit cards, taking on gigantic mortgages, shopping for fun, vacationing in exotic places we can't afford: these might once have seemed instances of certifiable madness; now they seem quite normal. After all, seeking pleasure is a rational activity, isn't it?

Shopping is now considered glamorous, not utilitarian. The consumer is encouraged to declare his and her worth by spending money on items that will help them look like, play like, or in some other way, be like, someone else. That someone else is the celeb, or more likely, celebs with whom they feel or want to feel an attachment.

So, how do celebrity *athletes* specifically prompt us to shop? The kind of global changes we have covered in Chapters 15 and 16 have had many effects, one of which is to turn sports into entertainment. Yet there is more drama in sports today. You might suppose that it no longer shares any DNA with its 4,000-year-old ancestor. But it does. The crucial *indeterminacy* that makes sports exciting and which we emphasized in Chapter 1 will always ensure it's never completely absorbed into pure entertainment. Yet celebrity culture has left its fingerprints all over sports and the people who play them.

THE GAP BETWEEN CELEBRITIES AND REAL PEOPLE

Celebrity athletes have much in common with other celebs, including their ability to make us shop. Replica shirts and baseball caps are just the start. Sports celebs come into view in just the same way as other celebrities: through the media. How and what they consume is now staple fare for the magazines and tv shows. They are every bit as potent as Hollywood stars when it comes to advertising the good life. Seeing Serena Williams step out of a $200,000 Lamborghini wearing a $3,000 Balenciaga dress may not send people rushing to balenciaga.com, but that $150 necklace she's wearing is the same one you can get at the mall. And it's a Bvlgari. Well, not quite: her's actually cost $18,500, but the one at the mall looks just the same and, to authenticate our attachment, we'll get some Bvlgari perfume and Bvlgari sunglasses, which will set us back another couple of hundred or so.

Strange as it seems, we used to respect the gulf between the stars and us. We'd happily wait for those airbrushed pictures of the Hollywood crowd and their like wearing the best clothes and in the best hair and makeup money could buy. They had an otherworldly quality about them that we loved. It was Them and Us. There's still a gulf, of course. It's just that celebrity culture has narrowed it. The stars-at-their-best pictures are still printed in glossies like *Marie Claire*. But, *Star*, *Heat*, and the newer publications specialize in photos of celebrities in unguarded moments, looking rough, picking their noses, or just being seen in a way they would sooner not be made public.

The celebrity-magazine has succeeded stunningly in showing celebrities appearing and behaving as ordinary people. Aided by reality tv shows, mags have closed the space between Them and Us though sometimes it's apparently possible to imagine Them as fundamentally different. Even Marie O'Riordan, editor of the aforementioned glossy, misjudged the ontological status of celebs when she advised, "the gap between celebrities and real people is diminishing" (in *The Independent Review*, August 2, 2004: 7).

A new type of consumer identification has been set up, involving what Charles Fairchild recognizes as "trust," not just in Williams, Sharapova, and other sports celebs, but in the integrity of the whole sporting enterprise. Celebrity athletes, to be effective endorsers, can't just rely on winning; they need to engage with fans, "constructing and mobilizing their loyalty and trust" (2007: 358).

Looked at in this way, shopping offers a way to strengthen our bonds with the people we admire and the good life in which they appear to luxuriate. Shopping in the age of celebrity has undergone something of transformation (compare Dittmar's account in 1992 with Goldberg *et al.*'s 2003 study).

Potentially, anything can induce us to shop. Watching a cookery program featuring a celebrity chef on tv, or a home improvement show, or even one of those "how to keep your house clean" series: they're not just there to be enjoyed. They also make us spend. There's a marvelously convenient "fit" between the requirements of the global media, the demands of a culture that turns celebrities into commodities, and the imperatives of consumer society. We watch, listen to, and, in many other ways, follow celebrities in the multiple media we have at our disposal, then go out and shop away our disposable income.

The importance of the equivocal alliance between celebrity and media can't be overemphasized, the latter feeding off celebrities and the former needing the so-called oxygen of publicity to survive. Another example of the symbiosis we covered in Chapter 16. Theoretically, it might seem that athletes could survive without it. They could insist that only their sports performance is open for public exhibition and that their private life is strictly their own business. Whether or not this would be a successful strategy we don't know: nobody's tried it.

Most athletes are too concerned about sinking like stones as they swim toward the shores of the good life. They grab every endorsement contract available, exploit every photo opportunity and turn up to every opening (of club, restaurant, movie etc.) imaginable. Fame, money, and adulation may not be the initial motivation for a career in sports. But who would pass on them? Foregoing a private life seems a modest sacrifice.

For the others who actually do want to keep a portion of their lives private, this is not good news. The media is so habituated to probing the crust of outward appearances that they can't or won't discriminate. A withdrawn athlete is just as much fair game as an exhibitionist *Big Brother* contestant.

Consider two cases. (1) In the late twentieth century, the vigilant mediawatch on David Beckham worked as straightforwardly as cause→effect in turning him into the world's most famous athlete since Michael Jordan. That status earned him more comprehensive surveillance in the twenty-first century and stories of his playing away from home, so to speak, were reported not just to his wife but to the entire population of the world. What might, in many other circumstances, have been a private matter became very public, with resounding repercussions for Beckham's professional life, too.

(2) In 2009, Martina Navratilova was sued by a former lover, Toni Layton, who claims the former tennis player dumped her after nearly eight years, causing her "emotional, mental and physical trauma." The lawsuit meant Navratilova, who dominated women's tennis in the 1970s and 1980s, had her private life exposed in court for a second time: another former lover, Judy Nelson, who left her husband and two children to live with Navratilova, sued for $7.5 million in 1991. During her playing days, Navratilova was open about her sexuality, but sought to retain a semblance of a private life. By the time of Layton's legal action, she had, in 2008, at the age of 52, consented to participate in *I'm a Celebrity . . . Get Me Out of Here!* She came second.

Like other celebrities, athletes today gladly receive the attention while they're on the rise and remain appreciative at their peak. So, when they moan about the persistent intrusions into their private life and their inability to move without a retinue of photographers, we suspect they are either pretending they don't enjoy it, or unwilling to accept that, when you become public property, you lose the right to a private life. Unless, of course, the courts rule otherwise, as they sometimes do. Despite the successful legal claims to privacy of Naomi Campbell in England, Michael Douglas and Catherine Zeta-Jones in the United States, and Princess Caroline of Hanover in the European Court of Human Rights, there is little evidence that the media's love affair with celebrities has gone cold.

Still, we need to remind ourselves: athletes, unlike the more ephemeral celebrities, who flit in and out of our attention monitors, do something other than just appear. They perform. Admittedly, celebrity status can often overpower athletic performance. Mike Tyson was still a pay-per-view performer in his late thirties when his time-eroded skills were all but gone. In his retirement, he appeared in films, such as James Toback's feature length documentary *Tyson* (2008) and Todd Phillips' 2009 comedy *The Hangover*. Other celebrities whose status originated in sports have used that status to transfer into film: Dwayne "The Rock" Johnson and Vinnie Jones, for example, have appeared in over 50 films each. The expansion of televised sports has also made it possible for celebrity athletes to prolong their sports careers long after retirement by becoming media commentators or pundits.

The point is that, while athletes are different in some respects from other celebs, they're very similar in others, including their equivocal relationships with the media. In his *Illusions of Immortality*, David Giles writes: "The proliferation of media for publicizing the individual has been reflected in a proliferation of celebrated individuals. As the mass media has expanded, so individuals have had to do less in order to be celebrated" (2000: 32).

Giles is right in his first point: there *are* more celebrity athletes today. But does his second point apply to athletes? Some might argue that athletes of only modest abilities could become celebrities as long as the media take notice of them. They will probably point to Anna Kournikova as a prime example. Others? Well, there are probably other celebrity athletes whose status disguises their playing limitations. But athletes who become *somebodies* usually distinguish themselves competitively.

It's difficult to garner media attention without substance. Wearing outrageous clothes, looking like a supermodel, behaving aggressively or raising hell in nightclubs are some of the ways athletes grab the headlines. But, if they're not good athletes as well, who cares? We should remember that, Kournikova apart, we are hard-pressed to name an athlete who has become a celebrity despite an absence of sporting prowess: most have earned initial recognition with something other than just well-knownness. Even Maria Sharapova, whose plentiful endorsements and modeling assignments made her the highest paid female athlete of the 2000s, won three grand slams by the end of 2010.

CLOSER TO THE GODS

What's in it for the fan? When Marina Sejung Choi and Nora J. Rifon point out, "consumers are constantly transporting symbolic properties out of products into their lives to construct their self," they suggest a mechanism through which celebrities transmute into commodities: "Celebrity emulation may take the form of purchasing and using the product endorsed by the celebrity, thereby obtaining the celebrity-conveyed meanings and constructing a satisfying self-concept" (2007: 309).

This is not quite as airy as it sounds. Shopping might be gratifying. Using our purchases might be enjoyable, perhaps even rapturous. Every step we take toward the world of Them might fill us with pleasure. But, in a way, all this could be just a big con, designed to separate us from our money and maintain our dependence on commodities. Surely, there's something else? Following celebrities must satisfy us in a – dare we say it? – deeper way.

At least two contemporary writers, Chris Rojek and John Maltby, have discerned the resemblance between spiritual devoutness and celebrity culture. Rojek's sociological approach yields parallels between following celebrities and ritual, shamanism, and experiences of ecstasy (the exalted state, not the class A drug). Secularization has not led to the replacement of religion by science, but it has meant a displacement of religious activities and beliefs into other areas, such as animal rights campaigns and ecology movements. On Rojek's account, there has also been a "substantial convergence between religion and consumer culture" (2001: 57).

A godless world leaves a "terrifying meaninglessness" and celebrities help fill the void. Of course, you could argue that following celebrities is meaningless in its own right: it seems trivial, pointless, unimportant and insignificant to an outsider. To someone who is involved in it, on the other hand, it can be tantamount to a religious experience.

BOX 17.7 SECULARIZATION

From the Latin *saeculum*, meaning an age, or generation, this refers to the growth in skepticism of religious knowledge and the corresponding decline in social significance of religion. Several influential theorists of the nineteenth and twentieth centuries, including Sigmund Freud, Max Weber and Karl Marx, predicted that the emergence of industrial society and the rise of science would make religion marginal and lead to a secular society, i.e. one in which sacred and ecclesiastical, or church affairs, are subordinated to worldly, or profane matters. (A *secularist* is someone opposed to religious education.)

Maltby's psychological research complements this. Celebrity worship syndrome is the expression Maltby uses to describe the condition of fans who adore celebrities. "Syndrome" isn't entirely appropriate, as it suggests a pathological condition that needs treatment. Maltby is not so judgmental: he is conveying an important point about the manner in which young people try to associate themselves with or affix themselves to their chosen celebs. There is a depth of devotion that mere observers just can't understand.

Giles traces the origins of the term "parasocial interaction" to a 1956 article in the journal *Psychiatry* (Horton and Wohl, 1956). The 1950s was the decade of growth for television: at the start, few households had a tv; by the end over 90 percent of household in the United States and the United Kingdom had at least one set. Viewers were forming unusual attachments. They were developing "friendships" with television characters, some fictional and others real (like announcers, or weather forecasters). Familiarity led to a sense of intimacy. Viewers actually thought they knew the figures they saw on their screens. They interacted with them parasocially.

It's called parasocial because *para* means beyond, as in paranormal. The attachment might only have been as strong as a beam of light from a cathode ray tube. Yet it was experienced as strong and meaningful. Consumers actually felt they knew people they had never met, probably never seen in the flesh and who knew nothing of their existence. So there is no actual interaction (*inter* means between): it's one way. This doesn't stop the consumer's feeling like there's a genuine interaction.

We often hear about fans who become stalkers after hearing a hallowed celebrity's voice commanding them. Fans regularly accost actors who play loathsome characters in the soaps. As we noted in Chapter 12 ("Not for the fainthearted") a devotee of the singer Björk believed he was acting out her will when he videotaped himself committing suicide. Of course, the celebs contribute to the feelings through their public performances but have no way of gauging the depth of fans' feelings toward them apart from fan mail or website conversations.

The point about parasocial interaction is that it's more relevant today than it was in the 1950s. At a time when there are more celebrities than ever, there are more fans experiencing feelings of emotional closeness and perhaps organizing parts of their lives around such feelings. A couple of films have dramatized this nicely. In

Gurinder Chadha's 2002 movie *Bend it Like Beckham* the central character Jess confides in no one, not even her closest friends. Yet David Beckham is her oracle: his face graces a poster on her bedroom ceiling and, at night, she lies in bed pouring out her heart to him, as ancient Greeks would once consult their deities for advice or prophecy. In Ken Loach's 2009 *Looking for Eric*, a worshipful Cantona fan conjures up his icon and instigates life-altering changes as a result of what he supposes is advice.

Although, in the original meaning, parasocial interaction was unilateral, we need to revise it to allow for the possibility of bilateral interaction. Fans can really interact. It's almost become part of the celeb's job definition: interacting with fans, however fleetingly (like signing an autograph), however cursorily (in a radio or tv phone-in) or however remotely (through cyberspace, maybe), there is always a chance it will happen.

There are certainly parallels between religious devotion and the exaltation of gods, on the one hand, and the reverence and worship of today's celebrity culture. This is most evident in obsessional fans, including stalkers and those who are either deluded or fixated by fans to the point of becoming pathological. It's also apparent in organized groups of fans, such as Elvis devotees and those longstanding Trekkies (see Jindra, 1994). So there is support for the idea that celebrities help relieve the "terrifying meaningless" of secular society, though we should guard against regarding celebrity culture as a kind of functional equivalent of religion.

For a start, it's possible that secularization has been exaggerated. The United States and Western Europe, have often been cited as secular, but they have far from abandoned religion. And the post-communist resurgence of organized religion in eastern European countries suggests a spiritual comeback. Combine these with the Islamic revival that has swept across the world in the early twenty-first century, the emergence of New Age beliefs, the evangelical revival that swept through Latin America and the widespread ethno-religious conflicts in international affairs and you are left with an image of what we might call a de-secularization.

BOX 17.8 PARASOCIAL INTERACTION

Interaction with imaginary, fictitious, legendary, or illusory beings, such as cartoon characters, or dramatic figures, these are unilateral (one-sided), affecting only one party. Film, television, and radio fans enter into relationships with figures with whom a bilateral (two-sided) relationship is improbable, though not impossible, as the Martin Scorsese 1982 movie *The King of Comedy* illustrated. In it, Rupert Pupkin obsesses over getting his own tv show, creating his own mock studio, complete with cutout guests, at his apartment. Not only does he follow the stars: he uses them as his own, imagining he's with them, that he has what they have, that he can do what they do. It's a triumph of fantasy. At least, until he decides to buttonhole a real tv presenter, then fraudulently gain entrance to his home.

Far from disappearing, religion has acquired a new role in what Ronald Inglehart and Pippa Norris call "existential security." In their 2004 book *Sacred and Secular: Religion and politics worldwide,* they argue that, during the second half of the twentieth century, all advanced industrial societies moved toward a secular state, but the world as a whole now has more people with traditional religious views than ever before. That's because, secularization has a substantial effect on human fertility rates. So, while Inglehart and Norris don't dismiss secularization, they marshal convincing evidence that it's not a straightforward process and that religiosity (being religious) persists, particularly in poorer nations and in failed states facing personal survival-threatening risks. Exposure to risks drives religiosity. The decline of religious practices, values and beliefs is restricted to the more affluent sections of the most prosperous nations.

Also, we have to consider that, when we describe celebs as godlike, or divine we are using similes, not explicit descriptions. Our enthusiasm for celebs might look like the devotion many have to a deity or deities. But that's as far as it goes; as we've seen, celebrities have become more available to us in recent years. In our eyes, they've become more flesh-and-blood and less godlike as the gap between Them and Us has closed.

But is this as true of sports as it is of other areas of entertainment? After all, athletes were latecomers to the celebrity parade. Even at the end of the 1980s, they were sportsmen and sportswomen, not celebrities. High-earners, to be sure. Watched, followed, imitated, and a source of inspiration for many, certainly. But still "real people," to repeat Marie O'Riordan.

Fashion models, rock stars and Hollywood actors might have occupied a position on the celestial equator, but athletes were down here on earth, organic parts of real, not imagined, communities, their roots in the same earth as ours. We weren't interested in their entire lives: just their conduct on the field of play. The term "superstar" was applied to a few overachieving athletes, but they were, almost by definition, a tiny minority. Only in the 1990s, did the transference begin in earnest and sports became showbusiness. In the process, the leading lights of sports became bone fide celebrities.

Yet there is a paradox. Because, long before the age of celebrity, sports had a spiritual dimension. It inspired writers like W. P. Kinsella to write *Shoeless Joe Jackson Comes to Iowa,* the source novel of *Field of Dreams* in which farmer "Ray Kinsella" hears a Voice whispering, "If you build it, he will come." Kinsella is able to resurrect the suspended players from the notorious 1919 Black Sox series. It inspired former Liverpool manager Bill Shankley to suggest that soccer was more important than life itself. It still inspires dozens of thousands to write into their wills requests that their ashes be scattered on the field of their favored ball club. The curiously positive and uplifting effect that sports have on its followers has an ethereal quality that bears resemblance to that of faith.

So, even if we allow that *worship* might exaggerate the adoration, honor, and respect afforded celebrities today, it still seems an appropriate way to describe how fans regard athletes. The word worship comes from *worth+ship* (as in scholarship or friendship) and has no necessary link with religion. Yet, in the case of sports, there does seem to be a religion-like fire that ignites passions. The sacrifice of money, time, and energy might be the equivalents of burnt offerings. The manner in which fans defer to celebrity athletes, buying their memoirs, seeking their autographs, wearing shirts with their names across the back, is reminiscent of suppliants humbling themselves at the feet of holy men. And, if we really want to stretch it, we should remember the point made earlier: that one interpretation of the source of the word fan is *fanaticus*, meaning "of a temple."

As faith brings its own sense of empowerment, so being a fan confers feelings of personal power on the otherwise dispossessed subordinates who feel deprived in many other areas of life (empowerment, in this sense, is close to the self-efficacy we discussed in Chapter 6 a belief in their capacity to produce sought-after results making individuals or groups believe they have the capacity to bring about the results they want out of life). At least that's the view of several researchers, including Cheryl Harris (1998) and Henry Jenkins (1992): fans feel stronger and more confident. Though some take this to bizarre extremes. The kind of weirdness that sometimes manifests in stalking and other forms of obsessive behavior evokes comparisons with the religious zealotry displayed by those seeking precisely the kind of empowerment sought by fans.

When Rojek concludes, "Celebrity culture is a culture of faux authenticity, since the passions it generates derive from staged authenticity rather than genuine forms of recognition and belonging," he surely confuses the theatricality of sports with fakeness (2001: 90). Faux means artificial. Of course, sports are staged events and, as such, provide showcases for the entertainers. This doesn't diminish the actuality or the verity of the experience and the passion aroused. In any case, aren't the rituals that are so integral to religious worship staged?

Who can say whether the parasocial attachment fans have to sports celebrities are more or less substantial or significant than those felt by acolytes, apostles, devotees, disciples, or zealots? Why is sport any more a "cult of distraction," as Rojek calls the assembly of celebrities, than religion, whether denominational, sectarian or cultic? Celebrity culture can't produce "transcendent value" on this account. If by transcendent value, we mean a quality that serves as both a guiding principle and an explanation of earthly matters, then celebrity culture fails. But do contemporary religious figures, including rabbis, evangelists, imam, ministers, preachers, priests, or any other type of cleric provide any more succor, euphoria, and contentment than sports figures? Affirmation, unity, sense of belonging? Or grief, sadness, and disconsolation?

Sports celebrities may not knowingly engender these kinds of emotions in their devotees. They may not even care. They frequently absolve themselves from responsibility if such emotions lead to unfortunate consequences (like drinking, fighting, or even killing). Yet this doesn't make them any less potent. Remember: the parasocial relationship needs only one active party; the other can be oblivious – yet still evoke experiences, behavior and, importantly, satisfactions in the follower.

Parallels between celebrity culture and religion may be strained, but, in the specific portion of that culture reserved for sports, the correspondence is compelling. Sports celebs are closer to the gods than they seem to recognize.

NO GUARANTEES

Has it all changed since the turn of the 1980s into the 1990s? Or, has there always been a celebrity culture, without its actually being called a celebrity culture? In the introduction to their edited collection *Sports Stars: The cultural politics of sporting celebrity*, David Andrews and Steven Jackson write: "Although at one point in time the emergence of celebrity figures was a haphazard and arbitrary voyage of discovery, today the process is considerably more proactive in its focus on the cultivation of potential celebrities" (2001: 4).

Over Chapters 14–16 we've seen how an entire sports industry has developed, principally around the demands of television. Without the commercial benefit of having sports relayed globally, there would be little point in calibrating the demands of competitive sports with those of other divisions of the sports industry. And, of course, it is, as we've seen, a proper industry: it provides habitual employment for millions, involves trade and manufacture, requires a high degree of organization, control, and regulation and runs on rational principles. In fact, the only thing about sports that isn't rational is the actual competition, as we noted in the opening chapter. For the duration of the competition, unpredictability, spontaneity, and sheer luck prevail; everything else is calculated, planned, and designed to minimize randomness.

Andrews and Jackson's point is that, in recent years, the industrial process that has steadily turned sports from an inchoate assembly of games into a fully-fledged business sector has affected not only the structure of sports, but the athletes. "As with any cultural product, there is also no guarantee that celebrities will be consumed in the manner intended," caution Andrews and Jackson (2001: 5). Music and movie stars and fashion models can be manufactured like products to meet the specific requirements of a market.

Athletes can't be produced to such fine tolerance. Their representations in the media, including advertising, tv talk shows, and other public appearances can be shaped according to an image. But, unlike actors, singers, models, and other members of the entertainment industry, athletes have to perform in an unscripted drama. If they don't compete well, their public presentations will eventually be seen as fraudulent. Consider the previously mentioned Anna Kournikova in the early twenty-first century. While she enjoyed unprecedented media attention and a bounty of endorsement contracts, consumers spied the deception when she failed to win any major tournaments.

Far from being "consumed in the manner intended," as Andrews and Jackson put it, she was sneered-at or lusted-after – but never respected, admired, or honored as an athlete. Some might maintain that this was never the objective, of course. But, looker that she was, there were any number of trained models who could outmatch here in the looks department. Her uniqueness was that she was a promising athlete. When her promise didn't translate into trophies, she was seen more as an artifice than a real player.

Consumers simply won't stand for frauds. Not consumers of sports, anyway. They're a far cry from the "one born every minute" suckers famously mocked by the great nineteenth-century showman, P. T. Barnum. Today's fans are mostly astute, canny, knowing, and enthusiastic partners in the celebrity production process. Partners? Yes, that's the conclusion of Joshua Gamson, who explodes the idea that fans are helpless dupes who get taken in by the slick celebrity production. The closing gap between Us and Them means that fans are now able to examine the mechanisms of celebrity production: "Seeing evidence of the publicity machinery and marketing behaviors . . . increases [fans'] confidence in the fairness of their tacit 'agreement' with the celebrity industry," writes Gamson (1994: 124).

In other words, consumers know all about the maneuvers involved in producing a celebrity and are quite willing to accept rather than rebel against them. The reason is: they rather like being parts of the industry. Knowing that celebrities are made or broken, in the last instance, by them, is a source of satisfaction to audiences. Recall Gamson's point: fans are simultaneously "voyeurs of and performers in commercial culture" (1994: 137). To outsiders, they're dupes, but, in actuality, they're accomplices.

Gamson's is a vision of the fan as inquisitive, investigative, and perceptive. Quite the opposite of the typical picture of a jerk who just soaks up all the hype without pausing for even a moment's reflection. Gamson discovered that fans are highly reflective, recognizing the façade of celebrity, but aware that they are integral to the façade's manufacture.

While Gamson's study concentrates on consumers of television and film celebrities, most of his points seem to hold good for sports fans. If anything, they are more self-reflective than Gamson's subjects. After all, they must realize that, the celebrities they follow are susceptible not only to their fickle tastes, but to changes of form, injuries, capricious coaches, and several other contingencies that might not

BOX 17.9 IMAGE RIGHTS

These refer to the legal rights associated with using the image of a person in marketing and promotional activities. In sports, the rights typically include his or her name or nickname, their photograph, or likeness (for example, cartoon or caricature) and their performance. Reproductions of performance are, of course, difficult to protect, particularly when clips are readily available on the net. But images are controllable. An advertiser can't, for example, simply use someone's picture alongside a commercial product to imply an endorsement: they negotiate payment in advance. Similarly, a name or signature is protected. Some British football players, such as David Beckham and Paul Gascoigne, have actually registered names as trademarks (Gascoigne registered his nickname, "Gazza"). Laws relating to image rights differ. For example, in the United States individuals have a legal right to control their own image and can allow this to be appropriated by a third party (the club to which they are contracted, for instance). In Britain, individuals rely on intellectual property and other rights to prevent the unauthorized exploitation of their names and images: libel, trademarks, copyright, and passing off especially.

sweep a well-planned showbusiness career off course. Celebrity athletes survive, prosper or perish in a fast-changing and unstable environment, where the reference points are constantly shifting.

They sometimes shift in totally unexpected ways. Think back to "Eric the Eel," the inept swimmer at the 2000 Olympics, or the hapless "Eddie the Eagle" of the 1988 winter Olympics. Both leapt to eminence thanks to cutely ironic nicknames and the penchant of the media to laud abject incompetence. They proved that celebritydom beckons not only for winners; but also for willing failures. Neither athlete made much of a lasting impression, though they probably made a nice packet of money in the immediate aftermath of their "triumphs."

Celebrity culture has in some way affected every feature of sports. Skim back over the past chapters and imagine the impact it has had on, for example, the mental approach of athletes (Chapter 6). Are prospective sportsmen and women motivated by success in sports, or is success in sports the means to another end? Young people dream about becoming the next Woods or Beckham. Would they settle for being a champion golfer, or the England soccer captain? Or are they really aspiring to the adulation and zealotry inspired by these athletes?

The emasculation of sports, as we called it in Chapter 9 is very much in harmony with celebrity culture. Celebrity culture emphasizes aestheticism, that is, an appreciation of the beauty, or art of a performance, rather than its functionality or end result. Sports in which women have traditionally excelled were often regarded as borderline sports, not because they didn't involve skill, but because they were evaluated on aesthetic performance rather than goals, touchdowns or tries. Synchronized swimming, ice dancing, gymnastics. Men participate in all of these and many other sports in which women compete, of course. Yet, they have strong associations with women and this had the effect of maintaining their marginal status, a status that has undergone a revamp in recent years.

Celebrity culture has ushered in celebrity athletes whose ethnic identities might, at a different time, have limited their prospects of attracting the big endorsement deals that are so vital to celebrity status. It barely needs stating that the first genuinely global celebrity athlete was, of course, Michael Jordan, whose well-planned route to the top was mapped in Chapter 16 Celebrity culture would simply not have been possible without the advent of the global media and the intricate circuitry it established with sports (Chapters 14 and 15).

Has celebrity culture had an impact on doping, as discussed in Chapter 11 There's no obvious connection. But think: the prizes now available to elite athletes go far beyond medals and trophies, even far beyond the cash, much of it as there is. The risks are there, but the benefits are colossal. The difference between first and fourth place was once a variance, a margin by which the most excellent surpassed the very, very good. By the twenty-first century, it meant the difference between world renown and obscurity. Do you remember the men's Olympic 100-meter winner? Of course. How about the fourth placed runner? Or the third, or even second? Winners are fêted and revered in a way once reserved for showbiz stars. Is it any wonder, with such incentives on the line, athletes succumb to temptation?

Celebrity culture is all-pervasive and, though, I've dedicated a chapter to its inspection, it actually permeates the book. There's no facet of sports today that remains untouched by celebrity culture. Perhaps this helps explain why so many premier athletes are coopted into a world in which political issues are nullified or suppressed. It's difficult to imagine a figure like Muhammad Ali, who so stridently opposed the war in Vietnam in the 1960s, or a renegade like Tommie Smith, or even a friend of Fidel Castro, like Diego Maradona, surfacing today.

There is one more facet of celebrity culture that we should flag: that is, the body. The changing human body has, of course, been a central theme in this book and we will return to it yet again in the concluding chapter. One of the byproducts, or perhaps main products, of celebrity culture has been what we might call an organized dissatisfaction with the body. In its infancy, the cosmetics industry, as we have seen, fastened on to the insight that they way to sell products was by infusing them with values rather than actual things. It didn't take long for them to personify these values, largely through Hollywood stars, who were signed up to all manner of products that were supposed to make consumers look like them. This has been an enduring convention in the cosmetics industry, of course.

Prior to the 1980s, advertisers were involved in promoting an organized dissatisfaction with the human body, encouraging discontent with appearances and instilling concerns about personal hygiene. The plethora of products from toothpaste to deodorants to makeup was aimed at meeting this dissatisfaction. In the age of celebrity, there was less need for direct advertising. As we noticed before, the celebrities themselves were moving advertisements for the good life. Living that life involved having symmetrical features, full lips, clear skin, lustrous hair, narrow waists, and, of course, no cellulite. For women, ample breasts were favored; for men slab-like pecs and a six pack. There are products to fix most of these; and, failing that, surgical procedures. If the arrangement had been designed, it would have been inspired: celebrities unwittingly promoting an entire industry – just by being there, being watched and being admired.

We consume products that deliver desirability, sexual attraction being the main one, but also friendship, masculinity, health, and so on. Every celebrity that sashays across our tv screen doesn't necessarily personify all of these, but, in a sense, they are all purveyors of one or more of these appealing properties; if only because they are seen as successful – we're watching them, not vice versa.

OF RELATED INTEREST

Claims to Fame: Celebrity in contemporary America by Joshua Gamson (University of California Press, 1994) proposes the fascinating argument that fans "participate more actively in the commodification and management of celebrities" than we typically acknowledge. They are, in fact, co-producers.

Sports Stars: The cultural politics of sporting celebrity edited by David A. Andrews and Steven J. Jackson (Routledge, 2001) is a collection of essays, each isolating a celebrity athlete. *Beckham*, 2nd edition (Polity, 2004) and *Tyson: Nurture of the beast* (Polity, 2004) are my own contributions to this area of study.

Consuming Sport: The consumption spectacle and surveillance of contemporary sports fans by Garry Crawford (Routledge, 2004) examines how fans engage with and experience sports. It traces how people become involved in sports and how it affects them over a life course. Tradition and locality might once have been important, but they have been overwhelmed by media and merchandising in their influence on fans.

"The habitus of Elizabeth Hurley: celebrity, fashion, and identity branding" by Lee Barron (*Fashion Theory,* 2007) is the interesting article cited earlier in the chapter and can be profitably read in conjunction with "Avoiding 'Star Wars' – celebrity creation as media strategy" by Egon Franck and Stephan Nüesch (in *Kyklos*, 2007), who argue: "the well-knowness [sic] of celebrities has become a viable commodity all by itself."

"Building the authentic celebrity: the 'idol' phenomenon in the attention economy" by Charles Fairchild (*Popular Music and Society*, 2007) uses the concept of "the attention economy" as a discussion of how advertisers vied for consumers' interests. Also valuable in this context is: "Who is the celebrity in advertising? Understanding dimensions of celebrity images" by Sejung Marina Choi and Nora J. Rifon (in *Journal of Popular Culture*, 2007).

Fame: From the Bronze Age to Britney by Tom Payne (Vintage, 2009) is one of a number of books devoted to exploring the reasons for the rise of celebrity culture and its consequences. Among the others are Graeme Turner's *Understanding Celebrity* (Sage, 2004), Chris Rojek's *Celebrity* (Reaktion, 2001), and David Giles' *Illusions of Intimacy: A psychology of fame and celebrity* (Macmillan, 2000). Other works include P. D. Marshall's *Celebrity and Power: Fame in contemporary culture* (University of Minneapolis Press, 1997) and my own *Celebrity/Culture* (Routledge, 2006).

ASSIGNMENT

You are a sports agent. One of your clients is a leading football player who is eager to expand his portfolio of endorsement contracts. A new men's magazine, specializing in sports, sex, and cars requires the services of your client and he agrees to do a photoshoot. Weeks later, you receive the relevant issue and discover that your client is featured with a case of beer swinging from his penis. You call your client and he informs you that he happily consented to the shot. The circulation of the magazine soars. You are subsequently inundated with solicitations for him to do advertising spots for internet porn sites, condoms, and sex toys. He is agreeable, but you equivocate: while you'll gladly take your commission from all his earnings, you wonder if his long-term interests are best served by involvement in these kinds of promotions. Email him a message, explaining how the rewards of celebrity culture can often turn to punishment and why you are dubious about the abundance of offers.

Morals and Medals

KEY ISSUES

▌ How can we learn anything from sport?

▌ What is the morality of sport?

▌ When was winning less important than competing?

▌ Where does the devil take the hindmost?

▌ Why is sport about rights and wrongs?

▌ . . . and what's the difference between morals and ethics?

THE VALUE OF TAKING PART

Were Thomas Edison (1847–1931), whose most famous contributions include practical electric lighting, to return from the dead, he would see still in place much of his work on power generation and distribution. On the other hand, his fellow inventor Alexander Graham Bell (1847–1922), who pioneered a method for transmitting speech electrically, would discover the telecommunications landscape altered beyond recognition.

Henry Ford (1863–1947), the pioneer of the Ford Motor Company, might not see his famous Model T, which he introduced in 1909, on the streets any more; but he would see billions of similar machines practically everywhere he looked. And Alexander Fleming (1881–1955), who discovered the effects of penicillin, would be overwhelmed to learn how many millions of lives have been saved thanks to antibiotics. But what of Baron Pierre de Coubertin (1863–1947)?

The visionary behind the modern Olympic Games, Coubertin, in 1894, founded the first International Olympic Committee, and, two years later, watched over the first games in Athens, Greece. There were only nine sports and the tournament received little attention. Were he to return, he would see a sporting spectacle rivaled only by the quadrennial World Cup: thousands of athletes competing in over 300 events, television and radio cameras relaying images and sounds to all corners of the world, and brand names frescoed on every visible surface. He would wonder what happened to his project and someone might tell him about the Nazi propaganda in 1936, Black Power protests in 1968, the killing of 11 Israeli athletes in 1972, the boycotts of 1976 and 1980, the drugs scandal in 1988, the introduction of professional basketball players in 1992, and the bomb attack in 1996.

The Baron might recognize features of the games he created: the gold, silver and bronze medals are still awarded, the track is the same size and, even though the fencers' épées and the archers' bows have changed drastically, they resemble the originals. But would he identify any remnant of the *moral atmosphere* he tried to create? After all, Coubertin was "committed to the ideal of sport as a social and moral endeavor," as Jeffrey O. Segrave puts it. And, as if to cement this commitment, he famously declared: "The important thing in the Olympic Games is not winning but taking part."

"Over time," writes Susan Birrell, the "*meaning* of sporting activities may have been lost, yet the *form* of those activities remains, ready to take on new meanings" (1981: 354). While Courbertin was inspired by the ancient Greek games, he never intended his revival to have comparable religious significance, though he wanted to unify communities and involve different nationalities in a shared experience, as the original Olympics did. So he used similar architecture to accommodate broadly comparable aims, leaving the form, or shape, of the games intact. Even today, a great many of the events look like their ancestors. But the context in which they take place is, of course, completely different, as are the ambitions, motivations, and perceptions of the competitors.

What of the *values*? The principles or standards of behavior, the judgments of what is truly important, the codes of conduct, the ideals – these are constituent parts of any sport. They provide it with a morality.

Morality and sports sounds an odd pairing. But think about it: principles concerning the distinction between right and wrong, or good and bad behavior are actually central to all sports. In fact, morality gives meaning and force to competition. Sport is considered to be good: about this, humans have been in basic agreement for centuries. We benefit from sport. Precisely how we benefit is subject to change. Coubertin believes that the Olympics would function as an affirmation of the oneness of humanity. Mutual respect was integral to this and healthy competition in the pursuit of excellence was an effective way of communicating it.

When Coubertin was distributing his goodwill, a big sporting event didn't occasion global reverberations as it would today. And competitors, though committed to doing their utmost to win, would never divest rivals of their dignity. "Taking part," to repeat Coubertin, was what counted: the gratification lay in contributing to a good, honestly fought competition, and the way to do that was to bring opponents to their mettle. Sport was ideal: it artificially created a demanding situation in which someone was forced to cope with difficulties. In doing so, they proved their excellence.

Losing was as valuable as winning in the sense that, if the loser had stayed within the rules and performed to a maximum level, he (and it would have been mostly men back then) would have contributed to the conditions that helped others reach their own peaks. A competition was more of a transfer of fortitude than a dog-eat-dog contest. Each contestant complemented the others and to hold back or in some way fail to put everything into the competition was an insult. There was no disgrace in losing; but there was shame for those who didn't squeeze out every drop of effort.

So how come we hear the American football coach Vince Lombardi's motto "Winning isn't everything; it's the only thing" so often? And why do people still quote former Liverpool manager Bill Shankly, who, when asked whether football was a matter of life and death, answered, "No, it's more important than that"? When we hear the phrase "nice guys finish last," we realize it's being uttered in jest, but we also know it contains a deeply held sentiment about the value we place on finishing first.

BOX 18.1 MORALITY AND ETHICS

Morality is concerned with the principles of right and wrong behavior. Ethics describe the code, rules, or guidelines that reflect morality and are intended to direct behavior. By following the guidelines people affirm moral principles. For example, the ethical codes governing the use of violence in sport reflect wider social practices and traditions and, as such, have a quality that surpasses sport. William Morgan defines these as part of the "moral sphere," which is concerned with abstract notions of humanity and universal issues. He contrasts this with the "ethical sphere," which is concerned with the practices that shape particular communities and confer goodness and value on the actions we undertake. So, when Rainer Martens writes, "I use the term *ethics* to mean the rules or standards governing the conduct of the members of society," he alludes to the fact that they are designed to validate morality (1993: 120). Morality means the principles; ethics are the rules for conduct that support those principles.

Competing, not winning, was the purpose of sport at the end of the nineteenth century. At least that's how Coubertin saw it and, for the first few decades of the twentieth century the same morality permeated Olympic competition and most other sports, even those that were already professional, like baseball and association football. Yet, gradually this value gave way to a more straightforward emphasis on winning alone. The tension between the two values is nicely illustrated in the 1981 Hugh Hudson film *Chariots of Fire*, which tells of British track athletes as they approach the 1924 Olympics. Harold Abrahams, in particular, is a prototype: his fellow students at Cambridge University are scandalized by his cutthroat approach to the then strictly amateur competition.

The more leisurely approach of Abrahams' colleagues is epitomized by his teammate and fellow Cambridge student, Lord Andrew Lindsay, who balances full champagne glasses on the edge of hurdles, then proceeds to sail over them at speed without spilling a drop. By contrast, Abrahams is grinding out the miles under the watchful eye of a professional coach whom he had hired specifically to enhance his chances of winning. Having a coach to assist in training was permissible, but a professional coach was dubious, and a coach who taught his charges to dip at the tape in order to gain a slight advantage was *persona non grata* – he was not allowed into the Olympic stadium to watch Abrahams race.

In the film Abrahams' motive for winning has its source in anti-Semitism: he reminds his friend that he has "felt the cold reluctance in a handshake." So when he declares, "I run to win," it's shocking though understandable: he wants to strike a blow for Jews. But the disdain of his colleagues is still apparent.

The film was based on actual events in the 1920s and Abrahams, who died in 1978, became the first Englishman to win the 100 meters at the Olympic Games. Subsequent developments have disguised the furor caused by his unorthodox approach. Entering an Olympic competition for any purpose other than wishing to take part seemed tantamount to immoral behavior. Of course, competitors were obliged to try their utmost and were disgraced if they were sparing in their efforts. But the point of sport was to *compete*, not just to win.

Abrahams' transgressions could have been worse. After all, 12 years before his triumph, Jim Thorpe, the American athlete, had won two golds at the Stockholm Olympics and was then stripped of the medals after it was discovered he had played professional baseball. In both cases, the morality of Olympic competition had been damaged. Unlike Thorpe, Abrahams broke no rules; his attitude was the principal cause of offense. Today, that same attitude is a prerequisite for sport. But, in the 1920s the moral tone was different: Abrahams' single-minded, self-serving, and perhaps egotistical attempt to win was scandalous. The fuss created by Abrahams reminds us that sport is a fundamentally moral enterprise: it may appear as if it's completely neutral: a pursuit of medals, titles and records. But there is a moral dimension: sport is always *for* something – something concerned with the principles of right and wrong.

THREE VIEWS ON CHARACTER

In *Chariots of Fire* days, the adage "sports build character" was popular. It's still invoked to justify sport, though we rarely reflect on whether or not it's true, or, indeed, what it means. What precisely *is* character and how does sport contribute to it? Rob Boddice attends to the first question, tracing the concept to the nineteenth century: "In Victorian terms this [character] included 'pluck,' 'spirit,' honor, courage, piety, and honesty" (2008: 3). Pluck means courage, guts, or to be more current, *cojones*.

We can add to these "resolve", though the third and last of Boddice's qualities are the ones that have occupied academic researchers on the subject. "The ability to promote and or prescribe fair and impartial moral action" is how C. Jones and Mike McNamee grasp "moral character" after reviewing research since the 1920s (2000: 132).

Character, in this sense, is less to do with willpower or the ability to withstand punishment and more to do with integrity and uprightness. So does sport actually help build it? After all, athletes are hardly incorruptible. Jones and McNamee throw up the possibility that being honest depends on circumstances rather than the individual's personal disposition. So maybe being involved in sport makes us more – or less – honest.

BOX 18.2 COMPETITION

The word itself provides a clue as to its original meaning: it comes from the Latin *com*, meaning for, and *petere*, seek; it shares a common source with the word *competence*. In the nineteenth century, the aim of competition was not to destroy or eliminate rivals: it was to try to excel by beating them. If they paid you the respect of trying their level best and you did likewise, it would bring all parties to their mettle – mettle being a person's ability to cope in a spirited way with a demanding situation. Winning was incidental to the main requirement, which was to strive as hard as possible and demonstrate proficiency. There was no disgrace, embarrassment, or regret in losing; the only cause for shame was if you didn't try to your utmost. If you held back, it was a sign of disrespect for your rivals.

Theory and research into the relationship between morality and sport emphasizes how training and competing with others within a framework of rules affects the way we develop as moral beings. That is, as people who know right from wrong and, as such, don't simply pursue our own best interests with disregard for other humans.

Peter J. Arnold divides views on the relationship between sport and morality into three: (1) *Positive*. There is "a clear, if unproven, connection between the playing of team sports and the development of social and moral values" (1994: 75). Note: he restricts this connection to team sports, though individual sports, such as boxing and running were thought to have similar qualities. It's a view that has its origins in the elite public schools of nineteenth-century England and it chimes perfectly with Boddice's observation. It would still have been widely held at Cambridge University when Abrahams was a student. Arnold argues that there were two theories emerging from this view: (a) participation in sports "led to desirable social and moral outcomes"; (b) training for sports could double as military training, producing a generation of fit young men who "could be called upon if necessary in battle" (1994: 75).

(2) *Neutral*. "What goes on in sport . . . is relatively inconsequential," making sport "morally unimportant." I'll return to this. (3) *Negative*. "Competitive sport is antithetical to moral education [and] detracts from rather than enhances moral development." Arnold appeals to empirical studies that show not only that cheating and foul play are pervasive, but success in sports is contingent on having undesirable qualities, such as dominance and assertiveness.

Arnold's own view is that "sport is not only just but (despite its breakdown from time to time) essentially moral." Competing involves judging what is right or wrong about an action, evaluating conflicting interests, and taking into consideration the needs of other participants. As such, participating in sport insinuates competitors in to a moral education: they learn to make judgments, take action, and care for others.

Arnold is convinced that players of any sport behave benevolently, not malevolently, toward rivals. "Sportspersonship," as he calls it, develops through cooperation, "conviviality and social harmony." In fact, there is a "logical connection" between sports and morality in the sense that "fairness, honesty, courage" and other qualities that are valuable in society generally are all encouraged and developed during competition. Arnold goes so far as to conclude "sport is inherently concerned with the moral," presumably meaning that conceptions of right and wrong are permanent parts of sport's essence.

To support his claim, Arnold invokes perhaps the most influential theory of moral development, that of Lawrence Kohlberg, for whom the principle of justice for all was the highest stage of moral reasoning and the basis for all moral judgments. Arnold argues that engaging in sport hastens the capacity for moral judgment and hence overall development – what C. R. Rees describes as "the changes in moral reasoning by individuals as they move through different levels of moral growth" (2001: 54).

BOX 18.3 THEORIES OF MORAL DEVELOPMENT

Kohlberg's theory rests on the premise that moral judgments emanate from stable and universal cognitive structures that develop through three levels: *preconventional*; *conventional*; and *postconventional*, or *principled*. (Universal in this usage means affecting all people in the world regardless of place and time.)

At the first level of development, a human being judges all matters in terms of its worth to him or herself, while at the second, there is conformity to norms, rules, and obligations. Only at the third level does a person fully understand the "why" of those obligations: here, he or she appreciates the moral injunctions of society and behaves not out of conformity but out of respect for and consideration of others – hence Kohlberg's term "principled."

An alternative model proposed by Norma Haan also incorporates developmental levels of moral maturity but in a rather different way. In Haan's version, the levels reflect different understandings of the way people think about, or reason through moral conflicts in attempts to establish "moral balance." This describes a position in which all parties agree about their own and each other's rights and obligations. If they don't agree, then there is an imbalance and they enter into "moral dialogue."

We mature through moral dialogue, employing negotiating skills, exchanging perspectives, and arriving at agreements. Haan is less abstract than Kohlberg and recognizes that morality is a product of social interactions, but shares his view that we develop morally. In other words, we grow, mature, and advance through certain stages.

While Arnold doesn't quote him, the British author of *1984* and *Animal Farm* George Orwell (1903–50) clung to the negative view and, in his essay "The sporting spirit" observed: "Serious sport has nothing to do with fair play. It is bound up with hatred, jealousy, boastfulness, disregard of all rules and sadistic pleasure in witnessing violence" (http://www.orwell.ru/library/articles/spirit/english/e_spirit).

Notice how Orwell, writing in the 1940s, stipulates "serious" sport, by which I take him to mean professional. Money has always had a presence in organized sport – and I mean sport as it became organized in the late nineteenth century. Association football, baseball, boxing, and several other sports that have survived to the present day paid their competitors. While the integrity of all these has been compromised by scandals, none has sustained irreparable damage and all remain major sports.

William J. Morgan argues that, in the late twentieth century, there was a qualitative shift: "It is not until relatively recently that it [money] has become a truly pernicious factor, one no longer content to be an occasional, on-again-off-again complement to sports, but its main driving force," he writes in his *Why Sports Morally Matter* (2006b: 58).

Morgan accepts that sport once had a morally redemptive value: it emphasized fair play, equal opportunity, and a form of egalitarianism. But the onset of commercialism, the rise of coaches and managers preoccupied with winning, and the withdrawal of support by liberals and radicals alike led to an "unraveling." Sport became just like any other commodity: at the mercy of market forces.

Perhaps the fundamental changes came earlier than Morgan suspects: when sport became paid work for some, or when it became a spectacle keyed to the interests of fans rather than players, or when the whole institution started being run as an industry. Double-dealing, fraud, profiteering, and miscellaneous other kinds of wrongdoing have probably been as inherent in professional sports as the morally uplifting qualities Arnold proposes.

Then there is Arnold's neutral view in which sport is seen as having little or no impact on the moral well-being, development, or functioning of its participants. The view is predicated on the triviality or inconsequentiality of sports, though these are not quite the same. Sport pales into insignificance when compared to global issues such as war, famine, climate change, or child abuse, and, considering the aim of any game is utterly arbitrary, all sports *are* trivial. The neutral view is that it's also inconsequential: it's a kind of self-contained sphere in which separate values and principles operate, none of which has much impact on the world outside. This is not such a naïve prospect as it first appears.

Consider the concept of "bracketed morality." A bracket is a category that sets limits: behavior deemed acceptable within the limits of sport wouldn't be acceptable outside, according to David L. Shields and Brenda J. Bredemeier whose investigations indicates that athletes justify competitive behavior that overrides the moral obligation to consider the views, needs, and interests of opponents (1995: 122).

In other words, we make decisions and execute actions in sport that we would shudder at in everyday life. But, in the context of a game, we "bracket" away the moral reasoning behind those decisions and actions. This isn't exactly support for the neutral view of sport as a self-contained sphere, but it gets close. Then Shields and Bredemeier add complicating evidence.

First, they break down moral action into four parts: interpreting a situation; judging the right thing to do; making decisions; and executing the action. Each process may be affected by contextual factors, personal competences, and ego processes, such as the ability to focus attention or to reciprocate with others.

So the link between context and cognitive evaluation appears to be crucial to how we respond morally to given situations. For instance, in a study described by C. R. Rees as "the first research program in the area of morality and physical activity" (2001: 54), Shields and Bredemeier discovered that basketball players and competitive swimmers respond differently to moral predicaments thrown up by their sports. Basketball players, unlike swimmers, come into frequent physical contact with rival players and perform as part of a team (I'm excluding swim relay teams). Young people, male and female, are likely to demonstrate low levels of moral reasoning and a willingness to behave aggressively toward opponents if they compete in a contact sport.

One of the severe limitations of Shields and Bredemeier's research is that it wasn't conducted on professional athletes, but their finding that the level of contact involved in a sport influences moral functioning is interesting all the same. Extrapolating from this, we could suggest that being involved in a contact or collision sport from an early age retards our ability to reason maturely and behave in a way that reflects our consideration of and sensitivity to others – showing recognition of right and wrong. Even more interesting is the finding that belonging to a group and depending on others impacts on our own moral behavior. This highlights the effect of group norms, which, as we will discover next, further complicates the question of whether or not sport builds character.

NORMS IN CONTEXT

Collectively, norms coalesce into a mood, tone, or moral atmosphere, that pervades a roster, squad, or team of individuals and affects thoughts and behavior. Maria Kavussanu has investigated this in several contexts: "Many inappropriate actions occurring in the sport realm may be the result of certain social norms that become predominant in each time over time" (2007: 271).

BOX 18.4 NORM

A standard or pattern of behavior that's typical or expected of members of a group. It doesn't necessarily support a moral position, but it may. Normative behavior derives from the standard of the group or wider society. For example, football players are not expected to go out and drink alcohol the night before a game; the norm prescribes that they stay in and go to bed early and this would be normative behavior, even though out-of-season and at other times in the week, they might deviate from this standard. The norm supports no moral directive: it just has practical benefits. So, if a player decides to breach the norm, he fails to observe a code of conduct but doesn't behave immorally. Unless, amid the night's excesses, he abuses a woman, in which case he contravenes another norm, this one with clear moral implications.

Much of Kavussanu's research examines "unsportsmanlike" or "unsportsperson-like" conduct, such as deliberately injuring an opponent, harassing a referee, or playing recklessly to procure a competitive advantage. This behavior has moral repercussions: it involves prioritizing one's own goals over all others, paying no respect to one's opponent, and exhibiting a preparedness to break rules, often surreptitiously, thus challenging the integrity of the game. "The importance of the social context in influencing moral judgment," as Kavussanu and Christopher M. Spray put it, is difficult to exaggerate: its impact is colossal (2006: 16).

Dawn E. Stephens' research confirms this: she found that "players' perceptions of their teammates' likelihood to aggress, or team norm, was the strongest predictor of player' own likelihood to aggress . . . moral decisions, especially regarding appropriate behavior in a particular context, are profoundly influenced by the context or norm of the situation" (2004: 72).

Sports participants are, like everyone else, affected by the prevailing morality of their own family, circle of friends and culture; but the sports context exerts very specific pressures to conform to different and perhaps unfamiliar norms. Motivational goal orientation also plays a part. A task-oriented competitor, such as a marathon runner who seeks personal best times rather than money or medals, is unlikely to approve of anything but the most scrupulous adherence to rules. But how about an ego-oriented athlete, who measures success by where she finishes in the field, regardless of whether she returns a fast or slow time? According to David Tod and Ken Hodge's research: "Individuals whose goal profiles were dominated by an ego orientation tended to use a less mature level of moral reasoning that was influenced by self-centeredness and a win-at-all-costs attitude" (2001: 307).

Athletes who prioritize winning are likely to condone rule-breaking behavior if it's necessary to win the competition (see also Kavussanu and Roberts, 2001; Jones, 2005). Although Tod and Hodge add a small but important caveat: "All participants' moral reasoning was influenced by situational variables."

We begin to understand why an easygoing, honest-to-goodness soul, who is otherwise placid, turns into a feral thug or a sly trickster once a competition starts. Ian D. Boardley joined Kavussanu to explain the mechanisms through which this kind of "moral disengagement," as they call it, works. One involves reclassifying harmful behavior as "respectable" in the cut-and-thrust of a competition. Another involves displacing or diffusing responsibility so that the individual understands his or her action as a result of teammates' pressure or a coach's instructions. The other is arguably the most revealing: dehumanizing opponents, which, according to Boardley and Kavussanu means, "cognitively depriving opponents of human qualities or attributing animalistic qualities to them [so that] transgressive behavior becomes excusable" (2007: 610).

Does this teach us more than it intends? Often we'll read about acts of violence in and out of sport and express both revulsion and incredulity: "How can somebody *do that* to another human being?" If we accept Boardley and Kavussanu's point, "The similarity one feels with another has an effect on how he or she treats that person" (2007: 610), it becomes more comprehensible: the less like us we think they are, the easier it becomes to treat them brutally.

Moral functioning is adjustable according to norms and achievement orientations, leading Jones and McNamee to conclude that individual dispositions, personal integrity, or stable personality traits have been less than useful in understanding morality in sports: "Honesty seemed more dependent on contextual influences" (2000: 132).

With this in mind, we should listen to one of the respondents of Sharon F. Kemp: "I am a professional. A professional is willing to do whatever it takes to win, willing to sacrifice anything to reach the goal. The goal is more important than anything in life. You need to have desire – competitiveness" (1999: 85).

The affirmation of moral position is interesting not because it is typical of professional athletes – though doubtless it is – but because it is spoken by a competitor in a sport that, as Kemp points out, depends, perhaps more than any other professional sport, on "co-operative and altruistic values": dogsled racing (drivers of the dogsleds are called mushers). "Whatever it takes": it's a phrase transparently free of moral ambiguity, or ethical uncertainty; the goal is all that matters. In this instance the goal is to win. Remember: dogsled racing has few celebrities, and little sense of its own importance; it is, however, professional and highly competitive.

The moral functioning of its competitors is, as Kemp confirms, determined by the singular environment in which they train and compete: they live where the dogs live in the snowbound wilderness of Minnesota. The morality of racing isn't something that they agonize over, or even think about. They notice it, to use Annette C. Baier's expression, "as we notice air, only when it becomes polluted" (1994: 98).

Kemp records how a winner of the Beargrease marathon – a kind of grand prix of dogsledding – appeared "cocky and arrogant, an upstart in the field of distance racing who wants to win at almost any cost" and was criticized accordingly (1999: 92). A steely determination to win was not equatable with wanting to win "at almost any cost." It's a fine distinction that may escape outsiders, but it's germane to the particular culture of dogsledding and, when combined with other research, issues two lessons.

First, that there is no single sports morality: the principles that govern the distinction between right and wrong, good and bad behavior, the values that follow from them, and the codes of ethics that affirm them are particular and specific. Second, if there is no overarching morality in sports, how can it be sensible to ask whether or not it builds character? Perhaps the notion of character needs rehabilitating in the light of evidence: more realistically there are many characters, each appropriate to the specific context in which a sport is practiced. Some sports, particularly professional sports, espouse a morality that approaches Orwell's description, while others embody the kind of noble standards that wouldn't have been out-of-place in the *Chariots of Fire* era. Still others, especially Olympic sports, struggle to align the ideals of Coubertin with the ruthless competitiveness that professionalism has ushered in.

CAN WE LEARN ANYTHING FROM SPORT?

A clown breezes into a hospital while patients are waiting for treatment. He's unnecessary, doesn't help a little bit and, for some people, unwelcome, if not downright annoying. But, for others, he's an amusing distraction and takes their minds off the procedures that lie ahead, some of which may be unpleasant. And, in time, everybody at the hospital treats him as a fixture and perhaps looks forward to his arrival. Is it asking too much of him to request that he should teach us something too?

Like the clown, sports are absurd, a point made by Morgan who writes: "When sports are objectively compared to all the other activities humans pursue, they look downright trivial and irrational . . . absurd human undertakings" (2003: 52). Distractions. Still, there may be "lessons sports can teach us about how to deal with failure, virtues like courage that sports frequently call upon, and a sense of justice and respect for others that sports often encourage" (2003: 54).

Douglas R. Hochstetler is convinced "sport is a viable means for promoting moral education, even though, at times, individuals and groups involved with sport act in unethical ways" (2006: 37).

The point is supplemented by M. Andrew Holowchak who suggests sports offer, "opportunities for reflection on moral education and moral development" (2003: 387). They embody a morality in the sense that they exhibit abstract qualities, such as vice, virtue, honor, disgrace, wealth, poverty, power, and subjugation. We can learn about these through participating and even just following sports.

Both views are entirely consistent with the original Olympian ambition. After all, "Coubertin revived the ancient games as an expression of his profound belief in the enduring educational values inherent in competitive sport, what he called *la pédagogie sportive*," writes Jeffrey O. Segrave (2006).

Judy Polumbaum and Stephen G. Wieting believe there are other lessons too: "Every society articulates boundaries that separate the acceptable from the unacceptable, insiders from outsiders, laudable acts from contemptible ones" (1999: 72).

These constitute the boundaries of the "moral order." When athletes break through those boundaries, they create scandals and controversies. Polumbaum and Wieting name the famous cases of Mike Tyson, Tonya Harding, and Latrell Sprewell, though there are a great many others that have elicited debate and which seem to offer a processed version of moral wrongdoing. There are so many drugs cases that Michael Atkinson and Kevin Young use the term "moral epidemic" to convey the infectious disease-like quality attributed to doping in sport (2008: 105).

Polumbaum and Wieting contend that sport captures "the pervasive moral sentiments of societies [and offers] a vocabulary for discussion of good and evil, virtue and vice, right and wrong, honor and disgrace" (1999: 74). (By sentiments, they mean widespread feeling or opinion.) Their theory is that sports provide narratives, or stories that communicate morals; fables, in other words. And fables contain lessons.

The story of Tiger Woods' rise to power, for example, reminds us about the goodness of multicultural society, how it's possible for an individual with talent or prowess to triumph without breaking rules or violating norms. Woods represented the goodness of the moral order.

Wood's ascent to the top of the sports world and a yearly income of $101 million/£65million is certainly the stuff of fable. It's easy to understand how Woods could be understood as a representative of the moral order. He even delivered media homilies on his own decency. The twist in this fable came when Woods changed from a model of wholesomeness and decency to a purulent philanderer with enough women to fill a Pirelli calendar. "Knowledge about what sports stars like Tiger

Woods . . . mean is necessarily supplied by the consumer," write Eileen Kennedy and Laura Hill (2009: 123). Their point is that the information is fed through the media, but we ultimately interpret it and decide whether it occasions commendation or disgrace.

On Kennedy and Hill's account, Woods' womanizing, in a different context, might prompt congratulations. Were he not known for his familial virtues and clean-living ways, and had a different kind of reputation, there would have been no story. But, of course, he was; and it was his Icarus-like fall that reminded us of the perils of hypocrisy.

Sport can be instructional in the way suggested by Morgan and Holowchak: as a method of imparting virtue or virtuous qualities, such as respect, courage, and honor. Also in the manner outlined by Polumbaum and Wieting: as a moral blueprint for how to progress through society. But it can also issue warnings about the pitfalls that await those who imagine they are above moral codes. As Woods himself admitted, he didn't think the rules that bind the rest of us applied to him.

Sport can be instructional in the way suggested by Morgan and Holowchak: as a method of imparting virtue or virtuous qualities, such as respect, courage, and honor. But also in the manner outlined by Polumbaum and Wieting: as a moral blueprint for how to progress through society.

There is a third and arguably more effective way: as a Socratic dialogue. The ancient Athenian philosopher Socrates taught through discussion, talking-through dilemmas in attempts to reach understanding and ethical resolutions by exposing and dispelling errors. Reasoning was the instrument of learning.

BOX 18.5 SOCRATES (469–399 BCE)

The Greek thinker philosopher had no interest in inquiring into the origins of the universe or the nature of humanity: his focus was on practical moral problems, specifically how people should conduct their everyday lives. The way he did this distinguished him from earlier philosophers. Instead of contemplative theorizing, Socrates introduced his students (the most celebrated of whom was Plato) to dialogue, asking commonplace questions and eliciting answers before exposing the students' failings then posing alternatives, which were then contradicted. The process was known as dialectic and the term is now applied to any method of reasoning or discussion aimed at discovery.

The German philosopher Georg Wilhelm Friedrich Hegel (1770–1831) used the term dialectic to describe the process of reasoning in which an initial argument called a thesis was challenged by an alternative called an antithesis, which, in turn, yielded a truer argument called the synthesis. Socrates, on the other hand, saw his task to stimulate teaching and enlightenment through dialogue rather than the revelation of truth.

Sports have been dialoguing in attempts to solve moral conundrums for years. We will look at just three.

Conundrum #1

In the early 1800s, cruelty to animals posed one such conundrum. The beneficial attributes of hunting were manifest: skill in horseriding, fresh air, and, as Rob Boddice emphasizes, "the pluck necessary *to ride to the death*" (2008: 15).

But did the benefits outweigh the pain and suffering of the quarry? Foxes were ripped to shreds and, while they were called pests, there were more humane ways of extirpating them. Hunters in Britain insisted that foxhunting was a traditional pursuit and resisted comparisons with other animal sports, such as dogfighting. The first law designed to prevent unnecessary cruelty to animals came in 1822, though the traditional sport of the gentry continued long after and fired fierce debate. Moral issues were always at the center of the to and fro between those who believed the human interests outweighed the cruelty involved and those who opposed the pain and suffering inflicted in the name of sport.

Conundrum #2

Bizarrely, a comparable debate surrounded mixed martial arts, which, when introduced in 1993, "were initially promoted as brutal, no-holds-barred contests," as Gregory H. Bledsoe *et al.* observe (2006: 139). By 2007, women fighters were in the cage, prompting *Time* magazine writer Sean Gregory to report that their "brutality is sometimes hard to watch" (2007: 40).

In this instance, the dialogue was over whether MMA was the human equivalent of a blood sport, a primitive throwback to a time when audiences took pleasure from watching bulls being tormented and dogs fight each other. Advocates argued that the fighters willingly consented to participate and that discipline, bravery, and a considerable degree of skill were preconditions. On this account, MMA, in common with other combat sports yields benefits as well as costs. But ultimately the debate was about morality: do we judge cage fighting to be good, or bad?

Holowchak has a definite answer: "By condoning aggression in sport, it seems we condone aggression (perhaps even violence) in society" (2003: 397). Before continuing his argument, we should be clear about the meaning of *condoning*: it means accepting or allowing behavior that's considered morally wrong, not positively approving of it. In some sports – not just combat sports – aggression and some degree of violence is actively encouraged and applauded.

"By condemning violent aggression in sports (e.g. fighting in hockey) and banning those sports that are excessively aggressive (e.g. boxing or tough-man brawling), we take a huge step toward moral reform and help sport to be an instrument of social improvement, not social disintegration," concludes Holowchak (2003: 397).

Holowchak urges harmony between the morality represented by sport and that upheld in the rest of society: there is no such harmony in a culture that rewards aggression and, in some contexts, violence, when they manifest in sport, but criticizes them most other places. So MMA and, for that matter, all combat sports and several others that require aggression, are reprehensible, not virtuous.

Most advocates of sport over the years have been much less inclined to take sports so literally: just because people fight in competition doesn't mean they should fight in the streets, or in wars. Sports are figurative representations of abstract principles. Combat requires the kind of qualities Morgan includes in his roll call "how to deal with failure . . . courage . . . and respect [for opponents]." To which we might append fortitude in adversity, and physical resilience, not neglecting the old-fashioned pluck required by any sport.

Preparing for combat sport involves discipline, both physical and mental, and a willingness to endure punishment and pain. The same goes for the analogous sport of boxing, which still is known in some circles as the Noble Art, meaning it displays high moral principles and fine personal qualities.

Conundrum #3

In February 2008, the swimwear manufacturer Speedo introduced the LZR Racer, a hydrodynamically designed outfit. Over the next 10 months, 74 world records were broken. Fair play? No, said 15 European nations, which, in December, protested to Fina, the international swimming federation. Yes, replied Fina, pointing to its relevant regulation that states that no "device" should aid buoyancy, speed, and endurance. According to Fina rules, the LZR (pronounced LAY-zer) was a suit, not a performance-enhancing device.

Forced to deliberate on the revolutionary attire, Fina, in 2009, declared it perfectly fair, though it made stipulations about head-to-toe body suits. Then in July amid a world swimming championships in which world records were not so much broken as annihilated, Fina re-thought its position and banned not only the LZR, but the all-polyurethane suits produced by Speedo's rival manufacturers (polyurethane is a synthetic resin chiefly used in paint, varnish, and adhesive, and which, when used in swimwear, minimizes drag). Fina's ruling that textile swimwear was to be used meant that every world record on the books was set using "illegal" methods. Even when official rules define fair play, cries of "foul!" can test the limits.

Similar protests have been heard about hypoxic chambers, or tents, which are oxygen deficient and simulate sleeping at altitude and induce an increase in erythrocytes, or red blood cells, in an athlete; erythrocytes contain hemoglobin which transports oxygen and carbon dioxide to and from tissues. In 2006, the World Anti-Doping Agency (WADA) made a decision to allow their use. Altitude training is also considered fair, though other means of stimulating hemoglobin production, such as blood doping or synthetic erythropoietin (EPO) are not.

David Cruise Malloy *et al.* disclosed that WADA's decision-making was based on the cautious acknowledgement that hypoxic chambers, while certainly an aid to performance didn't pose a health risk and, crucially, did not violate "the spirit of sport." "WADA was clear about its stance on the spirit of sport, claiming that the passive use of technology was lacking in virtue and thus was not in line with its perspective of the spirit of sport," write Cruise Malloy *et al.* (2007: 290).

Invoking the so-called "spirit of sport" is the equivalent of turning to an overarching morality for instruction and, as Cruise Malloy and his colleagues point out, "the spirit of sport must demonstrate that it will result in the greatest pleasure or happiness or least amount of pain or unhappiness for the greatest number . . .

must foster our sense of duty, both in a universal sense of respect for the dignity of others and to our adherence to establish socially acceptable norms, rules, and laws . . . ought to provide a medium through which individuals may develop authentically." (2007: 293).

The first two criteria are unexceptional, though the provision of a medium through which athletes can develop "authentically" is open to conjecture. WADA cautiously allowed hypoxic chambers, while noting that they involved a passive technology and, as such, didn't facilitate an authentic development. But as Cruise Malloy *et al.* point out, athletes in the twenty-first century (and before) habitually used passive technologies, such as iPods, stopwatches, lights to adjust sleep patterns, and countless other kinds of kinds of equipment. In their *Applied Physiology, Nutrition and Metabolism* article, Cruise Malloy *et al.* expose the "spirit of sport" as uneven and self-contradictory, leading to conclusion that morality in sport isn't fixed: it changes as the environment changes.

For this reason alone, sport is limited for those who expect a set of ethical prescriptions set in stone. But the dialogues prompted by the introduction of new forms of competition and new technologies are instructive. They are often complex, demanding, subtle, and rewarding for those who relish the challenge of Socratic-style debate. Earlier in this book, we have encountered conundrums over the eligibility of athletes with prosthetics and those who have undergone sex reassignment surgery in major sporting events. These and other issues will continues to tax inquiring minds. Sports, to repeat Holowchak offer "opportunities for reflection" on moral issues.

RACE FROM THE DEVIL

If forced to summarize a moral code in contemporary sport, we could do worse than invoke the proverb, "full speed ahead and the devil take the hindmost," which means everyone should or does look after their own interests rather than consider those of others, the allusion being to a race from the devil in which the fastest escape and stragglers get caught. This moral reasoning would have raised a few hackles in the early twentieth century, as Harold Abrahams can certify.

The morality fits nicely with Darwin's theory of natural selection – the process whereby those better adapted to their environments survive and the others perish. But a serviceable morality for evolutionary purposes is not necessarily appropriate for human civilizations. While healthy competition is sometimes seen as a natural state of affairs (see the ethnological theory on sport in Chapter 5), human culture isn't so much an expression of nature as evidence of our control, or dominion over nature.

Think about applied mathematics and science, writing, and education, medicine and law, politics and citizenship: these are products of a human willingness to cooperate, share, unite, pool resources, make common causes, assist each other to achieve aims, comply with others' requests for favors, and behave with selfless concern for the well-being of others. These qualities aren't totally absent from sport, but it seems fair to suggest that they are not often visible. If they were, sport would be less popular – except *korfball* maybe. (In *korfball*, there is no physical contact and no opportunity for individual skills: all movements are based on teamwork.)

While all sports depend to an extent on cooperation, the final contest is struggle. Competition is rife in society too, of course: conflicts over scarce resources of one kind or another have been a feature of human history since at least 1700 BCE when Aryan invaders destroyed the ancient southern Asian civilization of the Indus Valley. But historically, advances are made through cooperation. This is why human societies have evolved a morality based as much on altruism as on self-interest. So, once more: is there a consistency between sports moralities and social moralities? Let's approach this by reminding ourselves of the ridiculousness of sport.

All sports events are arbitrary; there is no reason for them. Ask yourself these questions. Why is there an offside rule in association football? What's wrong with a forward pass in rugby league? Why should a tennis shot be ruled in when it hits the line? Where's the logic in calling a batsman out if he's caught?

The rules strike us as commonsensical: based on sound judgment and forming part of the character of the respective sports. But they're still arbitrary in the sense that they have no value outside the laws of the sports; they're the products of human designs. Often, the design is mimetic, imitating practices that were once vital to our survival as a species. But we don't need to hunt or flee from predators today – at least not as a subsistence practice.

We all know this: sports are irrelevant to practically every important matter in society. The Lakers may win, but the global economy won't be buoyed, hostages won't be released, a cure for dementia won't be found, and 8,000 children will continue to die of malnutrition every day.

Most of us know deep down that sports are not serious matters, but prefer to regard them as, to recall the dogsled musher, "more important than anything in life." Admittedly, there are some who don't get the irony of this and treat competition as if it was for real. But for the most part, we keep sport in perspective. This is why we can accept sporting rivalries as deadly serious, yet still appreciate why rivals embrace each other at the end of the contest. And why we're outraged when one of those rivalries engenders real injury.

We realize that, unlike a genuine Darwinian struggle, sporting conflicts are bound by rules, arbitrated by officials and concluded without long-lasting enmity, or damage to either opponent (usually). We also realize that open competition is actually amoral – it's unconcerned with rightness or wrongness. Sport on the other hand has rules: it's organized around and practiced in accordance with the principle of fair play. Let's briefly anatomize a concept that many believe lies at the core of sports morality.

Fair: just, equitable, reasonable or acceptable in given circumstances; from the Latin *feriae*, meaning holy days on which markets for the sale of goods ("fairs") were convened. *Play*: engage in activity for enjoyment rather than a serious or practical purpose; from the Old English *plega*, meaning brisk movement. *Fair play*: respect for rules, impartial action or treatment for all concerned parties.

Some scholars, including the author of *Fair Play: Ethics in Sport and Education* Peter McIntosh, believe the concept of fair play has a timeless quality and has always been at the "moral center" of sport. Others, like William Morgan, counter that the idea of fair play is not such an archaic principle. America's "democratic experiment to wean itself of [*sic*] the patrician manner and class-driven social hierarchy of the motherland, England" gave rise to a conception of openness and fairness that spread into sports. "So, the moral, cultural and linguistic roots of fair play are unmistakably American ones, and equally unmistakably bound up with its rich sporting culture" (2006a: 179).

Both cases have their points. It's barely possible to conceive of any kind of human sport in which some version of fair play did not operate. Blood sports are a different matter, though some of those, cockfighting included, stipulated some form of equity (between the rival birds). Yet, in its migration to North America, sports shed some of their class distinctions: gentlemen and players were no longer recognized. The Land of Opportunity recast sports in its own image.

Morgan has a point, though we should remind ourselves that up till the 1964 Civil Rights Act, which outlawed racial discrimination, America's sporting landscape, like the rest of society, was largely segregated. The country may not have had a "class-driven hierarchy" like England's, but its racial hierarchy militated against fair play in any social sense of the term.

Is there one definition of fair play that holds good across time and, for that matter, space? Yes and no: if we mean a respect for and observance of rules, then the answer is yes; but, if we presume the rules themselves never change, then no – obviously. Rules in all sports change from time to time. Yet there are other rules that do seem to have value beyond sports. Those restricting the amount and type of physical violence, for example, are not arbitrary: sports test skill, proficiency, and other qualities, not the power to wound or injure someone so that they are permanently damaged.

In the midst of a particularly ferocious and physical game of rugby, an undisguised and unprovoked action that incapacitates another player violates the terms of fair play. Even combat sports impose limits on the type and degree of permissible punishment. Not even instrumental violence, which is directed toward achieving some advantage in the process of play, is condoned. But beyond this prohibition there are few common features that allow us to conclude: fair play is observed regardless of historical context or social convention.

The problem with this is that what counts as fair changes and, while all competitors should receive equal treatment, some are rewarded a great deal more than others. If someone used performance-enhancing drugs in the 1960s, they would be competing fairly, within the rules and, for intents and purposes, with the agreement of their rivals. Now, they would be subverting both the technical rules and moral code as well as generating the critical opprobrium of almost everyone. Records broken by swimmers wearing the LZR may, in years to come, be dismissed as inauthentic.

Let's briefly return to the Harold Abrahams case: Abrahams would now be admired for the same qualities that drew the disapproval of his teammates. From J. S Russell's perspective, this is progress: "Abrahams' innovations led us to refine and bring into greater coherence our knowledge of sportsmanship and of sport more generally" (2004: 156).

The key word is "coherence": Russell believes there is a unity in sports morality and that the changes are part of a logical progression. We might look back and wonder why the competitors and fans alike were disrespectful of Abrahams' "morally perilous compulsion to win at all costs" in the 1920s, but they eventually realized that his mentality was not as inconsistent with morality as they first supposed. Although it was questioned at the time, Abrahams' adherence to fair play is not in doubt. In *Chariots of Fire*, Abrahams unconvincingly denies that his attitude is "win-at-all-costs" by avowing that he abides by fair play. He does; at least in the sense of abiding by rules and observing protocols of amateur athletics.

Morgan's take on the Abrahams case is fundamentally different to Russell's: Abrahams' departure from existent standards was a truly radical break. In a sense, Abrahams could be seen as a harbinger, heralding the arrival of a new type of athlete who introduced discipline into his preparation, trained systematically, and experimented with tactics.

Morgan argues that there is no consistent morality that unites competition in the 1920s with its contemporary equivalent. When we compare the Abrahams episode with today we are presented with nothing less than "two different conceptions of sport itself" (2004: 173). For Morgan, comparing standards of sporting excellence in Victorian (1837–1901) and Edwardian (1901–10) eras with today is like comparing apples and pears: we have a vocabulary that allows us to call them both fruit and recognize the similarities; but they are completely different in many ways (actually, Abrahams was competing in the reign of George V, 1910–36, anyway).

Both Russell and Morgan would probably agree that Abrahams stuck dutifully to the principle of fair play. Their difference lies in the concept itself: is it eternal and changeless or time-bound and chameleonic?

Russell acknowledges that there have been and always will be changes in the complexion of sport. He argues that sports have an "internal principle," which "operates to foster the context in which certain human excellences can be displayed" (2004: 156). Safety equipment, improved medical facilities, rule changes designed to protect the well-being of competitors (for example, protective padding, restricted target areas) would be products of this internal principle.

There are also "external principles of sport morality" that have influenced the progress of sport. These are what provide sports with their constancy. For example, sport would simply not be sport without the consent of its competitors. How could fair play exist if one or more competitors did not compete voluntarily? Morgan would probably reply that "voluntarily" is a philosophically loaded adverb: can we act of our own freewill at all times, or do circumstances incline us one way or another? Does money influence the degree of freedom we exercise? Are our actions entirely of our own volition? Can we ever truly say that we behave willingly, intentionally and deliberately, or are we products of our backgrounds and present situations?

Similar questions could be asked about fair play itself. How can a competition ever be genuinely fair between competitors from different social circumstances? Some might have been provided with state-of-the-art training facilities from the get-go, while others had nothing but an able body. Is it realistic to assert the existence of fair play in a professional sphere in which money has become the decisive force and foul play has become the norm. Morgan believes the imperatives of professional sports "underwrite and legitimate such rule breaking."

The moral quandaries in sport are by no means exhausted in this chapter. In fact, they are inexhaustible: just as soon as one moral question is answered, another crops up. That's simply the way morality changes – in line with changes in the surrounding culture. There's no single lesson to be drawn from this chapter. Sport has no morality:

it has several moralities and these mutate from sport to sport and from epoch to epoch, just like other moralities. Notions of goodness and badness, right and wrong, are not nearly as inflexible as we might intuitively think.

Still, there are certain qualities that are deemed as morally desirable and being involved in sports might promote them. But there's simply no straightforward answer to the question, "do sports build character?" They can in some circumstances. In others, they can have a detrimental effect. Or, as the concept of bracketed morality shows us, there may be no effect either way. It all depends on the context – the circumstances that form the setting, including time, place, surrounding people, preceding episodes and expectations for the future. Contexts generate their own norms and these, as we have learned, are crucial in making moral decisions and executing moral actions.

We can learn from sport, but perhaps not in the direct ways assumed by some scholars: sport hasn't bequeathed to us a rulebook on how to live correctly or how to treat our fellow humans. And while its stories can be taken as fables, the more telling moral lessons to be learned from sport are in the dialogues that take place when conundrums test the official guardians of sport. Sports dilemmas are often deep and challenging and, more often than not, yield solutions that elicit further disagreements. We can learn more from moral arguments than we can from moral prescriptions.

Even the notion of fair play that many regard as sacrosanct can be argued over. We can't just assume the principle of fair play undergirds all sports, past and present. Instead, we can interrogate its meaning, its application, and implications for sport. Or indeed whether it's even relevant in activities that have long ago ditched Coubertin's ideal and prioritized winning as the their ambition.

OF RELATED INTEREST

"Moral realism in sport" by J. S. Russell (in *Journal of the Philosophy of Sport*, vol. 31, 2004) is a robust defense of moral realism, a philosophy that proclaims moral terms such as good, fair, and wrong, refer to natural facts about the world, and that our inquiries and reasoning are methods for improving our moral knowledge. Research is oriented to the discovery of "moral facts" that are independent of contexts. Morgan opposes this position in his "Moral antirealism, internalism, and sport" (in *Journal of the Philosophy of Sport*, vol. 31, 2004) where he argues against general moral principles that remain through history.

"The moral worth of sport reconsidered: Contributions of recreational sport and competitive sport to life aspirations and psychological well-being" by Nikos L. D. Chatzisarantis and Martin S. Hagger, (in *Journal of Sports Sciences*, vol. 25, no. 9, 2007) reports on an empirical investigation into the value of sports participation: "Is sport participation worth doing?" ask the researchers, their conclusion being, "the moral worth of sport lies in the goals and values people express through sport participation."

"Whose Prometheus? Transhumanism, biotechnology and the moral topography of sports medicine" by Mike McNamee (in *Sport, Ethics and Philosophy*, vol. 1, no. 2, 2007) is an example of how to respond to a moral conundrum in sport, in this case biotechnology, which promises (or threatens) to transform "our very nature as humans."

Why Sports Morally Matter by William J. Morgan (Routledge, 2006b) is effectively an ethical critique of American sports and, by implication, American culture. Jeffrey Fry's review (in *Sport, Ethics and Philosophy*, vol. 1, no. 3, 2007) argues that it's possible to "appreciate the author's social criticism without necessarily adopting his communitarian ethical framework." Communitarians emphasize the responsibility of the individual to the self-governing community and the importance of the family unit.

"Fatness, fitness, and the moral universe of sport and physical activity" by Cathy Zanker and Michael Gard (in *Sociology of Sport Journal*, vol. 25, 2008) is an unusual study on the moral value of exercise, which has become "a kind of medicine or tonic we take to improve our moral or medical health." The authors believe contemporary culture has concocted "an unhealthy cocktail: the hatred of fat bodies mixed with the moral certainty that physical activity makes you a better person."

ASSIGNMENT

Choose three moral conundrums, such as those covered in this chapter, and subject them to similar treatments, paying particular attention to the rights and wrongs of the cases. The conundrums should be actual cases that have occupied sports, either in history or in contemporary society. Then ask whether "fair play" has been observed in all three.

Same Rules, Different Game

THE DAY THE INNOCENCE DIED

"The world will begin hearing us. We are, for twenty-four years, the world's largest refugee population. Our homes taken from us, living in camps, no future, no food, nothing decent for our children." Mahmoud Hamshari (1938–73), the leader of the Palestine Liberation Organization (PLO), speaks in measured terms in Steven Spielberg's film *Munich* (2005).

Hamshari is reacting to the events of September 5, 1972, when members of the PLO splinter group Black September invaded the Olympic village in Munich and killed 11 members of the Israeli team. The Olympic Games were already in progress and, despite demands that they be aborted, the International Olympic Committee insisted they continued.

Spielberg's drama focuses on the Israeli intelligence agency Mossad's covert operation to assassinate each of the Palestinians involved in the massacre, though it shows in flashback the eight tracksuited Black September members carrying AK-47 rifles, Tokarev pistols, and grenades, scaling a fence and taking the Israeli athletes and coaches hostage before shooting them dead.

Hamshari's pitiless verdict suggest he sees the value of the atrocity in the context of the world's premier global sporting event. Since 1948, when the state of Israel had been established in what was traditionally Palestine, the political rights of displaced Palestinian Arabs had been disregarded. After Munich, the world would take notice, he speculates. In a sense he is right: despite the condemnation and the vilification of Black September, the event itself magnified the Palestinian cause. Kristine Toohey underlines its historical importance:

The Munich attack was so notorious its implication reached far beyond the area of sport, to the extent that it has been described as the defining moment in the growth of modern terrorism. The global attention it received demonstrated that terrorism could be an effective tactic in challenging governments and raising international awareness of a political cause.

(2008: 433)

Surprisingly, there was just a single day's mourning following the siege. Then competition resumed. Avery Brundage, at the time president of the IOC, famously announced: "We cannot allow a handful of terrorists to destroy this nucleus of international cooperation and goodwill we have in the Olympic movement." Brundage is featured making this declaration in Kevin MacDonald's 1999 documentary *One Day in September*. "The games must go on," he concludes (also quoted in Reeve, 2001; and Toohey, 2008*)*.

Earlier, in 1956, Brundage when IOC vice-president, observed: "Sport is completely free of politics."

It was a view colored by idealism, optimism, or possibly just ignorance. Brundage (1887–1975), was responding to the withdrawal of six Olympic member countries from the Melbourne games in protest at the military conflicts in Hungary and Suez.

It wasn't the first time a political pulse had throbbed in the Olympics. In fact, since 1956, every summer Olympics has been implicated in some sort of political controversy. The most common form of political gesture has been the boycott. Countries absenting themselves from competition either as a sign of protest, or because of exclusion, have been a feature of Olympic history and, indeed, as we will see in this chapter, of much of modern sports history.

Boycotts usually make headlines and attract the rhetoric of interested parties who talk regretfully about how unfortunate it is that sport and politics have become mixed up. In fact, sports and politics are not just mixed up, but entwined so closely that they will never be separated: sport is an effective vehicle for promoting or publicizing causes, principles, and aims, as well as full-blown ideologies. Presumably, this was on the minds of Black September when it planned what turned into a bloodbath. The group's demands for the release of 200 Palestinian prisoners were not met, precipitating a sequence of killing. William Graham's 1976 film *21 Hours at Munich* recreates the incident.

The Olympic Games have the kind of generic relevance that makes them a perfect theater in which to play out political dramas. Ostensibly sporting occasions, the games have continually managed grandly to capture tensions, protests, and sometimes atrocities that encircle the world. By celebrating the alleged unity, at least in spirit, of the world's population, Olympic Games have sought temporarily to suspend terrorism, racism, imperialism, ideological differences, and other "worldly" matters that are the bane of our age. Instead, they have been hijacked by them.

The setting and imagery of the games have been used to sensationalize events seemingly unconnected with sports. So many of the themes inherent in sports have political and ideological potential: nationalism, competition, the pursuit of supremacy, the heroism of victory; all have a wider application. Differences between the contrived competition of the track and field events and the real conflict in the streets have often melted in the spectacle of the Olympics.

BOX 19.1 IDEOLOGY

A complex of beliefs, ideals, and philosophies that form the foundation of political and economic systems and policies, real or putative. While they may be visionary, ideologies often support and inform social structures. An example is the communist ideology that underpinned the former Soviet Union and which was inspired by Marx's theories that declared all property should be publicly owned. Ideologies may also be more abstract or even utopian; these are usually held by groups that resist the prevalent social arrangements and argue for change, though sometimes without consensus over methods. For example: "Much of the PLO's history is defined by ideological disputes over means and ends in the struggle against Israel," writes Aaron Mannes. "The major debates about means have been over the armed struggle and the use of terrorism and of particular terror tactics, such as airline hijackings" (2004: 269).

When political factions, or even whole nations, consciously manipulate events to make their points decisively and dramatically, they often opt for sports, in the safe knowledge that the rest of the world will be so outraged that it will take immediate notice. For example, a press conference in New York to announce that civil rights in the United States have amounted to nothing and that the majority of African Americans and Latinos are still struggling in poverty will gain a response from the media of "so what?"

Announce the same message, this time silently and symbolically, with just two African Americans disdaining the U.S. national anthem and wait for the media to go to work. You have a political event on a near-epic scale. The difference? In the latter example, the two people in focus are Olympic track medalists and the moment they choose to make their gesture is after being awarded their medals on the victory rostrum at the 1968 Olympic Games in Mexico City. Sport worked as an instantly effective vehicle for what was obviously a political statement. The unspoken protest was louder and clearer than any other in the post-civil rights era.

The event itself has a place alongside Martin Luther King's "I have a dream" speech as one of the most potent messages about racial inequality. The image of the two Olympians, their heads bowed to avoid looking at the stars and stripes, their fists pointed upward in an unequivocal act of defiance, is one of the most famous sporting representations of the twentieth century.

For Tommie Smith and John Carlos, the U.S. athletes on the rostrum, and the organization behind them that orchestrated the protest, the Olympic Games were perfect: an effective vehicle for publicizing an openly political statement. The massive publicity it received and the fact that people still remember it today underscores the point: sport *is* political, if only because of its proven utility. It draws attention to particular issues, disseminates messages internationally, and occasionally eases or exacerbates diplomatic relations. Repugnant as the Munich incident was, there is no denying Hamshari's point, even if it was composed for him by *Munich* scriptwriter Tony Kushner: the world did begin taking notice of a conflict that had been in gestation for over two decades.

In this chapter, we'll see the diverse – and, to some, perverse – ways in which the development of sports has been and will continue to be influenced by political considerations. We will also see how sports are just too useful not to be used politically. Denials of this slip freely from the lips of those who have interests in presenting sport as an independent, transcendent force, one of few jewels decorating a tarnished crown. But, as we will also see later sport is political. Anyone with a grasp of the history of sport knows this. The question is: political *how*?

Another question could be: are there people who prefer sport to remain political? All the excitement, the media interest, the controversies and the scandals that thrum around sport: why wouldn't anyone or any organization with a political point to make want to take advantage? Outside the context of sports, politics can be boring. As we'll soon discover, politics can be adrenalized by sports.

Those who have argued against the penetration of sport by politics are often the biggest culprits and their messages have been subterfuge, covering up their own misdemeanors.

IDEOLOGY AND THE OLYMPICS: #1 – NAZISM

In his book *Sport and Political Ideology*, John Hoberman makes the point: "Sport is a latently political issue in any society, since the cultural themes which inhere in a sport culture are potentially ideological in a political sense" (1984: 20). Nationalism, competition, and segregation are just three of the more obvious themes that spring to mind. They all came together in 1936: the Berlin summer Olympics were an occasion for Nazis to flex their Aryan muscles and demonstrate the physical supremacy of the "master race." Adolf Hitler had expressed his doctrine of racial superiority and sought an international stage on which to reveal tangible evidence of this.

In his original conception, Pierre de Coubertin saw the Olympics as having bridge-building potential. He wanted to bring nations of various political ideologies together in a spirit of healthy competition. Participation was considered to be more important than winning and the only politics that mattered were the politics of unity. Hitler's visions were as ambitious, though less noble. The political ideology he wished to propagate concerned the dominance of one nation, or more specifically, one race, over all others; his philosophy was of the disunity rather than oneness of humanity.

While the blatant use of sports as a propagandist tool was roundly denounced, subsequent hosts of the Olympics weren't slow to realize the potential of the games and often turned them into jingoistic extravaganzas. Still, it seems fair to suggest that the particular utility Hitler found in sports warrants special attention, if only as the benchmark against which to gauge later expressions of nationalism.

Friedrich Ludwig Jahn's gymnastics *Turnen* movement of the nineteenth century was partly designed to prepare German youth to wage war against Napoleon. Jahn was a significant figure in fostering the "volkish" thought, which eventually gained political expression in Nazism, with its *leitmotif* of an overarching German essence. This was to be made visible through displays of physical control and strength, "a spectacle of masculine power." His sexism was complemented by racism. "Every real man must choose a mother from among his own people for his children," he asserted. "Any other marriage is an animal coupling" (quoted in Kühnst, 2004: 77).

Hitler had no interest in sports other than this: to express national superiority and internal unity. The Weimar Republic had assisted the growth of sports in Germany as part of the general morale restoration after World War I. But, under Hitler's National Socialism, it came to mean much more. "Fitness was declared a patriotic obligation," writes historian Richard Mandell in his *The Nazi Olympics* (1971).

BOX 19.2 NAZISM

The term represents an abbreviation of *Nationalsozialist*, or National Socialist. The Nazi Party was formed in Munich after World War I and was based on an anti-Semitic ideology of the superiority of Aryans and a commitment to authoritarian nationalist government. Adolf Hitler (1889–1945) was elected Chancellor in 1933 and established a totalitarian dictatorship. He rearmed Germany in support of expansionist foreign policies in central Europe and thus precipitated World War II.

Sports surfaced as a perfect showcase for Nazism. During the 1920s, its potential for drawing not just audiences, but masses, had convinced organizers and promoters that the concept behind the Olympics could be adapted. Association football, in particular, had been exported from England and become *fútbol* in Spain, *voetbal* in Holland, *futebol* in Brazil and *Fußball* in Germany. After the success of the inaugural World Cup in 1930, Italy, then under the Fascist rule of Benito Mussolini, staged the 1934 tournament. It was a colossal triumph: not only did Italy win the trophy, beating favorites Austria in the process, but the slickness of the organization and the prestige associated with the competition reflected well on Mussolini's regime.

Encouraged by this, Hitler sought an even more dramatic exploitation of a sporting event for political ends. Hosting a global event like the Olympics would, he anticipated, confer legitimacy on Nazi Germany, symbolizing his own importance in international terms.

The anti-Semitism that characterized Nazism affected sport. In 1933, Hitler pulled Germany out of the League of Nations, an organization formed in 1920 in response to the destruction of life during the 1914–18 war. Its purpose was to stop war and disputes liable to lead to war (in 1946, its functions were taken over by the United Nations). When a boycott of Jewish businesses came into effect in Germany, the organizing bodies of sport excluded Jewish performers and officials.

Two years later there was complete segregation in German sport, something that clearly contradicted Olympic ideals. In the United States, an abortive boycott campaign targeting the proposed 1936 Olympics failed to command support. Brundage, the then president of the American Olympic Committee, warned that: "Certain Jews must now understand that they cannot use these Games as a weapon in their boycott against the Nazis" (quoted in Hain, 1982: 233).

Germany reassured the world that the extent of anti-Semitism and segregation had been exaggerated and, to underline this, included the fencer, Helene Mayer, who was "half-Jewish," in the national team.

Newsreel depicts Hitler's leaving the Berlin stadium in apparent disgust as African American athlete Jesse Owens shook the ramparts of the Nazi's ideological platform by winning four gold medals. Doctrines of racial supremacy seemed ridiculous. Yet Hitler's departure was an uncomfortable moment in what was in other respects a satisfactory and rewarding Nazi spectacle. Not only did Germans lead the medal table, they "demonstrated to the whole world that the new Germans were administratively capable, generous, respectable, and peace loving," as Mandell puts it (1984: 244).

"Hitler, particularly, was greatly emboldened by the generally acknowledged, domestically and internationally, triumph of this festival grounded on the pagan (though very new) rituals of modern sport" (1984: 245).

In terms of propaganda, the entire Olympic project was of value to the Nazis: as the world acknowledged Germany's arrival as a modern international power, Germany stepped up its rearmament program.

Repercussions went beyond the Olympic movement. Before the games, in December 1935, an international game of soccer between England and Germany in London was opposed by Jewish organizations, supported by the Trades Union Congress and the Communist Party.

In the event, the match went ahead and, in a subsequent international game in 1938, this time in Germany, the England team was instructed to give the Nazi salute as the German national anthem was played before the match. Thanks to newsreel, the moment will live on as one of English sport's most mortifying moments, coming as it did so close to the outbreak of the Second World War.

BOX 19.3 PROPAGANDA

Information, usually misleading, used to promote or publicize a political cause or ideological viewpoint. The term shares the same root as the verb *to propagate*, that is, to spread and reproduce.

Only in retrospect was the full resonance of the "Nazi Olympics" realized. No single games since has approached it in terms of ideological pitch. Its sheer scale deserved the posterity afforded it by the openly propagandist film directed by Leni Riefenstahl, *Olympia*, which idealized German sportsmen as *Übermenschen*, or supermen, as we saw in Chapter 13.

It could be argued that the 1936 Games provided a blueprint for other nations seeking a method of validating their status. Seventy-two years later, China's Communist Party was eager to stage a successful Olympics and the Chinese people, at least those living in urban areas, appeared as enthusiastic about holding the Games. China regarded the event as a coming-out party to highlight its economic rise and emergence as a world power. The games took place 19 years after government troops opened fire on and killed 2,000 unarmed pro-democracy protesters in Tiananmen Square in the center of Beijing. I'll return to the Beijing games later in the chapter.

IDEOLOGY AND THE OLYMPICS: #2 – PROTEST

After 1936, no summer Olympics meeting escaped political incident. The defeated nations of Germany, Italy, and Japan were excluded from the first games after the war in London in 1948. Holland, Egypt, Iraq, and Spain boycotted the 1956 games in protest at the British and French invasion of Suez. In 1964, South Africa was suspended and subsequently expelled from the Olympic movement (in 1970).

In 1965, the white minority government of Rhodesia, a former British colony in southeastern Africa, issued a unilateral declaration of independence (UDI) under prime minister Ian Smith. Despite United Nations sanctions, illegal independence lasted until 1979. Rhodesia operated a similar system of stratification to apartheid and was expelled from the Olympic movement. New Zealand maintained sporting links with South Africa in the face of world opinion and the fact that it too wasn't expelled from the Olympics spurred 20 African nations to boycott the 1976 games in Montreal. Boycotts have since proliferated. Taiwan also withdrew after it was refused permission to compete as "China."

The U.S. team pulled out of the Moscow games in 1980 after the Soviet invasion of Afghanistan. British Prime Minister Margaret Thatcher exhorted British athletes not to go, but the British Olympic Association went ahead. Soviet bloc countries (except Romania) and their allies replied by steering clear of Los Angeles in 1984, though China sent a limited delegation of 200 athletes. The LA games were the most shamelessly nationalistic Olympics since 1936, though, as Rick Gruneau argues, "in no way a significant departure from practices established in earlier Olympics" (1984: 2).

In 1988, Cuba stayed away from Seoul after the South Korean government refused to share events with North Korea (which itself pulled out). In 1992, the political tensions were primarily internal, Barcelona, the host, being a municipality with a strong conservative tendency and nationalist Catalonian feelings. Its problem was in maintaining its autonomy while seeking the assistance of Spain's central government in Madrid. As Christopher Hill commented in the first edition of his *Olympic Politics*: "The political affinity one might expect it [Madrid] to have with Barcelona seems often to be strained by the rivalry between the two cities, as well as by the different traditions from which the national and local socialist parties spring" (1992: 219–20).

Apart from boycotts, incidents internal to the games sometimes led commentators to suggest that the Olympics themselves were hemorrhaging so badly that they would have to be either stopped, or scaled-down drastically. The original purpose as envisioned by Coubertin had long since been abandoned and, by the 1970s, the games had been exploited by all manner of political causes.

Ask anyone old enough to recall two events from the Mexico Olympics of 1968 and they will name Bob Beamon's barely believable 29 feet, 2½ inches leap across the long jump pit, or the demonstration of Tommie Smith and John Carlos on the victory rostrum. Smith had won the 200 meters, while Carlos took third position. They received their medals and, as the Star Spangled Banner played, dropped their heads as if in shame. Each thrust a black-gloved fist upwards. The meaning of their defiant gesture was clear. Vilified by the media and banned from participating in sport, Smith and Carlos became instant pariahs. But their action was of historical importance.

The massacre in Munich in 1972 opened up a new dimension of horror: Black September demonstrated how easily and – repulsive at it seems – effectively, the Olympics could be utilized and with such tragic consequences. As we noted previously, the games were interrupted for only one day. Munich 1972 remains the most memorable Olympics in history, it's longevity guaranteed by a perverse logic: there has not been comparable carnage at any sporting event. It was sport's equivalent of Columbine, 1999, or Mumbai, 2008.

The Atlanta Olympics of 1996 *could* have caused even more bloodshed, though, in the event, a pipe bomb explosion in the Centennial Olympic Park caused 2 deaths and over 100 injuries. According to the *New York Times*, "someone moved the bomb so that its main impact was skyward instead of horizontal" and this massively reduced the effects of the explosion ("A bomber, but not your usual suspect," by Janet Maslin, November 9, 2006).

The incendiary was a former U.S. Army explosives expert with neo-Nazi links, who objected to the liberalization of American abortion laws and wanted to, as he put it, "confound, anger and embarrass the Washington government in the eyes of the world for its abominable sanctioning of abortion on demand." He made this known only nine years after the bombing.

In 2008, the 85,000-mile, 130-day torch-carrying odyssey from Ancient Olympia in Greece to Beijing – the longest in Olympic history – was strewn with conflict, activists demonstrating against China's human rights record and that country's occupation of Tibet, which, it claims, is part of China. In 1959, the Dalai Lama and 100,000 Tibetans were forced to flee from their homeland. The year after the Olympics on February 25 – the beginning of Losar, the Tibetan new year – three men in a vehicle parked in Beijing set themselves on fire. While the event was reported in the West, it remains relatively obscure. One wonders how a triple self-immolation protest might be remembered if it was staged a year before in the lead-up to the Olympics, or even during the games themselves.

BOX 19.4 POLITICAL OLYMPICS

1936, Berlin: Usually seen as the first games used for propagandist purposes. Hitler showcased his political regime with the most spectacular and well-run games to date.

1948, London: The defeated nations of Germany, Italy, and Japan were excluded from the first games after the war

1952, Helsinki: The first games attended by a team from the communist Soviet Union. The differences in political ideology between the East and the West was reflected in the domestic arrangements: the Soviet team was housed in a separate village from teams representing western nations.

1956, Melbourne: Boycotts from Spain, Switzerland, and Holland over the Soviet invasion of Hungary and from Egypt, Lebanon, and Iraq over the takeover of the Suez Canal.

1960, Rome: The last games for 32 years for a team from South Africa. The IOC imposed its ban because of South Africa's maintenance of apartheid.

1964 Tokyo: South Africa suspended from the Olympic movement and subsequently expelled (in 1970).

1968, Mexico: The "black power" Olympics, where Smith and Carlos signaled their protest with heads bowed and defiant fists during the medals ceremony for the 200 meters.

1972, Munich: Eleven members of the Israeli team taken hostage and killed by the Palestinian Black September group. Southern Rhodesia made Unilateral Declaration of Independence from the Commonwealth and was excluded.

1976, Montreal: The most significant boycott to date: 30 African nations withdrew over New Zealand's inclusion in the games. The Kiwis had earlier toured South Africa. A year later, the Gleneagles Agreement blacklisted South Africa.

1980, Moscow: The Soviet invasion of Afghanistan prompted U.S. president, Jimmy Carter, to pull the U.S. team from the games, prompting several other nations to follow suit.

1984, Los Angeles: Retaliating for 1980, the Soviet Union withdrew its team, leading 13 other nations in a mass boycott.

1988, Seoul: The democratized South Korea was boycotted by its neighbors, North Korea as well as Cuba, Ethiopia, and Nicaragua.

1992, Barcelona: The first post-apartheid games, with the ban on South Africa removed. No boycotts for the first time since 1972.

1996, Atlanta: One immediate death, one related death, and 110 injuries after the explosion of a pipebomb in the year following the Oklahoma bombing.

2000, Sydney: North and South Korea marched under the same flag.

2004, Athens: U.S. team stays on an ocean liner rather than in Olympic village because of the perceived threat of attack from al Qaeda.

2008, Beijing: Protests against China's human rights violations, its restrictions of media freedom, and its occupation of Tibet started a year before the games began.

POSTCOLONIAL SOUTH AFRICA

During the colonial era, cricket, one of the world's oldest organized sports, was both a symbol of Britain's imperial dominance and a conduit for civilization. The belief was that, if you can teach subordinate groups of the Empire the rules, etiquette, and proprieties of the gentlemen's game, then you were helping civilize them out of their barbaric ways. For long, the administrative power of the sport, like that of the Empire, was in the grasp of England, though, in the post-colonial era, with the independence of what were formerly colonies and the replacement of the Empire by the Commonwealth, there were changes.

"Modern sport was adopted by many countries after decolonization for political, social and cultural purposes," writes Mahfoud Amara. "In the postcolonial period, sport became a tool par excellence for single-party states and monarchical regimes in their projects of mobilizing populations around nation-state building and integration into the international system"(2008: 68).

Amara is referring principally to Muslim states, traditionally suspicious of sport "because of its liberal and neo-imperial intentions," and I will return to the question of Islam and sport later when I consider the various protests that have been expressed through sports by Muslims and at least one directed against Muslims. For now, I want to open out Amara's point in a wider post-colonial context: sport was integral to national identity in many former colonies of European powers that sought to build independent nations. I'll begin with South Africa.

South Africa was declared a white dominion, that is, a self-governing state, in 1910. The majority black population was excluded from all areas of political influence. A rigid system of segregation known as apartheid was institutionalized in 1948 and vigorously enforced after 1958 under the leadership of Nazi sympathizer Hendrik Verwoerd (1906–66). In 1956, South Africa made a formal declaration of its sports policy program, which, it insisted, should stay within the boundaries of its general policy of apartheid.

Justifications, unnecessary as they were in a country utterly controlled and dominated by the numerically small white population, included the arguments that blacks had no "aptitude" for sport and the alleged potential for conflict in "mixed" teams and crowds of spectators.

On the second point: blacks, who constituted over 70 percent of South Africa's total population, were barred from a new rugby stadium in Bloemfontein in 1955. In the following year, Bishop Trevor Huddleston (1913–98), who was to become a prominent member of the anti-apartheid movement, observed that sports may be South Africa's Achilles' heel, in the sense that its national teams were so obviously good in certain sports, particularly Rugby Union. To deny South Africa the opportunity to demonstrate its excellence would, as Huddleston put it in his *Naught for Your Comfort*, "shake its self-assurance very severely" (1956: 202). Robin Denniston's *Trevor Huddleston: A life* provides an interesting account of Huddleston's pivotal role in the attempt to use sport to attack apartheid.

BOX 19.5 APARTHEID

This describes the policy or system employed in South Africa from 1948 to 1991. It is an Afrikaans (i.e. language of Dutch settlers in southern Africa) term meaning literally "separateness." Initially adopted by the successful Afrikaner National Party as a slogan in the 1948 election, the term was later used to refer to the entire institutional arrangement of South Africa in which European-descended whites were separated physically and socially from black Africans and people of Asian origin, and "coloreds." Black people constituted about 72 percent of the country's population (of nearly 30 million); they were allocated 12 percent of the land on Bantu reserves. Segregation was enforced in all areas of personal and cultural life. Black people were denied civil rights and access to prestigious jobs; inter-marriage was prohibited. Despite rioting and resistance in South Africa and pressure internationally, the system stood until 1990 when Premier F. W. De Klerk authorized the release of Nelson Mandela and announced the transition from a fragmented society to a liberal, multiethnic, democratic nation. Released in 1990, Mandela, who had been sentenced to life imprisonment in 1964 as an activist for the African National Congress (ANC), negotiated with De Klerk and, in 1994, became the country's first democratically elected president.

Verwoerd's commitment to retain apartheid influenced his decision to withdraw South Africa's application for continued membership of the Commonwealth. In 1961, South Africa became a republic. Separate lands were apportioned to blacks and legislation in 1963 and 1964 ensured that black people were reduced to the status of chattels. The physical segregation was backed up by police brutality and a repressive state that dealt unsympathetically with any attempt to challenge its authority – as the slayings at Sharpeville in 1960 indicated. Individual athletes and teams visiting South Africa were expected to "respect South Africa's customs as she respected theirs," according to South Africa's policies (quoted in Horrell, 1968: 9).

Another world power in rugby, New Zealand, had traditionally selected Maoris in its national team, but capitulated to South Africa by picking only white players to tour. This opened up a national controversy in 1960, especially when a New Zealand tour went ahead despite the atrocities at Sharpeville. This event crystallized many fears about South Africa, and a cricket tour in Britain in its aftermath prompted demonstrations. Sporadic protests continued, both at street level and at official levels.

The integration-oriented South African Non-Racial Olympic Committee (SANROC) was launched in 1962 with the intention that it should apply for recognition from the International Olympic Committee and officially replace the whites-only Olympic and National Games Association. The government pre-empted matters by banning SANROC. As the 1964 Olympic Games drew near, the IOC, whose charter forbids racial discrimination, demanded large concessions from South Africa before its entry could be approved. Some compromises were made in the trials, but the South African government maintained its insistence that sport comply with "custom"; so South Africa was denied entry to the Tokyo games.

New Zealand continued to send touring rugby sides to South Africa amid negotiations aimed at allowing the entry of Maoris. But, in a key speech in 1965, Verwoerd reaffirmed that no Maori players would be allowed to enter South Africa. Coming from the country's leader, the message was filled with political significance. In 1966, New Zealand finally declined an invitation to tour, but accepted another extended in 1968 under a new South African premier, John Vorster.

In the interim, newly independent African states had begun to recognize South Africa's vulnerability to sporting boycotts and were strenuously trying to convince the rest of the world's sports organizations to expel South Africa. The Supreme Council for Sport in Africa, as the alliance was called, reminded the world that, while sport may conventionally have been regarded as trivial or unrelated to politics, "South Africans do not consider it minor" (quoted in Guelke, 1986: 128). Outbursts from Verwoerd and Vorster confirmed this. They left no doubt that what was at first glance a sports issue was also one on which nations' premiers were obliged to dispense judgments

BOX 19.6 SHARPEVILLE, 1960

A black township (plot of land reserved for black people) south of Johannesburg in South Africa that, on March 21, 1960, was the scene of a conflict that ended in 69 deaths (all black) and 180 wounded. It signaled the first organized black resistance to white political rule in South Africa. The Pan-African Congress (PAC) had asked blacks to leave their pass books at home and go to police stations to be arrested. They did so voluntarily, but refused to be dispersed by the police who, eventually, opened fire. Sharpeville triggered nation-wide demonstrations. The reaction of the government was to arrest leaders of PAC and the other main black organization, the African National Congress (ANC), and ban both movements. Neil Blomkamp's 2009 film *District 9* is an allegory of the Sharpeville massacre: an extraterrestrial race known locally as "prawns" are displaced from Johannesburg to detention camps and, in the process, conflict erupts.

THE BOYCOTT THAT CHANGED HISTORY

Basil D'Oliveira, a black cricketer who was originally from South Africa's Cape and who had settled in England in 1960, was playing superbly. Selected for the English national representative team, he scored a century against Australia at London's Oval in 1968 and was the in-form batsman at the time. Yet when the national team for the winter tour of South Africa was announced, D'Oliveira's name was missing.

David Sheppard, a former England captain, later to become Bishop of Liverpool, led a protest, accusing selectors of submitting to the requirements of apartheid. D'Oliveira, having relatively pale brown skin, was officially classed by South Africans as "colored" and so had no legal right to share facilities with whites. South Africa's team consisted of only white players. Several England team members threatened to resign as the protest gathered momentum, prompting the selectors to slip D'Oliveira into the squad as a replacement for an injured bowler, Tom Cartwright.

It was an act of unheard-of nerve as far as South Africa's premier John Vorster was concerned: he smartly denounced the squad as "not the team of the MCC [Marylebone Cricket Club – the English governing organization] but the team of the Anti-Apartheid Movement, the team of SANROC [the South African Non-Racial Olympic Committee, which had led campaigns to isolate South African sports]."

Peter Osborne's book *Basil D'Oliveira* reveals how the MCC was inclined to accommodate South Africa to begin with, though, perhaps wounded by the accusation and certainly refusing to be dictated to, the English team's governing organization called off the tour. Vorster's intransigence and the MCC's pull-out were crucial: the former in hardening South Africa's policy in the face of suspicions that Vorster himself was beginning to soften; the latter in showing the rest of the world's sports governing federations how they might in future react to South African policies.

The effects were not immediate and in the following January the MCC actually countenanced a projected tour by the South African cricket team in 1970. This was met with a "Stop the Seventy Tour" campaign and a series of disruptions of the Springboks' rugby tour of the U.K., which served as a reminder of what would happen to any attempted cricket tour by the South Africans. The cricket tour did not take place. Progressively, more sports minimized or cut contacts with South Africa, effectively ostracizing that country's sport.

The episode itself wasn't the first to surface: it simply captured the elements more dramatically with statements from South Africa, and the refusal of the MCC to be commanded by a regime that had been widely condemned. By grabbing the attention of the world's media, the D'Oliveira case made the sports–South Africa link a significant political as well as sporting topic and one that would press governments into action. The political significance of South Africa in sports had been realized for at least ten years before D'Oliveira forced it into the open.

At a different time in history Vorster's conclusion that the MCC's selection of D'Oliveira was designed, as he expressed it, "to gain certain political objectives," may have passed virtually unnoticed by all those cricket devotees and anti-apartheid campaigners. In 1968, a momentous year in which conflicting forces of protest gathered and collided all over the world, its effects were more far-reaching. The year had seen student demonstrations and protests from young people from all over Europe and the United States. Vietnam provided a focal point for the protests, though there was a more generic unrest underlying this. It was a time in history when people began to sense that collective efforts by "the people" could change world events. It was thought that not even apartheid was immune from "people power."

The relevance of the race issue in world events was underscored by the assassination of civil rights leader Martin Luther King. The IOC had withdrawn its invitation to South Africa to attend the Mexico Olympics of 1968. A threat of boycott from about fifty member countries and protests from the black members of the American team were factors in the decision. British Rugby Union, a sport reluctant to dissolve its relationship with South Africa, entertained a Springboks touring team in the

1969–70 season and every match was seriously disrupted by mass demonstrations. The message from the tour was that any future visit by South Africans was likely to be met with a show of force.

In May 1970, a planned cricket tour of South Africans to Britain was aborted quickly after the threat of uproar on the D'Oliveira scale in the lead-up to a general election. The same year saw the severance of more links with South Africa: expulsion from the IOC; elimination from the Davis Cup tennis competition; suspension from athletics; and a bar from gymnastics.

Isolation stirred Vorster into action and, in 1971, he announced what he called a "multinational" sports program in which "whites," "Africans," "coloreds," and "Asians" could compete against each other as "nations," but only in international competitions. This rather devious move effectively allowed black sports performers to compete, provided they were affiliated to one of the government's "national" federations. As such it served to divide blacks: some wishing to compete felt compelled to affiliate; others rejected the racist premise of the divisions and refused to affiliate. With international links receding, the government permitted domestic contests between "nations," and later club-level competitions between "nations."

Rugby Union resisted the international trend and, in particular, New Zealand set itself against world opinion by willfully maintaining contacts. During a tour of South Africa in 1976, the near-cataclysmic Soweto uprising (official figures: 575 dead, 2,389 wounded) prompted ever more searching questions. As New Zealand seemed intent on prosecuting links regardless of the upheavals, should it too be isolated? The answer from the black African Olympic member countries was affirmative and New Zealand's admission to the Montreal Olympics in 1976 caused a mass boycott. Thus the crisis deepened.

BOX 19.7 SOWETO, 1976

On June 16, 1976, South African police opened fire on protesting students in Soweto, a large African township near Johannesburg, killing two and injuring many. The students retaliated by attacking government property and officials. Police countered and soon violence spread to every part of the republic except Natal. For months, schools were closed. Students forced workers to stay away from their factories and offices in a series of one-day strikes. Some migrant workers refused and a battle between workers and students resulted in 70 deaths. The total number killed as a result of the conflict, which began in Soweto, was officially reported as 575 with 2,389 wounded – almost certainly an underestimate.

Commonwealth heads of governments met at Gleneagles in Scotland in 1977 to formulate a now-famous agreement "vigorously to combat the evil of apartheid by withholding any form of support for, and by taking every practical step to discourage contact or competition by their nationals with sporting organizations, teams or sportsmen from South Africa." The agreement was between governments not sports organizing bodies and, as subsequent events were to show, the ability of governments to overrule individual organizations was often tested.

Rugby's robust stance against governments gave rise to several anomalies. In 1979, Britain entertained a "mixed" Barbarians side (8 whites, 8 "coloreds," and 8 blacks). Critics dismissed the team, which was said to reflect the tripartite structure of South African society, as window-dressing. The British Lions' subsequent tours in which they competed with similarly composed teams, met with much the same skepticism. It was, so the argument went, a case of South Africa using sport to project a distortedly liberal image of itself while preserving its essential tyranny and oppression. The majority of black players belonged to the South African Rugby Union (SARU), which remained outside the aegis of the organization from which sides selected for international competition were drawn. Hence the sides were hardly representative.

It was a period of public relations initiated by Pretorian officials bent on convincing the world that every measure was being taken to desegregate sport – though not education, employment, and housing. For all its promises, South Africa fell short on delivery. Invitations went out to individual players of international repute who were drawn by the love of money to South Africa to engage in what were known as rebel tours. Cricketers, buoyant after the triumph of the individual over governing bodies, courtesy of Kerry Packer, went to South Africa in their scores, both to play and to coach, usually in contexts that were notionally "multiracial."

British soccer players took short-term contracts to coach, some, like Stanley Matthews, working exclusively with blacks. American boxing champions, like Bob Foster and Mike Weaver, both black, defended their titles in South Africa against whites. South Africa made no secret of the fact that it had an embarrassment of riches with which to lure top sports performers.

There were prices to pay, however. In 1981, the United Nations special committee against apartheid published its first "blacklist" (an embarrassing misnomer) of sports performers who had worked in South Africa. This served as an effective prohibition and ostracized South Africa further. Starved of decent-quality opposition, promising South Africans, like Sidney Maree, a black athlete, and Zola Budd, who was white, left to campaign abroad. Maree took U.S. citizenship, while Budd was rapidly granted

▌ BOX 19.8 GLENEAGLES AGREEMENT, 1977

The issue of sporting links with South Africa prompted government involvement at high levels and, in 1977, at Gleneagles, Scotland, Commonwealth heads of government unanimously accepted to override the autonomy of sporting bodies and "take every practical step to discourage contact or competition by their nationals with sporting organizations, teams or sportsmen from South Africa or from any other country where sports are organized on the basis of race, color and ethnic origin." Sanctions were to be applied to those ignoring the agreement. The Commonwealth Secretariat, London, published the full agreement.

British citizenship. Controversies followed both those leaving South Africa and those who continued to flout the prohibition by going there. British cricketer Robin Jackman, who had played in South Africa, was deported from Guyana in 1981 just as a test match against the West Indies was about to begin. The match was abandoned. Others, like Geoff Boycott and Graham Gooch, were banned for a number of years from test cricket.

It wasn't until 1989 that the International Cricket Conference (ICC) passed a resolution, in defiance of a crucial summons obtained by the right-wing Freedom Association, to formalize sanctions against players, coaches, or administrators who worked in South Africa. Automatic suspensions from test cricket were the penalty. It was the most unambiguous pronouncement on sport and apartheid since the Gleneagles agreement. The decision was reached after the cancelation of England's scheduled winter tour of India, when Indians refused to play a team that included players with South African connections. "A victory for sport over racism," was how the resolution was greeted by Sam Ramsamy of SANROC.

Norris McWhirter, the leader of the Freedom Association, described it as "a crushing blow against cricketers' freedom to trade" and exhorted individual players to take out civil injunctions to prevent the ICC carrying out its ban. It could be argued against this that the freedom of over 21 million black South Africans to trade – and not just in cricket – was of far greater significance than that of a relatively small number of cricketers.

The succession of Nelson Mandela to South Africa's premiership in 1994, and the collapse of apartheid that preceded it, effectively ended the isolation of South Africa in all senses and sporting relations were resumed. South Africa was readmitted to the Olympic movement, its rugby teams were allowed to tour and its cricket teams were permitted to play test series against the world's other major cricket powers. The West Indies cricket team was the first to tour South Africa after the announcement of apartheid's dissolution in 1991.

Post-apartheid South Africa's re-integration into world sport was completed in 1995, when the country hosted and duly won rugby's World Cup. The country fostered the image of the "rainbow nation." Few moments in sporting history have been more poignant that when Springboks' captain Francois Pienaar received the trophy from President Mandela, himself wearing the green and gold Springbok shirt. Rugby had been regarded as a symbol of South Africa's racially divided past, though Mandela, as John Carlin reveals in his account of the game and its surrounding events, genuinely believed the sport could embody the new spirit of South Africa (2008). He was heartened by 62,000 mostly white fans, who chanted "Nelson! Nelson!" throughout the match. On Carlin's account, the game encapsulated the victorious struggle for liberation from apartheid. The paradox was that the South African team consisted mostly of white players. Chester Williams was the sole black player.

After South Africa's apartheid had been consigned to history and the race issue seemed to have abated, another former colony contrived to torment cricket. Zimbabwe, like its neighbor South Africa, had once operated a political system in which segregation was legally enshrined. Also, like South Africa, Southern Rhodesia, as it was, incurred the wrath of the IOC after drawing up a constitution that allowed for white minority rule, then making a Unilateral Declaration of Independence from the Commonwealth in 1965.

Robert Mugabe, a guerilla fighter who served ten years in prison under the white minority regime, took power in 1979 with the promise of reversing the injustices of colonial rule. He installed his Zimbabwe African National Union–Patriotic Front (Zanu PF) in power and remained in command for over two decades. Yet, his policies were contested: quite apart from manipulating elections to ensure his own party's hold on power, he embarked on a land reclamation that displaced 3,000 white farmers. Critics were dismissed as "puppets of the western world" by John Nkomo, the Zanu PF chair (quoted in zwnews.com/issuefull.cfm, 2004).

From 1999, five straight years of recession left 80 percent of its 12 million citizens in poverty. Unemployment raced to 70 percent and inflation ran at a staggering 650 percent. Global reaction to Mugabe convinced him to take more control of the international media in 2003 and even Zimbabwe's own independent newspaper the *Daily Star* was closed down after mildly critical editorials. Mugabe's influence extended to all levels of society: when, in April, 2004, the Zimbabwe Cricket Union (ZCU) decided that its policy should be to develop black players, 15 senior white players refused to play in a home test series against Sri Lanka. A depleted Zimbabwean team was hammered continually in the series, prompting the England and Wales Cricket Board (ECB) to consider the rightness of pressing ahead with a planned tour six months on. Cricket's global governing organization, the International Cricket Council threatened international suspension and a $2 million fine if the ECB pulled out, specifying security concerns or an instruction from a national government as the only legitimate reasons for refusing to tour. The British government offered only a recommendation that the tour should not go ahead, but drew short of actually mandating this.

Parallels between this and the South Africa situation were far from exact. Sports was, as Trevor Huddleston noted, the Achilles Heel of South Africa and, after the fall of apartheid, many reflected that the ostracizing of sports made possible by the Gleneagles agreement had played its part. No one suggested that withdrawing from a tour of Zimbabwe would have remotely comparable effects. Nor was Zimbabwe in the grip of a centuries old colonial regime ruled by whites: it may have been a dictatorship, but a black African presided over it. This, in the eyes of many, made it more difficult to take action without precipitating a reaction from some other African states.

The Zimbabwe affair thrust the general issue of sporting links back into focus. Was it legitimate to compete with, tour, and enjoy cordial sporting relations with countries that may have poor human rights records, or tyrannical political regimes, or unsavory cultural prescriptions (for example, about women)? If so, the world of sport would shrink considerably. Western nations would immediately find objectionable features with a great many other nations, which would, conversely, find fault with the likes of Europe and the United States.

ISLAM, GOD, AND OPPRESSION

Mahmoud Abdul-Rauf, an American-born Muslim, playing basketball for Denver Nuggets started a *cause célèbre* in 1996 when he staged his own personal protest against the playing of the Star Spangled Banner at the start of an NBA game. Born Chris Jackson, he converted to Islam in 1993. Some nights he would stand with his hands in his pockets while the national anthem played, other nights, he stayed in the locker room. But when he decided to sit down, he began a controversy that, as *Sports Illustrated*'s Rick Reilly put it, "set up an ideological slam-dunk contest" (March 25, 1996).

The American Civil Liberties Union and the NBA players' union upheld the player's right to express his opinion, which was: "The flag represents tyranny and oppression" (quoted in Reilly, 1996: 76). He argued further: "This country [United States] has a long history of [oppression] . . . You can't be for God and for oppression. It's clear in the Koran. Islam is the only way" (quoted in Pipes, 2000: 40).

The first Gulf War in which an international coalition of forces assembled in Saudi Arabia and forced the withdrawal of Saddam Hussein's Iraqi forces from Kuwait, had officially ended some months before. The Israel–Palestine conflict continued, each suicide bombing bringing fresh retaliation. The United States was heavily involved in both conflicts.

The league suspended Abdul-Rauf and fined him $31,707 – the equivalent of 1.2 percent of his annual earnings. He soon changed his stance and began standing, at the same time silently praying "for those who are suffering," as he put it. Two years later, Abdul-Rauf left the NBA and went to play for Fenerbahce in Turkey, then in Russia, then Greece and then Saudi Arabia.

He was by no means the first American to protest his country of birth. We've seen how Tommie Smith and John Carlos grabbed the attention of the world in 1968. Nor was he the first Muslim to rail against the West: Cassius Clay proclaimed his allegiance to the Nation of Islam, an exclusively black movement proposing a separate black nation, and one which numbered Malcom X (1925–65) among its members. Clay's conversion and his change of name to Muhammad Ali prompted an outcry. Once the furor died down, other athletes – including Kareem Abdul-Jabbar and Mike Tyson – converted to Islam.

But Ali's change of faith was an act of defiance: he refused the draft, expressing his opposition to the Vietnam War in terms that spoke to a generation: "I ain't got no quarrel with those Vietcong. Ain't no Vietcong ever call me a nigger." Boxing commissions across the United States revoked his license while his lawyers appealed an initial conviction for draft evasion. In 1971, the Supreme Court overturned the conviction.

It was a widely reported denunciation. Less publicized was Ali's broadside on "the entire power structure" of the United States, which, he claimed was dominated by Zionists who "are really against the Islam religion," as Daniel Pipes quotes him (2000: 40). One shudders to think what reaction this, or, for that matter, Abdul-Rauf's comments, would prompt were they uttered after September 11, 2001.

The attacks on the World Trade Center brought an invitation for the West to re-evaluate its relationship with Islam and vice versa. Maybe it took a cataclysmic event to make it happen. The outrage, the fear, the gung-ho reprisal; they combined to create an atmosphere of suspicion. Were *all* Muslims against the West? Madrid, London, and Bali in Indonesia, were among the places targeted by violent groups considered to be part of the jihad, the holy war undertaken by Muslims against unbelievers. Depending on your perspective, newly radicalized hotheads or trepidatious hero-martyrs were aligning themselves with what appeared to be a revitalized onslaught against western and, in particular, American values.

The ideological chasm opened up, or perhaps just prised further open by 9/11, brought the Muslim antipathy toward the West into sharp focus. The West had been vexed by Islam's attitude toward women for many years before and had actually expressed this through sport. In 1995, a year before the Atlanta Olympics, a movement known as Atlanta Plus, consisting of several women's groups, reminded the IOC that its charter included the stipulation: "any form of discrimination with regard to a country or a person on grounds of race, religion, politics, sex or otherwise is incompatible with belonging to the Olympic Movement."

Atlanta Plus launched a campaign demanding that countries barring women from their Olympic delegations be excluded from participating in the Games. Iran was the only country explicitly banning women from most sports but others, including Pakistan and Kuwait, were heavily discouraging women's participation. In Iran women could participate only in those Olympic sports in which they can wear head-to-toe robes and veils.

Hassiba Boulmerka, the Algerian 1,500-meter Olympic and world champion, had emerged as a reluctant symbol of Muslim sportswomen. Hailed as a hero during her finest 1992–5 phase, she was also censured for revealing too much of her body during competition: she wore shorts and vest – loose-fitting, unlike the hugging outfits we see today. The criticism built to such a crescendo that Boulmerka was forced to relocate to Europe in order to train.

Atlanta Plus didn't succeed, though it made the painful truth clear. Muslim men were free to compete and praised when they succeeded: the Nigerian-born NBA player Hakeem Olajuwon, the world record breaking marathon runner Khalid Khannouchi, born in Morocco and based in New York, Nasser Hussain, the English cricket captain, whose mother converted to Islam, were among the hundreds of men acknowledged globally. Muslim women, by contrast, were discouraged from competing and sometimes reprimanded for their success. Sania Mirza, the Indian tennis player, was given extra security following a public reproach for wearing short skirts and sleeveless tops by Muslim clerics in 2005. There are about 130 million Muslims in India.

Islam's stance on sport is equivocal. "The Muslim world has, on the one hand, accepted modern sport as a symbol of modernization in Muslim societies and as a privileged tool for national-state building," writes Amara. "On the other hand, many Muslims – particularly representatives of Islamist movement – are wary of modern sport as a symbol of secularism and a deviation from the authentic societal concerns of the *Ummah* (nation of Muslim believers)" (2008: 67).

The latter believe the world is divided into Islam and *jahiliyya*, the latter describing not only the condition of the Western world, with its laxity and permissiveness, but also much modernized Islamic culture which has been affected by commerce with the

West. "The history of Islamism has been one of the battle against fun, playfulness, and diversion," Asef Bayat observes, noting that, "fun, just like any exercise of freedom, has the potential to become a social problem" (2007: 441).

As symbol of western culture, sport should be avoided, or somehow transformed. Tamir Sorek's case study of an Islamic football league in Israel, offers an example of the latter: "It [the league] incorporated soccer into its activities, and attempted to Islamicize the game" (2002: 467). This entailed eliminating the aggression and individuality from the sport, while retaining its excitement.

There are about 1.4 million Muslims living in the United States; about 53 million in Europe; they constitute about one-fifth of the world's total population. Their beliefs are opaque to some, transparent to others. Some Muslims are hostile to sport, believing it to be superfluous to civilization, a symptom of the West's preoccupation with frivolity, consumption, and material excess. Others enthuse over sports, prompting them to participate, identify, or just watch. Still others, as we've seen, tailor competitive sports to their own cultural requirements; the infinite pliancy of sports makes this possible. Whether they have accepted or repudiated sport, Islamic groups have found it a potent medium for expressing messages of dispossession, oppression, and racism. Munich, 1972, as we now know, was portentous, and, while subsequent protests in the name of Islam were nowhere near as calamitous, the significance of sport was signaled.

Conversely, human rights groups, outraged by what they considered the abuses and exploitation of women in Islamic countries, have used sport to communicate their disapproval.

THE CORRUPTING POWER OF MONEY

Before closing this chapter, we should remember that politics are of two kinds: external and internal. While I've concentrated on the various ways in which external politics have intruded on sport and how sport has been used as an instrument to express or decry particular beliefs or whole ideologies, internal politics also impact sport. Internal politics describe the activities within organizations that are aimed at furthering someone or some group's interests or improving their status.

Before we go on, let's be honest: we don't actually know *that much* about the internal politics of sport. Most of the operations are covert, often clandestine, and sometimes plain illegal. This is why we rarely get to know about them. But, every so often, a case surfaces to remind us that all our worst suspicions about sport are probably well founded.

It's possible to chronicle an alternative history of sport, one that highlights the corruption and venality rather than the glory and triumph. Sport is dirty: episodes of dishonesty have tainted it. If there was ever any purity in sports – and there's no way of knowing conclusively whether there ever was – it was when amateur ideas reigned supreme. As soon as money became involved, corruption followed with the same inevitability as night follows day.

As one of the first sports to professionalize, in the 1850s, baseball was always a prime candidate for a major corruption scandal. The 1919 World Series destroyed the image of athletic integrity, perhaps not just for baseball either. If Chicago White Sox players could be bribed to lose such a momentous and symbolic prize, who could be trusted? This was the first great corruption scandal and, as such, it's remembered as an iconoclastic case: one that destroyed cherished beliefs about the institution of sport. The most cherished was that the highest standards of decency would always prevail.

Shortly before the Chicago White Sox scandal, in 1915, there was a less publicized but no less significant case of fixing. Nine players were banned for life from football after Manchester United beat Liverpool 2–0. The prime mover in both cases appeared to be the eagerness of low-paid players to supplement their income with bribes. Gamblers were able to take advantage of favorable odds and bet on underdogs in both games. While both baseball and soccer grew throughout the remainder of the twentieth century and remain two of the world's most popular sports, neither has completely expunged bribery and corruption and periodic cases remind us that no professional sport can claim to be incorruptible. Not even the hallowed Olympic Games.

The International Olympic Committee was founded in 1894 as a self-appointed association of ambassadors from national sports governing organizations. Athletics was amateur and it was thought the best way to protect amateur sports from corrupting influences was to insulate its members from outside influences; members were not even supposed to accept instructions from their home countries.

The Belgian successor to Coubertin as president Henri de Baillet-Latour explained this ideal to Adolf Hitler during the 1936 Games. Baillet-Latour (1876–1942) later saw notices outside restrooms at all the venues warning that Jews and dogs were not allowed in. Hitler refused Baillet-Latour's request to have them removed on the grounds that no one who was invited to a friend's home would to tell him or her how to run it. Baillet-Latour's riposte was: "When the five-circled flag is raised over the stadium, it is no longer Germany. It is Olympia and we are the masters here" (quoted in Morton, 1999: 23).

The Olympic movement strove to remain independent for much of its history. The débâcle of Montreal in 1976, in which financial losses were punitive and kickbacks from construction contractors were rife, was a turning point. For a while it looked as if the games had reached an end. The cost of staging what had become a quadrennial extravaganza, each successive host trying to outdo its predecessor, had become too great for even the world's biggest cities to bear. Determined not to let the Games disappear, the IOC embraced commercialism, doing deals with sponsors, television companies, and, for many, sacrificing its original ideals.

Whispers of bribery and corruption at Olympian levels had been heard for some time before 1998, but events in December of that year confirmed that the Olympics had finally lost the ability to uphold its own ideals. Marc Hodler (1918–2006), then 81 and an IOC member since 1963 (he remained in office till his death) attended a routine meeting at the Lausanne headquarters of the organization. During press briefings, Hodler made allegations about bribery in the IOC. There were, he said, four agents who, for a commission of between $500,000 and $1 million, offered to deliver blocks of votes to cities bidding for the right to host Olympic Games. The agents, one of whom was an IOC member, charged the city that won the vote between

$3 million and $5 million. Subsequent inquiries, some by the world's media, others by the IOC itself (which produced a report on the subject within a month of Hodler's accusations) revealed a story that centered on the award of the 2002 winter Olympics to Salt Lake City, Utah.

After Salt Lake City had been turned down in its attempt to stage the 1998 winter Olympic Games, it began to examine why its bid had failed. All cities vying for the right to host the games give IOC members (whose numbers vary, but usually between 95–115) gifts, such as laptop computers, designer luggage, or *objets d'art*. In the run-up to the voting, Nagano, Japan, had employed Goran Takacs as a lobbyist for a fee of $363,000 plus bonuses if the bid succeeded. Goran's father, Artur Takacs, was a Yugoslavian entrepreneur, and a close advisor to IOC President Juan Antonio Samaranch; he sat near Samaranch at IOC meetings and was influential among IOC members. The meeting to determine the site of the games was held in Birmingham, England, in April 1991. Prior to the voting, Takacs made it known that the president favored the Japanese bid; he later apologized for this impropriety. Nagano won.

Salt Lake City's bid committee set about correcting its mistakes. Over the next four years, it gave away nearly $800,000 in inappropriate "material benefits" to 14 IOC members. The benefits included cash, free housing, medical treatment, scholarships, and jobs. Two rifles valued at $2,000 were given to Samaranch who defended himself by explaining that, as president, he did not take part in the voting. Salt Lake City won the right to host the 2002 games.

The IOC's hastily assembled report in response to Hodler's statements, confirmed that there was evidence that IOC members and their relatives had received "benefits" from Salt Lake City officials, in some cases more than $100,000. The report recommended disciplinary action, including expulsion for members involved. Among them were Jean-Claude Ganga, of the Congo, who was said to have made $60,000 profit on a land deal in Utah arranged by a member of the Salt Lake City bid committee. The committee also gave him $50,000 to help feed children in the war-riven Congo and paid for medical care for him and his mother. Another IOC member, Bashir Mohammed Attarabulsi, from Libya, had his son's education at Brigham Young University paid for by the committee, which also arranged living expenses.

The scandal surrounding Salt Lake City shook a few more skeletons out the closet. John Coates, the chair of the Australian Olympic Committee and leader of Sydney's bid for the 2000 Olympics, offered inducements estimated between $35,000-$70,000 to the Kenyan and Ugandan IOC members at a dinner in Monte Carlo in 1993 – on the eve of the voting which saw Sydney beat Beijing by two votes for the right to host the games. Coates maintained that the money was a contribution toward helping the development of sports in Kenya and Uganda, though he admitted: "We didn't get the Games because of our great facilities or beautiful location" (quoted by Swift, 1999: 34).

Melbourne failed in its attempt to host the 1996 Games even though its bid committee arranged for the daughter of a South Korean IOC delegate to play with the Melbourne Symphony Orchestra. Atlanta eventually won the vote after high-profile power broker Andrew Young cultivated links with African IOC members to whom the bid committee provided athletic gear and other sports-related aid. The lobbying for this event became intense after Athens had reportedly prepared a dossier with details of IOC members' sexual preferences. Berlin allegedly repeated the operation when bidding for the 2000 Olympics.

Evidence, actual or inferential, was found to tarnish the bidding process for every summer and winter Olympics since 1988. There's no reason to suppose that backroom political deals and dubious gifts marked the elections before that date, though the stakes went up appreciably after the stupendous commercial success of the LA Games in 1984. The huge costs of running the event are offset by a dozen key sponsors, including Coca-Cola and Kodak, which pay sums in the region of $14 million to use the Olympic five-ring symbol on its merchandise.

Added to this is the extra revenue generated by businesses in the city hosting the Games and, importantly, the slice of the television revenues. NBC paid the IOC $3.55 billion for the U.S. tv rights to all Olympics through 2008. The four-year Olympic cycle is estimated to generate some $10 billion. One can imagine, with this kind of money available to host cities, the temptation to leave no stone unturned is great. Perhaps we might also remember that the tv deal itself was not completely untainted by controversy: rival networks were not given the opportunity to submit proposals for the Games beyond 2000; rumors of multimillion dollar payments over and above the $3.55 billion circulated, though without substantiation.

BOX 19.9 CORRUPTION

Some form of deception or fraud has probably been present in all organized professional sports. Even amateur sports in which competitors officially receive no money are vulnerable: gambling has been integral to the sports experience and, while there are observers willing to wager on the outcome of a contest, the probability that they will try to control, manipulate, or determine the desired outcome will persist. In horseracing, this has been achieved through administering drugs to the horses, a tactic known as "nobbling." The most usual way of managing a result in a human sport is by bribing competitors, a practice that has been exposed historically in a number of sports, including baseball (Black Sox Scandal of 1919), boxing (the Jack Johnson–Jess Willard fight of 1916), and soccer (the Tony Kay case of 1963).

It would be too simple to interpret the whole saga of corruption as the product of human avarice and overweening power. Greed has certainly been a factor, but the conditions under which that greed has been fed must be noted. The Olympic movement's embrace of commercialism, the proliferation of logo'd merchandise, the exorbitant television contracts, the bonanzas enjoyed by host cities: these are some of the other factors that made possible the fulfillment of individual greed. Being awarded an Olympic Games was like being given a cow that produced money instead of milk for its owner.

I've detailed this case, not because its consequences were great: the IOC was shaken, but remained intact, and, of course, the Olympic Games, summer and winter, remained juggernauts of the sporting calendar. When Brundage declared, "The games must go on," he was right: not even the kind of scandal that would have brought corporations or governments to their knees interrupted the Olympics. And this is one of the two reasons why the case is so important: it showed just how invulnerable the IOC had become. Not even a well-documented exposition of the kind of fraudulence that was inimical to its ideals could wreck the august institution.

The second reason for the detail is to give some impression of its scope. This was not just a case of someone handing over an envelope stuffed with cash: it was a conspiracy to suborn people in power, a machination to subvert fair play; contemptible but perhaps less alarming than it would have been, say, fifty years earlier before we'd grown accustomed to the dirty internal politics of sport.

In a sense, fatigue has set in: we are no longer surprised when sports are used like political instruments; we are not shocked when individuals get caught up in issues that are far beyond their control; we are not really astonished when we hear that the guardians of sports are themselves debased and dishonest. Perhaps our expectations of sport have changed. No longer do we regard sports as rising above the vileness that dwells in much of political life: sport is part of that political life and cannot help but be affected. Strenuous as efforts may once have been made to protect the image of sport as independent and virtuous, the facts tell a different story.

OF RELATED INTEREST

The Lords of the Rings by Vyv Simson, Andrew Jennings, and Patrick Nally (Simon & Schuster, 1992) was a groundbreaking book on corruption at the highest levels of sport. Jennings, a BBC journalist, pursued his theme further, publishing further editions in the United States as *Dishonored Games: Corruption, money and greed at the Olympics* (with Simson, SPI Books, 1992), and following up with further disclosures in *The New Lords of the Rings: Olympic corruption and how to buy gold medals* (Pocket Books, 1996), and then *The Great Olympic Swindle* (Simon & Schuster, 2000), the latter showing how, despite its promises to reform after the Salt Lake City scandal, the IOC fell back into its old corrupt ways. Jennings followed the Olympic exposés with a detailed examination of the internal politics of association football's governing organization, *Foul! The Secret World of FIFA: Bribes, vote rigging and ticket scandals* (HarperCollins, 2007). Considered collectively, the books make a compelling antidote to Corinthian idealism.

Baseball Babylon: From Black Sox to Pete Rose by D. Gutman (Penguin, 1992) recounts baseball's catalog of crookedness; the book is complemented by Alan Wyke's dated but still impressive *Gambling* (Spring Books, 1964) which looks at the manner in which sports gambling has led logically to attempts to preordain results.

Studies of sports in Islamic cultures reveal different responses. Thomas B. Stevenson and Abdul Karim Alaug's "Football in newly united Yemen: Rituals of equity, identity and state formation" (in *Journal of Anthropological Research*, 2000, vol. 54, no. 4) examines how football was attached with symbolic national importance in Yemen, in the Arabian peninsula. Paul A. Silverstein's "Islam, soccer, and the French nation-state" (in *Social Text*, 2000, vol. 18, no. 4) showed how the same sport was used for completely different purposes: "Muslim youth in France have forged their own set of localized patriotisms that can and do draw on subnational, nation, and transnational references. In so doing, these young men *and women* have refused to become solely the French citizens or the Muslim believers or the free market consumers" (my italics).

Football and Fascism: The national game in the international arena under Mussolini by Simon Martin (Berg, 2004) is a historical account of the way in which football, or *calcio*, as it is called in Italy, was politicized as a way of enhancing Mussolini's international prestige, inculcate nationalist values and reinforce conformity in the 1930s.

"Terrorism, sport and public policy" by Kristine Toohey (in *Sport in Society*, 2008, vol. 11, no. 4) is a valuable overview of the intrusion of terrorism into sporting events. Tooey notes how the development of risk society and the corresponding culture of fear have contributed to the response of sports organizers. "Sports can be utilized as a vehicle for political sparring, and waging and disseminating forms of political violence. At an Olympic Games, security cannot exist without assistance from government agencies."

"Massacre in Munich: The Olympic terror attacks of 1972 in historical perspective" by David Clay Large (in *Historically Speaking*, 2009, vol. 10, no. 2) is a scholarly account of the pivotal event and its aftermath. It can be productively read with Simon Reeve's *One Day in September: The full story of the 1972 Munich Olympics massacre and the Israeli Revenge Operation Wrath of God* (2001).

The Politics of the Olympics: A survey edited by Alan Bairner and Gyozo Molna (Routledge, 2009) investigates political aspects of the Olympics and includes a glossary of famous and infamous Olympic athletes, Olympic movement personnel and events, and broader political issues. The collection can be read with the earlier *Power, Politics and the Olympic Games* by Alfred E. Senn (Human Kinetics, 1999), which is especially useful in exploring the way in which South Africa's apartheid impacted on several Olympic Games. Also recommended in this context: the 2nd edition of Christopher Hill's *Olympic Politics* (Manchester University Press, 1996).

ASSIGNMENT

You are a national volleyball manager-coach in the final stages of your squad's preparation for a major international tournament to be attended by the world's volleyball powers. In a newspaper feature profiling one of the squad's outstanding attacking players, he/she reveals that he/she is a member of the Order, a group opposed to what it calls ZOG (Zionist Occupation Government) and which, as the newspaper journalist uncovers, has links or sympathies with the Ku Klux Klan, the Posse Comitatus, the Nazi Parties of Britain and the United States, and other anti-Semitic and racist groups. What is the likely fall-out and how will you, as manager-coach, deal with it?

Things to Come

KEY ISSUES

▓ How will we consume
  sports in the future?

▓ What records are left to
  break?

▓ When will the Paralympics
  become superfluous?

▓ Where do we draw the
  line between technology
  and humanity?

▓ Why is sport more
  important than ever?

▓ . . . and can we make
  sense of the senseless?

▓ TECHNOLOGY AND THE BODY

To . . .   e.e.cashmore@staffs.edu
From . . .   h.g.wells@timemachine.org
Subject: human machines and machined humans

Hello prof: In my books, I anticipated how humanity would change. I speculated about machines that could perform tasks like humans, though one of my contemporaries Karel Čapek (1890–1938), the Czech writer, gave us the right word in his 1920 novel *RUR (Rossum's Universal Robots)*. I certainly suspected we would harvest spare parts from animals and, in *The Island of Doctor Moreau* (1896) anticipated fusions of humans and animals. But I never imagined humans and machines could join to form a single entity.

Back in 2008, Oscar Pistorius was ruled ineligible to compete in the Olympics because his prosthetic limbs were thought to give him an unfair advantage. We didn't realize that he was the first of many athletes to demand official recognition as athletes, not disabled or handicapped athletes or even Paralympians: just athletes. That was 40 years ago. Now, the biggest debate in sports is over whether disabled sports should be discontinued.

The inaugural National Wheelchair Games took place in 1958. As you know, this led to athletic tournaments specifically for disabled competitors, which eventually evolved into the Paralympics. By the turn of the century, international events for the blind and partially sighted, paraplegics, tetraplegics and amputees were commonplace. Some years ago, some competitors with handicaps demanded admission into the Olympics. Their times and distances were of the requisite qualifying standard and the IOC consented. It didn't take long before amputees (not a term that's used nowadays, by the way), were beating fully-abled rivals in events where you might not expect them to be competitive, such as cycling and the pole vault.

The reason for this is metal/bone integration. Prosthetists used to attach artificial limbs to the remaining portion of an athlete's arm or leg via a socket. We've known that bone melds with metal since the middle of the twentieth century, of course. But, the risk of infection was high. Once this was minimized, it was possible to affix titanium prosthetics in a way that allowed them to bond with human bone. Recently, neuroscientists have perfected a way of tapping into the brain's cerebral cortex with electrodes and using electrical currents to direct the movements of the limb. Effectively, the bionic athlete uses the limb just like any other athlete. Because there is no muscle involved, there is no depletion nor build-up of waste products, making the athlete more efficient in biomechanical terms. This is the reason for the debate. People are asking: is it fair? What do *you* think?

There are some certainties in sport. Runners will run faster and jumpers will jump higher. Sports stars will earn more and more money. Cheats will cheat as long as there is money to be made. Science will keep producing new technologies to aid sporting performance and sport itself will keep agonizing over whether those technologies are fair.

The application of any form of scientific knowledge for the practical purpose of improving sporting performance has always and will always provoke arguments. For the ancient Greek games, stonemasons carved and polished stone into thick-centered, ventricular shapes to provide the discus with aerodynamic features. It may seem primitive, but it was technology all the same. Sport has been using technology ever since, each application prompting questions about fairness. The discus wasn't delivered from the heavens with an instruction that it should never be defiled: so when it was changed to bronze, and, later wood with metal rims and covered in plastic, there were no accusations of heresy, though there were probably arguments.

There certainly were in 1894, when A. G. Spalding, in the United States, began producing footwear specifically designed for improving purchase when running: the sole of the shoes was punctured with metal spikes. Actually, spiked shoes had been around for over thirty years before, as Peter R. Cavanagh notes: "The first spiked shoes were not made for running at all. The patent, issued in England in 1861, was for that grand old game of cricket" (1980: 17).

Those track runners who opted to wear the new footwear held an advantage over those who opted to stick with flats. The Irish-born, American-based miler Thomas Conneff, who held the world record in the 1890s, was known to favor running spikes. The benefits were very apparent. Questions of fairness were eventually answered satisfactorily and everyone switched to spikes.

In a rapidly industrializing world, it had to happen: technology extended into all areas of social life, so how could sport go it alone and remain in the dark ages? Nowadays athletes compete in footwear worthy of Nasa. Usain Bolt favors Puma Complete TFX Theses 3 Pro spikes, made with microfiber uppers and a fiber sole, weighing 298 grams, or 10.511 ounces (the pair).

It might be assumed that sport will inevitably embrace technologies it initially resists. For example, it would be absurd to imagine sprinters in flats, as it would footballs with outer cases made of uncoated hide that absorbs moisture, or the 40 lb (18 kg) steel-tube framed bicycles that competitors rode in the early days of the Tour de France. Today, footballs have polyurethane cases covering carbon latex airchambers, and cycles are aerodynamically designed, made with carbon frames and typically weigh less than 16 lb (about 7.25 kg). Cycling's governing organization UCI stipulates a minimum weight for cycles of 15 lb, or 6.8 kg. This is an instance of a sport accepting technological advance, but only to an extent: it's possible to manufacture lighter cycles, but the UCI deems them inappropriate for competition.

BOX 20.1 CARBON FIBER

A material consisting of thin, strong crystalline filaments of carbon tightly woven, so that it is has great tensile strength without losing flexibility. Sometimes known as graphite fiber, and carbon graphite, it is used in F1 and Indy cars' bodywork. Sporting goods and recreational equipment account for 18–20 percent of the carbon fiber market: rackets, fishing rods, ski poles, snowboards, sailboard masts, softball and baseball bats, bows and arrows. Carbon fiber is chemically inert, or inactive, making it highly suitable for medical applications such as those involving hip and knee ligament replacements and prosthetics, as well as a constituent of implants. Oscar Pistorius' famous blades were made of carbon fiber.

Sharon Kay Stoll *et al.* illustrate how the whole shape and experience of sports could theoretically be perverted by technology. "Electronically guided darts, heat-seeking missiles for grouse-shooting, solar energy-enhanced bicycles, and golf balls with terrain-following mechanisms that automatically find the lowest elevation on a putting surface – the bottom of the hole" are some of the possibilities (2002: 72).

In these examples, the human is subordinated to technology. Sport is already challenged: in recent history it has been sorely conflicted by its own demands. Every sport wants to oversee improvements in performance; yet none wants to reduce the human element to an auxiliary of technology. Formula One motor racing is engaged in a constant struggle to prevent technology assuming paramountcy: its ban on refueling was one of a number of rule changes that effectively slowed-down cars and reinstituted a more central role for drivers' judgments. Elsewhere in this book, we've examined the moral quandaries posed by performance-enhancing technologies, from EPO to polyurethane swimsuits. Sport will remain suspicious of technology.

So, Geneviève Rail was only partly right when she predicted: "High performance sport is increasingly contingent upon computer-revealed genetic potentialities . . . absorption of chemical substances, individualized diet and training, and publicity and marketing. The body becomes a means of production" (1998: 148–9).

Sport – and all sport is basically "high performance" nowadays – is dependent on technology of some description and the preparation of most athletes relies on scientific advice. Rail is also right to point out the importance of publicity and marketing. But her suggestion that sport is "contingent" – by which she presumably means conditional on, or determined by – genetic engineering and other forms enhancement is off the mark.

A primitive form of genetic engineering has actually been used in sport. In the late seventeenth century, English racehorse owners imported Arab stallions but not Arab mares and were forced to breed the prodigiously fast studs with comparatively sluggish English mares. They mated the female offspring of these unions back to other Arab stallions. After a few generations, the breeders had almost eliminated the English stock, leaving them with prime Arab bloodstock. Today, that practice seems altogether too longwinded. It's also crude when compared to what breeders can do. And, in any case, producing a thoroughbred racehorse is one thing; but a human athlete?

If genetic material could be delivered to the body just like cutting-and-pasting, then it would be possible to recreate organisms almost to order. Remember: the gene consists of DNA, the twin spiral ladder-like structure that contains the codes for development. As we saw in Chapter 3, there are many other mediating variables that affect how the body builds, but the DNA provides the potential. So, if, for example the gene that signals the body to yield erythropoietin (EPO), which stimulates the body to produce red blood cells, could be identified and this could be transferred to, say, a virus, which could then be injected into a human being, the advantages to an endurance athlete would be many.

Having conducted the body-building experiments with mice, Lee Sweeney told the American Association for the Advancement of Science, in 2004: "The prospects are especially high that muscle-directed gene transfer will be used by the athletic community for performance enhancement, just as many drugs are used and abused today" (quoted by John von Radowitz, *PA News*, February 4, 2004).

Rail is right in suggesting the technology is in development. But the IOC has already issued its disapproval of gene doping. Jacques Rogge, of the organization's medical commission, in 2001, stipulated: "Genetic manipulation is there to treat people who have ailments, not there to treat a healthy person" (quoted in Swift and Yaeger, 2001: 87). Of course, one athlete's "ailment" might be another's pretext. And, if there's any doubt over whether athletes would be unnerved by the unknown longterm consequences of gene doping, consider these cases.

A female basketball player asked a doctor to break her arms and reset them in a way that might make them longer; pediatricians were being pressured by parents to give their children human-growth hormone to make them taller and perhaps more athletic; parents of football players asked doctors to provide steroids so their sons might gain college scholarships.

All three cases are reported by Jeré Longman in "The rise of the superathlete" (2001). In the future, athletes could conceivably choose to lose perfectly good limbs for stronger, faster artificial equivalents. And remember: there is the previously quoted study quoted by Bamberger and Yaeger: asked whether they would take a drug that would guarantee sporting success but bring certain death within twenty years, over half a sample of young athletes said yes. Athletes are risk takers.

It's a view predicated on a fundamental shift in the ethos of sports and it's shared by, among others, Andrew Blake, who in 1996 argued:

> Body-builders and weightlifters, in order to succeed, routinely take drugs, which drastically alter the physical structure and chemical composition of their bodies. There is no reason why other athletes should not equally resort to structural alteration, biochemical or microprocessor-based implants or the like.
>
> (1996: 161)

Actually, there are several perfectly sound reasons why they won't. Taking dope, even dope that may have long-term deleterious effects, is understandable. So is undergoing surgery, though resetting limbs sounds extreme even in the twenty-first century. There are predictable consequences. Not so for genetic engineering. Studies on mice carry no assurance for humans. The manifold uncertainty surrounding genetic engineering – and this is, after all, what gene doping is – will prohibit the kind of future envisaged by Rail and Blake.

Even the cyborgized, posthuman possibilities we entertained in Chapter 8, are going to meet with resistance. The Oscar Pistorius case in 2008 issued a reminder of how governing bodies are reluctant to stand back and reassess their definitions of humanity in a world full of people walking around with bodies containing or held together by titanium, Kevlar, or other biocompatible materials. For sure, minds will be exercised by the question of how to define the limits of humanity when technology is changing them constantly.

BOX 20.2 TITANIUM

A silver-gray corrosion-resistant metallic element that is half as light as steel, yet nearly a third stronger. It has widespread application in manufacturing, especially aircraft. It is also used in jewelry. In sports, its uses are many: its ability to absorb vibration makes it useful in the shafts of golf clubs and bike frames, for example. It is also used to make surgical implants. The name is taken from *titan*, a thing of very great strength, and *-ium* denoting the name of a metallic element (e.g. magnesium; uranium).

There's no Luddite movement in sport. At least not an organized group of people who oppose the use of new technologies (Luddites were bands of English cotton and woolen mill workers who, in the early nineteenth century, destroyed the industrial machinery they believed would make them redundant to production). But, as Pistorius' case and the swimwear and drugs bans as well as the various other performance-restraining policies indicate, there is no unconditional welcome for all kinds of technology in sport. The probability is that we will continue to witness the arrival of new technology that carries the potential to assist us in improving performance. Some of it will meet with a cautious welcome, but, since the 1970s, sport tends to meet technology with a challenge.

PERFORMANCE

Sports in the twenty-first century have veered away from the original Olympic motto: higher, faster, longer. Swimmers won't swim as fast in textile swimsuits; cyclists won't ride so hard without EPO. There are probably some performances that will never be equaled. At least, measurable performances. In sports where subjective evaluations are possible, there will continue to be disputes. Romantics might insist that, for example the Pittsburgh Steelers of the 1960s were superior to today's best NFL teams, or that the indomitable Liverpool teams of the 1970s and 1980s would overcome the best contemporary soccer teams.

The truth is that they wouldn't. In sports in which performance levels are measurable, the trend has been toward improvement by increments. It makes no sense to believe other sports have not progressed in a similar way.

In the first four editions of *MSS*, I paraphrased former Olympian Sebastian Coe's father and coach, Peter (1919–2008), who once ventured to suggest that there was no limit to how fast the mile could be run. "It's like taking a straight line, dividing it in two, splitting again, then again and again and so on *ad infinitum*," he argued. "The lines get smaller and smaller, but you're always left with something." In other words, there will always be the potential for improvement in competitive performances, but the improvements will be quantitatively smaller each time. I agreed with this prognosis, pointing out that it can be applied to any sport, not just track and field. Does this argument still hold up?

Huge improvements or long-standing records, such as Jarmila Kratochvílová's 1:53.28 for 800 meters, set in 1983, Marita Koch's 47.60 for 400 meters, set in 1985, or Randy Barnes' 23.12 meters shot, set in 1990, remain historically aberrant performances, explicable only in terms of freak atmospheric conditions, exceptionally fierce competition or some undisclosed form of assistance. But, records have more typically progressed smoothly and by decreasing increments in most events for most of the past century. But, in the mid-1990s, something unusual happened.

In August 1994, Algeria's Noureddine Morceli broke the world's 3,000-meter record when he ran 7:25.11, which equates to 8:01 for two miles. In other words, very, very fast; nearly four seconds faster, in fact, than the previous world record held by Kenya's Moses Kiptanui. In the 20 years immediately before Morceli's run, the record had been lowered by a yearly average of 0.307 seconds (6.14 seconds in total). Yet Morceli's was an ominous run.

The following year, Haile Gebrselassie, of Ethiopia, began to rewrite the record books. He lopped 1.55 seconds off the 2-mile record, which was more than it had been lowered between the entire 1972–94 period. He also destroyed Kiptanui's 5,000-meter record with 12:44.39, an improvement of 10.91 seconds, compared with an average improvement of just under 3.64 seconds every year between 1972 and 1995. The Ethiopian later reduced this to 12.41.86, in 1997, and to 12:39.36, in 1998. But Gebrselassie's most extraordinary run was over 10,000 meters, in 1995, when he recorded 26:43.53. In the previous year, William Sigel, of Kenya, had shaken the athletics world when he ran a remarkable 26:52.23, which itself took a gigantic 6.15 seconds off a world record that had been brought down by about 15 seconds in the previous 15 years. So, Gebrselassie's 8.7 seconds improvement seemed to defy rational analysis. So, when, in 2008, Gebrselassie completed a marathon in a world's fastest 2:03.59, there was no incredulity: it was another instance of the Ethiopian's facility for resisting reasonable expectations.

The sequence of events did not stop. Gebrselassie's records were beaten by Daniel Komen and Paul Tergat, both of Kenya, and Salah Hissou, of Morocco, only for him to respond by breaking them again and again. Gebrselassie took the 5,000 meters mark from 12:58.39 to 12:39.36 and the 10,000 meters from 26:52.23 to 26:22.75. Then, after a period of relative calmness, during which Gebrselassie's dominance seemed consolidated and analysts began to adjudge him the greatest track runner in history, Kenenisa Bekele appeared. In a 10-month period in 2003/4, Bekele shattered Gebrselassie's 5,000 meters outdoor and indoor records, as well as his 6-year-old 10,000 meters record (he clocked 26:20.31, covering the second half of the race faster than the world record for 5,000 meters at the time he was born, June 13, 1982).

Collectively, the middle-distance records produced a pattern. The athletics equivalent of the law of diminishing returns held good up to around 1995; then the returns started to expand. Even if the pattern hasn't been replicated in other areas, the sharp and unexpected upturn in performance forces us to reconsider the orthodoxy about athletic progression and ponder on possible reasons for the disproportionate improvement.

Highly paid athletes often say money is the last thing they are thinking of in the midst of competition. This may be so, but it's tempting to advance cash incentives as at least one factor in the improvement. At the start of the twenty-first century, Bekele would not take his tracksuit off for less than $50,000 a race, top marathon runners could take home four or five times that and top male sprinters could command upwards of $100,000 a race. Bekele's middle-distance predecessors like Lasse Viren and Henry Rono – both world record breakers – ran for expenses only in the 1970s. Money *is* a motivating force, however much people deny it, and it becomes an even greater force when you come from pestilential African countries. It is, of course, no coincidence that a growing number of soccer players from nations such as Ghana, Nigeria, and Sierra Leone are now playing at the highest levels of European competition and earning millions for their labors. Or those hockey players from war-ravaged or hard-up eastern European countries excel in the NHL.

A second factor is the knowledge we have about how to prepare athletes. We know more about diet and training cycles and, importantly, how to use technology to improve performance. Philosophies of training have changed. The brutal regimes instigated by Franz Stampfl in the 1950s now seem quite modest. Gebrselassie employed a version of Stampfl's philosophy, which was to slice up a distance and repeatedly attack just one portion of it during training. He prepared for longer distances by running 400 meters at about 90 percent of his maximum (e.g. 46 seconds) about 20 times, with a one-minute recovery between reps. Bekele would typically do an even pace 8,000 meters training run in about 21:23. At about 2,600 meters above sea level, this would elevate his haemocrit level (percentage of red blood cells) to 49 (Gebrselassie's was usually about 42).

This reflects in actual performance. For example, distances up to a mile are now typically run quite evenly at about 96–7 percent capacity. Runners try to distribute their efforts in a way that replicates hard training. The first three laps of a fast 1,500 meters may each be run at even splits of 56 seconds, with the final three-quarter lap taking 41 seconds (equivalent of a 54.66 lap). This means that all distances up to 3,000 meters are likely to be less tactical affairs and more of sustained sprints.

Performance such as this requires training that accentuates quality as well as quantity. Combine better training with better nutrition and the supplementary aid of massage, acupuncture, and assorted methods of modifying cognition and you have potent factors that explain the improvements. But, there is perhaps one other we need to contemplate.

APPROACHING THE LIMITS?

In no other area of track and field has there been such a dramatic improvement as in men's middle distance. In some areas, there has actually been deterioration in measurable performance. Few women's records are challenged nowadays, either in track and field, or swimming. The accepted reason for this is that many, probably most, records set by athletes from the former Soviet bloc countries were involved in state-run programs, which involved taking performance enhancing substances for which there were no rigorous tests.

Anabolic steroids would have had an impact on virtually all strength-related performances, including throwing, field events, and track races up to 800 meters. Women have only recently begun to contest middle- and long-distance races. In men's events, the deterioration in power-based events is not so marked, though it is worth remembering that the best 21 throws in shot putt history were all made before 1991, after which systems of gas chromatography and mass spectroscopy made it possible to check a compound found in urine against 70,000 held in a computer's database.

But, in the late 1990s, when the men's middle-distance records went tumbling, there was no effective test for EPO. The genetically engineered substance is a more convenient and more efficient alternative to blood doping, which was known to be favored by some middle- and long-distance men in the 1970s.

The sharp upturn in distance records coincided with the greater availability of EPO. In his *Sports Illustrated* article "Distance thunder," Tim Layden quotes former marathon runner Alberto Salazar, of the United States: "I can believe that there can always be that one great person, that Superman who can run 45 seconds faster than Henry Rono . . . But all these people running so fast? That's incomprehensible to me" (1998: 37). (Gebrselassie's 1998 record for 10K was actually just under a minute faster than Rono's best of 20 years before.)

Perhaps it will become more comprehensible in years to come. The staggering achievements of the East German swimming team at the 1976 Olympics – described in chapter 11 – seemed less staggering after 1989. Some will hold that the exponential improvement in middle-distance running was the product of the genuinely gifted Superman referred to by Salazar, who inspired his rivals to greater and greater achievements. After all, rivalries tend to bring the best out of competitors. Others will dismiss it as a historical deviation. Cynics – and one suspects Salazar is among them – will wish to wait and see what happens when further tests for as-yet unknown substances comes into force. If there is a tapering-off in times, then we can draw obvious conclusions.

Brendan Foster, the British runner who held the 3,000 meters record, 1974–8, is also quoted by Layden: "You'd have to think these guys are approaching the limits of human endurance" (1998: 34). John Smith, who coached Maurice Greene, Ato Bolden and others, disagrees. "I don't think a limit exists," he said to Mike Rowbottom, of the *Independent* (July 5, 1999).

Ben Johnson's now-expunged time for the 100 meters at the 1988 Olympics was 9.79 seconds. It took only 11 years before the same time was clocked by Greene without the enhancement used by Johnson; although, in 2008, Greene himself was asked by the IAAF to provide an explanation about allegations from a government informant who claimed he gave athletes performance-enhancing drugs, according to Duff Wilson, of the *New York Times* ("I.A.A.F. Seeks an Explanation From Greene About Drug Allegations", April 17, 2008). By 2008, the record was down to 9.69 seconds.

The record-breaking sprinter was, of course, Usain Bolt, in every way as extraordinary an athlete as Gebrselassie. A year later, Bolt reduced the world record to 9.58 seconds. In 1968, Jim Hines became the first person to break the 10-second barrier, when he recorded 9.95 seconds Between then and 2009, the world record time improved by 3.7 percent, or less than 0.1 percent per year.

It seems my original forecast is in need of revision. The bit-by-even-smaller-bit progression I envisaged is interspersed with periods of rapid and perhaps explosive improvements. Perhaps we have witnessed them in some sports, but have not been able to measure them. For example, the ascendant Chicago Bulls team of the 1990s may have taken the sport to new heights because of its special combination of coaching and playing staff, and appreciable cash incentives. Without these, it may have taken basketball another 10 or 15 years to produce a team capable of elevating the game to the same level.

BOX 20.3 PROGRESS

Progress in sports is a uniquely human phenomenon, based more on mental abilities than physical ones. For example, over 1,500 meters, Hicham El Guerrouj in the early twenty-first century consistently ran about 40 seconds faster than his counterpart of 120 years previously. Yet, if we compare the Kentucky Derby or Grand National winner over a similar period, today's horses run only about 10 seconds faster. The reason for the difference is that a trained racehorse will maintain between 85–95 percent of its maximum speed, metabolizing anaerobic energy, which is, as we have seen, counterproductive in the long term as it produces lactic acid and retards muscle contraction.

Humans have improved their performances through advances in technique, training, rivalries, and supplements. They will run at between 70–75 percent of maximum speed for most of a middle distance race, kicking over the final phase e.g. 5,000 meters: 11 laps @ 61.5 seconds + 1 lap @ 56 seconds = 12:43.25. This requires timing, anticipation and a tactical awareness, as well as the capacity to assimilate stress and discomfort – features that are built into training.

There is also incentive: a horse has only a whipped flank to motivate it in the final stretch, whereas a human has rewards for which he or she is prepared to suffer pain. Apart from the intellectual stimulus, we should note that humans are physically inefficient at running and have modest locomotion capabilities compared to horses, whose capacity for running is an evolutionary adaptation, probably resulting from their relative lack of defense. The human desire to run fast over distances and, indeed, achieve in any competition, is a product of self-induced challenge.

Historically, we can identify intervals of superabundance in particular sports. The Duran/Hagler/Hearns/Leonard epoch of boxing in the 1970s stands out; there has been no evidence of such a sustained level of competition in the years since. Salazar's Superman theory seems to apply perfectly to Jean-Claude Killy, the best all-round ski racer in history, who glided to previously untouched planes of achievement and whose technical command has probably not been matched since (though fans of Alberto Tomba may wish to argue that point). But Michael Schumacher? For some, his achievements distinguish him as the greatest Formula One driver ever; for others, Schumacher's cars made him great.

Technological changes often disguise progress: motorcars have been slowed up; tennis balls have been deflated; javelins have been made less aerodynamic. The changes have usually been made in the interests of safety or spectacle, but, in both cases, their effect has been to mask quantifiable progress. In Bolt's case, the only piece of tangible technology that contributed to his time was his Puma Complete TFX Theses 3 Pro spikes.

In other words, several sports may have passed through the kind of stage that middle-distance running went through in the late 1990s. But, because they are either not objectively measurable in the same way as track or they have changed the conditions of competition, the periods have not been acknowledged as exponential jumps forward.

Perhaps, these are the equivalents of Norbert Elias's "civilizing spurts" we encountered in Chapter 5: relatively short, but transformative bursts of activity in which human conduct is significantly affected. As we saw, Elias budgets for a reverse gear. Traditionalists maintain that sports also have that facility. It probably only seems that way. While there may be less intense rivalry and/or less talented individuals in some eras, it is unlikely that overall standards reverse; more likely that our retrospective interpretations deceive us. Jordan, Leonard, Killy and many, many other athletes stand out as parts of "golden ages" in sports and, as I have argued, they were parts of periods of accelerated progress. But, the sports in which they participated would not have remained unchanged by their presence. They defined new standards of excellence in much the same way as Gebrselassie and Bolt did in track running.

So, the revision to my prediction is simple. We need to allow for the fact that sports typically progress smoothly without denying the possibility of rapid spurts that violate all accepted criteria. The trick is to identify the conditions under which those spurts take place. A sharp upturn in the financial incentives on offer seems to help. There has always been money to made in boxing; but in the 1970s, million dollar purses became commonplace. Would money alone explain Bolt's progress? No. But let's crunch numbers, anyway.

Mark McDonald, of the *New York Times* reported that Bolt's "annual earnings, pre-Beijing [August, 2008], have been estimated at $5 million. And that's not counting the $1 million bonus Speedo is paying him for tying Mark Spitz's record of seven golds" ("Phelps avoids commercials, but Bolt does not," August 18, 2008). Puma paid Bolt $1.5 million/£908,000 per year (and had a sales growth of 4 percent in the 6 months following Bolt's 2008 World Championship wins; Puma has 6 percent of the sportswear market).

Writing in the *NYT,* Jeré Longman observed of Bolt, "by the 2012 Summer Games in London, or soon after, he wants to become the first track star to earn $10 million a year in prize money, appearance fees and endorsements" ("Bolt, track's biggest star, looks to revitalize sport," April 11, 2009). This comparatively modest amount wouldn't push him into sport's top 20 "rich list" but it would obviate any need to clip discount coupons for the grocery.

Even if it doesn't explain the exponential improvement in sprint and middle-distance running, money remains an incentive. For most of its history, track and field athletics has been an amateur sport: the 1985 IAAF Grand Prix was the first meet to award official prize money. After that, money has poured in from sponsors and media companies. Gold medals are just one part of the motivational mix (see Table 20.1).

THE WORLD IN OUR HANDS

Overheard while waiting in line at a supermarket in 2002: "I just got this amazing new phone: it takes pictures – just like a camera!"

This was 2002, remember. Before phones and cameras became effectively the same thing, phones were mainly for talking to each other, their other main function being for texting. Now, they are for controlling computers remotely, checking football scores, playing a game of *Pro Evolution Soccer*, recognizing whatever music is playing in the background, shooting videos and streaming them onto the internet and . . . well, the list is endless. Anything you can do on your laptop, you can theoretically do on your phone. And more: if you get lost and want to know where you are, your phone will probably have an app that will tell you your exact longitudinal and latitudinal position on the planet.

When, in 2004, David Rowe wrote, "It is little wonder that the relationship between sport and the media (especially television) is commonly described as the happiest of marriages," he couldn't have known how the marriage he described would have got even happier. Of course, he was writing about traditional media when he suggested that there would be "an increasingly extensive and expensive exchange of exposure and rights fees for sport in return for compelling content and audience capture for the media" (2004: 32).

Sport still provides "compelling content" and television continues to pay lavishly for the rights to screen it. But, how will we view it? The traditional conception of viewing televised sport is at home, or more recently, in a bar or clubroom. This is how most people consume sports. They move to where there is a screen showing the event; mostly on big flat screens in high definition. Soon they'll be watching in 3D. But for how much longer will we organize our lives around a static receiver that picks up the broadcast signals and coverts them into visible and audible forms?

Now we have any number of portable devices capable of detecting signals and delivering to us content through countless applications. In 2009, the film director Sally Potter debuted her *Rage* not in a cinema or on DVD, but through phones and MP3 players. It was the first film to be distributed in this format, and for free.

There was logic in this: the concept of sitting in a cinema for 2+ hours, silently immersed in a movie is vaguely old-fashioned. Viewing media is not a passive activity and, as I've argued in Chapter 14, whether watching a program or a film, we are involved in a creative, interpretive activity. But nowadays people communicate at multiple levels simultaneously: watching, listening and staying in touch wherever and whenever we want. They do it for over seven hours a day, watching tv, surfing the net, using phones, listening to the radio; and they do it in combinations. It's perfectly possible to watch a movie, while listening to music, downloading other music, talking to someone on the phone, and taking breaks to message friends on a social media site.

This is broad focus activity, concentrating on several interests in different modes all at once. It's the kind of activity that doomsayers in the 1960s predicted would be beyond our scope: they imagined that television (then in its relative infancy) would squeeze our attention spans and kill off our imaginations. Even if that were the case (which it wasn't), the arrival of new forms of media has elicited new adaptations and

Table 20.1 Unbreakable records

Event	Record	Breaker	Representing	When	Why this record is special?
Women's 800 meters	1:53.28	Jarmila Kratochvílová	Czechoslovakia	1983	Since then no female has gone under 1:54 seconds. In fact the second fastest time ever recorded was three years before Kratochvílová's record-breaking time. In 2008, Pamela Jelimo ran 1:54.01, the third fastest women's race in history, but still 0.73 seconds slower than the then quarter-century-old record.
Women's 400 meters	47.60 secs	Marita Koch	East Germany		Kratochvílová's 47.99, set two years before, still stands as the second fastest 400 meters of all time. No other athlete has gone under 48 seconds, the closest being Marie-José Pérec, who ran 48.25 in 1996.
Men's hammer	86.74m	Yuriy Sedykh	Soviet Union	1986	Although Ivan Tsikhan came within 0.01 meters in 2005, no one else has seriously challenged the record this century.
Men's discus	74.08m	Jürgen Schult	East Germany	1986	The record was threatened in 2000 by Virgilijus Alekna's 73.88 meters; and, in 2006, by Gerd Kanter's 73.38, but has otherwise looked ominously indestructible.
Women's 100 meters	10.49 secs	Florence Griffith-Joyner	USA	1988	No other woman has got under 10.6, let alone 10.5. Carmelita Jeter's wind-assisted 10.64 in 2009 is the closest any woman has run to the late Griffith-Joyner's record. Third fastest is Marion Jones' 10.65 in 1998.

Event	Record	Athlete	Country	Year	Note
Women's Discus	76.80m	Gabriele Reinsch	East Germany	1988	No woman this century has gone beyond 73 meters.
Men's shot	23.12m	Randy Barnes	USA	1990	The four closest putts were all recorded before that time; since, no one has gone beyond 23 meters, the closest being 22.67 by Kevin Toth in 2003.
Men's long jump	8.95m	Mike Powell	USA	1991	On the day Powell broke Bob Beamon's freakish 23-year-old record, Carl Lewis jumped 8.87 and it seemed the 9-meter mark would soon be reached. In fact, Powell's jump now looks as prohibitively long as Beamon's.
Women's 10,000-meters	29:31.78	Wang Junxia	People's Republic of China	1993	Since then, the next fastest is 29:53.80 i.e. over 22 seconds slower.
Men's javelin	98.48	Jan Zelezný	Czech Republic	1996	The record was set with the post-1986 model javelin: since, just one man, Aki Parviainen, has thrown over 93 meters, and only two over 92 meters.

new multidimensional, multidirectional skills. So maybe this is how many people will view televised sports in future: on the densely pixelated screens of their personal electronic devices, while traveling and attending to several other communication tasks at the same time.

Would they still be watching television? Not in the way we understand it today. But the consumer would still be watching an event from great distance, and that's what television means: *tele* is Greek, meaning at a great distance, and vision is, of course, the faculty of being able to see.

How does this square with my earlier arguments about consumption? One of the themes in this edition of *MSS* is that we have all become sophisticated consumers and that consumption is inescapable. Whatever we do implicates us in some way with consuming commodities. In the above example, we would be consuming in a number of modes: we pay for the right to communicate and, at the same time, eat, drink, or ingest other consumables, and watch advertisements for other consumables, some of which we'll later purchase and use. To repeat myself: consumption is inescapable. Sport is now another portal through which we consume.

None of this contradicts Rowe's point: sport is compelling content and its compulsive qualities are unlikely to diminish in the foreseeable future. What is likely to be different is the way we consume sport. Smaller and lighter versions of television are already available; we won't have to wait long before the content is easily transferred to our personal devices.

BOX 20.4 VIDEO/COMPUTER GAMING

Video/computer gaming refers to playing electronic games with a specialized device or console, and/or a computer loaded with gaming software. Games in the 1970s consisted of the following: arcade cabinet games, dedicated "plug and play" devices, and consoles that used ROM (read-only memory) based cartridges that interfaced with cathode-ray tube televisions, or computer games played on mainframe or personal computers, amongst others. Today's video game consoles are typically powered by operating systems and central processing units (CPUs).

Games are now adapted for several platforms, these being architectures of hardware that allow the software to run, for example Xbox 360, PlayStation 3, or Wii. (Note: The term platform is also used in a more generic sense to describe technologies such as web operating systems or digital television distribution systems, i.e. not products in themselves but systems that can be adapted and customized by users, whether companies or individual consumers.) While several games are designed for multiple players, who compete or cooperate with each other using a computer over a local area network (LAN) or the internet, offline solo gaming remains popular.

Historically, the use of sports as a model for gaming dates back to the 1950s. William A. Higinbotham's *Tennis For Two* designed on an oscilloscope (a device for viewing oscillations of electrical voltage or current by a display on the screen of a cathode-ray tube) at Brookhaven National Laboratory, New York, in 1958, and Atari's arcade game *Pong* from 1972 are two examples of the table tennis or ping-pong based games.

Atari Football, a two-player arcade game based on the American game was introduced in 1978, and is credited with being the first arcade game actually to emulate the action of a real sport. Atari's *Pelé's Soccer*, released in 1981 for the Atari VCS console, was the first game based on the name and likeness of an actual athlete and EA's (Electronic Arts') multi-platform basketball-themed *Dr J and Larry Bird Go One on One* followed.

In 1980 Mattel's Intellivision launched a series of sports games based on, among others, the NBA, NHL, and NASL Soccer. In 1983, it released *World Series Major League Baseball*, though the game didn't use the names of actual players. By the early 1980s, there were titles for home consoles based on boxing, wrestling, racing, and many other sports.

EA struck up licensing deals with sports governing organizations such as FIFA and the NFL and tv companies, including ESPN in subsequent years. EA's *Fifa Soccer's* market hegemony was challenged in 2001 by the introduction in Europe of Konami's *Pro Evolution Soccer* (PES), though, in the 2000s, the former consistently outsold all other games globally. EA's *Fifa* series incorporated the world's major leagues, including England's Premier League, Italy's *Serie A*, Spain's *La Liga*, and German's *Bundesliga*, as well as World and European Cup competitions.

THE BIG BEAST

However we define television – a system for transmitting visual images and sound and reproducing them on screens, perhaps – we just can't hope to understand sports without it. For that matter, we can't understand television without examining its partnership with sports. As we saw in Chapter 14, television has enjoyed a productive relationship with sports virtually since it became a source of domestic pleasure in the 1950s. From the late 1980s, sports became increasingly important as content to fill the channels that multiplied at an almost bewildering rate. Already expensive, sports began to charge the television companies even more.

But there is still a mutual dependence. Sports needs tv: without it, the sponsorships dry up, and salaries drop with the probable consequence that interest would wane. Without sports, television struggles to find content that draws viewers to their screens so consistently. For commercial television, losing sports means losing advertising revenue. The problem is: what happens if the symbiosis becomes less beneficial to one of the parties?

Some people must already think tv is overdoing sport. It's barely believable, but sports governing organizations were once hesitant about deepening their involvements with tv, fearing that extensive coverage would hurt its appeal as live action and depress attendance. It was a justifiable fear in the 1960s. Eventually, the money on offer was serious enough to dispel them. Even if attendance figures dropped, there was enough tv money to compensate amply. Now, attendance is almost incidental. Admission money is a minor source of revenue when compared to the amounts sports draw from sponsors, games companies, advertisers as well as the media, which provides the lion's share of any major sport's income today.

Faced with growing demands from major sports, television has responded with alternatives to free-to-air transmission. Subscription, pay-per-view and other methods of enticing viewers to pay directly for live televised sports have exposed elasticity in the demand for sports. Viewers, who once felt entitled to get sports delivered free of charge to their tv sets, now seem prepared to pay to watch sports. The day may not be far away when free-to-air sports will be outdated.

Even with pay television, the tv networks might not want to bear all the risks. Genuine partnerships, with both parties agreeing to a profit- or loss-sharing arrangements are already looming. Media companies will probably seek ways of involving major sports financially. Instead of just paying for the rights to televise football or boxing, for example, it might say to the league or the promoter: "You arrange the competition and we'll handle the production and distribution. We'll add up how much revenue we take from advertising and ppv sales, subtract your costs and ours, and divide what's left over – or, in the event of a loss, split the deficit."

However sports and television modify their arrangements, one thing is sure: sports will remain on our screens – whatever shape or size those screens may be, and wherever we decide to take them. This alone will ensure its centrality in popular culture. Just being seen guarantees importance, culturally speaking.

In Chapter 17, we saw how celebrity culture was made possible by the media's remorseless pursuit of content for the ever-multiplying channels. Reality tv shows, in particular, were a kind of televisual equivalent of watching paint dry. But billions watched and new celebs came into being. The point is: exposure makes bland people interesting, trivial information important, banal, tedious and boring events engaging, exciting and perhaps even fascinating. In the highly improbable event of sports moving off our screens, it would cease to be the compelling feature it currently is.

Television won't drop sports, of course. It can't. It needs a continual supply of new celebs to take our attention. Sport is a conveyor belt of such beings: every year, it delivers a new batch ready for our consumption. They appear in *Heat* and *People* as well as the sports publications. Their dirty little secrets are aired by tabloids. And, although we eventually tire of them, for a while, they enthrall us, perhaps infuriate us and certainly inspire us to buy into the world of accessible luxury they portray. We consume sports stars as keenly as we consume movie and rock stars. They're all commodities now.

The consequence of this is that, as Rowe puts it, "every sentient human being . . . willingly or unwillingly, must in some way come to terms with the sports behemoth" (2002: 1). A behemoth is an enormous beast, so Rowe's point is presumably that we have to live peaceably with it rather than fight it.

Those readers of this book who are using it for a university course won't be able to remember, probably not even imagine a time when sports was equated with leisure. Sports were activities we engaged in during our leisure hours, whether watching or doing. It's now laughable to think that there was a virtual synonymy between sports and leisure. They're no more equivalent than clocks and grapefruit – some clocks are about the same diameter as grapefruit, but that's about the only thing they have in common. Now people watch sports during their leisure time – and their work time too, actually.

Sport is a sphere of such colossal cultural importance that it needs analysis on its own terms. It's never been such a central component of popular culture. Its influence has never been so pervasive. Its intrusions into people's lives never so invasive. Its impact on high finance and national economies never so great. It perplexes, infuriates, enraptures; it elicits conflict, harmony, delight, and despair. It does this not because it's intrinsically important: but because we attribute it with importance. Those who argue that it really is, when all's said and done, just playful diversion have a point. But they're wrong about the "just" part. Playful diversion it might be, but it's many, many other things besides.

To close, we should consider the subject that obviously occupies much of our attention: you wouldn't have got through 20 chapters unless you had a commitment to the study of sports. Over the final two decades of the twentieth century, sports studies and sports science were, sometimes grudgingly, accepted as legitimate academic pursuits. This reflected a more general recognition of sport as a central institution in contemporary society. Its historical association with frivolity, recreation and leisure is virtually over. A lot of this recognition has grown not so much out of an appreciation of sports, but of a concern with the problems sports seemed to generate. Fan violence, racism, sexism, drugs: these were some of the issues that forced analysts to take sports seriously.

In 1996, I wrote in the second edition of *MSS* that a book such as this would not have been written ten years ago. The fact that it's now in its fifth edition is testimony to the success of sports as a field of academic inquiry and scholarly endeavor. The growth of sports-related degrees and programs of study strengthens the view that the study of sports is as relevant to today's curriculum as studies of crime, education, industry, religion, technology and any number of other traditional subjects.

There are still areas of bewilderment: the apparent irrationality of some aspects of sports, the near-maniacal following they command, the almost suicidal tendencies of some of its participants and the inexplicable political controversies they are prone to provoke. The finances of sports seem set to go out-of-this-world: the numbers multiply at a rate that's difficult to understand, let alone justify. How can a guy, like Kevin Garnett, who plays basketball for a living, earn over 60 times more than the U.S. President?

Among the many media deals the NFL has brokered, one alone –with DIRECTV – is worth $1 billion (£613 million) yearly. For this, you could build a state-of-the-art hospital, like the $773 million Palomar Medical Center West in Escondido, California, feed the 31.1 million Americans living in poverty a Burger King Whopper and fries (@ $2.99), costing almost $83 million, donate $10 million to saving the endangered Arakan Forest Turtle, and contribute the remaining $174 million to relieving the estimated $7 billion external debt of Ethiopia, a country where normal life expectancy is 42 years, 47 percent of children under 5 suffer from malnutrition and only 24 percent of the population have access to water.

If you call a book *Making Sense of Sports*, you might reasonably be expected to offer some way of figuring out why some things are considered more important than others. For many, the order of priorities reflects the brazen irrationality of sports. As I pointed out in the Introduction sports will never take us any nearer finding a cure for cancer or any of the other malevolent sicknesses. Celebrity athletes often align themselves with environmental or peace movements, though the activities for which they are best known do nothing to advance great causes.

The sports business is clearly run on rational, practical, pragmatic lines. Yet the activity around which it's organized is fundamentally without rhyme or reason. When a player like the above-mentioned Garnett earns the same as 710 averagely paid American men combined, you know there must be a sound business organization behind sports. After all, what does Garnett do? Throw a 30-inch circumference ball through an 18-inch diameter hoop 10 feet off the ground. How arbitrary is that? Where is the purpose?

The importance we give sport today, the amount we spend on watching and in myriad other ways consuming it, and, of course, the money earned by players would have been unbelievable to readers in the 1980s. Sport was significant back then: now it is close to overshadowing music, theater, and even movies. We value it, probably more than those other forms of entertainment.

Sport has always been an entertainment-of-sorts. Since our agricultural predecessors started to re-enact the hunts 10, or 12,000 years ago, we've been agreeably engaged by competitive challenge. Our enthusiasm and seeming insatiable thirst for sport is a consequence of watching or doing sports – assisted, of course, by global media corporations, purveyors of merchandise, event organizers, and advertisers of multifarious commodities, all united by a common interest – to part consumers from their money.

Sport has never been so aggressively marketed as it is today and only a fool would underrate the influence of commercial factors in shaping our interests and preferences. Our taste for sport has many sources. But, as Alan Warde points out, we consume "neither as sovereign choosers nor as dupes" (2005: 146).

Warde means that we don't have supreme, unrestricted power to pick our interests, practices, and pursuits; they are often offered to use in a way that's hard to refuse. But, we can refuse all the same: we're not brainless dummies that just take whatever the market provides. So when we try to understand the elevated importance we have attributed to sport, we have to move to a level that allows us a degree of choice, though always within the limitations set. Set by whom? By us and by institutions that we have helped, perhaps inadvertently, support.

Every person who reads this book has been rewarded by sports. I don't just mean winning a trophy or earning money. Not many readers will own an Olympic medal, or a Super Bowl ring, but all will have access to the expansive social landscape of sport. And all will derive satisfaction, perhaps from an enhancement of status or recognition from peers, or the fellowship sports foster. Everybody will benefit in some way from the identities conferred by and expressed through sports.

This is effectively how I began my attempt to make sense of sport. After 20 chapters, we're hopefully in a better position to comprehend why this is so. For all their supposed lack of reason, sports are too important not to be understood. Making sense of sports is now a matter of obligation rather than choice.

OF RELATED INTEREST

The Sport Business Future by Hans Westerbeek and Aaron Smith (Palgrave Macmillan, 2004) is already a bit dated – underlining how quickly sports are changing. This analysis suggests that technology will change the business side of sport. The authors discuss human–computer interfaces and gene therapy, though their main interest is in how competitors of the future will relate to large business corporations.

"The future of sports" by Tom Van Riper (in *Forbes.com.*, March 4, 2009) predicts that sports "are building out their own networks [and] will control increasing amounts of coverage in the future." This means trouble for the established television networks which "may be left scrambling to find a niche beyond live programming [possibly] settling for the secondary role of supplying things like statistics, analysis and fantasy-league access" (http://www.forbes.com/2009/03/04/nba-nhl-mlb-nfl-sports-business_future_sports.html).

ASSIGNMENT

France, 1568: You are calling for your friend Michel de Nostredame on your way to a big *torneiement* in nearby Provence, where a visiting court from Burgundy is due to appear. As he goes to grab his coat, you peer at de Nostredame's desk and read his scribbled notes. "Are you making more prophecies, Nostradamus?" you ask. "Yes, those are about the tournaments of the twenty-first century," he replies. You are dismayed: "Not again. Didn't you get into enough trouble when you predicted King Henry's death in a joust?" "I was right, wasn't I?" he says. "Well, you might have got that one right, but all this business about a revolution in France in a couple of hundred years time and a Great Fire in London and this whatsisname, Hister or Hitler or something in the twentieth century . . . it's ridiculous. People are laughing at you. Take that one you wrote recently:

> In the seventh month of 1999
> From the sky will come a great King of Terror
> He will resurrect the great King of Angolmois
> Before and afterward war reigns happily

"What was that supposed to mean? The end of the world?" Nostradamus responds: "Not at all: it refers to a type of tournament, except the riders will have mechanical beasts with wheels instead of legs and they will charge not at each other but in unison all over France and with a fury that resembles a war. And when they descend from the mountains, it will seem as if they come from the sky and the swiftest shall be a King." "Yeah, right," you scoff. "So, the tournaments will still be around in 2018." Nostradamus answers: "Not quite. But, the spirit that moves them will be." As you leave, you smile: "You don't seriously think people are going to be reading this stuff in 450 years time, do you? " He just shrugs. What was Nostradamus writing?

BIBLIOGRAPHY

Aasved, Mikal (2003) *The Sociology of Gambling*, Springfield, IL: Charles C. Thomas.

Abbas, Andrea (2004) "The embodiment of class, gender and age through leisure: A realist analysis of long distance running," *Leisure Studies*, vol. 23, no. 2, pp. 159–75.

Abernethy, Bruce, Hanrahan, Stephanie, Kippers, Vaughan, Mackinnon, Laurel, and Pandy, Marcus (2005) *The Biophysical Foundations of Human Movement*, 2nd edn, Champaign, IL: Human Kinetics.

Adams, John (1995) *Risk*, London: UCL Press.

Addison, Heather (2002) "Capitalizing their charms: Cinema stars and physical culture in the 1920s," *Velvet Light Trap*, no. 50, Fall.

Alaug, Abdul Karim (2000) "Football in newly united Yemen: Rituals of equity, identity and state formation," *Journal of Anthropological Research*, vol. 54, no. 4.

Alderman, R. B. (1974) *Psychological Behavior in Sport*, Philadelphia, PA: Saunders.

Allain, Kristi (2008) "'Real fast and tough': The construction of Canadian hockey masculinity," *Sociology of Sport Journal*, vol. 25, pp. 462–81.

Alvito, Marcos (2007) "Our piece of the pie: Brazilian football and globalization," *Soccer and Society*, vol. 8, no. 4, pp. 524–44.

Amaechi John, with Bull, Chris (2007) *Man in the Middle*, New York: ESPN Books.

Amara, Mahfoud (2008) "The Muslim world in the global sporting arena," *Brown Journal of World Affairs*, vol. 14, no. 2, pp. 67–75.

Anderson, D. F. and Cychosz, C. M. (1995) "Exploration of the relationship between exercise behavior and exercise identity," *Journal of Sport Behavior,* vol. 18, pp. 159–66.

Anderson, Elijah (1999) *Code of the Street: Decency, violence, and the moral life of the inner city*, New York: Norton.

Anderson, Eric (2005) *In the Game: Gay athletes and the cult of masculinity*, Albany, NY: State University of New York Press.

Andrews, David L. (2006) "Disneyization, Debord, and the integrated NBA spectacle," *Social Semiotics*, vol. 15, no. 1, pp. 89–102.

Andrews, David L. and Jackson, Steven J. (eds) (2001) *Sports Stars: The cultural politics of sporting celebrity*, London: Routledge.

Andrews, David L. and Ritzer, George (2007) "The grobal in the sporting glocal," *Global Networks*, vol. 7, no. 2, pp. 113–53.

Andrews, John (1998) "The world of sport: Not just a game," *The Economist* (June 6).

Andronicus, M. (1979) "Essay and education: The institutions of the games in ancient Greece," in *The Eternal Olympics: The art and history of sport*, edited by N. Yalouris, New Rochelle, NY: Caratzas Brothers.

Anonymous (1994) *Cyclist's Training Diary*, 7th edn, Chambersberg, PA: Alan C. Hood & Co.

Anshel, Mark H. (1997) *Sport Psychology: From theory to practice*, 3rd edn, Scottsdale, AZ: Gorsuch Scarisbrick.

Arms, R., Russsell, G., and Sandilands, M. (1987) "Effects on the hostility of spectators of viewing aggressive sports," in *Sport Sociology*, 3rd edn, edited by A. Yiannakis, T. McIntyre, M. Melnick, and D. Hart, Dubuque: Kendall/Hunt.

Armstrong, Gary (2003) *Football Hooligans: Knowing the score*, Oxford: Berg.

Armstrong, Ketra L. (1999) "Nike's communication with black audiences," *Journal of Sport & Social Issues*, vol. 23, no. 3.

Armstrong, Lance and Jenkins, Sally (2000) *It's Not About the Bike: My journey back to life*, New York: Putnam.

Arnold, Peter J. (1994) "Sport and moral education," *Journal of Moral Education*, vol. 23, no. 1, pp. 75–90.

Arsenault, Darin J. and Fawzy, Tamer (2001) "Just buy it – Nike advertising aimed at *Glamour* readers: A critical feminist analysis," *Tamara: Journal of Critical Postmodern Organization Science*, vol. 1, no. 2, pp. 63–77.

Ashe, Arthur R. (1993) *A Hard Road to Glory: A history of the African-American Athlete*, 3 vols, New York: Amistad Warner.

Atencio, Matthew and Wright, Jan (2008) "'We be killin' them': Hierarchies of black masculinity in urban basketball spaces," *Sociology of Sport Journal*, vol. 25, pp. 263–80.

Atkinson, Michael (2007) "Playing with fire: Masculinity, health and sports supplements," *Sociology of Sport Journal*, vol. 24, pp. 165–86.

Atkinson, Michael and Young, Kevin (2008) *Deviance and Social Control in Sport*, Champaign, IL: Human Kinetics.

Azzarito, Laura and Solmon, Melinda A. (2006) "A feminist poststructuralist view on student bodies in physical education: Sites of compliance, resistance, and transformation," *Journal of Teaching in Physical Education*, vol. 25, pp. 200–25.

Bachner-Melman, Rachel (2003) "Anorexia nervosa from a family perspective: Why did nobody notice?," *American Journal of Family Therapy*, vol. 31, pp. 39–50.

Baier, Annette C. (1994) *Moral Prejudices: Essays on ethics*, London: Harvard University Press.

Bairner, Alan and Molna, Gyozo (eds) (2009) *The Politics of the Olympics: A survey*, London: Routledge.

Bakhtin, Mikhail (1981) *The Dialogic Imagination*, Austin, TX: University of Texas Press.

Bale, John and Christensen, Mette Krogh (eds) (2004) *Post-Olympism? Questioning sport in the twenty-first century*, Oxford: Berg.

Balsamo, Anne (1996) *Technologies of the Gendered Body: Reading cyborg women*, Durham, NC: Duke University Press.

Bamberger, M. and Yaeger. D. (1997) "Over the edge: Aware that drug testing is a sham, athletes seem to rely more than ever on banned performance enhancers," *Sports Illustrated*, April 14, p. 6.

Bandura, A. (1973) *Aggression: A social learning analysis*, Englewood Cliffs, NJ: Prentice-Hall.

Bandy, Susan and Darden, Anne (1999) *Crossing Boundaries: An international anthology of women's experiences in sport*, Champaign, IL: Human Kinetics.

Bane, Michael (1997) *Over the Edge: A regular guy's odyssey in extreme sports*, New York: Gollancz.

Barber, Benjamin R. (2008) "Shrunken sovereign: Consumerism, globalization, and American emptiness," *World Affairs*, vol. 170, no. 4, pp. 73–81.

Barber, Heather and Krane, Vikki (2007) "Creating inclusive and positive climates in girls' and women's sport: Position statement on homophobia, homonegativism, and heterosexism," *Women in Sport and Physical Recreation Journal*, vol. 16, no. 1, pp. 53–5.

Barker, Chris (1997) *Global Television: An introduction*, Oxford: Blackwell.

Barnett, S. (1990) *Games and Sets: The changing face of sport on television*, London: British Film Institute.

Barron, Lee (2007) "The habitus of Elizabeth Hurley: Celebrity, fashion, and identity branding," *Fashion Theory*, vol. 11, no. 4, pp. 443–62.

Bartlett, Roger (2005) *Introduction to Sports Biomechanics*, 2nd edn, London: Routledge.

Bauman, Zygmunt (1979) "The phenomenon of Norbert Elias," *Sociology* vol 13.

—— (2001) "Consuming life," *Journal of Consumer Culture*, vol. 1, no. 1, pp. 5–29.

Bayat, Asef (2007) "Islamism and the politics of fun," *Public Culture*, vol. 13, no. 3, pp. 433–59.

Beal, Becky (1996) "Alternative masculinity and its effects on gender relations in the subculture of skateboarding," *Journal of Sport Behavior*, vol. 19, no. 3, pp. 204–21.

Beaudoin, Christina M. (2006) "Competitive orientations and sport motivation of professional women football players: An internet survey," *Journal of Sport Behavior*, vol. 29, pp. 201–12.

Beck, Ulrich (1992) *Risk Society*, London: Sage.

Becker, Boris (2004) *Boris Becker – The Player: The autobiography*, London: Bantam.

Beisser, Arnold (1967) *The Madness in Sport*, New York: Appleton-Century-Crofts.

Bell, Barbara (2009) *Sport Studies*, Exeter: Learning Matters.

Bengry, Erwin (2000) "Nike," in *Sports Culture: An A-Z guide*, edited by Ellis Cashmore, London: Routledge.

Bergan, Ronald (1982) *Sports in the Movies*, Proteus Books.

Berger, Arthur Asa (2003) *Ads, Fads and Consumer Culture*, Lanham, MD: Rowman & Littlefield.

Biddle, S. J. H (1997) "Cognitive theories of motivation and the physical self," in *The Physical Self: From motivation to well-being*, edited by K. R. Fox, Champaign, IL: Human Kinetics.

Birke, Lynda and Vines, Gail (1987) "A sporting chance: The anatomy of destiny," *Women's Studies International Forum*, vol. 10, no. 4.

Birrell, Susan (1981) "Sport as ritual: Interpretations from Durkheim to Goffman," *Social Forces*, vol. 60, no. 2, pp. 354–76.

Birrell, Susan and Cole, Cheryl (1990) "Double fault: Renee Richards and the construction and naturalization of difference," *Sociology of Sport Journal*, vol. 7.

Birrell, Susan and Cole, Cheryl (eds) (1995) *Women, Sport and Culture*, Champaign, IL: Human Kinetics.

Birtley, Jack (1976) *The Tragedy of Randolph Turpin*, London: NEL.

Blackshaw, Tony and Crabbe, Tim (2004) *New Perspectives on Sport and 'Deviance': Consumption, performativity and social control*, London: Routledge.

Blaine, Bruce and McElroy, Jennifer (2002) "Selling stereotypes: Weight loss infomercials, sexism, and weightism," *Sex Roles*, vol. 46, nos 9–10, pp. 351–7.

Blake, Andrew (1996) *Body Language: The meaning of modern sport*, London: Lawrence & Wishart.

Blanchard, Kendall (1995) *The Anthropology of Sports: An introduction*, Westport, CT: Bergin & Garvey.

Bledsoe, Gregory H., Hsu, Edbert B., Grabowski, Jurek George, Brill, Justin D., and Li, Guohua (2006) "Incidence of injury in professional mixed martial arts competitions," *Journal of Sports Science and Medicine*, published online, July 1, 2006, pp. 136–42.

Blue, Adrienne (1987) *Grace Under Pressure*, London: Sidgwick & Jackson.

—— (1995) *Martina: The life and times of Martina Navratilova*, New York: Birch Lane Press.

Boardley, Ian D. and Kavussanu, Maria (2007) "Development and validation of the moral disengagement in sport scale," *Journal of Sport & Exercise Psychology*, vol. 29, pp. 608–28.

Boddice, Rob (2008) "Manliness and the 'morality of field sports': E. A. Freeman and Anthony Trollope, 1869–71," *The Historian*, vol. 70, no. 1, pp. 1–29.

Bolin, Anne (1996) "Body building," in *Encyclopedia of World Sport: From ancient times to the present*, vol. 1, edited by D. Levinson and K. Christensen, Santa Barbara, CA: ABC Clio.

Boorstin, Daniel (1961) *The Image: A guide to pseudo-events in America*, New York: Harper & Row.

Bourdieu, Pierre (1986) *Distinction: A social critique of the judgement of taste*, London: Routledge.

Bower, Glenna G. (2008) "Career paths and advice for women wanting to obtain a management position within the health and fitness industry," *Women in Sport and Physical Education Journal*, vol. 17, no. 1, pp. 29–37.

Bowerman, William and Harris, Waldo E. (1967) *Jogging: A physical fitness program for all ages*, New York: Grosset & Dunlap.

Boxill, Jan (2006) "Football and feminism," *Journal of the Philosophy of Sport*, vol. 33, pp. 115–24.

Brailsford, Dennis (1997) *British Sport: A social history*, Cambridge: Lutterworth Press.

Braudy, Leo (1997) *The Frenzy of Renown: Fame and its history*, 2nd edn, London: Vintage.

—— (2003) *From Chivalry to Terrorism*, New York: Alfred Knopf.

Brill, A. A. (1929) "The why of a fan," *North American Review*, vol. 22.

Brohm, Jean-Marie (1978) *Sport: A prison of measured time*, London: Ink Links.

Brookes, Rod (2002) *Representing Sport*, London: Arnold.

Brooks, Robert, Bussière, Luc F., Jennions, Michael D. and Hunt, John (2004) "Sinister strategies succeed at the cricket World Cup," *Proceedings of the Royal Society, B: Biological Sciences*, vol. 271, pp. 1–3.

Brower, Jonathan (1976) "Professional sports team ownership," *Journal of Sport Sociology*, vol. 1, no. 1.

Burdsey, Daniel (2007) *British Asians and Football: Culture, identity, exclusion*, London: Routledge.

Burke, Michael D. and Roberts, Terence J. (1997) "Drugs in sport: An issue of morality or sentimentality?," *Journal of the Philosophy of Sport*, vol. 24, pp. 99–113.

Burns, Jimmy (1996) *Hand of God: The life of Diego Maradona*, London: Bloomsbury.

Burton, Rick (1999) "Sports advertising and the Super Bowl," in *The Advertising Business*, edited by John Philip Jones, London: Sage.

Cahn, Susan K. (1994) *Coming on Strong: Gender and sexuality in twentieth-century women's sport*, New York: Free Press.

Callois, Roger (2001) *Man, Play, and Games*, translated by Meyer Barash, Urbana, IL: University of Illinois Press.

Canter, D., Comber, M. and Uzzell, D. (1989) *Football in its Place: An environmental psychology of football grounds*, London: Routledge.

Čapek, Karel ([1921] 2004) *RUR (Rossum's Universal Robots)*, New York: Penguin.

Cardinal, Bradley J. and Cardinal, Marita K. (1997) "Changes in exercise behavior and exercise identity associated with a 14-week aerobic exercise class," *Journal of Sport Behavior*, vol. 20, pp. 377–87.

Carless, David and Douglas, Kitrina (2008) "The role of sport and exercise in recovery from serious mental illness: Two case studies," *International Journal of Men's Health*, vol. 7, no. 2, pp. 137–56.

Carlin, John (2008) *Playing the Enemy: Nelson Mandela and the game that made a nation*, London: Atlantic Books.

Carlson, Brad D. and Donavan, D. Todd (2008) "Concerning the effect of athlete endorsements on brand and team-related intentions," *Sport Marketing Quarterly*, vol. 17, pp. 154–62.

Carty, Victoria (2005) "Textual portrayals of female athletes: Liberation of nuanced forms of patriarchy?," *Frontiers*, vol. 26, no. 2, pp. 132–55.

Cash, T. C. and Pruzinsky, T. (1990) *Body Images: Development, deviance and change*, New York: Guilford.

Cashmore, Ellis (2002) *Sport Psychology: The key concepts*, London: Routledge.

—— (ed.) (2003) *Sports Culture: An A-Z guide*, London: Routledge.

—— (2004a) *Beckham*, 2nd edn, Cambridge: Polity.

—— (2004b) *Tyson: Nurture of the beast*, Cambridge: Polity.

—— (2006) *Celebrity/Culture*, London: Routledge.

—— (2007) "Gambling and sport," in *The Blackwell Encyclopedia of Sociology*, edited by George Ritzer, Blackwell Reference Online.

—— (2008) *Sport and Exercise Psychology: The key concepts*, 2nd edn, London: Routledge.

Cavanagh, Peter R. (1980) *The Running Shoe Book*, La Jolla, CA: Anderson's World Books.

Chandler, Joan (1988) *Television and National Sport: The United States and Britain*, Urbana, IL: University of Illinois Press.

Chapman, Gwen E. (1997) "Making weight: Lightweight rowing, technologies of power, and technologies of the self," *Sociology of Sport Journal*, vol. 14, no. 3.

Chatzisarantis, Nikos L. D. and Hagger, Martin S. (2007) "The moral worth of sport reconsidered: Contributions of recreational sport and competitive sport to life aspirations and psychological well-being," *Journal of Sports Sciences*, vol. 25, no. 9, pp. 1047–56.

Chenoweth, Neil (2001) *Virtual Murdoch: Reality wars on the information highway*, London: Secker & Warburg.

Choi, Sejung Marina and Rifon, Nora J. (2007) "Who is the celebrity in advertising? Understanding dimensions of celebrity images," *Journal of Popular Culture*, vol. 40, no. 2, pp. 304–24.

Clasen, Patricia R. W. (2001) "The female athlete: Dualisms and paradox in practice," *Women and Language*, vol. 24, no. 2.

Clay Large, David (2009) "Massacre in Munich: The Olympic terror attacks of 1972 in historical perspective," *Historically Speaking*, vol. 10, no. 2, pp. 2–5.

Coad, David (2008) *The Metrosexual: Gender, sexuality, and sport*, Albany NY: State University of New York Press.

Coakley, Jay (2009) *Sports in Society: Issues and controversies*, 10th edn, New York: McGraw-Hill.

Coakley, Jay and Dunning, Eric (eds) (2000) *Handbook of Sports Studies*, Newbury Park, CA: Sage.

Cohen, Greta (1993) *Women in Sport*, Newbury Park, CA: Sage.

Coleman, Dorian Lambelet and Coleman, James E. (2008) "The problem of doping," *Duke Law Journal*, vol. 57.

Collins, Tony (1999) *Rugby's Great Split: Class, culture and the origins of rugby league football*, London: Frank Cass,

Commoner, Barry (2002) "Unravelling the DNA myth," *Harper's*, vol. 304, no. 1821, pp. 39–47.

Connell, Robert (1994) *Masculinities*, Cambridge: Polity.

Coombs, David (1978) *Sport and the Countryside*, Oxford: Phaidon.

Cooper, A. (1998) *Playing in the Zone: Exploring the spiritual dimensions of sport*, Boston: Shambhala.

Cooper, Kenneth H. (1969) *Aerobics*, New York: Bantam.

Cooper, P. J. (1996) "Eating disorders," pp. 930–49 in *Companion Encyclopedia of Psychology*, vol. 1, edited by A. M. Coleman, London: Routledge.

Coren, Stanley (1992) *Left Hander: Everything you need to know about left-handedness*, London: John Murray.

Coren, Stanley and Halpern, Diane F. (1991) "Left-handedness: A marker for decreased survival fitness," *Psychological Bulletin*, vol. 109, pp. 90–106.

Cosper, Amy C. (2001) "The curious Murdoch factor," *Satellite Broadband*, vol. 2, no. 9, pp. 22–6.

Costa, Margaret and Guthrie, Sharon (eds) (1994) *Women and Sport: Interdisciplinary perspectives*, Champaign, IL: Human Kinetics.

Côté, J. (2001) "Coach and peer influence on children's development through sport," pp. 520–40 in *Psychological Foundations of Sport*, edited by J. M. Silva and D. E. Stevens, Boston, MA: Allyn & Bacon.

Cowens, Steve (2001) *Blades Business Crew*, Lytham: Milo.

Craig, Peter and Beedie, Paul (2008) *Sport Sociology*, Exeter: Learning Matters.

Crawford, Garry (2004) *Consuming Sport: The consumption spectacle and surveillance of contemporary sports fans*, London: Routledge.

Cruise Malloy, David, Kell, Robert and Kelln, Rod (2007) "The spirit of sport, morality, and hypoxic tents: Logic and authenticity," *Applied Physiology, Nutrition and Metabolism*, vol. 32, pp. 289–96.

Csikszentmihalyi, M. (1990) *Flow: The psychology of optimal experience*, New York: Harper & Row.

Cunningham, Hugh (1980) *Leisure in the Industrial Revolution*, London: Croom Helm.

Curtis, J. and Loy, J (1978) "Race/ethnicity and relative centrality of playing positions in team sport," *Exercise and Sport Sciences Review*, vol 6.

Daniels, Danya B. (2005) "You throw like a girl: Sport and misogyny on the silver screen," *Film and History*, vol. 35, no. 1, pp. 29–38.

Daniels, Elizabeth, Sincharoean, Sirinda and Leaper, Campbell (2005) "The relation between sport orientations and athletic identity among adolescent girl and boy athletes," *Journal of Sport Behavior*, vol. 28, pp. 315–32.

Danielson, Michael N. (1997) *Home Team: Professional sports and the American metropolis*, Princeton. NJ: Princeton University Press.

Dauncey, Hugh and Hare, Geoff (eds) (1999) *France and the 1998 World Cup*, London: Cass.

De Kruif, Paul (1945) *The Male Hormone*, New York: Harcourt, Brace.

De Wachter, Frans (1985) "The symbolism of the healthy body: A philosophical analysis of the sportive imagery of health," *Journal of the Philosophy of Sport*, vol. 11, pp. 56–62.

Deal, William E. (2006) *Handbook to Life in Medieval and Early Modern Japan*, Oxford: Oxford University Press.

Deneen, Sally (2001) "Designer people," *E: The Environmental Magazine*, vol. 12, no. 1, pp. 26–33.

Denham, Bryan E. (2009) "Hegemonic masculinity in sport," pp. 143–52 in *Sociology of Sport and Social Theory*, edited by Earl Smith, Champaign, IL: Human Kinetics.

Denham, David (2004) "Global and local influences on English Rugby League," *Sociology of Sport Journal*, vol. 21, no. 2, pp. 206–19.

Denniston, Robin (1999). *Trevor Huddleston: A life*, London: Macmillan.

Depasquale, Peter (1990) *The Boxer's Workout*, New York: Fighting Fit.

Despres, Renee (1997) "'Burn baby burn': At what point does the quest for ultimate fitness turn into an unhealthy obsession?," *Women's Sports and Fitness*, vol. 19, no. 4, pp. 38–44.

Dillon, Kathleen M. and Tait, Jennifer L. (2000) "Spirituality and being in the zone in team sports: A relationship?," *Journal of Sport Behavior*, vol. 23, pp. 91–100.

Dittmar, Helga (1992) *The Social Psychology of Material Possessions: To have is to be*, Hemel Hempstead: Harvester Wheatsheaf.

Dittmar, Helga, Beattie, Jane and Friese, Susanne (1995) "Gender identity and material symbols: objects and decision considerations in impulse purchases," *Journal of Economic Psychology*, vol. 15, pp. 391–511.

Dollard, J., Doob, L. W., Miller, N. E., Mowrer, O. H. and Sears, R. R. (1939) *Frustration and Aggression*, New Haven, CT: Yale University Press.

Downes, S. and Mackay, D. (1996) *Running Scared: How athletics lost its innocence*, Edinburgh: Mainstream.

Draeger, John, Yates, Alayne and Crowell, Douglas (2005) "The obligatory exerciser: Assessing an overcommitment to exercise," *The Physician and Sportsmedicine*, vol. 33, pp. 13–23.

Dubos, René (1998) *So Human an Animal: How we are shaped by surroundings and events*, Piscataway, NJ: Transaction.

Dunning, Eric (1999) *Sport Matters: Sociological studies of sport, violence and civilization*, London: Routledge.

Dunning, Eric and Rojek, Chris (eds) (1992) *Sport and Leisure in the Civilizing Process*, Basingstoke: Macmillan.

Dunning, Eric and Sheard, Kenneth (1979) *Barbarians, Gentlemen and Players*, Oxford: Martin Robertson.

Dunning, Eric, Murphy, Patrick, and Williams, John (1988) *The Roots of Football Hooliganism*, London: Routledge & Kegan Paul,

Dweck, C. S. (1980) "Learned helplessness in sport," in *Psychology of Motor Behavior and Sport – 1979*, edited by C. H. Nadeau, W. R. Halliwell, K. M. Newell, and G. C. Roberts, Champaign, IL: Human Kinetics.

Eaton, Warren O., Chipperfield, Judith G., Ritchot, Kathryn F. M., and Kostiuk, Joanna H. (1996) "Is a maturational lag associated with left-handedness? A research note," *Journal of Child Psychology and Psychiatry and Allied Disciplines*, vol. 37, no. 5, pp. 613–17.

Edwards, Harry (1970) *The Revolt of the Black Athlete*, New York: Free Press.

—— (1973) *Sociology of Sport*, Homewood, IL: Dorsey Press.

Eitzen, D. Stanley (ed.) (1993) *Sport in Contemporary Society*, 4th edn, New York: St Martin's Press.

Eitzen, D. Stanley and Sanford, D. (1975) "The segregation of blacks by playing position in football," *Social Science Quarterly*, vol. 5, no. 4.

Eitzen, D. Stanley and Yetman, N. (1977) "Immune from racism?," *Civil Rights Digest*, vol. 9, no. 2.

Elias, Norbert (1982) *The Civilizing Process*, 2 vols, New York: Pantheon.

—— (1986a) "An essay on sport and violence," in *Quest for Excitement*, edited by Norbert Elias and Eric Dunning, Oxford: Blackwell.

—— (1986b) "Introduction," in *Quest for Excitement*, edited by Norbert Elias and Eric Dunning, Oxford: Blackwell.

Elliott, Richard and Maguire, Joseph (2008) "Thinking outside of the box: Exploring conceptual synthesis for research in the area of athletic labor migration," *Sociology of Sport Journal*, vol. 25, pp. 482–97.

Engström, Lars-Magnus (2004) "Social change and physical activity," *Scandinavian Journal of Nutrition*, vol. 48, no. 3, pp. 108–13.

Entine, Jon (2000) *Taboo: Why black athletes dominate and why we're afraid to talk about it*, New York: Public Affairs.

Evans, Marc (1997) *Endurance Athlete's Edge*, Champaign, IL: Human Kinetics.

Fairchild, Charles (2007) "Building the authentic celebrity: the 'idol' phenomenon in the attention economy," *Popular Music and Society*, vol. 30, no. 3, pp. 355–75.

Faludi, Susan (1999) *Stiffed: The betrayal of the modern man*, London: Chatto & Windus.

Fangio, Juan Manuel and Carrozzo, Roberto (1990) *Fangio: My racing life*, Wellingborough: Thorsons.

Fasting, Kari (1987) "Sports and women's culture," *Women's International Forum*, vol. 19, no. 4.

Fazey, J. and Hardy, L. (1988) *The inverted-U hypothesis: A catastrophe for sport psychology?*, British Association of Sports Sciences, Monograph no. 1, Leeds: National Coaching Foundation.

Featherstone, Mike (1991) "The body in consumer culture," in *The Body: Social process and cultural theory*, edited by Mike Featherstone, Mike Hepworth, and Bryan S. Turner, London: Sage.

Featherstone, Mike, Lash, Scott, and Robertson, Roland (eds) (1995) *Global Modernities*, London: Sage.

Feshbach, Seymour (1984) "The catharsis hypothesis, aggressive drive, and the reduction of aggression," *Aggressive Behavior*, vol. 10, pp. 91–101.

Festle, Mary Jo (1996) *Playing Nice: Politics and apologies in women's sport* New York: Columbia University Press.

Field, John (2003) *Social Capital*, London: Routledge.

Finch, Laura (2001) "Understanding individual motivation in sport," pp. 66–79 in *Psychological Foundations of Sport*, edited by J. M. Silva and D. E. Stevens, Boston, MA: Allyn & Bacon.

Fixx, Jim (1977) *The Complete Book of Running*, New York: Random House.

Fonda, Jane (1981) *Jane Fonda's Workout Book*, New York: Simon & Schuster.

Forman, Pamela J. and Plymire, Darcy C. (2005) "Amélie Mauresmo's muscles: The lesbian heroic in women's professional tennis," *Women's Studies Quarterly*, vol. 33, nos 1/2, pp. 120–33.

Fowles, Jib (1996) *Advertising and Popular Culture*, Newbury Park, CA: Sage.

Franck, Egon and Nüesch, Stephan (2007) "Avoiding 'Star Wars': Celebrity creation as media strategy," *Kyklos*, vol. 60, no. 2, pp. 211–30.

Frank, Thomas (1997a) "The new gilded age," pp. 23–28 in *Commodify Your Dissent: Salvos from* The Baffler, edited by Thomas Frank and Matt Weiland, New York: Norton.

—— (1997b) "Alternative to what?," pp. 145–61 in *Commodify Your Dissent: Salvos from* The Baffler, edited by Thomas Frank and Matt Weiland, New York: Norton.

Franklin, Bob (1997) *Newszak and News Media*, London: Arnold.

Fraser, George MacDonald (1997) *Black Ajax*, London: HarperCollins.

Freud, S. (1963) "Why war?," in *Freud: Character and culture*, edited by P. Reiff, New York: Collier.

Freund, Peter and Martin, George (2004) "Walking and motoring: Fitness and the social organisation of movement," *Sociology of Health & Illness*, vol. 26, no. 2, pp. 273–86.

Fry, Jeffrey (2007) "Review essay," *Sports, Ethics and Philosophy*, vol. 1, no. 3, pp. 378–80.

Furedi, Frank (1997) *Culture of Fear* London: Cassell.

Gallafent, Edward (2006) "Violence, actions and words in *Million Dollar Baby*," *Cineaction*, vol. 68, January 1, pp. 45–52.

Gallagher, Catherine and Laqueur, Thomas (eds) (1987) *The Making of the Modern Body: Sexuality and society in the nineteenth century*, Berkeley, CA: University of California Press.

Gallagher, Richard (2005) "The straight dope on gene doping," *The Scientist*, March 14, p. 6.

Gamson, Joshua (1994) *Claims to Fame: Celebrity in contemporary America* Berkeley, CA: University of California Press.

Gardenfors, Peter (2003) *How Homo Became Sapiens: On the evolution of thinking*, Oxford: Oxford University Press.

Geertz, Clifford (1972) "Deep Play: Notes on the Balinese cockfight," in *The Interpretation of Cultures*, edited by Clifford Geertz, New York: Basic Books.

George, Christeen, Hartley, Andrew, and Paris, Jenny (2001). "Focus on communication in sport: The representation of female athletes in textual and visual media," *Corporate Communications*, vol. 6, no. 2, pp. 94–102.

Geschwind, Norman and Galaburda, Albert M. (1987) *Cerebral Lateralization: Biological mechanisms, associations and pathology*, Cambridge, MA: MIT Press.

Gibson, K. and Ingold, T. (eds) (1993) *Tools, Language and Cognition in Human Evolution*, Cambridge: Cambridge University Press.

Giles, David (2000) *Illusions of Intimacy: A psychology of fame and celebrity*, London: Macmillan.

Gill, Diane (2000) *Psychological Dynamics of Sport and Exercise*, 2nd edn, Champaign, IL: Human Kinetics.

Gill, Diane and Williams, Lavon (2009) *Psychological Dynamics of Sport and Exercise*, 3rd edn, eBook, Champaign, IL: Human Kinetics.

Giulianotti, R. and Robertson, R. (2007) "Sport and globalization: Transformational dimensions," *Global Networks*, vol. 7, no. 2, pp. 107–12.

Giulianotti, R., Bonney, R., and Hepworth, M. (eds) (1994) *Football, Violence and Social Identity*, London: Routledge.

Glassner, Barry (1989) "Fitness and the postmodern self," *Journal of Health and Social Behavior*, vol. 30, pp. 180–91.

Goffman, Erving ([1956] 1971) *The Presentation of Self in Everyday Life*, Harmondsworth: Penguin.

Goldberg, Marvin E., Gorn, Gerald J., Peracchio, Laura A., and Bamossy, Gary (2003) "Understanding materialism among youth," *Journal of Consumer Behavior*, vol. 13.

Goldlust, John (1987) *Playing for Keeps: Sport, the media and society*, Melbourne: Longman Cheshire.

Goldman, Robert and Papson, Stephen (1999) *Nike Culture: The sign of the swoosh*, London: Sage.

Gorman, J. and Calhoun, K. (1994) *The Name of the Game: The business of sports*, New York: Wiley.

Gorn, Elliott J. (1986) *The Manly Art: Bare-knuckle prize fighting in America*, Ithaca, NJ: Cornell University Press.

Gorski, Roger A. (1991) "Gonadal hormones and the organization of brain structure and function," in *The Lifespan Development of Individuals: Behavioral, neurological and psychosocial perspectives*, edited by D. Magnuson, Cambridge: Cambridge University Press.

Gottdiener, Mark (1997) *The Theming of America: Dreams, visions and commercial spaces*, Boulder, CO: Westview Press.

Gould, Daniel, Dieffenbach, Kristen, and Moffett, Aaron (2002) "Psychological characteristics and their development in Olympic champions," *Journal of Applied Sport Psychology*, vol. 14, pp. 172–204.

Gould, Stephen Jay (2002) *The Structure of Evolutionary Thought*, Cambridge, MA: Harvard University Press.

Gouldner, Alvin W. (1965) *Wildcat Strike: A study in worker–management relations*, New York: Harper Torchbooks.

Govier, Ernie (1998) "Brainsex and occupation," in *Gender and Choice in Occupation and Education*, edited by John Radford, London: Routledge.

Grainger, Andrew and Jackson, Steven J. (2000) "Sports marketing and the challenges of globalization: A case study of cultural resistance in New Zealand," *International Journal of Sports Marketing and Sponsorship*, vol. 2, no. 2, pp. 111–15.

Grano, Daniel A. (2007) "Ritual disorder and the contractual morality of sport: A case study in race, class, and agreement," *Rhetoric and Public Affairs*, vol. 10, no. 3, pp. 445–74.

Grant, R. W. (1988) *The Psychology of Sport: Facing one's true opponent*, Raleigh, NC: McFarland Jefferson.

Gratton, Chris and Taylor, Peter (2004) *The Economics of Sport and Recreation: An economic analysis*, London: Routledge.

Gray, Chris Hables (2001) *Cyborg Citizen: Politics in the posthuman age*, London: Routledge.

Green, Ken (2004) "Physical education, lifelong participation and 'the couch potato society'," *Physical Education and Sport Pedagogy*, vol. 9, no. 1, pp. 73–86.

Green, R. G. (1996) "Social motivation," pp. 522–41 in *Companion Encyclopedia of Psychology*, edited by A. M. Coleman, London: Routledge.

Greenwood, Jim (1998) *Total Rugby: Fifteen-man rugby for coach and player*, London: A. & C. Black.

Gregory, Sean (2007) "It's Ladies' Fight," *Time*, vol. 17 no. 5, pp. 40–3.

Griffin, Pat (1998) *Strong Women, Deep Closets: Lesbians and homophobia in sport*, Champaign, IL: Human Kinetics.

Groff, Diane G. and Zabriskie, Ramon B. (2006) "An exploratory study of athletic identity among elite alpine skiers with physical disabilities: Issues of measurement and design," *Journal of Sport Behavior*, vol. 29, pp. 126–41.

Groves, D. (1987) "Why some athletes choose high-risk sports?," *Physician and Sportsmedicine*, vol. 15, no. 2.

Grow, Jean M. (2008) "The gender of branding: Early Nike women's advertising a feminist antenarrative," *Women's Studies in Communication*, vol. 31, no. 3, pp. 312–43.

Gruber, Thibaud, Muller, Martin N., Strimling, Pontus, Wrangham, Richard, and Zuberbüler, Klaus (2009) "Wild chimpanzees rely on cultural knowledge to solve an experimental honey acquisition task," *Current Biology*, vol. 19 (November 17), pp. 1–5.

Gruneau, Richard (1983) *Class, Sports and Social Development*, Amherst, MA: University of Massachusetts Press.

—— (1984) "Commercialism and the modern Olympics," in *Five Ring Circus*, edited by Alan Tomlinson and Garry Whannel, London: Pluto Press.

Gruneau, Richard and Whitson, David (1994) *Hockey Night in Canada: Sports, identities, and cultural politics*, 2nd edn, Toronto: Garamond Press (originally 1983, Amherst, MA: University of Massachusetts Press).

Guelke, A. (1986) "The politicisation of South African sport," in *The Politics of Sport*, edited by Lincoln Allison, Manchester: Manchester University Press.

Gutman, D. (1992) *Baseball Babylon: From Black Sox to Pete Rose*, London: Penguin.

Guttmann, Allen (1978) *From Ritual to Record: The nature of modern sports*, New York: Columbia University Press.

—— (1986) *Sports Spectators*, New York: Columbia University Press.

—— (1996) *The Erotic in Sports*, New York: Columbia University Press.

Haan, Norma (1978) "Two moralities in action contexts: Relationship to thought, ego regulation, and development," *Journal of Personality and Social Psychology*, vol. 36, pp. 286–305.

Hain, Peter (1982) "The politics of sport and apartheid," in *Sport, Culture and Ideology*, edited by John Hargreaves, London: Routledge & Kegan Paul.

Halberstam, David (1999) *Playing for Keeps: Michael Jordan and the world he made*, New York: Random House.

Halberstam, Judith (1998) *Female Masculinity*, Durham, NC: Duke University Press.

Hall, M. Ann (1996) *Feminism and Sporting Bodies: Essays on theory and practice*, Champaign, IL: Human Kinetics.

Hall, Steve, Winlow, Simon, and Ancrum, Craig (2008) *Criminal Identities and Consumer Culture*, Cullompton, Devon: Willan.

Hannigan, John (1998) *Fantasy City: Pleasure and profit in the postmodern metropolis*, London: Routledge.

Hansen, Cheryl J., Stevens, Larry C., and Coast, Richard J. (2001) "Exercise duration and mood state: How much is enough to feel better?," *Health Psychology*, vol. 20, pp. 267–75.

Haraway, Donna J. (1991) *Simians, Cyborgs and Women: The reinventon of nature*, New York: Routledge.

Hare, Nathan (1973) "The occupational culture of the black fighter," in *Sport and Society*, edited by J. Talamini and C. Page, Boston: Little, Brown.

Hargreaves, Jennifer (1994) *Sporting Females: Critical issues in the hisotry and sociology of women's sports*, London: Routledge.

Hargreaves, John (ed.) (1982) *Sport, Culture and Ideology*, London: Routledge & Kegan Paul.

—— (1986) *Sport, Power and Culture*, Oxford: Polity Press.

Harrington, Austin, Marshall, Barbara L. and Müller, Hans-Peter (eds) (2006) *Encyclopedia of social theory*, London: Routledge.

Harris, Cheryl (1998) "A sociology of television fandom," in *Theorizing Fandom: Fans, subculture and identity*, edited by Cheryl Harris and Alison Alexander, Cresskill, NJ: Hampton Press.

Harris, Daniel (2008) "Celebrity bodies," *Southwest Review*, vol. 93, no. 1, pp. 135–45.

Harris, John and Parker, Andrew (2009) "Afterword: Sport and social identities reconsidered," pp. 168–77 in *Sport and Social Identities*, edited by John Harris and Andrew Parker, Basingstoke: Palgrave Macmillan.

Harris, Lauren J. (1993) "Do left-handers die sooner than right-handers? Commentary on Coren and Halpern's (1991) 'Left-handedness: A marker for decreased survival fitness'," *Psychological Bulletin*, vol. 114, no. 2.

Harris, Marvin (1997) *Culture, People, Nature: An introduction to general anthropology*, 7th edn, New York: Addison-Wesley.

—— (1998) *Theories of Culture in Postmodern Times*, Walnut Creek, CA: Alta Mira.

Hartmann, Douglas (2000) "Rethinking relationships between sport and race in American culture: Golden ghettos and contested terrain," *Sociology of Sport Journal*, vol. 17, pp. 229–53

—— (2004) *Race, Culture, and the Revolt of the Black Athlete: The 1968 Olympic protests and their aftermath*, Chicago: University of Chicago Press.

—— (2006) "Bound by blackness or above it? Michael Jordan and the paradoxes of post-civil rights American race relations," pp. 301–24 in *Out of the Shadows: A biographical history of African American athletes*, edited by David K. Wiggins, Fayetteville, AK: University of Arkansas Press.

Hartmann, Douglas and Massoglia, Michael (2007) "Reassessing the relationship between high school sports participation and deviance: Evidence of enduring, bifurcated effects," *Sociological Quarterly*, vol. 48, pp. 485–505.

Harvey, Adrian (2005) *Football: The first hundred years: The untold story*, London: Routledge.

Hausenblas, Heather A. and Downs, Danielle Symons (2002) "Relationship among sex, imagery, and exercise dependence symptoms," *Psychology of Addictive Behaviors*, vol. 16.

Hauser, Thomas (1997) *Muhammad Ali: His life and times*, New York: Pan Books.

Heaton, A. W. and Sigall, H. (1989) "The 'championship choke' revisited: The role of fear of acquiring a negative identity," *Journal of Applied Social Psychology*, vol. 19.

Henderson, Edwin (1949) *The Negro in Sports*, Washington, DC: Associated Publishers.

Henry, Ruth, Anshel, Mark A., and Michael, Timothy (2006) "Effects of aerobic and circuit training on fitness and body image among women," *Journal of Sport Behavior*, vol. 29, pp. 281–303.

Hepworth, Julie (1999) *The Social Construction of Anorexia Nervosa*, London: Sage.

Hill, Christopher (1996) *Olympic Politics*, 2nd edn, Manchester: Manchester University Press.

Hill, John S. and Vincent, John (2006) "Globalisation and sports branding: The case of Manchester United," *International Journal of Sports Marketing and Sponsorship*, vol. 7, no. 3, pp. 213–30.

Hill, Karen L. (2001) *Frameworks for Sport Psychologists*, Champaign, IL: Human Kinetics.

Hoberman, John (1984) *Sport and Political Ideology*, Austin, TX: University of Texas Press.

—— (1992) *Mortal Engines: Human engineering and the transformation of sport*, New York: Free Press.

—— (1997) *Darwin's Athletes: How sport has damaged black America and preserved the myth of race*, New York: Houghton Mifflin.

Hoberman, John and Yesalis, Charles E. (1995) "The history of synthetic testosterone," *Scientific American*, vol. 272, no. 2.

Hoch, Paul (1972) *Rip Off the Big Game: The exploitation of sports by the power elite*, New York: Anchor Doubleday.

Hochstetler, Douglas R. (2006) "Using narratives to enhance moral education in sport," *Journal of Physical Education, Recreation & Dance*, vol. 77, no. 4, pp. 37–44.

Hoffer, Richard (1998) *A Savage Business: The comeback and comedown of Mike Tyson*, New York: Simon & Schuster.

Hoffman, Shirl (ed.) (1992) *Sport and Religion*, Champaign, IL: Human Kinetics.

—— (2009) *Introduction to Kinesiology: Studying physical activity*, Champaign, IL: Human Kinetics.

Hoffman, Tyler (2002) "The umpire is out," *The Advocate*, no. 877 (November), pp. 9–18.

Hoggett, Paul (1986) "The taming of violence," *New Society*, vol 36 (October 17).

Holowchak, M. Andrew (2003) "Aggression, gender, and sport: Reflections on sport as a means of moral education," *Journal of Social Philosophy*, vol. 34, no. 3, pp. 387–99.

Holt, Richard (1989) *Sport and the British*, Oxford: Oxford University Press.

—— (1990) *Sport and the Working Class in Modern Britain*, Manchester: Manchester University Press.

Hönekopp, Johannes, Bartholomé, Tobias, and Jansen, Gregor (2004) "Facial attractiveness, symmetry, and physical fitness in young women," *Human Nature*, vol. 15, no. 2, pp. 147–67.

Hornby, Nick (1996) *Fever Pitch*, London: Indigo.

Horner, M. S. (1972) "Toward an understanding of achievement-related conflicts in women," *Journal of Social Issues*, vol. 28.

Horrell, M. (1968) *South Africa and the Olympic Games*, Johannesburg: Institute of Race Relations.

Horsman, Mathew (1997) *SkyHigh: The inside story of BSkyB*, London: Orion Business.

Horton, D. and Wohl, R. R. (1956) "Mass communication and parasocial interaction," *Psychiatry*, vol. 19, pp. 215–29.

Houlihan, Barrie (1994) *Sport and International Politics*, Brighton: Harvester Wheatsheaf.

—— (1997) *Sport, Policy and Politics: A comparative analysis*, London: Routledge.

—— (ed.) (2003) *Sport and Society: A student introduction*, London: Sage.

Hubbard, Guy (1998) "Sports action," *Arts and Activities*, vol. 123 (March).

Huddleston, Trevor (1956) *Naught for Your Comfort*, London: Collins.

Huggins, Mike (2003) *Horseracing and the British, 1919–39*, Manchester: Manchester University Press.

Hughes, K. C. (2005) "A lesson learned: Post traumatic stress disorder," *Armor*, July/August, pp. 15–16.

Huizinga, Johan (1955) *Homo Ludens: A study of the play-element in culture*, Boston: Beacon Press.

Husman, B. F. and Silva, J. M (1984) "Aggression in sport: Definitional and theoretical considerations," pp. 246–60 in *Psychological Foundations of Sport*, edited by J. M. Silva and R. S. Weinberg, Champaign, IL: Human Kinetics.

Ian, Marcia (2001) "The primitive subject of female bodybuilding: Transgression and other postmodern myths," *Differences*, vol. 12, no. 3.

Inglehart, Ronald and Norris, Pippa (2004) *Sacred and Secular: Religion and politics worldwide*, Cambridge: Cambridge University Press.

Isberg, L. (2000) "Anger, aggressive behavior, and athletic performance," pp. 113–33 in *Emotions in Sport*, edited by Y. L. Hanin, Champaign, IL: Human Kinetics.

Jackson, S. A. and Csikszentmihalyi, M. (1999) *Flow in Sports: The keys to optimal experiences and performances*, Champaign, IL: Human Kinetics.

James, C. L. R. (1963) *Beyond a Boundary*, London: Hutchinson.

Janis, Lauren (2001) "Murdoch expands his global empire," *Columbia Journalism Review*, vol. 40, no. 4, pp. 100–1.

Jarvie, Grant and Maguire, Joseph (1995) *Sport and Leisure in Social Thought*, London: Routledge.

Jenkins, Henry (1992) *Textual Poachers*, London: Routledge.

Jennings, Andrew (1996) *The New Lords of the Rings: Olympic corruption and how to buy gold medals*, New York: Pocket Books.

—— (2000) *The Great Olympic Swindle: When the world wanted its games back*, London: Simon & Schuster.

—— (2007) *Foul! The Secret World of FIFA: Bribes, vote rigging and ticket scandals*, London: HarperCollins.

Jhally, Sut (1989) "Cultural studies and the sports/media complex," in *Media, Sports and Society*, edited by Lawrence A. Wenner, Newbury Park, CA: Sage.

Jindra, M. (1994). "*Star-Trek* fandom as a religious phenomenon," *Sociology of Religion*, vol. 55, pp. 27–51.

Jiobu, R. (1988) "Racial inequality in a public arena," *Social Forces*, vol. 67, no. 2.

Johnson, Roy S. and Harrington, Ann (1998) "The Jordan effect," *Fortune*, vol. 137, no. 12.

Jones, C. (2005) "Character, virtue and physical education," *European Physical Education Review*, vol. 11, no. 2, pp. 139–51.

Jones, C. and McNamee, Mike (2000) "Moral reasoning, moral action, and the moral atmosphere of sport," *Sport, Education and Society*, vol. 5, no. 2, pp. 131–46.

Jones, Dave and Rivers, Tony (2002) *Soul Crew*, Lytham: Milo.

Joyal, Steven V. (2004) "A perspective on the current strategies for the treatment of obesity," *Current Drug Targets – CNS and Neurological Disorders*, vol. 3, pp. 341–56.

Kane, Martin (1971) "An assessment of black is best," *Sports Illustrated*, January 18, pp. 72–83.

Katz, Donald (1994) *Just Do It: The Nike spirit in the corporate world*, Holbrook, MA: Adams Media.

Kauer, Kerrie J. and Krane, Vikki (2006) "'Scary dykes' and 'feminine queens': stereotypes and female college athletes," *Women in Sport and Physical Recreation Journal*, vol. 15, no. 1, pp. 42–54.

Kavussanu, Maria (2007) "Morality in sport," pp. 265–77 in *Social Psychology in Sport*, edited by S. Jowett and D. E. Lavallee, Champagne, IL: Human Kinetics.

Kavussanu, Maria and Roberts, Glyn C. (2001) "Moral functioning in sport: An achievement goal perspective," *Journal of Sport and Exercise Psychology*, vol. 23, pp. 37–54.

Kavussanu, Maria and Spray, Christopher M. (2006) "'Moral atmosphere, perceived performance motivational climate and moral functioning in male youth footballers: An examination of their interrelationships," *The Sport Psychologist*, vol. 20, pp. 1–23.

Kemp, Sharon F. (1999) "Sled dog racing: The celebration of co-operation in a competitive sport," *Ethnology*, vol. 38, no. 1, pp. 81–95.

Kennedy, Eileen and Hill, Laura (2009) *Sport, Media and Society*, Oxford: Berg.

Kerr, John (1994) *Understanding Soccer Hooliganism*, Philadelphia, PA: Open University Press.

—— (2004) *Rethinking Aggression and Violence in Sport*, London: Routledge.

Kerr, Robert (1982) *The Practical Use of Anabolic Steroids with Athletes*, San Gabriel, CA: Kerr Publishing.

King, Billie Jean and Deford, Frank (1982) *Billie Jean*, New York: Viking.

King, Colin (2004) *Offside Racism: Playing the white man*, Oxford: Berg.

King, John (2004) *The Football Factory*, London: Vintage.

Klatell, David and Marcus, Norman (1988) *Sports for Sale: Television, money and the fans*, Oxford: Oxford University Press.

Klein, Alan M. (1986) "Pumping irony: Crisis and contradiction in bodybuilding," *Sociology of Sport Journal*, vol. 3, pp. 112–33.

Klein, Naomi (2001) *No Logo*, London: Flamingo.

Knight, Jennifer and Giuliano, Traci (2003) "Blood, sweat, and jeers: The impact of the media's heterosexist portrayals on perceptions of male and female athletes," *Journal of Sport Behavior*, vol. 26, no. 3.

Kohlberg, Lawrence (1981) *Essays on Moral Development, vol. 1: The philosophy of moral development*, San Francisco, CA: Harper & Row.

—— (1984) *Essays on Moral Development, vol. 2: The psychology of moral development*, San Francisco, CA: Harper & Row

Kohn, Marek (1996) *The Race Gallery*, London: Vintage.

Kornspan, Alan S. (2009) *Fundamentals of Sport and Exercise Psychology*, Champaign, IL: Human Kinetics.

Krane, Vikki, Waldron, Jennifer, Michalenok, Jennifer, and Stiles-Shipley, Julie (2001) "Body image concerns in female exercisers and athletes: A feminist cultural studies perspective," *Women in Sport and Physical Activity*, vol. 10, pp. 17–33.

Kremer, John and Moran, Aidan P. (2008) *Pure Sport: Practical sport psychology*, London: Routledge.

Kühnst, Peter (1996) *Sports: A cultural history in the mirror of art*, Dresden: Verlag der Kunst.

—— (2004) *Physique: Classic photographs of naked athletes*, London: Thames & Hudson.

LaFeber, Walter (1999) *Michael Jordan and the new global capitalism*, New York: Norton.

Laland, Kevin N. and Janik, Vincent M. (2006) "The animal cultures debate," *Trends in Ecology and Evolution*, vol. 21, no. 10, pp. 542–7.

Lambelet Coleman, Doriane and Coleman, James E. (2008) "The problem of doping," *Duke Law Journal*, vol. 57, pp. 1743–94.

Landay, Lori (1999) "Millions 'Love Lucy': Commodification and the Lucy phenomenon," *NWSA Journal*, vol. 11, no. 2.

Lapchick, Richard (1986) *Fractured Focus*, Lexington, MA: Heath.

Laqueur, Thomas (1990) *Making Sex: Body and gender from the Greeks to Freud*, Cambridge, MA: Harvard University Press.

Lasch, Christopher (1979) *The Culture of Narcissism*, New York: Norton.

—— (1991) *The True and Only Heaven: Progress and its criticis*, New York: Norton.

Lavallee, David, Kremer, John, Moran, Aiden, and Williams, Mark (2003) *Sport Psychology: Contemporary themes*, London: Palgrave.

Layden, Tim(1998) "Distant thunder," *Sports Illustrated*, vol. 89, no. 3.

Leaman, Oliver (1988) "Cheating and fair play in sport," in *Philosophic Inquiry in Sport*, edited by William J. Morgan and Klaus Meier, Champaign, IL: Human Kinetics.

Leapman, Michael (1985) *Arrogant Aussie: The Rupert Murdoch Story*, New York: Carol Publishing.

Lenskyj, Helen (1986) *Out of Bounds: Women, sport and sexuality*, Toronto: The Women's Press.

Leonard, David J. (2004) "The next M.J. or the next O.J.? Kobe Bryant, race, and the absurdity of colorblind rhetoric," *Journal of Sport and Social Issues*, vol. 28, no. 3, pp. 284–313.

Leonard, Wilbert (1988) *A Sociological Perspective of Sport*, 3rd edn, New York: Macmillan.

Levenson, Eugenia (2008) "Citizen Nike," *Fortune*, vol. 10, pp. 165–78.

Levine, Lawrence (1977) *Black Culture and Black Consciousness*, New York: Oxford University Press.

Levine, Peter (1985) *A.G. Spalding and the Rise of Baseball: The promise of American sport*, New York: Oxford University Press.

Levinson, Daniel and Christensen, K. (1996) *Encyclopedia of World Sport: From Ancient times to the present*, Santa Barbara, CA: ABC-Clio.

Levy, J and Reid, M. (1976) "Variations in writing posture and cerebral organization," *Science*, vol. 194, no. 4262, pp. 337–9.

Lin, Carol (2003) "Interview with Lance Armstrong," *CNN Saturday Night Show*, October 18, LexisNexis Academic: Transcript # 101804CN.V88.

Lindsey, Linda (1990) *Gender Roles: A sociological perspective*, Englewood Cliffs, NJ: Prentice-Hall (London: Routledge, 1998).

Llaurens, Violaine, Raymond, Michel, and Faurie, Charlotte (2009) "Why are some people left-handed? An evolutionary perspective," *Philosophical Transactions of the Royal Society, B: Biological Sciences*, vol. 364, pp. 881–94.

Loland, Nina Waaler (2000) "The art of concealment in a culture of display: Aerobicizing women's and men's experience and use of their own bodies," *Sociology of Sport Journal*, vol. 17, pp. 111–29.

Longman, Jere (2001) "Rise of the superathlete: Altered genes could lead to gigantic football players, towering basketball centers, and huge risks," *New York Times Upfront*, vol. 134, no. 1.

Lorenz, K. (1966) *On Aggression*, New York: Harcourt Brace Jovanovich.

Louganis, Greg (1995) *Breaking the Surface: A life*, New York: Random House.

Loumidis, Konstantinos and Wells, Adrian (2001) "Exercising for the wrong reasons: Relationships among eating disorder beliefs, dysfunctional exercise beliefs and coping," *Clinical Psychology and Psychotherapy*, vol. 8.

Love, Christopher (2009) *A Social History of Swimming in England, 1800–1918: Splashing in the serpentine*, London: Routledge

Lukas, Gerhard ([1969] 1976) *Die Körperkultur in frühen Epochen der Menschenentwicklung*, East Berlin: Sportverlag.

Lüschen, G. (1976) "Cheating," in *Social Problems in America*, edited by D. Landers, Urbana, IL: University of Illinois Press.

MacGregor, Jeff (1999) "Less than murder," *Sports Illustrated*, vol. 90, no. 12.

MacKinnon, Kenneth (2003) *Representing Men: Maleness and masculinity in the media*, London: Hodder Arnold.

Magdalinski, Tara (2009) *Sport, Technology and the Body*, London: Routledge.

Malson, Lucien (1972) *Wolf Children and the Problem of Human Nature*, New York: Monthly Review Press.

Maltby, J., Houran, J., Lange, R., Ashe, D., and McCutcheon, L. E. (2002) "Thou shalt worship no other gods – unless they are celebrities," *Personality and Individual Differences*, vol. 32, pp. 1157–72.

Mandell, Richard (1971) *The Nazi Olympics*, New York: Macmillan.

—— (1984) *Sport: A cultural history*, New York: Columbia University Press.

Maney, Kevin (1995) *Megamedia Shakeout: The inside story of the leaders and the losers in the exploding communications industry*, London: Wiley.

Mannes, Aaron (2004) *Profiles in Terror: The guide to Middle East terrorist organizations*, Lanham, MD: Rowman & Littlefield.

Mansfield, Alan and McGinn, Barbara (1993) "Pumping irony," in *Body Matters*, edited by Sue Scott and D. Morgan, London: Falmer.

Manzo, L. (2002) "Enhancing sport performance: The role of confidence and concentration," in *Psychological Foundations of Sport*, edited by J. M. Silva and D. E. Stevens, Boston, MA: Allyn & Bacon.

Markula, Pirkko (1995) "Firm but shapely, fit but sexy, strong but thin: The postmodern aerobicizing female bodies," *Sociology of Sport Journal*, vol. 12, pp. 424–53.

Marqusee, Mike (1999) *Redemption Song: Muhammad Ali and the spirit of the sixties*, London: Verso.

Marsh, Peter (1979) *Aggro: The illusion of violence*, London: Dent.

Marsh, Peter, Prosser, Elizabeth, and Harré, Rom (1978) *The Rules of Disorder*, London: Routledge & Kegan Paul.

Marshall, P. D. (1997) *Celebrity and Power: Fame in contemporary culture*, Minneapolis, MN: University of Minneapolis Press.

Martens, Rainer (1993) "Business, ethics, and the physical activity field," *Quest*, vol. 45.

Martin, Beth Ann and Martin, James H. (1995) "Comparing perceived sex role orientations of the ideal male and female athlete to the ideal male and female person," *Journal of Sport Behavior*, vol. 18, no. 4.

Martin, LeAnn Tyson and Chalmers, Gordon R. (2007) "The relationship between academic achievement and physical fitness," *Physical Educator*, vol. 64, no. 4, pp. 214–21.

Martin, Simon (2004) *Football and Fascism: The national game of the international arena under Mussolini*, Oxford: Berg.

Martinez, Michael A. (2006) "What is metacognition?," *Phi Delta Kappa*, vol. 87, pp. 696–9.

Mason, Tony (1988) *Sport in Britain*, London: Faber & Faber.

Matza, David (1969) *Becoming Deviant*, Englewood Cliffs, NJ: Prentice-Hall.

Mayr, Ernst and Diamond, Jared (1998) *What Evolution Is*, New York: Free Press.

Mays, Willie and Sahadi, Lou (1989) *Say Hey: The autobiography of Willie Mays*, New York: Pocket Books.

McCalman, Iain and Perkins, Maureen (2001) "Popular culture," pp. 214–22 in *An Oxford Companion to the Romantic Age: British culture, 1776–1832*, edited by Iain McCalman, Oxford: Oxford University Press.

McCrone, Kathleen (1988) *Sport and the Physical Emancipation of English Women, 1870–1914*, London: Routledge.

McDonald, Mary G. and David L. Andrews (2001) "Michael Jordan: Corporate sport and postmodern celebrityhood," in *Sports Stars: The cultural politics of sporting celebrity*, edited by David L. Andrews and Steven J. Jackson, London: Routledge.

McGinnis, Lee, Chun, Seungwoo and McQuillan, Julia (2003) "A review of gendered consumpion in sport and leisure," *Academy of Marketing Science Review* www.amsreview.org/articles/mcginnis05–2003html.

McGinnis, Peter M. (1999) *Biomechanics of Sport and Exercise*, Champaign, IL: Human Kinetics.

McGregor, Jeff (1999) "SI view: Air and space," *Sports Illustrated*, vol. 90, no. 13.

McIntosh, Peter (1980) *Fair Play*, Oxford: Heinemann Educational.

McNamara, Lawrence (2000) "Tackling Racial Hatred: Conciliation, reconciliation and football," *Australian Journal of Human Rights*, vol. 6, no. 2, pp. 5–31.

McNamee, Mike (2007) "Whose Prometheus? Transhumanism, biotechnology and the moral topography of sports medicine," *Sport, Ethics and Philosophy*, vol. 1, no. 2, pp. 181–94.

McRae, Donald (2003) *In Black and White: The untold story of Joe Louis and Jesse Owens*, New York: Scribner.

Messier, Mark, Gretzky, Walter, and Hull, Brett (1998) *Wayne Gretzky: The making of the great one*, Dallas: Beckett Publications.

Messner, Michael A. (1992) *Power at Play: Sports and the problem of masculinity*, Boston: Beacon Press.

—— (2002) *Taking the Field: Women, men and sports*, Minneapolis, MN: University of Minnesota Press.

Miah, Andy (2004) *Genetically Modified Athletes: Biomedical ethics, gene doping, and sport*, London: Routledge.

Miah, Andy and Rich, Emma (2006) "Genetic tests for ability? Talent identification and the value of an open future," *Sport, Education and Society*, vol. 11, pp. 259–73.

Michener, James (1976) *Sports in America*, New York: Random House.

Miles, Steven (1998) *Consumerism as a Way of Life*, London: Sage.

Miller, Stephen G. (2004) *Ancient Greek Athletics*, New Haven, CT: Yale University Press.

Miller, Toby, Rowe, David, Lawrence, Geoffrey, and McKay, Jim (2001) *Globalization and Sport: Playing the world*, London: Sage.

Miller, Wayne C. (1999) "Fitness and fatness in relation to health: Implications for a paradigm shift," *Journal of Social Issues*, vol. 55, no. 2, pp. 207–19.

Moir, Anne and Bill (1998) *Why Men Don't Iron: The real science of gender studies*, London: HarperCollins.

Monaco, James (ed.) (1978) *Celebrity: The media as image makers*, New York: Delta.

Monaghan, Lee F. (2001) "Looking good, feeling good: The embodied pleasures of vibrant physicality," *Sociology of Health & Illness*, vol. 23, no. 3, pp. 330–56.

—— (2007) "Body Mass Index, masculinities and moral worth: Men's critical understandings of 'appropriate' weight-for-height," *Sociology of Health & Illness*, vol. 29, no. 4, pp. 584–609.

Money, Tony (1997) *Manly and Muscular Diversions: Public schools and the nineteenth-century sporting revival*, London: Duckworth.

Morgan, W. P. (1979) "Prediction of performance in athletics," pp. 173–86 in *Coach, Athlete and the Sport Psychologist*, edited by P. Klavora and J. V. Daniels, Champaign, IL: Human Kinetics.

Morgan, William J. (1994) *Leftist Theories of Sport: A critique and reconstruction*, Urbana, IL: University of Illinois Press.

—— (2003) "Why the 'view from nowhere' gets us nowhere in our moral considerations of sports," *Journal of the Philosophy of Sport*, vol. 30, pp. 51–67.

—— (2004) "Moral antirealism, internalism, and sport," *Journal of the Philosophy of Sport*, vol. 31, pp. 161–83.

—— (2006a) "Fair is fair, or is it? A moral consideration of the doping wars in American sport," *Sport in Society*, vol. 9, no. 2, pp 177–98.

—— (2006b) *Why Sports Morally Matter*, New York: Routledge.

Morgan, William J. and Meier, Klaus V (eds) (1995) *Philsophic Inquiry into Sport*, 2nd edn, Champaign, IL: Human Kinetics.

Morgan, William J., Meier, Klaus V., and Schneider, Angela J. (eds) (2001) *Ethics in Sport*, Champaign, IL: Human Kinetics.

Morris, Desmond (1981) *The Soccer Tribe*, London: Jonathan Cape.

Morton, Cole (1999) "The flame that died," *Independent on Sunday,* Focus section (January 24).

Morton, Oliver (1999) "As the Tour de France begins, it's time to rethink the way we treat drugs in sports," *Newsweek* (international edition), July 12, p. 4.

Mottram, David (2003) *Drugs in Sport*, 3rd edn, London: Routledge.

Munro, P. and Govier, E. (1993) "Dynamic gender-related differences in dichtotic listening performance," *Neuropsychologia*, vol. 31, no. 40.

Muris, P., Kop, W. J., and Merckelbach, H. (1994) "Handedness, symptom resorting and accident susceptibility," *Journal of Clinical Psychology*, vol. 50, no. 3.

Murphy, P., Sheard, K., and Waddington, I. (2000) "Figurational sociology and its application to sport," pp. 92–105 in *Handbook of Sports Studies*, edited by Jay Coakley and Eric Dunning, London: Sage.

Muster, Georg (1985) *Murdoch: A paper prince*, Harmondsworth: Penguin.

Naison, Mark (1972) "Sport and the American empire," *Radical America*, vol. 6, no. 4.

Nauright, John (2004) "Global games: Culture, political economy and sport in the globalised world of the the 21st century," *Third World Quarterly*, vol. 25, no. 7.

Nelson Burton, Mariah (1994) *The Stronger Women Get, the More Men Love Football: Sex and sport in America*, New York: Harcourt, Brace.

Newfield, Jack (1995) *Only in America: The life and crimes of Don King*, New York: William Morrow.

Niednagel, J. (1994) *Your Keys to Sports Success*, Nashville, TN: Nelson.

Noble, William and Davidson, Iain (1996) *Human Evolution, Language and Mind: A psychological and archaeological inquiry*, Cambridge: Cambridge University Press.

Novak, Michael (1976) *The Joy of Sport*, New York: Basic Books.

Oates, Tina and Clark, David A. (2004). "Sociotropy, body dissatisfaction and perceived social disapproval in dieting women: A prospective diathesis-stress study of dysphoria," *Cognitive Therapy and Research*, vol. 28, pp. 715–31.

Ogilvie, B. and Tutko, T. A. (1966) *Problem Athletes and How to Handle Them*, London: Pelham.

Olins, Wally (2003) *Wally Olins on Brand*, London: Thames & Hudson.

Oliver, Paul (2001) *What's the Score? A survey of cultural diversity and racism in Australian sport*, Sydney: Human Rights and Equal Opportunities Commission.

—— (2007) "Racism and cultural diversity in Australian sport," *Alternative Law Journal*, vol. 32, no. 2, pp. 116–17.

Olsen, Jack (1968) *The Black Athlete*, New York: Time Life.

Orbach, Susie (1978) *Fat is a Feminist Issue: The anti-diet guide for women*, New York: Galahad.

Orwell, George (1950) *Shooting an Elephant and Other Essays*, London: Secker & Warburg.

Osborne, Peter (2004) *Basil D'Oliveira*, London: Little, Brown.

Ostler, Scott (2008) *How to Cheat in Sports: Professional tricks exposed!*, San Francisco, CA: Chronicle Books.

Otten, Mark (2009) "Choking vs. clutch performance: A study of sport performance under pressure," *Journal of Sport & Exercise Psychology*, vol. 31, no. 5, pp 583–601.

Oudshoorn, Nelly (1994) *Beyond the Natural Body: An archeology of sex hormones*, London: Routledge.

Overman, Steven J. (1997) *The Influence of the Protestant Ethic on Sport and Recreation*, Aldershot: Avebury.

—— (2000) "The Protestant Ethic," in *Sports Culture: An A-Z guide*, edited by Ellis Cashmore, London: Routledge.

Page, Michael (1988) *Bradman: The biography*, Sydney: Pan Macmillian Australia,

Park, Roberta J. (2005) "Muscles, symmetry and action. 'Do you measure up?' Defining masculinity in Britain and America from the 1860s to the early 1900s," *International Journal of the History of Sport*, vol. 22, no. 3, 365–95.

Parker, Andrew (2009) "Sport, celebrity and identity: A socio-legal analysis," pp. 150–67 in *Sport and Social Identities*, edited by John Harris and Andrew Parker, Basingstoke: Palgrave Macmillan.

Pass, K., Freeman, H., Bautista, J., and Johnson, C. (1993) "Handedness and accidents with injury," *Perceptual and Motor Skills*, vol. 77, no. 3.

Patterson, Orlando (1971) "Rethinking black history," *Harvard Educational Review*, vol. 41 (August).

Paulsen, Gary (1994) *Winterdance: the fine madness of Alaskan dog-racing*, London: Gollancz.

Payne, Tom (2009) *Fame: From the Bronze Age to Britney*, London: Vintage.

Pearlman, Jeff (1998) "Bare knuckles," *Sports Illustrated* vol 89, no 17.

Pelé and Fish, Robert (1977) *Pelé: My life and the beautiful game*, New York: Doubleday.

Penhollow, Tina, Young, M., and Denny, G. (2009) "Predictors of quality of life, sexual intercourse, and sexual satisfaction among active older adults," *American Journal of Health Education*, vol. 40, pp. 14–22.

Pepperell, Robert (2004) *The Posthuman Condition: Consciousness beyond the brain*, 3rd edn, Bristol: Intellect.

Perrig, Walter J. (2000) "Intuition and levels of control: The non-rational way of reacting, adapting, and creating," pp. 103–23 in *Control of Human Behavior, Mental Processes, and Consciousness: Essays in honor of the 60th birthday of August Flammer*, edited by Walter J. Perrig and Alexander Grob, Mahwah, NJ: Lawrence Erlbaum.

Perry, Clifton (1983) "Blood doping and athletic competition," *International Journal of Applied Philosophy*, vol. 1, no. 3.

Petrie, Trent, A. (1996) "Differences between male and female college lean sport athletes, nonlean sports athletes, and nonathletes on behavioral and psychological indices of eating disorders," *Journal of Applied Sport Psychology*, vol. 8, no. 2.

Petróczi, Andrea and Aidman, Eugene (2008) "Psychological drivers in doping: The life-cycle model of performance enhancement," *Substance Abuse Treatment, Prevention, and Policy*, vol. 3, no. 7, pp. 1–12.

Phillips, Barbara J. (2005) "Working out: Consumers and the culture of exercise," *Journal of Popular Culture*, vol. 38, no. 3, pp. 525–51.

Pieterse, Jan Nederveen (1992). *White on Black: Images of Africa and blacks in Western popular culture*, London: Yale University Press.

Pipes, Daniel (2000) "In Muslim America: A presence and a challenge," *National Review*, February 21, pp. 40–1.

Poliakoff, Michael B. (1987) *Combat Sports in the Ancient World: Competition, violence, and culture*, New Haven, CT: Yale University Press.

Polley, Martin (2007) "History and sport," pp. 56–74 in *Sport and Society: A student introduction*, edited by Barrie Houlihan, London: Sage.

Polumbaum, Judy and Wieting, Stephen G. (1999) "Stories of sport and the moral order: Unraveling the cultural construction of Tiger Woods," *Journalism and Communication Monographs*, vol. 1, no. 2, pp. 67–118.

Prendergast, Mark (1993) *For God, Country and Coca-Cola: The unauthorized history of the great American soft drink and the company that makes it*, New York: Collier.

Prichard, Ivanka and Tiggeman, Marika (2005) "Objectification in fitness centers: Self-objectification, body dissatisfaction, and disordered eating in aerobic instructors and aerobic participants," *Sex Roles*, vol. 53, nos 1–2, pp. 19–28.

Pritchard, Mary E. and Wilson, Gregory S. (2005) "Factors influencing body image in female adolescent athletes," *Women in Sport and Physical Activity Journal*, vol. 14, pp. 72–8.

Pronger, Brian (1998) "Post-sport: Transgressing boundaries in physical culture" pp. 277–98 in *Sport and Postmodern Times* edited by Geneviève Rail, Albany, NY: State University of New York Press.

Puglise, M., Lifshitz, F., and Grad, G. (1983) "Fear of obesity," *New England Journal of Medicine,* vol. 309.

Putnam, Douglas T. (1999) *Controversies of the Sports World*, Westport, CT: Greenwood Press.

Rader, Benjamin (1984) *In its Own Image: How television has transformed sport*, New York: Collier-Macmillan.

Rail, Geneviève (1998) "Seismography of the postmodern condition: Three theses on the implosion of sport," pp. 143–61 in *Sport and Postmodern Times*, edited by Geneviève Rail, Albany, NY: State University of New York Press.

Ravizza, Kenneth (1984) "Qualities of the peak experience in sport," pp. 452–61 in *Psychological Foundations of Sport*, edited by J. M. Silva and R. S. Weinberg, Champaign, IL: Human Kinetics.

Raymond M., Pontier, D., Dufour, A.-B., and Møller, A. P. (1996) "Frequency-dependent maintenance of left handedness in humans," *Proceedings of the Royal Society, B: Biological Sciences*, vol. 263, pp. 1627–33.

Real, Michael R. (1998) "MediaSport: Technology and the commodification of postmodern sport," in *MediaSport* edited by Lawrence A. Wenner, London: Routledge.

Reber, Arthur S. (1995) *Dictionary of Psychology*, 2nd edn, Harmondsworth: Penguin.

Rees, C. R. (2001) "Character development, moral development, and social responsibility in physical education and sport: Towards a synthesis of subdisciplinary perspectives," *International Journal of Physical Education*, vol. 38, no. 2, pp. 52–9.

Reeser, J. C. (2005) "Gender identity and sport: Is the playing field level?," *British Journal of Sports Medicine*, vol. 39, pp. 695–9.

Reeve, Simon (2001) *One Day in September: The full story of the 1972 Munich Olympics massacre and the Israeli Revenge Operation Wrath of God*, New York: Arcade.

Regen, Richard (1990) "Neither does King," *Interview*, vol. 20 (October 10).

Reilly, Rick (1996) "Patriot Games: Mahmoud Abdul-Rauf caused an uproar when he sat out the national anthem," *Sports Illustrated*, vol. 84, no. 12, pp. 76–7.

Reiterer, Werner (2000) *Positive: An Australian Olympian reveals the inside story of drugs and sport*, Sydney: Pan Macmillan Australia.

Reith, Gerda (1999) *The Age of Chance: Gambling in western culture*, London: Prometheus Books.

Rescher, Nicholas (1995) *Luck: The brilliant randomness of everyday life*, New York: Farrar Straus Giroux.

Rhodes, Reilly (ed.) (1990) *Sport in Art from American Museums*, New York: Universe.

Richards, Renee and Ames, J. (1983) *Second Serve*, New York: Stein & Day.

Ridley, Matt (2001a)"Sex, errors, and the genome," *Natural History*, vol. 110, no. 5, pp. 45–51.

—— (2001b) "The genome is decoded: be happy," *Wall Street Journal*, February 14, p. A22.

—— (2003a) "Listen to the genome," *The American Spectator*, vol. 36, no. 3, pp. 59–65.

—— (2003b) *Nature via Nurture: Genes, experience and what makes us human*, New York: HarperCollins.

Riemer, Brenda A. and Visio, Michelle E. (2003) "Gender typing of sports: An investigation of Metheny's classification," *Research Quarterly for Exercise and Sport*, vol. 74, no. 2.

Rigauer, Bero (1981) *Sport and Work*, New York: Columbia University Press.

—— (2000) "Marxist theories," pp. 28–47 in *Handbook of Sports Studies*, edited by Jay Coakley and Eric Dunning, London: Sage.

Rinehart, R. (1998) "Born-again sport: Ethics in biographical research," in *Sport and Postmodern Times*, edited by Geneviève Rail, Albany, NY: State University of New York Press.

Ritzer, George (1998) *The McDonaldization of Society*, 2nd edn, Newbury Park, CA: Pine Forge.

Roberts, Johnnie L. (2008) "Murdoch, Ink," *Newsweek*, vol. 151, no. 17, pp. 40–5.

Robertson, Roland (1992) "Glocalization: Time-space and homogeneity-heterogeneity," pp. 25–44 in *Global Modernities*, edited by Mike Featherstone, Scott Lash, and Roland Roberston, London: Sage.

Robins, David (1982) "Sport and youth culture," in *Sport, Culture and Ideology*, edited by John Hargreaves, London: Routledge & Kegan Paul.

Robinson, Sugar Ray and Anderson, Dave (1992) *Sugar Ray: The Sugar Ray Robinson story*, London: Robson Books.

Rojek, Chris (2001) *Celebrity*, London: Reaktion.

Rosentraub, Mark (1997) *Major League Losers: The real cost of sports and who's paying for it*, New York: HarperCollins.

Rosner, Scott and Shropshire, Kenneth L. (eds) (2004) *The Business of Sports*, Boston: Jones & Bartlett.

Rowe, David (2002) "Taking the sports brief: a review essay," *Theory and Event*, vol. 6, no. 1.

—— (ed.) (2004) *Sport, Culture and the Media*, 2nd edn, Maidenhead: Open University Press.

Russell, J. S. (2004) "Moral realism in sport," *Journal of the Philosophy of Sport*, vol. 31, pp. 142–60.

Russell, W., Pritschet, B., Frost, B., Emmett, J., Pelley, T. J., Black, J., and Owen, J. (2003) "A comparison of post-exercise mood enhancement across common exercise distraction activities," *Journal of Sport Behavior*, vol. 26, pp. 368–83.

Ryan, Joan (1998) *Little Girls in Pretty Boxes: The making and breaking of elite gymnasts and figure skaters*, London: Women's Press.

Sakellarakis, J. (1979) "Athletics in Crete and Mycenae," in *The Eternal Olympics: The art and history of sport*, edited by Nikolaos Yaloris, New York: Caratzas Brothers.

Sammons, Jeffrey (1988) *Beyond the Ring*, Camden, NJ: University of Illinois Press.

Sandford, B. (1987) "The 'adrenaline rush'," *Physician and Sportsmedicine*, vol. 15, p. 184.

Sandrock, Michael (1996) *Running with the Legends*, Champaign, IL: Human Kinetics.

Schaap, Jeremy (2007) *Triumph: The untold story of Jesse Owens and Hitler's Olympics*, Boston, MA: Houghton Mifflin.

Schiebinger, Londa (1987) "Skeletons in the closet: The first illustrations of the female skeleton in eighteenth-century anatomy," in *The Making of the Modern Body: Sexuality and society in the nineteenth century*, edited by Catherine Gallagher and Thomas Laqueur, Berkeley, CA: University of California Press.

—— (1989) *The Mind Has No Sex: Women in the origins of modern science*, Cambridge, MA: Harvard University Press.

Schinke, Robert and Hanrahan, Stephanie (eds) (2009) *Cultural Sport Psychology*, Champaign, IL: Human Kinetics.

Scott, Jack (1971) *The Athletic Revolution*, New York: Free Press.

Scully, Gerald W. (1995) *The Market Structure of Sports*, Chicago, IL: University of Chicago Press.

Segrave, Jeffrey O. (2006) "Olympics," pp. 3262–5 in *The Blackwell Encyclopedia of Sociology* (12 vols, online), edited by George Ritzer, Oxford: Blackwell. http://www.blackwellreference.com/subscriber/tocnode?id = g9781405124331_chunk_g978140512433120_ss1–10.

Seligman, M. E. P. (1975) *Helplessness: On depression, development and death*, San Francisco, CA: W. H. Freeman.

Senn, Alfred E. (1999) *Power, Politics and the Olympic Games*, Champaign, IL: Human Kinetics.

Shawcross, William (1992) *Rupert Murdoch*, London: Chatto & Windus.

Shea, B. Christine (2001) "The paradox of pumping iron: Female bodybuilding as resistance and compliance," *Women and Language*, vol. 24, no. 2.

Sheard, Michael and Golby, Jim (2006) "The efficacy of an outdoor adventure education curriculum on selected aspects of positive psychological development," *Journal of Experiential Education*, vol. 29, pp. 187–209.

Sherman, Len (1998) *Big League, Big Time: The birth of the Arizona Diamondbacks, the billion-dollar business of sports, and the power of the media in America*, New York: Pocket Books.

Shields, David L. and Bredemeier, Brenda J. (1995) *Character Development and Physical Activity*, Champaign, IL: Human Kinetics.

Silva, J. M. and Weinberg, R. S. (eds) (1984) *Psychological Foundations of Sport*, Champaign, IL: Human Kinetics.

—— (1984) "Motivation," pp. 171–6 in *Psychological Foundations of Sport*, edited by J. M. Silva and R. S. Weinberg, Champaign, IL: Human Kinetics.

Silva, J. M. and Stevens, D. J. (eds) (2002) *Psychological Foundations of Sport*, New York: Allyn & Bacon.

Silverstein, Paul A. (2000) "Islam, soccer, and the French nation-state," *Social Text*, vol. 18, no. 4, pp. 25–53.

Simson, Vyv and Jennings, Andrew (1992) *Dishonored Games: Corruption, money and greed at the Olympics*, New York: SPI Books.

Simson, Vyv, Jennings, Andrew and Nally, Patrick (1992) *The Lords of the Rings: Power, money and drugs in the modern Olympics*, London: Simon & Schuster.

Smart, Barry (2007) "Not playing around: Global capitalism, modern sport and consumer culture," *Global Networks*, vol. 7, no. 2, pp. 113–34.

Smith, D. (1988) "Femininity as discourse," in *Becoming Feminine: The politics of popular culture*, edited by Leslie G. Roman, Linda Christian-Smith and Elizabeth Ellsworth, Philadelphia, PA: Falmer.

—— (2003) "A framework for understanding the training process leading to elite performance," *Sports Medicine*, vol. 33, pp. 1103–26.

Smith, D. and Hale, B. (2005) "Exercise dependence in bodybuilders: Antecedents and reliability of measurement," *Journal of Sports Medicine and Physical Fitness*, vol. 45.

Smith, Earl (ed.) (2009) *Sociology of Sport and Social Theory*, Champaign, IL: Human Kinetics.

Smith, Ed (2004) *On and Off the Field*, London: Viking.

Smith, Michael D. (1983) *Violence and Sport*, Toronto: Butterworth.

Smith, Pamela M. and Ogle, Jennifer Paff (2006) "Interactions among high school cross-country runners and coaches: Creating a cultural context for athletes' embodied experiences," *Family and Consumer Sciences Research Journal*, vol. 34, pp. 276–307.

Smith, R. E. (2006) "Understanding sport behavior," *Journal of Applied Sport Psychology*, vol. 18, pp. 1–27.

Smith, R. E. and Smoll, F. L. (1996) *Way to Go, Coach*, Portola Valley, CA: Warde.

Snyder, E. and Spreitzer, E. (1983) *Social Aspects of Sport*, 2nd edn, Englewood Cliffs, NJ: Prentice-Hall.

Solnit, Rebecca (2004) *Motion Studies: Time, space and Eadweard Muybridge*, London: Bloomsbury.

Solomon, Henry A. (1984) *The Exercise Myth*, New York: Harcourt, Brace, Jovanovich.

Sorek, Tamir (2002) "The Islamic Soccer League in Israel: Setting moral boundaries by taming the wild," *Identities: Global Studies in Culture and Power*, vol. 9, no. 4, pp. 445–70.

Sowell, Thomas (1994) *Race and Culture: A world view*, New York: Basic Books.

Spears, Betty and Swanson, Richard A. (1995) *History of Sport and Physical Activity in the United States*, 4th edn, Dubuque: Brown & Benchmark.

Spivey, Nigel (2004) *The Ancient Olympics*, London: Oxford University Press.

Staffo, Donald F. (2001) "Strategies for reducing criminal violence among athletes," *Journal of Physical Education, Recreation & Dance*, vol. 72, no. 6, pp. 38–42.

Staudohar, Paul and Mangan, James (eds) (1991) *The Business of Professional Sports*, Urbana, IL: University of Illinois Press.

Steele, Bruce C. (2002) "Tackling football's closet," *The Advocate*, no. 877 (November 26), pp. 30–7.

Stephens, Dawn E. (2004) "Moral atmosphere and aggression in collegiate intramural sport," *International Sports Journal*, vol. 8, no. 1, pp. 65–75.

Sternberg, Robert J. (1996) "Intelligence and cognitive styles," pp. 583–601 in *Companion Encyclopedia of Psychology*, vol. 2, edited by A. M. Coleman, London: Routledge.

Stevenson, Thomas B. and Karim Alaug, Abdul (2000) "Football in newly united Yemen: Rituals of equity, identity and state formation," *Journal of Anthropological Research*, vol. 56, no. 4, pp. 453–75.

Stoddart, Brian (1988) "Sport, cultural imperialism and colonial response in the British empire," *Comparative Studies in Society and History*, vol. 30 (October).

—— (2008) *Sport, Culture and History: Region, nation and globe*, London: Routledge.

Stoll, Sharon Kay, Prisbrey, Keith A., and Froes, F. H. (2002) "Advanced materials in sports: An advantage or ethical challenge," *USA Today Magazine*, vol. 130, no. 2684, pp. 72–6.

Stone, Alan A. (2004) "Million Dollar Baby," *Psychiatric Times*, vol. 22, no. 9, p. 63.

Stone, Linda, Lurquin, Paul F., and Cavalli-Sforza, L. Luca (2006) *Genes, Culture, and Human Evolution: A synthesis*, Oxford: Wiley-Blackwell.

Stotlar, D. K (2000) "Vertical integration in sport" *Journal of Sport Management*, vol. 14, no. 1, pp. 1–7.

Strasser, J. B. and Becklund, Laurie (1993) *Swoosh: The unauthorized story of Nike and the men who played there*, New York: HarperBusiness.

Strelan, Peter and Boeckmann, Robert J. (2006) "Why drug testing in elite sport does not work: Perceptual deterrence theory and the role of personal moral beliefs," *Journal of Applied Social Psychology*, vol. 36, no. 12, pp. 2909–34.

Sundgot-Borgen, Jorunn (1994a) "Eating disorders in female athletes," *Sports Medicine*, vol. 17, no. 3.

—— (1994b) "Risk and trigger factors the development of eating disorders in female elite athletes," *Medicine and Science in Sports and Exercise*, vol. 26, no. 4.

Suter, P. M. and Ruckstuhl, N. (2006) "Obesity during growth in Switzerland: Role of early socio-cultural factors favouring sedentary activities," *International Journal of Obesity*, vol. 30, pp. S4–S10.

Suttles, Gerald (1968) *The Social Order of the Slum: Ethnicity and territory in the inner city*, Chicago: University of Chicago Press.

Swift, E. M. (1999) "Breaking point" *Sports Illustrated*, vol. 90, no. 4.

Swift, E. M. and Yaeger, Don (2001) "Unnatural selection," *Sports Illustrated*, vol. 94, no. 20.

Sykes, Heather (2006) "Transsexual and transgender policies in sport," *Women in Sport and Physical Activity Journal*, vol. 15, no. 1, pp. 3–13.

Symons, Caroline (2009) *The Gay Games: A history*, London: Routledge.

Szabo, A. (2000) "Physical activity as a source of psychological dysfunction," in *Physical Activity and Psychological Well-being*, edited by Stuart L. Biddle, K. R. Fox, and S. H. Boutcher, London: Routledge.

Tatz, Colin (1995) *Obstacle Race: Aborigines in sport*, Sydney: University of New South Wales Press.

Taub, Diane and Benson, Rose (1992) "Weight concerns, weight control techniques, and easting disorders among adolescent competitive swimmers: The effect of gender," *Sociology of Sport Journal*, vol. 9, no. 2.

Taylor, Aaron (2007) "'He's gotta be strong, and he's gotta be fast, and he's gotta be larger than life': Investigating the engendered superhero body," *Journal of Popular Culture*, vol. 40, no. 2, pp. 344–60.

Taylor, Ian (1971) "Soccer consciousness and soccer hooliganism," in *Images of Deviance*, edited by Stanley Cohen, Harmondsworth: Penguin,

Taylor, J. and Demick, A. (1994) "A multidimensional model of momentum in sports," *Journal of Applied Sport Psychology*, vol. 6.

Taylor, Phil (1997) "Center of the storm," *Sports Illustrated*, vol. 87, no. 24.

Tenenbaum, Gershon, Stewart, Evan, Singer, Robert N., and Duda, Joan (1996) "Aggression and violence in sport: An ISSP position stand," *International Journal of Sport Psychology*, vol. 27, no. 2, pp. 229–36.

Tevis, Walter S. (1959) *The Hustler*, New York: Thunder's Mouth Press.

—— (1984) *The Color of Money*, New York: Thunder's Mouth Press.

Thogersen-Ntoumani, C., Lane, H. J., Biscomb, K., Jarrett, H., and Lane, A. M. (2007) "Women's motive to exercise," *Women in Sport and Physical Activity Journal*, vol. 16, no. 1, pp. 16–28.

Thrash, Todd M. and Elliott, Andrew J. (2002) "Implicit and self-attributed achievement motives: Concordance and predictive validity," *Journal of Personality*, vol. 70, pp. 729–55.

Tillyard, Stella (2005) "Celebrity in 18th-century London," *History Today*, vol. 55, no. 6, pp. 20–7.

Tod, David and Hodge, Ken (2001) "Moral reasoning and achievement motivation in sport: A qualitative inquiry," *Journal of Sport Behavior*, vol. 24, no. 3, pp. 307–27.

Todd, Jan (1987) "Bernarr Mafadden: Reformer of the feminine form," *Journal of Sport History*, vol. 14, no. 1.

—— (1998) *Physical Culture and the Body Beautiful: Purposive exercise in the lives of American women, 1800–1875*, Macon, GA: Mercer University Press.

Todd, Terry (1987) "Anabolic steroids: The gremlins of sport," *Journal of Sports History*, vol. 14, no. 1.

Toohey, Kristine (2008) "Terrorism, sport and public policy in the risk society," *Sport in Society*, vol. 11, no. 4, pp. 429–42.

Torres, Angela N., Boccaccini, Marcus T., and Miller, Holly A. (2006) "Perceptions of the validity and utility of criminal profiling among forensic psychologists and psychiatrists," *Professional Psychology: Research and Practice*, vol. 37, no. 1, pp. 51–8.

Tortora, Gerard J. and Derrickson, Bryan H. (2006) *Introduction to the Human Body: The essentials of anatomy and physiology*, 2nd edn, New York: Wiley.

Turner, Bryan S. (1992) *Max Weber: From history to modernity*, London: Routledge.

Turner, Graeme (2004) *Understanding Celebrity*, London: Sage.

Van Schoyck, S. and Grasha, A. (1981) "Attentional style variations and athletic ability: The advantages of a sports-specific test," *Medicine and Science in Sport and Exercise*, vol. 26.

Vandervell, Anthony and Coles, Charles (1980) *Game and the English Landscape: The Influence of the chase on sporting art and scenery*, London: Debrett's Peerage.

Vanwalleghem, Rik (1968) *Eddy Merckx: The greatest cyclist of the twentieth century*, Allentown, PA: Velo Press.

Vasili, Phil (1998) *The First Black Footballer, Arthur Wharton, 1865–1930: An absence of memory*, Portland, OR: Frank Cass.

Vealey, R. S. (1986) "Conceptualization of sport-confidence and competitive orientation: Preliminary investigation and instrument development," *Journal of Sport Psychology*, vol. 8.

Venditti, Robert and Weldele, Brett (2009) *The Surrogates*, Portland, OR: Top Shelf Productions.

Verma, Gajendra and Darby, Douglas (1994) *Winners and Losers: Ethnic minorities in sport and recreation*, London: Falmer.

Vertinsky, Patricia (1987) "Exercise, physical capability, and the eternally wounded woman in late nineteenth century North America," *Journal of Sport History*, vol. 14, no. 1.

—— (1990) *The Eternally Wounded Woman: Women, doctors and exercise in the late nineteenth century*, Manchester: Manchester University Press.

Vincent, Martin (1995) "Painters and punters," *New Statesman & Society*, vol. 8.

Voy, Robert and Deeter, Kirk (1991) *Drugs, Sport and Politics*, Champaign, IL: Human Kinetics.

Waddington, Ivan (1996) "The development of sports medicine," *Sociology of Sport Journal*, vol. 9.

—— (2000) *Sport, Health and Drugs: A critical sociological perspective*, London: E. & F. N. Spon.

Walsh, Michael (1983) "Make way for the new Spartans: Fitness addicts are changing images as well as bodies," *Time*, vol. 122 (September 19), pp. 90–3.

Wankel, L (1982) "Audience effects in sport," in *Psychological Foundations of Sport*, edited by J. Silva and R. Weinberg, Champaign, IL: Human Kinetics,

Wann, Daniel L. and Grieve, Frederick G. (2005) "Biased evaluations of in-group and out-group behavior at sporting events: The importance of team identification and threats to social identity," *The Journal of Social Psychology*, vol. 145, pp. 531–45.

Warde, Alan (2005) "Consumption and theories of practice," *Journal of Consumer Culture*, vol. 5, no. 2, pp. 131–53.

Waters, Malcolm ([1995] 2001) *Globalization*, 2nd edn, London: Routledge.

Watkins, James (2009) *Structure and Function of the Musculo-skeletal System*, 2nd edn, Champaign, IL: Human Kinetics.

Webb, William M., Nasco, Suzanne A., Riley, Sarah, and Headrick, Brian (1998) "Athlete identity and reactions to retirement from sports," *Journal of Sport Behavior*, vol. 21, pp. 338–62.

Weber, Max (1958) *The Protestant Ethic and the Spirit of Capitalism*, translated by Talcott Parsons, New York: Scribner & Sons.

Weeks, Jeffrey (2003) *Sexuality*, 2nd edn, London: Routledge.

Weinberg, Robert S. and Gould, Daniel (2004) *Foundations of Sport and Exercise Psychology*, Champaign, IL: Human Kinetics.

Weintraub, Arlene (2004) "Commentary: Can drug-busters beat new steroids?," *Business Week* (online), June 14, businessweek.com:/print/magazine/content/04_24/b3887096_mz018.htm?tc.

Weir, J. and Abrahams, P. (1992) *An Imaging Atlas of Human Anatomy*, St Louis, MO: Mosby-Wolfe.

Wellard, Ian (2006) "Able bodies and sport participation: Social constructions of physical ability for gendered and sexually identified bodies," *Sport, Education and Society*, vol. 11, no. 2, pp. 105–19.

Wenner, Lawrence (ed.) (1998) *MediaSport*, London: Routledge,

Wenner, Lawrence and Ganz, Walter (1998) "Watching sports on television: Audience experience, gender, fanship, and marriage," in *MediaSport* edited by Lawrence Wenner, London: Routledge.

Westerbeek, Hans and Smith, Aaron (2002) *Sport Business in the Global Marketplace*, London: Palgrave Macmillan.

Whannel, Garry (1992) *Fields in Vision: Television sport and cultural transformation*, London: Routledge.

—— (2000) "Sport and the media," in *Handbook of Sports Studies*, edited by Jay Coakley and Eric Dunning, Newbury Park, CA: Sage.

Wheaton, Belinda (2000) "New lads' masculinities and the 'New Sport' participant," *Men and Masculinities*, vol. 2, April, pp. 434–56.

Whitehead, Stephen M. and Barrett, Frank J. (2001) "The sociology of masculinity" pp. 1–26 in *The Masculinities Reader*, edited by Stephen M. Whitehead and Frank J. Barrett, Cambridge: Polity.

Whitson, David (1994) "The embodiment of gender: Discipline, domination and empowerment," in *Women, Sport and Culture*, edited by Susan Birrell and Cheryl Cole, Champaign, IL: Human Kinetics.

—— (1998) "Circuits of promotion: Media, marketing and the globalization of sport," in *MediaSport*, edited by Lawrence Wenner, London: Routledge.

Wiggins, David (1995) *Sports in America: From wicked amusement to national obsession*, Champaign, IL: Human Kinetics.

—— (1997) *Glory Bound: Black athletes in a white America*, Syracuse: Syracuse University Press.

—— (ed.) (2006) *Out of the Shadows: A biographical history of African American athletes*, Fayetteville, AK: University of Arkansas Press.

Williams, Alexandra (2007) "Culture, community and commitment," *Fitness Journal*, July/August, pp. 62–8.

Williams, Christa (2004) "Fitness, beauty, supplements, and money," *Journal of Professional Exercise Physiology*, vol. 2, no. 8, pp. 1–10.

Wilmore, Jack and Costill, David (1994) *Physiology of Sport and Exercise*, Champaign, IL: Human Kinetics.

Wilson, Neil (1988) *The Sport Business*, London: Piatkus.

Wilson, Wade and Derse, Edward (eds) (2001) *Doping in Elite Sport: The politics of drugs in the Olympic movement*, Champaign, IL: Human Kinetics.

Wolf, Naomi (1991) *The Beauty Myth: How images of beauty are used against women*, New York: Morrow.

Wolff, Michael (2008) *The Man Who Owns the News: Inside the secret world of Rupert Murdoch*, London: Bodley Head.

Woods, James (2001) *History of International Broadcasting*, vol. 1, London: Institute of Engineering and Technology.

Woodward, Kath (2004) "Rumbles in the jungle: Boxing, racialization and the performance of masculinity," *Leisure Studies*, vol. 23, no. 1, pp. 15–17.

Wu, Ping (2008) "Sport and the media," pp. 148–63 in *Sport Sociology* edited by Peter Craig and Paul Beedie, Exeter: Learning Matters.

Wyke, Andrew (1964) *Gambling*, London: Spring Books.

Yaloris, Nikolaos (ed.) (1979) *The Eternal Olympics: The art and history of sport*, New York: Caratzas Brothers.

Yesalis, Charles E. (ed.) (1993) *Anabolic Steroids in Sport and Exercise*, Champaign, IL: Human Kinetics.

Yesalis, Charles and Cowart, Virginia (1998) *The Steroids Game*, Champaign, IL: Human Kinetics.

Young, Eric (2000) "Sport and violence," in *Handbook of Sports Studies* edited by Jay Coakley and Eric Dunning, Newbury Park, CA: Sage.

Zajonc, R. (1965) "Social facilitation," *Science*, vol. 149.

Zanker, Cathy and Gard, Michael (2008) "Fatness, fitness, and the moral universe of sport and physical activity," *Sociology of Sport Journal*, vol. 25, pp. 48–65.

Ziegler, Paula J., Kannan, Srimathi, Jonnalagadda, Satya S., Krishnakumar, Ambika, Taksali, and Nelson, Judith A. (2005) "Dietary intake, body perceptions, and weight concerns of female US international synchronized figure skating teams," *International Journal of Sport Nutrition and Exercise Metabolism*, vol. 15, pp. 550–66.

Zimbalist, Andrew (1992) *Baseball and Billions*, New York: Basic Books.

—— (2006) *The Bottom Line: Observations and arguments on the sports business*, Chicago: Temple University Press.

Zimmer, Carl (2005) *Smithsonian Intimate Guide to Human Origins*, New York: Harper Collins.

Zimniuch, Fran (2009) *Crooked: A history of cheating in sports*, Lanham, MD: Taylor Trade.

Zolberg, Vera (1987) "Elias and Dunning's theory of sport and excitement," *Theory, Culture and Society*, vol. 4.

Zona, Louis A. (1990) "Red Grooms," in *Sport in Art from American Museums*, edited by Reilly Rhodes, New York: Universe.

Zucker, Harvey M. and Babich, Lawrence J. (1976) *Sports Films: A complete reference*, HM & M Publishers.

NAME INDEX

SUBJECT INDEX

TITLE INDEX